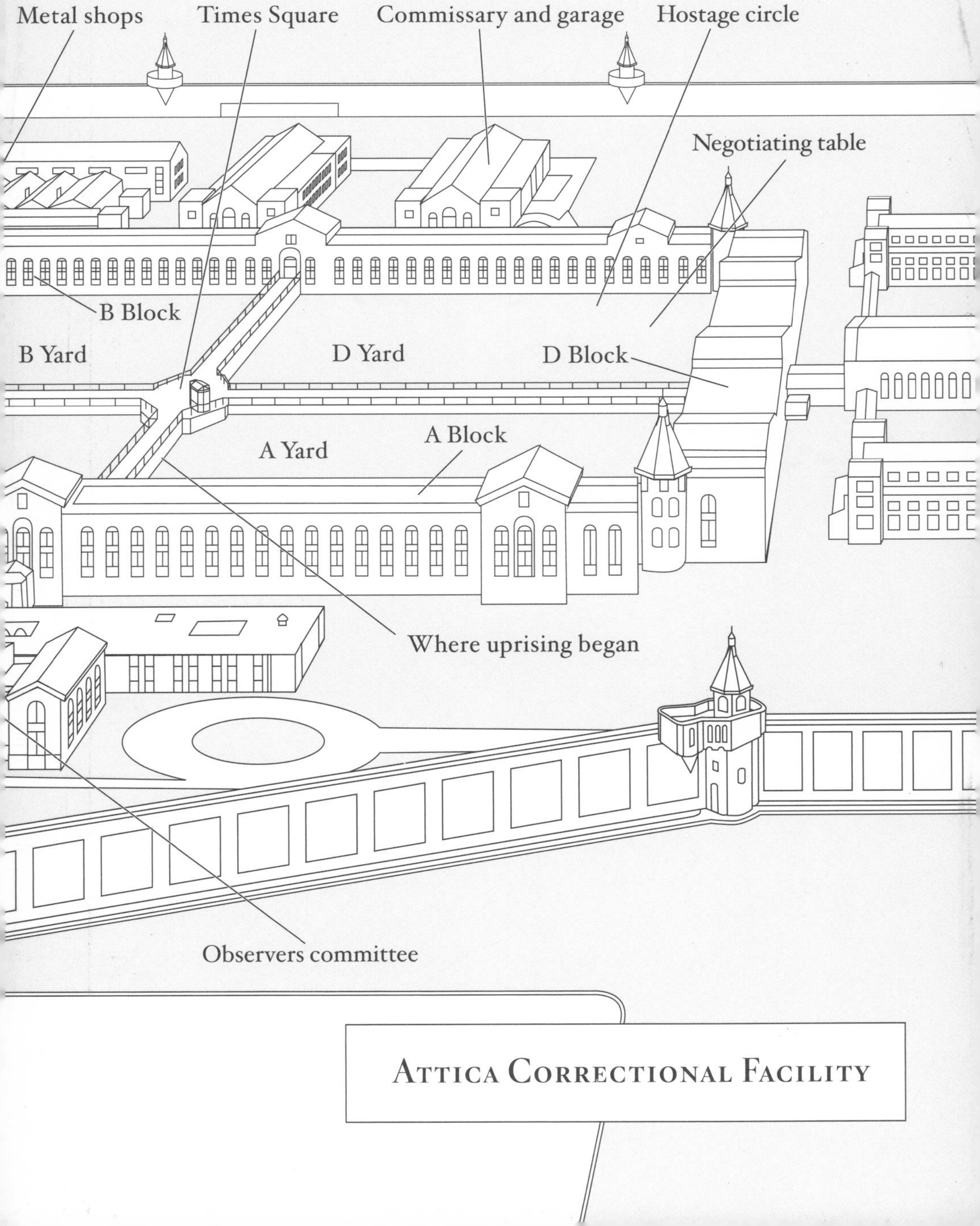

Metal shops

Times Square

Commissary and garage

Hostage circle

Negotiating table

B Block

B Yard

D Yard

D Block

A Block

A Yard

Where uprising began

Observers committee

ATTICA CORRECTIONAL FACILITY

ALSO BY HEATHER ANN THOMPSON

*Whose Detroit?:*
*Politics, Labor, and Race in a Modern American City*

(as editor)

*Speaking Out:*
*Activism and Protest in the 1960s and 1970s*

# BLOOD in the WATER

# BLOOD in the WATER

## The Attica Prison Uprising of 1971 and Its Legacy

Heather Ann Thompson

PANTHEON BOOKS NEW YORK

 Published in the United States by Pantheon Books, a division of Penguin Random House LLC, New York, and distributed in Canada by Random House of Canada, a division of Penguin Random House Canada Limited, Toronto.

Pantheon Books and colophon are registered trademarks of Penguin Random House LLC.

Library of Congress Cataloging-in-Publication Data
Name: Thompson, Heather Ann [date], author.
Title: Blood in the water : the Attica prison uprising of 1971 and its legacy / Heather Ann Thompson.
Description: New York : Pantheon, 2016. Includes index.
Identifiers: LCCN 2016000477. ISBN 9780375423222 (hardback).
ISBN 9781101871324 (ebook).
Subjects: LCSH: Prison riots—New York (State), Attica Prison.
BISAC: HISTORY/United States/20th Century. LAW/Criminal Law/General.
POLITICAL SCIENCE/Political Freedom & Security/Law Enforcement.
Classification: LCC HV9475.N716 T46 2016. DDC 365/.974793—dc23.
LC record available at lccn.loc.gov/2016000477

www.pantheonbooks.com

Endpaper drawing by Robert Bull
Jacket image: Prisoners during the uprising at the Attica Correctional Facility in Attica, New York, on September 9, 1971. AP Photo.
Jacket design by Kelly Blair
Book design by Cassandra J. Pappas

Printed in the United States of America
First Edition
6 8 9 7

For all who were killed at the Attica Correctional Facility
more than four decades ago

---

*William Allen*
*Elliot Barkley*
*John Barnes*
*Edward T. Cunningham*
*John D'Arcangelo*
*Bernard Davis*
*Allen Durham*
*William Fuller*
*Melvin Gray*
*Elmer Hardie*
*Robert Henigan*
*Kenneth Hess*
*Thomas Hicks*
*Emanuel Johnson*
*Herbert Jones*
*Richard Lewis*
*Charles Lundy*
*Kenneth Malloy*
*Gidell Martin*
*William McKinney*
*Lorenzo McNeil*
*Samuel Melville*
*Edward Menefee*
*Jose Mentijo*
*Milton Menyweather*
*John Monteleone*
*Richard Moore*
*Carlos Prescott*
*Michael Privitera*
*William Quinn*
*Raymond (Ramon) Rivera*
*James Robinson*
*Santiago Santos*
*Barry Schwartz*
*Harold Thomas*
*Carl Valone*
*Rafael Vasquez*
*Melvin Ware*
*Elon Werner*
*Ronald Werner*
*Willie West*
*Harrison Whalen*
*Alfred Williams*

---

And for all who were wounded, maimed, tortured, and scarred
on September 13, 1971. A list too long to recount here.

"You have read in the paper all these years of the My Lai Massacre. That was only 170-odd men. We are going to end up with 1500 men here, if things don't go right, at least 1500."

—ATTICA CORRECTION OFFICER EDWARD CUNNINGHAM

"The officer pulled out a Phillips screwdriver and told the naked inmate to get on his feet or he'd stab the screwdriver into his rectum. . . . Then he just started stabbing him."

—NATIONAL GUARDSMAN JAMES O'DAY

"You just wake up in the night sweating. It was just so overpowering, to see that much trauma."

—NEW YORK STATE TROOPER THOMAS CONSTANTINE

"I could see all this blood just running out of the mud and water. That's all I could see."

—ATTICA PRISONER JAMES LEE ASBURY

# *Contents*

# *Introduction*

## State Secrets

One might well wonder why it has taken forty-five years for a comprehensive history of the Attica prison uprising of 1971 to be written. The answer is simple: the most important details of this story have been deliberately kept from the public. Literally thousands of boxes of documents relating to these events are sealed or next to impossible to access.

Some of these materials, such as scores of boxes related to the McKay Commission inquiry into Attica, were deemed off limits four decades ago—in this case at the request of the commission members who feared that state prosecutors would try to use the information to make cases against prisoners in a court of law. Other materials related to the Attica uprising, such as the last two volumes of the Meyer Report of 1976, were also sealed back in the 1970s. Members of law enforcement fought hard to prevent disclosure of this report in particular. Although a judge has recently ruled that these volumes can now be released to the public, the redaction process that they first will undergo means that crucial parts of Attica's history will almost certainly remain hidden.[1]

The vast majority of Attica's records, however, are not sealed, and yet they might as well be. Federal agencies such as the FBI and the Justice Department have important Attica files, for example, but when one requests them via the Freedom of Information Act (FOIA), they have been rendered nearly unreadable from all of the redactions. And then there are the records held by the state of New York itself—countless boxes housed in various upstate warehouses that came from numerous sources: the state's official investigation into whether criminal acts had been committed at Attica during the rebellion, its five years of prosecuting such alleged crimes, and its nearly three decades of defending itself against civil actions filed by prisoners and hostages. In 2006 I was able to get an index of these files, which made clear that this is a treasure trove of Attica documentation: autopsies, ballistics reports, trooper statements, depositions, and more. It constitutes ground zero of the Attica story.[2]

Everything that the state holds in these warehouses can also be requested via FOIA, but here as well it is difficult to get documents released. As this book goes to press, and after waiting since 2013 for some explanation of whether my latest FOIA request would net me important documents, I just received word that state officials will not be giving me those materials. I know the items that I requested are there, according to the state's own inventory, and I also know that I did not ask for any grand jury materials that would be protected, and yet my request is still being denied.

But thanks to so many who lived and litigated the Attica uprising, as well as so many others who took the time to chronicle or to collect parts of this history in newspapers, in memoirs, and in archives outside the control of the state of New York, I was still able to rescue and recount the story of Attica.

And, because of two extraordinarily lucky breaks I had while I was trying to write this book, the history you are about to read is one that state officials very much hoped would not be told.

First, in 2006 I stumbled upon a cache of Attica documents at the Erie County courthouse in Buffalo, New York, that changed everything. I had, for two years, been calling and writing every county courthouse and coroner's office and municipal building in upstate New York in order to find any Attica-related records that had not been placed under lock and key by the Office of the Attorney General or sealed by a judge. I had little to go on in these early years—I didn't have case numbers to search, I knew few names to inquire about. But one day I hit pay dirt. I was on the phone with a woman from the Erie County courthouse who thought that a bunch of Attica papers had recently been placed in the back room there. They had been somewhere else, but had been moved to the Office of the Clerk, perhaps after suffering some water damage. I headed to Buffalo.

When I walked into that dim file room at the courthouse I was taken aback. In front of me, in complete disarray on floor-to-ceiling metal shelves, were literally thousands of pages of Attica documents. In this mess was everything from grand jury testimony, to depositions and indictments, to memos and personal letters. Most stunningly, though, I found in this mountain of moldy papers vital information from the very heart of the state's own investigation into whether crimes had been committed during the rebellion or the retaking of the prison. In short, I had found a great deal of what the state knew, and when it knew it—not the least of which was what evidence it thought it had against members of law enforcement who were never indicted. I took as many notes as I could take, and Xeroxed as many pages as they would let me, and, finally, had much of what I needed to write a history of Attica that no one yet knew.

Then, in 2011, I had another incredibly lucky break. I had just published an op-ed in *The New York Times* on the occasion of Attica's fortieth anniversary when I received an email from Craig Williams, an archivist at the New York State Museum who wanted help making sense of a new trove of materials he had received from the New York State Police.[3] Troopers had just turned over an entire Quonset hut full of items they had gathered from the prison yards of Attica immediately after the four-day standoff there in 1971—items that the state considered evidence in the cases that it might make against prisoners or troopers. I was thrilled to hear this, and soon headed to Albany.

When I got to the museum's cavernous warehouse, I was glad to be joined by Christine Christopher, a filmmaker making a documentary on Attica with whom I had been working closely. Together we just stood for a while, staring at rows and rows of cartons, boxes, bags, and crates of materials that had been removed from the prison forty years before. And what had been gathered and hidden away for those many decades turned out to be grim indeed. In one particularly mangled container lay a heap of clothing—the dirty, rumpled pants and shirt of a slain correction officer, Carl Valone. His clothing wasn't soiled merely with decades-old mud from Attica's D Yard. It was stiff and stained with blood. I had met two of Carl Valone's kids who were still desperate for answers regarding what, exactly, had happened to their father on September 13, 1971.

And this was just one box. Next to it sat another in which I found the now rigid, blood-soaked clothing of Attica prisoner Elliot "L. D." Barkley. Like Carl Valone, L. D. Barkley had been gunned down during Attica's retaking. I had met one of his family members too—L.D.'s younger sister, Traycee. She, like every one of the Valone kids, was also still haunted by Attica.

Although the detritus of Attica that the NYSP had saved in these many boxes revealed little new about why this event played out as it did, it was a harrowing reminder of its human toll. There was a dog-eared red spiral

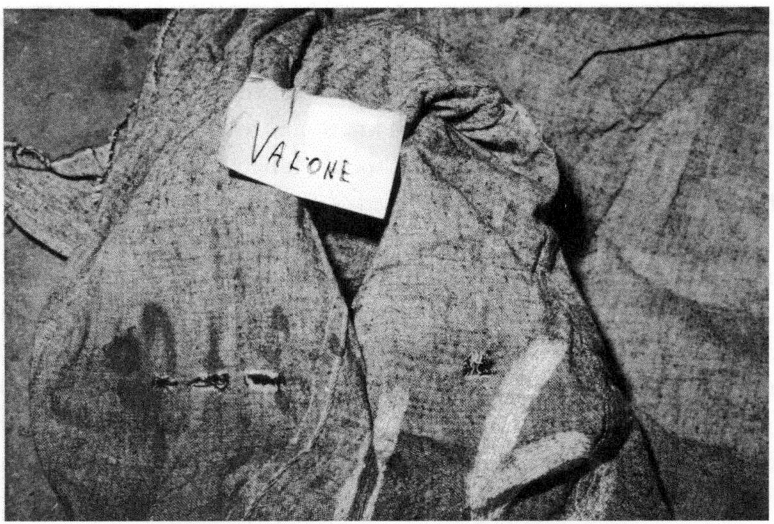


Carl Valone's clothing *(undated, from the Elizabeth Fink Papers)*

notebook filled with messages written by the prisoners who had survived the retaking, men who had hoped these pages could somehow be smuggled out so that their families and friends might know that they were still alive. There were also cartons of torn and faded photographs of prisoners' loved ones, countless legal proceedings that the prisoners had painstakingly copied, and even their Bibles and Qurans—all of which had been ripped out of cells in the aftermath of the rebellion.

All of the Attica files that I saw in that dark room of the Erie County courthouse have now vanished, and all of the Attica artifacts that the New York State Museum had been willing to share have also been removed from anyone's view.[4] But all that I learned from those documents back in 2006 can't be unlearned, and all of the boxes of bloody Attica clothes and heartbreaking letters written by Attica's prisoners that I saw back in 2011 can't be unseen.

And I have decided to include all that I have learned and seen in this book.

That said, this decision was agonizing. Although my job as a historian is to write the past as it was, not as I wished it had been, I have no desire to cause anyone pain in the present. I am well aware, and it haunts me, that my decision to name individuals who have spent the last forty-five years trying to remain unnamed will reopen many old wounds and cause much new suffering. That old wounds were never allowed to heal, and that new suffering is now a certainty, however, is, I believe, the responsibility of officials in the state of New York. It is these officials who have chosen repeatedly, since 1971, to protect the politicians and members of law enforcement who caused so much trauma. It is these officials who could have, and should have, told the whole truth about Attica long ago so that the healing could have begun and Attica's history would have been just that: history, not present-day politics and pain.

Of course, even this book can't promise Attica's survivors the full story. The state of New York still sits on many secrets. This book does vow, however, to recount all that I was able to uncover, and by doing that, at least, perhaps a bit more justice will be done.

# PART I

# The Tinderbox

# FRANK "BIG BLACK" SMITH

*Frank "Big Black" Smith wondered if he would ever get used to being locked up. His cell felt like a casket with the lid left off just far enough for noise, bugs, and weather to get in, and conditions outside of that cage were also grim. Green Haven Correctional Facility was no place for human beings to live.*

*Frank Smith had been born in Bennettsville, South Carolina, on September 11, 1933, to Henry Parker and Millie Smith. Millie spent long days laboring in the same fields that her family members had been forced to work under slavery. As her son grew older, however, Millie became determined to leave the South to forge a better life. When Frank was five years old she and Henry finally found the courage to move to Brooklyn. However, jobs were hard to find and poorly paid in this vast Northern city, and the family struggled there as well. Frank's father eventually turned to gambling and other street hustles to make ends meet, and by the time Frank was a teenager, he like his father had mastered the art of running numbers on the streets of Bedford-Stuyvesant. In 1969, and not for the first time, his luck ran out. That was the year he discovered that the problem with running games was that eventually someone owes money that they can't, or won't, pay. When Frank burst into a dice game with a loaded gun and took money that he felt he was owed, the next thing he knew he was bunking behind cement walls in one of the most rural parts of New York State.*

*The other prisoners at Green Haven tended to leave Frank Smith alone. Smith was a huge, thick-necked man with closely cropped hair and a deep booming voice. He was not political, so the Black Panthers, the various Muslim organizations, the antiwar rebels, and the Maoists in the prison had little use for him. Big Black, as he was known by all there, wasn't particularly religious, either, so the various Christian cliques also kept their distance. Big Black was just a man doing his time. His goals were simple: keep a low profile, tick off the days, and get back to Brooklyn.*

*In 1970 Big Black found himself transferred to Attica Correctional Facility, where he spent his days pulling smelly, soiled garments out of the massive rolling carts that crowded its steamy laundry room. All around him that summer and into the fall, Attica's prisoners were buzzing with the news that there had been a series of dramatic rebellions in New York City's jails. From the notorious facility known as the Tombs to the Queens House of Detention, thousands of prisoners had been taking over their facilities and demanding major reforms. Teams of sympathetic observers were sent to negotiate with them, which included two U.S. representatives from New York, Shirley Chisholm and Herman Badillo, and the mayor of New York City himself, John Lindsay. Some of these rebellions ended quietly after intensive discussions. Others ended when guards retook the prison with their nightsticks. There were no fatalities. Afterward, city officials decided that the quickest way to deal with one of the most obvious prisoner complaints—severe overcrowding—was to send as many men as possible to upstate facilities. In other words, to push the problem up the line rather than solve it. Rumor had it that many of these men were being sent to Attica. As Big Black sorted through the piles of dirty shirts and sheets before him—sent over from Superintendent Vincent Mancusi's mansion—he wondered wearily just how much more crowded Attica could get before it too would blow.*

## 1

# Not So Greener Pastures

If a man had lived his whole life in Brooklyn or the Bronx, the journey to Attica was profoundly disorienting. Within an hour of boarding one of the Department of Correctional Services' many vans ferrying newly sentenced prisoners upstate, all he could see out of the scratched-up bulletproof window was miles and miles of cows, barns, and land.

After getting off the highway in Batavia, the vans headed down the two-lane road connecting this small town to the even smaller village of Attica. Here the faces were all white. Here the men drove pickup trucks rather than pushed their way through subway turnstiles. Here the landscape consisted of rolling hills, not bodegas and burned-out buildings. The sign welcoming visitors to Attica, New York, boasted a population of less than three thousand—fewer people than lived in many of the urban neighborhoods that Attica's prisoners called home.

Attica, New York, was a part of America that for most of these prisoners existed only on TV. The town's tiny storefronts were quaint. It had a pretty park, complete with a gaily adorned bandstand, a Little League pitcher's mound, and a sparkling public pool, all straight out of a Norman Rockwell painting. Yet just beyond this slice of Americana loomed a massive and most forbidding fortress, one of New York's most notorious maximum security prisons.

Less than a mile from the village was the Attica Correctional Facility, enclosed by massive gray walls. Each thirty-foot slab was cemented twelve feet deep into the ground and on each corner perched a gun tower from which guards could scan the fifty-five-acre penal complex for any trouble. From the parking lot, newly arriving prisoners could make out the shapes

Approaching the Attica prison *(Courtesy of the* Democrat and Chronicle*)*

of the men who paced within those red-tiled towers, ready to fire either into or outside the prison in the blink of an eye.

The contrast between this colossal and intimidating facility and its bucolic environs was something to behold. As men were delivered to Attica's front entrance, and just before they were ushered through its massive doors, most could not help but steal one final glance back across the road. Even as guards yelled at them to get inside, it was hard not to be lulled by the rhythmic hum of a million crickets echoing from the tall grasses of the neighboring wildflower-sprinkled pasture.

Entering this high security prison was another jolt. The building was archaic, hardly modernized since it first opened during the Great Depression. And it was crowded with bodies—jam-packed with anxious and angry men, young and old, from cities and small towns all across the state of New York. Attica's 2,243 prisoners were overwhelmingly young, urban, under-educated, and African American or Puerto Rican.[1] More than two thirds of the men at Attica had been incarcerated at least once before arriving there.

That is not to say, though, that Attica's men were all hardened criminals. Many had been sent to Attica simply because they had violated parole, including some who were much too young to navigate life in a maximum security prison. James and John Schleich were nineteen-year-old twins who had landed in Attica for parole violations. John's original conviction had been for the "unauthorized use of a motor vehicle" and his brother James had come before the court for "cutting a hole in a lady's convertible top." Even though he had "bought the lady a new top," he still got time.[2] Another young Attica prisoner, twenty-one-year-old Elliot "L. D." Barkley, had been sent to Attica for violating his parole by driving without a license.

Increasingly younger men also had been landing in Attica because of their drug addiction. One seventeen-year-old Puerto Rican kid, Angel Martinez, had become an addict after shooting heroin to try to alleviate the pain of polio. When he then committed a crime to feed his habit, the judge sent him to Attica.[3] Ending up in this particular New York state prison was especially rough on prisoners like Martinez since they could neither speak nor understand English. There was one Spanish-speaking Puerto Rican correction officer on staff, but his fellow officers insisted that he only use English with the men in his charge.[4]

Whatever brought someone to Attica, once there his routine varied little. After passing through the entrance in the massive concrete facade, officers would assign each prisoner to a housing block. Attica had five main housing blocks: A, B, C, D, and E. There was also Housing Block Z, an area of the prison known as HBZ, or "the Box," where officers placed men for disciplinary reasons. Each of the five main housing blocks held five hundred prisoners. Each block had its own exercise yard, and each was divided into twelve different groups of forty to forty-five men known as "companies." All of the cell blocks save E were three stories high and divided into two wings. The cells in these wings looked in 1970 just as they had when the prison was built in the 1930s, except that by 1970 the bars had become thick with rust and layers of peeling paint.

Even though Attica's cell blocks were equally uninviting, which one was assigned to could make a big difference. For one thing, the cells in some blocks had bars, while others were enclosed by steel doors with small viewing slots. The former offered little privacy but the latter were claustrophobic. While some of Attica's cell blocks had little to no heat and the wind howled through the cement walls, others were so hot one could barely breathe. Where one bunked also determined where one worked.

Attica's most menial and hardest jobs, such as shoveling the endless piles of snow in the harsh winter months, were done by the so-called grading companies. The best jobs were those in the commissary, the laundry,

Cells at Attica *(Courtesy of the* Democrat and Chronicle*)*

and the hospital. Being a clerk or a messenger in the administration building was also considered a step up. No matter what the job, few of Attica's prisoners earned more than 6 cents a day in 1970. The lucky ones were paid $2.90 for a full day's work, which was still much less than a man needed to survive at this facility.

The men needed money at Attica because the state offered them only a few items gratis. These included a thin gray coat, two gray work shirts, three pairs of gray pants, one pair of shoes, three pairs of underwear, six pairs of socks, and one comb. Then, every month, prisoners would receive one bar of soap and one roll of toilet paper, which meant that men were forced to limit themselves "to one sheet per day."[5] The state's food budget allotment was also meager. At a mere 63 cents per prisoner per day, it was insufficient to meet the minimum dietary standards as determined by federal guidelines.[6] The reality was that many men at Attica went to bed hungry.[7] For this reason jobs in the kitchen or the mess hall, while more arduous than others given their seven-day-a-week schedule, were some of the most coveted. At least on those jobs a man could eat leftovers.

To get anything beyond the supplies given them—warmer clothes, more food, toiletries like toothbrushes, toothpaste, deodorant, shampoo, razors, and extra toilet paper—prisoners needed money.[8] Being able to buy deodorant was no luxury since these men were allowed only one shower a week and were given only two quarts of water a day. With this water prisoners were expected to wash their socks and underwear, shave, brush their teeth, and clean the cell to a correction officer's exacting standards.[9]

Attica's men could rarely rely on their families to send funds to meet their basic needs because they too were usually impoverished. Nearly half of Attica's prisoners came from the New York City area. To visit them, it would cost family members $33.55 for a bus ticket to Batavia, the city nearest to Attica with a depot. Since there was no public transportation to and from that bus depot, they would also need cab fare. For loved ones who did manage to come up with the more than $100 of travel expenses and twenty hours of time away from a job required to visit the prison, there was rarely money left over to buy food for themselves, let alone assist the relative they had come to see.[10]

The constant hustling for adequate supplies took its toll on prisoners' morale and went a long way toward escalating tensions at the facility. Attica's men spent fifteen to twenty-four hours of every day in their cells. They were bored, frustrated, and on edge. Crammed into each tiny cell was a bed, a toilet, and a basin, which left barely enough room for a man to move around. Most of the men were allowed thirty-one to one hundred minutes a day in one of the prison's four exercise yards to run or stretch their muscles. Unfortunately, many months of the year, the temperature was well below freezing, so even a break from one's cell could be most uncomfortable.[11]

One benefit of being inside the cell, even if oppressive, might have been the opportunity to read or listen to the radio. And, yet, Attica had no newspapers, very few books to share, and nothing at all to read in Spanish. Attica did subscribe to a few magazines, including such unlikely selections as *Outdoor Life, Field and Stream, American Home,* and *House Beautiful.*[12] If a prisoner wanted anything else to read, he had to have it sent to him from the outside. And even then he might not actually receive the publication since administrators confiscated a great many books and newspapers they considered inappropriate. As for listening to the radio, the prison piped in only three static-ridden stations, which all stopped broadcasting at 11:00 p.m. Since the men were forbidden from talking in their cells after 8:00 p.m., evenings passed very slowly.[13]

There were scores of rules governing the daily behavior of Attica's prisoners that were, on the whole, petty and thus netted men frequent punishment. Breaking rules usually resulted in a man facing "keeplock"—a slang term for being confined to his cell, twenty-four hours a day, for an indefinite number of days. Often this sanction was imposed for trivial violations, such as talking on the way to the mess hall. Yet the "no talking" rule that was supposed to be in effect when a company walked from one part of the prison to another was enforced by some guards and ignored by others.

Many of Attica's prisoners coped with their living conditions creatively. In order to heat water to make hot drinks and thus ward off the chill, for example, they devised their own electrical units called "droppers." They would take two razor blades, put matchsticks between them, and wrap them in thread or string. By using paper clips to hook a piece of lamp cord to this contraption, and then placing the entire mechanism into water, they could generate heat via electrolysis. Even though the prison administration had deemed these heaters contraband, and being caught with one could land a man in serious trouble, nearly every cell had one, and for the most part they were tolerated. The bottom line, according to one outsider who later interviewed over 1,600 of Attica's prisoners, was that almost all of the men at Attica, "including the acclimated ones," were deeply "frustrated by the inconsistencies."[14] The fact that keeplock was used to force their labor also generated anger. When teenager Angel Martinez begged off work for two days because he was in intense pain from his polio, guards confined him to his cramped cell for a full month.[15]

The men at Attica worried a great deal about remaining as healthy as possible while serving their time, not only because they had to work even when ill. This vast facility had just two doctors: Selden T. Williams and Paul G. Sternberg. The pair came to Attica between 8:00 and 8:30 every morning to address the medical needs of the 100 to 125 prisoners who showed up for "sick call" each day. Dr. Williams had worked at Attica since 1949, Dr. Sternberg since 1957. These physicians usually required prisoners to describe their problems through a mesh screen and rarely gave them a physical examination. Most men were sent away with an aspirin. For prisoners with chronic health issues, like Big Black Smith, who had serious dental problems, this meant that initially minor issues often grew acute. During his few years at Attica, Big Black lost almost all of his teeth because Attica's doctors had refused to give him a referral to a dentist.[16]

Dr. Williams and Dr. Sternberg were particularly unresponsive to the medical needs of Attica's Puerto Rican population. Neither of them spoke Spanish, and neither ever asked correction officials for interpreters. The only way Angel Martinez was able to communicate to the doctors the intense pain in his legs was to roll his pants up to show them the swelling. Even so, they did nothing to help him.[17] These doctors did even less for the men who had been placed in Housing Block Z. One man in this segregated unit had broken bones in his hand and was in such pain that he couldn't move his fingers. When he begged Dr. Sternberg to help him, Sternberg turned his back and told him to write a letter to a different doctor.[18]

Attica's doctors were so regularly unresponsive to the medical needs of the prisoners that at one point in 1969, the civilian staff of E Block actually tried to take action. That year a thirty-year-old E block prisoner had died under Dr. Williams's care, and the staff decided to have a meeting to discuss holding the doctor accountable. They debated a couple of options, including picketing the doctor's private practice, writing the newspaper with details of the prisoner's death, and writing to a congressman and/or having prisoners write their congressmen. Another wanted to go much further and bring Dr. Williams before the district attorney of the county to have him charged with malpractice.[19] But in the end, nothing came of these plans, and Dr. Williams changed nothing about the way he dealt with the prisoners in his care.

From time to time prisoners' family members tried to intervene to get better medical care for their loved ones. One woman was so distressed by her son's lack of needed treatment at Attica that she enlisted the aid of one of the leaders of FIGHT, a community organization in Rochester. This minister in turn wrote to the deputy commissioner at the Department of Correctional Services (DOCS) to let him know that "unless the situation is taken care of by your staff, we will be forced to send our own doctors in to examine [the prisoner]."[20] Rather than investigate the situation, however, this prison official took umbrage and merely responded, "There is nothing in any law giving you permission to send doctors in to examine any prisoner."[21]

Although prison officials weren't eager to press Attica's doctors to provide prisoners better care, they were willing to allow medical experimentation on them. One physician, employed by both Rochester and Strong Memorial hospitals, conducted "studies of the immune response system to a viral infection" at Attica.[22] The doctor knew that he needed volunteers for his ongoing research, but finding a stable population of volunteers was "not easy," therefore he was most grateful when he got permission to use Attica's men.[23] Because becoming a test subject offered the men in Attica some needed money, more than a few agreed to be exposed to the test virus.[24] Although the doctor made sure that prisoners signed an informed consent agreement, as he later conceded, one "could argue about how informed they were."[25]

The overwhelming disregard for the health of the men in Attica certainly eroded their morale, but so did other things about the way the state's correctional system operated, such as the workings of the parole process. Being allowed to leave Attica early on parole was of course the dream of every prisoner, but the way in which a man might earn parole was shrouded in mystery. Once a month the parole board came to Attica, but it was never clear why some men qualified for early release and others didn't. As one prisoner noted, "It's so arbitrary."[26]

Even for those who did somehow make parole, their elation was usually short lived since they could not actually leave Attica until they secured a job on the outside. To make this happen, the men were handed a long-outdated phone book so that they could find the addresses of businesses they might contact in order to secure employment. Because many of the prisoners could barely write, and all had to pay for both paper and postage, trying to find a job in this manner proved extremely difficult. Prisoners were known to save their money and to write as many as two or three hundred letters, and stay imprisoned long past parole was awarded, before any response was received.[27] So capricious was Attica's parole process that even correction officers recognized the problem. Having prisoners face repeated disappointments and feel cheated out of earned time off made their own jobs much harder.[28]

Prison life was also made unnecessarily tense because administrators routinely cut corners. A number of correction officers thought that prisoners should be offered more vocational and educational training opportunities instead of just being warehoused, but the DOCS always cited its severe budgetary constraints as barriers.[29] Administrators also failed to provide the prisoners sufficient food because they were told to watch the bottom line. As one correction officer put it frustratedly, "if you can spend an extra dollar on feeding, it would solve a lot of our problems."[30] But according to state officials, even for obvious necessities, money was in short supply. Only 6.19 percent of Attica's operating budget was allotted to food, 0.69 percent to medical supplies, 1.6 percent to academic and vocational training, and 1.65 percent for clothing.[31]

Though resources were limited for all of the prisoners, it was obvious that some of them suffered worse hardships than others because of the highly discriminatory way that prison officials ran the institution. While everyone at Attica had to work and run various cons to supplement his basic supplies, African Americans and Puerto Ricans had to hustle a great deal more because their work usually paid much less. Even though only 37 percent of the prisoner population was white, whites held 74 percent of the jobs in Attica's power house, 67 percent of the coveted clerk positions, and

62 percent of the staff jobs in the officers' mess hall. By contrast, 76 percent of the men in the dreaded and low-paid metal shop, and 80 percent in the grueling grading companies, were African American or Puerto Rican.[32] Even when whites worked the worst jobs, it was common for them to start off at a higher pay rate.[33]

Sometimes racial discrimination operated in ways that hit the men at Attica particularly personally. For instance, although all prisoners were, theoretically, subject to mail censorship, in practical terms it was disproportionately the black and Puerto Rican inmates who suffered most from the policy. Every month an administrative committee would review which publications should be censored, but overwhelmingly it was the titles requested by the prisoners of color that made it onto the prohibited list. Whether it was a black community newspaper such as the *Amsterdam News* or the *Buffalo Challenger,* or a religious publication such as *The Messenger* or *Muhammad Speaks,* rarely would the reading materials requested by nonwhite prisoners make it past the mail room.[34] For reasons they never had to justify, prison officials considered these materials too dangerous to allow. As one lawyer for the DOCS put it, the rules for "the Black Muslims" were "in general the same as those applied to other religious sects except that you should exercise greater caution and vigil with this group."[35] Meanwhile, any letter written in Spanish, or any Spanish-language publication, did not even have to be considered inflammatory to be confiscated. If something was not in English, it was thrown out.

Puerto Rican and African American prisoners were subject to far more stringent rules when it came to family visitation as well. Twenty-six point six percent of all Puerto Ricans and 20.4 percent of all blacks at Attica were in common-law relationships, but prison policy was clear that no common-law wives or children from those unions were allowed to visit.[36] Even letters between common-law partners were confiscated. In one such letter a prisoner wrote to the mother of his child and told her how she might try to reach him while he was incarcerated at Attica. "Darling, I know you'll be surprised to get this, so please read it carefully several times. I had it smuggled out. . . . When you write, make sure that you don't make a mistake and write your name."[37] In case her letters still didn't get through, he went on, "I listen to WMYR, Rochester, from 6:30 to 7:30 in the evening after supper. You call in and he will give requests. I will be able to hear your voice on the earphones. Ask him to play 'I'm so afraid of losing you' and say hi to me. I will start listening as soon as I mail this."[38] So obvious was the racial discrimination at Attica that white prisoners readily agreed that guards applied rules differently to blacks and Puerto Ricans.[39]

While such discrimination did its part to escalate tensions at Attica, so too did the deepening problem of overcrowding that increased stress for prisoners and correction officers alike.[40] As Attica grew ever more crowded during the late 1960s, rather than hire more officers, prison management instead decided to put existing employees in charge of ever greater numbers of prisoners. Officer John Stockholm couldn't believe when he came to Attica in 1971 and realized he was "in charge of approximately 60 to 70 inmates at one time . . . sometimes we would take up to 120 inmates to breakfast."[41] The fact that prison administrators expected a single officer to accompany two or even three companies of men to the mess hall, to their jobs, and to the exercise yards several times a day, completely on their own and with only a nightstick at their side, generated enormous anxiety for those guards and made prisoners fearful as well.[42]

The truth was that the only thing that kept the prison running smoothly under these circumstances was that the prisoners usually followed the rules and did what the officer in charge asked them to do. But as the number of men at Attica grew, order and calm were harder to come by. Significantly, the profile of the average prisoner coming to Attica had changed. Many more prisoners were young, politically aware, and determined to speak out when they saw injustices in the facility. These were black and brown youth who had been deeply impacted by the civil rights struggles of this period as well as by the writings of Malcolm X, Mao, and Che Guevara. These younger men made it clear that they were more willing to stand up for themselves—less likely to put up with poor treatment than were Attica's veterans. Correction officers found this new type of prisoner alarming and their fear and suspicion of these more outspoken men further exacerbated tensions. Time and again Attica's COs, believing they had to start coming down harder on these younger, more militant prisoners, resorted to the very intimidation, verbal abuse, and petty rule enforcement that virtually guaranteed a militant prisoner response.[43] These increased "expressions of solidarity and inmate militancy" in turn made Attica's correction officers even more aggressive.[44] While most officers knew deep down that their own safety depended on making sure that prisoners felt, as one put it, "a sense of respect and a feeling that all the legitimate grievances . . . are being attended to," many COs were too bitter, angry, and even frightened to put those principles into practice.[45]

The truth was that most of the correction officers at Attica had little familiarity with African Americans or Puerto Ricans and little connection to the cities where these prisoners had grown up. The officers were from small towns across western New York—overwhelmingly white, Catholic villages like Attica where high school graduates had few job prospects save a career in corrections. In 1970 Attica prison employed 398 locals ranging in age from twenty-two to sixty. A young man starting out as a CO earned between $8,500 and $9,600 per year, and after fifteen years on the job he was still making under $12,000.[46] Many officers had to work two jobs to make ends meet, and thus were always bone tired in addition to being on edge.[47] Perhaps most significantly, these men had received virtually no training for their jobs at the prison.[48] When new hires first reported for duty they were handed a stick, a badge, and a uniform, and then put in charge of a company of forty or so prisoners. With only nineteen supervisors, the nearly four hundred men who made up the CO staff were left mainly to their own devices to figure out how to deal with the ever-growing number of prisoners.

The lack of training and direction from the prison administration frustrated and angered the COs a great deal. They blamed their superiors for the fact that they were working in an increasingly dangerous and hostile workplace. COs began demanding that their union, Council 82 AFSCME (American Federation of State, County and Municipal Employees), negotiate more pay for their work as well as more hires to walk the cell blocks so that they would be safer.

Yet even in the wake of the uprisings in the New York City jails in the summer and fall of 1970, Attica's administrators and the prison officials in Albany did virtually nothing to address either the COs' or the prisoners' concerns.[49] If anything, administrators at Attica had begun to clamp down even more on the men in their charge, and to turn an even deafer ear to the complaints of their COs, as the year 1970 wore on. In no small part this was because Attica's prisoners had initiated their own very bold protest to improve conditions even before the New York City jails had erupted.

On July 29, 1970, prisoners working in Attica's hated metal shop had sat down and refused to work until someone raised their wages, which, they insisted, were "so low that working at Attica is tantamount to slavery."[50] These men had been making between 6 cents and 29 cents per day, but prison officials were then keeping back half of that pay until the men were released, which meant that they had too little each week to buy necessities at the exorbitant commissary prices.

The men locked up at Attica had long been sensitive about the exploitation of their labor; particularly once one of them, a white prisoner named Sam Melville, did some research into the economics of the metal shop, the commissary, and the prison laundry and then wrote a mini-treatise, "Anatomy of the Laundry." By mid-1970 copies of his short exposé could be found in many an Attica cell.[51] Had the men also known that Attica netted the state of New York almost $1.2 million in sales off of their labor between 1969 and 1970 they might well have been even more outraged than they already were.[52]

The July 1970 protest started out quietly. The prisoners sent a small delegation of men to meet with their supervisor. However, this effort at peaceful negotiation failed. Superintendent Vincent Mancusi had the members of the delegation put into keeplock, and then arranged for other men he suspected of stirring up trouble to be transferred out of Attica altogether.

Mancusi's actions so enraged the metal shop workers that they called for a full-scale strike. At first it was only B Block prisoners who refused to work, because it was men from their block who had been keeplocked. But when Mancusi locked down that entire cell block for striking, the next day almost all 450 of the men in the metal shop refused to work. Flustered, Mancusi called the commissioner of correction, Paul McGinnis, to make sure he knew of this prisoner recalcitrance. Rather uncharacteristically, Commissioner McGinnis decided not to further punish the strikers, and

The prison metal shop *(Courtesy of the* Democrat and Chronicle*)*

instead agreed to talk with them once they had elected two representatives to present their position. Thanks to those discussions, those who were making 6 cents in Attica's metal shop got a raise to 25, and the maximum allowable hourly rate went from 29 cents to $1 per day.[53]

But the metal shop strike of 1970 proved a pyrrhic victory. Even though the metal shop workers had protested peacefully, and had assured COs when they began that they intended no harm and "merely wanted to demonstrate the extent of their grievances," Superintendent Mancusi was determined to make them pay for their actions. In the wake of this rebellion, once Commissioner McGinnis had returned to Albany, Mancusi suddenly transferred a number of the strikers whom he had previously keeplocked over to the dreaded Housing Block Z.[54]

Mancusi viewed prisoner activism as the work of black militant troublemakers who needed to be watched with particular care and shut up the instant they spoke out.[55] His perspective mirrored that of an increasing number of state and national politicians by the year 1970. It was past time, they believed, to get tough on anyone who bucked authority, and even tougher on anyone who had broken a law.

# 2

# Responding to Resistance

In the early 1960s, Northern cities including Philadelphia, Rochester, and New York, were the sites of particularly intense urban rebellions against seemingly intractable discrimination and the lack of jobs, as well as against the abusive actions of law enforcement.[1] Although Northern politicians had been relatively sympathetic when such racial uprisings rocked Southern cities like Birmingham, Alabama, when they witnessed upheaval in their own downtowns they were greatly unnerved. Northern politicians very quickly began responding to the unrest and anger they saw on their city streets just as their Southern counterparts had: they sought to discredit these protests as the behavior of a criminal element bent on destruction. By 1965, politicians from both North and South, and from both major political parties, were routinely equating urban disorder with urban criminality. All agreed not only that crime was fast becoming the nation's most serious problem, but also that it was well past time to wage a major new war against it.

Although the election of Richard Nixon in 1968 is commonly assumed to have signaled the beginning of America's "law and order" moment, the dramatic shift in focus from liberalization and reform in the first half of the 1960s to maintaining civic order and fighting crime had actually first begun during the administration of Lyndon Johnson.[2] With the same enthusiasm that led him to authorize the Office of Economic Opportunity and sign the Civil Rights Act of 1964, President Johnson, a liberal Democrat, created the Office of Law Enforcement Assistance (OLEA) in 1965, not only granting a wholly new level of funding to law enforcement and prisons, but also creating the bureaucracy necessary to wage a historically unprecedented War on Crime. The Law Enforcement Assistance Act of 1965 and the Omnibus Crime Control and Safe Streets Act of 1968 lavished even more federal funds on fighting crime. In addition, landmark Supreme Court decisions such as *Terry v. Ohio*—which gave the police virtually unlimited powers to stop and frisk citizens without probable cause—intensified the policing of poor neighborhoods and people of color, which, in turn, resulted in record arrest rates. Before long, prisons like Attica were bursting at the seams.

This profound shift in public policy—a watershed moment that would eventually lead to the United States imprisoning more people than any other country on the globe—had depended upon a serious misperception regarding just how just dire America's "crime problem" really was. In 1964, when federal and state officials first embraced the more punitive laws and more aggressive policing, the nation's crime rate was historically unremarkable. Indeed, the national murder rate was only 5.1 per 100,000 when Johnson created OLEA, whereas in 1921 it had been 8.1 and in 1933 was 9.7.[3]

As the 1960s wore on, governors and mayors, from conservative Republicans to liberal Democrats, committed themselves to waging a major War on Crime in America's most fragile communities. However, just because support for America's new War on Crime was bipartisan didn't mean its origins weren't politically complex. This was perhaps most or particularly true for Nelson Aldrich Rockefeller, New York's governor since 1959, when he decided to get tougher on crime. Rockefeller had been a lifelong Republican, but he had routinely found himself in the liberal wing of his own party. Historically, this had benefited him mightily. He was, for example, one of the few of his party to survive the Lyndon Johnson landslide of 1964. But Rockefeller had ambitions beyond New York. A savvy politician, he increasingly realized that the liberal reputation that had earned him such a following in New York was fast becoming a liability—especially if he hoped to win his party's nomination for the presidency. Throughout the 1960s he had watched Richard Nixon slowly but surely steal his political thunder across the nation. And so, by the close of the decade, Rockefeller had begun to craft a more conservative and more traditionally Republican image for himself. In 1970, Rockefeller made no bones about the fact that he too would be "tough on crime." This had suddenly become *the* platform that could get a man elected.

However, when Rockefeller put a new commissioner in charge of administering the state's corrections apparatus in 1971, he chose an outspoken reformer named Russell G. Oswald. Oswald had run the parole systems of both Wisconsin and Massachusetts before coming to New York, and he also held a degree in social work. As cochair of the Special Committee on Criminal Offenders, a panel described as having "grown out of the governor's concern about the increase in the crime rate and out of his intention to search for new solutions,"[4] Oswald had been instrumental in pushing for the 1970 legislation that created the New York Department of Correctional Services (DOCS), a new unified department to deal with both those who were incarcerated and those who were on parole.[5] In January of 1971 Rockefeller appointed him its head.

When Oswald took the reins from Paul McGinnis, the commissioner who had helped negotiate the end of the Attica metal shop strike the preceding year, he was determined to lead his DOCS in a bold new direction. Oswald, a squat, portly man who always looked harried and slightly unkempt, came across as kind-hearted. He considered his new job an opportunity to improve the lives of prisoners and parolees. By renaming prisons, jails, and reformatories "correctional facilities," redubbing prison guards as "correction officers," and calling prisoners "inmates," Oswald felt that he was sending a message about his intention to professionalize and humanize prisons.[6] Governor Rockefeller may have viewed Oswald's role as providing "safety and security for the law-abiding citizen," but Oswald himself wanted to make a bigger mark, intending, as he put it, "to move towards nothing less than the marked reduction of men in the traditional prisons" and toward "an atmosphere of community lifestyle even though in a confining situation."[7] As he saw it, one could not expect an individual to "adapt to a normal setting when he is placed for long periods of time in a totally abnormal setting."[8]

Shortly after taking over as commissioner of corrections, Oswald wrote a memo to the governor in which he pushed for reforms as well as the funding to institute them. He made clear that prisoners across the state had been "clamoring for meaningful changes," and that, in his opinion, doing nothing "would lead to uncontrollable frustrations, hostility and anger."[9] Having men locked "twelve or more hours a day in their cells is unacceptable to them and me." He added, however, that "to attempt to bring about change with no new positions and seriously restricted funds is courting big trouble."[10] Oswald was acutely aware that there were a few specific "trouble spots" in New York's prison system—places that were "more potentially explosive" than others—and he insisted that the governor allocate more funds to avert any disaster.[11]

To assist his efforts Oswald had hired a deputy commissioner who seemed to share his views on the need for penal reforms. Walter Dunbar was a pipe-smoking man with horn-rimmed glasses and a long and impressive résumé. He had served on the U.S. Board of Parole as the director of California's Department of Corrections and had been president of the American Correctional Association.[12]

Governor Rockefeller agreed with his new commissioner that prison problems should be dealt with forthrightly and immediately. The prisoner rebellions that had erupted in jails and prisons across New York in the summer and early fall of 1970 had persuaded him that something had to be done, but he tended to believe the answer was to coddle prisoners less. Whereas New York City's mayor, John Lindsay, had been willing to concede that the jail protesters had some legitimate demands and had even agreed eventually to meet with them, Rockefeller, a Cold Warrior to his core, viewed any prisoner agitation as part of a larger leftist plot, just "one more step toward the ultimate destruction of the country."[13]

Still, Rockefeller could see the merit of endorsing some reforms. First and foremost it might undercut support for the prison "revolutionaries" and thus might halt what his former commissioner had termed "an acceleration of the postwar incidence of social deviants and protests."[14] Since at least 1960, Rockefeller had been hearing from his then-Department of Corrections board that some serious reforms were needed—particularly in the "provision of medical care" and with regard to prisoner morale as a result of "incipient overcrowding."[15] Now it seemed more prudent than ever to deal with these concerns.

Rockefeller was glad to have Oswald in charge. He had met few penal professionals with such optimism about tackling correction's myriad problems. But even Oswald's bright outlook began to dim almost immediately after taking the helm. On his predecessor's watch there recently had been a major prisoner rebellion at the Auburn Correctional Facility, one of upstate New York's largest and most troubled prisons. Whereas Oswald had been hoping to work on new programs for prisoners, he was instead forced to deal with the fallout from that uprising.

# 3

# Voices from Auburn

Located thirty miles west of Syracuse, Auburn was another forbidding-looking complex of prison buildings surrounded by imposing walls and anchored by gun towers at its corners. Auburn's historical claim to fame was that it had hosted the country's first execution by electrocution, and in 1970 it was known for being one of New York's most overcrowded facilities. Three months after the metal shop strike at Attica, a group of Auburn prisoners asked their superintendent to let them commemorate "Black Solidarity Day." Just as Attica's prisoners had become more politically aware and active, so had Auburn's. There were various political organizations at Auburn, and two of the most organized of these were the Black Muslims—affiliated with either the Nation of Islam or some off-shoot group—and the Black Panther Party. As one of the leading Black Panthers at Auburn explained the men's desire for a Black Solidarity Day celebration, "You have days for all your white heroes, we want our days."[1] The superintendent told the men to write to Commissioner McGinnis, but the commissioner punted the decision back to Auburn's superintendent. By the time the day arrived, November 2, no decision had been made, so the Black Muslim prisoners grabbed a microphone in the exercise yard and announced that in honor of Black Solidarity Day, "no black man should work today."[2]

Following this announcement, three or four men blocked the doors to the yard so that COs could not enter. For the next six hours much of Auburn's African American workforce remained in the yard listening to speeches instead of showing up for their assigned jobs.[3] Aside from a few minor scuffles as the men were ushered back to their cells for the evening head count, the day's work stoppage had been peaceful and seemed cathartic for the participants. Feeling that things had ended well that day, and also to ward off any possible eruption as prisoners headed inside from the yard, Auburn's correction officers assured them that prisoners would not be punished for their actions. But then Auburn administrators overrode the rank-and-file officers and decided to place fourteen men they identified as leaders of the protest on indefinite keeplock.

This betrayal was like a flame to kindling. The following morning four hundred Auburn prisoners, both black and white, refused to line up to report for work and demanded the release of those in keeplock. Meanwhile others gathered in the main yard to see what prison officials would do. After consulting with correction officials in Albany, Auburn prison administrators refused to meet with these men to discuss their demands. Chaos ensued, and amid the cacophony of shouting, yelling, and smashing glass, groups of men in the yard began arming themselves with makeshift weapons while taking hostage approximately fifty COs and civilian personnel. While the prisoners protected most of these men, some were not so fortunate. In addition to four men being badly beaten up, one was cracked over the head with his own nightstick when he refused to surrender it.[4]

Eventually the prisoners brought all of the hostages to the center of the yard where, to prevent further assaults, the Black Muslims formed a protective circle around them. To keep them warm in the cool November air, other prisoners gave these terrified men blankets. Then, as all of the men began settling in for the night, the prisoners composed a list of demands that included the following twelve items:

1. More Spanish-speaking correction officers and counselors.
2. More black culture courses.
3. Better medical care and treatment.
4. Fire incompetent psychiatric staff.
5. Better quality commissary items and lower prices.
6. Improved parole proceedings.
7. Better clothing; for example, rubbers for wear in the muddy yard.
8. Better food and sanitary conditions.
9. Better "good time" programs.
10. Improved law library.
11. More frequent review by parole board of life sentence prisoners.
12. Protection from reprisals.[5]

After a six-hour standoff, prison officials promised these men that if they surrendered peacefully and released the hostages, they would be able to meet with a correction official to discuss their demands. More important, they gave their word that no prisoners would suffer reprisals. While the former pledge was fulfilled, the latter was not.

Not only were Auburn's prisoners beaten and forced to run gauntlets of angry COs with batons after their surrender, but 120 of these men were then rounded up and taken to Auburn's Special Housing Unit or segregation area, where they would wait indefinitely to learn their fate for having participated in the November uprising. Eventually, six of those men faced criminal indictments. Word that the Auburn protesters had surrendered peacefully but had still been beaten, placed in segregation, and charged with crimes quickly spread throughout the prisoner grapevine.

This history of broken pledges and unresolved disciplinary hearings is what awaited Russell Oswald when he began his new job as commissioner of corrections. As he put it to Rockefeller, regretfully, "It seems that this entire period has been spent working on the problems at the correctional facilities of Auburn."[6] As Oswald also pointed out worriedly to his boss, Auburn's prisoners being held in segregation had managed to get the attention of some lawyers who, in turn, were now initiating "an action" against the DOCS in federal court claiming that the prisoners "were being beaten by correction officers and county deputies (with tree trunks, etc.)."[7]

In addition to filing a lawsuit against the DOCS alleging guard brutality, organizations including the NAACP Legal Defense Fund and the New York City ACLU as well as a number of individual lawyers had banded together and obtained a federal order instructing the Auburn administration to "show cause" as to why it was holding 120 men in segregated housing indefinitely. Two of these attorneys, Lewis Steel and Herman Schwartz, were already representing prisoners who had been charged just months earlier with instigating riots in New York City's jails, and wanted to be sure that men from Auburn were not going to face similarly serious charges without representation. Nor were they going to let prison officials keep more than a hundred other men locked up in segregation forever. These two lawyers would later play important roles at Attica.

Thanks to the myriad legal efforts of men such as Steel and Schwartz, Auburn's brass was forced to release most of the 120 men in segregation back into the general population. These administrators were incensed. As lawyer Herman Schwartz pointed out, "This was one of the first times that the prison had lost a disciplinary matter."[8] It also set Oswald on edge. Not only did he realize that he was up against a determined group of prisoner advocates in his prison system, but he was also dealing with substantial pressure from their allies in the court of public opinion. When an assemblyman from Buffalo, Arthur O. Eve, took an impromptu tour of Auburn's segregated Special Housing Unit and declared that those still being held there (six men the DOCS had decided were the real leaders of the rebellion) were not just receiving inhumane treatment, but were actually "fearful for their lives," a media storm ensued.[9]

Sensing that the situation at Auburn was fast becoming a public relations disaster, Commissioner Oswald assured Governor Rockefeller that he would go to the prison personally to see if things were as bad as Assemblyman Eve had claimed. He would meet with staff, with prisoners in the general population, and with any prisoner remaining in segregation who was willing to talk.[10] Before embarking on this visit, however, Oswald sent a letter to the six still confined to segregation pledging penal improvements, but only if they gave up their "deliberately contrived harassment tactics."[11]

Oswald's hostile reception when he visited Auburn that March seriously tested his earlier view that New York's prisoners had legitimate grievances. Oswald was used to the incarcerated seeing him as the good guy, the one who would help them when others wouldn't. Here at Auburn, however, it was clear that many prisoners despised him and it took him completely aback. In their view Oswald had had the power to stop Auburn administrators from harming them once they had surrendered and also could have kept them from so many months in segregation, but he had done nothing. Rather than try to explain himself to these men, or try to repair his relationship with them, the commissioner instead dismissed them as part of the lunatic fringe. As Oswald reported to Rockefeller, "The so-called 'Auburn 6,' those indicted for their part in the riot, impressed me as being emotionally sick individuals. They yelled and screamed during our discussion, called me a 'racist pig' and much less complimentary things, threw water at me and 'cussed out' all the correctional personnel."[12]

Oswald's personally wounding visit to Auburn had left him increasingly sympathetic to Rockefeller's long-held belief that prisoners had become unreasonably militant. The commissioner still remained hopeful that some of his planned reforms would "ultimately break down the offenders' negative attitude toward institutional personnel."[13] Making sure that Auburn's men were allowed to take daily showers, for example, could be "a real breakthrough" in his view. But Oswald's worry that "the new prison revolutionaries" now posed the greatest threat to the stability of the correction system was beginning to consume him.[14]

Oswald wrote to Republican assemblyman Frank Walkley in May 1971 to explain his concern: "Recent court decisions in favor of offenders, greater leniency on the part of the courts, and an increase in the militancy of the offenders—which goes along with the militant and aggressive attitude of many individuals in our society—has without a doubt, brought about increased disrespect."[15] Prisoners' use of the courts particularly irked him. He hated, for example, that attorney Lewis Steel from the National Lawyers Guild was continuing to tell reporters that guards still felt "free to abuse the prisoners."[16] Oswald also resented, as he put it, the "daily legal harassment [that] continues from the American Civil Liberties Union staff and other legal aid groups." He also felt "deluged" by the huge volume of mail he was receiving from ordinary citizens regarding problems in New York's prisons.[17] In his view he had done his very best "to ensure that procedures regarding: use of force, use of gas, visitation by justices and judges, mailed-visitation privileges in common-law relationships, disturbance control plans and programs" were clarified and adhered to religiously.[18] And yet, as he reported to Rockefeller, "a hard core group" of prisoners seemed bent on disrupting their facility and "failed to respond to all conventional methods of treatment."[19] And to his astonishment, those in segregation at Auburn "continued to demonstrate in their cells, smashed everything they can, throw food, and excrement and obscenities."[20]

Other state officials largely disagreed with Oswald and Rockefeller that the actions of a handful of revolutionary troublemakers could explain the tension and violence in jails and prisons across New York. On May 26, 1971, a special legislative committee comprised of three Republican and two Democratic assemblymen toured Auburn and talked directly to prisoners there to get a sense of what was going on. They subsequently issued a five-page report on prison conditions that confirmed, among other things, that there had been a great deal of prisoner harassment at this facility, as well as evidence of injury. Still the head of DOCS clung to the idea that certain troublemakers behind bars and their lawyers on the outside were causing the most serious problems.

By the summer of 1971, Oswald had so fully adopted the "militant troublemaker" analysis of the problems at Auburn and other prisons in his system that he decided the only way to restore peace in a given facility was to remove the "problem" prisoners. So he closed Auburn's Special Housing

Unit and transferred all the "militant troublemakers" who were still awaiting court dates. The so-called Auburn 6 were sent to Attica. Once they were moved, he ordered that these men stay in segregated housing "until they give evidence of being amenable in other parts of the institution."[21]

In the wake of the transfer of men out of Auburn, Oswald felt that a weight had been lifted off his shoulders. Refreshed and recommitted to his initial reform agenda, the commissioner wrote to Rockefeller, "We must convince all that we do not countenance disinterest in prisoners or brutalizing of any kind by anyone and that we will make opportunities for rehabilitation available." Most important, he went on, "by showing that we care" the image of correction would start "changing for the better."[22]

But the Attica Correctional Facility, already severely overcrowded and now home to the Auburn 6, had seen no positive change. Still facing harsh conditions, capricious rules, and racial discrimination, Attica's men were more frustrated than ever.[23]

# 4

# Knowledge Is Power

In the summer of 1971 Attica's prisoners weren't just frustrated, they were, as prison officials like Oswald worried, becoming much more politically aware. Not only had these men been developing a powerful critique of poor prison conditions, but they also had begun to discuss how they might reform their institution—what they might do, concretely, to get the state to treat them as human beings who were serving their time, not as monsters deserving of abuse and neglect.

One key reform that the incarcerated had already managed to secure in this period was in the area of education. Although they were not granted eligibility for Pell Grants until 1972, by the late 1960s prisoners were taking a variety of courses in penal facilities across the country. By 1970 Attica had hired quite a few teachers, including several reading instructors, one who taught math, and a few who offered courses in history and sociology. Officially hired to help men get their high school equivalency, these instructors were instrumental in inspiring Attica's incarcerated to see the world both within and outside of Attica's walls as inexorably linked.[1]

During one English course offered at Attica in the summer of 1971, two "outspoken streetwise thinkers," Kenny Malloy and Tommy Hicks, were particularly vocal about "their feelings about race, economics, politics and crime and justice."[2] Both were members of the Black Panther Party and had participated in Auburn's November 1970 Black Solidarity Day uprising.[3] But as politically savvy as these two students were—Hicks could "quote black poets, writers and historical black figures . . . [and] speak Swahili fluently and Spanish well enough to be understood"—they were by no means the only men at Attica who were articulating potent critiques of the injustice.[4] As one of Attica's men put it, there were many prisoners there who were determined to get as much education as they could with the goal of "bettering [their] lot and [their] family's lot."[5]

Sociology classes were particularly popular with Attica's men in the summer of 1971. In one weekly class, a racially mixed group of fifteen prisoners read authors ranging from Adam Smith to Marx and Mao. Each week these men challenged one another to think about how these texts might apply to their own experiences. Several of the students in this class could share practical experiences that helped them to think about how marginalized people might empower themselves. Two students in the class, Samuel Melville and Herbert Blyden, had both been in the Tombs in New York City when it had erupted the summer before. Both had a lot to say about the importance of taking action if one really wanted to change things for the better.

Sam Melville (born Sam Grossman before he chose the literary moniker) looked more like an absentminded professor than the "Mad Bomber" the media had dubbed him. Melville had landed at Attica after having been sentenced to eighteen years for setting explosives in government buildings in protest against the war in Vietnam. As he saw it, the war would never end until the United States experienced firsthand the destruction it wrought abroad. Being incarcerated at Attica, where officials, in Melville's view, also acted brutally and with impunity, only solidified this Brooklyn-born white radical's conviction that society had to be overhauled by any means necessary.

Herb Blyden was also persuaded that the United States needed to undergo some major changes. Blyden had been born on the island of St. Thomas, but in his thirty-three years this broad-shouldered and tall black man had had more than his share of run-ins with the police in New York City. For Blyden it was crucial to read as much as one could about everything from American colonialism and imperialism to how the legal system operated. Blyden had been one of the most outspoken men during the Tombs jail rebellion, and the aftermath of that uprising had shown him firsthand how prisoners who took on the state needed as much information as they could get about how the law might eventually be used against them.

The presence of these men offered Attica's otherwise apolitical men—like Big Black Smith—a new understanding of their discontents and a new language for articulating them. But contrary to what state officials such as Russell Oswald thought, adding experienced activists like Blyden, Melville, Malloy, and Hicks to the general population at Attica is not what riled up the prisoners. No one had to be persuaded that things at Attica were bad or needed remedy. The men at Attica were well aware of how brutal America's prisons could be—particularly if those incarcerated remained silent and state officials were allowed to do anything they liked with no public scrutiny.[6]

The fate of the Auburn rebels transferred to Attica had been most instructive in that regard. Although Oswald's decision to close Auburn's dreaded Special Housing Unit convinced many outsiders that he was committed to penal reform, those on the inside knew that the alleged leaders of the rebellion had been sent straight to another segregation unit, HBZ, when they arrived at Attica.[7] Auburn transferee Jomo Joka Omowale later described their reception: "The guards were big and . . . they said they would try to kill us. . . . We were scared."[8]

Notably, because the Auburn transferees had educated themselves about the law, they didn't stay in HBZ forever. These men knew that the state had no legal grounds to hold them in this place indefinitely, and, thanks to the round-the-clock efforts of their advocates (including Lewis Steel, Herman Schwartz, and a young lawyer named Elizabeth Fischer), they were, after six months, released into Attica's general population.[9] Central to that victory was the decision of federal district judge John T. Curtin—a man who would be asked to rule on prison officials' actions at Attica many more times over the coming year.

The prisoners well knew that any legal activism on their part infuriated Attica's superintendent, Vincent Mancusi. They had already butted heads with him in the metal shop strike, and it was clear that he was determined to fight the Auburn transferees' release from HBZ with everything he had. Whereas Mancusi feared the Auburn prisoners would set about brainwashing the entire prison population and turn everyone into a radical troublemaker, it was in fact how DOCS officials had treated these Auburn transferees that ended up further radicalizing many men at Attica. Not only had they been beaten, but they had also been subjected to the harrowing experience of the Box for six whole months, *after* they had been promised no reprisals. That the word of prison officials meant nothing increasingly angered and agitated most of the men locked up at Attica.[10]

Even while they misunderstood its origin, by the summer of 1971 prison officials were well aware that they were sitting on a powder keg. As Commissioner Russell Oswald noted, that summer, "the focus of our anxieties moved from Auburn to Attica."[11]

# 5

# Playing by the Rules

Although Judge John T. Curtin forced administrators to let the Auburn transferees out of HBZ, prisoner frustration remained high. Few among them believed that prison administrators had been chastened into treating them with greater dignity or humanity, and one group of prisoners decided that it was now time to articulate a specific list of all that needed to happen at their facility to address this most important issue. On June 16, 1971, a surprise cell search turned up a draft of demands—one that greatly alarmed Attica superintendent Mancusi and the COs who had confiscated it. Two weeks later, Commissioner Oswald received the same set of demands in a letter signed by a group of five men calling themselves the Attica Liberation Faction. There actually wasn't much of an Attica Liberation Faction to speak of, but, as one prisoner later explained, "when the Manifesto was written up, there was obviously a need for a name on behalf of all inmates . . . [even though] as far as a strict organization, there was no such thing."[1]

The letter unnerved Oswald—especially since it was also cc'd to the governor—but it was not the vitriolic attack the commissioner might have expected from an entity calling itself a Liberation Faction: "Dear Sir, Enclosed is a copy of our manifesto of demands. We find it is necessary to forward you said copy in order for you to be aware of our needs and the need for prison reform. We hope that your department don't cause us any hardships in the future because we are informing you of prison conditions. We are doing this in a democratic manner; and we do hope that you will aid us."[2]

If Oswald was relieved that the letter's opening was neither threatening nor abusive, he was still greatly unsettled by the passion of its attached manifesto. "We the inmates of Attica Prison," that document began, "have come to recognize that because of our posture as prisoners and branded characters as alleged criminals, the administration and prison employees no longer consider or respect us as human beings but rather as domesticated animals selected to do their bidding and slave labor and furnished as a personal whipping dog for their sadistic psychopathic hate." The manifesto went on to list twenty-eight demands for reform, including changes in the parole system, religious freedom for Muslims, improvements in the working and living conditions, and a change in medical staff and medical policy and procedure.[3] The five men writing as the Attica Liberation Faction—Herbert Blyden, Frank Lott, Donald Noble, Peter Butler, and Carl Jones-El—closed by reminding Oswald that they were playing by the rules. "These demands are being presented to you. There is no strike of any kind to protest these demands. We are trying to do this in a democratic fashion."[4]

Oswald reacted with a mix of caution, suspicion, and conciliation. Caution first: now that the "alleged representatives of inmates at Attica Correctional Facility have submitted a long list of demands," he wrote to Rockefeller, "concern over lodging the 'Auburn 6' at Attica becomes magnified."[5] Would it just call more unwanted attention to their case to move them to a nearby county jail to await their day in court on the charges they faced from the November uprising, he wondered, or would it be worse to keep them in the general population at Attica where they could further agitate the other prisoners?

Then suspicion: the more times he read the manifesto, the more cynical Oswald became about its provenance. Oswald was sure that he had seen a treatise just like this not too long ago and it hadn't come from a New York prison, but from California. After investigating he reported to Rockefeller, "We have since discovered that these demands are almost entirely copied from demands issued at Folsom Prison in California as developed by Black Panther leadership there some time ago."[6] The commissioner found it particularly "interesting" that Attica's "July Manifesto"—as it was now being called by the prisoners—had demanded "religious freedom." In his view this was a dead giveaway that radicals were stirring up trouble in this prison from as far away as California, and worse, that "the Black Muslims were involved."[7] He found it equally disturbing that one of the signers of the manifesto was Herbert Blyden, who he knew had been a key participant in the New York City jail rebellion of 1970.

By doing simple acts of kindness for others, we can't help but lift ourselves up too.

It was true that these five Attica prisoners had modeled their call for prison reform on a manifesto that had been drafted by men in California's Folsom State Prison.[8] The dramatic prisoner protest at Folsom the year before had been a big news item, and copies of those inmates' grievances could be found in countless cells across the country. But that did not negate the legitimacy of the cry for reform coming out of Attica; nor was Blyden's involvement indicative of any incipient rebellion. Blyden could see clearly that conditions at Attica were just as dreadful as at the Tombs, and he simply felt it necessary to speak out.

Prison officials at Attica itself expended little effort trying to understand the real reasons Attica's July Manifesto read so similarly to Folsom's. Having grasped instead at sinister explanations for the penning of this document, administrators decided that the best response to it was to clamp down even harder on the prison population. Things became so grim at Attica in the wake of the July Manifesto that, as prisoner Sam Melville reported in a long handwritten letter to his lawyer, men were now ending up in segregation—getting a "60-day box bit"—simply for having the manifesto.[9]

But while Superintendent Mancusi opted to punish those who were sympathetic to the July Manifesto, over in Albany Oswald had decided on a strategy of conciliation. To Rockefeller he explained that he intended to "investigate all demands with a view toward responsive action where possible and beneficial."[10] Oswald had spent his life as a prison reformer and it was still important to him that the prisoners at Attica feel that he had their best interests at heart. This, he believed, might be their only hope in trying to thwart the designs of outside agitators.

On July 7, 1971, Oswald replied to the authors of Attica's July Manifesto and assured them that he would "give careful consideration to the entire list."[11] He also reminded them of their stated intention to proceed in a democratic fashion, adding pointedly, "I applaud this as a rational approach."[12] Suspecting that his letter would be read in every cell block, Oswald also informed the men that he had already been hard at work to address penal problems. "You may have . . . noted that some change has already come about and I assure you that greater change toward a more progressive, humane and rehabilitative system is in the planning state."[13]

On July 19 Oswald received a response, this time penned solely by Frank Lott, expressing appreciation for the dialogue that had now begun, as well as the Attica prisoner population's faith in the commissioner's "sincerity."[14] He added, though, that with the exception of management having placed water pitchers on the lunch tables for the first time, "the conditions listed in the last two pages of our manifesto still exist," and he then went on to enumerate those.[15]

A month went by. Hearing nothing from the commissioner after this moment of good-faith back-and-forth made Attica's self-appointed spokesmen nervous. On August 16, 1971, Lott wrote again on behalf of the men calling themselves the Attica Liberation Faction, this time to bring the commissioner's attention to the fact that Superintendent Mancusi was still censoring the newspapers that prisoners read even though the courts had recently ruled that such censorship was not legal, and also to impress upon Commissioner Oswald how desperate the men were to see signs of change. "We are anxiously awaiting your evaluation of our manifesto," he wrote. "I do hope that you will drop me a few lines and let me know what is happening."[16] Still, Lott did not want the commissioner to feel threatened. Despite the fact that conditions had grown even more oppressive for the men in Attica since they first contacted the commissioner—with the escalation of cell searches, the confiscation of writing and reading materials, and the increase in disciplinary lockups—Lott promised Oswald, "we will continue to strive for prison reform in a democratic manner."[17]

This time Oswald replied to Lott. He reiterated that much was already being accomplished in the area of prison reform and again assured him that he would continue to study improvements that needed to be made.[18] But Attica's prisoners needed to be realistic, he chided. "Complete change cannot be brought about in just a short time."[19] They knew that. But they also knew that the sorts of things they were asking for—"such simple changes as providing clean trays from which to eat in the mess hall, or allowing more than one shower a week during the hot summer months"—did not require "complete change."[20]

# 6

# Back and Forth

By mid-August 1971, as the temperatures hovered around 90 degrees in the day and never dipped below 68 at night, a sense of futility and frustration hung in the stale air of Attica's five sweltering cell blocks.[1] The optimism that the men had allowed themselves to feel only a month earlier, when there was a belief that the commissioner of the Department of Correctional Services might do something for them, now seemed naive. The stench of nearly 2,300 sweaty men hovering like a poisonous cloud over the cell blocks could persuade even the most patient prisoner that Oswald had played them.

There was, however, at least one very tangible and ultimately significant product of the prisoners having put on paper the concrete things they needed to humanize Attica. For the first time in this institution's history, the desire for change had prompted usually antagonistic prisoner factions to talk with one another, and soon a number of shaky, but nevertheless potentially powerful, alliances had been forged across ethnic, racial, and political lines. The CO staff saw this happening and it worried them. As one correction officer noted anxiously, "the particular make up of these groups changed. . . . A group would have three or four of the different factions involved . . . which, you know, wasn't normal."[2]

That an unusual unity had developed between various prisoner groups became particularly obvious the morning of August 22, 1971. As Attica's various companies were marched in their neat lines to the mess hall in silence, the COs immediately noticed that most of the prisoners were wearing a strip of black cloth as an armband. As notably, rather than lining up behind the two tallest men, as was customary, each company followed two stony-faced black prisoners of varying height. Then, even more unnerving to the officers, no one ate a thing once they sat down in the mess hall. As the COs looked across that cavernous room for some clue as to what was going on, a prisoner finally explained to one of them that the men were staging a "spiritual sit in" to protest the murder the previous day of a fellow prisoner, George Jackson, out in California's San Quentin State Prison.[3]

George Jackson had become famous in prison systems across the United States for his extensive writings from the inside—expositions on just how racist and brutal America's penal institutions were, particularly for prisoners of color.[4] His killing touched a nerve among the incarcerated everywhere. The story put out by prison officials in California was that Jackson had been trying to escape and had "pulled a 9mm automatic pistol about five inches long out of a wig that he snatched off his head when a guard reached to examine it."[5] He then ran across the yard and was shot.

To Attica's prisoners this story rang false, even absurd.[6] How in the world could the most closely monitored man in the entire California prison system have had a wig on in the first place, let alone hidden a heavy, bulky gun in it? As one of Attica's prisoners put it, there was simply no way that "anybody hid it in their hair . . . then got back to the box without being searched."[7] Prisoners everywhere were convinced that whatever had happened at San Quentin must have involved trigger-happy guards, and now George Jackson was dead. Former Auburn, now Attica, prisoner Jomo Joka Omowale was particularly dismayed to learn of Jackson's death because he had recently been corresponding with Jackson about the prison life in New York. Jomo was alarmed that CO aggression—itself quite common—could lead to the outright murder of such a famous prisoner.[8] As another prisoner put it, the men at Attica "had always generally been aware that in the past, [guards] could get away with killing inmates . . . but nobody ever really expected it to happen [now] . . . until it happened to Jackson."[9] That so many prisoners, black, white, and Puerto Rican, stood together on August 22, 1971, and refused to eat, indicated that Jackson's death had not only shaken them, but had rallied them as well.

Riding the wave of this new unity, the men in A Block decided then to engage in a mass "sick-in" on August 30. Specifically they hoped to call attention to the dire state of the prison's medical facilities that day because it was rumored that Commissioner Oswald would be making a visit to Attica.

As it turned out, the commissioner canceled his visit, so he never saw the crowd of protesting prisoners crammed into Attica's antiquated infirmary. But he did hear about their action and sent word to Governor Rockefeller and Superintendent Mancusi that he would visit Attica the very next week. He was worried. As he explained it to Rockefeller, "While it is not characteristic of me to 'cry wolf,' the recent tragedy at San Quentin has made it all too apparent that anything can happen when dealing with the kinds of idealists and fanatics housed in our facilities."[10]

By August's end Attica's correction officers had also grown increasingly concerned. They began expressing to their wives and co-workers a reluctance to go to work. Some had even started leaving their wallets at home in case anything "jumped off" at the prison. CO William Quinn also felt compelled to make sure that his financial affairs were in good order. One night, after putting his daughters, Deanne and Christine, to bed, Quinn showed his wife, Nancy, where all the insurance papers were and how to deal with the household bills.[11] He worried that an explosion at Attica was inevitable and perhaps even imminent.

Like Commissioner Russell Oswald, many of the COs at Attica blamed the new level of tension they were experiencing on the courts—feeling in particular that Judge Curtin had weakened their authority when he ordered the release of the Auburn detainees into Attica's general population.[12] Most also believed, however, that the DOCS had made the situation worse. Officials in Albany had left them too understaffed and undertrained to meet the challenges posed by the angry and newly empowered prisoners. Oswald agreed to discuss the issue of guard security in his upcoming visit.

Although the commissioner and the officers feared that prisoners might be planning an insurrection, they were not. While prisoners remained deeply skeptical that state officials could be counted on to help them, Oswald's willingness to correspond with the Attica Liberation Faction had been encouraging. As one prisoner summed it up, in the summer of 1971 many men genuinely felt that Oswald might do something positive for them, and even the more cynical were at least willing to "wait and see."[13]

# 7

# End of the Line

In some ways the men at Attica couldn't believe that the head of the entire New York State Department of Correctional Services was coming to talk with them. They hoped that the recent rebellions at Auburn and in New York City jails had taught officials like Oswald a lesson—that prisoners would never stop demanding to be treated as human beings. They wanted him to see the wisdom of really listening to prisoners rather than ignoring their needs. As inspiring as it was to read the broader critiques of injustice found in George Jackson's *Soledad Brother: The Prison Letters of George Jackson,* Eldridge Cleaver's *Soul on Ice,* or in Mao's *Little Red Book*—which Attica's prisoners read and discussed passionately—they also prayed that having Oswald's ear might net them needed changes now.

All waited with great anticipation for September 2, the day when the commissioner was to arrive. Once there, he was to meet with staff, meet with representatives from the Attica Liberation Faction, and then speak to all of the other prisoners in the facility via the prison address system. That evening, men sat in their cells and placed headphones over their ears, the ones they usually listened to static-filled radio songs on, waiting to hear what Oswald would say. Word had it that he had met, face-to-face, with some reps from the Attica Liberation Faction earlier that day, which was a good sign, but everyone really wanted to hear what reforms would be coming to Attica from the commissioner himself. First the men in A, B, and C Blocks were to hear Oswald speak through their headphones from 7:00 to 7:09, and then, from 9:18 to 9:27, he would speak to the men in E Block. Finally, from 9:44 to 9:53 the commissioner would once again take to the microphone and talk with the metal shop's prisoners in D Block.

Instead of talking with the prisoners in person, though, Oswald had left them a taped message. The recording began with the commissioner explaining why he was not addressing them live as he had said he would. "I had originally planned to spend two days here," he intoned, "but unfortunately an emergent situation in the office, plus the fact that my wife had been taken to the hospital, dictates my early return to Albany."[1]

As a low rumble of disbelief began to spread through the cell blocks, Oswald's voice played on. He told the prisoners that he had already taken key steps to bring reforms to Attica and that he had done this, despite "facing the worst fiscal crisis in remembered state history."[2] As important, he continued, the DOCS was planning to "implement several new programs and projects," such as adding a law library, and a new "program for training in meaningful rehabilitative methods for all personnel . . . [as well as] extending our programming into the community."[3]

Not until the tail end of his message did Oswald address any of the issues that the men had raised in the letter sent to him back in July. Oswald said only that he and his staff "are reviewing, and will continue to review, the numerous aspects of each single item" and that his office would make changes that were "reasonably possible."[4]

As Oswald's message ended, a few of Attica's men were still able to muster some measure of optimism about the possibilities of reform. One twenty-one-year-old even felt compelled the next week to write to the commissioner that he had "listened intently to the recorded speech," and believed that there was "sincerity" in his words.[5] He went on, "I have a strong faith in you Sir, for you want to give us back our pride and self-respect in as many ways as you can find, and I know that eventually you will succeed."[6] Another man also wrote to Oswald expressing not only gratitude for his efforts, but also hope for his wife's speedy recovery. However, most of Attica's men felt betrayed by Oswald. Although he was not there to hear it, no sooner did his taped speech end than the sound of "earphones hitting the wall and men shouting, 'That's a cop out, that's a cop out!' " began echoing through Attica's cell blocks.[7] He also never saw those men who could only sit despondently with their heads in their hands in the wake of his recorded message, nor those who found themselves pacing their cells in despair. In the words of one man: "He didn't do nothing. . . . He didn't so much as make one concession, such as giving a man soap or giving a man an extra shower."[8]

Over the coming days, Attica's prisoners engaged in intense debates about what the commissioner's taped response signified and what they might do next to get him to act. To most, it seemed clear that their foray into the democratic process and their patience as well as pledge of nonviolence had produced not a single improvement in their living conditions. If anything, it had resulted in more censorship, more cell shakedowns, fewer minutes outside the dismal blocks, and an administration even more suspicious and watchful of their every move. As Sam Melville wrote to his lawyers on September 4, "All rules are now strictly enforced. Attire, haircuts, lining up, not talking, no wearing hats—everything."[9]

And yet, even those prisoners who had some experience with direct action, including some veterans of Auburn and the New York City jail riots, still very much hoped that something so dramatic might be avoided at Attica. On September 8, 1971, Herb Blyden wrote one more letter—this time to John Dunne, a Republican state senator who had been involved in negotiating a peaceful end to the uprising at the Tombs in New York City, where Blyden had been, and who also chaired the Standing Committee on Crime and Correction in Albany. In some ways, Blyden saw Dunne as their last hope. "We need more visits from your Committee on the immediate future as the situation at prisons is rather fluid," Blyden wrote.[10] "All we received were promises of change. . . . I thank you in advance—Respectfully, Herbert X Blyden."[11]

Others expressed the need for immediate outside intervention far more desperately and passionately. As Sam Melville put it in a frantic letter to his lawyer, "For Christ's sake, do something!"[12]

PART II

# Power and Politics Unleashed

# MICHAEL SMITH

*Michael Smith couldn't quite figure how he had wound up working as a correction officer. The twenty-two-year-old wore sideburns, had a mustache, and looked a bit more like a scruffy college student than an employee of the New York Department of Correctional Services. But like so many other small town boys who had grown up in rural New York Mike needed to make a living, and prisons were the going industry in that part of the state.*

*Shortly after graduating from high school, Mike had enrolled in Genesee County Community College. There he met a girl named Sharon and was so smitten that he decided to leave school and get a job so that he could ask Sharon to marry him. Soon after they got engaged, Mike took a position in a local machine shop. It didn't take long, though, before he began to think that he needed a better job. It dawned on him that he could take the civil service exam and start working for the prison system like several of his cousins. The pay was stable, the benefits were fine, the job was secure, and these were the things that mattered, since what Mike wanted most was to be able to provide for a family.*

*On September 3, 1970, two weeks after his wedding, Mike started his first guard job at the Eastern Correctional Facility in Napanoch, New York. Another young CO, John D'Arcangelo, offered to show him the ropes, for which Mike was grateful. He had been given no other training for the job. Mike and Sharon soon became close to John and his wife, Ann, a bond made closer because both women were expecting babies. When Mike then transferred to Attica in order to be near his extended family, he hoped John would also transfer there. To his delight, within a few months John joined him.*

*Mike thought that he could be happy at Attica. Archaic as it was, it was more modern than Napanoch and seemed more secure.*[1] *Also, he thought he might actually have a knack for prison work. As far as he was concerned, it was all about mutual respect. Whereas most of his fellow guards called prisoners by their number or, maybe, by their last name, Mike addressed every prisoner as "Mr." To be sure, this irritated several of his colleagues, who saw him as too soft and easygoing. To Mike, though, there were many decent men in prison who had simply made bad choices or had some tough luck. He had been quite touched when two Napanoch prisoners wrote him a letter thanking him for the way he had treated them. Mike was so proud of this letter that he held on to it.*

*Mike had not been at Attica long, however, before he became troubled by the way the other COs treated the prisoners, and this weighed on him. It bothered Mike that every time a Puerto Rican prisoner got a letter, his fellow guards threw it into the trash simply because they couldn't read it.*[2] *The practice of strip-searching every new prisoner also struck Mike as unnecessary and demoralizing. He was fairly certain that he would have considered suicide had he been forced to undergo this ritual.*[3]

*So Mike Smith was not surprised that dissent was on the rise at Attica. When he was placed in charge of one of Attica's metal shops, it became clear to him that the prisoners there had legitimate gripes and that they were growing more determined to voice them. He believed that it was important for prisoners to be allowed to speak up.*

*One day in July 1971, Mike was approached by Don Noble and two other prisoners at the end of their shift. They wanted his opinion on a letter they had drafted to the commissioner of corrections—this was the letter that they had signed as the Attica Liberation Faction. After reading it carefully, Mike thought they had expressed their concerns clearly and rationally, and told them he thought that writing it was the right thing to do.*[4]

*When the letter only elicited a taped message from Oswald, Mike was nearly as dismayed as the prisoners. He was also worried. Mike had been walking through one of Attica's cell blocks when Oswald's tape had been broadcast, and he could tell immediately that the administration's decision to handle things this way was disastrous. Mike could feel the air around him begin to crackle with a new fury.*

# 8

# Talking Back

While the men at Attica hoped that powerful people such as State Senator John Dunne still might do something on their behalf, there was little consensus regarding what to do if this effort also failed to bring some meaningful improvements to their facility. The disparate political factions in the yard had been talking about this very question for some time now—activists like Sam Melville from the Weather Underground (a revolutionary organization committed to fighting racism and imperialism), Black Panthers like Tommy Hicks, Black Muslims like Richard X Clark, and men like Mariano "Dalou" Gonzalez from the Young Lords Party (a grassroots activist organization working in cities like New York and Chicago to improve conditions for Puerto Ricans).[1] Still, no new strategy had been agreed upon. By early September 1971, however, and after Oswald's taped message, all of them could agree on one crucial point: most men at Attica were now at a breaking point. Just about anything might cause this place to explode.

Correction officer Mike Smith believed this as well. Although he had a good relationship with the men in his company, as he walked them to mess on the morning after the debacle of Oswald's taped speech he could see that they were unusually on edge and he disliked the idea of so many prisoners all together in one room with tensions so high. Nothing happened that day. But a week later, on September 8, 1971, an incident confirmed his worst fears about how strained things had become at Attica.

At about 3:30 that afternoon Mike Smith was assigned to A Yard, where almost five hundred men from the A Block companies were on their rec break. In one corner of the yard near the handball court, Mike noticed two men sparring with each other. To Mike it seemed obvious that they were just playing, so he felt no need to intervene. Another CO came to a different conclusion, however, and went to get his superior, sixty-one-year-old Senior Lieutenant Richard Maroney. One of the men disappeared into the yard before he could be brought over to Maroney, leaving only the other, Leroy Dewer, to explain what had been happening.

Dewer was a slightly built twenty-three-year-old from New York City, serving a five-year sentence. He had just been released from his cell after seven days of keeplock for disobeying an officer's order. After all the long hours of being cooped up in his tiny cell, he had really been enjoying the release of horsing around out in the open air. When Dewer reached Maroney, he tried to explain what he had been doing, but the lieutenant insisted that he leave A Yard immediately and return to his dreaded cell.

Incredulous, Dewer asked, "What for?"

Maroney replied, "I said, get inside."

A ten-year veteran of Attica, Maroney was used to being obeyed.

Dewer countered, "I asked you for what, why? I haven't done anything."

Maroney repeated, "I said, get in there."[2]

Furious, Dewer turned his back on Maroney and started to walk away. Then Maroney reached out to grab him. In a shocking move, Dewer spun around and hit Maroney in the middle of his chest. Again the lieutenant repeated his order, and again Dewer hit Maroney, before running out into the middle of the yard, with Maroney hard on his heels. As this highly unusual scene played out, a crowd of almost two hundred gathered around. Some of Dewer's supporters began threatening Maroney with assault if he took Dewer anywhere. In response, Maroney tried to assure the crowd that Dewer would not be harmed—he just needed to leave the yard. By the summer of 1971, however, COs' promises meant virtually nothing to the men at Attica, and many were certain that Dewer would suffer a serious beating the moment he was out of their sight.[3]

All of a sudden, another prisoner, a white twenty-eight-year-old named Ray Lamorie who had been playing football in another section of the yard, burst into the circle that had formed around Dewer and Maroney. Later, no one could agree whether Lamorie tried to hit Maroney, or was just calling him names. But at that moment another Attica officer, forty-nine-year-old Lieutenant Robert Curtiss, looked out of A Block corridor and saw what he felt was an escalating confrontation between prisoners and guards, and immediately moved in to try to cool things down. Curtiss entered A Yard and told Maroney and the other COs to walk away; they would deal with Dewer and Lamorie later.

When Lieutenants Maroney and Curtiss walked out of A Yard without Dewer in tow, it was hard to say who was more surprised, they or the prisoners who looked on warily as they departed. Curtiss returned to his post at "Times Square," a very small, dark room enclosed by massive steel gates at the very center of the prison—the command center where the halls to A, B, C, and D Blocks all converged and where a tiny stairway led up to Attica's catwalks. Although Curtiss had decided to walk away from the altercation in A Yard, he felt it vital to report what had just happened to Superintendent Mancusi and Mancusi's deputy superintendent, Leon Vincent.[4]

Curtiss finally located both Mancusi and Vincent in the Parole Hearing Room of the administration building located nearest to A Block, where they, along with Assistant Deputy Superintendent Karl Pfeil, were in a tense meeting with the Attica guards' union, Council 82 AFSCME. This meeting had been going on since 10:00 a.m. and, as it happened, the issue that had kept all parties there for so long was none other than officer safety.[5] Union rep Captain Frank "Pappy" Wald argued that prison administrators were not taking the employees' concerns seriously. It was the second time in two days that Attica's union had confronted prison management with an urgent request to do something to guarantee safety on the job. The previous day, COs had met with Mancusi and were so concerned about safety that they had asked that the prison be placed on total lockdown to avert a possible crisis. Nothing seemed to get through to management. Even now, as Curtiss reported what had just transpired in A Yard, Mancusi just stared impassively. In his view, the fact that some prisoners had acted up earlier that day just meant that they needed to be punished. He instructed Curtiss to wait until the men in Dewer's and Lamorie's companies had been locked up for the night, and then to take the two offenders to HBZ.

This was most men at Attica's worst fear, and all of the men in the A Block companies were especially worried about what might happen to Dewer or Lamorie once they were placed in segregation. For starters, no man had ever hit an Attica lieutenant, and the punishment for such an act was sure to be harsh. Even worse, however, both Dewer and Lamorie had come to Attica from Auburn because both had been in the rebellion there the previous November.[6] Everyone knew that this too would make them a target of Attica guards still furious that their Auburn counterparts had been taken hostage in that uprising. That night, when the men of A Block's 3 Company heard Maroney and three other COs heading to Dewer's cell, all grew silent and wary.

Dewer stalled at first, asking for time to gather his books to give to another prisoner. When the guards refused, Dewer announced that he wouldn't go, and the men came in after him, tearing up the cell.[7] Those in the cells nearby could hear the sounds of furniture breaking and glass shattering and began banging on their bars while yelling, "Leave that kid alone!" None of them could actually see what was happening inside Dewer's cell, so they imagined the worst. When they saw Dewer being carried out motionless, one guard holding each of his extremities, the other prisoners thought he was dead. Stunned silence reigned after Dewer was taken away. "It was like a member of the family had just died," recalled one prisoner. Everyone was now very frightened.[8]

Then, mere minutes later, the sound of another confrontation could be heard coming from the floor below, where Ray Lamorie's group, A Block's 5 Company, was locked down for the night. Even though Lieutenant Curtiss was not sure what Lamorie's offense was, he and four other COs had dutifully followed Mancusi's instructions and had ventured over to cell 24 to take this man to HBZ. Terrified after having just heard the commotion that accompanied the removal of Dewer, Lamorie had already picked up a stool to defend himself. However, he soon saw the futility of this act, and even though he found it unbelievable that Curtiss could not tell him exactly why he was being disciplined, Lamorie went peaceably with the officers.

Because 5 Company was a so-called grading company, and the men on it were relegated to doing the absolute worst kind of scut work at the prison, they had their own lengthy list of established grievances against Attica's guards and the removal of Lamorie and Dewer was like a match to kindling. As the COs walked Lamorie out of the gallery, men flung various objects at them from their cells while screaming obscenities. One of them, William Ortiz, hurled a soup can and managed to strike an officer, which landed him on keeplock until he could be taken before the adjustment committee the next day.[9] Word that Ortiz too was now being disciplined only escalated the men's outcries, so Lieutenant Curtiss sent the other officers with Lamorie to HBZ, while he himself stayed for a while to make sure things did not get any more out of control. Feeling the situation still most unstable, Curtiss called for backup. Soon, eight more officers were walking the gallery that night.[10]

Curtiss had reason for concern. The forty men in 5 Company were some of Attica's angriest prisoners, and they were also some of the most vocal of them. The group included Sam Melville, the white radical who had bombed buildings in protest of the Vietnam War and had written the treatise on how badly Attica's prisoners were being exploited in the laundry. Also in this company was Tommy Hicks, the Black Panther and Auburn transferee who had been one of the leaders of the rebellion there; and L. D. Barkley, another young member of the Panthers who was not only very well read, but also most outspoken about his politics. Eventually, though, A Block did grow quiet. Lieutenant Curtiss decided to head back to the room where Attica's upper-level administrators were still meeting with the union. Breaking into their meeting yet again, Curtiss told Mancusi that he felt that "inmate unrest had reached a point of crisis."[11] Given that this pronouncement didn't even prompt his boss to adjourn the meeting, Curtiss was not at all sure that he had conveyed the true volatility of the situation.[12]

Taking a different tack, Curtiss decided to ask if his superiors might at least allow the late shift to stay over into the next morning in case there was trouble. He also requested permission to bring in the next day's 10 a.m.–7 p.m. shift three hours earlier.[13] That way, he reasoned, the period of the day when COs would be most at risk—the breakfast hour, when every company was going back and forth from their cells to the mess hall—would be well covered. Deputy Superintendent Leon Vincent responded curtly, "Who in the hell is going to pay the overtime?"[14] Giving up, Curtiss left the room. As he walked away, he decided that he would keep at least the current shift over for an hour while the hall captains made their usual late night rounds, and deal with the overtime consequences later.[15]

That night the lights were extinguished in Attica's cell blocks without further incident, but Curtiss couldn't relax. He knew that many of the prisoners in A Block believed that Leroy Dewer was dead, and he was aware that no amount of reassurance would convince them otherwise.[16] Worse, he knew that the uproar that had accompanied the removal of both Dewer and Lamorie had traveled through the radiators and ventilators throughout every one of A Block's galleries.[17] And, indeed, it had. Before the clock struck midnight on September 8, the rumor that "they beat up both guys," and that Dewer might be in a coma or dead, had circulated through the prison. As dawn broke, prisoners and COs alike greeted the new day with dread.[18]

# 9

# Burning Down the House

At 7:00 a.m. on September 9, 1971, Attica's lights came on, rousing all of the men in A Block from their fitful slumber. Throughout the night, speculation had raged regarding Leroy Dewer's fate. Many couldn't sleep, fearing that COs might again descend upon their galleries. The silence was deafening as the men lined up by their cell doors, waiting for the hall captain to disengage the master lock so they could step out for the routine head count before breakfast.[1] When the doors did unlock, a number of the men just stood there, afraid to exit their cells or to leave the block.[2] But eventually they did, and as they walked to the mess hall, peering nervously from side to side, each seemed to "sense that just a sigh, a cry, or maybe a spark, anything" could send the place up in flames.[3]

The correction officers felt the same way. As COs Richard Lewis and William Quinn prepared to leave home for their 7:00 a.m. shift, neither of them wanted to alarm their families but both were deeply apprehensive. After patting his Great Dane and Doberman pinscher on their heads, and waving goodbye to his twelve-year-old daughter, Patty, and fourteen-year-old son, David, CO Lewis, who wished that he could call in sick, headed to work. Quinn was also reluctant to leave that day. After checking in on his still sleeping daughters, Deanne and Christine, he slipped out the door and hoped for the best.

When Quinn and Lewis arrived at the prison, they joined other jumpy day shift officers getting ready for a briefing from Lieutenant Robert Curtiss, who clearly had not had much rest. Curtiss tried his best to apprise them of everything that had happened in A Yard and A Block over the past thirty-six hours, and then he told his men he would make sure to place an extra officer in the mess hall for the 7:15 breakfast sitting, just in case anything went down. He wished them luck as they filed out the door.[4]

Officer Gordon Kelsey had been assigned to take 5 Company to the mess hall that morning, which worried him since he had no experience with this company and he knew that the events of the previous evening would have left their mark. When it was time to lift the lever that released the locks on the cells, Kelsey made sure to keep William Ortiz's cell bolted since he had been informed that this man was to stay there—under keeplock—for having struck an officer the night before. While Kelsey was trying to get the other men to leave the gallery, many of them demanded to know exactly what would happen to Ortiz in their absence. Other than the fact that Ortiz was slated to meet with the adjustment committee, Kelsey knew nothing about what prison officials had in mind, but his perceived evasiveness only agitated the men in his charge. Abruptly, several declared that they weren't leaving the gallery unless Ortiz was with them, and they headed back to their cells. Unruffled, Kelsey proceeded with the remaining men out to A Block corridor. Unbeknownst to Kelsey, however, as these men passed by the central lockbox, one of them managed to throw the switch that was keeping Ortiz locked in. When his door slid open, Ortiz, along with the men who had hung back in solidarity with him, rushed to join the larger group heading to the mess hall.[5]

The hall captain of 5 Company raced to the phone to report this security violation. It was relayed to Lieutenant Curtiss, who was in the administration building finally writing up his report on the Dewer-Lamorie incident. Superintendent Mancusi sent Curtiss to A Block to investigate; he confirmed that the gallery was empty and that all the men, including Ortiz, had gone to breakfast. When Curtiss returned to the administration building, Mancusi was gone. Curtiss asked Mancusi's assistant deputy superintendent, Karl Pfeil, what he should do.

Pfeil ordered that Ortiz be returned to keeplock and all of 5 Company returned to their cells after breakfast. None of them would get rec time in A Yard today. Though he was fearful of what this might set off, Curtiss dutifully telephoned William Quinn, who was manning Times Square. He told Quinn to lock the A Gate to Times Square as soon as 5 Company passed through on the way back from the mess. Quinn knew immediately that something must be wrong, since it was standard practice to leave all the gates surrounding Times Square open during high-traffic times, such as meals.[6]

Meanwhile, at breakfast, the men of 5 Company were oblivious to all of this. With Ortiz eating alongside them, it looked as if all had been forgiven and, for the first time since leaving the cell block, they relaxed, just a bit. The men remained in a fairly good mood as Kelsey led them in a neat double line from the mess hall through C Tunnel to Times Square and then out into A Tunnel, where they assumed they would exit into A Yard. Right behind 5 Company was 2 Company, another grading company, and behind it was 9 Company. The men in all these companies were lined up peacefully, waiting to be let out for their rec time. None of them, including CO Kelsey, knew that the door leading from A Tunnel out into A Yard had been locked ahead of their arrival. No one had bothered to inform CO Kelsey of the change to regular procedures.[7] The prisoners looked on, puzzled, as Kelsey, equally mystified, tried the door. Finally he gave up and, leaving the men in line, headed toward the gate at the far end of the tunnel from Times Square that led into A Block. Halfway there he met Lieutenant Curtiss, who was heading into the tunnel to inform 5 Company that they were being taken back to their cells.[8]

Just as Curtiss came abreast of the first four prisoners in line, the men closest to the A Yard door realized that they had been locked into A Tunnel on purpose. They panicked. Coming toward them in A Tunnel was the man they believed had played the central role in the beatings of Dewer and Lamorie the night before, and within seconds the 5 Company line began to break down as the men at the front began backing away from Curtiss, unsure what he might do. Suddenly, one of them decided to fight rather than flee, landing a blow to Curtiss's left temple. Several others then jumped him.[9]

While these men were hitting Curtiss, the rest of the men in the 5 Company formation, and those in the two companies behind it, stared on in confusion and terror. As Curtiss later described it, "I looked over my left shoulder [and] . . . the men were standing there with a dumbfounded look on their faces. The back end of the company, I would say probably 40 men, still stood in a column of two's in perfect formation."[10] All of a sudden, it seemed to dawn on them too that they were little more than sitting ducks locked in the tight confines of this ill-lit tunnel. As prisoner Richard X Clark put it, "We expected the goon squad any minute."[11] Sheer chaos ensued as men began grabbing anything they could find to protect themselves.

In this melee some of the men broke off, trying to hide. Others, however, saw this bedlam as an opportunity for revenge on officers whom they particularly hated, or on fellow prisoners against whom they had grudges. Still others wanted to head for the commissary and loot it for food, or go to the prison pharmacy to score drugs. Within mere minutes A Tunnel had disintegrated into a blur of flying fists, breaking windows, and screaming men.

William Quinn, who was safe behind locked gates in the Times Square command center, was one of a number of COs who were witness to this pandemonium. Others watched what was happening from where they stood, waiting their turn to enter Times Square to head to B, C, and D Tunnels with their companies after morning mess. All were unnerved, but most felt that whatever was happening in A Tunnel could be contained.

Meanwhile, more than one hundred A Block prisoners who had been on the earlier breakfast shift were already in A Yard having their rec time. When they heard the shouting and glass smashing in A Tunnel, they crowded around the windows of the tunnel to see what was going on. Word spread like wildfire through A Yard that a riot was under way. These men began arming themselves with anything they could find—rakes, boards, football helmets, and other pieces of sports equipment. The two COs watching over the A Yard group, John D'Arcangelo and Walter Zymowski, felt their knees go weak as a group of prisoners approached them and snatched their rings of keys. These officers watched helplessly as the group went over to the door to A Tunnel and, after struggling a bit to open the lock, flooded into the already cramped space to join in the fracas.

In Times Square, the guards on the outside of the command center could see that William Quinn was growing more nervous. As he began double-checking to make sure that all the gates were still secure, he looked up and saw his friend Gordon Kelsey with blood streaming down his face. Taking an enormous risk, Quinn opened the gate a crack to let Kelsey in to safety. He then did the same for CO Don Melven, who was waiting in C Tunnel with the men he was bringing back from breakfast. The prisoners in C Tunnel still hadn't quite figured out that a full-scale riot had engulfed A Tunnel, but Quinn feared that once they did, Melven would become a target.

Seeing that Quinn had opened the gates for the two guards, a number of terrified prisoners from 9 Company begged to be let in to Times Square so that they would be safe. One beseeched, "Let me in . . . I didn't have nothing to do with it."[12] But Quinn was too afraid to chance opening Times Square one more time. He told the men in 9 Company to stand quietly alongside the wall, and urged them not to get involved in any of this craziness. Then he picked up the phone and frantically tried to reach the administration building.[13]

The phone didn't work. Attica's telephone system was so archaic that only one party at a time could make a call, and the lines were now overloaded with people trying to reach the administration building to find out what the commotion was near Times Square. With no way of communicating with anyone, Quinn had little choice but simply to wait for help. He had no idea what he was supposed to do in a riot situation. There were no plans, no procedures—as the correction officers had been complaining to management all summer. As one guard put it, "[While] the superintendent . . . took [our request] under advisement in each instance, nothing was really done as far as I could see."[14]

In A Tunnel, most of the prisoners originally under Kelsey's command were desperately trying to get out of the claustrophobic space that was growing more dangerous by the minute. If they could not somehow open a gate, they would be trapped and thus an easy target for the scores of police officers and guards they imagined had by now assembled in the administration building. Driven by both fear and fury, a large group descended upon the massive gate at Times Square and several men began shoving various keys they had taken from the A Yard guards into its lock. They tried key after key, as Quinn, Kelsey, and Melven watched in terror. But none of the keys worked, and for a brief period it appeared that the COs would be safe.

But the A Block prisoners were desperate. Giving up on the keys, they began trying to force the gate open. Working furiously at its hinges, they called out to the still stunned men watching from C Tunnel, urging them to try to open their gate to Times Square. None of those men made any move to follow suit.

Nevertheless, the gate separating A Tunnel from Times Square A Gate began to groan. Someone had handed the men a long piece of pipe that appeared to have been ripped from the backboard of A Yard's basketball net. Thanks to the force of dozens of men behind this makeshift battering ram, the massive gate between A Tunnel and Times Square suddenly gave way.[15] One of the bars that secured the gate to the cement, which had long needed replacing, broke in half about fifteen inches down from the ceiling.[16] Apparently this bar had broken before, been improperly rewelded, and then painted over so many times that its weakness had become invisible.[17]

At 9:05 a.m., as the massive gate separating A Tunnel from Times Square finally gave way, scores of prisoners flooded that tiny space and demanded William Quinn surrender his keys and nightstick. No sooner had Quinn handed them over, however, than he was hit on the head with tremendous force by someone wielding what was later described as either a two-by-four or a "heavy stick." Quinn fell to the ground, where others set upon him and trampled him as men continued to pour into Times Square. Soon this young CO was lying motionless, with blood streaming down his head and face.[18] Within minutes, both Gordon Kelsey and Don Melven were also knocked to the floor, where they too were kicked and beaten. All three COs were soon covered in blood, fading in and out of consciousness.

Meanwhile the scores of men who now crowded into the nerve center of Attica began trying to use Quinn's keys to open the gates to the rest of Attica's cell block tunnels. In no time, they had access to all four tunnels and cell blocks, as well as to the set of stairs leading from Times Square to the catwalks above. From this height they could evaluate what was happening in all four courtyards of the prison at once. As important, the roof of Times Square was where the officers kept several gas guns as well as tear gas grenades and they soon had commandeered these as well.[19]

Ten minutes after the collapse of A Block gate at Times Square, the prison alarm whistle finally sounded. Until that point, most of the 116 correction officers and 78 civilian employees who were on shift at Attica had no clue that all hell had broken loose at the very epicenter of the prison. Each time a group of prisoners burst into another area of the prison, they caught the officers there completely unprepared. Anyone in a white CO shirt or blue shirt worn by civilian employees was fair game for retaliation from prisoners deeply angry at the abuses they felt they had too long endured at Attica.

Standing guard in the metal shop, Mike Smith heard the prison whistle, but he had no idea what it meant; all he had ever been told was that an alarm would sound if a prisoner escaped. Heading to the windows that looked down to the first floor of the shop, the garage area, which was under the supervision of CO Eugene (G. B.) Smith, he saw that something was seriously wrong: prisoners were running around and arming themselves. Mike Smith hurriedly decided to lock the civilians in the metal shop office to protect them, and watched as the now terrified prisoner workers in his shop began trying to squeeze themselves into lockers or hide under tables.

Mike ran to the phone in the office. But it was dead. As he frantically dialed, trying to reach someone in authority, Mike could hear men breaking through the steel doors at the bottom of the stairs. He heard them climbing the stairs, then beating on the doors leading to his part of the shop. Mike could only stand still, his keys in one hand and his nightstick in the other, praying that the doors would hold. To his shock, a prisoner inside the shop suddenly came out of hiding, took Mike's keys, and opened the door. Scores of men rushed in, knocked him down, and set upon him with a pipe.

As Mike lay there trying to protect his head, two other prisoners who had been hiding, July Manifesto author Don Noble and another man, threw their bodies over him, telling the men to leave him alone because he was "a good guy." Correction officer Donald Almeter, who was also in the metal shop that day, didn't fare so well. Twenty-three-year-old Almeter had a reputation as a tough guy, and prisoners gladly gave him a beating. "They looked like Watutsis comin' in," Almeter later recounted. "I got hit so hard and spun around I thought I was in A yard."[20]

The prisoners then broke into the metal shop office and dragged the civilian employees down the stairs and out of the shop. Mike Smith was still in the shop with prisoner Don Noble and the other man who had protected him. These men now fretted about what to do with the CO. They considered hiding Smith in the paint shop, but feared what would happen to him if he were discovered later on. So they escorted him out of the metal shop as their "prisoner," hoping to get him through A Block and out to the administration building, where he would be safe.

Although many of Attica's COs experienced violence and wrath as the prison fell, Mike Smith was by no means the only guard to be protected by prisoners. G. B. Smith, the guard in the downstairs part of the metal shop, had watched in terror as the eighty men in his charge began to arm themselves. He asked one of them why he had grabbed a metal pipe. The man replied, "That is for my protection, Mr. Smith, I am not planning on using it on you."[21] Another group of men from outside the shop smashed through the steel door by driving an electric forklift through it. It appeared that the workers in G. B. Smith's shop were abandoning him when they stepped aside, though he later reflected that stepping aside was "exactly what I would have done."[22] The intruders forced G. B. Smith to strip, but one of the men who worked for him grabbed the CO away from them and escorted him out the door, shouting at any prisoner who came near that this was his "motherfucking hostage."[23] When they were almost to Times Square, this man said quietly, "Don't worry, Mr. Smith, I am going to try to get you to the yard as easy as possible."[24]

In B Yard, correction officer Dean Wright had a similar experience. Soon after it became clear to him that a full-scale riot was under way, he and Mike Smith's friend John D'Arcangelo barricaded themselves in the yard toilet, piling pillows, cushions, and other items that were stored in there up against the door. After several hours of hearing nothing but smashing glass and screaming and, at times, utter silence, the two were discovered by prisoners, who threatened to burn them out if they did not open the door. They surrendered to this ragged group of men wearing football helmets and wielding baseball bats. They were subsequently stripped, roughed up, and forced out into D Yard. But as Wright recalled, one guy then ran over, grabbed him, told the others to leave him alone, and said to him, "You were always fair with me and I'm going to try to see that you don't get hurt."[25]

While Dean Wright, John D'Arcangelo, Mike Smith, G. B. Smith, and Don Almeter were being taken hostage, back in Times Square William Quinn still lay motionless on the floor. Don Melven and Gordon Kelsey were coming to, and two other officers whom prisoners had beaten, Paul Rosecrans and Alton Tolbert, were huddled on the floor. When prisoner Richard X Clark happened upon this scene, he could see that Quinn was in bad shape; the four other guards weren't doing well either. He knew he had to do something to get them help.

Clark was twenty-five years old and had been sent to Attica after his addiction to drugs led him to stealing and a conviction for robbery and petty larceny. Clark had acquired his drug habit while serving in the Navy. He had managed to contain it for a while, even receiving an honorable discharge in 1968 and returning home to his wife, Celeste, and their one-year-old twin sons. But he soon became addicted again.[26]

Being in prison had been a wake-up call for Clark. He'd become a devout Muslim, and by 1971 had risen to a leadership position within Attica's Black Muslim community. As a leader he felt compelled to do whatever it took to secure the safety of the five men who lay injured in Times Square. Within an hour, Clark and several of his men had taken COs Kelsey, Melven, Rosecrans, and Tolbert through A Tunnel to A Block, and for their own protection had locked them in two cells where 8 Company was usually housed. When he returned to A Tunnel, Clark came upon another battered guard, CO Royal Morgan, nicknamed "Tree Trunk," and a prisoner, who were trying to carry CO William Quinn somewhere safer—although Morgan himself seemed to be in shock and had on nothing but his shoes and socks.[27] It was obvious that Morgan's hand had been badly shattered and that he was having a hard time carrying Quinn's unconscious body, so Clark called some other prisoners over to assist. They moved Quinn into an office on the ground floor of A Block, and then locked up Morgan on the second floor gallery of A Block with the other guards from Times Square so that he would be spared further assault.[28] Returning to Quinn, Clark realized that this CO was in urgent need of medical attention. He was, as Clark recalled, "still unconscious, flat on his back. He was bleeding from the nose and mouth . . . he also had a bad head injury."[29] With great trepidation, Clark walked to the gate that separated A Block from the administration building. Facing nervous officers with shotguns behind a second gate a mere fifteen feet away, he called out, "There's a hurt guard in here, can you send in a doctor?" Their first response was cold stares.[30] "Damn," Clark thought, "here is one of their own men and they won't even come to help him."[31] Finally, someone shouted that he should bring Quinn to them.[32]

Shaking his head in disbelief, Clark went back into A Block and recruited five of his fellow Black Muslims to help him lift Quinn's limp body onto a mattress and carry him down one flight of stairs to the gate.[33] Along the way one of the men known as Brother Sharif slipped on some blood and fell with such force that he chipped his tooth. The others somehow managed to keep Quinn upright, and they placed him carefully on the floor so that the guards behind the second gate could see him. Still no one came for Quinn. Thinking that prison officials might rescue Quinn if he left the area, Clark walked up the stairway to A Block. From there, he watched as someone finally came to take the severely injured CO away.

As soon as they shut the gate behind them, Clark yelled out to the officers on the other side of the gate that there were other guards upstairs who also needed medical attention. In addition to the COs he had secured on 8 Company, Clark had come upon Robert Curtiss and two other COs, Elmer Huehn and Raymond Bogart, hiding in a cell. It was clear that Bogart needed medical care.[34] Clark told all of the men in the 8 Company cells that he was going to try to get them out. As CO Gordon Kelsey remembered, "He said he was going to try . . . [but] he didn't know whether they were going to make it or not."[35] In fact, by 10:00 a.m., Clark had managed to get Kelsey, Tolbert, Rosecrans, Morgan, Melven, and another guard, Carl Murray, down to the first floor, where other COs got them out of the prison and to safety.[36] By that afternoon, prisoners had managed to get four more officers out of the prison: Raymond Bogart, James Clute, Richard Delaney, and Ken Jennings. Some of them were well enough to go home; others needed to go to the hospital. No CO was as seriously injured as William Quinn. Not only had he been badly beaten by prisoners, but prison administrators had left Quinn alone on a mattress, on the ground by the front door, with no prison doctors or nurses anywhere in sight.[37] When ambulance driver Richard O. Merle finally arrived at Attica to pick up Quinn, he couldn't believe his eyes. He was shocked by how bad Quinn's injuries were. If he hadn't known Quinn his whole life, he wouldn't have recognized him.

Outside Attica's walls William Quinn's wife, Nancy, had been hearing the relentless shrieking of the prison's whistle from 9:15 until 10:30 that morning and had no idea what was happening over there. It wasn't until many hours later that Nancy was notified that her husband was injured and had been taken to St. Jerome's Hospital in nearby Batavia. When she finally saw him, she was horrified by the "bruising and swelling all over his arms and large bandages over his hands."[38] Doctors told her that he had two open skull fractures and would need to be transferred to Northside, a larger, better-equipped hospital in Rochester, almost an hour away.[39] Nancy could barely process what she was seeing and hearing. Even much later that night Nancy Quinn still had no idea what had happened over at Attica to cause the injuries to her husband.

# 10

# Reeling and Reacting

No one in the town of Attica, not the family members of Attica employees, nor even the COs who usually worked there, had any idea why police cars were racing to the prison as the siren there blared on the morning of September 9, 1971. Lieutenant Richard Maroney, the Attica CO who had been struck by prisoner Leroy Dewer the day before, had been in his house when Attica's whistle began to sound and, though he wasn't that surprised that things had blown up the next day, it bothered him that he had no idea what had happened to cause someone to sound the alarm. No one called and no one he tried to reach seemed to have a clue what was going on.[1]

Correction officer John D'Arcangelo's wife, Ann, also had no idea why the prison whistle kept sounding, but the longer it did, the more frightened she became. She tried to remember what John had told her about that whistle. From what she could recall, it was only sounded when a prisoner had escaped. Since Ann was home alone with their three-month-old daughter, this thought was itself terrifying. She eventually gleaned that a riot had erupted, but that was all she knew. No one had called her to let her know if her husband was all right. Finally, many hours later, she learned that he was one of the COs taken hostage but that was it. She had no idea what might happen next.

Prisoners' family members who were waiting in the visitor's area to see their loved ones the morning of September 9 also had no clue why all hell seemed to be breaking loose just past the room they were in.[2] Eventually, they realized that a riot was under way inside when they saw Attica's clerical staff running out the front gate in a panic. The visiting family members also left the building, but they did so sick with fear for their loved ones still inside. Over the next few hours, the parking lot around the prison filled with the cars of family members of prisoners and prison employees alike—all desperate to know what was happening.

But Superintendent Mancusi was loath to release any information to anyone regarding why his prison was in complete chaos. Not only had he been reluctant to sound the whistle, even once he realized that things truly had gotten out of hand, but he also did not want officials from DOCS or local enforcement to get involved. Mancusi wanted to handle this crisis himself and regain control of Attica with his own men. To that end, he began calling his off-duty officers back to work. Still, Mancusi knew that he had to at least apprise his bosses in Albany of what had happened at his facility. At 9:15 that morning, he managed to reach DOCS deputy commissioner Walter Dunbar, who, in turn, alerted Commissioner Russell Oswald. Deeply alarmed, Dunbar told Oswald that he believed they both should leave immediately for Attica. At around 1:00 p.m., the two boarded a twin-engine Beechcraft King Air in Albany. Wim Van Eekeren, another deputy commissioner of corrections, was told to make sure that all other state prisons were kept under tight watch.[3] The National Guard was alerted. Governor Rockefeller's office was also contacted, but the governor himself was at a meeting of the Foreign Intelligence Advisory Board in Washington, D.C. Oswald spoke instead with the governor's first assistant counsel, Howard Shapiro, who communicated with Rockefeller's personal attorney, Michael Whiteman, who in turn relayed this intelligence to Rockefeller's close advisor, Robert Douglass. Whiteman also alerted Rockefeller's personal secretary, Ann Whitman. It was time for her to interrupt his meeting to tell the governor what was going on.[4]

While various officials were being briefed about the quickly deteriorating situation, and around the same time that William Quinn was being taken to the hospital, Mancusi's off-duty COs began arriving at Attica. They armed themselves with guns from the prison arsenal as well as baseball bats and axes from a shed behind the prison.[5] Eager to get inside to help their fellow officers, these men made some forays into Attica's chaotic cell blocks but quickly retreated when it became clear that the prisoners were in full control. Mancusi eventually advised his men to stand down and await backup from the New York State Police, whom his deputy superintendent, Leon Vincent, had contacted despite Mancusi's reservations. A mere fifteen minutes after hearing from Vincent, Major John Monahan of the NYSP's Troop A in Batavia contacted his division headquarters to let his superiors know that he was readying a battalion of men to go to the prison.[6] Governor Rockefeller's attorney, Michael Whiteman, was alarmed to learn this. There seemed to be no clear plan for reestablishing order at the prison, and yet the NYSP was already on the scene, eager to go in.

Major John Monahan, a formidable-looking man with silvery hair and a long bulbous nose, was indeed determined to retake the prison as soon as possible. Word had reached him that E Block was on fire with people still inside. Wasting no time, he ordered one of his lieutenants into that area of the prison with fire apparatus, a detail of thirty men, and a fifteen-man backup.[7] This battalion managed to put out the flames in E Block, which had already been abandoned by all but two sick inmates. The NYSP men were able to secure the area, so at least one section of the prison was now back under DOCS control.

Retaking the other cell blocks was another matter entirely. This mission was undertaken initially, at Mancusi's behest, by two contingents of correction officers, armed with tear gas canisters as well as weapons ranging from rifles to .38 caliber revolvers and even a Thompson submachine gun. Normally, it was forbidden for guards to carry a gun when confronting prisoners since guards might lose their weapons to the prisoners, but normal rules no longer applied. One contingent of COs was later joined by about one hundred state troopers, and by noon this group had swept through and eventually managed to regain control of B mess hall as well as A and C Blocks. C Block was an easy recapture, because scores of men there had chosen the safety of their cells over the chaos of the corridors.

With more than half of the prison secure by mid-morning, COs and troopers alike assumed they were going to retake the rest of it. Major Monahan, however, said no. Even though extra troopers and COs had already arrived, he considered their numbers insufficient. Helping Monahan think through the next steps was Troop A's Captain Henry "Hank" Williams, who had also arrived at Attica. Williams, a large man who sported a severe buzz cut and kept his eyes hidden behind dark glasses, had been a trooper since the age of twenty-one, and he now oversaw an eight-county region of the Bureau of Criminal Investigation of the NYSP in western New York.[8] Both he and Major Monahan spent most of that morning making sure that NYSP brass was apprised of all that was happening at the prison. George Infante, lieutenant colonel of the NYSP's Bureau of Criminal Investigation, was one of these high-ranking officials who wanted to be kept in the loop, and he too would soon be on the scene.

New York State Police gather outside the prison. *(Courtesy of* The New York Times*)*

By noon on the 9th, one hundred men from Troop A had shown up in front of Attica, as had a hundred men from Troops E and D. Word had it that Troop C was nearby, staging another fifty men.[9] There was nothing for these men to do, so they paced and fretted. No one seemed to know what should happen next. As prison officials looked from the windows or roofs of A or C Block they could see that rebelling prisoners were getting themselves organized—mostly all moving into D Yard. They could also see that these men had taken guards and civilians hostage, but how many or where they were was unknown.

# 11

# Order Out of Chaos

To the relief of the 1,281 prisoners who found themselves suddenly in charge of their own facility, and to the horror of prison officials and the police who had been watching their actions from the outside, by the afternoon of September 9 Attica's D Yard had become the scene of a highly organized and remarkably calm protest. Whereas the early morning hours had been filled with the sounds of men screaming and windows being smashed, a few hours later the incarcerated at Attica were bringing some remarkable order to what had been utter chaos.

Prisoner Carlos Roche very much liked the freedom of movement that the morning's upheaval had netted him, but he also found the lack of structure worrisome. Roche was part of 48 Company in D Block and like the thirty-nine other men in his company, including his friend Frank "Big Black" Smith, he was assigned to work in the laundry.[1] The morning of September 9, he was at his job when he realized that the metal shop just above the laundry was on fire. The phone was ringing behind him—Superintendent Mancusi's wife was, at this very moment, calling down to the laundry to order clean sheets for the warden's mansion—but all Roche could focus on was the smell of smoke, the sound of men yelling, and then, once he'd stepped out into the corridor, the utter chaos.[2] When a forklift driven by a prisoner came barreling down the corridor, he finally understood: a riot was in progress.

Not knowing where to go, Roche took off for D Yard, since that seemed to be where everyone else was running. On his way, he saw a seventy-five-year-old prisoner known as "Old Man Perry" leaning over a drum of prison-made wine, passing out big cups to men who were grabbing cartons of cigarettes and rolling big boxes of juice out of the commissary. Roche was more than ready to join the party, but he couldn't shake his wariness. This couldn't last, and it felt dangerous that no one seemed to be in charge.[3]

Roche was right to be concerned. While some prisoners like Old Man Perry were living it up in a relatively harmless way, others were engaging in much more vicious activities. Two prisoners, the nineteen-year-old twins John and James Schleich, who had landed at Attica on parole violations, experienced this firsthand. In the bedlam of that morning, John had gotten separated from James and then watched, horrified, as he saw someone walking his brother toward the bathroom. John ran to his brother's rescue, but before he knew it another man was holding a knife on him and ushering him into the same bathroom.[4] He was surrounded by a group of five or six men who repeatedly raped him.[5] Meanwhile John could hear and see his brother "up against a wall, some guy behind him," also being attacked.[6]

Others who found themselves wandering Attica's corridors unsupervised were actually more dangerous to themselves than to others. One prisoner who tried to go into a bathroom near Times Square came upon "a whole bunch of guys in there, all shooting up."[7] They'd taken advantage of their initial moments of freedom to raid the prison hospital for drugs.

Roger Champen, a well-respected jailhouse lawyer from D Block, "stood dumbfounded" by the free-for-all he was witnessing around him in the early hours of September 9.[8] When Champ, as his friends called him, walked into D Yard, it was pandemonium. There were cigarettes from the commissary and food scattered everywhere. Overwhelmed, Champ realized that order had to be established soon or else this situation was going to escalate into something scary.[9]

But the men running around the prison on the morning of September 9 seemed to know that they should stick together in one place and by midday had come to D Yard.[10] Still, Champ worried about having so many men in one open space with no one in charge. There were racial as well as political divisions, and it was unclear to Champ how everyone would behave in this unprecedented situation. The racial divisions particularly worried Champ, because he could clearly see from the looks on the faces of the whites, and from the way they had set themselves apart from the rest of the men, that they feared that a racial conflict might be brewing.[11] To his mind, this would be an utter disaster. Of the nearly 1,300 men still loose in the prison who decided to congregate in D Yard, nearly two thirds were African American, about a quarter were white, and almost 10 percent were Puerto Rican.[12] Some were affiliated with organizations such as the Black Panther Party or the Young Lords Party, while others were not at all political and wanted largely to be left alone. Champ hoped that someone would step in soon to ease tensions and encourage prisoner unity.

Champ wasn't the only prisoner out in D Yard who recognized that he needed to do something to prevent clashes and bring some calm in D Yard. Richard X Clark and his fellow Black Muslims took the initiative. They first worked to make sure that the hostages, who had been blindfolded and gathered in one area of D Yard, were protected from further assault. They formed two circles around them, inner and outer, then linked arms and faced outward to ward off any possible attack from other prisoners.[13] The way they saw it, without healthy hostages, the prisoners would have nothing to bargain with, nothing to dissuade the authorities from retaking the prison by deadly force.

Although some of the COs who'd been taken hostage were fairly well liked by the prisoners, including Mike Smith and John Stockholm, others, like Lieutenant Robert Curtiss, were not. According to one of his fellow officers, Curtiss was, in fact, "one of the most unpopular officers in the prison. . . . He was famous for his 14-day keep-locks."[14] Attica's Black Muslims not only succeeded in preventing any revenge attacks against the unpopular COs who now were being contained in what was being called the "hostage circle," but they also tried to make them as comfortable as they could be under the circumstances.[15] They gave clothing to all of the hostages who'd been stripped.[16] CO hostage G. B. Smith asked one of the men if he would tie his arms in front rather than behind to alleviate the terrible pain in his shoulders, and to his great relief, he did as asked.[17] Gary Walker, an unpopular CO who'd been grabbed out of the metal shop, stripped, and made to run through a gauntlet of prisoners, found himself grateful when the security team surrounded him.[18]

As the Muslims protectively encircled the hostages, Champ impetuously grabbed a bullhorn he had seen lying near Times Square, jumped up on a table, and issued an appeal for unity.[19] While Champ spoke to his fellow prisoners of the need to stand by one another across political and racial lines, a hush fell over D Yard. Everyone was clearly listening to his plea to "eliminate fights among ourselves and focus our hostility outside."[20] Champ was in a good position to make this pitch, because he was well known to many of the men at Attica as a fair man, someone who had been holding free classes in the yard concerning law and politics since 1968.

He had a way of speaking that was authoritative without being threatening, and his overall message—that they should work together—seemed sensible.[21]

As Champ spoke, several other men made their way to the table. Leading the way was L. D. Barkley, whom Champ had earlier asked for help. He was joined by Herbert X Blyden, Don Noble, and Frank Lott. Blyden's Auburn experience had taught him something about how to negotiate with prison authorities, and Noble and Lott, two authors of the original July Manifesto, had great credibility as well. Shortly thereafter, white radical Sam Melville also made his way to the table, as did Muslim Richard X Clark, Black Panther Tommy Hicks, and Young Lords leader Mariano "Dalou" Gonzalez. Together these men formed a committee that would help bring order to the yard. The addition of Dalou to this group was an important sign that all of Attica's men would be included in what happened next. His job was to make sure that discussions held at the table would be translated for Attica's Spanish-speaking prisoners.

In time, Champ's bullhorn was being used not just to spread calm and unity, but also to get practical things accomplished in D Yard. A prisoner skilled in electrical work managed to set up a speaker system, and everyone was soon listening as instructions were issued to immediately cease all drug taking, sexual acts, and hoarding of food and cigarettes. They were told to bring any and all weapons—crowbars, iron pipes, knives—and put them under the table where the speakers stood.[22] Dalou translated every directive into Spanish.[23]

L. D. Barkley, although the youngest man at the table, quickly became one of the most mighty speakers in the yard. Thanks to him, tensions were eased between various political factions because he insisted that his own group, the Black Panthers, work cooperatively, even with other organizations they might not like, because, as he put it, "everybody was in this thing together."[24]

Although there was remarkable good will among the men in the yard, the committee up at the table suspected they might still need a security detail. A call for volunteers netted about fifty men. Blyden and Clark went out into the yard to actively recruit more security guards, aiming for a mix of blacks, whites, and Puerto Ricans. Targeting some of the most respected—and largest—men in the group, they recruited a dedicated group, including Frank "Big Black" Smith.

Because of his size and strength, because he was one of the best players on the D Block football team, and because everyone knew he had no political allegiances that would lead him to favor some prisoners over others, Big Black was chosen to head up the security force. His friend Carlos Roche begged him not to do it, fearing the price he would pay when the takeover inevitably ended, but Big Black agreed to accept the position. Along with Herbie Scott Dean (aka Akil Al-Jundi), another well-liked man who routinely refereed the basketball and football games, he took charge of almost three hundred fellow prisoner security guards. They made sure that food was evenly distributed, that personal violence was kept in check, and that anyone who threatened another prisoner was removed from the yard. Specific security guards were also given particular tasks in the yard. A prisoner by the name of Bernard Stroble (known by all as Shango) was assigned to guard the entrance to D Block, while former Auburn prisoner Jomo Joka Omowale, known simply as Jomo, was put in charge of guarding the entrance to Times Square.

Though the task of keeping everyone safe seemed monumental, Big Black was determined to ensure that "anyone in the yard could feel like they could be in the yard without any bodily harm coming to 'em."[25] The Schleich brothers were especially glad to see men with security armbands roaming around and keeping watch over things. When Richard X Clark heard about the attack on them, he and Champ organized a security team to take the brothers on a flashlit search that night to find their rapists.[26] Although the young men were unable to identify their attackers, they nevertheless were grateful for the support.[27]

Another urgent problem facing the men in D Yard was finding some way to deal with prisoner and hostage injuries, as well as chronic maladies such as diabetes and asthma. Blyden called for anyone in the yard with medical experience to come forward.[28] Once again, volunteers headed up to the table in the corner of D Yard and began offering their services. Some went to the prison hospital to bring out bandages, and others negotiated with personnel on the outside to obtain additional supplies. One man, forty-seven-year-old Tiny Swift, became the chief prisoner administering medical care. By day's end he and his fellow volunteers had set up a fully functioning medical station, designated by a makeshift cross and a large white sheet draped over the area. Painkillers were dispensed to the injured, and medications like insulin were given to those who needed them.

As the afternoon wore on, moves were made to house people by setting up tents using cell block sheets and also to make sure that everyone got fed. The men who had assumed leadership asked a group of prisoners to go to the commissary to get its remaining supplies, and then directed that all

The organized medical station *(Courtesy of the Associated Press)*

the swiped foodstuffs and other goods the men had grabbed be deposited in a community kitty. After some discussion about how most efficiently to feed nearly 1,300 people, they decided that men would be called up to eat by cell block, and then served each meal by designated volunteers. Canned goods like Spam were among the offerings, as were sandwiches and coffee.[29]

Once basic needs were attended to, the men at the table began discussing how a more democratic decision-making body might be formed. Eventually, it was agreed that an election should be held—one in which the members of each cell block would elect two men to vote on all important decisions. Addressing the men in the yard, they asked for everyone to group together by cell block to decide which man would then "talk for the group."[30] This wasn't a speedy process, but D Yard was being transformed from anarchy into an organized tent city with democratically elected representatives, a security force, a dining area, and a fairly well-equipped medical station.

In many cases, it was the most politically engaged and outspoken prisoners who were elected. A Block chose Black Muslim leader Richard X Clark and Black Panther L. D. Barkley; B Block's men selected former New York City jail activist Herbert X Blyden to represent them. C Block elected a man named Jerry "the Jew" Rosenberg, who was highly respected for his legal knowledge, as well as Flip Crowley, who was very good at articulating a position. Champ was one of the leaders elected out of D Block. In addition to the officially elected leaders, others were eager to participate, including Sam Melville, Frank Lott, and Tommy Hicks. These men gathered around the table to be available in case anyone wanted their assistance on matters of strategy and organization.

Once it was decided who would represent the nearly 1,300 men now gathered in D Yard, the bullhorn was up for grabs, and everyone who wanted to speak could line up to voice their opinions and concerns. Free speech had come to Attica. As Richard X Clark later recalled, "a lot of rhetoric was spoken at that time," and the speeches were pointed and powerful.[31] Most focused on the many things that needed to be changed at Attica. With so many important issues being raised, it was soon clear to the leadership that they needed to draft an official statement of demands to present to prison officials. Although they had not planned this prison uprising, the men who found themselves in the middle of it wanted to make sure that they used the opportunity to make their grievances known.[32] A call for typists went out over the bullhorn, and after an hour-long cacophony of shouts, impassioned pleas, and indignant outbursts, two white and two black prisoners had tapped out a list of the major things the men in the yard wanted to accomplish.[33] Votes were taken in order to reach consensus on each point, and the leaders worked hard to help the group prioritize their demands and distinguish between issues that were urgent and those that could be dealt with later.[34]

The leadership committee also compiled a list of people they hoped would come to Attica to serve as witnesses to their uprising. They were eager to receive individuals, as Clark explained, who they felt would help them get the word out about conditions inside the prison and hold the prison officials accountable: "We wanted these individuals to come in as observers, to keep an eye on us and keep an eye on the department of correction."[35]

# 12

# What's Going On

It was clear to anyone watching Superintendent Vincent Mancusi pace his office on the morning of September 9, 1971, that he was furious. Mancusi could not believe the position he'd been put in. Here he was, fifty-seven years old with a college degree from the State University of New York at New Paltz and a high position within the state bureaucracy, and he had to go hat in hand to a bunch of thugs to ask them what in the hell they wanted. Although he thought this was outrageous, it was unavoidable. Mancusi believed that he had done all he could do to protect his staff—he had, for example, sent all of the female staff home by 10:00 that morning—but now he had to figure out how to wrest his prison back from the men inside.[1] The only way forward was to find out what the prisoners wanted and let them know, in no uncertain terms, that they had better surrender immediately.

At 11:30 on the first morning of the rebellion, as the prisoners were getting themselves organized, Mancusi grabbed a bullhorn and headed down to the gate leading to A Tunnel, the tunnel closest to the administration building. He shouted that someone needed to come and tell him what was going on. Eventually, four or five prisoners appeared in the dark recesses of the tunnel. Mancusi was unnerved to see that "they had football helmets on, towels around their head so that they were not recognizable [and] everybody was talking at once, hollering."[2] "Shut up and talk one at a time," he barked at them, as though they were ill-behaved children.[3]

They stared icily at Mancusi and, without missing a beat, one of these men, Richard X Clark, stated that "they would have nothing more to do with [him] and would only talk to the commissioner or the governor."[4]

Mancusi stormed back to his office. He was not happy to hand the problem off. In fact, he still hoped that he would be able to send Major Monahan in to take back the rest of his prison as soon as there was sufficient manpower, but that idea was nixed when Commissioner Oswald finally arrived from Albany at 2:00 p.m. with his team of officials, including his deputy commissioner, Walter Dunbar; the chief inspector of the New York State Police, John C. Miller; and Gerard Houlihan, director of public information for the Department of Correctional Services.

During a briefing in Mancusi's office on the second floor of the administration building that afternoon, Oswald made clear that he wasn't willing to approve a forcible retaking of D Yard because he was worried about the potential loss of life.[5] Instead, Oswald hoped they could find a peaceful resolution through negotiations.[6] One thing the commissioner was insistent about, however: the prisoners would have to release the hostages before he would agree to talk with them.[7]

Meanwhile, there were other parties showing up at the prison who also wanted to make sure that this riot's end was negotiated peacefully. One of these was Herman Schwartz, the practicing attorney and law professor at the University of Buffalo who had managed to get the Auburn 6 out of HBZ after their transfer to Attica. As soon as he heard on the local radio that this prison had exploded, he'd called Deputy Commissioner Dunbar in Albany and offered his assistance. Though he was told that Dunbar's office would be in touch with him should his services be needed, he decided to go to the prison anyway, just in case.[8]

As he pulled up to Attica in the early afternoon of September 9, Schwartz was taken aback by the number of spectators, reporters, and policemen already gathered there. On one of his business cards, he wrote a message—"Mr. Commissioner: I'm out here on the grass in front if I can help"—and handed it to an officer at the main door.[9] When he received it, Oswald had mixed feelings about Schwartz's offer of assistance. He had been at odds with this prisoner rights attorney on more than one occasion. That said, Oswald believed Schwartz to be "a man of warmth and convictions," and agreed to let him in.[10] As Schwartz entered through the massive door, he found himself shocked by the number of "Tommy carrying troopers and guards."[11] Unnerved, he nevertheless proceeded to the A Tunnel gate, where a group of prisoners standing guard agreed to let him come into D Yard to receive their demands.[12] Schwartz said that this was okay with him, but he would first have to talk to Commissioner Oswald.

The prisoners saw this as encouraging news—perhaps some negotiations could now begin.

Thirty-five miles away in Buffalo, Assemblyman Arthur Eve, the legislator who had visited Auburn the previous November and had been distressed with how prisoners were being treated following the rebellion there, had also heard about the uprising via an AP radio broadcast. He drove straight to the radio station to read the full transcript of what the station had gotten off the wire. Soon he too was on his way to Attica.[13] Since 1966, Eve had been one of the few African Americans in the New York State Assembly, and given how many of his constituents experienced intensive policing and high rates of arrest, prison issues had always been close to his heart. Over the years, he had found himself visiting many New York state prisons to follow up on the complaints of those locked inside.[14] Eve's reputation as a reformer, and his outspokenness on behalf of the Auburn rebels, had earned him the respect of many of the Attica prisoners. As he edged through the ever-growing crowd in Attica's parking lot on the early afternoon of the 9th, he hoped that being an elected official would allow him entrance. He knew that the prisoners had paid a high price for rebelling at Auburn, and he very much wanted to be an advocate for them before this latest uprising came to its inevitable end.

By 3:00 p.m., while the men in D Yard were still hashing out what demands they might make of prison officials, Assemblyman Eve and lawyer Schwartz were in Attica's administration building, being briefed by Oswald. Schwartz made the case that he should go into the yard as the men had requested, and Eve was eager to go in as well. Oswald agreed to send them both, asking that they set up a meeting between him and prisoner representatives contingent on the release of the hostages. At 3:25 p.m., Schwartz and Eve made their way to the A Block gate via the administration building, where they were met on the other side by a formidable-looking group who frisked them and then led them into D Yard, straight to the leadership table.[15] Schwartz was offered juice and was then asked to get up onto the table and introduce himself. Though he was well known to some of the men in the yard, others were clearly skeptical that this white lawyer in a button-down shirt could really be on their side.

Their suspicions only intensified after Schwartz asked to go over their typewritten list of "Immediate demands" and then offered his comments. The list that Schwartz reviewed included six items (reprinted here verbatim):

1. We want Complete Amnesty. Meaning Freedom for all and from all physical, mental and legal reprisals.
2. We want now speedy and safe transportation out of confinement, to a Non-Imperialistic country.
3. We demand that the Fed. Government intervine, so that we will be under direct Fed. Jurisdiction.
4. We demand the reconstruction of Attica Prison to be done by Inmates and/or inmates supervision.
5. We urgently demand immediate negotiation thru Wm. M. Kunstler, Attorney at Law—588 Ninth Ave., New York City, Assemblyman Arthur O. Eve, of Buffalo, New York. The Solidarity Prison Committee, Minister Faerrekhan of M.S. Palante, the Young Lords Party Paper, the Black Panther Party. [Clarence Jones, of Amster News]. Tom Wicker, of the New York Times, Richard Roth from the Courier Express, The Fortune Society., Dave Anderson of the Urban League of Rochester, New York., Blond Eva-Bond Nicap., and Jim Ingram of Democratic Chronicle of Detroit, Mic.
6. We intensely demand that all Communication will be conducted in "OUR" Doman "GUARANTEE ING SAFE TRANSPORTATION TO AND FROM."[16]

Schwartz felt that some of these demands were feasible. However, he made clear that he did not think that either the demand for passage to another country nor the demand for the prison to come under federal jurisdiction was likely to be met. Many in the yard became hostile, meeting his comments with boos. Confused, Schwartz felt that he was helping these men, but some saw him as "project[ing] a superior-type of attitude," and others "had this feeling that he was talking down to them" and that he was "a racist like all the others."[17]

Fearing that the situation might rapidly deteriorate, Arthur Eve stood up, introduced himself, and gave Schwartz his heartiest endorsement. This had the desired effect. Things soon calmed down. Deep down the men in D Yard knew they needed Eve and Schwartz—to communicate their demands, to set up a meeting with Oswald, and hopefully to arrange for television cameras to be brought into the prison. This last desire was important because, as Champ later explained, we "were trying to reach . . . the poor working-class people, the people who have sons and daughters and uncles and fathers and husbands and nephews in places like these. . . . Then, hopefully they can reach those in political office to get some changes made."[18] The prisoners also wanted more transistor radios so that every man sitting in D Yard would be able to hear what was being reported about their rebellion.

Twenty-five minutes after they had been escorted under heavy guard into the yard, Schwartz and Eve were back at A Tunnel gate. As they parted company, the prisoners gave them the names of three more people they hoped would come right away to Attica to act as observers: State Senator John Dunne, U.S. Congresswoman Shirley Chisholm, and Federal Judge Constance Baker Motley.

Although Oswald was obviously relieved to see Eve and Schwartz emerge from A Tunnel unharmed, he was most unhappy to learn that the issue of releasing the hostages had never come up. Worse, he was told, the prisoners wouldn't discuss anything further until the commissioner met with them personally. Superintendents Mancusi and Dunbar were adamantly opposed to this idea, fearful that Oswald might be killed or held hostage.[19] Oswald agreed to talk with the men in D Yard, but only if they would meet him on more neutral ground. Oswald proceeded to walk out onto one of the catwalks overlooking the yard and shouted down to the prisoners that he would speak with them from up there. To Oswald's astonishment, his offer was refused. If the commissioner was going to talk with the prisoners, the men shouted back, he was going to have to meet with them on the same level, man-to-man.

When the commissioner returned, he was so upset that he considered sending the state troopers in immediately. It astonished Herman Schwartz that Oswald "seemed to think that the matter had to be resolved within a few hours," because it seemed clear to him "that this situation demanded time and a lot of it." But after Schwartz and Eve reminded him that there were nearly forty hostages' lives at stake, he looked down and said softly, "I've got to go in."[20]

Together, the trio descended into A Tunnel, now referred to ominously by both sides as "No Man's Land" or the "DMZ." Schwartz, Eve, and Commissioner Oswald were met by Richard Clark and a team of prisoners charged with protecting these visitors. When they stepped into D Yard, they were surrounded by an even larger security force. Oswald was pulled and pushed along toward the table at the corner of the yard, keenly aware of the tension and anger radiating from the men on all sides. As he continually wiped the sweat from his balding head, the security force tried to calm him. Big Black Smith, for example, took care not to frisk Oswald too aggressively before bringing him into the yard, and other security men shouted, "Don't let anyone near him! Don't let anyone near him!" as the commissioner made his way forward.[21] When Oswald saw who some of the men were up at the makeshift negotiating table just ahead, however, he was unsettled all over again. Jerry "the Jew" Rosenberg, a convicted cop-killer, and L. D. Barkley's angry eyes took him aback. He was glad to see that Frank Lott and Herbert Blyden, two of the July Manifesto's authors, were also there, however, because he remembered them as seeming genuinely interested in discussion and had always written to him respectfully.[22]

To Oswald's surprise, from the moment he sat down at the negotiating table every one of the men who spoke to him began politely. In fact, as soon as he took a seat, one man offered him a drink of Grapeade, while another assured him that "they had no animus against him, but against the local prison administration."[23] Nevertheless, the men were eager to get some answers regarding why Oswald had not responded in any meaningful way to their July Manifesto. He answered that he had taken their needs seriously but had viewed the manifesto as little more than a copy of the one rebel inmates had produced at Folsom prison, sparking some angry outbursts and a chorus of boos. The men insisted that their document described conditions at Attica, and accused the commissioner of dodging their concerns. As this back-and-forth continued, Oswald kept trying, unsuccessfully, to turn the discussion to the issue of the men over in the hostage circle.

By 5:00 p.m. on this first day of the rebellion, the meeting between Oswald and the men in D Yard was coming to an end. To the commissioner's dismay, he had not secured the release of the hostages, and yet the prisoners made clear that no further discussions would take place until he fulfilled a number of their requests. So he did. Oswald agreed to, among other things, send in more food and water, remove some of the armed state troopers and COs who were watching D Yard from the roofs of other cell blocks, and check on Ray Lamorie and Leroy Dewer—whose mistreatment had helped to spark this rebellion—to make sure they were unharmed. He pledged also to look into conditions in C Block to ensure that the prisoners who had been returned to their cells there were not being beaten. Finally, and very importantly, Oswald agreed to the prisoners' request that the media be allowed into D Yard so that the world could hear what they were trying to accomplish in this protest.

As he was being handed off at the gate, one of the prisoners reminded Oswald that he had indeed been given safe passage: "You see, we kept our promise."[24] This mattered to the commissioner. He saw himself as an honorable man, and he would attempt to resolve these men's concerns to the best of his ability.

This was not at all what Major Monahan wanted to hear. By the time Oswald exited the yard, Monahan had marshaled sufficient troops to regain control of the prison.[25] In addition to his own men, by 2:30 that afternoon 250 additional troopers had arrived from other areas of the state, joining at least forty sheriff's deputies and 350 on-duty COs, all ready to storm the prison.[26]

But Oswald had already committed himself to talks with the prisoners and refused to be talked into an assault on Attica, at least for now. Over the angry objections of the growing crowd of law enforcement officers now thronging Attica's outside lawn, the commissioner set about contacting a team of newsmen to go into D Yard. He then personally toured HBZ and C Block to check on the safety of the prisoners. He also began working to contact people to serve as observers to the negotiations he hoped would soon commence. Fulfilling the prisoners' request for water turned out to be a more difficult task since many of the water lines in the prison had been damaged in the riot, but Oswald persevered. He began by contacting General Almerin C. O'Hara—known to all as Buzz. If anyone could make this happen, Buzz O'Hara was the likely candidate. Commissioner of Rockefeller's Office of General Services as well as a former commander of the New York Army National Guard who had been very effective during the Rochester, New York, riot of 1964, O'Hara did manage, by day's end, to get many large cans of water to the prison to be distributed in D Yard.[27]

At 5:48 p.m., Oswald was pleased that he had responded to the prisoners' demands so quickly and was therefore optimistic about what the next round of discussions would yield. He returned to D Yard—this time accompanied not just by Eve and Schwartz but also by two newsmen from *The New York Times* and the *Buffalo Evening News*, as well as a handful of local reporters. This group was then joined by some national broadcast and print reporters—from NBC, UPI, and ABC.[28]

From that moment on, Attica entered history. For the first time ever, Americans could get an inside look at a prison rebellion and watch it unfold. Notably, the media weren't the only ones filming inside. Since that afternoon, the New York State Police had been monitoring every move the prisoners made via a portable television camera and a videotape recorder. They were looking for any acts of potential "evidentiary value," making sure to film who was doing damage to the prison, who seemed to be in charge of the negotiations, and who was keeping the hostages in one place.[29]

The men in D Yard were thrilled to see the newscasters and cameras coming across the grass toward the negotiating table. Once the television cameras started filming, a hush fell over the yard as L. D. Barkley first took to the bullhorn. Addressing himself to "the people of the United States of America," Barkley told how the state had promised the men at Attica "many things [but] they have given us nothing, except more of what we already got, brutalization, murder inside this penitentiary. We do not intend to accept . . . this situation again. . . . Therefore we have composed this declaration to the people of America, to let them know exactly how we feel and what . . . we want." He went on to say, passionately:

> We are men: We are not beasts and we do not intend to be beaten or driven as such. The entire prison populace, that means each and every one of us here, has set forth to change forever the ruthless brutalization and disregard for the lives of the prisoners here and throughout the United States. What has happened here is but the sound before the fury of those who are oppressed.[30]

Although the men in D Yard had, as Herman Schwartz suggested, written and voted on a revised list of demands prior to the media's arriving, Barkley concluded his speech by repeating some of the prisoners' original demands, including safe transit to a "non-imperialist country" and intervention by the federal government to bring the prison under its jurisdiction. When Barkley finished his soliloquy, he received thunderous applause from the crowd of prisoners in the yard.

As Barkley spoke, Oswald and those who had come in with him sat and listened like an audience at a play. Looking at the scores of men surrounding him, Oswald said: "I've complied with the several things I said I would do as my part. I saw the three individuals you told me to see; I've brought the press and other media in here to listen as we talk. I earlier promised you there would be no reprisals other than what any law enforcement district attorney might take in terms of any crimes that might have been committed. And now, my question is . . . when will you release the hostages?"[31] To that, he heard no affirmative response.

Every man at Attica remembered what had happened at Auburn once the prisoners agreed to give up their hostages and surrender in exchange for a promise of no reprisals: they had been beaten and put into segregation. The men in D Yard reminded Oswald that his solemn assurance that

Elation in D Yard *(Courtesy of the Associated Press)*

no harm would come to them meant little. Oswald countered by reminding them that he had not been the commissioner when the men at Auburn had ended their protest. "I am a man of my word. If I say I'm going to do it, I'm going to do it!"[32] A sea of skeptical faces looked back at him. They doubted that Oswald had the authority to make decisions pertaining to any physical or legal backlash they might suffer after surrendering.

Feeling that they were reaching an impasse, Oswald decided to leave the yard. Before escorting him to A Tunnel, however, the prisoners handed him something to think over: their new list of fifteen "practical proposals" that they had prepared in response to Schwartz's critique:

1. Apply the New York State minimum wage law to all State Institutions. STOP SLAVE LABOR.
2. Allow all New York State prisoners to be politically active, without intimidation or reprisals.
3. Give us true religious freedom.
4. End all censorship of newspaper, magazines, letters, and other publications coming from the publisher.

5. Allow all inmates at their own expense to communicate with anyone they please.
6. When an inmate reaches Conditional Release, given him a full release without parole.
7. Cease administrative resentencing of inmates returned for parole violation.
8. Institute realistic rehabilitation programs for all inmates according to their offense and personal needs.
9. Educate all Correctional Officers to the needs of the inmates, i.e. understanding rather than punishment.
10. Give us a healthy diet, stop feeding us so much pork, and give us some fresh fruit daily.
11. Modernize the inmate educational system.
12. Give us a doctor that will examine and treat all inmates that request treatment.
13. Have an Institutional delegation comprised of one inmate from each company authorized to speak to the Institution Administration, concerning grievances (QUARTERLY).
14. Give us less cell time and more recreational equipment and facilities.
15. Remove inside walls, making one open yard and no more segregation or punishment.[33]

Though Oswald agreed to consider this new list of demands, he was now the skeptical one. Oswald could see that the demands on this list were quite different from those laid out by Barkley's fiery speech, which led him to worry that there was no consensus in the yard as to what it would take to end the standoff.

In the administration building that evening, Oswald briefed the prison and law enforcement officials waiting for him and then he called Governor Rockefeller's attorney, Michael Whiteman, to update him. The commissioner wanted everyone in the governor's office to have faith in his decision to negotiate with the prisoners, but seeing how suspicious of him the men in D Yard had been had sapped some of his own enthusiasm for the process. As had happened earlier in the year when he dealt with the aftermath of the Auburn rebellion, his feelings of personal affront were slowly morphing into a powerful suspicion that prisoners were not in fact calling "for prison reform" but rather "for revolution and anarchy beginning in the prisons."[34] Whereas Governor Rockefeller believed that "discussions could prove counter-productive" at Attica, Oswald still resisted fully adopting this view.[35]

Notably, Rockefeller's lawyers in Albany, Michael Whiteman and Howard Shapiro, did not count on Oswald's meetings with the prisoners to resolve the crisis at hand and spent the first day of the rebellion at Attica trying to get the governor to weigh in. It had taken until 6:00 p.m. for Whiteman to reach the governor to brief him. Rockefeller instructed Whiteman to continue monitoring the situation and also to keep an eye out for the possibility of outside agitators coming to Attica. Like all of the other uprisings that had taken place recently in his state's penal facilities, the governor refused to believe that this one was born of the genuine grievances of prisoners on the inside. To prevent further rabblerousing from outside militants, Rockefeller told Whiteman to stay in touch with local law enforcement and to invoke the state's "emergency powers to cordon the area off."[36] According to Rockefeller attorney Howard Shapiro the State Police had in fact informed him that "a black organization from Buffalo" was "planning to go to Attica," so he alerted Deputy Commissioner of Corrections Wim Van Eekeren to this news and instructed him to watch this situation closely.[37] Shortly afterward Van Eekeren received his own police briefing to the effect that "25 Panthers were en route from Buffalo to Attica."[38] An hour later, Shapiro again called the Department of Corrections, this time to ascertain whether the DOCS would be willing to close all roads leading to the prison should any "outsiders attempt to get near" it.[39]

Rockefeller's men were not the only ones interested in monitoring the response of grassroots and civil rights organizations to the Attica uprising. So was the Federal Bureau of Investigation (FBI). In fact, it was remarkable that federal agencies were so involved in what was happening in this one state prison in the middle of rural New York. Immediately, the FBI stepped up its already extensive surveillance of groups suspected to be sympathetic to prisoners and leaned on its informants in New York, Chicago, and San Francisco to gather information on the Attica rebels. Even more astoundingly, whatever intelligence the FBI gathered, credible or not, was then relayed to authorities at the highest levels of the United States government, including President Richard Nixon, Vice President Spiro Agnew, and U.S. Attorney General John Mitchell, as well as the Defense Intelligence Agency, the Department of the Army, the Department of the Air Force, the Naval Investigative Service, the Secret Service, and the National Security Agency.[40] The Albany office of the FBI alerted other bureau directors that Rockefeller's right-hand man, Robert Douglass, also wanted to be kept apprised of any "information bearing on the Attica situation" that they gleaned from their "extremist informants."[41]

Troublingly, the various reports disseminated by the FBI were often misleading if not outright inaccurate. In one teletype sent to the director of the Domestic Intelligence Division of the FBI, as well as to the White House and the U.S. attorney general, at 11:58 p.m. on September 9, the Buffalo office reported that during the riot "the whites were reportedly forced into the yard area by the blacks" and Black Power militants there were rounding up not just employee hostages but also all white prisoners, which was misleading in that it suggested a race riot was unfolding.[42] More inflammatory still, the FBI's Buffalo office stated that the prisoners "have threatened to kill one guard for every shot fired [at them]"; that they "have threatened to kill all hostages unless demands are met"; and that all of the hostages "are being made to stand at attention" out in D Yard.[43] None of this proved to be the case.

During the tumultuous 1960s and 1970s the FBI was deeply invested in destabilizing and undermining grassroots organizations that it considered a threat to national security—as were the politicians, such as Nixon, Agnew, and Mitchell, who supported its efforts and relied on its briefings.[44] One of the FBI's counterintelligence programs in this period—COINTELPRO—was notorious for using rumor and outright fabrication stories in an attempt to destroy leftist, antiwar, and civil rights groups from within. For this reason Commissioner Oswald's determination to keep negotiating with the men in D Yard infuriated much of the Bureau. As one internal FBI memo put it, state officials had "capitulated to the unreasonable demands of prisoners."[45] And these weren't just any criminals; as the FBI noted on multiple occasions, "The majority of the mutinous prisoners are black."[46] As dusk fell over D Yard on the first day of the Attica uprising, FBI and State Police rumors about black prisoners' threats and outrageous actions only multiplied. But no matter how hostile everyone else was to the idea of the state negotiating with the prisoners, Commissioner Russell Oswald insisted even more forcefully that he was going to see these talks through.

# 13

# Into the Night

As much as Commissioner Russell Oswald wanted his negotiations with the men in D Yard to bring a speedy end to the rebellion that was now making news across the country, he was also determined to get some concessions from those men quickly, lest his superiors pull the plug. When his deputy commissioner, Walter Dunbar, offered to go in to talk to the prisoners, Oswald agreed and, at 7:30 p.m.—still on this first day of the Attica uprising—Dunbar, accompanied by Herman Schwartz, Arthur Eve, and a Republican state assemblyman named James Emery, made a fourth outsider visit into D Yard.

But Deputy Commissioner Dunbar was not the sort of person to win anyone over in a situation as charged as this one. When the prisoners handed him a copy of the same list of demands they had already given Oswald, Dunbar let himself be derailed by his concerns about proposal number two: "Allow all New York State prisoners to be politically active, without intimidation or reprisals." What, Dunbar asked the men, peering at them over his horn-rimmed glasses, did they mean by politically *active*? And he proceeded to debate them on the point. But the men soon changed the subject to focus on the issue at the heart of the matter, as far as they were concerned: the rebellion itself and what it would take to end it. They could not release any hostages, let alone surrender, they told Dunbar, if they were not given some sort of guarantee that there would be no reprisals.

As the discussions in D Yard grew increasingly tense, prisoner Jerry Rosenberg suddenly produced a handwritten legal document he'd been working on during the previous hour entitled "Inmates of Attica Prison

v. Nelson Rockefeller, Russell Oswald, and Vincent Mancusi." If a federal judge was willing to sign this, Rosenberg explained, it would act as a court injunction forbidding the state from engaging in any reprisals when the men surrendered. The men in the yard were glad to hear this and soon discussion turned to the question of which judge might be willing to sign this document. The name of Judge Constance Baker Motley kept coming up because she was well known among prisoners as one who had been willing to rule in favor of Martin Sostre, a prisoner who had sued the Department of Corrections for keeping him locked in solitary confinement for a year.[1]

Herman Schwartz, who had accompanied Dunbar into the yard, jumped in with an offer to get the injunction signed—though not by Judge Motley, as she presided over the Southern District of New York, and thus Attica was not in her jurisdiction. Instead, he suggested approaching Judge John T. Curtin of the Western District. The men liked this idea. Judge Curtin had forced Mancusi to let the Auburn 6 out of HBZ, which suggested he too was a jurist sympathetic to prisoners. This, though, would take time, Schwartz pointed out. Curtin, along with every other New York judge who might help them, was currently in Vermont attending a conference. As he explained these complications, which many of the men viewed as just another delaying tactic, Schwartz was booed. But one prisoner's voice broke through the denunciations to say that there really was such a conference taking place, he'd read about it in the *New York Law Journal*. When Schwartz then offered to go to Vermont to try to see Curtin that very night, the men again turned enthusiastic.[2]

Discussion in the yard now turned to the question of whether the men in C Block were being beaten. Although both Oswald and Arthur Eve had together looked into this and reported that all was fine earlier that evening, the men's fears had not been allayed. Deputy Commissioner Dunbar could sense that this issue was not going to go away unless they could see the cell block for themselves. He agreed to take three prisoners on a tour of the wing to confirm that their fellow prisoners were okay. Dunbar also agreed, after being pressed hard, to allow a doctor into D Yard. He had to concede that there were people there, prisoners as well as hostages, who needed more professional medical care than the self-appointed caregivers at the medical station could provide. As the men in the yard had made clear to him, it reflected very poorly on state officials that they had not yet allowed a physician to enter the yard.[3]

At 8:00 p.m. Dunbar left D Yard to update Oswald, while Arthur Eve took Champ, Richard Clark, and a third prisoner on the promised tour of C Block. This was an extremely frightening experience for the trio of prisoners because, as Clark recalled, "You could just feel the hatred of the troopers there . . . you could look into their eyes and feel the hate and see all the restraint they had to put on themselves to keep from pulling the trigger."[4] Once in C Block, though, they felt the trip had been worth it. The men locked up there were indeed unharmed.

At around 9:00 p.m. after the tour of C Block, Champ, acting in his capacity as jailhouse lawyer, went with Assemblyman Eve to Mancusi's office to work with Herman Schwartz on finalizing the language of the injunction. After a number of drafts, Champ was finally satisfied that the injunction covered the necessary points. Schwartz called Judge Curtin at his hotel in Manchester, Vermont, to explain what he needed and the judge gave his word that he would sign the injunction as soon as Schwartz arrived. Schwartz persuaded Commissioner Oswald to affix his signature of consent to the document as well, then had a state trooper drive him the twelve miles to the nearest airport, in Batavia.

At 11:30 p.m., while he waited for his flight to leave, Schwartz called Judge Motley to see if she too would sign the injunction. He explained that he had already told the prisoners that Attica was not in her jurisdiction, but they still wanted her endorsement of this document. Despite his rather lengthy plea, Schwartz was unable to persuade Motley to sign the injunction. It was clear to him that "she simply didn't want to do any irrelevant and idle act."[5] Schwartz felt that Motley's signature would have been very helpful, even if just symbolically, but he retained hope that having both Curtin's and Oswald's endorsement would be enough.

As Schwartz boarded the plane to Vermont to see Judge Curtin, Walter Dunbar was returning to D Yard, this time with a physician, Dr. Warren Hanson. Dr. Hanson, a surgeon at the Wyoming County Community Hospital fifteen miles south of Attica, had responded to the Wyoming county sheriff's call for physicians to come to the prison in case they were needed. Although Dr. Hanson had been outside Attica for hours, along with several other doctors simply hovering around "the Red Cross stand drinking coffee and eating donuts," no one had called for medical assistance or bothered to explain anything about the medical situation inside.[6] Hanson and other doctors found this incredible given the rumors that were flying around "about the hostages being either dead or seriously wounded."[7]

After being given assurance of safe passage by the prisoners in the DMZ, Hanson was assigned a personal security guard who told him, "Doctor, I am responsible for your safety. . . . I don't want to be holding and pushing you around [so] why don't you hold my arm and let me kind of lead you, and you just follow me."[8] Once in D Yard, Hanson saw two long lines of prisoners who were wearing white armbands, had linked elbows, and faced each other. These men had, in effect, formed a secure human tunnel for him to walk through. He was very grateful.[9]

Hanson met with the leadership group, and then was escorted to the medical station, which consisted of three tables and a chest with some medications and bandages. After being briefed by the prisoners' medical team, Hanson headed over to the hostage circle. The hostages, who were still surrounded by the security team of Black Muslims, were huddled together in an oval-shaped space, some of them sitting up, others lying down.[10] By now the hostages had been blindfolded for almost ten hours and Hanson found them in a state of severe emotional distress. He did his best to try to calm them down, and was "pleased to find that they were in quite good shape."[11] The prisoners had already tried to tend to the hostages, in several cases splinting possible fractures as well as doing some emergency suturing, and while a number of the hostages had various wounds and injuries, none of them were life-threatening.[12]

Although the prison administration had sent Dr. Hanson in to check on the health of the hostages, when the leaders in D Yard asked him to look at the prisoners who were also in need of care, he readily agreed. Returning to the medical station, he held a sick call attended by approximately twenty-five to thirty men. Some had been injured during the takeover, but others sought his help for long-standing problems. As Richard Clark explained, "We had sick prisoners who had never received any medical attention in Attica."[13] In need of more supplies, Hanson asked permission to send prisoner Tiny Swift out of D Yard to get medicine and splints. Swift had been sent to Attica on a life sentence for murder, but Hanson found him to be a dedicated caregiver in this stressful situation. Hanson was in fact so impressed with Swift's dedication to patient care that when he returned with the supplies, the doctor decided to give him some additional on-the-spot medical training so that he could do more good once Hanson left.[14]

After taking care of the ambulatory patients, Dr. Hanson began making rounds, accompanied by a security detail of four or five prisoners. As they walked through the now dark yard, one of the men worked a bullhorn: "Anybody want a doctor? Anybody want a doctor?"[15] Hanson grew somewhat fearful, especially when he noticed that the leaders were no longer keeping tabs on him. "It was dark, and people were guiding me around with flashlights, and all these menacing people were carrying clubs and weapons of all kinds." But eventually he realized he had nothing to worry about.[16] After also taking a trip through two tiers of D Block, where some of the elderly or infirm prisoners who might need care had chosen to sleep, Hanson was escorted out of the yard by the same man who had brought him in four hours earlier. He shook the doctor's hand and thanked him "on behalf of his brothers."[17]

Around the same time that Dr. Hanson was leaving the prison, two top aides to Governor Rockefeller were coming in: General Buzz O'Hara, who earlier that day had facilitated getting water to the men in D Yard, and T. Norman Hurd, New York's state budget director.[18] Oswald briefed the governor's men and took them on a tour of A Block, then invited them to a meeting with Dunbar, Mancusi, and Major John Monahan and Chief Inspector John C. Miller from the NYSP. Everyone at the meeting was gratified to learn that Oswald, while still insisting on seeing negotiations through, was at least willing to discuss what would be required to retake the prison.[19] Major Monahan felt that with five to six hundred troopers assembled outside, ready to move in as soon as they received the go-ahead, they now had everything they needed. General Buzz O'Hara disagreed; in his view, CS gas (a kind of tear gas) was essential for success in such an operation, and they had neither the gas nor the plane with which to disperse it over the prison yard. So O'Hara reached out to his contacts in the National Guard, who worked through the night to secure a CH-34 helicopter with an M-5 chemical dispenser and enough gas to incapacitate everyone in D Yard.[20]

Back in D Yard, prisoners and hostages alike were still counting on successful talks. Both groups were grateful to have seen Hanson, but some felt fearful when he left. This was particularly true of the men over in the hostage circle. These men had been glad of the security afforded them so far, yet were worried about whether "the Muslims could really protect us."[21] On this score, hostage Don Almeter felt "more scared than I ever was in Vietnam," and hostage John Stockholm was so scared that he could not even go to the bathroom when his captors gave him the chance to do so.[22] As he recalled, his "body just shut down."[23] As the hours passed, though, these men began to feel much better about their prospects. In the middle of the night, a number of prisoners went into D Block's cells and dragged out mattresses for the hostages to sleep on as well blankets to keep them covered.[24]

The prisoners knew that the hostages were all that stood between them and what they believed would be a bloody assault on the prison. Despite the bravado they had displayed in their discussions with prison officials throughout the day, the men in D Yard were also terrified. They were not at all sure they could trust Schwartz to get them an injunction against reprisals and they worried mightily about the sharpshooters that the NYSP had been placing on the cell block roofs above them. For this reason, as one prisoner explained, "most of us slept right out there in the yard."[25] At least out in the open they'd know if an attack was starting.

Despite the sense of foreboding, there were moments of levity and, for some, even a feeling of unexpected joy as men who hadn't felt the fresh air of night for years reveled in this strange freedom. Out in the dark, music could be heard—"drums, a guitar, vibes, flute, sax, [that] the brothers were playing." This was the lightest many of the men had felt since being processed into the maximum security facility.[26] That night was in fact a deeply emotional time for all of them. Richard Clark watched in amazement as men embraced each other, and he saw one man break down into tears because it had been so long since he had been "allowed to get close to someone."[27] Carlos Roche watched as tears of elation ran down the withered face of his friend "Owl," an old man who had been locked up for decades. "You know," Owl said in wonderment, "I haven't seen the stars in twenty-two years."[28] As Clark later described this first night of the rebellion, while there was much trepidation about what might occur next, the men in D Yard also felt wonderful, because "no matter what happened later on, they couldn't take this night away from us."[29]

# 14

# A New Day Dawns

Early in the morning on Friday, September 10, the second day of the Attica rebellion, Herman Schwartz arrived back at Attica prison from Vermont. He was proud of himself; he'd managed to drag Judge John T. Curtin out of his cozy bed at the Equinox Hotel at 3:30 a.m. to sign a document that read simply, "Upon consent of defendants, it is hereby ORDERED that: Defendants, their agents and employers, are enjoined from taking any physical or other administrative reprisals against any inmates participating in the disturbance at the Attica Correctional Facility on September 9, 1971."[1] By getting Commissioner Russell Oswald's signature at the bottom, Schwartz felt that he had secured the "consent of the defendants" and that this was what the men in D Yard really needed to be protected.[2]

At around 8:00 a.m., Schwartz was able to hand the now rather crumpled legal document over to the prisoners at the gate that separated A Tunnel from A Block. Since Oswald had promised them the night before that he would be back by 7:00 a.m. and he hadn't yet shown up, many were clearly tense but Schwartz hoped that this injunction would improve moods. Much to his astonishment, soon after he handed over a copy of the document, he and Arthur Eve were summoned back to the A Block gate where, looking at him with hard eyes, Richard Clark proclaimed it "worthless."[3] "Why?" Schwartz asked incredulously. "Because it has no seal on it," Clark replied.[4] Schwartz explained to Clark that the judge could not have had his seal with him in Vermont at 3:30 in the morning but that, if the men demanded one, he would now try to get one affixed at Curtin's office in Buffalo.[5] Schwartz beat a hasty retreat to get the original of the document driven to Buffalo to affix the judge's seal to it. He personally felt that Curtin's signature on the original document was wholly sufficient, but very much wanted to ease the minds of the men in D Yard that this injunction was indeed binding.

At 8:45, with still no sign of Oswald, Clark sent word to the administration building that the commissioner needed to come to meet with the men immediately. Clark also indicated that Black Panther Bobby Seale should be added to their list of people who might come to Attica to be an observer to the negotiations. Originally the men had hoped Black Panther Huey Newton would come to Attica, but if Seale came instead they wanted to be sure he was admitted. Having now waited more than two hours to resume negotiations with the commissioner, the men feared that an assault on them could come soon and believed it crucial to have as many outside eyes on this situation as they could get.

Oswald had been delayed precisely because he was hard at work trying to get the observers whom the prisoners had asked to appear. He also was making sure that there were men in that group whom the state would also be happy with—men on this committee who saw the state's side of things. To that end, he enlisted the aid of Norman Hurd and Buzz O'Hara from the governor's office, who in turn contacted Rockefeller attorney Michael Whiteman, to see who might be interested in coming to Attica.

After some deliberation, Whiteman and others in the governor's office came up with a list of possible observers they thought would temper the influence of the more liberal, and in some cases radical, observers requested by the prisoners. The key, as they saw it, was to choose men who were sympathetic to the state, but not so obviously that the prisoners would reject their participation. On their list were two African Americans who had worked closely with Dr. Martin Luther King Jr.—the Reverend Wyatt Tee Walker, senior pastor of Canaan Baptist Church of Christ in Harlem, and Clarence Jones, the editor of the black paper the *Amsterdam News*. They also suggested approaching Puerto Rican congressman Democrat Herman Badillo, as well as moderate Republican state senator John Dunne, since both had had experience in resolving the prison crises in the New York City jail system the previous summer. They insisted, however, on a conservative presence as well, and chose former police officer, district attorney, and now Republican state senator Thomas F. McGowan, as well as Republican New York state assemblymen Frank Walkley and Clark Wemple.

Meanwhile, state assemblyman Arthur Eve was also feverishly trying to reach the men and women the prisoners wanted for the observers committee. His staff successfully reached not only Jim Ingram, the black reporter from Detroit, and Tom Wicker from *The New York Times*, whom the men had requested, but also contacted men from the prisoner reform organization, the Fortune Society, as well as two men from the Young Lords. Eve reached out personally to leaders of the Black Panthers, who agreed to send someone after they consulted further. By that afternoon, Eve was glad to learn that Lewis Steel, the attorney who had represented the Auburn 6 with Herman Schwartz, was already outside Attica prepared to offer his services to the group. Eve still wanted to reach famed leftist lawyer William Kunstler, as the prisoners had asked for him particularly.

As the men in D Yard waited anxiously—but peacefully—for some sight of the commissioner, rumors of prisoner atrocities ran rampant outside the prison. After having seen the prisoners bring mattresses out from cells and place them in the hostage circle (so that these men would have beds), rumors flew among the troopers that the hostages were being "surrounded by gasoline soaked mattresses."[6] Again insisting that it was imperative they get into the prison, state troopers began to ready themselves for a forcible retaking. By 12:45 p.m., all State Police personnel were on standby in front of the administration building, waiting for the green light.[7] There remained, however, a tactical problem: the tear gas and the

An aerial view of D Yard *(Courtesy of the* Buffalo News*)*

helicopters necessary for this undertaking had yet not arrived. A few hours later the helicopters were finally available, but the men whom the commander of the New York National Guard had tagged to fly this mission still needed "a period of ten hours or more . . . to prepare gas canisters and primer mechanisms."[8] A forcible retaking was again forestalled.

So focused was Oswald on assembling the observers committee and resuming negotiations that he seemed almost oblivious to the fact that law enforcement was still planning to storm the prison as soon as they had all of their ducks in a row. And yet, his ability to gather this group of impressive individuals in the prison was, unbeknownst to him, thwarting those same retaking plans. Observers and other outsiders had been arriving throughout the day and they were a diverse group. There were Republican senators, but also well-known black clergymen such as Marvin Chandler, Raymond Scott, and Franklin Florence who worked with the anti-poverty group FIGHT. These pastors wanted to be at Attica to gather information for the many prisoners' families they knew in nearby Rochester. Once Oswald learned from Eve that they were there, he decided that they too should be official observers. As Marvin Chandler saw it, "I think they just wanted us to give it legitimacy."[9]

Oswald had spent so much time on getting observers to Attica that when he finally contacted the men in D Yard, they had been waiting to hear from him for four hours. There was a flurry of heated exchanges about where the meeting would take place, with Oswald proposing it be held in the A Block tunnel and the prisoners unyielding in their insistence that it be held in the yard. Oswald capitulated.[10] As they had made clear to him, "This is a people issue, not a group, therefore you must bring your observers, etc., to the people."[11]

At 11:25 a.m.—now Friday, the second day of the uprising—Oswald, along with five observers, Arthur Eve, Herman Schwartz, Lewis Steel, Raymond Scott, and Marvin Chandler, as well as almost a dozen members of the media, trekked through A Tunnel and back into the yard for a fifth visit. Oswald, Schwartz, and Eve could immediately feel that the mood of the men had turned considerably grimmer since their last visit, as evidenced by how much more aggressively they were frisked. Schwartz, who was uncertain how the prisoners would react to the still unresolved issue of the injunction, was particularly nervous.[12] Rightly so, as it turned out.

As soon as their group arrived at the negotiating table, lawyer Herman Schwartz was startled by "the harangues and tirades and bitterness spewed out against Oswald."[13] And it wasn't just the more high-profile men in the yard—L. D. Barkley, Champ, Herb Blyden, Richard Clark, Sam Melville—who were hurling invective at the commissioner. The anger in the yard was widespread. Oswald sat silently through the abuse, looking dazed and weary as epithets like "racist pig" and "vicious dog" rained down on him. And then it was Schwartz's turn. Once the men's attention returned to the injunction, Schwartz tried to explain that, even without the seal, the document gave them protection against both physical and administrative reprisals, but nevertheless someone was on his way to get a seal placed on the original injunction as they had demanded. Somehow his defense only intensified the group's suspicion of the injunction.[14]

To the men in D Yard this court order was absolutely crucial to their ability, as prisoner Flip Crowley explained, to get "out of the yard with some type of dignity [and] without getting hurt."[15] For this reason Schwartz was bombarded with questions about the injunction—its meaning, its power, etc. "Why was Oswald's signature on it? What good would that do? . . . Why wasn't [Rockefeller's] signature on it, if a signature was necessary?"[16] Then, suddenly, one of the elected leaders, jailhouse lawyer Jerry Rosenberg, grabbed the microphone and with a great flourish ripped a copy of the injunction all had been reviewing to shreds. Not only did the injunction have no seal, Rosenberg shouted, but it referred specifically to the events of September 9 and thus did them no good *now*. Furthermore, it did not prevent prison officials from exacting retribution on the prisoners by charging them with crimes after their rebellion ended. Without criminal amnesty, he argued, they really had no protection whatsoever. Schwartz was incredulous that the injunction he had worked so hard to obtain, and at the prisoners' request, was now rejected outright by them. The roar of approval touched off by Rosenberg's speech was enough to persuade him to remain silent, however.[17]

The men at the table then turned their anger back to Oswald. Although they kept trying to go over their list of "practical proposals" with the commissioner, it only infuriated them more when he explained that he had not yet accomplished any of them. He needed more time. Worse, in their view, Oswald then kept trying to turn the discussion back to a freeing of the hostages. The way the prisoners saw it, they had already released many of their hostages—eleven men, COs as well as civilians. Some, like Gordon Kelsey and William Quinn, had been hurt and clearly needed care, but they had released others as well. But Oswald was unappeased. He had just learned that two other COs had been found hiding in a bathroom that morning, so he was not at all certain how many men were even being

Commissioner Russell Oswald (seated, lower left corner) faces the prisoner leaders at the negotiation table, including Frank "Big Black" Smith (wearing sunglasses) and L. D. Barkley (second from right). *(Courtesy of* The New York Times*)*

held in D Yard and this troubled him mightily.[18] "How many hostages are there? Thirty-eight?" he asked. At which point someone yelled out, "Now thirty-nine!" and, turning to the men in the yard, said, "Why don't we keep him here?"[19] Now Schwartz was really scared. The yard had suddenly erupted into a cacophony of yelling, screaming, and arguing. Prisoner leaders Herb Blyden and Richard Clark also seemed overwhelmed by the situation, helpless to turn it around.[20] But just when it looked like Oswald might be in serious danger, Big Black Smith "stepped up in front of Oswald, put his arm around him, and said, 'Don't worry, there's nothing going to happen.'"[21]

Although one leader, Dalou, had been in favor of taking Oswald hostage, the vast majority seemed committed to keeping the commissioner safe from harm. And when Herb Blyden tried to regain order by calling for a vote on the question, asking those in favor of taking the commissioner hostage to stand, almost no one did. That settled it.[22]

It was nearly 1:00 p.m. on this second day of the uprising when Oswald and the others walked safely out of D Yard and back to the administration building. The prisoners said that no further discussions would happen until all the observers they requested had arrived, and Oswald was in no mood to continue talking either. He was so shaken that he decided he was going to leave all further interactions with the men in D Yard to the observers. To observer Marvin Chandler, one of the clergymen, the whole situation was not so much scary as heartbreaking. As he was leaving the yard, he heard someone call to him, "Reverend . . ."[23] It was Big Black Smith. "Yes, sir," Chandler replied, and then, to his surprise, Big Black said, "Reverend, they gonna whip ass, but thank you so much for comin'."[24] Black's comment brought tears to Chandler's eyes.[25]

Chandler and the rest of his group vowed in that moment that they were not willing to let the ugliness they'd just witnessed in the yard jeopardize a peaceful resolution to the standoff. To that end, Arthur Eve and Lewis Steel were newly determined to get the commissioner to understand just how crucial the issue of legal amnesty had become to the prisoners. If their encounter in D Yard that morning had told them nothing else, it was now clear that, without criminal amnesty, the men would never feel secure enough to give up the hostages.

As soon as he left the yard that afternoon, Oswald attended another meeting to discuss the logistics of ending the rebellion. At the table were some top brass of the NYSP including Chief Inspector John Miller, as well as Major Monahan, the head of the local Troop A out of Batavia. Prison officials Vincent Mancusi and Walter Dunbar were also there, as was Rockefeller's man, Buzz O'Hara. Bluntly, and clearly reflecting how spooked he had been by his recent visit to the yard, Oswald asked the men assembled whether they thought conditions were now right for "retaking the institution by force."[26] The more they all hashed this over, however, the more the commissioner kept coming back to one hard truth: he simply couldn't allow a retaking now that he had not only authorized, but actually facilitated, the process of bringing more than two dozen well-known individuals to Attica to oversee and observe the negotiation process. Even the officials gathered at this meeting understood that this made a retaking dicey at best.

Back in D Yard, the knowledge that more observers were on the way was helping to lift the spirts of prisoners and hostages alike. The hostages were allowed more freedoms—some were exercising that morning in their circle area—and they had been given coffee and cigarettes in addition to their regular food. One hostage asked if he could have some Marlboros instead of the Camels he'd been given, and the man guarding him came

The prisoners in D Yard are undaunted, raising the Black Power salute. September 10. *(Courtesy of the Associated Press)*

back with three packs.[27] State officials had also allowed Dr. Hanson to make a second trip into the yard that day, and when he did so, "he found that the hostages were feeling much better; they were being well cared for and their blindfolds were off."[28] He noticed that the prisoners had given the hostages better shelter by draping some sheets over some boards so that they would be protected from the sun.[29]

Even though they were all more hopeful once they realized that negotiations were going to proceed, and with outside observers, the disastrous meeting with Oswald had unnerved everyone. Sleeplessness was also taking its toll. Big Black Smith had, for example, asked Dr. Hanson if he could give him some sort of amphetamines because he knew he needed to stay alert and "awake for the negotiations."[30] He and most of the other prisoners also wanted to be alert should state officials suddenly change their minds and decide to retake the prison by force. In many ways their long history with prison authorities led them to expect betrayal and so, even as they waited for the negotiations to recommence, the men also devoted considerable time that day to constructing barricades at various doors in the yard as well as on the catwalks above.[31] If the police should begin an assault, the men in the yard wanted as much protection as possible.

As the hours passed following Oswald's departure from the yard, the prisoners began worrying that they were perhaps now being set up. What if no one was coming to negotiate again? By that afternoon, slight unease was once again turning to paranoia. Stewart Dan, a television reporter from WGR-TV in Buffalo, saw this firsthand. Prisoners and prison officials had given Dan and his cameraman permission to walk around the yard to interview people. They spent some time talking with two white inmates who had become friends while in prison, twenty-six-year-old Barry Schwartz, who'd been at Attica for about three years by then, and Kenny Hess, a twenty-two-year-old who had only been there for four months and was eligible for parole in a mere six more.[32] When Dan asked the two how they were handling the crisis, they regaled him with dramatic tales of the uprising. As Dan furiously scribbled in his small reporter's notebook, a large shadow fell across it, and he looked up to see Herb Blyden, who, without preamble, took his notebook, saying, "Let's see what you have."[33]

But Blyden was unable to read Dan's notes—the reporter used his own version of shorthand—and insisted that Dan, Schwartz, and Hess accompany him to the negotiating table.[34] Once there, Dan had to read his notes aloud to a group that included Champ, Flip Crowley, Richard Clark, Dalou, Jerry Rosenberg, Jomo Joka Omowale, Bernard Stroble (Shango), and others. All three of the men who'd been brought to the table protested vehemently that they'd done nothing wrong.[35] But after Oswald's visit to the yard, the men were so on edge that the existence of seemingly mysterious notes only stoked suspicions. "While we are trying to work things out, this is what's going on!" one of the men shouted at Barry Schwartz.[36] Flip Crowley, who had befriended Barry Schwartz while in prison counseling sessions together, asked him what was going on—why hadn't he gone through the proper channels to talk to the media?—to which Schwartz replied sincerely that "he didn't know he was supposed to."[37]

As Dan looked on with increasing dread, one of the men at the table called for a vote regarding what should be done with Hess and Schwartz. With almost no deliberation, the approximately six men at the table handed down the group's verdict: Hess and Schwartz had been undermining prisoner solidarity in the yard. They couldn't be trusted. They needed to be watched now. Trying to defuse the situation, the reporter offered to leave the yard right away, and even to leave his notes with the committee if that was what they wanted. "No," said Blyden, "you don't have to go . . . you're only doing your job."[38] But, Dan pressed, what would happen to these men? To his relief, he was told that "nothing would happen to them," and that Hess and Schwartz would just be moved to a different part of the prison.[39]

Dan wanted to believe this. He retrieved his notebook and left the yard, but did not tell any prison officials what had just transpired. He decided that he would just have to trust what Blyden told him.[40] But things did not go well for Hess and Schwartz after Dan left. Both were forced to strip and then, according to one prisoner, four members of the security team "marched them out of D Yard into the corridor [of D Block]," where they were subsequently locked in cells.[41]

Meanwhile, the tension in D Yard continued to crackle—there still had been no word from the administration building and the recent scene at the negotiating table had gotten ugly. Were outsider observers in fact coming to D Yard to oversee a peaceful resolution of their rebellion, the men wondered, or were they being set up for an attack? They needn't have worried yet. The observers were indeed on their way, and later that night everyone would once again feel that anything was possible.

PART III

# The Sound Before the Fury

# TOM WICKER

*In 1971 forty-four-year-old Tom Wicker was one of the most respected journalists at* The New York Times. *This son of a railroad conductor had traveled more, studied more, and experienced more than most of the folks he met at swanky parties in Washington, D.C., or New York City. Wicker had not only seen the world, he had also taken the time to think deeply about it, to probe many of the social and political issues that were now dividing the nation. Chief among them was the state of American race relations. Wicker had grown up in the tiny town of Hamlet, North Carolina, largely oblivious to the ways in which segregation structured his town and undergirded all of its social and political institutions.*

*But as a young man Wicker became acutely aware of the immoral laws and inhumane practices that defined his region of the country. By the time he landed his job as a newspaper columnist in New York, he had decided to use his platform to call attention to social injustice, and to the people and organizations committed to fighting it. If this slightly pudgy newsman with an open face and a deferential demeanor couldn't be the great novelist that he secretly wanted to be, then he would be a damned good social critic.*

*The year before the Attica uprising Wicker had written about a New York state prisoner who had filed suit against the Department of Correctional Services for locking him in solitary confinement for an entire year. Wicker had been horrified by what he learned of Martin Sostre's ordeal, and impressed by federal judge Constance Baker Motley's ruling that the treatment Sostre endured was cruel and unusual. Wicker admired jurists like Motley who were brave enough to take on state officials when they were not following the rules or doing their jobs humanely. Stories like this cemented Wicker's faith in the transformative power of simple truth telling. In his heart he believed that ordinary Americans would do the right thing if they just had all of the facts in front of them.*

*At noon on September 10, 1971, Wicker was sitting down to lunch in the lush dining room of the National Geographic Society a few blocks from the White House. He felt honored to be breaking bread with dignitaries as impressive as the ambassadors of New Zealand and Italy. Then he was told he had a phone call. On the line was his secretary with surprising news: Wicker was being summoned to Attica.*[1] *A state assemblyman had called to let him know that rebellious prisoners had requested that Wicker act as a witness to their negotiations with the state of New York.*

*Wicker agreed to go. If nothing else, this would give him something to write about in his weekly column. So far his green spiral notebook, the one that he always carried with him to jot down ideas, contained only uninspired possibilities: "New York Stories: traffic, Giants, CUNY open admissions" and "Taxis—doing well?"*[2]

*He retrieved his jacket, made his way to the airport, and flew to Buffalo. There he was met by a state trooper who drove him to the prison. Over the next hour the two men chatted companionably, but as they neared the ominous-looking structure, the mood in the car shifted. The building was surrounded by hundreds of heavily armed state troopers, which alarmed Wicker. And yet, weirdly, the scene in the parking lot could also have passed for a state fair or carnival. The Lions Club had set up a stand where members were busily passing out hot coffee and sandwiches; children "ran and played in front of the prison's main gate"; and across the street from a row of port-a-johns people were tapping a keg.*[3]

*As Wicker drew closer, though, it was clear that no one here was in the mood for games. Grim and unsmiling faces watched him as he made his way through the crowd to Attica's remarkably ordinary-looking front door, which was flanked by troopers. This was a makeshift military base, complete with families awaiting news of loved ones and platoons preparing for battle. "Every officer," Wicker noted, "seemed to have a pistol at his side, a heavy club; many carried rifles and shotguns; some had tear-gas launchers; others had gas masks swinging at their belts."*[4] *There were also "military-looking trucks, stacks of boxes, extended fire hoses"—everything one would need to take down a small country.*[5] *Wicker found himself questioning the wisdom of making this trip. He had absolutely no idea what role he was expected to play in the drama unfolding at Attica.*

# 15

# Getting Down to Business

Although not every luminary whom the prisoners wanted at Attica agreed to come—Minister Louis Farrakhan of the Nation of Islam, for example, declined the invitation, explaining that his leader and mentor, Elijah Muhammad, had instructed him not to go—many others welcomed the opportunity.[1] Among these were William Kunstler, the fifty-two-year-old attorney who was well known as a tireless advocate for human and civil rights, as well as two representatives from the Young Lords Party, and several liberal prison reformers from the Fortune Society.[2] In the mix too were two well-known black journalists, Jim Ingram from the *Michigan Chronicle* and Clarence Jones from New York's *Amsterdam News*. Although the Black Panther Party minister of self-defense, Huey Newton, had not yet agreed to help out, word had it that Bobby Seale, the BPP chairman, would make the trip.[3]

Commissioner Oswald and the governor's staff were comfortable with the group that had been assembled, but were especially glad to see that Arthur Eve had persuaded reporter Clarence Jones to be a part of it, since Rockefeller had a good personal relationship with him. They were also delighted when U.S. representative Herman Badillo accepted their invitation to be an observer, and were pleased as well when he brought two other moderate Latinos with him—State Senator Robert Garcia of the Bronx and Bronx school superintendent Alfredo Mathew.[4]

The ranks of the observers group continued to swell into Friday evening, not just as these men began to arrive, but also because others kept showing up uninvited. One of these was a man named Jabarr Kenyatta, a former prisoner who now led a mosque. No one really knew who

Kenyatta was, but because he had somehow attached himself to reporter Jim Ingram, and because he had long flowing African robes, prison officials finally let him in—assuming, according to Oswald, that he must be "the highly regarded black nationalist leader Charles 37X Kenyatta of New York City"—an impression Kenyatta did little to dispel.[5] Later that evening three public interest lawyers from Washington, D.C., including a man named Julian Tepper, showed up and were admitted as well. By the end of Friday night, a total of thirty-three observers would be on the scene at Attica.

On Friday afternoon, as the men in D Yard were growing concerned that talks had been abandoned, the many observers already at Attica had sat down with Commissioner Oswald and Deputy Commissioner Dunbar and pressed these state officials on the specifics of what was now expected of them. As Tom Wicker put it, they had to push, because everyone was at a total loss "as to precisely what we should do, what role we should be playing, were we to view ourselves as representatives of the prisoners, were we to view ourselves as representative of the state. Were we purely neutral go-betweens. Were we in fact negotiators?"[6]

From these officials, the observers learned two crucial facts: one, the prisoners had no intention of giving up; and two, Oswald and Dunbar had no intention of going back into the yard again to persuade them to do so. This was to be the observers' task—to enter the prison and talk with the men in the yard. More specifically, Oswald said, they were to go into D Yard to ascertain exactly what it would take to reach a settlement, and then they were to negotiate an agreement that would put an end to the rebellion.[7] The observers were taken aback. Tom Wicker, for example, had just assumed he was going home to his own bed that night and hadn't even bothered to pack a toothbrush or a clean shirt.[8] The responsibility just handed them was daunting, to say the least. But the group assembled was impressive and at least some within it were happy to be negotiators and had faith that they would be able to make a difference. Congressman Herman Badillo had not only spent the previous summer hammering out a relatively peaceful end to the New York City jail riots, but when he saw the list of prisoner demands, he, for one, believed that a settlement was possible. As he noted, the prisoners were well aware "that some things could be negotiated and some things could not."[9]

Observers Clarence Jones and Lewis Steel weren't so confident about the chances of reaching an agreement. Jones's paper, the *Amsterdam News,* ran a column called "Behind Prison Walls" written by prisoners, and he was familiar with the grievances at issue here.[10] What wasn't clear to him, however, was what position the state would take in addressing those concerns. Jones pushed Oswald to clarify how the state intended to respond to the various demands, arguing "vehemently that he would not enter D-yard as the bearer of mixed and inconclusive tidings resulting from Oswald's 'yes, yes, yes' and occasional 'no' " with the prisoners.[11]

Lewis Steel raised an even thornier, deeply prophetic, concern. "The issue here is amnesty," Steel told the assembled group. "Those guys in there know what happened after Auburn. They know inmates were indicted that time for everything the prosecution could think of, even stealing a guard's keys. . . . They know there could be charges up to kidnapping, and if that guard dies [referring to William Quinn, the CO severely beaten in Times Square in the first hours of the uprising], there's a murder rap for somebody. Maybe for a lot of them. Those guys have to get amnesty. If they can't get it, there won't be any negotiated settlement."[12]

Commissioner Oswald listened attentively to the various concerns raised by the men gathered in the administration building and agreed right then and there to place a call to the Wyoming County district attorney, Louis James, to get his thoughts on the issue of amnesty. Putting down the phone, the commissioner reported somberly, "James says he does not have the authority to grant criminal amnesty [and] if he did, he wouldn't do it. So, there's not going to be any amnesty, gentlemen. Absolutely not."[13]

Silence fell over the room as the men considered what this meant. If there was not going to be amnesty, then what? Still, Tom Wicker and most of the other observers simply took it for granted that no one wanted "the irrationality of bloodshed and death," and that surely "reasonable men could find a formula that would, for all practical purposes, mean something close to amnesty without men like James and Oswald having to admit that it *was* amnesty."[14] Clarence Jones also felt strongly that "the resolution of amnesty was not a legal question, not a constitutional question. It was a moral humanitarian question" and thus things would eventually work themselves out.[15] As he later put it, it was obvious that "if you are a chief executive officer of the State, you consider the preservation of human lives more important than the risk of breaking the symmetry of law. . . . Human lives are far more important."[16]

Sensing that, for now, there wasn't more they could do about the amnesty issue, and with the daylight fading, the observers decided that it was time to go into D Yard and meet the prisoners. Almost six hours had passed since Oswald's last tense meeting in D Yard, and Badillo, for one, thought it would be a good idea to try to see these men before much more time passed—especially given that the media was now in D Yard and, therefore, everyone knew that at least some of the observers were there and eager to help.[17]

Notwithstanding the warnings, such as those offered by one of Attica's prison chaplains that "the more rabid inmates in the yard might attack [the hostages] at any time," a group that included State Senators John Dunne and Robert Garcia, journalist Tom Wicker, Congressman Herman Badillo, school superintendent Alfredo Mathew, lawyer Lewis Steel, Reverend Walker, Reverend Chandler, Minister Scott, newspaper editor Clarence Jones, and State Assemblyman Arthur Eve entered the yard at 7:00 Friday evening.[18] Most soberingly, on their way down to A Gate for this sixth visit of outsiders into D Yard, a trooper wrote down each of their names just in case any of them were captured.

Many in the observers group were genuinely scared. Tomblike quiet surrounded them as they made their way through the No Man's Land of A Tunnel, where prisoners, carrying an assortment of makeshift weapons, stood. Some of the prisoners wore football helmets, some wore shirts over their heads with eye holes cut out, and others wore bandit masks over the

A group of prisoners wearing homemade protective gear keeps watch on Times Square. *(Courtesy of the Associated Press)*

lower half of their ill-lit faces.[19] To the great relief of the observers, though, the prisoners were clearly happy to see them. When one prisoner greeted them with an enthusiastic "Right on, Brother!" others immediately echoed his hearty salutation. Everyone breathed a huge sigh of relief.[20]

Once the observers left A Tunnel, they were escorted into the yard through a human tunnel comprised of two long lines of men, two deep, facing outward. The yard was eerily silent. Tom Wicker could almost feel the masses pressing in on the chain of men surrounding his group, many simply trying to get a glimpse of the new arrivals. Although he knew that there were just over a thousand men in the yard, it looked to him like many more than that.[21]

Since the last meeting with Oswald, Attica's elected prisoners had moved their base of operations closer to the wall in D Yard and had built a lighted wooden gazebo-like structure over their table. They had also added additional speakers in the yard so that everything said at the negotiating table could be heard by all. As they arrived at the table, L. D. Barkley extended his hand to greet each of the observers in a formal and guarded manner. Though Barkley wanted these men to be here, he was uncertain of their motives. When Wicker nervously asked him, "How's it going?" L.D. bluntly replied, "You tell me."[22] Interrupting this frosty exchange, Blyden grabbed a microphone pilfered earlier that day from the room where the prison band kept its equipment and exclaimed, "Brothers! The world is hearing us! The world is seeing our struggle! And here is the proof before your eyes!"[23] The crowd roared its appreciation. Optimism had returned to D Yard. Blyden then asked each of the visitors to come to the mic for introductions. When it was John Dunne's turn to speak, the inmates let out a deafening cheer, standing and clapping for him. He was stunned, realizing for the first time just how much these men were counting on him.

After all of the introductions had been made, Arthur Eve explained that they were still waiting for other observers to arrive before the full discussions began, but that they had wanted to come in for a brief meeting now to get a sense of what stage the negotiations process had reached. They also wanted to check on the hostages. It was clear that Champ and Richard Clark, among others, were not happy to hear that there would be another delay. They had been waiting for hours to resume talks. They had little choice, however. So, after a bit more speech making, the observers walked over to see how well the hostages and the other prisoners in the yard were holding up.

It was apparent that the waiting game, as well as lack of sleep, had taken its toll on the hostages. They all looked fairly healthy, but they were deeply stressed, and they too were counting on the observers to bring a peaceful end to their nightmare. Seeing them reminded the observers just how important it was for them to keep the state at the negotiating table. If either the prisoners or state officials decided that these talks were pointless, they feared, these men would be in immediate jeopardy.

That there were also nearly 1,300 anxious prisoners scattered around the rest of the rutted and muddy yard also showed the observers how important it was that they help to end this standoff with the state peacefully and with clear protections for the rebels should they surrender. The observers were startled to see just how worried the men in D Yard were about their future safety as well as that of those men in C Block still in state custody. Some of the prisoners, recounting past experiences with retaliation by COs, feared that the men in C Block were being made to pay for the actions of the men in D Yard. There had even been some talk earlier in D Yard of trying to spring the men in C Block, but as Blyden and Clark firmly reminded everyone, "the block was fully secured by State Troopers and correctional officers, and this would be a deadly effort to try to take the block back."[24] So powerful was this concern for the men in C Block that Clarence Jones and Arthur Eve asked Wicker, Dunne, Badillo, and some of the others to go with them on yet another inspection of this area before heading back to the administration building to await the arrival of the rest of the observers.

To Tom Wicker, this area of the prison was far more frightening than D Yard had been. Everywhere there were heavily armed guards, and they all seemed to be in an abysmal mood. As Wicker commented to Congressman Herman Badillo next to him, "We got better treatment inside from the men without guns than we did from those outside with guns."[25] Evidence of the previous day's riot was everywhere—pools of water from broken pipes covered the floor, and debris littered the walkways. Even more unsettling was the desperate sound of the men calling out to the observers from the moment they stepped inside the cell block. Some were trying to get attention for medical needs. Others reported that they were being starved and beaten.[26] Still others begged the observers to help them "join the brothers in D Yard."[27]

The observers were shaken by the stories they heard and saw as they walked from cell to cell. Unlike the earlier report given of C Block, it was obvious that these men were terrified, some had clearly been injured, and all were begging for help. Even the men who seemed to be in good shape physically told stories about all they had endured as prisoners at Attica. One man Wicker spoke with had been locked in his tiny cell for twenty-seven years. Another, he learned, had arrived in this hell hole because he was an alcoholic, couldn't get help, and had one too many DUIs. These sorts of offenses were not, Wicker later told his fellow observers, what he had always thought landed men in this notorious maximum security prison, and he was stunned by the small cages they were forced to live in for decades on end. When it was time to leave, the observers were sickened and felt enormously guilty having to extricate themselves from the imploring gazes and desperate pleas of the men they left behind. To Wicker's surprise, as he passed one cell he felt a prisoner slip him a note, whispering his hope that it could be taken to the men in D Yard. It read in part:

> *Brothers, please don't give up! This is new for them and they don't know how to react!*
> *We are ok.*
>
> *Hold on as long as you can*
> *Big Black*
> *Bro. Herb*
> *Bro. Richie*
> *Carlos*
> *and all of you*
>
> *Right on!*[28]

While Wicker's group was touring C Block and the other observers had headed back to brief Oswald, Herman Schwartz was on his way to the airport. He had decided that there was no way he was going back into D Yard after the injunction debacle, but he would go pick up lawyer William Kunstler. A graduate of Yale and Columbia, Kunstler was respected both as someone who had served in the Pacific Theater during World War II and as someone who had long been committed to a fiery defense for activists in numerous high-profile civil rights and social justice cases. Schwartz didn't always agree with Kunstler but he was grateful he was coming to Attica in no small part because his presence would give the public even more reason to pay attention.[29]

When he arrived at Attica, Kunstler had to push his way through the throngs of anxious townspeople now crowding the front lawn and then past the hundreds of heavily armed state troopers who lined the prison's inner courtyard and inside hallways. Finally arriving in the Steward's Room he was introduced to the assembled observers. Arthur Eve had now stepped into the position of meeting chair and facilitator and, after briefing Kunstler on the state of the discussions between the prisoners and officials thus far, he asked to hear the lawyer's reaction. Without preamble, Kunstler stated unequivocally, as had Steel earlier, that the only issue that really mattered in terms of ending the rebellion was amnesty. Wicker wearily agreed: "That was the demand that really mattered out of them all."[30]

Every observer could see that Kunstler was going to be an entirely new force with whom the state would have to reckon. He was assertive, unapologetic, and damned certain of himself. As important, he was connected. When Eve mentioned that neither Huey Newton's nor Bobby Seale's arrival at Attica was yet a certainty, Kunstler simply picked up a phone at one end of the room and said, "I'll get Bobby." After a quick call he turned to the group and announced that Bobby Seale would be there the next day. Kunstler had also successfully leaned on Oswald to let a prisoner rights activist by the name of Tom Soto join the observers group despite the commissioner's misgivings about adding any more radicals.

Soto was a young Puerto Rican activist from New York City who had been instrumental in a takeover of City College of New York and had come to prison solidarity work through his affiliation with Youth Against War and Fascism (YAWF). Not all of the observers knew Soto, but they knew about the dramatic protest at City College. The more moderate among them were as concerned about his joining the group as Oswald had been. Eve, in particular, worried that he'd be trouble—especially since earlier that day he'd seen Soto telling the press that the injunction Schwartz had gotten would not offer the prisoners in the yard any real protection because the state could appeal it. Seeing this, Schwartz had been furious; he went outside to the parking lot where Soto was speaking and shouted that he had no idea what he was talking about. An injunction, he spat coldly, was by consent and therefore wasn't appealable.[31]

But Kunstler believed that Soto could be an asset to the negotiations. As he pointed out to the commissioner, while it was true that Soto had not been asked for by name, the prisoners had asked for his organization, YAWF. As important, since Soto had been giving interviews outside the prison, they would know that a YAWF representative was on the premises and would expect to see him. Although Oswald caved, Eve still felt compelled to insist that Soto promise to make no more renegade statements to the public or to the prisoners in D Yard. Summoned to the Steward's Room, Soto agreed to abide by these conditions. Soon thereafter, the entire observers committee now at the prison, plus members of the press, entered D Yard for what was to be the seventh visit of outsiders and the most important set of discussions to date.

It was now 11:30 Friday night, still the second day of the uprising, and the men in D Yard could hardly believe their eyes as they saw the observers, now a remarkable cohort of national figures, important people, and powerful men, walking to the negotiating table to hear their demands and bear witness to their struggle. It had been an excruciatingly long day for these men and emotions were raw. Since daybreak there had been some tense moments over the injunction Herman Schwartz brought back from Vermont and with Commissioner Oswald. And Kenny Hess and Barry Schwartz had been removed to D Block after that dramatic scene with reporter Stewart Dan up at the negotiating table. Now, however, with attorney William Kunstler there, and with television cameras rolling, it was time to get down to business.

The very first observer to grab the mic was Tom Soto. "Power to the People!" he roared with his fist raised high in the air. "Power to the People!" the men in D Yard bellowed back.[32] Next was Kunstler, whose reception dwarfed Soto's. "Pa'lante—Power to the People!" he shouted out in greeting, and the men in D Yard jumped up, yelling and clapping with an enthusiasm that stunned the other observers.[33] This was clearly what Attica, at its core, was all about. These disfranchised and seemingly disposable men were determined to stand together, in unity, to make some concrete changes to their lives. Seeing this solidarity and passion took Tom Wicker's breath away. When Kunstler could again be heard, he apologized to the men that there was not yet a member of the Black Panther Party present but he assured them that Bobby Seale would be there tomorrow. "Many of us love you," he told the men, "and many of us understand what a shitty decrepit system we have here in New York and elsewhere. . . . We are your brothers, we hope."[34] There was a loud cry of appreciation.

Kunstler explained to the men that they needed to be clear about what exactly they wanted from the state, and that it had to be what *they* wanted and not what outsiders wanted for them. Taking the mic next, Herb Blyden impulsively asked, "Brother Bill, will you be our lawyer? Will you represent the brothers as only you can?"[35] Looking a bit surprised but clearly honored, Kunstler responded, to thunderous applause and cheers, "Yes I will."[36]

Kunstler's affirmative response worried at least one observer, Senator John Dunne. Dunne was well aware that Oswald had placed a great deal of hope in his ability "to negotiate the real demands for prison reform—while splitting off from the revolutionary demands," and yet one of his fellow observers would now be legally representing the very men who might insist upon just such demands.[37] On the other hand, Dunne remembered, from the beginning it had been the prisoners, not state officials, who had stressed their desire for "communications and understanding." What is more, most of their demands so far had been as basic as the right to be treated as human beings rather than "as statistics and numbers."[38] In addition, these men had clearly been taking care of the hostages and had also protected the observers and the prison officials each time they entered the yard.

Before any of the observers could think too much about Kunstler's new role as D Yard prisoner lawyer, the sudden sounds of a violent commotion came from C Block and sheer panic set in. "They're coming in!" someone yelled. Springing into action the security men in the yard surrounded the observers to protect them. The leaders at the table cut off all the lights in the hope that this would make it more difficult for attackers to see them. With D Yard plunged into darkness, observer Tom Wicker found himself barely able to see his hands in front of his face and was trembling with fear.[39] To ward off any harm that might come to him, one of the prisoners had jumped up on the table in front of Wicker and assumed a rigid military posture—"his legs spread one arm behind his back, the other holding the butt of a tear gas launcher against his hip." Wicker was almost overcome by the poignancy of it. Here were prisoners, men deemed animals by society, who were putting their own lives at risk in order to honor their commitment to protect the men they'd asked to come help them. Still, he could nearly taste his own terror, "as sour as vomit" in his mouth.[40]

Gradually, in the deathly silence that followed, all eyes began to adjust and it no longer seemed that D Yard was under attack. Calm descended over the yard once more. Something had definitely gone wrong over in C Block, however, so John Dunne and Arthur Eve agreed to go see what it was. When they returned they brought unwelcome news: a prisoner in C Block had indeed been beaten, but they had the name of the CO who'd done it and said they would report him. Before everyone could get inflamed by this new incident of officer violence, Eve noted to the group that some additional observers had just arrived: two men from the Young Lords Party, three men from the Fortune Society, and Minister Jabarr

Kenyatta, complete with turban, flowing robes, and a prayer rug draped over his arm.

As if nothing had happened, the meeting then resumed. At the three tables that were now squeezed together for negotiations, each of the new observers took his turn introducing himself. It turned out that Kenyatta, not Soto, would be the real rabble-rouser—exhorting the men assembled before him to engage in a violent uprising against "the Man" and "the Pig." His message, however, was out of sync with the mood of brotherhood and unity that had enveloped everyone in the yard during those harrowing minutes in the dark. Although he received applause from some isolated pockets in the yard, the vast majority seemed uncomfortable with his message. One prisoner even chastised him publicly for sowing the seeds of disunity, and another exclaimed, "I'm not here to die; I want to live. I don't want to hear any more of that kind of talk; we're all brothers."[41] Clarence Jones, the observer known by the men in the yard as the editor of one of their favorite publications, the *Amsterdam News,* actually grabbed the mic from Kenyatta's hands. He then reminded everyone of the need to focus on concrete concessions from state officials.

Following Jones's lead, Kunstler looked down at the detailed notes he had been taking and commented that there were now multiple versions of the demands floating around. Taking the mic next himself, Kunstler called for a final list—one that all the prisoners, not the observers, could endorse. He and Eve both felt that the prisoners' decision-making autonomy was sacrosanct since it was their lives on the line. As Eve put it, "We were never, ever to make any decisions for them. I mean, they made that absolutely clear."[42]

To everyone's relief, one of the more controversial demands was dispensed with relatively quickly. Although a small number of prisoners, including Dalou and L. D. Barkley, had really hoped that the original demand for transportation to a "non-imperialist" country would be a top priority, when the men voted on it, very few thought it should be on the list and the two advocates conceded.[43] As Herman Badillo later marveled, "Listening to the news reports one would have thought that the demand for transportation out of this country was an unalterable position of the inmates. But when the demand came up for a vote, it received support from fewer than 20 of the 1200 prisoners. It was not a substantial question in the negotiations."[44] The one hot-button demand that the prisoners were still unanimously committed to, however, was full amnesty.[45]

Soon dawn began to break on Saturday, September 11. It had taken that long, almost the full night, for the observers to ascertain which demands were most crucial to the prisoners. At 5:00 a.m. all of the observers except for Soto, Kenyatta, and the two observers from the Young Lords Party (who wanted to "rap" with the men in the yard still longer) trudged, exhausted but wired, back up to the Steward's Room in the administration building to compare their notes and draft a final list of demands for Commissioner Oswald's consideration.[46] This would be no easy task since there were now some serious tensions among the observers themselves. Bronx school superintendent Alfredo Mathew, for example, was furious at Kenyatta and Soto for, in his view, trying to inflame the passions of the prisoners rather than trying to defuse them. It was at William Kunstler, though, that Mathew directed his real venom. Kunstler, he insisted, was giving prisoners the false, unrealistic impression that if they held out for anything that was "just," they could in fact get it. Mathew's diatribe seemed to unleash a stream of vitriol among the rest of the observers for a variety of often conflicting reasons, and the group's early morning meeting soon disintegrated into recriminations.

Ultimately, after much back-and-forthing, it was decided that an executive committee of six should create the document for Oswald: Eve, Kunstler, Jones, Kenyatta, Dunne, and Badillo, with Eve acting as chair. Since the prisoners had made it clear that amnesty was the main issue, the committee turned its attention first to the question of whether in fact Wyoming County's DA, Louis James, could help on this matter. It was true that James had said that he would never grant amnesty, but maybe he could be persuaded. As Wicker saw it, "Perhaps if James knew the gravity of the situation, the danger of wholesale bloodshed," he would be moved to do something. Most agreed with this reasoning, so Eve suggested that while the rest of the observers caught a few hours of sleep, Tom Wicker, Clarence Jones, and the public interest lawyer, Julian Tepper, should pay a visit to James in Warsaw and try to change his mind.

But while the observers committee was operating under the assumption that the Attica rebellion might still be resolved peacefully, those in charge of the New York State Police, the National Guard, and even many in Rockefeller's office continued to agitate for an immediate retaking of the prison. At 10:43 the night before, just before the observers entered the yard for their marathon negotiations session, Chief Inspector Miller of the NYSP was waiting by the phone in the Batavia Holiday Inn because he was certain that his men were going to be called into action very soon. General O'Hara had also ordered eight hundred National Guardsmen to be at the ready. From what they had been hearing from FBI intelligence as well as various individuals in the Department of Correctional Services, things were falling apart in D Yard and there was no way the observers were going to change that. As one member of law enforcement put it, "There was no way that large amount of 'brain power' gathered at one location, debating every issue could be effective."[47] Most of the many hundreds of troopers now marshalled outside the prison agreed that something was seriously "wrong with Oswald" for allowing these outsiders to get involved.[48]

There was a new hitch to retaking the prison right away, however. Both John C. Miller and General O'Hara had been informed in confidence that the governor himself might come to the prison Saturday morning.[49] In fact the governor was not planning to make a visit to Attica, in no small part because his own attorney, Michael Whiteman, had been reporting, via conservative observer State Assemblyman James Emery, that the radical observers were making the situation in the yard much worse. In one instance, Whiteman told Rockefeller, "the mood of the inmates had changed radically, that they were now defiant and insistent on all of their demands, including safe passage to a non-imperialist country."[50] Although this briefing to the governor was utterly inaccurate, it would have a huge, and tragic, impact on the way state officials would handle the crisis at Attica. While prisoners and observers spent hours painstakingly coming up with demands that were not only reasonable but would make life better for both COs and prisoners, Nelson Rockefeller's suspicions of these men were only being fueled.

## 16

# Dreams and Nightmares

At 6:30 on Saturday morning, September 11, the third day of the uprising, leaders at the negotiating table in D Yard decided to awaken everyone in the yard. They felt good about the progress that had been made in the previous hours with the observers, but they nevertheless thought it prudent that everyone still needed to make preparations to defend themselves in case negotiations fell through. In a forcible retaking, COs and troopers would undoubtedly come in with clubs flailing, as they had at Auburn and in several of the New York City jail riots. Thus, everyone in the yard was to "take all precautions, either dig a hole, pile up mattresses or anything you can get a hold of to protect yourself."[1] Some twenty or so prisoners were commissioned to dig an L-shaped trench in which the men could take shelter—an arduous task that would take them until almost 3:00 that afternoon to complete.[2]

As head of security, Big Black Smith felt the weight of planning for a worst-case scenario. One thing on his mind was making sure he protected one specific CO with whom he'd been business partners of sorts: while Big Black ran various moneymaking schemes in order to make ends meet, this CO had always watched his back, in exchange for a cut. They had developed a mutual respect, even a friendship of sorts. Big Black could see that the hostages would be sitting ducks should the state decide to attack. Quietly, Big Black told this guard to feign a heart attack and he would do his best to have him evacuated. That Big Black expended this effort, and actually succeeded in getting the CO out later that afternoon, made the rest of the hostages feel better about their prospects. At least the prisoners, be it for selfish or unselfish reasons, wanted to make sure they stayed alive.

Two of the hostages, Gary Walker and Ron Kozlowski, were actually having a kind of celebration on this chilly Saturday morning. As the prisoners went about their frenzied defensive maneuvers—"building makeshift housing, digging holes, making bunkers, making weapons"—Walker and Kozlowski realized it was both of their birthdays. Kozlowski was turning twenty-three, Walker thirty-four.[3] They shared a cup of coffee and spoke about how much they looked forward to the goulash they had heard the men were cooking up for the evening's supper—a prisoner-made concoction of "elbow noodles with spaghetti sauce and chunks of ham."[4]

That same morning, with rumpled shirts and eyes burning from lack of rest, three of the observers, Wicker, Jones, and Tepper, were making their way down a maze of rural roads. Wyoming County district attorney Louis James had agreed to meet with them at his home in Warsaw. When they arrived, James and his wife greeted them warmly with hot coffee and a bacon and eggs breakfast.

Dabbing his mouth with a napkin, James cut to the chase. He could not and would not authorize any sort of criminal amnesty for the prisoners. Period. In Wicker's opinion, James did seem to grasp what was at stake and really did want to help in some way, so he tried a new tack: Would the DA be willing to put in writing the specific terms under which he *would* prosecute, for example, only specific individuals linked to specific crimes by conclusive evidence, as well as pledge on paper that he *would not* allow any mass reprisals?[5] Yes, James said he'd be willing to do this. For the first time in many hours, the three observers felt optimistic. They followed James to his office in downtown Warsaw where, as a team, they drafted the document.[6]

The trio was eager to bring the signed agreement back to the Steward's Room, where the rest of the observers were awaiting news of their visit. However, when they arrived back at Attica, a large contingent of troopers refused them entry. Wicker was incredulous. He'd assumed that prison officials were waiting on tenterhooks for word of what had happened with the DA, and now they couldn't even get in to see the commissioner.[7] It wasn't until nearly 1:30 p.m. that the door opened for them, and then only because Badillo and the other legislators intervened and forced law enforcement to let them pass.[8] These three weren't the only observers to have been barred, either. Herman Schwartz and William Kunstler had also been kept outside for an extended period of time when they tried to reenter that morning. Such a hostile reception made all of them wonder if this suggested "a substantive hardening" in the state's position.[9]

William Kunstler, Tom Wicker, and Clarence Jones confer outside the prison. *(Courtesy of* The New York Times)

By the time the observers did manage to reconvene inside that afternoon, everyone was out of sorts. No one had gotten enough rest, and the obvious deepening of law enforcement hostility had raised the stakes of their job immeasurably. Under these fraught circumstances, Wicker, Tepper, and Jones nevertheless recounted their visit with James and made the case the observers should take the document he'd signed into D Yard. The statement read:

> I have been asked by Mssrs. Clarence Jones, Tom Wicker and Julian Tepper, representing the Committee of Observers at Attica Correctional Facility, to express my views as to possible prosecutions that might arise from recent events at the Facility.
>
> First, I deem it to be my duty as a prosecuting attorney to prosecute without fear or favor ALL substantial crimes committed or apparently

> committed within this county, if sufficient evidence exists to warrant prosecution.
>
> Second, in prosecuting any crime, I do and would endeavor to prosecute fairly and impartially and for the sole purpose of attempting to see that justice is done.
>
> Third, under the circumstances of the present situation at Attica, I deem it to be my obligation to prosecute only when in my judgment there is substantial evidence to link a specific individual with the commission of a specific crime.
>
> Fourth, in this particular instance at Attica, I am unalterably opposed to the commencement of indiscriminate mass prosecutions of any and all persons who may have been present, and to prosecutions brought solely for the sake of vindictive reprisals.
>
> Fifth, in the prosecution of any crime, in this as in every other situation, I would endeavor to prosecute honorably, fairly and impartially, with full regard for the rights of defendants.
>
> Finally, as prosecuting attorney, I regard it as my paramount duty to attempt to assure justice, both in the trial itself, the outcome of the trial, and in the possible sentence.[10]

Before anyone could make a comment, Jones jumped in to reiterate not only that "this was the best of all possible things which was capable of being achieved," but also to suggest that they present it to the prisoners as a major political victory.[11] Although a number of the others seemed to agree—among them Alfredo Mathew, John Dunne, and Reverend Walker—William Kunstler most emphatically did not. In Kunstler's opinion the document merely restated the law, was full of platitudes that did not in fact protect the men in any substantive way, and, of course, said nothing at all about the most important issue, amnesty. He was representing the prisoners' legal interests, as he had promised to do. Wicker, however, was flabbergasted. He immediately launched into a passionate defense of the district attorney's integrity, and that man's intention to do the right thing.[12]

And then Herman Schwartz entered the fray. Still smarting from the previous day's events when prisoners had rejected the document he'd gotten Judge Curtis to sign, he stated that there was no way the prisoners would accept this new mealy-mouthed document since the injunction he'd given them "was worded much more tightly than the statement from the D.A."[13] To the dismay of Jones, Tepper, and Wicker, the rest of the observers began debating whether they should even show the prisoners the James letter at all. Eventually they concluded that, given how nervous the men in the yard were undoubtedly becoming as they waited for some word from the state, it was better to show them the document. Even if it wasn't everything the men hoped for, at least this paper indicated that the observers were making a good-faith effort on their behalf.

Before anyone would be heading into D Yard, however, there was another document still to deal with: the list of demands that the executive committee had hammered out with Oswald in the early hours of the morning. To the surprise of the observers, Oswald seemed amenable to almost everything on the list. The commissioner went through the prisoners' thirty-three demands one by one, saying yes to most.[14] As Oswald later described the process, "We went over each word in the demand . . . and then attempted to rephrase it. And Mr. Kunstler and I, I think, did most of it, with some suggestions along the way from the others. But he and I did a good part of it. It took all afternoon, at least."[15]

Yet, when a final version was typed up and circulated for the observers' approval, not everyone was happy.[16] Lewis Steel, for one, was concerned that Oswald was unwilling to replace Mancusi, an important demand that would be easy to grant. Nor would Oswald budge on the amnesty question. Every time Steel tried to insist on how crucial this demand was, Oswald simply replied: "You've got the James letter."[17] Hours later, though, even Steel had to concede that they had in this meeting "pressed Commissioner Oswald as hard as [they] could."[18] Amnesty wasn't going to happen, but Attica's prisoners had gotten the highest-ranking official in New York State's Department of Correctional Services to agree to twenty-eight out of the thirty-three key demands they had submitted. This, everyone prayed, would be enough.[19]

| Observers' Proposals | Proposals Acceptable to Commissioner Oswald |
|---|---|
| 1. Provide adequate food and water and shelter for this group. | 1. Provide adequate food, water, and shelter for all inmates. |
| 2. Replace Superintendent Mancusi immediately. | 2. Inmates shall be permitted to return to their cells or to other suitable accommodations or |

| | |
|---|---|
| | shelter under their own power. The observers' committee shall monitor the implementation of this operation. |
| 3. Grant complete administrative and legal amnesty to all persons associated with this matter. | 3. Grant complete administrative amnesty to all persons associated with this matter. By administrative amnesty, the state agrees:<br>a. Not to take any adverse parole actions, administrative proceedings, physical punishment, or other type of harassment such as holding inmates incommunicado, segregating any inmates, or keeping them in isolation or in 24-hour lock-up.<br>b. The state will grant legal amnesty in regard to all civil actions which could arise from this matter.<br>c. It is agreed that the State of New York and all its departments, divisions, and subdivisions, including the State Department of Correction and the Attica Correctional Facility, and its employees and agents shall not file or initiate any criminal complaint or act on complaints in any criminal action of any kind or nature relating to property, property damage, or property-related crimes arising out of the incidents at the Attica Correctional Facility during September 9, 10, 11, 1971. |

| | |
|---|---|
| | d. The District Attorney of Wyoming County, New York, has issued and signed the attached letter as of this date. |
| 4. Place this institution under federal jurisdiction. | 4. Establish by October 1, 1971, a permanent ombudsman service for the facility staffed by appropriate persons from the neighboring communities. |
| 5. Apply the New York State minimum wage law to all work done by the inmates. STOP SLAVE LABOR. | 5. Recommend the application of the New York State minimum wage law standards to all work done by inmates. Every effort will be made to make the records of payments available to inmates. |
| 6. Allow all New York State prisoners to be politically active, without intimidation or reprisal. | 6. Allow all New York State prisoners to be politically active, without intimidation or reprisal. |
| 7. Allow true religious freedom. | 7. Allow true religious freedom. |
| 8. End all censorship of newspapers, magazines, and other publications from publishers. | 8. End all censorship of newspapers, magazines, and other publications from publishers, unless there is determined by qualified authority which includes the ombudsman that the literature in question presents a clear and present danger to the safety and security of the institution. Institution spot censoring only of letters. |
| 9. Allow all inmates on their own to communicate with anyone they please. | 9. Allow all inmates, at their own expense, to communicate with anyone they please. |

| | |
|---|---|
| 10. When an inmate reaches conditional release, give him a full release without parole. | |
| 11. Institute realistic, effective rehabilitation programs for all inmates according to their offense and personal needs. | 10. Institute realistic, effective rehabilitation programs for all inmates, according to their offense and personal needs. |
| 12. Modernize the inmate education system. | 11. Modernize the inmate education system, including the establishment of a Latin library. |
| 13. Provide a narcotics treatment program that is effective. | 12. Provide an effective narcotics treatment program for all prisoners requesting such treatment. |
| 14. Provide adequate legal assistance to all inmates requesting it. | 13. Provide or allow adequate legal assistance to all inmates requesting it or permit them to use inmate legal assistance of their choice in any proceeding whatsoever. In all such proceedings, inmates shall be entitled to appropriate due process of law. |
| 15. Provide a healthy diet; reduce the number of pork dishes; serve fresh fruit daily. | 14. Provide a healthy diet; reduce the number of pork dishes; increase fresh fruit daily. |
| 16. Reduce cell time, increase recreation time, and provide better recreation facilities and equipment. | 15. Reduce cell time, increase recreation facilities and equipment, hopefully by November 1, 1971. |
| 17. Provide adequate medical treatment for every inmate, engage either a Spanish-speaking doctor or interpreters who will accom- | 16. Provide adequate medical treatment for every inmate; engage either a Spanish-speaking doctor or inmate interpreters who will |

| | |
|---|---|
| pany Spanish-speaking inmates to medical interviews. | accompany Spanish-speaking inmates to medical interviews. (See point 11 above.) |
| 18. Provide a complete Spanish library. | |
| 19. Educate all officers in the needs of inmates. | |
| 20. Institute a program for the employment of black and Spanish-speaking officers. | 17. Institute a program for the recruitment and employment of a significant number of black and Spanish-speaking officers. |
| 21. Establish an inmate grievance delegation comprised of one elected inmate from each company which is authorized to speak to the administration concerning grievances, and develop other procedures for community control of the institution. | 18. Establish an inmate grievance commission comprised of one elected inmate from each company which is authorized to speak to the administration concerning grievances, and develop other procedures for inmate participation in the operation and decision-making processes of the institution. |
| 22. Conduct a grand-jury investigation of the expropriation of inmate funds and the use of profits from the metal and other shops. | 19. Investigate the alleged expropriation of inmate funds and the use of profits from the metal and other shops. |
| 23. Cease administrative resentencing of inmates returned for parole violation. | 20. The State Commissioner of Correctional Services will recommend that the penal law be changed to cease administrative resentencing of inmates returned for parole violation. |

| | |
|---|---|
| 24. Conduct Menechino hearings in a fair manner. | 21. Recommend that Menechino hearings be held promptly and fairly.[20] |
| 25. Permit other inmates in C block and the box to join this group. | |
| 26. Arrange flights out of this country to nonimperialist nations for those inmates desiring to leave this country. | |
| 27. Remove inside walls, making one open yard and no more segregation or punishment. | |
| 28. Expansion of work-release programs. | 22. Recommend necessary legislation and more adequate funds to expand work-release programs. |
| 29. End approved lists for visiting and correspondence. | 23. End approved lists for correspondence and visitors. |
| 30. Remove screens in visitation rooms as soon as possible. | 24. Remove visitation screens as soon as possible. |
| 31. Institute parole violation changes—revocation of parole shall not be for vehicle and traffic violation. | 25. Paroled inmates shall not be charged with parole violations for moving traffic violations or driving without a license, unconnected with any other crime. |
| 32. Due process hearing for all disciplinary proceedings with 30-day maximum. | 26. Institute a 30-day maximum for segregation arising out of any one offense. Every effort should be geared toward restoring the individual to regular housing as soon as possible, consistent with safety regulations. |

| | |
|---|---|
| 33. Access to facility for outside dentists and doctors at inmates' expense. | 27. Permit access to outside dentists and doctors at the inmates' own expense within the institution, where possible, and consistent with scheduling problems, medical diagnosis, and health needs. |
| | 28. It is expressly understood that members of the observers' committee will be permitted into the Institution on a reasonable basis to determine whether all of the above provisions are being effectively carried out. If questions of adequacy are raised, the matter will be brought to the attention of the Commissioner of Correctional Services for clearance. |

As the observers girded themselves to bring both this and the James document to the prisoners, Oswald reported to Rockefeller's aides some good news: he now felt optimistic that a reasonable end to this ordeal was in sight. As he mulled things over from his family estate overlooking the Hudson River, Rockefeller, however, wasn't so certain that Oswald's view of things was realistic—especially given what he had heard from his right-hand man, Michael Whiteman. In fact, it seemed to Rockefeller that it was now time to assert much more gubernatorial control over the situation. So he decided to send another one of his closest aides, Robert Douglass, to Attica. From the moment he arrived on the scene on Saturday, the third day of the uprising, Douglass kept in constant touch with his boss.[21] Douglass's interpretation of the events there would have an immeasurable impact on how the governor reacted to, and made vital decisions about, the standoff.

On Saturday, Black Panther Bobby Seale also headed to Attica. The observers in the Steward's Room were surprised to learn that Seale and his two bodyguards were en route to the prison. But the FBI was well informed of Seale's itinerary. At 11:15 a.m. Saturday morning the San Francisco bureau of the FBI had notified the agencies in Buffalo, Albany, Chicago, and New York City that Seale would be arriving at the Buffalo airport at 4:53 p.m. on United flight #412.[22] This despite the fact that Governor Rockefeller's office had informed the New York bureau that "it would be better" if representatives from the Black Panther Party were not allowed to appear at Attica and that "if anything can be done to prevent their appearance, it is believed that this would help the situation."[23] But the San Francisco office had been unable to prevent Seale from traveling to Attica, and now it was up to Commissioner Oswald to decide whether to let him in.

Although he was pretty certain Oswald wouldn't let Seale in, Herman Schwartz agreed to pick him up at the airport and drive him to Attica. Sure enough, Oswald wanted to bar Seale's entry, and Schwartz found himself arguing passionately for the commissioner to change his mind—to no avail, it seemed. Oswald had already been leaned on by the governor's men, Douglass, Hurd, and Shapiro, and he was loath to go against their wishes.[24]

What is more, Oswald feared that Seale would upset the progress that he felt had been made that day. The commissioner had also been hearing that "some sort of psychological deterioration [was] taking place" in the yard and in his view Seale's presence could only make it worse.[25] His concern was based on a report from Dr. Hanson, who, after returning from yet another medical visit to the yard, had stated his view that the men were becoming more anxious. As Hanson described it, "The prisoners were really uptight. I saw a number of people that had acute psychotic or hysterical reactions of various types. There was one husky one, one black male, that came up, and he was carrying a cross . . . and he was shouting about Black Power and about God and they were all going to die, and all sorts of gibberish."[26] The doctor also reported that he had come across "a couple of men that had sort of catatonic seizures, which is a hysterical reaction."[27]

In delivering these reports, Dr. Hanson had no intention of encouraging the state to take a more hard-line position with the men in the yard. He had made it crystal clear to Oswald that he "felt very sorry for these people."[28] Indeed, positive news—clear evidence of the prisoners' calm and humanity—had also been reported to the commissioner. Oswald had been informed by Hanson, for instance, that the prisoners willingly released another hostage (the CO who was Big Black's friend) who was apparently having a heart attack.[29] The doctor had also told Oswald that one of the hostages had slipped him a note to take out that said that they "hoped that every possible rebel demand would be granted" so that they could return home safely.[30] As notably, the hostages had sent out a list of items they wanted, which specifically included supplies they "intended to share with our security guards . . . [because] they have been sharing a lot of things with us and we would like to share these things with them."[31]

But prisoner acts of kindness barely registered with prison officials in this crisis situation, and Hanson had little control over how his words were interpreted. The doctor couldn't have imagined that when he mentioned that the prisoners had constructed a platform over and around the negotiating table, Rockefeller's men began fixating on the possibility that it was intended "to be a sacrificial altar and a hangman's platform."[32] Everything they were told just made Oswald worry that his efforts to resolve this situation peacefully were failing and made Rockefeller's people even more hostile toward the idea of continued negotiations.

And yet, despite the insistence of the governor's office that Seale not be allowed into the prison, Oswald began to think that it might be foolish to keep him out. Kunstler had expressed the view that this revered figure might actually be the one to persuade the men to accept the twenty-eight out of thirty-three points. This argument nagged at Oswald, particularly in light of the fact that the observers had already sent an emissary into No Man's Land with the news that Seale would soon be there. Given that the men had been asking to see a member of the Black Panther Party since day one of the rebellion, it wouldn't do for them to think that the state was refusing him entrance now. Getting Kunstler's assurances that Seale would not make any inflammatory remarks, the commissioner grudgingly, and with great trepidation, called downstairs to tell the troopers at the entrance to let him in.

However, Seale had already left. Furious that he'd been left to sit in Schwartz's car for over an hour while Oswald decided whether to admit him, he'd had Schwartz turn around to drive him back to the airport. Oswald had to send a New York state policeman to flag down Schwartz's car and bring Seale back to Attica—a move that left the observers enjoying a much needed moment of levity. As Wicker marveled, "Oswald dispatched a State Police car to bring back the famous Panther leader, who probably never before had been pursued by policemen whose purpose was to ask him politely to please come help the authorities restore the peace."[33]

But all merriment ended the moment the unsmiling Seale entered the Steward's Room.

The first order of business was to get Seale's response to the twenty-eight points. Silence fell over the room as his eyes scanned the pages. It did

Bobby Seale makes his way through the crowds outside Attica. *(Courtesy of Corbis)*

not take him long to say what many of the observers feared he might: in his view, the document didn't say much. More to the point, it contained absolutely nothing about the biggest sticking point in the negotiations: amnesty.

Into this discussion came some news that made clear to all assembled that this particular demand was now a must. William Quinn, the officer that had been taken to the hospital with severe head injuries, had just died.[34]

Attica superintendent Vincent Mancusi had learned of Quinn's death at the same time that Robert Douglass was arriving at Attica, around 5:00 Saturday afternoon. Once he learned of this tragedy, Douglass grabbed the phone and called District Attorney James. It was imperative, Douglass told James, that the public not find out about Quinn's death because it would harden both the observers' and the prisoners' insistence that criminal amnesty be granted.[35] Despite Douglass's wishes, news of Quinn's death somehow got out. Not only did the observers hear about it as they began hashing things over with Bobby Seale up in the Steward's Room, but word also reached, and seemed to electrify, the many hundreds of already agitated state troopers who had been waiting outside the prison, some since Thursday morning. For days now, the observers had been watching the troopers' hot anger building, and the news of a CO's death, combined with the presence of Bobby Seale, according to Tom Wicker "inflamed the troopers, deputies, and correction officers with more resentment and bitterness than they already felt."[36]

The troopers' fury was further fueled by the completely false version of Quinn's death that had, within minutes, become gospel: that this CO had sustained the terrible injuries that killed him when prisoners had thrown him out of a second floor window onto his head. Both the *Buffalo Evening News* and *The New York Times* ran stories containing this false report.[37] Rumors started flying that not only had Quinn been thrown to his death, but he may also have been castrated.[38]

Under these circumstances, it was clear that Bobby Seale could not endorse an agreement that did not include amnesty. All of the observers, even Herman Badillo, who had been arguing that they could surely work out an agreement short of amnesty, now saw that without the legal protection of amnesty, the men in D Yard would be in grave danger. Maybe worse, as he put it, the prisoners would now likely "find themselves at the mercy of furious correction officers once everybody else had gone away" and thus they also needed "unbreakable assurances against reprisals."[39]

Even if the state were to grant amnesty, Seale, as it turned out, had no intention of either endorsing or rejecting anything crafted by its officials. As he explained it, he alone could not endorse anything—only the Central Committee of the Black Panther Party had the power to do that. He would therefore leave in order to consult with that body.

Stunned by the idea that Seale might leave before going to see any of the prisoners, the observers begged him to go into the yard, if only for a brief meeting.[40] One of the observers tried to impress upon him how important a visit was by handing Seale a note that had been given to him in the yard a few hours earlier: "Brother Bobby . . . Our lives are in your hands—Come! Attica prisoners."[41] To everyone's surprise, however, Seale glanced at it only cursorily before tossing it onto a table dismissively, like a used napkin. Nevertheless, he finally, reluctantly, agreed to make a brief visit inside. Tom Wicker felt disgusted by the whole scene as the group made their way down to the A Gate. In his view, Seale's "absorption in an abstract if genuine cause had dulled in him the sense of humanity that first had drawn him to the cause."[42]

By now it had been a full sixteen hours since anyone from the administration or the observers committee had visited the yard. From Richard Clark's vantage point, state officials had been "stalling" all day. He had "kept going back and forth to the gate for word, but there was nothing."[43] Such lapses in communication always made the men in D Yard anxious. This day's delays had left even Roger Champen, usually one of the calmest men in the yard, on edge. To make things worse, the troopers posted on the rooftops had been taunting and jeering them for hours. Finally, though, the men got word that famed Black Panther leader Bobby Seale was on his way to speak to them. Many of the prisoners deeply admired "what Bobby stood for," and felt that his ferocity would make him a powerful advocate on their behalf.[44] As they prepared for what was to be the eighth visit of outsiders into the yard on this third day of the uprising, expectations were high.

As the observers made their way to the negotiating table this time, there was little trace of the ebullient mood of Thursday or Friday night. Even the sight of Bobby Seale generated much less excitement than anyone imagined it would. In part this was due to Seale's own lack of enthusiasm. Although he gave the Black Panther salute and yelled "Power to the People," he did so without much energy or conviction and, in turn, he received only a tepid welcome—quite a contrast to the standing cheers that Senator John Dunne and William Kunstler had received only the night before. This was worrisome to the observers. They were all counting on Seale to get a "tremendous ovation," which would help pave the way for giving the men in D Yard the two documents they had to decide upon.[45]

Not only was Seale's arrival shockingly "anticlimactic," but he then proceeded to give only a very brief speech.[46] In that speech he laid blame on the commissioner for delaying him and then told the men that Oswald had tried to make his entry conditional upon his directing the men to surrender.[47] This statement was patently untrue, but it did rile up some indignation, as he hoped it would.[48] They need not worry, Seale went on, because he was not going to do that. In fact, he wasn't going to make any judgment at all on what they should do. Instead he was going to leave to talk things over with Huey Newton and the Central Committee, and would return to report on their response the following morning. He then got up and started walking out of the yard.

The men in D Yard couldn't believe that Seale had only just arrived and was now leaving. They were clearly upset that he had given them so little time and none of his perspective. It was "very disappointing," Champ explained. "We had looked for a person [who] related to what was going on. And then he appeared very nervous . . . very apprehensive. . . . You really can't conclude anything in that short period of time, especially something of that magnitude. So, when he left . . . it was followed by disappointment."[49]

As Seale strode toward the exit Herman Badillo asked Wicker worriedly, "Aren't we all going out the way we promised? Isn't that the arrangement, that we all go out together?"[50] They had indeed made a commitment to Oswald that they would all leave together, and Wicker agreed that it was best to do so. John Dunne, sitting nearby, didn't even need to be asked. He had been in plenty of prisons in his life, and he could see that Seale's abrupt departure had made the situation in this one unstable.

Seeing that the other observers were also making moves to leave, even the usually mild-mannered Champ exclaimed angrily, "I don't understand!"[51] Over in the hostage circle, CO John Stockholm thought he understood just fine. His take on what he'd just seen was that "Bobby Seale was scared to death, couldn't get out of there fast enough," and now the observers were nervous too.[52]

Clarence Jones quickly jumped in to try to calm the situation down. He explained that the men were not being abandoned. The observers were leaving them with the fruits of their hard labor—two documents that they thought would meet most of their demands.[53] But nothing Jones said could stem the waves of disappointment crashing over D Yard. Deep down the men didn't really believe that Bobby Seale or anyone else was coming back.

And, indeed, when the observers who'd followed Seale out of the yard arrived on the state side of the A Block gate, many of them had already decided, as had State Senator John Dunne, that they were not going back in.[54] Oswald couldn't imagine why they were back so quickly, and he was alarmed that the group had split up. Dunne assured Oswald that it was fine and to be patient; it was good that nine of the observers had decided to stay in the yard to make sure the prisoners were given the James letter along with the list of demands that Oswald had agreed to. Also, Dunne explained, Seale was now going to consult with Huey Newton about a possible Panther endorsement. The Black Panther leader had assured the prisoners that he would relay Newton's position to them personally the next morning at 7:00. Somewhat appeased, Oswald nodded and bade farewell to Seale with a heartfelt handshake, murmuring his thanks that he had come to help. Then, seeing how furious state troopers were that Seale was anywhere near Attica, the commissioner again made arrangements for him to have a police escort for his own protection when he left.

Back in D Yard, the nine observers who had stayed—Eve, Jones, Steel, Tepper, Fitch, Kenyatta, and Soto, as well as the two representatives from the Young Lords Party, Juan Ortiz and Jose Paris—were unsure whether this had been a good idea. It had been Eve who had made the snap decision to stay, he later explained, because "the situation was so serious, the prisoners' nerves were so on edge and they were feeling so let down."[55] In his mind, he had little choice but to "go ahead and present the package."[56] He knew, though, this could be disastrous.

Arthur Eve could smell the fear of the prisoners as they talked worriedly among themselves in the darkening yard about the possibility that "the negotiations had broken down," which, to them, was a terrifying development.[57] When Eve mustered the courage to go to the mic to speak, he was showered with invective and cries of, "Where have you guys been all day?" At that point, Clarence Jones stepped to the mic and made his own attempt to talk calmly about the documents. He reminded them that they could never have expected to get all thirty-three of their demands met, and then of the real stakes here. It was all "well and good to quote Chairman Mao about power coming out of the barrel of a gun," he noted, but the men needed to be clear that the only ones with guns in this situation were the "men outside," and, in his view, "if the situation was not resolved by compromise, the 'Kent State psychology' would take over" and violence would ensue.[58] Although it was up to them to decide, Jones said, he felt that the package the observers had gotten the men was the best they could hope for. He then began to read through the twenty-eight demands that Oswald had signed off on.

The men listened quietly until they realized that Oswald had not agreed to an amnesty provision. When Jones began reading through the James letter, all hell broke loose once again. Sitting near Jones and watching him as he faced the crowd, Lewis Steel realized that he and the other observers were now facing "the most danger they had ever encountered."[59] As Jones was wrapping up, Steel could see that Bill Kunstler had come back into the yard and was making his way to the table. While he marveled at the man's courage, he wasn't sure that even Kunstler could dissipate the hostility. Kunstler quickly recognized that the situation had turned much uglier in the yard in the last thirty minutes. This worried as much as scared him since he had just come from seeing General Buzz O'Hara in the administration building and had been told "that what had been offered was the best they could get."[60]

Feeling tremendous pressure to ward off disaster, Kunstler rushed to the table and, grabbing the microphone from Jones, embarked upon a passionate speech in defense of the package Jones had just presented to them, not as something perfect, not even as something that they must accept, but as "the very best the state was willing to offer" and, very likely, "the best that they could hope to get."[61] Since he was after all their attorney, the men had at least some reason to trust what Kunstler had to say, and they did start to listen more attentively. Eve, Steel, and Jones all felt that, if nothing else had been accomplished that night, William Kunstler had just saved their lives.[62]

But just as quickly, the tide turned again. In his effort to make sure that he understood exactly what the men's position was so that he could render an accurate reporting of it to state officials, Kunstler unwittingly gave them news they had not yet heard. He really did understand their concern about forgoing amnesty, he said, "now that the guard has died."[63]

William Kunstler addresses the yard. *(Courtesy of the Associated Press)*

A hush fell over the yard, and gasps of fear and disbelief could be heard. It was in that split second that Kunstler realized, horrified, that they hadn't known about Quinn's death. Suddenly, all was different. These men had been terrified of giving up without amnesty all along, but now they well knew that the stakes were even higher. In short, after "the death of Quinn . . . everyone could be indicted and [those who had been] elected as spokesmen . . . were definitely going to be under prosecution."[64] As if to emphasize this point, Richard Clark grabbed the copy of the twenty-eight points, jumped up onto the negotiating table, and with a flourish ripped the document to shreds. The meeting was over.

Although no one had specifically said that the prisoners were rejecting the state's proposal, and no vote was taken, the message was clear. The hostages knew it too. As hostage G. B. Smith put it, when the "word got out that Billy Quinn had died . . . there was a great mood swing in both inmates and hostages. Everybody knew that was a whole new ball game now."[65] The observers, now back up in the Steward's Room, knew this, but at least a few of them still held out hope that Seale would come back in the morning, as promised, and help them to avert a tragic end to the prisoners' protest.

Leaving the prison to get a bit of sleep, Kunstler made sure that General Buzz O'Hara knew that both he and Seale might need transportation back to the prison the next morning. Herman Schwartz, who had dropped Seale off at the Holiday Inn earlier that evening, also made himself available should he be called to bring him back to Attica. Observers Wicker, McGowan, Badillo, Garcia, and Mathew were already at the Treadway Inn, having left earlier to make sure they could get a room. After grabbing a drink at the hotel bar and catching a bit of the Miss America pageant that was blaring on a TV screen above their heads, this group then headed over to a bowling alley–restaurant for a steak dinner. It wasn't until Lewis Steel joined them that they learned about the prisoners' rejection of the twenty-eight points, but Steel agreed with them: perhaps Seale could still turn things around. As Saturday ended it was clear that everyone was "waiting for Bobby."[66]

Commissioner Oswald refused to wait any longer, however. He couldn't imagine anyone or anything turning this situation around. Demoralized and exhausted, in his heart Oswald believed that he had walked the last mile to meet the prisoners' demands. As even he knew, some of the twenty-eight points he had committed himself to—such as the minimum wage and changing the penal code on parole—he personally had no power to implement, and, equally important, he knew that he had deliberately inserted words such as "reasonable," "true," and "adequate" to allow for some wiggle room regarding what he had in fact agreed to. Still he was devastated and even bitter that the prisoners hadn't accepted the twenty-eight points. He now agreed with Rockefeller's men that "instead of . . . the situation becoming better, it was worsening."[67]

Late Saturday night, when Oswald met again with Attica administrators, men from the governor's office, and Major Monahan, even Oswald was willing to talk in earnest "about the possibility . . . or the desirability of taking the institution Sunday."[68] They settled on a plan. Unless something changed with the "unsettled state of 'negotiations,'" an all-out assault on D Yard would likely commence at 6:00 the next morning, on Sunday, September 12.[69]

Meanwhile, back in D Yard on that pitch-black Saturday night, a cold drizzle was soaking through the prisoners' ragtag tents and shelters and no one knew whether they should sleep or remain vigilant. Deciding to make the hostages more comfortable, some prisoners went over to the men in the circle to make "sure they had extra blankets" and then scanned the night sky for any sign of trouble.[70]

Blankets or no, the hostages in the circle were as anxious as the other men in D Yard. The same was true for their families and friends in the village of Attica. No one knew what was happening with the negotiations, and even the mayor, Richard W. Miller, whose brother Edward Miller was a civilian hostage, could get no news out of any state official. Hostage wife Paula Krotz, like many of the families, felt that she "might as well have been invisible," since "the only person who spoke to us during all those days was Father Marcinkevich."[71] In fact, so desperate were locals to learn something from officials about their loved ones that they had been descending on Attica's front lawn demanding answers for the last three days. So many people had crowded the grass by Saturday afternoon that according to reporters, "Salvation Army workers had served 32,510 cups of coffee and cold drinks, 750 dozen donuts, 6,500 sandwiches, 3,000 cups of hot soup, 300 bottles of milk and an unknown quantity of sliced pizza."[72] Hostage Carl Valone's wife, Ann, a nurse at St. Jerome's Hospital, was one of those who parked for hours in front of Attica in her station wagon hoping in vain for some news; up until then, all she had been doing was "praying, and listening, and watching television," but she had learned nothing.[73]

Attica's tiny streets were also swarming with outsiders seeking information. Scores of newspaper and television men had arrived, there was a steady stream of cars bearing prisoner supporters, and there were throngs of gawkers from nearby towns as well. Many of Attica's townspeople felt as though they too were under siege.[74] Hearing little news except for stories about the comings and goings of various observers only fueled locals' fears, encouraging them to imagine the very worst. By Saturday, the town's men were arming themselves while their wives kept vigil at living room windows to defend against any intruders.[75] State troopers had also begun going door-to-door asking Attica's residents to park their cars to block the side streets, so that any protester or prisoner sympathizer who might show up wouldn't be able to dodge police roadblocks.[76] In response to a rumor that prisoner supporters were coming to Attica via the Tonawanda Creek, troopers came to people's houses that bordered streams, including that of hostage John Stockholm, to ask if they could take a dog along their property looking for outside agitators. Stockholm's wife, Mary, agreed and for a while she enthusiastically helped a trooper patrol her yard.[77] On every major street corner stood men armed with rifles and, responding to wholly unfounded rumors that black militants were coming to town to kidnap white children, the village of Attica closed its schools.[78]

The townspeople weren't just fearful, they were also hostile—particularly toward the observers who were staying at local hotels and eating at local restaurants. Some resented that these outsiders had more access to men like Commissioner Oswald than they did, and hated that these men were better informed about what was happening in the yard than the family members of the hostages. Most also believed that all of the observers were militantly pro-prisoner and would never be able to do right by the correction officers being held in D Yard. One afternoon, Congressman Badillo tried to get a hot dog at a food tent that the local Lions Club had set up in front of the prison, but he was told in no uncertain terms that "This food's not for you."[79] Arthur Eve likewise found himself unable to order a meal at an Attica eatery because the staff refused even to acknowledge his presence.

The families of the prisoners were equally unwelcome when they showed up in the village hoping for information, if they even were able to make the trip. For the families far downstate in boroughs like Brooklyn or the Bronx there was no way they could afford to head to Attica to stand vigil outside the prison, so they had to rely solely on television coverage and newspapers that had little new or meaningful to report. And, of course, for the many Spanish-speaking relatives of men in Attica, network news coverage was useless. Most prisoner families didn't even know whether their sons and husbands were in D Yard or whether they were among those still under state control in C Block.

In this respect L. D. Barkley's mother, Laverne, was one of the lucky ones because she had at least seen her son on television. Like most mothers, Laverne Barkley didn't learn that the prisoners had seized Attica on September 9 until she saw the nightly news and realized that the young man on the screen trying to explain to the world why the men had rebelled was none other than her own son. It was bad enough that the state had sent her son, the second eldest of her eleven children, to a maximum security facility for a minor parole violation—driving without a license. But now, just as he'd almost served his time and was all set to begin college so that the baby he had on the way would have a good future, he was in the midst of a prison uprising.[80] She, her daughter Betty, and L.D.'s girlfriend had just visited L.D. on September 5. He had surprised them by showing them a book he'd been writing. L.D. had wanted his mother to take the volume home for him but she had persuaded him to hold on to it. "Elliot," she had said, "you're coming home in a few days, so you bring it with you when you come."[81] Laverne now deeply regretted not having taken that book.

By Saturday night, no one—no prisoner relative sitting in a far-off city nervously watching the TV news, no hostage family member pacing the parking lot under Attica's foreboding facade, no observer trying to get some sleep in a local motel, no trooper standing with arms at the ready on the prison's vast lawn, and no man huddling in a tent in D Yard—thought that this standoff could continue much longer. Someone, somewhere, was going to break.

17

# On the Precipice

To his great annoyance, as dawn broke on Sunday, the 12th of September, NYSP Major John Monahan, head of Batavia's Troop A, stood ready, but was not given the green light to commence a forcible retaking of Attica. Instead he was told to stand by. For him this was intensely frustrating because it seemed that every hour that state officials were talking with the prisoners, they were legitimizing their takeover. He firmly believed that had he been allowed to go in for a full retaking days earlier, this would all be long over.

Meanwhile, waking up in nearby hotels, the observers saw things very differently. To them the prisoners had tried to get their grievances addressed through proper channels and had gotten nowhere. While the eruption four days earlier was not good, it was to them understandable. Now, the observers felt, it was up to them to make sure that something positive came out of this unfortunate situation. They were, however, tired and highly stressed. On Sunday morning those who had managed to grab a bed or some floor space on the matted shag carpeting of the Holiday Inn or the Treadway blearily buttoned up their now rumpled, smelly shirts and tried to psych themselves up for another day of negotiations. Tom Wicker and Lewis Steel were in Bill Kunstler's room when he got the call that he had been waiting for from the Black Panthers in New York. Feeling desperate for some way to end the Attica standoff without violence, Kunstler had asked the Panthers to explore whether some of their contacts in countries such as Algeria might be willing to take some of Attica's prisoners, should they manage to secure transport to a "non-imperialist" country. Wicker didn't like hearing this. As he tried to remind Kunstler, the prisoners had already made it clear that this original "demand" in fact had very little support and, he went on, it would be a real distraction to bring it up again. In Wicker's view the focus now should be solely on getting Bobby Seale, somehow, to persuade the men in the yard to accept the settlement they'd been offered.

At 8:20 Sunday morning, Seale dutifully returned to Attica, but when Oswald told him he would not be allowed into D Yard unless he promised to endorse the twenty-eight points, Seale turned on his heel and left. Outside the prison, in front of a growing crowd pushing in to hear what he had to say, Seale read a statement he had just drafted:

> This morning, the commissioner and his aides would not let me in, saying that if I was not going inside to encourage the prisoners to accept the so-called demands made by the committee, they did not want me. I am not going to do that. . . . The Black Panther Party position is this: The prisoners have to make their own decision. I will not encourage them to compromise their position. The Black Panther Party position is that all political prisoners who want to be released to go to non-imperialistic countries should be complied with by the New York state governments.[1]

Back in the Steward's Room, a few of the observers, including Kunstler, were supportive of Seale's position and newly angry at Oswald. Others, however, were furious at Seale for what they believed to be dodging responsibility in the face of the crisis. Wicker, for example, felt strongly that Seale should have told the men in the yard, "Look, you've gone as far as you can. You've made a political point to the whole world. You've made The Man listen. Now a lot of you are going to get killed if you push it further."[2] Whatever their disagreements, however, all the observers agreed that they now needed a new plan.

As the minutes ticked by, consensus among the observers only was hard to come by. Some thought that the prisoners should be told that they had a clear choice—accept what the state had offered them or face the possibility of death in a forcible retaking. Tom Soto went so far as to say that "the acts of the prisoners are in the interests of all the working people and the oppressed people of the world, regardless of whether they get slaughtered."[3] And Jabarr Kenyatta seemed almost enthusiastic about the possibility of a confrontation with the state: "We've got to have a commitment . . . when the man comes we don't mind fighting."[4] Arthur Eve couldn't have felt more differently. He was concerned not just about what might happen to the prisoners and their hostages if the troopers went in, but how it would affect his constituents. "If they come in there and kill people, Buffalo gonna blow up. . . . If something happens here it's gonna mirror in every community all over the city," he worried out loud.[5]

But as every observer was well aware, Oswald was under increasing and "tremendous pressure from officials in other states, correctional officers, organizations such as the PBA [Police Benevolent Association], the families of hostages and people on the street to use force." The mayor of Auburn wrote to Rockefeller how "utterly dismayed and angered" he was by Oswald's "permissiveness."[6]

Thanks to this pressure, on Sunday morning, the commissioner announced to the observers that unless the prisoners agreed to send a team of negotiators to Attica's mess hall to meet with him and a team of observers, he was done talking. No one paid much attention to his new line in the sand, though, because all were too busy venting their own frustrations and opinions. When Clarence Jones ventured that it was high time to clarify the observers' "role in relation to the prisoners," it became clear just how differently they all now saw this.[7] Republican state assemblyman Frank Walkley thought their task was to convince the men to give up on the demand for amnesty. Kunstler was incredulous that anyone could think that the prisoners would be adequately protected by what they'd been offered, and said the idea that anyone thought that made him feel like he was in *Alice in Wonderland*. He then stated unequivocally, "They must be told the absolute, utter truth as to what this situation is."[8]

Clarence Jones agreed that the prisoners needed to be told the full facts, as did Wicker, who argued that the observers had "the responsibility to give them [the] chance to make a clear choice." Yes, agreed one of the representatives from the Young Lords, they needed the opportunity to think through whether they really needed "a confrontation with the state."[9] All in the room recognized, though, that time was in short supply. Shaking his head, Kunstler said despondently, "I am utterly sick at heart that those men will die and they'll die because of me."[10] Suddenly realizing exactly what had to be done, he stated firmly, "The Bobby Seale episode is irrelevant. . . . Whatever reason he gives to the public is immaterial. . . . We should all go down and tell them the truth."[11]

Observer Julian Tepper looked shaken by this pronouncement. Quietly he shook his head and said to the group, "I'll be completely honest. I'm afraid to go back in."[12] He elaborated: "There's going to be no resolution [because the] Administration puts us in an untenable position [and]

Bobby Seale has put us in an untenable position."[13] Most in the room seemed to agree with him. As the group grew more desperate about its diminishing options, Clarence Jones came back to the question of whether prison superintendent Mancusi might be transferred out of Attica. Might that be a significant enough concession to persuade the prisoners to abandon their demand for amnesty? Others suggested asking the governor to come to Attica to personally assure the prisoners that he would allow no reprisals. And then the group returned to the importance of amnesty—full stop.[14] But this simply wasn't on the table, State Senator John Dunne reminded everyone. The prisoners must be made to understand, he went on, that "a political point has been proven. . . . More has been accomplished in terms of penal reform in the last three days than ever before."[15] With this pronouncement, and at the request of his fellow observers, the state senator headed out at 10:35 a.m. to find Robert Douglass. Maybe they could work on him to get the governor to Attica. Rockefeller could at least offer his word that the men wouldn't be harmed if they surrendered.

Less than ten minutes later, Senator Dunne returned to the Steward's Room, but with Norman Hurd, not Douglass, in tow. They were met with a great deal of grumbling since no one believed Hurd had any power to do anything at Attica, to which Oswald, still sitting at the table, said defensively, "Hurd is sent here as the Governor's personal representative."[16] Even Dunne felt the need to press the commissioner on this. Did the commissioner feel that Hurd "has as much power as Douglass?"[17] Clearly offended, Hurd told the group that he was Rockefeller's official representative and Douglass was there only "to be of assistance."[18] "Maybe," said Herman Badillo, but "Douglass got me here, [so it's] important to have him."[19]

By 10:50 Sunday morning, Robert Douglass was finally standing before the observers and found himself inundated with their questions and concerns. Arthur Eve explained to Douglass that the observers were unanimous in their conviction that, at the very least, the governor should come to the prison because without a peaceable resolution, "hundreds and possibly thousands will be killed."[20] Badillo also tried to persuade Douglass how important it was for Rockefeller to come to Attica. He echoed Eve's concerns, telling Douglass he feared how places like Harlem and the Bronx would respond to a retaking, and assuring him that they did not expect the governor to go into the yard and talk to prisoners; they just wanted him to come, because doing so would underscore his commitment to protecting the men when they surrendered.

Kunstler put the matter more bluntly: "If the governor does not come, he is condoning a massacre."[21] Other observers agreed. The members of law enforcement assembling outside of the prison are "no more than animals . . . straining at the leash. . . . There will be a bloodbath . . . when those beasts are turned loose on the people out there," one said.[22] Clarence Jones also believed that a "massacre of prisoners is about to take place," and he implored Douglass to "spend time instead of lives."[23] "I hear you, I understand," Douglass told the group as he headed out the door, presumably to call his boss.[24]

Badillo was still unsettled and suggested that, since Douglass might not persuade the governor how imperative it was that he come to Attica, perhaps it was time for the observers to enlist the aid of the American people. In a press release, they could explain just how dire the situation had become, and then ask citizens to put pressure on the governor to oversee personally a peaceful end to the standoff. Secretly, Dunne doubted that even this pressure would make Rockefeller budge. In his opinion, the governor had his eyes on the presidency of the United States, and for that reason he couldn't afford to look soft on "criminals" in this standoff at Attica.[25] Nevertheless, Dunne did not stand in the way of those trying to pen a national press release.[26] By 11:00 a.m. a draft had been finalized, which they agreed must also be taken to the gate in A Block in order to get the prisoners' approval of its wording:

> The committee of observers in Attica prison is now convinced a massacre of prisoners and guards may take place in this institution. For the sake of common humanity, we call on every person who hears these words to implore the Governor of this state to come to Attica to consult with the observer committee, so we can spend time and not lives in an attempt to resolve the issues before us. Send the following telegram immediately to Governor Nelson Rockefeller in New York City: "Please go to Attica to meet with the observers committee."[27]

The men in D Yard did approve, but the observers could see the desperation on their faces and agreed to take their subsequent request immediately back to Oswald: that one black and one Puerto Rican reporter come to the yard within a half hour, along with five observers, one of whom should be a man with "real credibility" with the outside world to show that the hostages were still okay and that the men really wanted to end their uprising safely, as well as with meaningful changes to the institution.

Few had much faith that the press release would make a difference.

Nevertheless, as Wicker put it, it was important to make "the last effort, even if it proved only a hopeless gesture to decency and humanity."[28] Wicker's own commitment to making "the last effort" was quickly tested when it became clear that he and Dunne were the observers the group as a whole agreed met the criterion of "credibility with outsiders." It would be up to them to go back in the yard at the prisoners' request. Senator Dunne said, unequivocally, that he would not go. That left Wicker, the *New York Times* journalist, and though he felt he had to do it, he was petrified. Seeing his fear, Clarence Jones stepped up and said that he would go with him. Wicker felt relief wash over him at this "considerable gesture of courage and friendship."[29] No sooner had each man made his peace with the decision to walk into a terrifyingly uncertain situation than Oswald arrived to inform them that absolutely no more visits to the yard would take place. Moreover, he had already sent Deputy Commissioner Walter Dunbar to the A Tunnel gate with his final statement to the prisoners in D Yard, which read:

> As Commissioner of Correctional Services, I have personally met with you several times in areas under your control for the purposes of insuring the immediate safety of employee hostages, and the safety of all others concerned during the difficult situation. As you all know, food, clothing, bedding, water and medical care have been available to you. You have been able to meet with outside observers of your choice and representatives of the news media. A Federal Court Order was obtained promptly to guarantee that there would be no administrative reprisals; your representatives have been able to ascertain that no mistreatment of inmates has occurred.
>
> I urgently request you to release the hostages unharmed, now, and to accept the recommendations of the committee of outside observers which recommendations were approved by me, and join with me in restoring order to this institution.
>
> Only after these steps are taken am I willing to meet with a five member committee chosen by you to discuss any grievances you may have and to create a mechanism by which you can be assured that the recommendations I have agreed to are implemented.
>
> All possible efforts have been made to deal fairly with your problems and grievances and to resolve the present situation. All good faith is embodied in the proposed agreement I signed which is in your hands.

> It is in the interest of all concerned that you now respond affirmatively to this request.[30]

Dunbar handed the statement to Richard X Clark through the A Tunnel gate, telling him the men had fifteen minutes to respond.

Clark walked back into D Yard with a bad feeling and handed the statement to the men with microphones at the negotiating table, whereupon they read it in both English and Spanish to the restless crowd. As the words of Oswald's statement sank in, particularly the sentence "I urgently request you to release the hostages unharmed, now, and to *accept the recommendations of the committee of outside observers* . . . [which] were approved by me," the men in D Yard felt blindsided. As Clark later explained, "what hurt us most was that the observers had agreed to it without consulting us. . . . Instead of reporting our word to the outside, we saw that they were allied with the state."[31]

As soon as the observers back in the Steward's Room read Oswald's statement they too exploded. Arthur Eve was particularly incredulous. Shaking his head, he demanded to know why Oswald had told the prisoners such a thing; why had he suggested that the observers and the state were in cahoots, and thereby jeopardized the safety of the observers? Eve was so overwrought he broke down into tears.[32]

Despite feeling that Oswald had made an observer trip into the yard even more dangerous than it already was, Eve and the others now insisted that they be allowed back in to make things right. Forced by the sheer passion in the room to listen to one eloquent plea after another about how important it was to honor their commitment to the men in D Yard, to do anything they could to avoid further angering a group of men holding other men's lives in their hands, the commissioner finally agreed to consult with his higher-ups about the possibility of one last visit. A few minutes after he left, however, the observers began to sneeze and their eyes watered as the faint smell of tear gas entered the room. Panicked, they ran to the windows, wondering if Oswald had just been stalling them and the dreaded attack was actually beginning.

It was another false alarm; someone had dropped a canister of gas while unloading a truck outside.

The observers sat back down, to worry and to wait. Talking among themselves, they returned again and again to the importance of getting Rockefeller to come to Attica. Tired of waiting on word from Douglass,

Badillo said that, somehow, they had to speak with the governor directly. That was their only hope. Wicker agreed, but couldn't imagine how they would pull it off. At which point John Dunne pulled a small black address book from his breast pocket, saying, "I've got his number." Within minutes, Wicker, Badillo, Dunne, and Clarence Jones managed to reach the governor at his lush Pocantico Hills estate in Westchester County.

To Wicker's surprise, Rockefeller greeted each of them warmly, and after a few pleasantries, the foursome launched into their pitch: the observers were extending the governor an official invitation to come to Attica to meet with them. Wicker took pains to make clear to Rockefeller that he was being asked to meet with them and them alone, not the prisoners. Rockefeller's visit would serve two critical purposes: first, it would show the men in the yard—prisoners and hostages alike—that the governor cared for their plight; second, it would indicate to the men in D Yard that they had the governor's personal assurance that the twenty-eight points would be honored and that they would come to no harm if they surrendered. Both of these things would immeasurably bolster the observers' efforts to end the stalemate peacefully.[33] But as Wicker and the others made this case, Rockefeller's "ebullient manner vanished to be replaced by a crisp executive style."[34]

Even Republican state senator Dunne couldn't budge Rockefeller. "I can't grant amnesty, so why come, Johnny?" the governor asked. "Come for the psychological reason; it might tip the scales," Dunne urged.[35] But this argument went nowhere. After more than an hour of conversation that ranged from the logical to the emotional to outright pleading and begging, it was finally clear to the observers that, although he never came out and said it, Rockefeller was not going to come to Attica. According to Wicker, his "tone was brisk, his argument carefully organized, as if his mind had been made up."[36]

That was, in fact, the case. The observers' call had come just as Douglass had been discussing this very issue of a visit to Attica with the governor. After summing up the observers' various arguments for the importance of the governor's presence at the prison, Douglass had then expressed his own opinion that he did not think this was a good idea. Douglass knew that there had been some talk, "confidentially," back on Friday night that the governor might go to Attica on Saturday, but he had been dissuaded then and must be again.[37] Trusting his advisor, Rockefeller had spent the rest of the phone call with Douglass discussing how to word an official statement explaining his decision not to visit, and not to grant amnesty either.[38] It was just as Douglass signed off with the governor that the call came in from the four observers.

Knowing their options were running out, the observers once again began pressuring Oswald to let them back in the yard. At 2:45 p.m. Sunday, Eve, Kunstler, Kenyatta, Ortiz, Paris, Soto, Florence, Wicker, and Jones made their way to A Gate. With them came two newsmen, Rudy Garcia of the New York *Daily News* and Dick Edwards of Jones's *Amsterdam News,* as well as their camera crews. A harried Oswald met them there and, after fifteen minutes, finally agreed to let them enter the yard. First, however, they were each handed waivers they had to sign to the effect that neither they, nor their "heirs and estate," could hold the state of New York liable "for any and all physical injuries or damages to me personally which may result from my voluntary participation in these negotiations."[39] "Suddenly, I was scared to death," Arthur Eve later remembered. "I saw what the state was willing to do. Sacrifice me, a state legislator."[40]

At 3:45 p.m., the locks on the gate to A Tunnel and No Man's Land finally disengaged, and the group met up with Richard Clark. They could feel the animosity thick in the air. Jabarr Kenyatta opened nervously with a hurried explanation that the observers had not known anything about the statement that Commissioner Oswald sent in earlier that day. "Nothing at all," Wicker chimed in. Without even looking at the men, Richard Clark said in a tight voice, "Some of the brothers would love to kill you guys."[41] But once the observers arrived at the negotiating table, it seemed to them that the masses awaiting their arrival were not all that hostile; in fact, they seemed grateful just to be hearing news from the outside. Clark opened the proceedings by stating that the observers had assured him that they had not been behind the Oswald document. He read the statement aloud to his fellow prisoners and asked if these men would agree to Oswald's most recent terms of surrender. "Hell, no!" they roared back at him from the muddy yard.[42]

The crowd's real interest now was in the reporters who had arrived. These men were here not only to capture what the men in the yard felt needed saying, but also to interview the hostages so that the public could see they were alive and well and, therefore, that state officials needed to keep the talks going.[43]

Prisoner Richard Clark joined reporter Rudy Garcia as well as Tom Wicker as they went from hostage to hostage. The first officer Wicker

The hostages, standing near their mattresses and sleeping bags provided by the prisoners, speak to the news team. CO Frank "Pappy" Wald is in the foreground. *(Courtesy of the Associated Press)*

approached, Captain Frank "Pappy" Wald, minced no words as he looked into the camera. "We've had nothing but fine treatment, this is both medically, food, and we're living as good as the rest of the people in the yard, if not a little better at times."[44] When he was asked if he wanted to say anything to Governor Rockefeller, he did. Passionately, in fact. He pleaded with the governor to do "anything you can" to try to save lives.[45]

Then hostage Frank Strollo, whose brother Tony Strollo was among the armed state troopers surrounding the prison, chimed in: "We all have been treated 100 per cent, been fed well, gave us blankets, slept on mattresses while they slept on the ground, medication was given to us when they didn't get any." Strollo went on, "He [the governor] should give them complete amnesty, that's one thing we've got to have, complete amnesty. . . . We talked it over, the 38 of us, we all agree, we'd give them complete amnesty, that's what we want Rockefeller to give them."[46]

Sergeant Edward Cunningham, a CO who had a reputation of being particularly hard on prisoners, almost yanked the microphone from Wicker's hand to express his agreement on this point and to remind anyone listening of the stakes in this standoff:

> [The governor] must give them clemency. He must give them clemency from criminal prosecution. . . . I mean this is cut and dry. That is all there is to it. . . . This is not a joke. This is not some kind of little tea party we have here. You have read in the paper all these years of the My Lai massacre. That was only 170-odd men. We are going to end up with 1500 men here, if things don't go right, at least 1500.[47]

Cunningham also said:

> I wish you would take any of the men that belong to us off the roof and any of the troopers out of here, because you get these shaky guys shooting off or getting up in a group or something, someone is going to get excited and we are all going to pay.[48]

The prisoners were heartened by Cunningham's candor and his willingness to stand up to his employers, particularly when reporters raised the issue of Rockefeller and amnesty. He stated emphatically, "If he says no, I am dead."[49] Champ was incredulous: "And that is the toughest fuckin' sarg't on the job. He is the *brute*. Put more guys in keep-lock than any 40 hacks around. And you hear what *he* say now?"[50]

CO Mike Smith, the hostage who had read over the men's initial letter to Oswald asking for reforms back that July, was also unequivocal about the need for Rockefeller to make an appearance at Attica. He told the reporters that the governor "should get his ass here now," and gesturing toward the prisoners in the yard, he stated firmly, "We're not scared of any of you people. We know it's not you, it's the people outside."[51] Casting his eyes upward, Smith went on, "Anybody with a weapon, anybody with anything of a militant manner, leave. Just get them off the roof."[52] Then the reporters turned to listen to a young white prisoner, Blaze Montgomery, whose Southern accent was as thick as Wicker's. Montgomery said solemnly, "I want everyone to know we gone stick together, we gone get what we want, or we gone die together."[53]

While the interviews with hostages continued, so did the speeches up at the negotiating table. Kenyatta kept trying to take the microphone, but was forced time and again to hand it back to others, such as the still very upset and nervous assemblyman Arthur Eve, who spoke openly with the prisoners of his feeling that Oswald had betrayed the observers and that securing amnesty was still important to them all. William Kunstler suddenly found himself the center of attention when Herb Blyden asked him pointedly if there were indeed foreign countries that would take in rebel Attica inmates who wanted to leave. Kunstler was ready for this question per his earlier call to the Black Panther Party. Yes, he said, there are four "third-world and African" countries that were in fact "prepared to provide asylum for everyone who wants to leave this country from this prison."[54] This was, of course, an exaggeration. No country was ready simply to whisk prisoners away from D Yard, but Kunstler was desperately trying to impress upon the men that the world was watching their struggle and that they were not alone. As important, Kunstler wanted the men in the yard to know that he had in fact worked hard on their behalf and, personally, was on their side. To drive that point home, he closed with a flourish, telling the crowd that Bobby Seale wanted them "to know that in every city with a black, Chicano, Puerto Rican poor community" the people were "watching Attica Prison. The Gringos talk about Remember the Alamo. Remember Attica."[55]

The longer Kunstler spoke, the warier some of the other less radical observers grew. First Eve's reemphasis on amnesty, then Kunstler's talk of foreign political asylum might have bolstered these men's reputations with the prisoners, but these observers worried that such talk could also be dangerous in that it might raise false hopes. On the other hand, it was clear that the men very much appreciated Kunstler's words. Hardly shy to express the opinion that fellow observers such as Kunstler might be going "too far," reporter Tom Wicker this time did not think that either Eve's or Kunstler's speeches had given the prisoners "any cause to believe that if they just hang on a bit longer, they were going to get amnesty and go home free."[56]

With little more left to discuss, at 6:00 Sunday night the observers made their way back to the administration building. This time the goodbyes seemed foreboding and final. No one was certain how this crisis would end, but all suspected that it wouldn't go smoothly. As the observers took their final walk across the now fetid, rutted, and filthy D Yard, the prisoners expressed a deep gratitude for what the observers had tried to do for them. Big Black Smith, who had spent the preceding four days in a state of steely and wary alert, felt an unexpected and powerful surge of warmth toward the team he was escorting out of the yard. He reached out to Tom Wicker and gripped his hand tightly. Feeling overwhelmed, Wicker managed, "Good luck. Good luck, Brother."[57]

Since he was the one to have just interviewed the hostages, Wicker felt that it was his duty to go out into Attica's parking lot to update the anxious

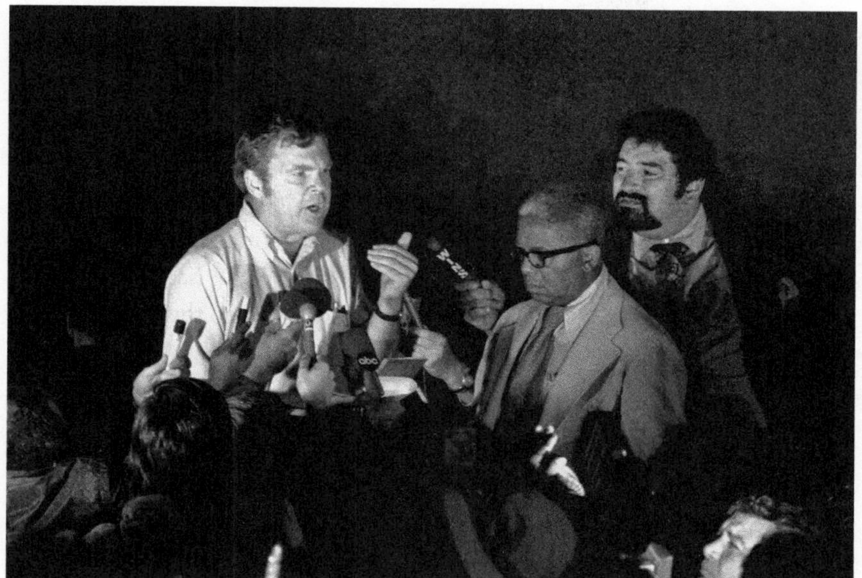

Wicker addresses the crowd. *(Courtesy of* The New York Times*)*

crowd about their relatives and townspeople. His reception there immediately confirmed his worry that Big Black Smith and the other men in D Yard would need all the luck they could get. As Wicker climbed on top of a car so that he could be seen by the crowd, a cold drizzle was again falling. Trying to read the ever-dampening notebook in his hand, he began to summarize his interviews. All the hostages, he said, "requested strongly that as much consideration as possible be given to granting full amnesty to the prisoners."[58] He added that they had all "requested strongly that Gov. Rockefeller come here physically" and finally that "they urged the prison authorities here at Attica and Commissioner Oswald not to allow any troops to [make a] show of force on the roof or anywhere inside."[59] He was clear that everyone—the observers, the hostages, and the prisoners—now feared a massacre should the governor not step in.

His audience erupted. "What about my son?" Steven Smith, hostage Mike Smith's father, yelled up at Wicker with tears on his face and rain soaking his body.[60] "We have to go in and bring those people out!" he continued in anguish.[61] "Wet nursing those convicts won't do it!"[62] Galvanized by Smith's impassioned outburst, other townspeople surged toward Wicker hurling epithets and demanding that the state step in. "I'd like to show them a little brutality," screamed one woman; another cried out, "Those troopers should have gone in there for them!"[63] Hostage Frank

Strollo's brother Tony, one of the hundreds of state troopers standing by and also listening to Wicker, couldn't have agreed more. He was certain that this observer was spinning tales about what the hostages really thought, and he was more eager than ever to end this riot once and for all by going in. Others, like hostage John Stockholm's wife, Mary, were more scared than angry once they heard Wicker speak. They were alarmed by Wicker's dire message about possible bloodshed should someone not step in. "Until that point," Mary Stockholm remembered, "I had believed this would end peacefully."[64] As the crowd grew moblike and the noise became deafening, Mary fainted. Wicker looked out at the desperation and chaos feeling more disheartened and helpless than he could ever remember.[65]

Wicker returned to the administration building, where he and the other observers debriefed Oswald about their most recent visit to D Yard. It soon became clear that Oswald had no remaining faith that he could still make a difference in how this standoff ended. They even played Oswald a taped message from Richard X Clark, which made clear the prisoners' view that "anything that results will be the result of the commissioner moving—not us."[66] Oswald just stared at the wall for a moment, then got up, told the observers that no one would be going back into D Yard, and on his way out said forlornly, "I've given everything."[67] From there, the commissioner went back to his office. At 7:20 p.m., he instructed that the phone in the Steward's Room be cut off immediately. He worried that some of the observers had somehow been sending "code messages that the rebels would pick up on their transistor radios."[68] It was only a matter of time, Oswald knew, before his superiors were going to order this prison protest ended once and for all.

# 18

# Deciding Disaster

By Sunday night, the fourth day of the Attica uprising, troopers filled the swath of lawn between the prison's gate and the administration building, as well as the asphalt that ringed the prison walls. There were so many men that it was hard for them to move without running into one another. And they were fed up.[1] As one trooper later bluntly explained, "Everyone was getting frustrated by the length of time it was taking to resolve the riot. We just wanted to get it over with and get on with our lives."[2] Technical Sergeant F. D. Smith, a state trooper who'd been filming the goings-on in D Yard from the catwalks since the afternoon of the first day of the uprising, felt that "an attitude of disgust was apparent among troopers and guards on Sunday, the 12th. . . . A number of our people were heard to be wishing for 'something to happen even if it's the wrong thing.' "[3] The COs felt the same way. They had come from counties near and far to retake the prison and they were tired of the waiting.

It was obvious to anyone who was at Attica that members of law enforcement were so riled up that it would be difficult, if not impossible, for them to do their job dispassionately should they be sent in to retake the prison. Yet, by deciding that negotiations were now over, Oswald ensured that these were exactly the men who would be sent in to end the rebellion. As if feeling that he needed to make it clear that this was out of his hands, and that the governor himself had, in fact, made the decision to stop all discussions with the prisoners, Oswald began distributing copies of the statement that Rockefeller had drafted earlier in the day with Douglass:

> From the beginning of the tragic situation, involving riots and hostages at the Attica Correctional Facility which imperils the lives of many persons, including 38 innocent citizens and dedicated law enforcement officers, I have been in constant, direct contact with Correction Commissioner Russell Oswald and my representatives on the scene.
>
> Every effort has been made by the state to resolve the situation and to establish order, hopefully by peaceable means. I have carefully considered the request conveyed to me by the committee of citizen observers for my physical presence at Attica, as well as the demands of the inmates that I meet with them in the prison yard.
>
> I am deeply grateful to members of the committee for the long and courageous efforts to achieve a peaceful settlement. The key issue at stake, however, is still the demand for total amnesty for any criminal acts which may have occurred.
>
> I do not have the constitutional authority, because to do so would undermine the very essence of our free society—the fair and impartial application of the law.
>
> In view of the fact that the key issue is total amnesty—in spite of the best efforts of the committee and in spite of Commissioner Oswald's major commitments to the inmates—I do not feel that my physical presence can contribute to a peaceful settlement.
>
> Commissioner Oswald has offered 28 major proposals recommended by the inmates and the committee of citizen observers. I fully support the Commissioner's proposals and concur with the considered opinion of the Commissioner that the inmates must now be offered a direct opportunity to respond to his offers.
>
> I join personally with the Commissioner in an urgent appeal to the inmates that they now:
>
> 1. Release the hostages without harm
> 2. Cooperate in the peaceful restoration of order
> 3. Accept the Commissioner's good-faith commitment to the 28 major proposals offered to the inmates[4]

Rockefeller's statement only reiterated what Oswald had been saying to the observers all along. Many of these men had hoped that Rockefeller's mind would be changed by the newsmen's interviews with the hostages, since they had talked about how important it was for the governor to come. The prisoners had also placed great faith in these interviews—everyone could now see for themselves that the hostages were safe. They too had hoped desperately that the governor would appear, since, as one of them explained, such a visit would have given the men "a way for us to get out with some dignity and real assurance with muscle behind it that we'd not be physically hurt."[5] In lieu of amnesty, said another, the governor's visit "could have insured that only the individuals responsible with a particular act, you know, would be prosecuted."[6]

But State Senator Dunne had been right when he predicted that Rockefeller would decide it was too politically costly to make the trip to Attica. Several observers, including Dunne, suspected that the governor had been persuaded by Robert Douglass not to come, and that Douglass was really the one who was deciding that the Attica rebellion must be ended.[7] One thing was certain: by refusing to visit the prison, the governor had pleased the men whose approval he most wanted: the leaders of his own political party. "After issuing the statement," said a confidential report written by the governor's closest aides, "Rockefeller spoke with the President [Nixon], who expressed strong support for the Governor's position."[8]

Some of the observers clearly hadn't given up hope that Oswald might be able at least to sway the governor on the amnesty issue. For quite some time Sunday evening, back in the Steward's Room, a number of them had made extremely emotional pleas to the commissioner to do something, anything, to forestall an assuredly disastrous attack. And, unbeknownst to the observers, Oswald did communicate these pleas to Governor Rockefeller later that night. As he explained it to the governor, "Kunstler argued vigorously for amnesty, drawing on the British response to the seizure of hostages by Arab guerrillas. . . . Kunstler also suggested that one hostage could be released every week and talks extended over a longer period. Wicker made an impassioned plea quoting from the Bible."[9] But no amount of begging or cajoling or reasoning on the part of the observers or the commissioner could budge the governor.

And so the final decision to end the negotiations at Attica was indeed the governor's. By 10:35 p.m., the exhausted, bitter, and deeply discouraged men on the observers committee had heard nothing new from Oswald. They knew they had done everything they could to change the governor's mind and now had only to decide whether to leave or stay in the prison once an assault began. Most chose to leave, but nine decided to stay all night in case something more positive developed or, as they believed more likely, to be witnesses to the attack.

An assault was more imminent than even they understood. At 11:00 p.m. General Buzz O'Hara called Rockefeller and asked his permission to coordinate with others for an assault on the prison the next morning. "You have it," replied Rockefeller.[10] With the governor's go-ahead, Buzz O'Hara sat down with Oswald, Douglass, Rockefeller lawyer Howard Shapiro, Norman Hurd, State Senator John Dunne, and State Assemblymen Clark Wemple and James Emery to inform them of what would now happen. For all of the flak that Kunstler took for being brought in as an impartial observer but then agreeing to represent the prisoners in D Yard, this meeting made clear that at least three other observers were also representing an interest—in their case, that of the state.

The actual dirty work of the retaking would fall "to the two local representatives of police and correction" at that meeting: Major John Monahan and Superintendent Mancusi.[11] That, in itself, was odd. Both of these men had far less expertise than many others in both the Department of Correctional Services and the New York State Police—even others in this very meeting. And, notably, another more obvious person to be in charge, the head of the NYSP, William Kirwan, was conspicuously absent not only from this meeting but from Attica itself. Superintendent Kirwan had been on vacation when Attica exploded, but for reasons unclear, he had been allowed to continue to enjoy Lake George as one of his state's biggest crises unfolded. That such a potentially disastrous assault on Attica would be overseen by Mancusi, and undertaken by Major Monahan, one of his lowest-ranking officers in the NYSP, strongly implied that Rockefeller had his own reservations about how this retaking might unfold.[12] Distancing his top-ranked NYSP and DOCS officials from the actual assault also meant being able to distance the governor's office from anything that might go wrong.

At least one of the men at this strategy meeting late Sunday night felt deeply uncomfortable at the way the plans to retake the prison were shaping up. John Dunne was well aware that the prisoners were counting on him, and yet, now, he was sitting there again discussing how their rebellion would be ended with force. Thanks in no small part to Dunne's influence, every previous plan to storm the prison had been stalled, including the most recent one that morning.[13] But it was now a certainty that a forcible retaking of the prison would commence the very next morning. In short, Rockefeller was done. In his opinion, Attica-like rebellions would likely "become epidemic in prisons throughout the state and the nation" in the future and he wanted his retaking of Attica to send a strong message of deterrence.[14] As an investigative body later put it, "The decision to retake the prison was . . . a decisive reassertion of the state of its sovereignty and power."[15]

And, notwithstanding what many would later claim, it was crystal clear to all at this late-night meeting—Dunne, as well as those charged with carrying out the retaking—that this assault would come at a staggeringly high price. Not only would there likely be many prisoner fatalities, but as Assemblyman Clark Wemple put it, "there was absolutely no doubt in anyone's mind that if we went in there, the guards would be killed."[16] General O'Hara concurred: "It was the general consensus of opinion by all the officials present that . . . if the prison was retaken by force the hostages would be killed."[17]

A bloody outcome was virtually guaranteed by the NYSP's choice of weaponry.[18] Two six-man teams of troopers would position themselves on the rooftops of A and C Blocks with rifles at the ready to provide cover for the men launching the assault below. The men leading the assault on D Yard would themselves be armed with .270 caliber rifles, which utilized unjacketed bullets, a kind of ammunition that causes such enormous damage to human flesh that it was banned by the Geneva Conventions.[19] Many of the other troopers and COs preparing to go in were also carrying other weapons that would have a particularly brutal effect, such as shotguns filled with deadly buckshot pellets that sprayed out in a wide arc. As all state officials knew, although there were some gas guns in the yard that could fire tear gas, no prisoner in the yard was carrying a firearm.[20]

Although the men in D Yard preparing for bed late Sunday night had no idea that the NYSP had been given the green light to storm the prison the next morning, they were by no means optimistic that a peaceful end to this standoff was imminent. It was clear to them that Oswald had no intention of removing Vincent Mancusi from his position at Attica, nor was Rockefeller budging on offering full amnesty in exchange for their surrender. And yet, it still wasn't easy to imagine surrendering. Earlier that day, Herb Blyden had gotten up before the men in D Yard and had made the implications of this crystal clear. Even after being transferred to Attica, he reminded everyone, he still faced "seventy-seven counts" for having rebelled at the Tombs the year before.[21] "All of this came about," he made clear, "after the Mayor and staff promised us, promised us no reprisals on the T.V. screen." Before he sat down Blyden said sadly to those looking up at him, "Man, I am not trying to scare you," but no matter what they say and promise here at Attica, "you're gonna still die."[22]

Roger Champen felt ill as Blyden's words rang in his ears. Then, later on that night when a prison chaplain suddenly showed up and asked that he be allowed to give the men huddled over in the hostage circle Last Rites, Champ thought he was going to be sick.[23] "I was afraid," he said. "I didn't want to die and I didn't feel it would serve a purpose to die for what was going on. Nothing concrete has happened then in terms of seeing some changes."[24] As he tried to bed down that night, Champ hoped against hope that Blyden was wrong about what would happen. Champ felt some peace, though, knowing that "if there are any lives lost in here, and if a massacre takes place . . . in the final analysis the world will know that the animals were not in here, but outside running the system and the government."[25]

# PART IV

# Retribution and Reprisals Unimagined

# TONY STROLLO

*Tony Strollo considered himself a staunch patriot as well as a devout Catholic who attended mass every Sunday, avoided meat on Fridays, and made the sign of the cross whenever he drove past a church. Tony's father had labored day in and day out at a Chevy plant in Buffalo and he, like so many other autoworkers of his generation, felt pretty certain that America's working stiffs could only trust the party of FDR. But Tony distrusted liberals. And while many kids of the 1960s found themselves leaning to the political left of their parents, Tony spent that decade growing considerably more conservative than his.*

*When Tony graduated from high school in 1962, he was eager to enlist in the Army. By 1966, Tony was married and had started a family. To support his kids, he decided to try his hand at being a prison guard—one of the few jobs available to young men seeking work in the rural areas of the state. Tony worked for a while at Sing Sing Correctional Facility and eventually landed a transfer to Attica, which allowed him to work closer to home as well as to be in the same prison where his brother Frank worked. Tony, though, did not want to collect his paycheck from a penal institution forever. His dream had always been to become a police officer, and after a few short months Tony got a call from the New York State Police.*

*In 1971 Tony was loving every minute of his job as a state trooper. Assigned to the Genesco barracks in Livingston County, about twenty-five miles from home, he patrolled the rural areas of the county, driving the highways and byways of upstate New York looking for speeders and drunk drivers. At night he attended classes at Erie County Community College in Williamsville.*

*On September 9, 1971, Tony's brother Frank had been on duty at Attica when it exploded in rebellion. Now, Frank sat in the hostage circle and Tony paced outside the prison's walls feeling utterly helpless. He was a member of law enforcement, yet he could do nothing to rescue his brother. So he, along with hundreds of other state troopers, did the only thing they could do, keep pressuring their superiors to be allowed to retake the facility from the rioters. After five days of waiting, and as Tony and the rest of his troop shivered outside Attica in the cold drizzly dawn, sleep-deprived and on edge, they finally got some good news. They were going in.*

*Tony was secretly troubled, though. He knew that troopers had a lot more experience stopping speeders than storming a prison. Tony had been assigned his own .38 sidearm, and about three times a year, he and his fellow "Staties" would go to the shooting range to practice just in case they ever needed to use their weapons with an unruly citizen. But they were also being handed .270 rifles. Tony had absolutely no training in the use of this weapon and he knew that was true of most of the other officers.*[1]

*In Tony's opinion it was strange that the New York State Police even had such weapons. They had ordered about one hundred of them a decade ago when it was time to update the arsenal. Most officers, however, were uncomfortable using a .270. Each gun had a scope on it and the slightest jostling could throw it off-kilter. What's more, the ammunition that came with these Model 70 Winchester bolt-action rifles consisted of silver-tipped bullets, which were, according to another trooper, "particularly explosive [and capable of] terrible damage to human tissue."*[2]

*But Tony just tried to shake off his misgivings. After all, the prisoners had started this—their possible injury was certainly nothing to lose sleep over. Still, he was finding it hard to get the words of one of his commanding officers out of his head. He had said to Tony gravely, "There is no chance that we can get to your brother in time."*[3] *Tony prayed he was wrong.*

# 19

# Chomping at the Bit

At 6:30 a.m. on Monday, the 13th of September, the fifth and what would be the final day of the Attica uprising, Commissioner Russell Oswald was locked away with Rockefeller attorney Howard Shapiro and Gerald Houlihan, the public relations director for the Department of Corrections, busily crafting the final statement they shortly would give to the prisoners. Oswald was feeling raw and ragged, having just returned to the prison after less than two hours of rest the night before.[1] He was dreading the task of presenting this particular message to the men in the yard. It seemed "paradoxical" to Oswald that he had "spent a lifetime in furthering, meeting the needs, human rights concerns, of disadvantaged people" and now had to "face up to this kind of decision against people I was trying to help."[2] He made peace with this by concluding that he couldn't have done any more than he already had. The real problem, he had decided, was the "some 3,000 people from the New York City system" who had been transferred to upstate prisons like Attica in the wake of the previous summer's jail rebellions.[3] The "hard core group . . . led in large measure by Maoists" that had sparked those riots, he reasoned, had been "constantly trying to radicalize" prisoners in the rest of the state and now here he was.[4] Maybe there was no way he could have ended the standoff at Attica peacefully. And anyway, the governor had indicated that "his decision was firm." Oswald decided he now had no choice but to follow orders.

So now there he sat, hunched over a typewriter next to Shapiro and Houlihan, getting the wording of the statement he would take to the prisoners at the A Gate just right. That there would even be a final communiqué to men in D Yard was in no small part thanks, again, to John Dunne.

As his fellow observer Tom Wicker remembered gratefully, once Dunne learned on Sunday night that the troopers were going in the next morning, he "argued for and obtained a pledge that at 7 a.m., before the resort to violence . . . one last appeal would be made to the inmates for a settlement."[5]

But the final missive that Oswald was drafting would not at all convey what Dunne had hoped it would—what the true cost of not surrendering immediately now would be. According to documents internal to the Rockefeller administration, Oswald had been told to "submit his final offer—not phrased as an ultimatum—to the inmates about 7:00 Monday morning, giving them one hour to respond . . . if the response was negative or if no answer was received within an hour, orders would be given to retake the facility."[6] The crucial caveat here, of course, was that the "final offer" would not be "phrased as an ultimatum." Rockefeller did not want to let the prisoners know that if they didn't comply, an assault would commence immediately.[7]

But the message was precisely that. As another internal memo makes clear, Deputy Superintendent Leon Vincent had already advised his correctional personnel via their supervisors, at approximately 6:00 on Sunday—the night before the assault—that a "move to regain control of the institution" was going to take place "during the morning hours of Monday September 13, 1971."[8] This was of course before any prisoners had been given any final opportunity to surrender. The New York State Police, the Monroe County Sheriff's Office, and Attica's correction officers and correction officials from as far away as the Great Meadow Correctional Facility in Comstock had also been informed Sunday night that the retaking would definitely happen Monday morning.[9]

As Oswald worked on the text of this appeal, Major John Monahan from Batavia Troop A of the New York State Police and Attica superintendent Vincent Mancusi held a formal briefing in the Attica head clerk's office to iron out the final details of a plan to commence at 9:00 a.m. Meanwhile, Captain Hank Williams, also of Batavia's Troop A, readied his troops; Lieutenant Colonel George Infante of the Bureau of Criminal Investigation (BCI) waited in the wings to make sure the assault went as planned; and Governor Rockefeller's right-hand man, Robert Douglass, reviewed the "surrender message" that was to be read to prisoners once the assault began.[10] Simultaneously, Major General John C. Baker, the chief of staff to Governor Rockefeller, began briefing the many National Guardsmen who had been summoned over the last few days to let them know that, contrary to standard protocol, Governor Rockefeller had decided that the New York State Police would be leading the assault, and the National Guard would only go into the prison later to administer any needed medical assistance.

This break in protocol was both surprising and problematic. Whereas the National Guard had a clear plan already in place for bringing civil disturbances in confined areas under control, known as Operation Plan Skyhawk, the New York State Police had virtually no formal training for this sort of action.[11] The hundreds of troopers gathered at Attica had never conducted any drills or mock assaults. They had no practice communicating with each other through gas masks, nor familiarity with handling the weapons. As one trooper by the name of Gerard Smith put it, troopers "weren't trained for this and . . . the position [they got put into] was a political football."[12]

That the Attica rebellion was so fraught politically might well be why Rockefeller did not ask his National Guard to end it. A dark cloud still hovered over the Ohio National Guard after its men had shot more than sixty-seven rounds of ammunition into an unarmed crowd of student protesters at Kent State University, killing four, little more than a year before, in May of 1970.[13] Neither Rockefeller nor the higher-ups in the Nixon administration (including John Mitchell, the attorney general) wanted to give America's liberal and left elements any more reason to focus attention on Attica than they already had.[14]

To National Guardsman Dan Callahan, however, the governor's decision to let the police troopers retake the prison was just stupid. Before his unit was called to Attica it had spent considerable time back at the armory discussing what weapons, if any, should be used in a retaking of this prison. Since there was no reason to believe the prisoners had firearms, maybe no guns were needed, but if firearms would be used, Callahan felt strongly that these must be chosen with great care. No weapon loaded with buckshot should be used, for example, because its wide scatter would cause many casualties.[15] Yet as Callahan could now see, not only were the troopers about to enter Attica heavily armed with buckshot-loaded shotguns, but they clearly were also angry as well as "haggard" and "exhausted."[16] For the life of him, Callahan could not understand why the governor would send such an unwieldy and clearly disintegrating group into an operation as delicate as a hostage rescue. "There was a way to do this," he later reflected, but unleashing hundreds of overwrought, fatigued, and excessively armed men was not it.[17]

How, exactly, the State Police would retake Attica was formalized in a handwritten agreement signed by Major John Monahan and Attica superintendent Vincent Mancusi in their early morning meeting.[18] That plan was then conveyed both verbally and in writing to Deputy Superintendent Leon Vincent and Assistant Deputy Superintendent Karl Pfeil of Attica, as well as to Captain Henry Williams of the State Police.[19]

First, all electricity to the prison would be shut off. Then, a helicopter, dubbed "Jackpot 1" and provided by the National Guard, would fly over the prison yard to drop CS tear gas, temporarily disabling the rebel prisoners gathered outside in D Yard. Another chopper carrying tear gas canisters would follow that one in case it should malfunction. Almost immediately thereafter two six-man teams of troopers, who, armed with .270 rifles and tear gas projectiles, had taken positions on the rooftops of A and C Blocks, would clear the catwalks of anyone in the way. Nearly two hundred troopers "armed with revolvers and shotguns" simultaneously would enter A and C Tunnels in small teams and converge on Times Square.[20] Once those troopers made it to Times Square, they would fan out to secure B and D Blocks, while a team of twenty-five men with guns and ladders would attempt to rescue the hostages in the circle.[21] For reasons not made clear, the entire operation would also be filmed. Since the day the Attica rebellion began, there had been several state troopers assigned to chronicle events at the prison. Those men would continue to operate both a television camera and a video recorder during the retaking.

As many details as this plan had, there were many crucially important ones missing. There was, for starters, no plan for telling troopers when to commence shooting nor a mechanism by which they would be informed when to stop. Indeed, "the decision on whether or not to fire thus passed directly to the riflemen themselves," which left much of the assault's fate in individuals' hands.[22] Since there was no clear way for an individual trooper to communicate with another, this lack of planning was potentially dangerous for all concerned. The troopers had not been equipped with radios, and specific troopers weren't charged with relaying commands from the higher-ups. Worse, each trooper sent into the prison was to wear a heavy gas mask, which would make it almost impossible for him to see through the gas fog. The noise of shooting was likely to make it impossible to communicate. Hand signals could have been agreed upon to deal with the other communication barriers, but this wasn't done either. Perhaps most important, the plan had no provision for giving either a surrender message or post-assault instructions to the prisoners in English or

Spanish, and no procedure was outlined for what to do with the prisoners once the state had regained control of the facility.

Not only did the state's retaking plan leave a great deal to chance, but troopers later claimed to have heard instructions very different from those that their commanding officers had been charged with giving them. Trooper Gerard Smith later testified that his captain had told his team that "firing was supposed to take place simultaneously when the helicopter came over to drop the gas" and that "everybody on the top catwalk was supposed to be eliminated."[23] Others later denied they had been given this charge.

While various battalions of troopers were being briefed, Attica's deputy superintendent, Leon Vincent, explained the attack plan to approximately 312 correction officers just as eager as the NYSP troopers to enter the prison. Although Vincent later insisted that he had made it clear to them that only state troopers, and no COs, were to go in, there is no corroboration of this claim.[24] To the contrary, according to later testimony by Superintendent Mancusi, Leon Vincent had actually "issued an order that correctional officers could participate in the armed retaking."[25] Even if Vincent had verbally banned these men from participating, they likely would not have been deterred. Some had traveled a great distance to lend their assistance. One CO's wife later described her husband as walking out the door "like John Wayne," armed with the personal gun he kept under his bed, as soon as he heard the news that the retaking was imminent. She desperately called out to him, "Don't do something you will regret," but he just "kept on going."[26]

A crowd of sheriffs and sheriff's deputies from a total of eight New York counties had also converged on Attica, and, like the COs, they had spent the last four days pacing restlessly outside the prison hoping to assist in the retaking. On the morning of the 13th, they had already donned "grey coveralls, and an assortment of helmets, riot batons, shotguns, and other weapons" in anticipation of being able to enter the facility.[27] Park police from Genesee and Schuyler counties were also there. As in the case of the COs, it is unclear whether they were told they could participate in the retaking or not. But to men of rank from numerous sheriff's offices, such as Sergeant Frank Hall from Monroe County, there seemed to be little question that they too would act.[28] They were armed and ready.

It was remarkable just how many weapons had been distributed to members of law enforcement trampling the grass around the prison. The way in which this process was conducted, particularly by the NYSP, was extraordinary as well. As early as the first day of the rebellion, .270 rifles were passed out to officers in every troop and—quite deliberately, it would later become clear—there was virtually "no effort made by anyone . . . to make a record by serial number or trooper" of who received which rifles.[29] Although four full days had passed during which those in charge could have ensured that all protocols regarding the distribution of weapons were followed, none of the weapons now being readied for the retaking had been formally recorded. And thus, the men who were about to go into Attica were accountable to no one.

# 20

# Standing Firm

On the morning of Monday, September 13, Governor Nelson Rockefeller and many of his aides were in Manhattan, "sitting down to scrambled eggs, bacon, toast and coffee" in his Fifth Avenue apartment, awaiting news of Attica's imminent retaking.[1] The troopers outside Attica were busily loading rounds into their guns, and the prisoners in D Yard were beginning to awaken in tents soaked from the previous night's cold rain.

Although the men in the yard had no idea that they were about to be attacked, things for them were already very grim. They had been in the confines of D Yard for five days now and it had become a mud slick with neither a working sewage system nor a source of clean drinking water. The night before, prison officials had cut off their water supply. As desperate as conditions had become, however, the prisoners and hostages clung however irrationally to the hope that Tom Wicker's interviews with the hostages the previous evening would bolster productive negotiations that day. As one man explained, they still hoped that outside pressure would convince Rockefeller to show up, and still "really believed we could get amnesty."[2]

To find out exactly when the negotiations would resume, Richard Clark went straight to A Gate when he awoke Monday morning. No one was there. Then, around 8:00 a.m., sentries from A Tunnel advised Clark that Oswald had sent word that he wanted to talk with him. By 8:25, Oswald, Dunbar, and General O'Hara were standing across the gate from Clark, ready to deliver the final version of the statement they'd drafted. The commissioner told Clark that he needed to persuade the men in the yard to let the hostages go, and he instructed him to make sure that they all heard this new missive. As he handed the message over to Clark, Oswald said to him beseechingly, "Mr. Clark, I earnestly implore you to give the contents of this memorandum your most careful consideration . . . *I want to continue negotiations with you.*"[3]

Clark looked carefully at the letter but was mystified by Oswald's solemn demeanor. He also was perplexed as to why Oswald was making such a big deal about this new statement, since, from what he could tell, it said the same thing as the note that had been given to him on Sunday that the men had already voted down. Still, he agreed to convey the message to the men in the yard, and he asked for thirty minutes to get their reaction and report back. Oswald said fifteen minutes. They compromised at twenty.

When Clark arrived back in D Yard he grabbed the loudspeaker and read out the latest message from Oswald:

> For four days I have been using every resource available to me to settle peacefully the tragic situation here at Attica. We have met with you; have granted your requests for food, clothing, bedding and water; for medical aid; for a Federal Court Order against administrative reprisals. We have worked with the special Citizen Committee which you requested. We have acceded to 28 major demands which you have made and which the Citizen Committee had recommended. In spite of these efforts, you continue to hold hostages. I am anxious to achieve a peaceful resolution of the situation which now prevails there. I urgently request that you seriously consider my earlier appeal that:[4]
>
> 1. All hostages be released immediately unharmed; and
> 2. You join with me in restoring order to the facility.
>
> I must have your reply to this urgent appeal within the hour. I hope and pray your answer will be affirmative.[5]

The yard erupted. Wasn't this exactly what Oswald had said the day before? What was different? Hadn't he paid any attention to the reporters' interviews with the hostages? Didn't he understand that even the hostages wanted him to grant amnesty so that there could be a peaceful end to this situation? As the minutes ticked away Clark reminded the group that they had to vote on whether to agree to Oswald's appeal or to reject it. To the question of whether they agreed to release the hostages and surrender now, the silence in the yard was deafening. Only one voice could be heard supporting this position. "Why not take it?" one man shouted, "You got

28 out of 30 demands . . . you can't get no better than that."[6] But in the wake of CO William Quinn's death, all understood that amnesty was a must. Any or all of them could be charged with felony murder and those who had acted as leaders and spokesmen would be particularly vulnerable.[7] As one man put it, he "just couldn't agree, you know, to throw the guys that . . . acted as spokesmen . . . to the wolves."[8]

Clark restated the question, asking whether the men were rejecting Oswald's request for surrender. The roar of approval that echoed through the yard was overwhelming. As hostage Frank Wald marveled, "From where I sat, it sounded almost as if everybody agreed to not accept it."[9]

However, the men in D Yard had no inkling that Oswald's request was in fact a demand. As prisoner Dalou Gonzalez said later, the vote might have looked very different "if they had said, either release the hostages or we're coming in shooting."[10] As important, especially after having brought newsmen in to interview hostages the night before, the men still could not believe that amnesty was not on the table. According to Gonzalez, "A lot of prisoners wanted to hear it from Rockefeller. . . . If he had said no amnesty and had given us an ultimatum, it would have made a lot of prisoners reconsider their position."[11]

Back in the Steward's Room, DOCS deputy commissioner Walter Dunbar handed out to the observers a copy of the statement that had just been delivered to Richard Clark.[12] He tersely advised them that the building was being cleared for the retaking. If they planned on staying, they would not be allowed to leave the room until it was over. Arthur Eve couldn't believe it had come to this. Eve declared that if Rockefeller wouldn't even come to the aid of the "38 men who are on his staff [referring to the hostages] . . . he's not fit to be the governor of this state."[13] As Dunbar backed out the door, eager to extricate himself from the bitter remarks and incredulous stares of the observers, one question did stop him momentarily: Would gas masks be available to them if they stayed? No, Dunbar replied, they would not.[14] A correction officer accompanying Dunbar added, with a cold stare, "The truck bringing your gas masks got lost."[15]

Senator Dunne already knew that he was going to stay. Now that he had become personally involved in the retaking—consulting with Attica's officials as well as with the governor's aides at the prison, he was no longer really a member of the observers committee. He, unlike the majority of the observers, had accepted the view that the prison had to be retaken by force, though he also felt that it was Rockefeller's refusal to come to Attica (a "most crucial mistake") that had made a forcible retaking the only option. His only hope now was that even this would end all right.[16] After all, as he had pointed out on more than one occasion in the last few days, the jail riot in Queens the year before had been forcibly ended and no one died.[17]

The other observers were not at all persuaded by Dunne's optimism, and most made no secret of the fact that they were terrified at the prospect of being in the prison when the hundreds of armed state troopers and correction officers they saw outside the window were unleashed. A vital difference between this and every other prison retaking, they reminded him, was that no firearms had been utilized in the others. From the moment that the door closed behind Dunbar, the observers struggled between their desire to flee and their feeling of responsibility to witness the retaking for the prisoners' sake. No one doubted that it would be violent, but some of them, including reporter Jim Ingram of the *Michigan Chronicle*, Congressman Herman Badillo, and D.C. public interest lawyer Julian Tepper, hoped that their presence in the prison might exert a tempering influence, although they too might be in danger. Too often they had experienced the hateful glares of the correction officers who periodically looked in on the group, and all had clearly heard the whispered threat of "we gonna get you motherfuckers" from one of these men.[18] As Ingram noted wryly, "They got guns and tension, we just got tension."[19] Still, the majority decided to stick it out.

Meanwhile, the sentries in A Tunnel sent word that Richard Clark wanted to see Oswald again. After making sure that the "State Troopers assigned to the assault were now in position and ready," Oswald, Dunbar, and General O'Hara headed back to the DMZ.[20] To their astonishment, however, Clark did not offer a response to their recent call to surrender. Instead he told them that "the inmates' committee did not understand certain aspects of the offer, particularly in reference to the 28 proposals" and, therefore, they wanted to meet again with the observers committee. Clark was doing his best to buy time, time to persuade Rockefeller of the importance of coming to the prison, time to persuade officials of how crucial amnesty was to any surrender. "Absolutely not!" Oswald exclaimed and Clark's heart sank. It began to dawn on him that this might, in fact, be the end of the line with the commissioner. All right, he said to Oswald, in that case, could he just have some more time to further discuss Oswald's request with the men in the yard? Disgusted, Oswald spat that he could have twenty minutes and, turning on his heel, he left Dunbar and a state trooper at the gate with a radio. They were instructed to alert him the moment that Clark returned with his final answer.[21]

Oswald made his way to Superintendent Mancusi's office to report back to Douglass and the rest of the governor's men awaiting word. Sheepishly, he had to admit that he had given the men a bit more time. Silence fell on the room as the clock ticked, and the deadline passed. After some discussion, the men assembled decided to move in at 10:00 a.m.[22] Robert Douglass got up to call Rockefeller. After reporting that the second deadline given the prisoners had just come and gone, Douglass handed the receiver to Oswald and then Hurd. When all three men had finished speaking to the governor, it was clear that he was done with any more discussions. Rockefeller's only parting instruction to the men was, "Keep me informed."[23]

Although Richard Clark thought it was possible that Oswald was bluffing, deep down he was scared. It was, he acknowledged, a bad sign that no observers had come that morning since the state likely would keep them out if an attack was imminent. Still, he didn't know and wasn't sure whether he should be sounding an alarm in D Yard or preparing the men for more talks. Uncertain of what to do, Clark and his compatriots decided that they somehow had to impress upon Oswald that if by any chance he was planning a forcible retaking that day, he should reconsider.

The centerpiece of their plan depended upon one critical thing: that state officials did indeed care what happened to the hostages. In the predawn hours of that morning there had already been some discussion of how to use more effectively the state's desire to protect its own employees. According to Big Black Smith, there had been "no escalation of anger toward hostages," but around 4:00 a.m. some of the prisoners had begun to wonder if it was now time to remind state officials that they did, in fact, have the ultimate power over their hostages so that these same officials wouldn't order an attack.[24]

As the clock ticked, hearing nothing that indicated the observers were on their way, the men in D Yard decided that they would randomly select a group of eight hostages to take up onto the catwalks. They would surround each hostage with at least three prisoners carrying homemade knives and spears to suggest to the state that if it chose to come into Attica with force rather than to negotiate, it was risking the lives of its own men. As Roger Champen explained, "We felt that by having hostages we would also have the ability to more or less force them to keep their word."[25] Killing these men "definitely was not" their intention. He went on, "We wouldn't even consider harming the hostages," because they "were our only means of negotiation."[26]

However, the very act of moving the hostages intensified anxiety in the yard. Within minutes prisoners were arming themselves with whatever they could find—pieces of lumber, baseball bats, anything. Others just began "lots of praying" and "looking for cover."[27]

Seeing prisoners suddenly making their way over to the hostage circle greatly alarmed those within it as well. "They started to tie our hands and feet, put blindfolds back on our eyes," Pappy Wald recalled, and then without explanation some of the hostages were walked over to the catwalks.[28] While he was worried about why he was being taken away, Wald was also well aware that his captors had, so far, been "protecting us" and that they had "done an excellent job of doing this" so he was more concerned about what was happening outside the prison walls to cause them to be moved.[29] Some of the prisoners did try to explain what their plan was. Hostage Mike Smith was slightly relieved to learn that the prisoners were simply "trying to get the time extended," but he also concluded by the panicked looks of some of the men surrounding him that they would indeed kill him if they thought it would save them, or if they were given the go-ahead to do so.[30] Civilian hostage Ron Kozlowski hoped it was true that the prisoners intended to use them "as insurance to deter anyone from trying to retake the prison."[31] Still he was worried, and didn't quite know what to think—whether he was being soothed or groomed for death—when his captor cut his wrist binding, combed his hair, and gave him a Tums as well as a cigarette while they waited for the state to register their presence on the catwalk.[32] As hostage Curly Watkins was being marched to the catwalk, he too was terrified but hoped for the best as he chatted nervously with his captor "about shared acquaintances."[33]

Even those hostages who believed their move to the catwalk was a bluff were petrified by how risky this all was. For one thing, they weren't sure that the men assigned to be their "executioners" understood that they really weren't to be harmed. One of the prisoners had actually scrawled the word "executioner" on the handmade weapon he now held up on the catwalk and it wasn't clear to the hostages if this was to deter the state or to indicate to the hostages what was in fact coming. More alarmingly, the hostages now wondered if the state really cared what happened to them. The governor had surely been shown the news footage of them begging for him to come to Attica; he had not come. Surely he had been told that they too supported amnesty and wanted him to reconsider his position. And yet, he had not done so. Now, they fretted, what made these prisoners think that seeing homemade knives at hostage throats or spears at their sides would prompt officials to do the right thing?

But the prisoners were desperate and could think of no other tactic to keep troopers out of D Yard. At 9:22 that morning, immediately after the hostages had been placed on the catwalks, a group of prisoners went into A Tunnel with a loudspeaker to tell state officials that they meant business about resuming negotiations. "We want the Citizens' Committee in D Block yard," they yelled out. "There are eight hostages up on the roof—it's up to you. Come in now with the Citizens' Committee and Oswald."[34] Walter Dunbar heard this, and then hinted that if they released the hostages such a meeting could take place. But when the prisoner reply came back "negative," Dunbar simply left.[35]

Up on the catwalk, prisoners and hostages alike waited with hearts pounding for what might happen next. Wobbling slightly because it was hard to keep one's balance while blindfolded, hostage Mike Smith began having a serious conversation with one of his so-called executioners, Donald Noble. Noble was one of the two prisoners who had gone to great

Waiting up on the catwalk *(From the Elizabeth Fink Papers)*

lengths to protect Mike from harm when the rebellion broke out five days earlier, and Mike was greatly relieved to hear this man's voice next to him once he had finally made it through D Tunnel and up onto the catwalk.

Mike had been worried for a few days now that the state might choose to sacrifice him and his fellow hostages, and he had felt the need to write a letter to his wife, Sharon, in case he didn't make it out of Attica alive. He had gotten hold of a pen from one of the other hostages, who had somehow managed to keep it hidden in his pocket, and secretly written her a note that he then secured deep in his wallet. With the minutes ticking by, Mike and Don both expressed deep sadness that the last four days had come down to this. Then, after telling each other how to reach their loved ones, they made a solemn pact that if anything happened to either of them they would find the other's family members and make sure they knew how

A helicopter heads toward D Yard as New York State Police file into the prison. *(Courtesy of the LIFE Picture Collection/Getty Images)*

much they were loved.[36] Mike told Don about the note to Sharon in his wallet, and Don promised to deliver it.

No sooner had Mike Smith and Don Noble finished exchanging their personal information than they heard a sound that sent a chill down their spines. It was the ominous roar of helicopter blades revving up. "Besides being able to hear it," Mike Smith recalled in horror, "you could actually feel the concussion of the propellers."[37] A Conservation Corps helicopter was flying over Attica in order to survey the situation in D Yard before troopers would go in.[38]

One of the prisoners holding Richard Fargo hostage up on the catwalk also quaked at the sound of the helicopter and he decided that the only way the state wouldn't attack was if it truly believed the hostages' lives were in jeopardy. Desperately trying to change the course of events, this prisoner then leaned over to give Fargo a nick on the neck—one that he hoped the men in the helicopter could see—while assuring the guard in a whisper, "It's a sham boss, it's a sham."[39] CO G. B. Smith wanted to believe that these new, more aggressive maneuvers were indeed for show. He very clearly "could hear somebody hollering, 'Stand the hostages up so they can see they are all right.' "[40] Nevertheless, he was nearly immobilized with fear. If the state was willing to risk the lives of the hostages, then this couldn't possibly end well.

## 21

# No Mercy

As the small Conservation Corps helicopter appeared directly above the prison walls, many of the nearly 1,300 men in D Yard and up on the catwalks watched for some indication of what it was going to do. Some continued casting about for a weapon; others just dove into and under anything that might offer them protection. Suddenly, everyone stopped in their tracks as the outline of an entirely different, much larger, helicopter became visible on the horizon. Since this might be just a way to intimidate them, one prisoner thought, it was important to be calm and "Stand your ground."[1] A few others wondered if the chopper might be delivering Rockefeller to the prison to finally meet with prisoners. Most men, however, had no such illusions, particularly when the second helicopter began dumping a thick powdery fog into the yard. It was obvious that an attack had begun. Within seconds the air in D Yard was opaque with a combination of CS and CN gas—a thick and powdery substance that quickly enveloped, sickened, and felled every man it touched. In fact CS gas, chemical name orthochlorobenzylidene, wasn't "really a gas at all, but a fine white powder. Once dispersed, it hangs almost suspended in the air, causing tearing, nausea and retching in those who inhale it."[2]

When the first helicopter flew over, Carlos Roche was one of the men who thought that it might actually be Rockefeller, and, as he remembered, some of the "guys started hollering, yelling, you know cheering."[3] But when the air began to vibrate anew as the second, much bigger helicopter began its tour over the yard, a deep fear seized them. Before they could run or hide anywhere, they found themselves engulfed in a white cloud that immediately made people throw up.[4] "I brought up everything that I ate . . . and then I . . . started bringing up blood," recalled Roche.[5] Another prisoner began vomiting violently when a canister of the gas exploded right next to him, and the powder also caused "his eyes to swell closed, and his lips, nose, and lungs to burn as if on fire."[6] So powerful was this substance that even the observers felt its effects over in the prison's administration building, in a room where the windows were completely shut.[7]

If the Rockefeller administration's goal had been, as General O'Hara later testified, to completely immobilize "persons exposed to the CS gas," so that prison officials could walk in and, with no one capable of stopping them, calmly retake control, they had succeeded in mere minutes.[8] This was, however, only the prelude to the much more aggressive assault. At 9:46 a.m., pursuant to both an official proclamation and an executive order issued by the governor, the New York State Police broadcast over its radio system the long-awaited command: "Tell all your units to move in!"[9]

As prisoners and hostages began stumbling and crawling through the thick, noxious air, phalanxes of gas-mask-shrouded troopers poured onto the catwalks with guns blazing.[10]

The troopers had removed their identification emblems—the badges affixed to their collars that indicated which troop they belonged to as well as their name and rank—just before they went in.[11] Trooper Captain William Dillon not only took off his nameplate and his captain's bars, but as he later recounted, he "told [his] people to take them off too . . . [because] we weren't stopping traffic where a citizen would have the perfect right to know who they're being stopped by . . . it was a different thing."[12] Trooper Gerard Smith explained it even more bluntly: "Everybody started taking off their things . . . so they couldn't identify what troop or identify to pinpoint the individual in case something happens."[13]

Whereas some of the troopers now heading into D Yard were excited finally to take control and to show the prisoners who was boss, Tony Strollo was going in for one reason and one reason only: to rescue his brother, hostage Frank Strollo. Either way, these were men with much ammunition and only the flimsiest of plans as to how they were going to secure the facility let alone actually retrieve the hostages unharmed. Worse, these were men who had spent the last five days being inundated with rumors about the "animals" inside who would kill them if they could.[14] According to later blotter entries and store clerk records submitted by the State Police, a total of thirty-three rifles had been sent to Attica in preparation for the retaking, and 217 shotguns had been passed out to the troopers from various troop supply trucks. There were also uncounted numbers of personal weapons. All this added up to an extraordinary concentration of firepower in the hands of members of law enforcement now buzzing from a toxic cocktail of hatred, fear, and aggression.[15]

On September 13, there was an astonishing number of men lined up to wield these weapons. In addition to the 550 uniformed men from the New York State Police, "augmented by BCI [Bureau of Criminal Investigation] personnel for a total force of approximately 600," there were "232 Sheriff's Deputies at Attica Correctional Facility" armed and ready to enter the prison, on top of which there were sheriffs from Genesee County and park police from Genesee and Schuyler counties.[16] Although state officials later insisted that these other members of law enforcement had joined the assault against the state's wishes, both sheriffs and park police insisted that they had been invited in. One officer from Genesee State Park explained that when "the state police found out we had rifles . . . they asked us if we would stand by a window there [in C Block] and be there if needed for any reason."[17] What is more, he explained, it was a NYSP trooper who gave them the okay "to pick a target" and to shoot to kill—to help them "to eliminate a threat to the hostages."[18] COs from Attica as well as some from Auburn also felt welcome to join the assault and, armed with personal as well as state-issued weapons, they stationed themselves on the second and third floors of A Block in firing position.[19]

Although it was reassuring to many of these men that they had so much firepower supporting them, they also realized that this also meant a very real danger of being caught in the crossfire. Troopers like Tony Strollo were especially concerned about this because so many were wielding shotguns loaded with buckshot, which, "because it scattered," could be disastrous.[20] Another real concern was visibility. For starters, there had been "no discussion of the amount of time that the gas was supposed to be allowed to work," and so the men all proceeded out into air so thick with powder it was hard to see a thing—particularly through the thick rubber of a gas mask. One trooper was so taken aback by the power and density of the gas that had just been dropped that, years later, he still couldn't believe his superiors had sent him in through such "a heavy fog."[21]

Despite the troopers' impaired vision, from the instant they entered the prison and began moving out onto the catwalks above Attica's yards, they began shooting.

The hostages up on the catwalks were right in the first line of fire. Hostage Richard Fargo felt almost faint with fear when he realized how wrong the prisoners had been to think that the presence of hostages on the catwalk "would prevent police from shooting in the area."[22] Civilian hostage Ron Kozlowski felt his stomach lurch as he heard the unmistakable sounds of guns fired all around him. Seconds before, there had been a prisoner right next to him with a handmade knife at his neck, and the next thing he knew that man had been hit and "wasn't there anymore."[23] As the bullets hit him, the prisoner's body jerked and fell backward and the knife that he had been holding sliced an erratic gouge from Ron's neck up to his hairline and then back down across the shoulder blade. Horrified, Ron "dropped to the floor, curled up in a ball and laid still" so that no one would shoot at him.[24] But to his dismay, "the bullets were coming like rain" and, because so many of them were ricocheting off the catwalk, his face was also being blasted by jagged shards of cement.[25]

Mike Smith felt the impact of the prisoner on his right being shot twice, the last shot literally catapulting him over the railing of the catwalk. In a futile attempt to save both himself and Mike from being hit, Don Noble pulled him to the left as the man immediately behind him received a fatal volley of gunfire. But the shots reached them anyway. Mike's abdomen was on fire as four bullets ripped across it in a straight line. He was also shot in the arm, which felt as if it had been torn from his body.[26] The bullets that entered Mike's stomach, dead center right between his navel and genitals, exploded upon impact, which sent shrapnel downward to his spine. One exiting slug took the base of Mike's spine along with it, leaving "a hole about the size of a grapefruit" in his intestines.[27] All Mike could hear around him as the shooting kept going on was "people crying, people dying, and people screaming."[28] As he lay curled up, bleeding profusely, Mike suddenly found himself looking up into the eyes of a trooper who had a shotgun pointed directly at his head. Somewhere close by, he heard a correction officer yell to the trooper, "He is one of us," and started to breathe a sigh of relief. Then, he realized sickeningly that the trooper had simply resighted his weapon on Don Noble, who also lay bleeding next to him. Weakly Mike tried to tell the trooper, "He saved my life."[29] To his relief, as he faded in and out of consciousness, he saw that Noble seemed to have been spared.

Nearby, hostage Dean Stenshorn tried desperately to see what was happening around him through the blindfold over his eyes. He wanted to get shelter from the bullets whizzing around him, but could only stand there frozen. He could hear a prisoner say "Don't kill him" and realized in that moment that he had much more to fear from the troopers barreling over the catwalk toward him than from the men who had counted on his life being a bargaining chip with the state.[30] As hostage Curly Watkins suddenly found himself on the ground with a prisoner lying heavily on top of him, it dawned on him as well that, though this prisoner could very well have killed him should he have wanted to, he was still alive. And yet, ironically, he still might die from so-called friendly fire.[31]

John Hill, known in the yard as Dacajewiah, was one of the prisoners holding a hostage on the catwalk of B Block when the gunfire erupted. In that second he realized how completely the men in D Yard had failed to grasp the state's intentions. "We felt somewhat protected by the presence of Dunne, and even the media. . . . We felt, I think, that there just couldn't have been a massacre with media watching."[32] As he came up from under a barricade the prisoners had built on B catwalk where he had been crouching for cover, he was shot. He was then hit with the butt of another trooper's weapon, which hurled him over the catwalk railing onto the cement handball court below.

As Hill fell all he could hear was "people screaming and crying"—people like Edward Kowalczyk.[33] In the first few seconds of the retaking, prisoner Kowalczyk was shot seven times as he tried desperately to find cover on A Catwalk.[34] After he fell to the ground in agony with gunshot wounds to the chest, abdomen, back, and base of his penis, he stared up in horror to see a state trooper looming over him.[35] The trooper threw him a knife and "ordered that I stab my fellow Brother, Carlos, who was a prisoner laying just to the right of me, and who appeared to be also seriously injured. When I refused to do so, the trooper laughed and tried to put the knife in my hand. But I wouldn't hold it and threw it back down. The trooper then picked up the knife, gave it to another trooper and left"—after which Kowalczyk passed out.[36]

Prisoner Jose Quinones was also up on a catwalk when the gas dropped and the shooting began. He couldn't believe what he was hearing and seeing. Even as bullets rained down into D Yard, with many hundreds of state troopers, COs, and officers from the BCI firing from the roof of A Block alone, a State Police helicopter hovered overhead, broadcasting a message through a loudspeaker: "Surrender peacefully. You will not be harmed. Surrender peacefully, you will not be harmed."[37] Suddenly, "someone grabbed the back of his neck and forced him to stand, then struck him with something behind his ear . . . [whereupon] State troopers tear gassed him directly in the face and began to beat him in the head," leaving him screaming in pain from second- and third-degree chemical burns.[38]

Even some of the troopers were overwhelmed by how quickly this retaking had disintegrated into chaos. Tony Strollo "just kept stepping over the bodies" as he tried to find his brother, while trooper Gerard Smith felt almost paralyzed by the sheer madness around him.[39] Smith found himself staring incredulously as men trying to avoid the fusillade of bullets "slid underneath the bottom rail" of the catwalks, dropping a full fifteen feet to the ground below.[40] Not that that took them to safety. Looking over the railing, Smith saw a trooper approach a prisoner who was lying still on the pavement and shoot him in the head.[41]

Strollo and Smith's fellow troopers, the correction officers, and the other members of law enforcement were just getting started. After clearing the catwalks so that there wasn't a single man left standing on any of them, the NYSP launched its ground assault. It was instantly clear to everyone huddled there that troopers and COs were no longer merely trying to regain control of the facility. This was already done. They now seemed determined to make Attica's prisoners pay a high price for their rebellion. A twenty-two-year-old prisoner who had remained locked in C Block for the duration of the uprising later recounted how two C Block guards came

The New York State Police in the fog of gas, out on the catwalk *(From the Elizabeth Fink Papers)*

to his cell as the retaking began simply to abuse him. According to this man, these COs "slammed his face against the window bars, and ordered him to watch 'and see what happens to fucking convicts who didn't obey the rules and try to run something.' "[42] As he was being hurt he was horrified also to learn that other prisoners out in the yard were "being shot in spite of the fact that they were waving their hands high in the air and begging that their lives be spared."[43]

Frank "Big Black" Smith simply couldn't believe the horror unfolding around him either. Big Black had suspected that the state might "come in there and knock some heads and bust some heads," but once he started "seeing people get opened up with shotguns," he understood that they never remotely anticipated this level of savagery.[44] To Jomo Joka Omowale it was "like a war zone"—a phrase that would be heard again and again in later descriptions from those who lived through the retaking—and the callousness of the shooters was hard for him to comprehend. "It was very painful to see all these old and crippled guys getting shot. . . . They were in D Yard because they had no place else to go."[45]

Carlos Roche was also overwhelmed by the horror of the assault. He looked over at "the negotiating tables, and everything over there was down," and then he could see wounded and dead men scattered around the yard and also piling on top of one another in the confusion.[46] One man spoke of falling on top of other men right after being hit with gunfire and then feeling other wounded men falling on top of him. "I couldn't breathe. . . . You know, people was on top of me and . . . they keep telling us, keep your head down, so I'm trying to crawl and I'm trying to get the person off of me."[47]

Nineteen-year-old prisoner Melvin Marshall just couldn't believe that he had landed in this nightmare simply for violating parole. He lay on the ground, gasping for breath in the gas that still hung like a heavy blanket over the yard, then a trooper kicked him and brought a gun butt crashing down on his head.[48] Prisoner Rodney Zobrist, who'd hit the ground for safety the minute he heard the choppers overhead, dared to peer out from under his arms only to see troopers all around him "shooting at random" and to watch as several men he knew were "hit by gunfire."[49] To his horror one of those troopers spotted Rodney, marched over to him, and shoved a shotgun in his mouth and then walked away.[50] Lorenzo Skinner, like Jomo, was caught "in an unbelievable barrage of gunfire that seemed to be coming from everywhere." As he fell to his knees and tried to cover his face against the tear gas canisters that still were exploding around him, a trooper pushed his "face down into a mud puddle and told him not to move or he would be killed." Forced to suck in "large amounts of water through his mouth and nose" in order to breathe, this young prisoner felt that he was drowning.[51]

Even the men who scrambled to surrender were subjected to unspeakable abuse. One prisoner who'd already been shot in the back was ordered "to stand up with his hands over his head. Because of the wound, he was unable to raise his hand to his head." Nevertheless, another trooper ordered him to remove the football helmet that he had been wearing for protection. When the wounded man couldn't do that either, the officer "proceeded to kick the helmet off of his head."[52]

As cruel as these events were, it was the acts of cold-blooded killing, and attempted killing, that made the scene especially terrifying. One prisoner watched in disbelief as two troopers aimed their guns at a man trying to take cover in a trench. The troopers instructed the man to climb out of the hole with his hands on his head, which he did. Then, "he was shot in the chest by the trooper who [had] told him to keep his hands on his head."[53] Another prisoner who had been shot in the abdomen and in the leg was ordered to get up and walk, which he was unable to do. "The trooper then shot him in the head with a handgun."[54] Trooper Gerard Smith watched his fellow officers storm through the tent city and happen upon foxholes that prisoners were trying to hide in, and then witnessed one of these troopers as he "just stuck the rifle into the hole and pulled the trigger."[55]

Twenty-one-year-old Chris Reed was gunned down with four bullets, including one that "exploded and took out a big chunk "of his left thigh. He listened in terror as troopers debated in front of him whether to kill him or let him bleed to death. As they discussed this the troopers had fun jamming their rifle butts into his injuries and dumping lime onto his face and injured legs, until he fell unconscious. When he awoke, he found himself "stacked up with the dead bodies."[56] "I never saw human beings treated like this," another prisoner later recalled. He couldn't understand: "Why all the hatred?"[57] But it wasn't just any hatred—it was racial hatred. As one prisoner was told by a trooper who had a gun trained on him: he would soon be dead because "we haven't killed enough niggers."[58] Everywhere there were cries of "Keep your nigger nose down!"[59] "Don't you know state troopers don't like niggers?"[60] "Don't move nigger! You're dead!"[61]

Underscoring just how much racial hatred was fueling trooper rage in D Yard, one prisoner, William Maynard, tried to carry Jomo to safety after he had been shot multiple times. As Maynard struggled along, a CO ordered him to stop and put his hands in the air. As he dutifully put his hands up, still trying to balance Jomo on his shoulders, the CO shot him twice in the forearms. As Maynard fell in a heap, with Jomo on top of him, this same officer "loaded up his gun and shot Jomo six times right on top of me and kicked me in the face and says both the niggers are dead and went on."[62]

To the shock of the hostages who had been left in the hostage circle and who were now, like the prisoners, trying to find cover, the prisoners were still trying to keep them protected even as their own were being shot. Minutes before the assault had begun, Herb Blyden had instructed Akil Al-Jundi and nine or ten other men to "stay in front of the hostages and not to let harm come to them."[63] Despite their terror at being left so exposed, these men held their ground, until they too were gunned down. Al-Jundi "was shot in the left hand by a .270 rifle while guarding the hostage circle," and suffered an injury "so serious that he could see through his hand." He was also hit by a bullet fragment under his right eye.[64]

The hostages fared little better. When CO Dean Wright, huddled into the smallest ball he could make, suddenly felt somebody reach down and turn him over, he was relieved, thinking he was finally being rescued. Then he panicked. As he looked up he found himself staring into the "barrel of a twelve gauge shotgun" in the hands of a New York state trooper who looked like he was about to pull the trigger. Had somebody else not yelled "He's one of ours, he's one of ours" just then, he realized, with sickening clarity, he would have been dead.[65] After being shot in the back, guard Robert Curtiss also felt the fear of imminent death when a trooper kept knocking him over every time he tried to sit up. He shouted as loudly as he could that he was an officer, but still had to beg the trooper not to shoot him.[66] Hostage G. B. Smith might also have been shot dead had it not been for fellow hostage John Stockholm. As Stockholm remembered, "GB started to get out of the pile and a trooper tried to level his gun at him until I said he's one of ours."[67]

So thick was the gunfire that morning that, just as Tony Strollo had feared, even members of the assault force couldn't avoid being shot by their own. Hostage Don Almeter was stunned to see "a state policeman who was down and bleeding."[68] Since the prisoners had no guns, clearly his own men had shot him. That trooper was Lieutenant Joseph Christian and he had been running toward the hostage circle when, he later maintained, a prisoner tried to hit him—in response to which, he said, troopers up on B Catwalk "let loose their guns to save him."[69] Thanks to prisoner Vergyl Horace Mulligan, however, at least one hostage was pulled out of harm's way when the bullets began spraying the circle. That hostage would later testify before Mulligan's parole board that he had saved his life.[70]

The overall situation in D Yard was astonishing devastation wrought in a remarkably short period of time. Prisoner James Lee Asbury recalled that merely ten minutes after the assault on the prison began, no matter where he looked, all he could see was blood and water.[71] One nineteen-year-old prisoner, Charles Pernasalice, recoiled from the sight and smell of so much blood and the sound of so much screaming.[72] Frank Lott, one of the authors of the original July Manifesto, shook his head in disbelief: "Guys were laying all over . . . they tried to get up and were shot down."[73]

Even though NYSP officials reported that Attica was fully secured by 10:05 a.m., the observers who had waited out the retaking locked in the Steward's Room could still hear shots being fired inside the prison as late as 10:24 a.m., and others reported hearing gunfire from inside the prison even an hour later.[74]

Ultimately, the human cost of the retaking was staggeringly high: 128 men were shot—some of them multiple times.[75] Less than half an hour after the retaking had commenced, nine hostages were dead and at least one additional hostage was close to death. Twenty-nine prisoners had been fatally shot.[76] Many of the deaths in D Yard—both hostages

Casualties on the catwalk *(From the Elizabeth Fink Papers)*

and prisoners—were caused by the scatter of buckshot, and still others resulted from the devastating impact of unjacketed bullets.[77]

The hostages, both those who'd been taken to the catwalks to serve as bargaining chips and those who'd been held in a circle in the yard, paid a terrible price for the state's excessive use of force. Correction Sergeant Edward Cunningham, a father of eight, lay dead, hit in the head by a buckshot pellet that then traveled and severed his cervical spinal cord.[78] Mike Smith's dear friend John D'Arcangelo, whose first child had just been born and who had transferred to Attica only seven weeks before, was killed by a .270 rifle wielded by a state trooper sniper who'd apparently been aiming at several prisoners.[79] Guard Carl Valone, father of four, died from "traumatic shock and laceration of the brain" caused by a gunshot wound to the head, as well as bleeding from his abdominal organs caused by a wound to the chest.[80] B Block captain Richard Lewis died when a bullet went through his back and destroyed his aorta.[81]

CO John Monteleone died when he took a bullet to the heart from a personal weapon—a .44 Magnum.[82] Among the civilian deaths were industrial foreman and father of eight Elmer Hardie, killed by a shot to the head, and senior account clerk Herbert Jones.[83] Principal account clerk Elon Werner, as well as his nephew, CO guard Ronnie Werner, both perished from internal bleeding caused by gunshots.[84] Ultimately, "five . . . died from Double-o buckshot. The rest of the group was shot by State Police snipers firing .270 cal. rifles from the roofs and upper floors of A and C Blocks."[85]

The hostages who survived the attack suffered significant injuries. In addition to the horrific wounds Mike Smith sustained, Lieutenant Robert Curtiss suffered a gunshot wound to his back, while civilian employee Gordon Knickerbocker suffered a gunshot to the head and fellow civilian Al Mitzel received bullet fragments in his back.[86]

The death and injury toll among the prisoners was much higher. Twenty-one-year-old William Allen had been killed, shot by bullets from a .38 caliber handgun as well as by .00 pellets, and Melvin Ware, age twenty-three, had died from multiple gunshots, including .270 caliber bullets from a trooper's gun and .00 buckshot from an officer who had fired at him two or three times with a twelve gauge deer slayer shotgun.[87] Twenty-nine-year-old Lorenzo McNeil died in D Yard after a trooper up on D catwalk shot him in the back of the head.[88] Twenty-five-year-old Milton Menyweather was shot to death, riddled with .270 bullets to his back, chest, and right lung. Twenty-two-year-old Charles "Carlos" Prescott was felled by the .00 buckshot that pockmarked his body on A Catwalk.[89] Perhaps no shooting was more brutal than that of Kenneth B. Malloy. Malloy was shot twelve times at close range, pumped full of bullets from both a .357 and a .38 caliber weapon, which led to "lacerations of the brain, and destruction of the lungs and heart."[90] Malloy was shot with such vicious abandon that his eyes were ripped apart from the shards of bone splintering in his head.

A number of prisoners killed had, according to several witnesses, actually still been alive after troopers had control of the facility. One of these dead men was thirty-five-year-old Samuel Melville, the so-called Mad Bomber who spent time trying to educate his fellow prisoners in Attica's classrooms and had penned the exposé of profits derived from prison labor in Attica's laundry. Prisoners maintained that Melville had been "alive following the assault," and had dutifully tried to surrender, but by day's end he'd been shot to death from a one-ounce lead shotgun slug that had entered the upper left part of his chest, fragmented, and subsequently ripped through his left lung.[91]

Then there was Thomas Hicks, who was riddled by .00 buckshot.[92] He had been shot in the back with ammunition that perforated his right lung and heart, and also suffered a gunshot wound to his right buttock.[93] Although his account was disputed by state officials, a National Guardsman who came into the prison to deal with the injured inmates in the immediate aftermath of the retaking insisted he saw Hicks alive after the prison was fully in the troopers' control.[94] He said that he remembered this prisoner in particular because he heard a correction officer grabbing him and saying to his fellow guards, "Look who we have here, we got Mr. Hicks," and then, after forcing Hicks to his knees and telling him to put his hands on his head, he threatened to kill him while at the same time kicking him in the throat.[95] Two prisoners, Larry Barnes and Melvin Marshall, also later described watching Tommy Hicks get shot "after the original shooting ceased."[96] According to Marshall, Hicks was "hit with a barrage of gunfire," after which he saw troopers walk over to Hicks's body, take "the butt end of the gun, pound the flesh in the ground, kick it, pound it, shoot it again."[97]

Twenty-one-year-old Elliot "L. D." Barkley, who had been in so many respects the face of Attica with his wire-rimmed granny glasses and his impassioned speeches, was also said by various accounts, including those of fellow prisoners Frank "Big Black" Smith, Frank Lott, Carl Jones, and

Melvin Marshall as well as New York Assemblyman Arthur Eve, to have been alive well after the police had ceased to have even a tenuous rationale for shooting anyone.[98] According to a later autopsy report, L.D. was killed by gunshot wounds to his back from "a tumbling .270 caliber slug in the Southeast quadrant of D Yard."[99] When exactly L.D. had been shot to death, and whether the bullet that killed him was in fact "tumbling" or had been shot at him point-blank, would become major issues of contention in the years that followed. Many prisoners at Attica believed strongly, though, that the state had "murdered him."[100]

Back in the administration building the observers and state officials had no real idea what was happening in D Yard, but the sounds of gunfire and the fog of the gas did not bode well. At 11:46 a.m., State Senator John Dunne demanded to be allowed in to see "results of the assault."[101] Walter Dunbar and Rockefeller's attorney Howard Shapiro reluctantly gave him a tour. What Dunne saw in the yard appalled him: "30 to 40 correction officers striking half a dozen inmates" who were being forced to run a gauntlet. As he recalled years later, "I observed naked men running in a direction toward me through a row of correction officers who were striking them with their batons on buttocks."[102] This abuse was so egregious that Dunne told Dunbar, "I shouldn't be seeing [this] and it had better stop right away."[103] He was assured that it would.[104]

The other observers did not hear any official news of the retaking until 12:16 p.m., when DOCS deputy commissioner Walter Dunbar finally came to the Steward's Room to update them. He painted a picture of success: the State Police and correction officers had handled prisoners "with excellent discipline and without brutality," he reported proudly.[105] When Tom Wicker asked whether they could now go and see the prisoners, however, Dunbar told him quite brusquely that a visit would not be possible while the operation was still under way.[106] Dunbar's report only intensified the unease in the room but, to everyone's relief, John Dunne, who had stayed with prison officials during the retaking, appeared about an hour later and also gave a relatively optimistic briefing, based on what he had been told by prison officials: the "place was completely under control," the wounded prisoners were now in the prison hospital, the wounded staff were in local hospitals, and the rest of the prisoners were now being rehoused in cells.[107]

There was, in fact, little reason to feel that this retaking had been a success or that things would now be all right. Although no numbers had yet been released—or would be for several days—everyone could assume from the sounds alone that the death toll must be high. Even from outside the prison, the cacophony of bullets hitting walls and flesh could be heard so loudly and clearly that African American reporter John Johnson found himself overcome with emotion as he tried to report the retaking to the nation far from Attica's walls. "It's an awful scene," he said into the camera as he choked up. "I think that people are dying in there."[108] The observers were also quite certain that something horrific had just occurred. Reverend Martin Chandler recounted: "I saw them bringing out bodies, bringing out folks and just kinda, puttin' 'em on the ground and . . . they were lined up all the way down the wall from the prison and from there to the gate."[109]

William Kunstler was sickened by what had just taken place inside Attica. He personally had experienced a level of hostility that left him stunned, including walking down the road outside the prison when "a car with four men in it came at us. They made a feint as if to run us down and I could see they were laughing."[110] He couldn't even fathom what the men in

NYSP troopers and state officials review slain prisoners atop the catwalk. *(From the Elizabeth Fink Papers)*

D Yard must have suffered when law enforcement came in. In the hours to come, still awaiting word from inside the prison, Kunstler found himself sitting alone, unable to speak, with tears running down his face.[111]

Inside the prison, Roger Champen also wept. Like many of his fellow prisoners, he couldn't understand why this had happened: "Why didn't someone say . . . they're going to come in with guns and shoot you people to death?"[112]

New York State Police troopers clad in gas masks and rain gear make their way to the prison entrance. *(Courtesy of Don Dutton/Getty Images)*

## 22

# Spinning Disaster

In contrast to the observers or prisoners like Champ, Rockefeller's men on the scene seemed a bit startled, but largely unmoved by the carnage of the retaking they had authorized. To be sure, they were taken aback by how quickly the operation went. But, overall, they were relieved that everything had seemed to go so well, and that the performance of the State Police had been "magnificent," as General O'Hara later described it to Rockefeller.[1]

Douglass delivered his report of the retaking to Rockefeller late on the morning of the 13th, complete with a tally of the number of hostages who had survived. The governor seemed concerned, above all, with making sure that the nation understood what a success the retaking in fact was.[2] Well aware that the assault he ordered could have resulted in all of the hostages being killed, Rockefeller was elated that so many had in fact managed to make it out of the prison alive.[3] Commissioner Oswald, however, was finding it much harder to conjure up anything positive about what had just happened. He would have to go speak to the large crowd of family members and reporters now gathered outside the prison and even he could smell the acrid scent of blood in the air. Though he still believed that morning's death and devastation unavoidable, it made him ill to think about it. "I think I have some feeling now of how Truman must have felt when he decided to drop the A-bomb," he remarked to those around him that morning.[4]

After consulting with Department of Corrections public relations director Gerald Houlihan and Deputy Commissoner Walter Dunbar about the wording, Oswald emerged from the prison to give a statement to the press at 10:40 a.m.[5] First he reiterated his version of what had led to the retaking in the first place—namely that negotiations had reached a stalemate and, therefore, the state had no choice but to go in. He also made clear what he felt had been at stake that morning. As he put it, "To delay the action any longer would not only jeopardize innocent lives, but would threaten the security of the entire correctional system of this state."[6] Becoming more passionate, he went on, "The armed rebellion of the type we have faced threatens the destruction of our free society. We cannot permit that destruction to happen. It has indeed been an agonizing decision."[7]

Almost two hours later, with the air around the prison still thick with tear gas and the periodic sounds of guns still being fired, Houlihan and Dunbar gave additional press statements. This time offering more specifics regarding the fate of the hostages, since, according to the Gannett News Service, what every reporter was demanding to know was "How did they die?"[8]

Without even blinking, Houlihan stated: "I understand several had their throats cut. . . . Some of their throats were slit."[9]

"How many?" the reporter pressed.

"Seven, seven or eight," he continued.[10]

DOCS public relations director Gerald Houlihan addresses the press. *(Courtesy of the* Democrat and Chronicle*)*

"Were they all killed by prisoners? All nine of them?"

"Yes," stated Houlihan unabashedly.[11]

A few hours later, Walter Dunbar provided his own bloodcurdling twist to the rumors of atrocities committed by the prisoners. During tours of the prison he conducted later that day with a group of legislators including Arthur Eve and Herman Badillo, and then with members of the press, Dunbar regaled everyone with a vivid tale of state officials yelling at the prisoners to "give up the hostages!" to which one of them responded, "This is your answer," and then proceeded to stick a "knife in the hostage's stomach."[12] After that, Dunbar went on, the awfulness only escalated. Not only did the other prisoners slit the throats of other hostages, but, worse, "one of them took a knife and grabbed young officer [Mike] Smith and castrated him . . . and took this man's organs and stuck them in his mouth in clear view of us all . . . we saw it. We saw it."[13] Then, with a final flourish, Dunbar "took pains to point out the particular inmate who had stuffed hostage Michael Smith's genitals in his mouth and slit his throat."[14] The prisoner he pointed to, now lying on a table and very obviously being tortured in full view of the group, was Big Black Smith. Arthur Eve and Herman Badillo, who had gotten to know Big Black during the time they spent in the yard, were dismayed but also so sickened by the tale they didn't quite know how to react. Eve at least mustered the strength to ask Dunbar how they knew it was this particular prisoner who had committed the atrocity. "We saw it," Dunbar replied. "We have it on film."[15]

Later that night, Dunbar sat down with several reporters, including Lawrence Beaupre of the *Rochester Times-Union,* and repeated this story, which had already been spreading like wildfire among the troopers who'd seen Mike Smith bleeding from the gut and then heard that this was because he had been castrated by the biggest black man in the yard. By that hour so-called eyewitness accounts included not only this castration, but claims as well about how the prisoners had also "mutilated faces with knives and . . . disemboweled a guard."[16]

These horrific stories electrified the press as much as the day's earlier news that all of the dead hostages had been murdered in cold blood by knife-wielding inmates.[17] And to top off these stories, according to a statement sent out on the AP wire by the end of the day: "A spokesman for Gov. Nelson A. Rockefeller said several of the hostages had been dead for several hours before State moved into the prison in force."[18] This news item from the highest office in the state of New York would turn out to have been based on nothing but the wholly unfounded opinions of at least five correction officials, who had called into a hotline set up by Wim Van Eekeren, a deputy commissioner of corrections based in Albany, to discuss their thoughts on the retaking. During one such call, Allen Mills, the director of the Department of Correction Industries, offered his opinion that the hostages had "been dead a long time," which indicated to him that the prisoners "never intended to release them."[19]

The inflammatory stories of prisoner depravity reported by New York state officials found their way onto the front pages of the nation's most highly regarded newspapers as dawn broke the morning after the retaking. "In this worst of American prison riots," *The New York Times* reported, "several of the hostages—prison guards and civilian employees—died when convicts slashed their throats with knives." The paper then went on to editorialize, "The deaths of [the hostages] reflect a barbarism wholly alien to our civilized society. Prisoners slashed the throats of utterly helpless, unarmed guards." The piece noted that the "inmates responsible for the killing of the hostages at Attica Prison will be liable for the death penalty under New York State law."[20] The New York *Daily News,* in an article headlined "I Saw Seven Throats Cut," recounted the ordeal of one trooper who experienced "the agony of witnessing the massacre etched into his sweating face," after seeing the "cons" "just slit throats."[21] After informing its readers that "nine hostages were killed by inmates," the *Los Angeles Times* quoted Governor Rockefeller's view that these were " 'cold-blooded killings' by revolutionary militants."[22] *The Washington Post* also reported "Convicts Kill Nine Hostages."[23] Thanks to the Associated Press wire service, the story of prisoner barbarism made headline news in the local newspapers of almost every midsized city and small town in America.[24]

Whipped into a frenzy by all the inflammatory press reports, citizen telegrams flooded state and prison officials from the governor on down, expressing both support for the strong stand they had taken for law and order and fury at the prisoners who had launched the rebellion. One of the more blunt messages read "Amnesty no, Smith and Wesson yes. Good job." Another writer expressed his opinion that "there should have been no surviving inmates after the cellblock was cleared."[25] The observers were also attacked: "Too bad [that] Wicker and Kunstler got out alive," read one letter jointly signed by a husband and wife.[26]

The "Letter to the Editor" sections of the country's magazines and newspapers were soon filled with equally virulent expressions of rage toward the "murderous convicts," those "desperately sick men whose . . . lawlessness cannot be tolerated," and those "evil, vicious enemies of society"—not to mention "the thoughtless idiots on the outside who support them."[27]

In the immediate aftermath of the retaking, though, not all citizens and media wanted prisoners to pay an even higher price than they already had for their uprising. Some felt that the nation needed to take more time to assess what had happened at Attica and openly questioned the violence of the retaking. A week after the retaking, talk show host David Frost, for example, scrapped his regularly scheduled 8:30 Monday night show on New York City's Channel 5 (WNEW) in favor of moderating a live ninety-minute discussion of Attica that offered some more critical perspectives on the way the rebellion had been ended. Those he invited to join him included Leo Zeferetti, head of Correction Officers' Benevolent Association of New York City, Attica observers Clarence Jones and Lewis Steel, and one guard who had been held during the Tombs rebellion the previous year.[28] After a heated discussion with various opposing views, Frost closed by saying gravely, "We end with a prayer for everybody who lost somebody."[29]

There were also those who went public with their feelings that the men in the prison might have rebelled for good reason and had shown remarkable humanity toward others throughout the siege. As one citizen wrote to *Time,* "The inmates, branded 'animals' by many, were animals only by virtue of the conditions under which they were forced to live. For a fact, zoo animals live better than do these prisoners, and zoo animals are not even supposedly being 'rehabilitated.'"[30] Several notable penal reformers also expressed their dismay at how law enforcement handled the retaking, as did several prison reform publications such as *Penal Digest.*[31] The NAACP also chimed in. Its official publication, *The Crisis,* referred to what had happened as "the awesome Attica tragedy." Mainstream black publications such as *Ebony* tried to focus on the necessity of finding the "cure for prison riots" rather than simply blaming them on depraved inmates.[32]

After the rebellion's end some members of Congress weighed in as well. Henry Bellmon, a Republican senator from Oklahoma, stated that he was "stunned and outraged" by the "violent and bloody episode at New York State's Attica State Prison . . . [a] slaughter of human life [that] was more horrifying than any such event in recent times."[33] To him prison riots were "inevitable as long as our prisons remain in the condition they are in" and, as important, "the Law Enforcement Assistance Administration [set up in 1964 by President Lyndon Johnson to offer substantial new support to both police and prisons] has not used its resources to change the system, but rather to perpetuate it."[34] Perhaps no congressman was more outspoken, though, than Attica observer Herman Badillo. He tried to make clear to his fellow members of the House that the retaking had been a tragedy of monumental proportions. There should have been no rush to end the rebellion in this violent way, particularly, he pointed out, since the prisoners were going nowhere and the hostages were being protected. Even the early demand for transport to "a non-imperialist country" had had "no support at all" as the rebellion wore on, he explained, which in his view was "extraordinary, because I understand there were more than 200 prisoners who had life sentences."[35]

While the state tried to focus Americans' attention on alleged prisoner depravity, younger Americans and those in the antiwar and civil rights movements also weren't buying it. An article that appeared in *The Nation* on September 27, 1971, summed up their views and concerns:

> Attica will evoke the bloodiest prison rebellion in U.S. history. It will take its place alongside Kent State, Jackson State, My Lai and other traumatic events that have shaken the American conscience and incited searing controversy over the application of force—and the pressures that provoke it. . . . Since most of Attica's prisoners are black, many blacks saw the event as yet another manifestation of America's deep-rooted racism. . . . White liberals—and not liberals alone—interpreted Attica as, at the very least, a measure of the bankruptcy of the U.S. prison system.[36]

People from all political persuasions and age groups could at least agree that the American prison system was in serious trouble. From the point of view of the left this stemmed from racism and neglect, whereas from the perspective of conservative power brokers like Nelson Rockefeller this was thanks to "the highly-organized, revolutionary tactics of militants."[37] Indeed, it was Rockefeller's deeply held belief that he had thwarted a revolutionary plot to destabilize the nation that allowed him to take such undiluted pride in how things had transpired on the morning of September 13. When the governor faced the media on the day after the retaking, he not only reiterated the falsehood that the prisoners had "rejected all efforts at a peaceful settlement, forced a confrontation, and carried out cold-blooded killings they had threatened from the outset," but he shared with the media his enthusiasm for how the Attica rebellion had ended.[38]

"We can all be grateful," he began, "that the skill and courage of the

Governor Nelson Rockefeller takes the podium at a press conference on September 15. *(Courtesy of* The New York Times*)*

state police and correction officers, supported by the National Guard and sheriffs' deputies, saved the lives of 29 hostages, and that their restraint held down casualties among prisoners as well."[39]

Rockefeller's positive feelings about the decision he had made to take Attica with force had everything to do with the reaction he had received from the White House. At about 11:30 on the morning of the 13th, he first recounted the events of the retaking to Nixon aide John Ehrlichman, who soon afterward conveyed Rockefeller's message to the president.[40] By 12:37 p.m. President Nixon was in the Oval Office discussing all that he had just learned about the retaking with fellow Republicans Robert Dole, Alexander M. Haig, Jr., and H. R. Haldeman.[41] "They killed seven of the guards. . . . A bloody business," Nixon told his aides, and worse, he went on, "one of [the guards] had been castrated."[42] Nixon was clear to the men assembled that, in his view, "Rockefeller handled it well" because, as the president put it, "you see it's the black business . . . he had to do it."[43] To a one, these men felt strongly that this rebellion was of a piece with the revolutionary plots that had recently been hatched in the California system by black activists such as Angela Davis, famed leader from the Communist Party. All those assembled in the president's office agreed that while the morning's events made a particularly "gruesome story," news of the slashings and castration would go a long way toward discrediting America's "bleeding hearts" like "the Tom Wickers of the world."[44] "I think this is going to have a hell of a salutary effect on future prison riots," Nixon said. "Just like Kent State had a hell of a salutary effect. . . . They can talk all they want about force, but that is the purpose of force."[45]

When the president finally spoke with Rockefeller at 1:38 p.m., he wanted him to know that the White House was behind him one hundred percent.[46] "I know you have had a hard day," Nixon greeted Rockefeller, "but I want you to know that I just back you to the hilt. . . . The courage you showed and the judgment in not granting amnesty, it was right. . . . I don't care what they say . . . you did the right thing."[47]

The governor was thrilled. Given the "castration of the guard," Rockefeller stressed, they did indeed need to go in with force.[48] When Rockefeller went on to report that, actually, the prisoners had killed some guards prior to the retaking, Nixon reacted more cautiously. "You can prove that can'tcha?" he said warily, to which Rockefeller gave his assurances.[49] Of course, the governor conceded, it was likely to be "a Catholic hospital" that would be dealing with the hostage deaths, and therefore, "it's outside of our jurisdiction" (implying that he might have had some sway over media reports had the hospital been a publicly run and funded institution), but he was confident that his information would nevertheless be corroborated.[50] The bottom line, Rockefeller confirmed for Nixon, was that the entire rebellion had been masterminded by African Americans. "The whole thing was led by the blacks," he said, and he assured the president that he had sent in the troopers "only when they were in the process of murdering the guards."[51] Rockefeller did warn the president that he was probably going to get some flak from New York City's mayor, John Lindsay (whom Nixon referred to dismissively as "the New Democrat . . . the convert" since Lindsay had recently changed political parties), and that the mayor would "probably say that I should have gone up and all these deaths would have been saved," but Nixon seemed unconcerned.[52] To the idea that Rockefeller should have gone to Attica he said, "No Sir, no Sir."[53] After Nixon reiterated how much everyone in Washington supported his moves at the prison that morning, Rockefeller thanked him profusely, and signed off by saying, "We'll do the mopping up now."[54]

As far as the families of the hostages as well as the prisoners were concerned, the "mopping up" was extremely slow, and didn't seem to take them into account. Although the families of several hostages had been at the prison when they heard helicopters swooping over the yard, they had

Family members of hostages wait outside the prison. *(Courtesy of the* Democrat and Chronicle*)*

had to leave, because, as Richard Fargo's wife, June, explained, "the tear gas was so bad we couldn't stay."[55] Still, they felt certain that as soon as there was word on the fate of their loved ones inside, someone from the Department of Corrections would call them and let them know where to go and what to do next. But in fact there was no system in place for communicating injuries and deaths to family members.[56]

Most of the news the hostage families received on the 13th came via the grapevine and rumor mill. Not surprisingly, much of it was inaccurate. As hostage wife Paula Krotz remembered it, "Early on the morning of the 13th I was at home and heard on the radio that they were going in. . . . I hurried to the prison."[57] When the tear gas was dropped, Paula crawled into "Mike Smith's father's car with a towel over my face, and still the gas was terrible."[58] While she was sitting there, however, she heard someone say that her husband had been taken to St. Jerome's Hospital so she drove off in a frenzy. Once there, though, she could learn nothing. Not locating her husband there left her "feeling so faint that I knelt down on the floor and held my head down."[59] Hours later she did find her husband, Paul, at Genesee Hospital, but by then she was so distraught she could barely believe that the man lying there was really her husband.

Hostage Mike Smith's wife, Sharon, passed an equally nightmarish morning. She had been at the prison when the shooting had commenced and, like June Fargo, had been so overcome by terror and by the effects of the CS gas that a member of the news media brought her into their Winnebago camper trying to calm her by telling her "Don't worry Mrs. Smith, they aren't shooting real bullets, they are using rubber bullets."[60] When the hostages who had survived were finally brought out, she had no idea if Mike was among them or, if he was, where they had taken him. Frantically calling hospital after hospital, she finally got word at 4:00 p.m. that he had been taken to St. Jerome's. When she met with a doctor in the intensive care ward there she was told, "Your husband is in critical condition. We will be lucky if he lives through the night."[61]

Ann D'Arcangelo, the young wife of guard John D'Arcangelo, was equally in the dark about what had happened to her husband. "I was at my apartment," she remembered, when, at about 10:30 that morning, she finally received a call from someone at Attica telling her the wonderful news that her "husband was out on his way to a hospital and to stay off the phone."[62] Elated, she thought, "Oh my god, they saved him," and then waited patiently for someone to call with more information.[63] She received no further news for several hours, and "finally, around two in the afternoon, I started frantically calling every hospital in the phone book from Buffalo to Rochester. . . . The hospitals had never heard of him. Then around four or five in the afternoon I received a call from Superintendent Mancusi. He told me that John was a casualty."[64] The prisoners had killed her husband, the warden told her, and now she was supposed to "go to some church basement to identify John's body." When she arrived, she felt so light-headed and ill that she could barely walk. "The place," she described, "smelled of blood and dirt."[65]

Ann Valone also spent all of Monday morning desperate to know what had happened to her husband, Carl. Finally, to her tremendous relief she received a call from a nun who told her "your husband is in Genesee Memorial ER."[66] Thrilled, she shared the news with their children, and daughter Mary Ann began planning a party at the house—calling all of the family's friends to share the great news.[67] Meanwhile, Ann rushed to the hospital. Once there, however, all was ominously quiet, and no one would tell her anything about where Carl was or how he was doing. "Then Dr. Jenks came out," she recalled. "He said I couldn't see him because he was dead. That was really traumatic for me. I just went to the chapel to pray."[68] She couldn't in that moment bear to think about going home. Her "kids were all at home celebrating," and she just couldn't imagine being the one to have to tell them, "No, he's dead!"[69] Deep down, she also wondered whether she could even believe the doctor. After all, someone had told her he was alive, and now this doctor was saying he was dead. Did he know what her husband looked like? Finally, though, she "got someone who knew him to ID him" and she realized that she now had to go home to break four children's hearts.[70] Break their hearts she did. Mary Ann just kept yelling, "No, no, no!" and, furious with her mother, insisted that she didn't know what she was talking about because on the phone they had told her "that my dad is alive."[71] But when she saw the priest at the door, she understood with a monumental sense of betrayal and despair that her father had indeed been killed.

For the families of the prisoners there was even less information available regarding their loved ones' fate. Hearing nothing at all from prison officials, approximately forty relatives of Attica prisoners from Rochester, "mostly women," converged on the Monroe County Medical Examiner's Office and "gathered in the drizzling rain . . . in a vain effort to get from the autopsy reports . . . the names of the dead and the hospitals to which the injured had been taken." Doris Session, the mother of three children, trying desperately to learn news of her husband, Josh, begged, "If they're in the hospital, why can't we know what hospital so that we can see them? They're people." Ethel Whitaker was frantic to know what might have happened to her brother. She first tried to call the prison and the police department but, she explained, "They hang up on us, they won't even call us." Prisoner relative Ella Greer had a similar account. "The police department cursed my mother-in-law out" when she had tried to get some news the previous night.[72] Families from Buffalo also grouped together to learn some news and, finding out nothing, they began dubbing the city of Attica "Up South."[73]

Feeling pressured, Commissioner Oswald announced that information on the prisoners at Attica would be made available via various state phone numbers.[74] The public was promised three phone numbers and were assured that "the numbers would be manned 24 hours a day." [75] Predictably, all of the lines were so jammed that it was almost impossible to get through.[76] Meanwhile, back in the prison, their loved ones were in a desperate situation—bleeding, terrified, and even being tortured.

## 23

# And the Beat Goes On

While President Nixon in the Oval Office reveled in the bold stand Governor Rockefeller had taken against the blacks trying to foment revolution, those who could actually see the devastation, and how traumatized the prisoners were from it, were sickened. Sergeant Frank Hall, a sheriff from Monroe County, was one of these who saw the retaking's aftermath firsthand. Early on the morning of September 13, Sergeant Hall had personally assisted in loading the canisters of tear gas into the helicopter that had dropped them into the yard and had stuck around in case he could be of assistance as a litter bearer. By mid-morning, however, he felt "numb at the sight of more than a hundred injured men lying on the ground."[1] Disturbingly, Hall could still hear rifle shots coming from within D Block.[2] And then he saw already injured prisoners being beaten so "unmercifully . . . it just brought tears to my eyes. I mean the prison riot was over and . . . they're taking out all of their aggression on these people that were naked. . . . It just really bothered me probably more than seeing some of the dead people because these people were alive [and] being subjected to this kind of abuse."[3]

National Guardsman Franklin Davenport, who had also come to offer assistance as a litter bearer, was equally shocked by the carnage in D Yard. Looking at the empty casings now strewn about the ground of the prison, he felt strongly that the retaking had been, from the beginning, all about killing. Deer slug bullets were not, he knew, "a controlling or a disabling thing."[4]

Another member of law enforcement on the scene was so stunned by the magnitude of the suffering and death in D Yard that he compared the

National Guardsmen carry an unidentified victim on a stretcher.
*(From the Elizabeth Fink Papers)*

scene he was witnessing—the dead bodies on the ground being labeled with toe tags and the screams of wounded men—to "wartime conditions in the Guadalcanal."[5] Even a seasoned captain from the National Guard on the scene struggled to process the bloodbath. He had worked before in a hospital where "mass casualty" was defined as three or four patients injured at once, this was, in his opinion, a full-fledged "disaster."[6]

According to a doctor who had been conducting medical research at Attica since 1960, even Superintendent Mancusi was "quivering" at the sight of so much trauma in D Yard.[7] As the doctor saw it, Mancusi had simply not understood that, when they were sent in to retake his prison, troopers and COs alike were going to "really open up and start killing people."[8] And not grasping this meant that neither Mancusi nor any other state officials for that matter had made any prior arrangements with paramedics, ambulance companies, or physicians from local hospitals to be on hand in the wake of that bloody assault.[9]

When the shooting officially ended, there was but the usual skeleton crew of medical personnel at Attica—the reviled Drs. Sternberg and Williams, as well as "two nurses, an X-ray technician, three orderlies from Batavia hospital, and two veterinarians."[10] Because there was so little medical care on hand, according to National Guard and other medical workers and witnesses, "the wounded were twitching and in convulsions," and eventually going "motionless."[11] Mancusi did not make any calls for additional medical assistance until after 11:00 a.m.—more than an hour after the assault was officially over. And, when he finally let some more doctors in, he was instructed by General John C. Baker, the governor's chief of staff, to make sure that the prisoners weren't going to "get priority" when it came to dispensing medical care.[12] This state official deemed trooper injuries—a "fractured finger, bruised knee," a "fractured toe," and "gas in eyes and inhalation"—a higher priority than the 128 prisoners who had been shot, many multiple times.[13]

Indeed, not taking prisoner injuries seriously meant that when Superintendent Mancusi finally contacted Meyer Memorial Hospital to ask for more doctors, he failed to convey the scope of the tragedy at his prison and thus the size of the medical team that would be needed. Meyer Memorial's Dr. Worthington Schenk cobbled together a tiny team consisting of himself and two medical residents to head to Attica a full hour later. As soon as Schenk saw the extent of the disaster awaiting him, he went to the prison administration building and spent another half an hour making calls to assemble a much larger team consisting of four mobile medical units as well as surgical supplies, blood, plasma, and other needed items. It took another three hours before this still insufficient medical team was in place. By the time the additional medical help arrived, numerous severely wounded men had lain for hours without treatment.[14]

The state of the suffering was hard even for these medical professionals to witness. One physician looked in dismay at the bodies lined up by Attica's fence and couldn't help but liken it to "a Civil War painting."[15] Another, a doctor who had seen combat care in World War II, stared in disbelief because "he had never seen people who were so badly neglected."[16] Members of the National Guard were equally appalled when they came in, reporting that "people had to be put everywhere, on the floors and in the corridors and in "every spare area," and that trying to treat "the most severely wounded first" simply "was not possible in all of the confusion."[17]

Dr. Robert S. Jenks of the hospital in Genesee County wasn't just appalled at the scene he came upon, finding it unconscionable, but he was also furious that no one from the prison had called doctors in until long after the injuries had occurred. Another doctor from a nearby hospital was equally appalled at this delay, and later reported that he had been "waiting in his fully equipped almost empty hospital for all the wounded he had heard there were . . . and wondering 'where are the prisoners?' . . . [And, finally], on his own initiative, he gathered up four other surgeons and set off for Attica."[18] When they arrived, there was nothing to work with. As Jenks described it, not only were "there inmates lying out there for hours without any kind of care," but in the area where he was trying to work, "there wasn't a pint of blood anywhere."[19] This, he felt, was completely "inexcusable; they just didn't ask for it, because I know plenty was available. There are several blood banks around here and they could have gotten all they needed beforehand."[20] Another doctor also reported that "it was chaos when he arrived."[21] "Nobody was directing anybody what to do," he went on, and the prison had none of the medical supplies he needed including vital things such as plasma.[22]

Because of this lack of planning and neglect prisoners with compound fractures received either no care or "nothing beyond primitive bandaging," and even the most severely wounded prisoners had no sedation and "were expected to suffer through the pain."[23] Worse, even after the reinforcements arrived, every doctor on the scene could see that it was going to be impossible to treat all of the men in serious need of care given the state of the tiny prison hospital. Treatment was also hindered by the tear gas still hanging in the air making medical personnel ill. Dr. David Breen, a third-year medical resident, recalled that at first he could only stay inside the facility for "about 60 seconds . . . because the tear gas bothered my eyes."[24]

Clearly the only way to deal with the large number of seriously injured inmates at Attica was to get them transferred out of Attica to local hospitals, but prison officials made that process almost impossible. As later testimony made clear, "Even when finally permitted entry, medical and legal personnel were severely hampered in discharging their professional responsibilities by the obstructionist correction officials . . . the refusal by correction officials, Warden Mancusi in particular, to permit certain injured inmates to be removed to a nearby Buffalo hospital for surgery and emergency medical care [that] doctors maintained they so urgently needed."[25]

By late in the afternoon on the day of the retaking, only two prisoners had been moved to a hospital; by day's end only six.[26] Among those men was Edward Kowalczyk, who'd been shot multiple times. He was transported to Meyer Memorial only because a National Guardsman kept insisting that he needed immediate emergency surgery. And still, as he lay in unimaginable pain in an ambulance, the wounded man noticed that the prison guard who was driving "took his time, no lights, no siren and stopped at stop signs."[27] A National Guardsman who was in the ambulance with them "got into it with him," saying to the guard that the guys "were no longer moving in back," but the guard refused to hit the accelerator any harder.[28]

For the lucky few who made it to a hospital for treatment, their care was compromised because even some of the most grievously wounded of the men were "shackled by one foot to the bed frame" by the correction officer in charge.[29] He maintained that, while he had "received no orders to shackle the prisoners," he "deemed it necessary because some of them were large and strong, and presented an assault and escape risk."[30] One of these alleged flight risks was Jomo, who'd been shot seven times and was barely alive.

Back at Attica, National Guard physician Dr. John W. Cudmore was overwhelmed as he tried to deal with the tremendous numbers of men in critical condition in the prison's tiny and archaic hospital. Because Mancusi was making the transfer of wounded prisoners to outside hospitals so difficult, Dr. Cudmore was forced to do serious trauma surgery under conditions that, at best, resembled a battlefield medic station. On September 13 alone his small crew of doctors on hand at Attica "were forced . . . to perform twenty-five operations, including three abdominal laparotomies," and at times were operating on multiple men simultaneously.[31]

What Cudmore was most upset by, however, was the way in which troopers and correction officers interfered with his attempts to help the injured men who lay in heaps all over D and A Yards. The surgeon saw one man staggering around, blinded by the river of blood running down his face, and as he approached him to try to treat his gushing wound, he "heard a voice from behind me telling me to stop, that he was a ring leader and I was not to treat him."[32]

Troopers and guards were so often getting in the way of medical caregiving that outside doctors found themselves more than once in open conflict with members of law enforcement in the midst of the chaos. In one case a Guardsman was told quite literally "to rub salt in the prisoners' wounds," and in another case a Guardsman who was trying to reassure prisoners that they were going to be all right was contradicted by an officer "shouting out how bad the wounds looked and how it looked as though the prisoners were going to die."[33] When one Guardsman "started to make a list of the wounded so that he could get in touch with their families a

A medic leaves the prison surrounded by press. *(Courtesy of the Associated Press)*

CO came over and told him he couldn't do that and then ripped a couple of names off the list because, the CO said, those two weren't wounded."[34]

Other members of law enforcement still in the prison after the retaking went beyond preventing prisoners from receiving care and were actively meting out additional pain to scores of already wounded men. Dr. Cudmore watched in horror while one young man with severe shotgun wounds was tortured by troopers "poking or kicking at him when he was on the ground."[35] One young doctor who was on the scene with Dr. Cudmore, David Breen, saw one Spanish-speaking prisoner trying to sit up so that he could ask someone to please contact his family and let them know that he was alive. After he tried repeatedly to get someone's attention, the prisoner "was struck on the head with a blunt object by a security guard . . . a very severe blow to the head."[36] Another hurt man "asked for some kind of . . . hospital assistance such as medication. He said I'm shot. You know, help me, please. He was pleading for his life. And the trooper turned around and put his foot on his neck."[37]

Some of the torture was so hideous that it literally nauseated those who happened upon it. One doctor "described a prisoner whom he saw on Monday between 2 and 2:30 pm" who was "cut up badly and raggedly around the rectum and genitals and it was not a gunshot wound but looked like it had been done with glass or a broken bottle."[38]

One equally barbaric incident witnessed by a National Guardsman occurred mid-afternoon on Monday the 13th. James O'Day, a young Guardsman, was on duty when he noticed a group of eight fellow Guardsmen carrying an injured man on a stretcher. The man looked badly hurt so O'Day asked what had happened to him and was told that he had gunshot wounds in his legs and buttocks. Suddenly, as O'Day looked on, a white CO standing nearby said that he didn't believe this man had really been hurt and reached over to tip the stretcher, "dump[ing] the prisoner onto the ground which was slimy and dirty. . . . He told the prisoner to go to his cell or he would stab him with a screwdriver, and before the prisoner had a chance to do anything he stabbed him five or six times in the anal area. The prisoner never stood up but just pushed back with his feet . . . and all this time he was on his back the man was walking between the prisoner's legs threatening him." O'Day desperately wanted to stop what he saw happening but he was terrified of the COs who were standing around nearby. He had the feeling "that if he had done anything his life would have been in danger."[39] O'Day was so disturbed by the incident that he tried to report it to the New York State Police several days after it occurred and, when no one believed him, eventually went to the FBI office in Buffalo. There agents took down his report and noted in writing that he appeared to be "a very level-headed individual and is not a long-haired hippie," which suggested that they saw his account as credible.[40]

And then there was the abuse inmates were suffering at the hands of Attica's own physicians, Selden Williams and Paul Sternberg. According to reports from other medical personnel, one injured man had a large lump in his throat, and when Dr. Sternberg saw the protrusion he "laughed and said, 'ha, ha, you swallowed your teeth,' and this was in fact what had happened."[41] Eyewitnesses on the scene reported hearing one of the prison doctors (either Sternberg or Williams) say about an injured inmate, "That nigger is a fucker and he should have died in the yard so we won't treat him."[42] Another prisoner was in the prison hospital with two gunshot wounds in his back when "two men in white coats, presumably doctors," approached him "and one of them stuck his finger into one of the holes and started wriggling it around. The prisoner was screaming with pain."[43] A National Guardsman reported seeing one prisoner who "had a deep hole in his head that looked like a gunshot wound. As he was being taken to the hospital his head was hanging down so the Guardsman picked it up and found it was in two pieces."[44] Later the same Guardsman checked on this person and found one of the prison doctors "playing with the head, joggling it up and down."[45] Another prisoner begged Dr. Williams for medication for his injuries, and allegedly Williams retorted, "I'm never going to give you no medication. I hope you all die."[46]

That troopers, COs, and Attica's staff physicians were largely unbothered by the barbaric treatment given these seriously wounded prisoners had everything to do with the vicious rumors about prisoner "atrocities" that they had been inundated with for days outside of Attica and now actively spread within its walls.[47] National Guardsman Dan Callahan, for example, saw terrible abuses of prisoners take place when he was sent into Attica right after the retaking, but he had also been told stories that made him cold to their plight—for example, "that [William] Quinn had been sodomized before he was deliberately killed."[48] Trooper Gerard Smith had heard the same sorts of tales of prisoner barbarism, which he could see "got the emotions really rolling. . . . [The COs were] real excited and they were doing some damage to the people."[49] This was also how the prisoner abuses that state legislators witnessed when they toured the facilities were justified. Arthur Eve, Herman Badillo, John Dunne, James Emery, Frank Walkley, Clark Wemple, and others had watched from catwalks as men lying on the ground in the yard were beaten with sticks and could see that certain inmates were being singled out for particularly harsh treatment from the troopers.[50] They had even seen the particular horror of Big Black Smith, totally naked, being tortured on a table below them.[51] None of them rushed to intervene.[52] Like National Guardsman Dan Callahan, who witnessed the torture, they later felt enormous regret that they did not try to help. At the time, however, each of them had "bought the whole argument."[53]

Even at the time, however, National Guardsman Callahan could see that the abuses happening to prisoners following the retaking were fueled by outright racism. Callahan overheard one trooper bragging of shooting a black inmate with a .357 and watched him then give a "White Power salute."[54] He also saw "a prison guard sergeant telling this very tall, yellow-skinned black to strip" and when the man refused, the sergeant "told others to hold him down and then kicked him in the head like a football—he went limp."[55] Another Guardsman overheard one trooper saying to another over by a food stand outside Attica's walls that it was "hot work killing niggers."[56] Racial hostility was in fact so intense that during the legislators' tour that morning, even Assemblyman Arthur Eve was showered with invective. "Guards [were] yelling at Eve—get your nigger ass out of here."[57]

Any white inmate who had stood with the black rebels in D Yard also suffered special abuse. Doctors from the National Guard reported hearing troopers and COs punctuate their beating of white inmates—the "nigger lovers"—with bitter refrains of "This is what you get for hanging around with niggers."[58]

So deep was the guards' and troopers' hatred of Attica's surrendered prisoners, and particularly the black men among them, that for days after the retaking they engaged not only in physical abuse but also in the wanton destruction of these men's most basic and necessary possessions. A trooper forced Jack Florence to pull out his dentures and hand them over, then threw them "on the ground and stepped on it."[59] In addition

Correction officers and New York State Police stand over the crowd of prisoners forced to crawl through the mud in D Yard. *(Courtesy of the Associated Press)*

to smashing the men's false teeth that they needed to eat, troopers and COs mangled eyeglasses and ground them into the dirt, and tore apart every necklace and smashed every wristwatch they happened to find on a prisoner.

What wasn't savagely destroyed was stolen. On the 14th of September men from the National Guard went into the prison armed with metal detectors and Dan Callahan noticed that one of his "sergeants had stolen a bunch of watches—all up and down his arm, he was proud."[60] Another Guardsman cheerily displayed "his own trophy—a set of false teeth with a bullet hole in it."[61]

From the moment that the shooting died down, officers had begun herding inmates violently up the half dozen steps into D Block, across D Tunnel, and then back down into A Yard. As the men were being rushed, pushed, and kicked from D Yard into A Yard, they had begun falling over one another, bodies on top of bodies. For the men on the bottom of this heap, it was almost impossible to breathe.[62] Barely able to get air, these men were then, as Herbert X Blyden remembered the ordeal, stripped naked and forced to "lay in the mud, face down . . . and crawl."[63]

During this entire process they encountered more and more "officers who beat them and tore their clothes off, took away glasses, watches, false teeth, etc., then herded them naked in a long snaking line that wound slowly through [A] yard," into A Tunnel, where a gauntlet of armed officers awaited them.[64]

Once inside the tunnel, with their feet bleeding profusely from the glass fragments that covered the prison's ground, the men were forced to run "for some 50 yards . . . [and] both sides were lined with officers with ax handles, 2 x 4s, baseball bats and rifle butts." When these naked and often severely wounded men stumbled or fell, they had to "crawl the length of the tunnel, while being struck and jabbed repeatedly."[65] One prisoner described the gauntlet this way: "Well, they stripped me and they told me to go and get in line. They had a line in the form of a snake and you had to get in line and they were moving [us] in one at a time. So this way . . . the officers [got the] chance to get their sticks ready. On both sides of the hall they had officers, you know, with sticks, correction officers."[66] John Cudmore and some of the other doctors saw with their own eyes what happened inside A Tunnel: "There were people on either side of the door and as men came to the door they'd aim at their legs or vicinity with clubs and, and hit them to knock them down."[67]

Prisoners are ordered to strip and line up in D Yard after the retaking, September 13. *(Courtesy of Corbis)*

Any prisoner who troopers or COs considered to be a leader was chalked across the back with a large white "X" and singled out for abuse. When these eighty men managed to make it through that first gauntlet, they were forced to run another when they were taken from A Block over to HBZ.[68] At the entrance to HBZ, where the men would all be placed in solitary, "six to eight COs . . . called to each one: 'you want your amnesty? Well come and get it.'" After they made it through that lineup, guards continued to beat them "severely with clubs."[69]

Big Black Smith was of course chalked as a leader and after enduring many hours of torture on the table in A Yard, he too was forced to run these gauntlets before being thrown, eventually, into an HBZ cell. Guardsman Dan Callahan was just inside A Tunnel when Big Black got to that first entrance. "The last inmate in the yard was Frank Smith. There was a sense of anticipation—this guy is going to get special treatment. The guards approached Smith and told him to get to his feet. He had been in that position [on the table] for 4–5 hours so he fell and they hit him repeatedly between the legs and in the anal area [as he was] pleading for mercy." Eventually he managed to crawl through A Tunnel and all Callahan could hear then "was the thrumming of night sticks against his body."

As five officers took turns hitting him, one of them managed to break his wrist while another, as Big Black recalled, "opened my head up and knocked me just about out." Big Black felt each blow. After this, he explained, "They took me to a room next to the hospital, laid me on the floor, spread-eagled me, and played shotgun roulette with me. Then they took me and dumped me on the floor in the [prison] hospital."[70]

As night descended upon Attica, "a skeleton force of troop A personnel assisting correction officers at the facility had managed to rehouse 1,240 of the prisoners who had been in D Yard into 540 cells—most in A Block.[71] The rehousing had been a brutal affair from start to finish. Guardsman Dan Callahan recounted that when some of his men went into a cell block "to help guards get an unruly inmate in the cell," he heard a commotion and then watched in disbelief as an officer dragged the man out of his cell and threw him down, whereupon "his head opened like a melon all over [the] concrete."[72] He also watched as naked, wounded, and terrified men were locked at times three to a cell in A Block. In the best-case scenario, there were "two men sleeping head to foot on a narrow bed, and the third one on the floor, with a blanket and no mattress," but usually all the men lay naked on the cold concrete floor of the cell with no covering or bed.[73]

Some men viewed being locked up even in these conditions with relief—after all, perhaps this meant that the cruelty of the day was over. Perry Ford was one of these. As the sound of gunfire continued to punctuate the night air, Ford now cowered in a cell with two white prisoners hoping that they would now be left alone.[74] But the correction officers who had tossed him into this cell were still seething with anger, having decided that Perry had been involved in the death of Officer Billy Quinn. Within fifteen minutes of locking him up, the officers came back and dragged him out of the cell, shouting, "We going to kill you because you killed Quinn," all the while calling Ford "a black slimy nigger."[75] As he was dragged down the stairs back into the yard he almost slipped and fell on a large puddle of blood with broken teeth in it. One of the officers told him that this was from the last "nigger" they had dealt with.[76] Now trembling from sheer terror, Ford was thrust out into the yard and placed against a wall, where he faced a trooper with a shotgun in hand. The trooper took all but one of the bullets out of his gun, cocked the gun at Ford, and said, "There's a bullet in here and you'll find out when you're hit" and then began pulling the trigger again and again. Each time, Ford "anticipated death."[77]

Russian roulette was a frequent practice of the night guards and troopers; so was telling thirsty, exhausted men cowering on the floor—like Carlos Roche—to "drink the urine of correction officers."[78] Officers spent the entire night of the 13th scraping the bars loudly with the butts of their guns, taunting, physically assaulting, and threatening to kill the men they had just rehoused. And during the following several nights as well, groups of COs visited the cell area and threatened inmates with death, pointing guns and clubs into the cells.[79] Some of the former hostages were taken aback by how relentless the attacks on prisoners were. Once hostage Donny Almeter heard about what had been happening at the prison, he said, shaking his head, "I understood the initial beatings but I never understood going back in a cell three days later and dragging a guy out of his cell to beat him."[80]

Superintendent Mancusi had ordered all the doctors from outside to leave the prison by 11:00 p.m., and the remaining prison doctor announced he was going to bed, so the men in cells were not only terrorized by officers, many of them were still also in serious medical trauma. Perry Ford described two of the men he saw that night: "One was shot 12 times or close to 12 times and he was in the cell. He had a bullet in his neck. There was another inmate with a bullet on his spine. And they were asking for medication, you know, could they get out to the doctor," to no avail.[81] Prisoner Jack Florence, whose dentures had been smashed, experienced this callous lack of treatment firsthand. "I keep begging for a nurse, don't get one," he remembered, shuddering. "Tuesday night, everybody come by, asked them for a nurse or a doctor. Don't get one. Wednesday came, I asked for a nurse, don't get one." Finally Florence saw that a member of the "brass" was coming by his cell so he then begged him to get a doctor up there. This official too "didn't say a word, kept on walking."[82] Even the postoperative patients got no follow-up care—a fact reportedly shrugged off by a physician leaving the prison on the 13th who said, "Well, they're young and strong; I guess they'll be all right."[83]

But there were many medical professionals who were deeply worried about these men, and who would have stayed to treat them or would gladly have entered the prison to treat them if only they were allowed. Waiting outside the prison doors that night was a medical team consisting of "nine doctors and three nurses from New York City, mostly from Lincoln Hospital in the Bronx, [who had] arrived at the prison saying they were answering the call for doctors, "but none were let in."[84] This team represented the National Medical Association, a group of about eight thousand doctors and nurses of color. They had gotten there earlier that day and, desperate to be allowed to render their services, had tried to enlist the aid of all medical personnel they saw at the entrance to the prison.[85] "They came running up to us," one doctor recalled, and asked that he tell Mancusi they were there and ready to help.[86] This physician promised to pass on the message but wasn't optimistic that the superintendent would want them there.[87] And Mancusi didn't. The reason they were barred, according to Dr. Michael Brandriss, was that Lincoln Hospital "was a well-known hotbed of activism, social activism and everything else."[88] One of the group from Lincoln Hospital, Dr. Howard Levy, had "gained fame in 1967 as the military doctor who was court-martialed for refusing to instruct Green Beret troops," but the clear need to have more doctors on hand to help should have made this a minor concern. Even when another group of doctors, residents, and nurses from Buffalo with no political associations showed up at Attica, hoping to be allowed to assist the medical personnel already there from Meyer Memorial Hospital and University of Buffalo Medical School, they too were denied entry.[89] The truth was that prison officials didn't really trust any doctors to see what was happening inside of Attica—particularly after two staff physicians from Meyer Memorial were now telling "the press of guards' brutality."[90]

For Mancusi, this was only the beginning of a years-long effort to prevent word from getting out about the abuses occurring behind Attica's walls throughout the day and into the night of September 13, and for weeks thereafter. But he was surely aware that these terrible violations of human rights were taking place—as were his deputies, Leon Vincent and Karl Pfeil, his boss, Russell Oswald, and various high-ranking State Police officials such George Infante, John Monahan, and Henry Williams. All were at the prison from the morning of the 13th onward, and all could not have helped but see the rampant abuse of prisoners reported by doctors, legislators, and even National Guardsmen.[91]

And yet, to a one, they all claimed that procedures were being adhered to. Indeed, the Department of Corrections described its officers as "dog tired and deeply concerned, dedicated correction officers and staff" who were working tirelessly to issue "clothing, bedding and the essentials of living to the population and housed them three to a cell under as comfortable living conditions as possible."[92] The troopers themselves were less politic about how they felt about the men they were now supposed to rehouse. Directly below a chalked inscription made by the D Yard rebels commemorating the beginning of the uprising on the 9th of September, members of law enforcement made their own inscription: "Retaken 9-13-71. 31 Dead Niggers."[93]

Outside the prison many people were working around the clock to ensure that law enforcement wouldn't be allowed to continue to hurt the men who had just been assaulted in the retaking of Attica. Besides their families and the medical personnel who volunteered, scores of prisoner rights lawyers set out for the prison to insist on proper medical care and immediate legal counsel. As Herman Schwartz put it, "Lawyers started to pour into upstate New York that night."[94] They didn't know much about what was going on yet, but they knew enough to know that Attica's prisoners were now at the mercy of troopers and correction officers who had been hoping to get at them for four long days; they also knew, from the death toll of the hostages and the stories told about how they died, that things were very likely to be ugly inside for anyone with a number.

William Hellerstein, a full-bearded, thirty-five-year-old attorney in charge of the criminal appeals board of the Legal Aid Society in New York City, set out for Buffalo the morning of the 13th with a group of other young attorneys, two of whom he had just hired. As he recalled it, "we didn't know exactly what we could do," but eventually they ended up at Herman Schwartz's house for a planning meeting and then headed to the University of Buffalo to discuss how they would get into Attica to check on the prisoners.[95]

Making that plan was fairly fraught. As Hellerstein remembered, it was a "big get-together. . . . Lots of yelling and screaming," between the lawyers such as himself and Schwartz and the younger, more radical attorneys and law students. At issue was how best to levy pressure on the state in order to protect the men inside.[96] All suspected that abuses were taking place but they didn't have concrete evidence. So what could they really do? Eventually it was decided that their best shot at helping the prisoners would be to get a federal order allowing them to enter the prison on the grounds of ensuring that the prisoners' Miranda rights were being observed.[97] Schwartz, who had long known U.S. district judge John Curtin and had just met with him days earlier to get the ill-fated injunction he had brought into D Yard, called the judge at his home that night. Curtin invited Schwartz, Hellerstein, and Stan Bass from the NAACP over to his house so that he could hear their arguments in person. Listening gravely, he finally decided that he would grant a temporary order granting them "the right to enjoin interrogation, granting us the right to see our clients, and allowing medical care."[98] Curtin personally phoned Mancusi to inform him of the order and to tell him that, if he had any questions, there would be a hearing to review the order in his chambers at 10:30 the following morning, September 14.

Relieved, a large group of the lawyers set out for Attica in the pouring rain. Hellerstein and his team, who were traveling in a rented station wagon and several other cars, found themselves caravanning with the band of doctors from Lincoln Hospital who were just then making their way to the prison by van from New York City. Right before reaching the prison these vehicles filled with lawyers and doctors stopped to gas up, when suddenly they were "surrounded by troopers with shotguns drawn" who demanded to search the doctors' van.[99] Hellerstein knew that it was a crime to interfere with the process of serving a federal court order, so, brandishing the Curtin order, he not only forced the troopers to cease harassing the van-ful of "hippie" doctors, but actually convinced the troopers to escort the caravan of lawyers and doctors to the prison.[100]

At approximately midnight the group arrived at Attica, showed the court order, and expected at that point to be let in to check on the prisoners. Warden Mancusi and Assistant Deputy Superintendent Pfeil, however, refused them entry. The minute that he learned of the court order, Pfeil had conferred with his superiors in the Department of Corrections and he felt confident that the Attica staff would be supported if they refused to follow Curtin's order.[101]

Schwartz and Hellerstein were incredulous. Even though they had with them "some twenty lawyers and twenty doctors, we were told that they would not obey the order, and at 3:30 in the morning that was confirmed."[102] Hellerstein set out to find a phone so that he could call Curtin to tell him that his order was being disregarded. Curtin was, he could tell, "very shaken up" that prison officials were so blatantly refusing to follow a federal court order. But Curtin didn't see that there was anything he could do until the next morning at the hearing he had scheduled.[103] Tired and dispirited, the lawyers marshaled their energies to try to prepare their arguments for later that morning.[104]

PART V

# Reckonings and Reactions

# ROBERT DOUGLASS

*Robert Douglass had spent a long week trying to help Governor Rockefeller resolve the situation at Attica and somehow, even though the uprising was over, the crisis was not. Douglass had worked for the governor as an attorney since 1965. He had an impressive pedigree. Born in Binghamton, New York, he had graduated with distinction from Dartmouth and earned an LL.B. from Cornell Law School. He then took a position with a prestigious law firm before coming on board with the Rockefeller administration. Douglass loved New York and knew its laws inside and out. It was an honor to serve as the governor's eyes and ears at Attica. He felt that Rockefeller's team on the ground had done a good job of trying to broker a peaceful settlement, and, when that had proved impossible, retaking the prison with as little loss of life as possible.*

*Douglass had never been persuaded that the prisoner conditions at Attica were that grave. In his view their grievances largely came down to "the number of showers and the amount of fresh fruit you got, and whether or not they had alternatives to pork in the diet."*[1] *What is more, he didn't think they were a sympathetic group. As far as Douglass was concerned, "These were . . . the most hardened, toughest of New York's criminal inmate population. These guys were there for long sentences, mostly murder, arsons, rapes. These were the worst of the worst." By Sunday it was clear in Douglass's mind that Attica's prisoners really just "wanted a confrontation. . . . The prison yard [was] starting to become barricaded with mattresses. They were fashioning weapons, they soaked mattresses in gasoline, and it looked like they were getting ready for some kind of a battle."*

*Now the battle was over. As Douglass saw it, "the gunfire [had] ended very quickly . . . [and] we got the hostages out." The state's job had been to restore order and so "they went in, they did it, and they restored order."*

*Still, he knew that what mattered was how the next few days would unfold. If the media began feeding on this thing, Douglass thought, then what should be "regarded as a reasonably successful effort to put down a terrible prison riot" might turn "into a bit of a nightmare for the governor."*

# 24

# Speaking Up

On the morning of September 13, as hostages began coming out of the prison, the retaking had initially seemed like a success to the men whom Rockefeller had sent to Attica on his behalf. But within twenty-four hours, it was beginning to seem like a major disaster—one that would require significant public relations maneuvering. When Wyoming County district attorney Louis James, the man who had the most immediate legal jurisdiction over Attica, arrived at the prison late that morning, even he was shaken by what he saw, and immediately made it clear to the men on the governor's staff that this was a far bigger mess than his office was equipped to address.[1] There were simply too many dead bodies, too many people inside who were in awful shape and might still die, and, frankly, too many questions looming about why things had happened as they had. As he said to them, "'Gentleman, the size of this thing, look out the window, you can just visualize the hundreds of possible cases that need to be investigated. I don't have the staff to cope with it.'"[2]

Alarmed, Rockefeller counsel Howard Shapiro hastened to confer with his other trusted legal advisors, Robert Douglass and Michael Whiteman, and it was decided they would ask the deputy attorney general, Robert E. Fischer, to give an early assessment of the legal situation at Attica. He was "to overlook the thing from a law enforcement point of view; that is, a prosecution of any of the criminal events."[3] In turn, Fischer sent his assistant attorney general, Anthony Simonetti, to the prison to suss things out. Simonetti arrived on the scene fairly early on the 13th as the chaos there continued to unfold.[4] It wouldn't be until several days later, on September 17, that Rockefeller made the official announcement that Fischer had

DOCS deputy commissioner Walter Dunbar surveys D Yard after the retaking. *(Courtesy of the* Democrat and Chronicle*)*

assumed direction of the investigation into the rebellion and retaking at Attica, but the governor had made sure to have his keen legal eyes on the ground well before that.[5] In fact, the call to Fischer, and Simonetti's almost immediate presence on the scene, were clear indicators that the governor had very quickly understood that his troopers' actions on the 13th might land him in hot water. That Rockefeller looked to Fischer's office to handle this potentially messy legal situation was significant. Fischer headed up the state's Organized Crime Task Force (OCTF), a unit that was set up to go after thugs and gangs. Rockefeller chose this unit to investigate the Attica uprising because he had from the beginning been convinced that it had been the result of a left-wing revolutionary conspiracy. He hoped that the same laws that Fischer used to prosecute organized crime might be applicable here.

As the Rockefeller administration readied itself for a backlash, and as civil rights lawyers from across the state were working any angle they could think of to get into Attica to see what was happening, the county morgues near the prison were receiving the bodies. The number of corpses lying on the floor of the prison's maintenance building was such that pathologists from three different counties were alerted of the many autopsies needed. Some bodies were in nearby hospitals in Batavia, some went to the office of the Erie County medical examiner in Buffalo, and the remainder—nineteen prisoners and eight hostages—went to Rochester to the Monroe County medical examiner's office of Dr. John Edland and his assistant, Dr. G. Richard Abbott.[6]

When Dr. Edland received the call requesting that his office take the bulk of the Attica victims, he agreed but had to put his office's disaster plan into effect, thus allowing for him to bring in three additional medical examiner physicians to assist with the work.[7] These doctors quickly made their way to the ME's office, only to have to wait until past midnight for the bodies to arrive. Edland and Abbott were speechless as they watched state troopers back two large trucks into the garage bay of their facility, lock the garage door, and proceed to unload stretcher after stretcher onto the cement floor.

By 12:20 Tuesday morning, September 14, the morgue's garage was full—crowded not just with dead bodies but with troopers and other state officials who insisted on remaining in the room. The state troopers, as well as various members of the Monroe County Sheriff's Office, were determined to watch as each body was undressed and autopsied, and State Police photographers were on hand to snap pictures. Members of law

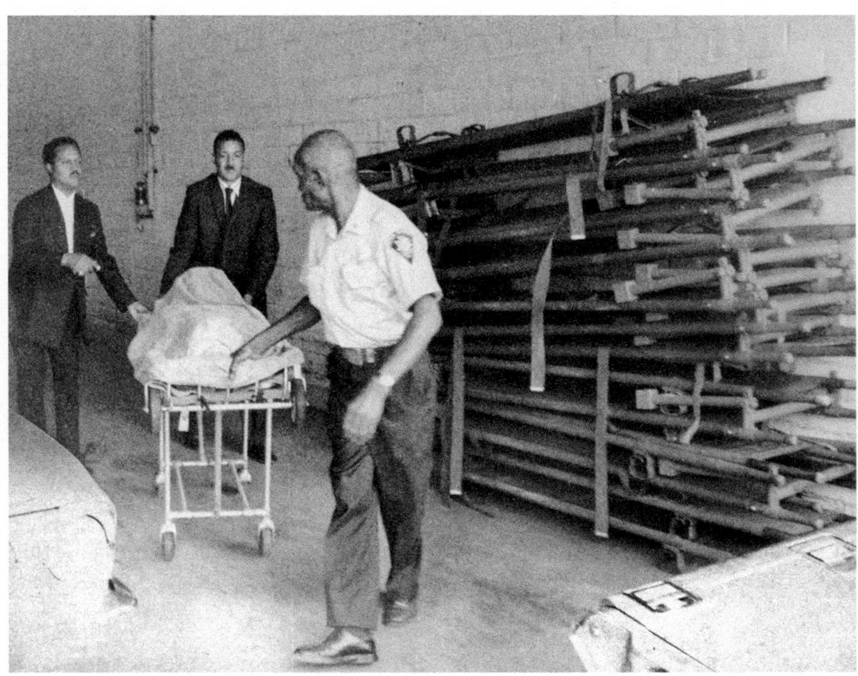

Another body is unloaded at the morgue. *(Courtesy of the* Democrat and Chronicle*)*

enforcement were clearly fearful of what the autopsy process might reveal, and like Rockefeller's men, they wanted to maintain as much control over the aftermath of the retaking as they could.[8] Dr. Edland had been the one to autopsy William Quinn on September 12, and in that case he had had no trouble ruling that the cause of death had been "severe head injuries" due to "alleged assault by prison inmates."[9] These deaths, however, were much more controversial.

But Dr. Edland was a consummate professional who did not think politics and medicine should mix. It wasn't that he had no interest in the world around him; indeed he was a registered Republican and had vacillated between a career in law or medicine—deciding to become a pathologist precisely so that he could have a foot in both arenas. He considered it his job to provide accurate answers about the cause of death to the family members of the deceased—whatever those causes were. How his findings might affect public opinion about the Attica retaking, or the political careers of those in charge, would have no influence on how he did his work.[10] He had been the chief medical examiner of Monroe County for three years and in that time had earned a solid reputation as both a hard worker and a decent man.

Dr. Edland and his assistant, Dr. Abbott, got to work immediately. First, they had to hose down each body because of their "heavy contamination with pepper gas," and then, before starting on any autopsy, the doctors made sure that the medical photographer, Ed Riley, took X-rays of the body.[11] Meanwhile, the fact that state troopers kept milling around and trying to oversee everything was unnerving to the morgue personnel. From the moment Riley turned on the X-ray machine, and they could clearly see the many bullets and buckshot pellets lodged deep in the prisoners' bodies, both Abbott and Edland understood why the troopers were so concerned. By 4:30 a.m. it was patently obvious that "the hostages had all been shot, and that there were no slashed throats or genital mutilations."[12] This, of course, was not at all what state officials had told the media and the doctors were aware of this. With more than forty troopers crowding the hallways, hovering over them and mumbling under their breath, the two pathologists continued to search dutifully for any signs of slashed throats as cause of death. But all that they could find were two knife cuts near hostage throats, and "the wounds [were] . . . on the back of the neck," and "less than a tenth-of-an-inch deep."[13] As both doctors knew, if someone is going to try "to seriously harm or kill somebody with a knife wound to the throat, he's going to do it from the front."[14]

Perhaps even more alarming to the troopers than the fact that none of the men had died from knife wounds was that everyone was well aware that the only people at Attica who had guns on the 13th of September were members of law enforcement.

Even with hostile stares boring into their backs, Edland and Abbott pushed on, trying to learn as much as possible about how each man at Attica had died. It was clear, for example, that hostage John Monteleone had died from a gunshot wound to the chest that had entered his body, then traveled downward until it perforated his "aorta and the left lung."[15] Deeply embedded in Monteleone's chest Dr. Abbott found "a mushroomed lead, partially jacketed bullet bearing numerous rifling grooves," which he identified as coming from a "forty-four caliber."[16] It was equally obvious that prisoner L. D. Barkley had been shot in the back, where there was "a 1 x ½ inch gunshot entrance wound with well-defined contact ring," and that this bullet had caused "extensive destruction of the lower lobe of the right lung." The bullet, "a badly fragmented jacketed bullet of slightly greater than 25 caliber," was lodged in his right fourth rib. Barkley had been shot at close range.[17] Sam Melville, whom police had particularly hated, died when bullet fragments tore up his lung, causing him to bleed to death.[18] Whether this supported later prisoner reports that Melville had been alive after the retaking with his arms up in surrender could not be settled by his autopsy.[19]

As the long hours dragged on, and still finding nothing but gunshot wounds, Edland and Abbott decided to go home to get a bit of sleep before finishing the fifteen autopsies they still had to do. The doctors and their staff had been up for over twenty-four hours, and by 6:30 a.m. they felt "that a break was necessary in order for us to complete our work in the careful objective manner that was required."[20] After what amounted to little more than a catnap, however, within ninety minutes the pair were back at it, and both were growing ever more unsettled. From the moment the bodies had arrived in his facility Edland in particular had felt intimidated by the presence of the troopers, and, once it became clear what the autopsies revealed, he felt that he was being "subjected to pressure" to change his findings.[21] He had also been told to pay special attention to the bodies of two prisoners, Barry Schwartz and Michael Privitera, whom troopers had found in D Block after the retaking and who had died, these same troopers insisted, under suspicious circumstances. Edland immediately knew why he had been instructed to focus on these bodies—these men had clearly been killed before the morning of the retaking—presumably by prisoners. The autopsies revealed not only that Schwartz had been badly beaten up, but his neck had been cut so deeply that it had severed both of his carotid arteries and his neck muscles were fully exposed, and his body had more than thirty-six stab wounds.[22] Michael Privitera's end hadn't been any prettier. His skull had been fractured, his throat slashed, and he had suffered twenty-one deep stab wounds.[23]

Although the troopers might have hoped that all future media attention would focus on these savage killings, not those of the hostages', it was clear to both doctors that the real news story here was how many of its own men the state had killed and how many prisoners had been shot to death when they themselves had no guns. Once the public knew how many men had died from trooper bullets, Edland suspected, all hell was going to break loose.[24] And, he also knew, it wasn't going to be long before this news broke given that newspaper reporters were "besieging" his office "with requests for more information."[25]

With each passing hour, Dr. Wendell Ames, the director of the Monroe County Health Department, grew more worried about the media. Indeed, he specifically asked Dr. Edland not to speak to reporters until something official was set up because, as he said, "We don't want a trial in the press in advance of the investigations that are to be done."[26] As soon as Governor Rockefeller's team heard what Edland was discovering they too panicked. The governor's office immediately sent its own directive that no news be leaked and made clear that Edland's autopsies were going to be reviewed before any news conferences were called.

To the dismay of all parties concerned, however, this news could not be contained. For starters, it was obvious to anyone who had been in the ME's office and had seen the bodies that they were riddled with bullets and buckshot. And as soon as the hostages' autopsies were completed and their bodies were released to funeral homes, countless other people would be able to see their wounds.[27] But what really forced their hand was that Edland's office supervisor leaked the autopsy findings to Dick Cooper, a reporter at a local paper, the *Rochester Times-Union*. Cooper ran back to his car and headed for the city room to file the story. "I knew the information I had was important but the weight of my knowledge did not hit me until I was on the road. If the hostages did not die from slashed throats and did in fact die of bullet and buckshot wounds then they must have been shot by the state police who were sent into Cellblock D to save them."[28] When Dick told his colleagues at the paper, they were stunned. Another *Times-Union* reporter, Lawrence Beaupre, recalled hearing the news. "I gasped. Everyone knew what that meant, since the prisoners reportedly had no firearms at all."[29]

Once Cooper broke the story of the gunshot wounds, suddenly "the shy, unassuming Dr. John Edland was thrust into the nation's spotlight."[30] At 3:00 p.m. Tuesday, September 14, Edland held a national press conference. In it he gave only brief statements regarding his autopsy findings and then he took a few questions.[31] Still, the effect of his words was electrifying. Attica observers like Arthur Eve, while appalled by Edland's revelations, could not have been more grateful for this ME's commitment to the truth. As he put it some months later, "Thank God for an honest medical examiner whose integrity was questioned for weeks by those whose integrity is questionable." With guilt Eve recalled that he too had "repeated those lies [about the throat slashings] that evening in reporting to a large black group in Buffalo. I did not conceive that the Governor would so debase the truth in order to justify his actions."[32]

Within minutes of Edland's press conference, the offices of Governor Rockefeller were bedlam. As Rockefeller attorney Michael Whiteman later put it, news of Edland's findings "staggered us."[33] They had watched in dismay as Dr. Edland stood in front of a bank of reporters and calmly stated, "The first eight autopsies were on the cases identified to us as hostages. All eight cases died of gunshot wounds."[34] He then went on to say that "only one hostage had a 'slight slash' on the back of his neck."[35]

Rockefeller heard the news at his Fifth Avenue apartment in New York, and "was tremendously upset" by what he later described as a "very unfortunate and embarrassing situation."[36] He knew that he had to get to his office right away. He was not yet ready, however, to talk to the press. He managed to elude throngs of reporters waiting outside for his reaction to Edland's report by "slipping through a side door when he left his apartment"; he escaped them once again "by entering a back door" of his office."[37]

But the governor's attempt to spin Edland's revelations had already begun, much of it focused on trying to cast doubt on the doctor's competence and integrity.

# 25

# Stepping Back

Before making any public statement, Governor Rockefeller wanted to find out if Dr. Edland's findings were correct. His main advisor at Attica, Robert Douglass, immediately advised George Infante, one of the top-ranking NYSP officials who had been on the scene during the retaking and its aftermath, to "make an extensive investigation and take notes on wound marks and so forth so that we would have a record to make sure that the coroner's findings were accurate."[1] Rockefeller also dispatched Assistant Attorney General Anthony Simonetti, the man who would be conducting Fischer's official investigation into what had happened at Attica, to meet personally with Edland about his autopsies.[2]

When Edland sat down with Simonetti it was clear to him that state officials were very upset about his findings, and that they were now planning to have someone double-check his work. Sure enough, by 7:30 p.m. on September 14, he was informed that Dr. Henry Siegel of the Westchester County Medical Examiner's Office would go to the various funeral homes where the hostages' bodies had been sent to reexamine them.[3]

Dr. Siegel wasn't the only state official to be visiting those funeral homes. Terrified about what might come out about the retaking, troopers went out to obtain affidavits from directors and employees of these morgues stating "that there were in fact no gunshot wounds" to the hostages.[4] Meanwhile on both the 13th and 14th troopers were themselves "running around to various morticians' parlors and attempting to look at bodies . . . to see whether or not they could discern injuries other than those which were reported to have been recorded by the medical examiner," and attempting to lean on funeral personnel to cover up the fact that gunshot wounds had killed the hostages.[5]

Carl Valone's widow, Ann, later recounted getting a call from the mortician at Gilmartin's Funeral Home who wondered what he should do because, as he told her in a hushed breath, "a bunch of State Troopers wanted to be alone with his body."[6] An employee of the H. E. Turner Funeral Home on Main Street in Batavia received his own visit at home from troopers who wanted him to certify that slain hostage Richard Lewis had "no visible bullet wounds on the body."[7] And when the widow of Edward Cunningham went to see her husband's body at Marley's funeral parlor in downtown Attica, to her surprise she was greeted by Mr. Marley himself. Looking harried and scared, Marley proceeded to take her into the room where her husband's body lay, put a finger to his lips, looked nervously around the area to make sure that none of the many troopers in the building were watching, and then slowly turned the body over so she could see for herself that he had been shot in the head.

The prisoners' bodies, unlike the hostages' bodies, had not been sent to funeral homes, nor would they be for several more days, because Simonetti prevented the medical examiner's office from releasing them. Sometime later that night, or early on the morning of the 15th, Edland was told that, in addition to Westchester County ME Henry Siegel, Dr. Michael Baden (the pathologist who years later would become well known as the chairman of the Forensic Pathology Panel of the House Select Committee on Assassinations that reinvestigated the John F. Kennedy assassination) would also be reviewing each of the autopsies.[8]

Before even getting results from the new autopsies they had ordered, officials from the Department of Corrections began a concerted effort to raise public concern about Edland's political views and, thus, his professional integrity. Gerald Houlihan, the PR director for DOCS, not only made sure that reporters knew that "a top pathologist was being flown up to check the findings of this clown the coroner, Dr. Edland," but others were also spreading the rumor that Edland was "a radical left-winger."[9] It soon became gospel both that there were eyewitnesses who saw the hostages being murdered by having their throats cut and also that "there were various types of arms in the possession of the inmates that could have inflicted bullet-type wounds."[10] Deputy Commissioner of Corrections Wim Van Eekeren, without any hard evidence, suggested in his own statement to the press that the gunshot-like wounds might have come from so-called zip guns made by the prisoners.[11] Then, DOCS announced that five National Guard teams would be going to Attica to sweep the yards for metal weapons that might have been buried by these same prisoners.[12]

The governor's office felt no need to comment publicly on much of anything pending verification of his autopsy results by outside experts. Throughout the afternoon and evening of September 14 the door to Rockefeller press secretary Ronald Maiorana's office remained locked even though at least "25 assembled newsmen waited outside in the adjacent press room."[13] Still, there was one man who would most definitely expect some sort of explanation of these new revelations: President Richard Nixon.

Before Rockefeller managed to reach the president, though, Nixon had already made the strategic decision to support the governor publicly. In fact, John Ehrlichman had already broken the news to him that troopers at Attica were the ones who had killed the hostages, to which Nixon could only gasp, "Oh God."[14] Since he had already decided that this was "a black business," though, Nixon still believed that Rockefeller had done exactly the right thing.[15] As he put it about the governor, "he's got a hellofa lot of guts," and, what is more, he felt that "we have got to be tough on this," because this involved "the Angela Davis crowd . . . the negroes."[16] Ehrlichman agreed. In his view what really drove Rockefeller's decisions at Attica was that "the word is around that this is a signal for the black uprising, that's got him a little worried."[17] In any case, as Nixon pointed out, by standing with the governor on this, Rockefeller "owes us one now; that is just a matter of fact."[18]

And, thus, when Rockefeller spoke to Nixon about the Edland revelations, all was fine. Nixon made it clear that he thought the governor had had to make "a very hard decision," and he gave him his assurances that he would "support him."[19] As the president pointed out to Ehrlichman in the Oval Office, "First, they started it all . . . second, they murdered one, there is no question. Third, they threatened to murder the others. . . . What the hell, it looked pretty good in my opinion."[20] Again Ehrlichman was in full agreement: if nothing else, he noted, the "4-1 kill ratio . . . is gonna give convicts in other prisons a second thought."[21]

Members of the press, however, were now far more critical of Rockefeller's actions. Indeed, from the second the *Times-Union* piece about the results of Dr. Edland's autopsies appeared, reporters from virtually all outlets were furious at having been misled because they too now had to scramble to explain why they had so readily printed outrageous stories of castration and throat slashings without a shred of corroboration. Many sought out Gerald Houlihan, the man who had first told them these tales, and began shouting at him angrily. Houlihan only escaped by promising them that Oswald would soon answer their questions.[22]

At 11:00 the night of Tuesday, September 14, Oswald found himself standing just inside the main gate of Attica talking to a crowd of reporters and conceding that the throat slashing stories were false.[23] But, he reminded reporters, "You know, I never told you this."[24] As for how the hostages might have been shot, the commissioner offered up the possibility that "hostages could very well have been used as shields or forced into the gunfire."[25] And, lest the reporters miss the real point about the dangers the State Police had faced, Oswald went on, "Approximately 400 homemade weapons were recovered in the prison area directly after the action to recover the prison. Today, additional hundreds of weapons were uncovered . . . [and] minesweepers are now being used to uncover other weapons."[26]

In the absence of any satisfactory answer from either the governor's staff or the Department of Correctional Services regarding how they could have given the press such serious misinformation, reporters began their own damage control. Some journalists insisted that they had done the best reporting they could have based on the evidence they were given. As Stephen Isaacs from *The Washington Post* put it, "Perhaps the press can go too far in self-flagellations" because it was the commissioner of corrections himself who, "slowly moving his head from side to side as if in mourning, and pointing to the prison yard below, told me that, yes, a hostage had been castrated 'right down there.' "[27]

Other reporters were willing only to admit that their coverage had been sloppy but maintained that it had not been at all dishonest.[28] There had been, many argued, a number of alleged eyewitness accounts to what they had reported. As the AP news service explained it, for example, its reporters had covered the events at Attica as they had because this was the story they had been told, had heard, and had good reason to believe. Indeed, it was not the case, as some critics of the coverage had suggested, that "the press was too ready to accept as fact the word of the officials."[29] According to the AP, it had "set up a coverage command post in a private home 150 yards from prison walls" and the very first stories reporters filed were not from DOCS but "were based on the sounds of the assault, the choking odor of tear gas that spread over the prison walls, and what some reporters were able to pick up monitoring police radio."[30] The first news of the hostages' deaths had, they maintained, come to them "in the gasping, choking voices of those who had been inside, in fragments of conversations as they stumbled, walked, or were led away."[31] The fact that an official representative from the state, Gerald Houlihan, had appeared at Attica's gate at 11:15 on the morning of the assault and had said categorically that "'several hostages had their throats slashed'" had only confirmed what they had been hearing firsthand.[32]

However, there were reporters who felt guilty about the lies they had perpetuated and sought to grapple in print with the reasons why they had proceeded with their stories when there had been virtually no hard evidence to support them.[33] As two reporters from the *New York Post* acknowledged ruefully, "Everyone—prisoners and prison officials, mediators, the Rockefeller people, the press—tended to believe whatever confirmed their own preconceptions, their own fears."[34]

More state-critical stories might have followed Edland's revelations had it not been for the attempts of editors to manage reporters' stories, if not outright censor them. The two reporters from the *New York Post* who had offered mea culpas were forced to redraft that particular piece countless times because their paper's editor in chief, Dorothy Schiff, felt strongly that each draft was "flagrantly biased in favor of the inmates and certain members of the Observers' Committee."[35] In her opinion, "our staffers reflect the opinion of the radicals and the liberals, who are inclined to confuse these hard-core criminals with rebellious students—the black ones, anyway."[36] In Schiff's view, a better story to write on Attica would be one that explored "why the individual committed whatever crime he was convicted of. . . . How does he feel now about what he did then? Is he defensive, or does he think it was a mistake or is he repentant?"[37]

Reporters were also under pressure from state officials. When *The Washington Post*'s Stephen Isaacs learned that a hostage at Attica had been hit during the retaking with a "dumdum—an expanding bullet considered so maiming that the 1906 Geneva Convention banned them from use in international warfare," he first corroborated the story and then decided to print it, only to receive a call from the press spokesman for Deputy Attorney General Robert Fischer, who denied that the story was true, and then, according to Isaacs, "asked me not to report the story. *The Washington Post,* he said, would be 'acting irresponsibly' to publish such unconfirmed, inflammatory material."[38]

While members of the press were trying to do their job of getting at the truth, so too was Dr. Michael Baden, whom state officials had hired to redo Edland's autopsies. When Dr. Baden first arrived from New York City on Wednesday, September 15, both Commissioner Oswald and Superintendent Mancusi stared at him "in dismay."[39] In vetting possible candidates, Walter Dunbar had demanded that whoever was chosen to do the autopsy reviews be someone who was "politically clean," as this was "not a medical matter . . . it's a political-administrative thing."[40] So Oswald and Mancusi accordingly expected someone older, buttoned-down, "someone more bureaucratic," yet there stood a man who was "thirty-seven, had long hair, and looked like a hippie."[41] Oswald was "certain there had been a mistake."[42] Still, both men tried to make the best of the situation. Oswald made it clear to Baden that Edland must have had some political agenda, "a communist plot of some kind," otherwise, "Why else would Edland lie?"[43] To Baden "the idea that Edland was part of a communist plot did not seem plausible." In fact, Edland was "known among MEs as a right winger," and, more to the point, "He was also very good."[44] But there was no use in arguing; all he could do was get to work.

Before he set out that morning Baden had called Dr. Edland to let him know that he was going to "view the bodies of some of the hostages and then come to [his office] at 5:00 p.m. for a critique."[45] At 9:00 a.m., an hour before his call from Baden, Edland had already met with Westchester County's ME, Dr. Siegel, who had viewed five of the eight hostage bodies the night before. To Edland's relief, but not surprise, Siegel "confirmed the presence of gunshot wounds."[46] Edland fully expected Baden to do the same.[47]

Baden, committed to reviewing all of the autopsy findings in person, proceeded to visit the various funeral homes where the hostages' bodies lay, and also scheduled time at the Monroe County morgue to reexamine bodies and go over previous autopsy findings.[48] The cause of death for all of the hostages was as clear to Baden as it had been to Edland: gunshot wounds.

When Baden's work concluded, days after Edland had first broken the news that all deaths were from gunfire, Deputy Attorney General Fischer called for all of the MEs who had worked on the bodies—Edland, Abbott, Baden, and Siegel—to meet with Anthony Simonetti, along with other members of the Task Force on Organized Crime, and members of the NYSP, back at Attica prison.[49] Nervously Edland and Abbott got into the car sent for them and soon found themselves, again, explaining the results of the autopsies they had conducted. Over six grueling hours the doctors answered questions regarding their findings; but no matter how the questions were posed, and how much the NYSP officials wished differently, the answers remained the same. "It was the consensus of the pathologists present that they agreed on the causes of death and that such a statement should be released."[50]

Still, the state officials present at Attica were unwilling to accept these conclusions, and ended the meeting with plans to hold another meeting on the subject on Thursday, September 23. Acting independently, Dr. Baden and Dr. Siegel went ahead and published their findings in their press releases, now a full week after the assault on Attica had ended. The doctors not only stood by Edland's original finding but, most disturbingly for state officials, Dr. Baden had stated that, in his opinion, six hostages had been shot in such a way that looked "like an execution."[51] This, he explained, was because a trooper had "discharged buckshot at a prisoner" and the spray of pellets had hit these hostages in their heads.[52] However, he also offered state officials one bit of good news. Under considerable pressure from state and police officials to consider scenarios other than deliberate homicide for how prisoners such as L. D. Barkley had come to be killed, Baden had reexamined Barkley's autopsy report and concluded that "the bullet had gone in sideways. It was a tumbling bullet [which] had hit something else first, which meant it hadn't been meant for Barkley originally."[53] This finding was crucial because it suggested that, contrary to the firsthand accounts of prisoners and state politician Arthur Eve's own firsthand report that Barkley had been alive a full hour after the retaking, he had not been deliberately killed by a state trooper after the incident was over but rather during the initial retaking. For many decades to come Baden's autopsy would stand as the definitive answer to the question of L. D. Barkley's death, seeming to exonerate the New York State Police of any wrongdoing.[54]

Edland felt a huge sense of relief that Baden's overall findings about the many deaths at Attica matched his own.[55] He had endured so many threatening phone calls, so many chilling sightings of trooper cruisers idling outside his home, and so much hate mail that he needed Baden's support. One handwritten, unsigned letter sent to him on September 14 had said, "May your throat be slashed and violence come upon you and your family."[56] As unnerved as Edland was, though, he never had any intention of backing down, because "you have to call them as you see them." Still, he considered the day he went public with his findings on the Attica victims "the worst day of my life."[57] Sadly, the threats and character assassinations would continue to plague Edland for many years to come.

Once Baden publicly confirmed that all deaths at Attica on the 13th had been caused by law enforcement, state officials had no choice but to acknowledge these facts. But, ever on the offensive, in the news conference held jointly by Deputy Attorney General Robert Fischer and Major John Monahan of the New York State Police, the state chose, as one later critic put it, "not to apologize for, or . . . correct the false press release about the stabbing and castration, but [instead] to show pictures of all the weapons found in D yard—clubs, knives, screwdrivers and hammers."[58] As for the large number of wounded and dead, none of whom had in fact died from any of these "weapons," the state explained simply that many of the men had been shot either accidentally in the crossfire or from ricocheting bullets.[59]

Now Rockefeller was ready to speak with the press too—only his second meeting with reporters since the retaking. The governor also promoted the "crossfire" explanation for the retaking-related deaths at Attica. And he returned to his central argument that he had had no choice but to order that the prison be retaken by force.[60] This time, though, he went much further, suggesting that there had been consensus among all parties, including the observers committee, that the retaking was necessary. Incredibly he said: "The decision to use force had not been made until after Tom Wicker of the *New York Times,* along with other committee members, had 'agreed no other move could be made.'"[61] Regarding his decision not to come to Attica, he maintained that it would have been irresponsible for him to meet with dangerous criminals, and it would have been bad public policy to set such a precedent. Rockefeller's statement followed the playbook set out for him by his speechwriter: he was to focus on "the philosophy of the actions taken: Initial reasonableness, willingness to meet legitimate complaints, the rejection of concessions that would tear apart the social order, the judgments to act before deterioration progressed further, the rejection of social change through violence, coercion, blackmail, etc."[62]

Those who had served as observers at Attica were stunned by Rockefeller's rewriting of such recent history. As Herman Badillo told anyone who would listen, "it was made absolutely clear to Rocky's staff that they were not asking the Governor to come in physical contact with the prisoners. . . . The idea was to have the committee act as a shuttle between the prisoners and the Governor and possibly have the Governor address the inmates over the public address system."[63]

Even members of the press were taken aback that, given recent reports regarding what had caused such carnage at Attica, Rockefeller was still claiming that he had done everything possible to avoid this ugliness and, perhaps worse, was now claiming that the deaths at Attica—due to "crossfire"—were "morally," if not legally, justified homicide.[64] *New York Post* columnist James A. Wechsler simply couldn't believe that the governor would make no concession to the fact that there had indeed been alternatives to a retaking with guns.[65] As he put it, the Tombs riots the previous year "were halted without a shot being fired, without a single fatality among hostages, prisoners or guards—and without general amnesty."[66] New York City mayor John Lindsay, who had faced not one but several major jail protests in his city the previous year, also criticized the governor's handling of Attica. Lindsay reminded the press that "he had met with rebellious prisoners [and] . . . he had finally quelled the insurrections at the Manhattan and Queens houses of detention with unarmed correction officers rather than armed policemen."[67] To drive home the point, Lindsay added, "Not a single firearm was permitted when correction officers went in."[68]

Still, many people sided with the state, including family members of the slain hostages. Juanita Werner, who lost two family members in the retaking, continued to insist that "the State Police did not kill all of those hostages" even after Edland's findings were confirmed.[69] As John D'Arcangelo's widow remembered, "My entire family believed that somehow, no matter what we were told, the inmates must have gotten guns. . . . Because it defies logic that anyone would be killed by their own employer."[70] Dead hostage Elmer Hardie's brother Jim said that he "could accept that some, but not all, of the eight were killed by police bullets."[71] Cindy Elmore, the daughter of an Attica CO, Lieutenant Elmore, agreed. "Townspeople do not believe troopers killed the hostages 'because it's just not true.' "[72] When guard John Monteleone's brother heard the news that officer bullets had killed John, he simply said, "Bull." He too worked at Attica but had decided to quit his job because he felt that there had been too much coddling of the prisoners from day one of the riot. As he put it, "I don't want to work there so long as this state is run by the Oswalds, the Dunbars and the niggers."[73] In fact, as one reporter noted after canvassing the various local towns near Attica, "Few people can be found on the rustic roads who accept the Medical Examiner's report that the hostages who died during the state assault on the prison were killed by gunshots," even though the governor himself had just conceded that those shots "had probably come from the weapons of state policemen."[74]

Whatever the rest of America may have thought, there was one group of people that was outraged by both the actions and the inaction of the state: family members of the prisoners at Attica. At the same time that Dr. Edland was being attacked for his autopsy findings on the hostages, many of the children, parents, and partners of the prisoners still had no idea whether their loved ones were alive or dead, injured or well. The state had yet to communicate with them in person, or even to release a list of the casualties. Their indignities and trauma would continue.

# 26

# Funerals and Fallout

In the days and weeks that followed the retaking of Attica prison, the volume of calls from "the worried relatives of Attica prisoners who [had] heard no word on whether their loved ones survived" continued to jam the switchboards at the prison and at DOCS in Albany.[1] Even Dr. John Edland initially hadn't any idea who most of the prisoners were on the slabs in his morgue. Recognizing that these were people with families who would want to know the fate of their loved ones, though, Edland had fingerprinted each of the bodies "for identification to be made on that basis."[2]

Edland was one of the few state employees who felt that these men needed to be treated humanely in death. When a DOCS official finally released "a full list of inmate casualties with their backgrounds" to the media outside Attica on September 16, indicating the crime each slain man had been convicted of after reading his name, according to reporters, "Prison guards threw up clenched fists . . . [and shouted] 'White Power.' "[3]

Still no one from the state of New York ever contacted the families of the dead prisoners by phone or personal letter to tell them the fate of their loved one. Most had to hear this terrible news over the radio and only then because Howard Coles, a popular African American radio personality from Rochester, had decided to dedicate his popular broadcast to providing his listeners with whatever information the DOCS released about the dead as soon as it was made available.[4] This was how Laverne Barkley finally found out what had happened to her son. For days she had been trying to reach someone at the prison for word of L.D., and when she got nowhere with state officials, she decided to drive across town to the headquarters of FIGHT—the social justice organization run by minister Franklin Florence, one of the observers—to see if she could get him to help her. But before she ever got to the office, while she was still circling the street looking for a parking space, she heard her son's name being read over the radio.[5] Her young daughter Traycee, who was sitting next to her in the passenger seat, watched in great distress as her mother almost lost control of the car, pulled over, and collapsed in grief.[6] Now that L.D. was dead, Mrs. Barkley berated herself for never having taken his complaints about his treatment at the prison seriously enough. Just before the uprising L.D. had said to her: "You can't imagine what it is like here. . . . I know that there is a possibility that I shall never leave here alive."[7]

Other parents had their own burdens of guilt. The grief-stricken parents of Lorenzo McNeil felt that they were in some way responsible for the death of their twenty-nine-year-old son because they had actually "persuaded him to give up his parole and return to prison for the last 18 months of his sentence" so that he would be guaranteed to keep away from trouble on the outside and be able to start fresh when his time was over.[8] Talking to reporters as she sat in her home in Queens, his mother recounted how he had "tried to keep a job, but every time they would find out he was a convict they would fire him. . . . We were afraid he would go out and steal some money again and it was better to send him back again than to let him do that. . . . We thought we were doing the best thing at the time."[9] Elizabeth Durham, the mother of twenty-year-old slain prisoner Allen Durham, was also grieving deeply, and also feeling that her son might still be alive if she had acted differently. Allen had just written to tell her that "he was taking up a trade in tailoring and did not want to be transferred from Attica until he finished," and she hadn't tried to talk him out of that decision.[10]

And then there were the families that didn't get the news via the newspaper or radio, but received notification via telegrams that eventually came from the prison. As one such notification read: "REGRET TO INFORM YOU THAT YOUR HUSBAND RAYMOND RIVERA NUMBER 29533 HAS DECEASED. THE BODY REPOSES AT THIS INSTITUTION."[11] As late as September 18, some inmate families had still received no notification.[12]

Even having official confirmation of a son's, brother's, or husband's death at Attica did not necessarily mean closure for many family members because it remained unclear where their loved one's body was or when the state was going to release him for burial. Arranging for funerals was thus most difficult. It wasn't until the afternoon of September 17 that Vincent Mancusi sent Dr. Edland a telegram finally authorizing him "to release all bodies in your establishment to the authorized undertakers," and then it took still more days before the bodies arrived at the places where they would be prepared for interment.[13]

Plans were made to send the bodies of Samuel Melville and Barry Schwartz to Parsky Funeral Home, L. D. Barkley's remains were to go to Latimer Funeral Home in Rochester, and other prisoner bodies to other places such as N. J. Miller's funeral parlor and Hauner Funeral Home. However, for seventeen dead prisoners still at the morgue there was no clear idea where they might go to be buried.[14] The Fortune Society had advised Mancusi that it would gladly "bury any inmates not claimed by family or anyone. Please advise," but the superintendent was not at all eager to talk about the logistics of prisoner funerals with this organization or any other.[15]

Once L. D. Barkley's mother learned of her son's whereabouts, she began planning his funeral, which turned into a community-wide memorial and celebration of his life. The event took place on September 20, and it brought the area around Rochester's AME Memorial Zion Church to a standstill.

The old red-brick church in the midst of an urban renewal project in Rochester's black community was crowded by a "throng of more than 1,000" overflowing into the surrounding streets, which were jammed with residents who had come to pay their respects to L.D.[16] Canon St. Julian Simpkins from St. Simon's Episcopal Church presided over the service, the congregation sang spirituals, including "Oh Freedom," and three powerful eulogies lauded L.D. as "a martyr to end man's inhumanity to man."[17] The congregation was reminded that L.D. had been in Attica only for a parole violation, and that the original "crime" for which he had been on parole consisted of forging a money order for $124.50.[18] Many local luminaries, including one of the Attica observers, minister Raymond Scott, president of Rochester's FIGHT, gave passionate speeches about Attica and L.D.'s struggle for human rights in that prison. At the conclusion of the service a hearse at the head of a long motorcade took L. D. Barkley's body to Mount Hope Cemetery for burial.[19]

Four days later the streets of Brooklyn, New York, were teeming with thousands of people who hoped to pay their respects to other prisoners killed at Attica.[20] Before the funeral began at the Cornerstone Baptist

Mourners raise the Black Power salute at L. D. Barkley's funeral. *(Courtesy of the Associated Press)*

Hearses bearing the bodies of six Attica inmates process through Brooklyn, September 25. *(Courtesy of* The New York Times*)*

Church, a sea of people surrounded the coffins of the six men as they were carried through the streets of Bedford-Stuyvesant.[21] Inside the church, the walls vibrated with the thunder of impassioned speeches. People were gripped with anguish and fury as the service proceeded. But outrage trumped all other emotions when the church officiants announced to the assembled crowd of mourners that the burials could not take place as planned. They had just been ordered to send three of the bodies back to the medical examiner's office in Rochester "because of a dispute over their identity."[22] At noon the bodies of three men were removed from the church as the crowds looked on from the packed sidewalks, wondering if the indignities would ever cease.[23]

Other prisoner funerals took place with far smaller crowds and much less fanfare. For some of the prisoners who'd been killed at Attica, there was no ceremony. Like the Fortune Society, other community groups in New York City felt they had to do something about this, and a number of groups came together for a series of meetings at Westminster Presbyterian, the church of Rev. C. Herbert Oliver. Reverend Oliver was a Brooklyn activist, known among African American and Latino parents in this neighborhood as a supporter and former chairman of the Ocean Hill–Brownsville Experimental School District. Oliver wanted to find a way to bury the unclaimed dead of Attica. As he explained, "the men who laid down their lives at Attica did a great service to me, you, the city, the state and the world." Oliver and another Ocean Hill–Brownsville activist, Sonny Carson, helped jump-start fundraising for those burials.[24]

Soon additional organizations and individuals began raising money to help those prisoner families who wanted to bury their loved ones but had no money to do so. The Urban League of New York and singer Aretha Franklin held a big fundraiser at the Apollo Theater in Harlem on behalf of victim families.[25] Student groups at various schools around the country also collected donations. Students from Cornell University managed to "collect $700 for families of deceased riot victims."[26] To the surprise of several prisoner families, the Gannett Newspaper group in Rochester included them when collecting funds for victims' families in its Lend-a-Hand program. Out of a total of $21,000 that was contributed for the families of those slain at Attica, however, the fund gave only $1,964 to three prisoner families and the rest went to the families of hostages.[27]

The families who had lost a guard or civilian employee at Attica were just as grateful as the families of the inmates for the financial help they received, and in many cases they were just as needy. Many of the wives and children of the prison employees who had been killed in Attica had been plummeted into poverty by the loss of the sole breadwinner in the family. Edward Cunningham, one of the guard hostages, was survived by his wife and eight children. Funds came to the families from a variety of sources, including other COs who contributed to the "Attica Family Memorial Fund." The families of William Quinn and nine of the slain hostages—Elon Werner, Ronald Werner, Elmer Hardie, Edward Cunningham, Herbert Jones, John Monteleone, Richard Lewis, Carl Valone, and John D'Arcangelo—were so grateful that on September 29 they took out a full-page ad in the local paper to thank "all who offered us aid and assistance."[28] "As people said to us," they wrote, "'We have no words to express our grief.' We now say to you, 'We have no words to express our gratitude.'"[29]

The first funeral to be held for a prison employee victim of the uprising was William Quinn's on September 15 at St. Vincent's in the village of Attica. Afterward, as his family sobbed and the community grieved alongside them at the gravesite, many also expressed their anger that Russell Oswald was nowhere to be seen at this commemoration of Quinn's life and his service to the state of New York. When asked why he had not attended the funeral, Commissioner Oswald said, rather sheepishly, that

An honor guard of four hundred men marches through downtown Attica for William Quinn's funeral. *(Courtesy of the LIFE Picture Collection/Getty Images)*

it was because he thought "there might have been resentments."[30] The following day John Monteleone was buried, leaving five children behind.

Just as with some of the prisoners' funerals, some of the funerals for the slain guards were delayed because of ongoing controversies about the cause of their deaths. The funeral of Richard Lewis was delayed when his body was sent back for a second autopsy, this time by Michael Baden.[31] And even though the funeral of John D'Arcangelo was held as planned on September 16, in Auburn at St. Mary's Church, his body was then returned to the Farrell Funeral Home to be examined by Dr. Siegel.[32] In some cases these delays meant that no family members were able to be present when the burials finally took place.[33]

September 17 was the day of the largest number of funerals for the slain hostages, when five men were buried: Elmer Hardie, Herbert Jones, Ronald Werner, Elon Werner, and Edward Cunningham. "From early morning until late afternoon . . . there was scarcely a moment without a funeral, a cortege or a graveside ceremony in progress," wrote a local reporter, and these commemorations "brought prison guards and police men from Maryland, Rhode Island, Pennsylvania, and around New York State to stand silently in ranks, saluting the coffins as they passed from funeral home to hearse, from hearse to church, from church to cemetery."[34] Those who drove down Route 98 to attend the funerals would have seen a road lined with "flags at half-mast in solemn tribute to the sacrifices made by the employees of the Attica Correctional Facility."[35] Local stores were closed to honor the killed hostages, and many posted "small signs printed in black ink, saying: 'In respect, closing Friday, Sept. 17.' "[36]

The day of mourning ended in the late afternoon at the gravesite of Herbert Jones, who had left behind a twenty-month-old daughter.[37] All of the funerals that day had been extremely emotional, but people were particularly struck by the senselessness of the death of Elon Werner—a humble man who had not been a guard but a senior accountant at Attica, and "was regarded by many . . . as a nonpareil, a man of gentle demeanor, quick to help others."[38] No one could make sense of his having died a violent death. Emotions had also run high the day before at the funeral of Carl Valone, where the clergyman who presided over the graveside ceremony at St. Joseph's cemetery delivered a fiery speech in which he "warned that major prison upheavals would recur in New York State prisons unless a separate institution was opened for inmates he described as 'hard core revolutionaries.' "[39]

The very last hostage funeral was not held until October when correc-

Carl Valone's funeral *(Courtesy of the* Democrat and Chronicle*)*

tion officer Harrison Whalen, after clinging to life for more than three weeks, finally died of his gunshot wounds. Whalen's passing increased to ten the number of guards and civilian employee hostages who had been killed because of the state's assault on the prison.[40]

Yet in all the weeks that had passed since the Attica uprising, and even after so many men had been laid to rest, no one from the state had ever come to explain to the families what had happened.

Ann Valone was so desperate to understand the circumstances of her husband's death that in October 1971 she made the quite extraordinary decision to write a heartfelt letter to former observer William Kunstler—whom most of Attica's townspeople reviled as a radical troublemaker—asking him, as someone who had been on the inside and seen so much firsthand, if he could help her to know what had gone so terribly wrong.[41] To her surprise Kunstler responded with his own emotional letter, trying, he said, to address "the very perplexing questions you raise," and to do his best to let her know how he felt "about the tragic events of last September."[42] Kunstler wanted Ann Valone to know that he, and all of those who had served "on the so-called negotiating committee wanted desperately to settle the controversy without further bloodshed. As varied as we were, we became convinced on Sunday that, had the Governor come and had we been given a few more days, we could have hammered out an agreement satisfactory to all sides. In fact, the only reason I insisted that Bobby Seale come was to aid us in convincing the inmates that proposals that were accepted by the commissioner on Saturday, as watered down as they were, were the best we could hope to get for them."[43]

Kunstler closed his letter by asking for her aid in calling for greater prison reform in America because, then, "not only will men like your husband be far safer than they are now, but they will surely find their jobs infinitely more rewarding and creative than they can possibly be under present conditions. Instead of supervising resentful, desperate inmates, they will be associating with men and women who at least feel that they possess some shreds of human dignity and who can see some hope for themselves in the future."[44] Whatever she decided, though, William Kunstler wanted Ann Valone to know that he grieved for her and he believed, in his heart, that together they could "do something, no matter how small or insignificant, to change places like Attica so that the pain you are now enduring, which must be duplicated in more than forty other homes, will never press down on any other human being," and so that "no person will ever have to write again a letter such as you have written to me."[45] He signed off, "In sorrow and hope."[46]

Nearly two months after Attica's retaking, Commissioner Oswald summoned "about 50 employees and wives at a meeting in a Presbyterian church, without anyone in the community notifying the press" to discuss what might lie ahead of them now that they were without a regular breadwinner.[47] Overall Oswald's message was a relief, albeit a bit strange. As June Fargo remembered it, the good news was that "Commissioner Oswald told the men not to worry, to take six months off" because it was implied that they would be taken care of.[48] Even better, each of the widows and the surviving hostages had already been given some checks, meager but most welcome, to help them get by. And yet, more ominously, they were clearly instructed in this meeting "not to talk about what had happened."[49] Although the CO families largely heeded this message, others in the nation were not so compliant. Many parties were determined not only to keep attention focused on Attica, but also to probe what was happening to the prisoners inside in the wake of the retaking.

## 27

# Prodding and Probing

Attorneys Herman Schwartz and William Hellerstein, who had obtained the temporary order from Judge Curtin late in the evening on September 13, remained determined to enter the prison to represent the prisoners and make sure they were safe. When Superintendent Mancusi violated that temporary order, refusing them entry into the prison, they feared the worst. The problem was, the lawyers weren't sure how to get Curtin to force the issue. As Schwartz put it, the lawyers were in "a true 'Catch-22' situation, since we couldn't show the need [to get in] if we couldn't get in and if we couldn't show the need [to get in], we wouldn't be able to get in."[1]

This is exactly what Attica's administrators were hoping for when they headed into the hearing that Judge Curtin had ordered for September 14, the day after the retaking. In the hearing, DOC Deputy Commissioner Walter Dunbar managed to persuade Curtin they were doing what was necessary to attend to the needs of the prisoners. No one was interrogating prisoners, he maintained, so there would be no need for their lawyers to come in. Curtain was sufficiently convinced.

The prisoners' attorneys, however, were undeterred, for they were convinced that abuses were still occurring at Attica and adamant that they be let in to ensure that the abuses were stopped. On Wednesday the 15th, they finally obtained some concrete evidence of abuse that they hoped would reengage Curtin. A National Guardsman named James Wilson came forward to provide excruciating and gruesome details that confirmed fears about how prisoners were being treated.[2] He had witnessed physical assaults and medical neglect of prisoners' wounds and injuries, as well as a violent, highly charged atmosphere in which guards hurled racial insults and obscenities at the prisoners.[3] And so Schwartz and Hellerstein got another meeting with Curtin the very next day to present this new evidence. The judge, however, was still unwilling to issue an order to admit them.[4] What he did suggest, however, was that it might be possible for them to get in under the auspices of the so-called Goldman Panel, an observational body created by Governor Rockefeller just the day before.

On the 15th, under great pressure to answer questions from many quarters about how the prisoners were being treated post-retaking, the governor had asked Presiding Judge Harry D. Goldman of the Appellate Division, Fourth Judicial Department, "to name a distinguished panel of impartial visitors to observe and report on this transitional period at the Attica State Correctional Facility so that the public may be assured that the constitutional rights of the inmates are being protected."[5] The panel included, among others, former Attica observer Clarence Jones; Dr. Austin H. MacCormick, executive director of the prisoner-friendly Osborne Association; and Luis Nuñez, national executive director, Aspira of America (an educational and leadership organization for the Puerto Rican community).[6]

Judge Curtin's instinct proved correct. Much to their surprise, the lawyers Schwartz and Hellerstein received a call later that same day telling them they would, in fact, be let in.[7] So, along with the just-appointed Goldman panelists, on Friday, September 17, a team of prisoner rights attorneys entered Attica. The Goldman panelists were told they'd be allowed in the prison twelve hours a day, seven days a week, "visiting cells, the hospital, halls, mess hall, and even HBZ block," yet somehow they then got restricted. On their first visit they were told they must leave by 5:00 p.m. and, thereafter, their hours of access were restricted to "between 9 a.m. and 3:30 p.m. Saturday and Sunday and from 9:00 a.m. to 5 p.m. weekdays beginning next Monday."[8] Given that they had to interview many hundreds of men, and also were allotted only four rooms in the prison for this purpose, these time limitations were frustrating. "At this rate," Schwartz noted dourly, "it would take us weeks upon weeks upon weeks to interview them."[9]

The restricted schedule was Mancusi's way of making sure that he could still limit the impact that prisoner rights lawyers might have. He had argued strenuously against admitting the Goldman panelists too, but Oswald made it clear he had no choice but to cooperate with them fully. The good news for the state was that the panelists and the prisoners' lawyers would be getting all of their "logistical and liaison information" from two people as interested in protecting the state as Oswald was—Rockefeller's lawyers, Michael Whiteman and Howard Shapiro. Even better, from the state's perspective, Whiteman had made it clear to the Goldman Panel that its job was time-limited—approximately thirty days—and that the "Panel was not an Investigative group"; rather, it was just there to monitor what was happening inside the prison.[10]

As soon as Goldman Panel cochairs Clarence Jones and Austin MacCormick began walking around Attica and also, eventually, visiting Attica prisoners now housed at Great Meadows on the 24th, Clinton on the 25th, and Green Haven on the 27th, it became clear that even the simple task of monitoring would be arduous. At least eighty-three of the inmates they encountered had been so severely injured that they "required surgical treatment, and some were wounded so badly, so hurt that they had to be interviewed at Meyer Memorial hospital."[11] Many men at Attica had not seen any medical personnel since the afternoon of the retaking—more than a week earlier—at which time doctors, including National Guardsmen and others, had insisted that their serious injuries not go untreated thereafter.

It wasn't until the morning of September 21 that a new team of doctors actually began conducting medical examinations in the prison. Trying to make the clearly scared prisoners feel more comfortable, the Goldman Panel had "requested that there be at least three black doctors and two Spanish speaking doctors on the Panel to carry out the examinations."[12] Eventually a group of nine doctors was assembled to examine 1,220 prisoners and to make an inventory of their medical needs, all in a mere four hours on the 21st. But even with such a cursory look at these men, it was clear to these physicians that they were still in terrible shape, that they were suffering ongoing abuse from the guards, and that conditions in the prison were still unacceptable. As one of the doctors, Lionel Sifontes, reported, prisoners were still suffering from numerous gunshot wounds as well as first- and second-degree burns from the tear gas they'd been covered with in the first minutes of the assault.[13] As noticeably, "most of the prisoners were observed to have multiple body bruises and this was true of all floors of Cell Block A."[14] Dr. Sifontes minced no words about these bruises when he spoke to federal officials a month later; they were "fresh, less than 48 hours old and received since Monday, September 13, 1971. The bruises were apparently inflicted by a long blunt instrument."[15] As important, the Goldman Panel–appointed doctors noted, prisoners were terrified of identifying who had been hitting them. "One prisoner with bruises to back and cheek and a head dressing told the doctor that 'he had fallen down the stairs.' "[16]

Despite reports from the physicians it had called to Attica, Goldman Panel members were more willing to call attention to the abuses that had already happened at Attica than ones still occurring. In its final report, for example, the panel noted that "of the inmates who had been a part of the uprising, 63% had suffered a reprisal immediately following the assault, from a mild injury, such as abrasions, to a severe injury, such as fractured ribs or a lacerated scalp, to lost glasses or dentures," but it said next to nothing about what physicians like Dr. Sifontes had witnessed.[17]

And when the Goldman Panel held its first press conference after canvassing prisoner injuries, they reported that their doctors had found no bruises or wounds inflicted since the 13th.[18] As one Goldman Panel monitor put it: "From our observations at Attica we are convinced that inmates are treated decently, with fairness, and without brutality by Correction Officers. Their physical needs are adequately met. Food is good, Cells are clean, medical attention is provided. Inmates appear to be washed, shaven and cleanly dressed."[19]

Such a conclusion struck many who knew anything about the retaking at Attica as dangerously dishonest. Various former Attica observers committee members including Herman Badillo, "demanded the resignation of the Goldman Committee," and said that it should be disbanded because, among other things, "it has been unable to . . . guarantee [the prisoners'] physical safety."[20] The composition of the panel had in fact bothered prisoner advocates from its inception since so many of the monitors, even if officially seen as prisoner advocates, were also close friends with Rockefeller. The potential conflicts of interest at work here were perhaps even worse than they suspected. Panel cochair Austin MacCormick had written a personal letter to Rockefeller indicating support for the actions he had taken at Attica on September 13. "I was disturbed and indignant over the unjust and unwarranted criticism you received for not going to Attica," he said. "If you would have gone to Attica," he continued, "you would inevitably [have] found yourself cheek by jowl with Mr. Kunstler and Bobby Seale, and some others little better than they."[21] The governor, MacCormick went on, was right to retake the prison as he did since the observers committee had "made rational negotiation well-nigh impossible" at Attica.[22]

And yet, even though some Goldman panelists were sympathetic to

Rockefeller, and the panel as a whole had been unwilling to mention the continuing and persistent abuses that their own doctors indicated were taking place, this monitoring body did insist that serious work needed to be done at Attica on behalf of the men locked up there. They called, for example, for a more permanent monitoring system to be set up in the prison and staffed by people unaffiliated with the prison, and, "in view of allegations by inmates of post-riot beatings," they called for improvements in prisoner rights, including prisoners' greater access to legal counsel.[23]

Some improvements were eventually made at Attica thanks to the panel's recommendations. By the panel's last visit on November 15, the prison had two dentists, two nurses, and two part-time psychiatrists on staff for two days a week. But while this was a welcome development, prisoners also needed help "securing replacement of [their] legal papers, necessary for appeals, parole applications, etc. which had been deliberately destroyed by the guards," as well as much more attention paid to their safety at the hands of these same guards.[24] As important, and as even the panel had to acknowledge publicly, the "danger of harassment of inmates" still loomed at Attica, as did "the likelihood of unjust retaliatory and inflammatory acts in parole and other areas."[25]

# 28

# Which Side Are You On?

While members of the Goldman Panel were insufficiently critical of state officials' treatment of prisoners at Attica, others across the country were much more outspoken in their outrage—taking to the pen and to the streets. Songwriters like John Lennon, for example, wrote powerful ballads to commemorate the prisoners at Attica, while activist James Foreman penned a poem to

> Attica, Attica, Attica. Black men, brown men, white men—shot down at Attica by the command of Nelson Rockefeller and supported by the Nixon administration. Black women, brown women, white women, families, friends, lovers, wives, millions of people mourning the loss of those slaughtered at Attica, killed on American soil by weapons developed in the Vietnam War.[1]

Prisoner rights activist Angela Davis also authored an opinion piece, in her case for *The New York Times,* arguing strongly that the men at Attica needed support—particularly since "in the aftermath, officials would resort to equivocation, untruths and myriad efforts to shift the blame onto the prisoners."[2]

In the wake of the Attica retaking, myriad rallies in support of the prisoners also took place across upstate New York: outside Elmira prison, at the African Studies and Research Center on the Cornell University campus, and also Cornell's Rockefeller Hall, where they demanded, among other things, that the building be renamed "Attica Hall."[3] Other demonstrations took place in Albany, the state capital and also the location of the Depart-

An Attica protest in Albany, 1971 *(Courtesy of the* Democrat and Chronicle*)*

ment of Correctional Services offices, which were in buildings known as the twin towers. The largest of the Albany protests involved "about 500 demonstrators [who] marched for three miles through this city . . . to the steps of the Capitol."[4] This group, described as "mostly young and white," joined at least three hundred others who had already congregated at the capitol.[5] "Run Rocky, run Rocky, run, run, run—People of the world are picking up the gun," they chanted, while carrying pictures of the governor with the words "Wanted for murder, the butcher of Attica."[6]

Such public protests made New York's commissioner of corrections, Russell Oswald, extremely nervous. He already felt he was "under tremendous pressure"[7] after the retaking, in no small part because there had been "at least 15 bomb threats at the twin towers that resulted in evacuation" since September 17.[8] According to the commissioner, "his wife was getting threatening calls" as well.[9] What is more, Oswald reported to Rockefeller, he felt personally harassed. "There seems to be a relatively well-organized group called the Prisoners Solidarity Committee," he explained, "which has decided to 'bird dog' all of my appearances" and, at one such appearance, "they tried to take over the luncheon meeting, grabbed the microphone, kept chanting 'murderer' and carried huge banners insulting you and me."[10]

Many months after the retaking, protests against Rockefeller were still going strong, including some particularly high-profile events in Manhattan. At a gala hosted by the Cerebral Palsy Foundation of New York City in December, where the governor was to receive a humanitarian award, more than a thousand people showed up to picket.[11] People from all walks of life came out against the governor's actions at Attica, including artists who paraded outside the Museum of Modern Art while demanding Rockefeller's resignation from the museum's board of trustees.[12]

Attica-related protests also exploded in other American cities right after the retaking. In Los Angeles at least 150 people crowded into downtown on a sticky 90-degree day in September to show solidarity with the Attica prisoners and to call for prison reform nationwide."[13] Over seventy-five African American students at the University of Oklahoma in Norman blocked a one-way street for several hours chanting and carrying signs, one which read "30 Brothers dead, and things go on as usual."[14] According to the National Student Association, the country's largest organization of college students, by October 1971 Attica "teach-ins on prisons and prison reforms" had been planned at "more than 20 college campuses."[15]

To be sure, not all of the protests were critical of the state of New York's actions at Attica. There were also rallies in support of Governor Rockefeller such as one held on Wall Street by a conservative student organization, Viva—Voices in Vital America—little more than a week after the retaking of Attica.[16] Members of law enforcement, correction officers, and townspeople in upstate New York were all grateful to see this support of the governor since they feared that the anti-Rockefeller types would soon be protesting against them. Some Attica residents had decided to arm themselves in case this happened and New York state troopers near the town were regularly "on the lookout for troublemakers."[17] They patrolled the highways into the big cities nearby as well, looking for anyone they thought might be a prisoner supporter. As entries in the NYSP's official call log read: "2:50 pm: Trooper had stopped two car loads of Blacks who claim they were en route to 'Panther Headquarters' in Buffalo," and then, two hours later, "4:26 pm: 4 Blacks were stopped on Thruway by patrol and advised they were en route to Panther Headquarters in Buffalo."[18] Troopers even kept tabs on former Attica observers Herman Schwartz and William Kunstler.[19] And every time there was word of some protest, troopers were alerted and they worked with city and town officials to monitor the gatherings if not prevent them from happening altogether. When rumors began circulating about a massive demonstration "by outsiders planned for Oct 2" and "approaching black invasions" in Attica, the village's five-man board of trustees called an emergency meeting to decide how to respond.[20] Among other things, they discussed arresting anyone parading without a permit as well as adding a curfew.[21]

Officials from the Department of Correctional Services were also worried about new protests erupting within their penal facilities, and at Attica itself.[22] "The situation at Attica continues to be tense," Commissioner Oswald wrote to Rockefeller in December of 1971, and worse, he went on, "the tension at Attica is seemingly an epidemic having spread to other facilities causing severe problems in overtime payment [to COs]."[23] Officials were particularly concerned about what might happen at Clinton prison, where many Attica prisoners recently had been transferred and which was already known to be a hotbed of discontent. Even before the rebellion at Attica, Herman Schwartz had observed that "Clinton looks very serious. It may blow up, although there are so many State Troopers there at the moment, probably that won't happen for a while."[24] In the wake of Attica's retaking the danger at Clinton had only grown, according to Oswald. Three months after Attica's end he was worrying about the fallout at Clinton, noting in a memo to Rockefeller that a recent cell search of this prison had "uncovered large numbers of hidden and buried weapons."[25]

Most of the prison protests in the wake of the Attica rebellion and in support of those wounded and dead took place in states other than New York. On September 15, about sixty men at the Fulton County Jail in Atlanta, Georgia, initiated a lunchtime protest, having "got the idea from the riot in New York."[26] Prisoner protests also erupted on that day at the Cuyahoga County Jail in Cleveland and in Baltimore's City Jail, where 180 inmates tried to take a hostage and "barricaded themselves in the Baltimore Jail cafeteria . . . in an apparent show of sympathy for inmates at Attica."[27] That same day in Detroit, Michigan, a phalanx of 1,140 guards at the Wayne County Jail seized 150 weapons after FBI tip-offs that there was a planned rebellion.[28] At Massachusetts Correctional Institution–Norfolk, 783 men began a four-day strike for prison reform that soon spread to a facility in Walpole.[29] Female prisoners also erupted in solidarity with the men at Attica. Sixty-six women at the Federal Reformatory for Women in Alderson, West Virginia, launched a four-day rebellion, which they described as having started out as "a memorial service for the dead inmates at Attica."[30]

In October 1971 there was an uprising at the Illinois State Penitentiary in Pontiac, a rebellion in a county courthouse jail in Dallas, Texas, a hostage-taking protest in a maximum security prison in Rahway, New Jersey, a hunger strike by 330 inmates at the Maine State Prison, and over the next months many other upheavals in jails and prisons throughout the country. The year 1971 ended with a dramatic ten-hour rebellion on December 28, launched by men in the New York City Jail system who were "demanding changes to detention rules."[31] This protest ended peacefully after city officials agreed "to automatic bail review after 30 days detention and [to] set a limit of 90 days for detention."[32] News of what had happened at Attica reverberated through prisons as far away as Europe. In Paris prisoners took hostages in their own Attica-inspired rebellion.[33]

COs were so terrified of prisoner rebellions after Attica that their unions again began to speak out loudly about the issue of workplace safety. The leadership of the main union for all state correctional employees in NY, AFSCME and its Council 82, believed that it had been DOCS policies that had led to the situation at Attica in the first place. As AFSCME president Jerry Wurf put it, "We believe that it is the obligation and the duty of government—in this case the state of New York—to provide secure and humane penal facilities," and yet, "the state prisons are mostly crowded, decaying relics of penal theories discarded long ago."[34] Indeed, he went further, the uprising there "happened only after reasonable requests from the inmates were ignored by the state administration. It happened after unheeded warnings by members of our union who work at Attica, who could see and hear evidence of impending trouble."[35]

Union officials were insistent that they meet with the governor about what Attica meant for them. They currently were "in negotiations with the state on several broad demands for changes in the prison system formulated by members of Council 82," and in their view the uprising at Attica only strengthened their arguments for "New York to bring about immediate and widespread change in the state's ill-administered prison system."[36] Five of the ten hostages killed at Attica had been members of AFSCME and, as far as their union was concerned, "the most tragic thing about the bloody riot and massacre . . . is that it could have been avoided. If the state had listened to warnings from correctional officers, if administrators had shown a modicum of sensitivity in providing for the inmates—if the state had just listened, the revolt might never have occurred."[37] So bad were tensions between the union and the DOCS following the Attica retaking that Oswald felt compelled to report to the governor, "The negotiations so far have served more as confrontations and have not resulted in any purposeful outcome to date."[38]

State officials failed to deliver a satisfactory response to the union's complaints about safety issues and, on September 22, "the union representing New York State's 8,000 prisoner workers, reacting to the Attica Prison revolt, said today that they would lock all convicts in their cells Oct. 7 unless Gov. Nelson A. Rockefeller implements immediate reforms." The union president pointed out, "We've been discussing these demands for 18 months with the administration and had nothing but lip service. . . . I guess it takes 40 men who did not need to die."[39]

After Attica, prison employees' wives also began to speak out about the need to take workplace safety seriously. These women had formed a statewide organization that planned on lobbying legislators to address their husbands' safety needs and to inform the public just how dangerous a job these men did.[40] Commissioner Oswald was particularly disturbed by this group's activities because he did not feel that they represented him at all favorably. The "information they pass along to various news media and legislators after these meetings," he told the governor, "does not reflect what I have considered to be a good relationship."[41]

The few African American correction officers working in the state system were also concerned about the problems at Attica, but they saw them from a different vantage point. A number of them became vocal that "the causes and lessons of the Attica uprising have been grossly misunderstood by white officers and policymakers."[42] In short, they felt that the DOCS was "moving in the wrong direction" in its desire to clamp down harder on inmates when it was such treatment that led to Attica in the first place.[43] They also expressed concern about the treatment that black guards received from their white co-workers. As one black CO observed nervously, since Attica, "he can feel a question hanging in the air when he is among white officers: 'Whose side are you on . . . our side or the inmates' side?' "[44]

The reality for the prisoners who had survived the assault on Attica prison on September 13 was that few from the Department of Correctional Services, or from the state more generally, were on their side. While it appeared from its announcement of Robert Fischer's appointment that the governor's office was organizing to go after those who had initiated the rebellion at Attica, it was doing virtually nothing to protect the men who survived it—the many still badly wounded from being abused—or to supply them with the medical care they desperately needed.[45] And a full month after state officials had regained full control of Attica, none of the men huddled in their cells had been allowed to contact their family members.

And so, the men at Attica tried their best to smuggle out word of their condition to their loved ones. As soon as some modicum of calm had returned to the prison, they began to circulate a tattered red spiral-bound notebook from cell to cell. In it, men wrote down the names and addresses of their loved ones and penned a brief message to them, in the hope that someone, somehow, would be able to get this notebook out of Attica and to any one of these addresses.[46] One prisoner, identified only as "James," wrote down the address of his sister, Ethel Walker, and next to it he scrawled, "Sis, I am alright as of now and I hope that things work out for the best." Charles Halley wrote to his mother, Lenora Halley, "We are OK." A note to Gladys Harris said, "Okay and in good health now. Call wife, etc."[47] The book was filled with similar missives reassuring family members that the prisoners were alive and in decent health. Even though several of these men were in fact still injured and suffered beatings on a regular basis, they didn't want their families to worry more than they already had.

But none of these notes reached their intended recipients. In one of the

Personal items, furniture, and other debris lined the cell blocks after the retaking. *(Courtesy of Corbis)*

many abrupt, violent sweeps of the prison that took place in the days after the rebellion, state troopers confiscated the notebook. As the members of the Goldman Panel observed the moment they got into Attica, raids such as this meant that the prisoners routinely suffered "the loss of personal property which it has taken months and years to earn, collect or create."[48] The troopers and guards who had been placed in charge of the prison in the hours, days, and weeks after the retaking seemed to take particular satisfaction in ruining prisoner property. As one National Guardsman noted in disgust, COs and troopers had fun tossing prisoner belongings in the air and smashing them for sport, "like you used to toss a ball in the air and hit it when you were a kid."[49]

A particularly egregious problem that continued at Attica, as noted by the Goldman Panel, was that state officials were not acting quickly enough to replace the prisoner eyeglasses and dentures that had been smashed by correction officers and troopers. As the panel had pointed out, these were needed for "eating and seeing" and, therefore, "involve fundamental human rights."[50] By Vincent Mancusi's own count at least seventy-eight prisoners were in need of new dentures "in connection with the problem of . . . dental prosthetics that were lost or destroyed during the riot."[51] Mancusi ultimately was forced to call upon the University of Buffalo School of Dentistry to replace the many dental appliances and dentures that had been destroyed as a "result of the September incident."[52] He was also pressured by the Goldman Panel to contact several optometrists to deal with "the backlog of requests for glasses."[53]

Beyond damaging prisoner belongings, troopers and COs had also worked hard to destroy anything in the prisoners' cells that they worried might be used against them. Particular attention was paid to the legal papers that had painstakingly been gathered by the prisoners over the years. These papers, literally thousands of pages of writs of habeas corpus, appeals, and legal briefs that the men in Attica had written out by hand, often in triplicate, were confiscated, thrown haphazardly into boxes, and hauled off to a Quonset hut at the barracks of NYSP Troop A.

At the end of September 1971 a portion of the more than two thousand prisoners still at Attica were allowed to receive visits from family members. Unsurprisingly, what the "more than 200 visitors [who] streamed through Attica prison's iron gates to spend an hour with inmate relatives" heard on that first visit was deeply upsetting. Dorothy Trimmer, for example, "emerged weeping" over her son Wayne's account of having been "savagely beaten about the genitals and elsewhere and . . . forced to walk over

Prisoners' families at Attica on the first day they were allowed to visit after the retaking *(Courtesy of the* Democrat and Chronicle*)*

broken glass."[54] When pushed to account for such stories, Walter Dunbar maintained that "correction officers in some instances firmly prodded inmates who were lagging as they were moving back to cells. To the best of my knowledge, no inmate received any physical force from Correction officers other than prodding."[55] He circulated this party line among the COs themselves in one of the prison's internal "Fact Sheet from Attica" publications.

In the first days after the retaking of Attica, a great many of the prisoners were transferred to other prisons, but none of their families were told that such a move was taking place. According to memos written between officials at Attica and other penal institutions around the state, on September 17, 1971, "A draft of 70 inmates is scheduled to leave Attica . . . for transfer to Green Haven [and] similar transfers were made on Tuesday and Thursday for Clinton and Great Meadow."[56] By Friday the 17th, 217 of Attica's inmates had been transferred out of that prison and another 150 were scheduled to go to Green Haven after that. Ultimately, by September, the last day of the transfers, 780 men had been moved out of Attica to other prisons around upstate New York.[57]

But even the men who had been transferred to other prisons were not exempt from continued harassment. Though none of the prisoners who had been moved were leaders of the rebellion, they were treated as radical agitators by those who ran their new facilities. Administrators at Great Meadow had to acknowledge that "some men have bullet wounds, burns, abrasions," but when these men asked for medical care, these same prison officials insisted that the men were troublemakers and that their injuries were "nothing too serious."[58]

The men who had been sent to Great Meadow were so upset that their injuries were being ignored and that they were being mistreated by guards that eighty-two of them launched a hunger strike within weeks of their arrival.[59]

Guard and trooper treatment of the Attica men who had been transferred to Clinton apparently was even worse than it had been for the men moved to Great Meadow. On October 29 the Legal Aid Society of Albany filed a $1.5 million class action suit against "Rockefeller, Oswald, and numerous Clinton guards and administrators" and sought a restraining order from Chief Judge James T. Foley of the Northern District Court against various abuses.[60] According to the suit, the men at Clinton were "frequently beaten, gratuitously tear-gassed and threatened, harassed and subjected to racial slurs as a matter of routine."[61]

By October, with lawsuits like this one, and with numerous citizens and even several congressmen calling for a closer look at what had gone so wrong at Attica more than six weeks after the retaking, it was clear that this controversy wasn't going to go away. Top officials in the Rockefeller administration recognized that it was time to get stories straight regarding exactly what had happened there.

# 29

# Ducks in a Row

Governor Rockefeller could see that the nation's attention on Attica was simply not dissipating and he was determined not to appear the villain in this story. To his core, he believed that rebellions such as the one he recently had put down at Attica were ominous warnings that the American way of life itself was under attack. As he first articulated it to one of his speechwriters, "Today there is a relatively new political problem, centering on the well-organized national effort of revolutionaries, within and without the prisoners, to wreck the penal system as one more step toward the ultimate destruction of this country."[1] In another draft he put his views even more pointedly: "I declared last Monday that 'the tragedy (at Attica) was brought on by the highly-organized, revolutionary tactics of militants. . . . Unfolding events since then have given me no cause whatsoever to alter that estimate; to the contrary."[2]

This was the view from the top, as well. President Nixon made it clear that he too saw Attica as part of a broader threat of black revolutionary foment, and so did members of his administration.[3] Vice President Spiro Agnew penned a piece in *The New York Times* entitled "The 'Root Causes' of Attica," which not only suggested that this rebellion had been caused by extremists bent on violence but that to imagine that the lives of felons were "of equal dignity with legitimate aspirations of law abiding citizens" was "absurd."[4] Attorney General John Mitchell had long held the view that radical groups were but breeding grounds for "violence-prone militants who seek only to destroy" and who have "no constructive objective; their sole aim is to disrupt. Their leaders brag about being revolutionaries and anarchists."[5]

That the nation's most powerful politicians viewed Attica as part and parcel of a revolutionary plot to destabilize the nation as a whole would have profound consequences for how officials, both state and federal, handled the official investigation into what happened there. When Rockefeller appointed Robert Fischer, head of the Organized Crime Task Force, to lead the state inquiry into the rebellion as well as the retaking, he was without question hoping to shape the scope of the investigation. In his words, he wanted the investigation "to determine the role that outside forces would appear to have played—including the role of certain individuals in persuading prisoners to hold out for completely unattainable political demands."[6] Basing the investigation in the Organized Crime Task Force unit would ensure a great deal of funding for it—as well as experience dealing with criminal conspiracies, in which he felt sure that Attica radicals had engaged.

Still, Rockefeller was no idiot. He was aware that in the blink of an eye Attica could become all about state wrongdoing. There were so many dead bodies following the retaking he had ordered, so much ugliness during the rehousing, and so many accusations of prisoners being executed as well as beaten. Therefore, it was vital that he and his staff have a chance to debrief those who'd been on the ground at Attica before any investigations (not only Fischer's, but any of the others that would surely be undertaken) got under way.

To make sure he was on top of all relevant information related to both the uprising and the retaking, the governor called a meeting for the morning of September 24 at his Pocantico Hills mansion.[7] As his attorney Michael Whiteman recalled, "The purpose was to get people to sharpen their recollections," especially because they were "likely to be questioned."[8] By 10:00 a.m. that day a large group had assembled around a table in the pool house of the estate. Those present at the meeting included the governor, his personal secretary, Ann Whitman, Robert Douglass, attorney Michael Whiteman and his assistants Harry Albright and Eliot Vestner, Howard Shapiro, Norman Hurd, General Buzz O'Hara, General John C. Baker, press secretary Ronald Maiorana, speechwriter Hugh Morrow, Russell Oswald, Walter Dunbar, Anthony Simonetti, and Major John Monahan.[9] According to Rockefeller, William Kirwan, the head of the New York State Police, who had been absent during the Attica uprising and retaking, was also there, as was Chief Inspector J. C. Miller of the NYSP.[10] Detailed notes were taken, later read into a tape recorder, and then formally typed up.[11]

Three more of these "debriefing" meetings were held at the Rockefeller estate, described by Russell Oswald as "three long weekend meetings," all of which were, according to Oswald, secret, and were intended, according to Robert Douglass, to nail down "our own executive chamber chronology."[12] In each of these meetings, one on October 25 from 9:30 a.m. to 2:00 p.m., another on October 30 from 9:00 a.m. to 2:00 p.m., and the final one for many hours on November 8, Rockefeller and his staff met not only with members of Fischer's office, but also with high-ranking officials from the New York State Police.[13] The very last meeting, however, was perhaps the most comprehensive and most problematic since it included both Major John Monahan and Captain Henry Williams of the NYSP—the two who had carried out the retaking that had killed thirty-nine men and wounded eighty-nine others and, therefore, whose men presumably face charges filed by Fischer's OTCF investigation into Attica—usually referred to as the "Attica investigation." These potential indictees were now at the home of the governor of New York working with the head of the Attica investigation to get a formal narrative of what had happened at Attica secured. Also there to help do this were other members of the State Police who had firsthand knowledge of exactly what had gone down in D Yard on the 13th. These included one trooper who had taken a series of 35mm slides from the roof of C Block during the assault, and another from the Office of the Counsel to the Governor who was there "to view a video tape, film and photographs and ask questions related to the role of the state police at Attica."[14]

This meeting, like all the others, was attended by Harry Albright and Eliot Vestner, whose job it was to record what was discussed and write it up in a report.[15] In the following decades state officials would repeatedly deny the existence of the so-called "Albright-Vestner Report," but it had served its intended purpose. Over the coming years, the retaking of Attica would come under extraordinary scrutiny, and the state officials who had spent so many hours in the fall of 1971 in that pool house corroborating their stories would be very glad they had.

PART VI

# Inquiries and Diversions

# ANTHONY SIMONETTI

*Tony Simonetti worked for Robert Fischer in the Organized Crime Task Force's Rochester office. He had come to the OCTF after first getting his BA at St. John's University and then his law degree from Fordham. He was admitted to the bar in 1964, was a former U.S. Marine, had been an FBI agent, and had even spent time in the South the previous decade looking into civil rights violations in that region. Simonetti had come to Robert Fischer's attention, though, as someone who worked for famed Manhattan DA Frank Hogan. Tony Simonetti had been a bit of loner in Hogan's office, but he had nevertheless earned the respect of staff lawyers and investigators alike. He got the job done. Not only did he investigate his cases carefully and methodically, but he was also extremely sharp in the courtroom. Everyone could see that Simonetti relished getting witnesses on the stand and then, with little fanfare and a penchant for simple but devastatingly direct questions, getting them to say exactly what he needed them to say.*

*When Tony Simonetti got the call from Robert Fischer to come to the Attica Correctional Facility on September 13, 1971, he had no idea how much his life was about to change. It soon became clear that most of the responsibility for investigating what had happened at Attica was going to fall on his shoulders. Even Simonetti's investigative and prosecutorial skills would be challenged. He would have power as "Attica Special Prosecutor Anthony G. Simonetti," but it would be hard to do his job without stepping on a lot of toes. The very man who was employing him, the governor of New York, had ordered the retaking of the prison that he was now supposed to look at carefully and critically. And, as awkwardly, New York state troopers who had retaken the prison were now collecting the "evidence" from Attica's yards that he would soon have to rely upon to make cases.*

# 30

# Digging More Deeply

Rockefeller's office worked hard to control all investigations into what had happened at Attica. Choosing Robert Fischer to head up the official inquiry—the OCTF's Attica investigation—was but one way. Devoting several meetings to creating a unified state version of what had taken place was another. Still, by mid-fall of 1971 there were many individuals, groups, and organizations calling for very different, and far more independent, probes into why the retaking of Attica had been so deadly. Those investigations would be much harder to direct.[1] Among those calling for an Attica inquiry were thirteen African American members of the House of Representatives, the New York Urban League, the National Legal Aid, the Defender Association, and the Buffalo Council of Churches. Additionally, "a group of 300 students at Harvard Law School signed a petition to President Nixon asking for assignment of a Federal Commission to investigate the country's penal system" more generally.[2] The Prison Reform and Justice Committee of Rochester's FIGHT organization also began calling for a statewide coalition to pressure for prison reform, and the committee's chairwoman was none other than Betty Barkley, L. D. Barkley's sister.[3]

So unhappy was Governor Rockefeller with these inquiries that he attempted to meet with legislative leaders in Albany "in an effort to consolidate the many investigations of the rebellion that have been called for."[4] This he was unable to do, and, worryingly, word had it that Attica's observers committee, the group that had been constituted during the uprising, had started meeting again in order to pressure legislators to order a totally independent investigation of the retaking.

The observers committee had in fact reconvened on Sunday, September 26, at the behest of Arthur Eve, who felt strongly that they should collect and preserve all the documents, papers, tapes, and records they had accumulated over the course of the five days they'd spent at Attica. His idea was that they could deliver a full and accurate report regarding how the rebellion had progressed—including the committee's many efforts to warn the Rockefeller administration how disastrous a forcible retaking would be—to any serious investigative body.[5] They even did some fundraising, collecting money for both "the families of the deceased inmates and hostages." In short, the reconstituted observers committee had "pledged not to let down either the inmates or the hostages who died at Attica."[6]

By May of 1972, however, and as other more formal investigations had gotten under way, only a few of the observers seemed interested in meeting anymore.[7] Some, such as Tom Wicker, had decided to keep Attica alive in a different way—in Wicker's case through his columns in *The New York Times*. Others had parted company with the committee because they now disagreed with its views. State Senator John Dunne, for instance, felt that the current committee consisted of men who took a one-sided pro-prisoner stance.[8]

Dunne did, however, join another committee—also created by Rockefeller—the Select Committee on Correctional Institutions and Programs. The governor tasked this group, known by all as the "Jones Committee" since it was chaired by Hugh Jones, president of the State Bar Association and former chair of the Board of Social Welfare, with looking into prison conditions at the Attica Correctional Facility and in New York more generally.[9] John Dunne was still the chairman of the state's Standing Committee on Crime and Correction, which prior to the Attica uprising had been calling attention to New York's prison overcrowding and other problems. He was eager to serve here, as were the dozen or so additional committee members, including state assemblymen, state senators, religious leaders, and officials from various state agencies. Governor Rockefeller's longtime friend Peter Preiser was appointed "Special Consultant to coordinate the work of the Select Committee" because, as Russell Oswald put it, "he knows most of you."[10]

Beginning in early October, the Jones Committee visited numerous correctional institutions across the state where they "explored . . . the experiences, feelings, and judgments of inmates, administrative staff, correction officers and other institutional personnel."[11] When the committee visited Attica, its members were horrified by accounts they heard from "at least 17–20 inmates . . . about excessive and continuing brutality," and detailed descriptions of episodes of "gauntlets and beatings."[12]

After what they had seen and heard at Attica and other prisons, the Jones Committee pulled no punches in the first report it submitted to the governor on January 24, 1972.[13] As it noted, "The committee is profoundly troubled by its impression of the present institutional system after making its initial assessment. There is substantial doubt as to whether the existing system offers any real hope of accomplishing the stated objectives."[14] At the very least, it went on, the Department of Correctional Services needed to invest in far "more training, more education, less profiteering, less warehousing, more attention to civil rights abuses, less censorship, greater mental health resources, adequate legal assistance supplied to inmates, brighter and cheerier prison facilities, better food, better medical and dental care."[15] To bring their recommendations about penal reform to a broader audience, the Jones Committee went on to hold three public hearings the following month, one in Albany, the second in Buffalo, and the third in New York City. Such hearings and the scathing final report that the Jones Committee issued were not at all what the Rockefeller administration had expected.

DOCS commissioner Russell Oswald was incensed. "It seems to me," he wrote Governor Rockefeller, "that this continuing negative emphasis by the Jones Committee is a disservice to the effort of Department and administration personnel who have worked so hard to bring about meaningful change."[16] The commissioner had been equally unhappy with the findings of the Goldman Panel. As he put it, "A disturbing situation has developed with the advent of the Goldman and Jones Commission reports. . . . [Both] have consistently failed to credit the efforts of the department in the very areas in which it has contributed so much."[17]

DOCS officials and the Rockefeller administration became more alarmed, though, once an even higher ranking committee really began looking into Attica—this one a federal investigative body chaired by Representative Claude Pepper, who also headed up the House Select Committee on Crime. Initially, at least, the governor's office felt pretty good about this particular inquiry, which had begun almost immediately after the retaking. On Friday, September 17, Pepper and five other congressmen, including Charles Rangel of New York, went to New York City to have an hour-and-a-half meeting with Rockefeller in order "to listen to the Governor's account of the uprising."[18] Afterward the governor flew them to Attica in his private jet so that they could see what conditions were like a

The Pepper Commission: Congressmen William Keating (OH), Sam Steiger (AZ), Charles Rangel (NY), Claude Pepper (FL), Frank Brasco (NY) *(Courtesy of Corbis)*

few days after the retaking.[19] After this initial trip Representative Pepper told the press that they had had "a most interesting and profitable visit."[20] Committee member Representative Frank Brasco elaborated a bit further, stating to reporters that, in his view, Commissioner Oswald had gone "as far as he could in negotiations."[21]

The next day, however, the Pepper Commission members spoke to some of the prisoners and COs, and had decided that they would stay at the prison "'for as long as necessary' perhaps the whole weekend" to get a full sense of conditions there.[22] According to *The New York Times* the commission was not at all pleased to hear prisoners tell of suffering much abuse after the retaking, and having had to run a gauntlet of officers wielding batons.[23]

The Pepper Commission went on to examine other prisons in the country that had also experienced uprisings—institutions that Rockefeller felt were also hotbeds of destructive revolutionary activism—which slightly buoyed the governor's faith in its mission. But once the commission hearings got under way, he realized that his office was going to get an earful that it didn't particularly want to hear.[24] Despite Claude Pepper's opening the hearings by stating that the committee was primarily interested in a "national inquiry into the American system for treating and rehabilitating criminal offenders" so that the nation could better deal with "the problem of crime," conditions at Attica were clearly going to dominate the agenda, taking up a full two and a half days of the five days of hearings.[25]

It appeared that the Pepper Commission intended to probe conditions at Attica fully—even arranging for Richard X Clark as well as other prisoners they had spoken to at Attica to come in to offer graphic testimony about severe and continuing abuse prisoners experienced at the hands of troopers and correction officers—but the prisoners ultimately were let down. Russell Oswald and Walter Dunbar refused to let Clark come, arguing that his visit would pose a security risk.[26] And, instead of prisoners testifying, the commission instead heard a great deal from Superintendent Mancusi as well as many of Attica's guards—all of whom "denied that any beatings or officially-sanctioned brutality occurred at the prison."[27]

These witnesses did get some pushback from committee members. Representative Charles Rangel, for example, refused to accept the viewpoint that prisoners were nothing more than militant troublemakers determined to destroy America. Rangel noted with disgust that this trope had gotten so out of hand that "there is talk right now from the governor's office right on down, that prisoners now will be labeled as to whether or not they are rebellious, they're revolutionists, or they're moderate, and they will be systematically segregated or removed from the general population."[28] Some of Rockefeller's own political friends, including John Dunne, also disagreed with his view of the Attica rebels. Dunne had steadfastly maintained that "there was 'no basis' for Warden Mancusi's belief in a conspiracy influenced by Marxists, Maoists, and far-leftists, enhanced by an atmosphere of permissiveness in the outside world."[29] One of the governor's closest advisors, attorney Michael Whiteman, indicated as well that he and Rockefeller had a stark difference of opinion about this.[30] Commissioner Oswald too rejected the idea that Attica's uprising had been a leftist plot. He testified before the Pepper Commission that he saw " 'no evidence' that a communist or a revolutionary conspiracy lay behind the Attica prison riot" and therefore, like Rangel, Oswald thought it far more productive to focus on "root causes, such as an obsolete prison system long starved by the state government for funds and trained personnel."[31]

Still, the first set of Pepper Commission hearings did little to further prisoner rights in America. Indeed the whole affair seemed relatively pointless to Congressman Badillo, who stepped in to testify at the last minute when Richard Clark was prevented from doing so. Badillo felt that no investigation of the rebellion at Attica prison, including the Pepper inquiry, got at the heart of the issues at hand in New York's prisons—this one had even managed to "obfuscate the fact that inmates' demands agreed to by state have not been implemented."[32]

Eventually the Pepper Commission did hear testimony from a few of Attica's prisoners. In a later set of hearings, held at the U.S. Customs House in February 1972, Richard Clark and Frank Lott, along with two white prisoners, took to the stand to report on what had led to the uprising at Attica, as well as how they had fared since. All four expressed their frustration that, despite having finally spoken to the men from the commission during their visit to the prison back in September, little had changed for them.[33] Clark was particularly dismayed by the commission's ineffectiveness. As he put it, "We had people come up and talk and talk about reform and rehabilitation and that's all it is is talk. . . . We've still got brothers being beaten up in here."[34]

While both the Jones Committee and the Pepper Commission expressed criticism of Rockefeller for not going to Attica, most prisoners, civil rights groups, and what remained of the observers committee felt that "all the committees appointed by the state to investigate the events of Attica would produce a 'whitewash.' "[35]

There was one investigative body that state officials had almost no influence over. In the wake of the retaking the public had persistently and loudly demanded a genuinely independent inquiry, and the governor was eventually pressured to create a fully independent citizens committee to conduct the investigation.[36] On September 21 he announced that Chief Judge Stanley Fuld would be in charge of appointing this committee, which would "investigate the facts leading up to, during and following the riot at Attica," and then file "a full, factual, and impartial report just as soon as possible."[37]

Chairing the citizen inquiry was Robert McKay, dean of New York University School of Law. The McKay Commission, which first met in November 1971, was comprised of judges and lawyers, members of the clergy, and leaders of various political and social justice organizations, who were all formally empowered by the State Supreme Court.[38] The commission's general counsel was Arthur L. Liman, an experienced lawyer who had worked as both a defense counsel and a prosecutor, and was currently a partner in the very prestigious New York firm of Paul, Weiss, Rifkind, Wharton & Garrison. This commission was one impressive body, to be sure, but as Liman himself put it, black and white alike they were all "save one . . . totally ignorant" of prisons. The exception was commission member Amos Henix, who had served several sentences as a young man and had become "a leader in the movement for the rehabilitation of addicts."[39]

The commission was sent to work with a budget of $250,000, and Liman was tasked with putting together a full-time staff, which eventually contained "36 full time attorneys, investigators, researchers and clerical personnel. . . . They were assisted by more than sixty part-time interviewers, student volunteers, and consultants in the fields of communications, penology, sociology, hospital and health services, psychiatry, pathology, and ballistics."[40]

Despite its official independence, however, members of the McKay Commission felt from the beginning that they had to fight to keep the governor's office from trying to control or undermine their inquiry.[41] The commission's goal was not to make general recommendations on penal reform—that had been the goal of both the Jones and Pepper commissions.[42] The McKay Commission was to focus solely on Attica—going over the rebellion and the retaking with a magnifying glass. From the moment he accepted his appointment as counsel for the commission, Arthur Liman constantly had to fend off Robert Fischer, who wanted to know everything the McKay Commission was learning and wanted access to all its files for the purposes of the state's inquiry into criminal acts committed at Attica during the rebellion and retaking. As Rockefeller attorney Michael Whiteman recalled, "After its formation [Fischer] complained and said, 'You know, I don't understand how these things are going to function together.' "[43]

Fischer tried to get Rockefeller to issue an executive order under Section 6 of the Executive Law indicating that investigations into corruption had ready access to any information that might be useful. Since the governor had placed Fischer's inquiry under the Organized Crime Task Force, Fischer reasoned that he should have unlimited access to the McKay findings. McKay and the rest of his commission, however, argued that this would be "totally unacceptable" and made this crystal clear to Rockefeller lawyer Michael Whiteman. When Whiteman was unable to get Fischer to back down from his efforts to get at the commission files, McKay called Rockefeller to inform him that "the Commission would resign" if he planned on doing what Fischer wanted.[44] In addition to threatening to disband the entire operation, McKay insisted that the governor stand by some ironclad principles so that commission members could do their work unhampered and unintimidated. These included the commission's right to hold public hearings, its right to the full cooperation of all state officials, and a guarantee that its files and witnesses would remain off-limits to any other state office or body.[45] If he would not agree to these conditions, Dean McKay informed Rockefeller, members of the commission "would give serious consideration to immediate resignation at the November 8th meeting."[46]

To the dismay of Fischer, and to the great consternation of prison officials, the governor gave in to McKay. Russell Oswald was particularly worried by what this would mean for his people. He wrote to Attica superintendent Vincent Mancusi, "Frankly I can see nothing but trouble ahead for you, Walter [Dunbar] and me, for the next several months with the manner in which this Commission is moving. You are undoubtedly aware of the fact that they have recruited law students from New York University, Columbia University Law School and Yale Law School to assist in their study. Need more be said?"[47]

Once the McKay Commission entered Attica in November of 1971, just after the Goldman Panel left, Mancusi had his hands full. The commission spent the next seven months trying to interview anyone who had any knowledge of the causes of the uprising, the day-by-day course of the uprising, the retaking by the state, and the immediate aftermath of the retaking. The commission members faced great difficulty in collecting this information. The COs they encountered were often hostile, doing their best to instill a serious fear of the prisoners in the interviewers, in particular the young ones. Recalled Arthur Liman, "The initial reaction of many guards to our visit was that even the male members of the Commission would be raped" and when a woman arrived to conduct interviews, they unnerved her by "constantly peering in the window to make sure that she was okay."[48]

Another serious barrier to the McKay investigators was that many prisoners were deeply suspicious of them—particularly because they were an overwhelmingly white group. Aware of this potential reaction, Robert McKay and Arthur Liman had tried to include black interviewers in the group; Liman had specifically met with members of the Black Law Students Association at Yale, but he ultimately recruited only four part-time students.

Ironically, these few black interviewers among so many whites became objects of suspicion for the prisoners. As a prisoner writing on behalf of the group of eighty men who were locked in Attica's HBZ segregation unit put it, "When the McKay Commission saw that the greater majority of us, who are black, were reluctant to talk to them (white), they went and got five or six blacks, hoping we would relate to them. As a result, we strongly feel that the Blacks appointed to this Commission compromised their principles and sold their Blackness to obtain information from us."[49] If the commission were really interested in "hearing about events leading up to the rebellion and its bloody climax," he went on, from the beginning it "should have been made up of our peers, of people who know how we live, who come from our communities, who are poor like us, who can relate to our struggle for survival in this society."[50]

These same prisoners had been willing to talk to congressmen as well as members of both the Goldman Panel and the Jones Committee, yet it had gotten them no improvements. They were understandably jaded. The real issue driving prisoner suspicion of the McKay Commission interviewers, however, was that for the past two months they had endured some particularly aggressive interrogations by Fischer's investigators—both State Police and state investigators—who had been grilling them and trying to get them to inform on their cell mates. The prisoners knew that Fischer was trying to find evidence of criminal wrongdoing during the rebellion and retaking, and it certainly appeared to the prisoners that his team was only looking at them. When the McKay investigators came in, it was hard for the prisoners to know how the McKay investigation might relate to the Fischer investigation, or which investigators belonged to which group. Even if the former was independent of the latter, prisoners feared that something they might say to investigators from McKay's office could end up twisted by Fischer's men to build cases against them. As a man in HBZ explained, it was the fear of what the state might do with McKay information that terrified prisoners who had participated in the rebellion and kept them from cooperating: "any and all information the Commission accumulates can be subpoenaed by the grand jury and used as evidence against us."[51]

Roger Champen was particularly concerned about the McKay investigators—as he put it, they "worried me to death."[52] Not only did they want him to make statements about the rebellion, but they wanted him to testify about his experiences in future public hearings. "He [Arthur Liman] was at my cell—I thought the man would move in there with me. I'm serious, he came up there one night just before the hearing and said, 'Are you sure you won't reconsider?' . . . And I said, 'Listen, I respect you, but I don't think you give me the same respect. I told you repeatedly I am not speaking to you or any member of the McKay Commission . . . because I am going to be indicted and the testimony I give you can be used in the trial. I'm not going to give it to you. . . . And he stood there trying to convince me, so much so that . . . I had to be rude and . . . ignore him."[53]

Richard X Clark also felt compelled to speak on behalf of the eighty prisoners being held in solitary. He issued an official statement to the McKay Commission in order to explain why so many didn't want to testify at any hearing. The commission had "spoken to 'thousands of inmates,'" he said, but had done "'nothing favorable for them.'"[54] More to the point, he continued, the commission "is solidly connected with the privileged class, which makes it a whitewash group."[55] Some prisoner rights advocates were so suspicious of the McKay Commission's true intentions that a group calling itself the "Ad Hoc Citizens Committee to Defend the Constitutional Rights of Prisoners in New York State" filed a case in U.S. District Court on December 22, 1971, on the prisoners' behalf, so that the commission would not be able "to go forward with its investigation."[56]

Although the McKay Commission in fact worked very hard to protect prisoners' rights and would be deeply critical of the state's retaking of the prison, its members sometimes behaved in ways that directly undermined their credibility with the prisoners. One day when Arthur Liman was on his way to speak with Richard Clark in his cell, it suddenly occurred to him that the fact that he was walking through the prison corridors accompanied by Vincent Mancusi might not be construed very favorably by the men, and asked the warden to "hide under a chair in the barbershop."[57] Of course for any prisoner who saw Liman's awkward effort to appear independent, it looked like he was trying to cover up a close relationship with the prison administration. From the prisoners' perspective, anyone who might be trusted by Mancusi couldn't be trusted, since they blamed his callousness for the reason there was a rebellion in the first place. Liman thought that prisoners were overreacting when it came to McKay Commission members talking with prison administrators. As he later put it, "It seemed so ludicrous that the warden of the prison institution should have to screen himself under a stool."[58]

Despite these barriers to trust, in one year the McKay Commission was able to collect information from more than 3,200 witnesses, "including 1,600 present and former inmates of Attica, 400 correction officers, 270 State Police personnel, 200 National Guardsmen, 100 sheriffs and sheriff's deputies, prison administrators at Attica and in Albany, doctors and other medical personnel who were called to the scene, residents of the town of Attica, and the wives of correction officers and inmates."[59] The commission also interviewed or took testimony from Governor Rockefeller and five members of his executive staff.[60] What is more, it collected an extraordinary number of documents, over two thousand, from the Department of Correctional Services, the New York State Police, the New York National Guard, "and other sources."[61]

What they found made it abundantly clear not only that the men locked in Attica had much to protest in the first place, but that they had also experienced terrible abuse in the wake of the uprising. This was the very reason that Robert McKay insisted on holding a series of public hearings on the commission's findings: he wanted the citizens of New York to hear all of this for themselves.

It was likely to be the same reason that Robert Fischer was determined to prevent such hearings from taking place. Just before the hearings were to commence on April 12, 1972, Fischer sought an eleventh-hour injunction against them.[62] Dean McKay immediately fired off a letter to Rockefeller reminding him of previous correspondence in which the governor had already agreed that the commission "would be empowered to hold public hearings and issue our report without any restrictions and without the approval of any court."[63]

Once again, McKay won his battle to keep the commission on track. During the month of April the commission went to the studios of local public television stations in Rochester and New York City and from there broadcast the hearings live.[64] Rockefeller, though, asked to testify privately in his Manhattan office, which he did for almost three hours. Having been carefully prepped by a special counsel who'd been brought on exclusively to get him ready for his testimony, the governor explained that he personally had little involvement with any decisions that had been made at Attica because of "his belief in delegating authority to subordinates in whom he had faith."[65] Rockefeller repeatedly dodged any personal responsibility for the debacle, but it was nevertheless clear to the McKay Commission—and to the public—that his office had had complete agency over the event. More important, he might have prevented the disaster there. Numerous witnesses told the McKay Commission that had Rockefeller merely come to the prison or, better yet, heeded the observers committee's warnings about the bloodbath that was sure to result from an armed retaking, the outcome of this prison rebellion might have been very different.

And the McKay hearings drove home to anyone listening that the outcome—the retaking of Attica—had been almost incomprehensibly barbaric. Powerful testimony by National Guardsman physician John W.

Cudmore made the room fall silent.[66] Speaking quietly, Cudmore summed up everything he had witnessed on September 13: "I think Attica brings to mind several things. The first is the basic inhumanity of man to man, the veneer of civilization as we sit here today in a well-lit, reasonably well appointed room with suits and ties on objectively performing an autopsy on this day, yet cannot get at the absolute horror of the situation, to people, be they black, yellow, orange, spotted, whatever, whatever uniform they wore, that day tore from them the shreds of their humanity. The veneer was penetrated. After seeing that day I went home and sat down and spoke with my wife and I said for the first time being a somewhat dedicated amateur army type, I could understand what may have happened at My Lai."[67]

This was not at all the story that state officials in New York had hoped the world would hear. More alarmingly for the state, Robert McKay announced on August 30, 1972, that his committee would be publishing a lengthy report on all of its findings—a report that could be purchased by the public—on the one-year anniversary of the retaking of Attica.[68] At 11:00 a.m. that day, at the New York University Law Center, McKay took questions from the media and informed the press that there also would be "a one-hour television special to be broadcast on public television" to discuss the main points of the report.[69] As it turned out, there was so much public interest in this story that New York City's public television station, Channel 13, decided to devote ninety minutes to the McKay Commission findings, followed by a thirty-minute panel discussion chaired by newscaster Bill Moyers. Panelists included William Vanden Heuvel, then chairman of the New York City Board of Correction, Leo Zeferetti, president of the Correction Officers' Benevolent Association, Tom Wicker, Arthur Liman, and two Attica prisoner survivors.[70]

The report, published by Bantam Books in mass-market paperback form as *Attica: The Official Report of the New York State Special Commission on Attica,* flew off the shelves. Widely available in bookstores and on newsstands, it was so riveting a read that the following year it was a finalist for the National Book Award. The McKay Commission's narrative of events unflinchingly and graphically exposed the mistreatment of prisoners that had led to the rebellion, and made it equally clear that its bloody end was both avoidable and unconscionable. In their conclusion, the authors of the report bluntly summed it up: "The decision to retake the prison was not a quixotic effort to rescue the hostages in the midst of 1,200 inmates; it was a decisive reassertion of the state of its sovereignty and power."[71]

Even New York political operatives who were in Rockefeller's camp, such as Senator Jacob Javits, were unsettled by what they learned from the McKay Commission report. Javits publicly stated, "There will be more Atticas until federal and state governments and the American people accept their responsibility to establish minimum standards of decency and respect for human rights in our prisons. We cannot afford to wait for new explosions."[72] One of his aides described the report more bluntly still as "an incredibly shocking story of maladministration, bad judgment and total disregard for human life."[73]

Anthony Simonetti, now fully in charge of Fischer's inquiry, reacted to the release of the report by redoubling his efforts to access everything the McKay Commission had collected over the course of its investigation. He wanted to have as much information as possible about the Attica uprising and aftermath at his fingertips. He suspected the McKay book would reveal a great deal he needed to see. He had his investigators go through the book line by line, listing every key fact about each event that had taken place during the rebellion or the retaking alongside what his investigation did or did not know about that same event.[74] On the basis of this analysis, Simonetti was certain that the McKay Commission had evidence that his men needed if they were going to bring indictments against those who had committed crimes during the course of Attica's rebellion and retaking.

Arthur Liman held firm to the commission's position that if it was compelled to release its documents, the governor would have "violated his commitment to the Commission that its records of interviews (confidential statements of inmates, guards and others) would not be subject to the subpoena of the State Attorney General for criminal purposes."[75] Liman publicly stated that "he [would] go to jail first, rather than hand them over."[76]

Drawing this line in the sand was not enough to make the issue of state access to the McKay files go away—particularly since, according to one political aide, "the Governor's people [were] apparently saying that no such commitment 'as such' was made."[77] Fischer refused to back down from his belief that he had a right to these files. He particularly wanted any information that would allow him to prosecute whoever had killed correction officer William Quinn. In a bold move, New York State attorney general Louis Lefkowitz, who when Fischer moved on in 1973 would be the main person overseeing Anthony Simonetti's ongoing criminal investigation, decided to subpoena top McKay officials to come before a grand jury, testify to what they had learned in the course of their investigation, and then turn over all of their investigative files.[78] As far as McKay was concerned, however, the files remained protected. As he reminded everyone, "In carrying out our task we made statements to inmates, state police and correction officers that their confidentiality would be respected. . . . If the records are given over to the grand jury, the credibility of the state and the commission would be compromised and it would be another justified instance where the inmates could not trust the establishment."[79]

Eventually, Judge Lee P. Gagliardi settled the matter in a hearing on October 17, 1972, ruling that the McKay files would remain protected.[80] Rockefeller had been pressured not to play a public role in the dispute, likely making it easier for the judge to rule in favor of the McKay Commission. As Rockefeller attorney Michael Whiteman later recalled, the men charged with running the Attica investigation were, in the end, "quite embittered (a) that we wouldn't support them in their demands to get the McKay records, and (b) that they lost."[81] Not getting to see the McKay files, however, did not prevent Simonetti's office from moving forward in its investigation.

31

# Foxes in the Hen House

Simonetti's investigation of criminal wrongdoing at Attica was not at all disadvantaged by its inability to see the McKay Commission's files. The reality was that Simonetti's office had unfettered access to every person involved in the rebellion as well as the retaking—better access than the McKay investigators had had—and was asking questions of prisoners well before anyone from the McKay Commission ever set foot in Attica.

Before the gas had even cleared over Attica, Anthony Simonetti had "complete access to the prison yard." He was also present when the prison was sealed so that investigators could "gather evidence such as ballistics information, blood tests, weapons, fingerprints and preparation of diagrams."[1] Incredibly, the investigators that Simonetti was relying upon to collect that evidence were from the New York State Police's Bureau of Criminal Investigation (BCI). Troop A's Captain Henry Williams, who had been instrumental in overseeing the retaking, was the main BCI man now collecting evidence and at least one other BCI investigator, Vincent Tobia, had used his weapon in the retaking. Indeed, during the first critical weeks of the Attica investigation—the weeks in which evidence was secured and troopers' statements about the shots they had fired were taken—the main investigators of crimes at Attica were those who may well have committed them.

It was not odd or unusual for an investigation being run out of New York's Organized Crime Task Force to use the State Police's Bureau of Criminal Investigation unit—in fact, it was standard practice. However, in the earliest days of the Attica investigation even Robert Fischer realized relying on them in this case was going to raise eyebrows. To try to ward off criticism, Fischer told Rockefeller attorney Michael Whiteman up front that BCI investigators would have to report directly to him, and not, as they normally would, to their State Police superiors. In fact, back in September 1971, Fischer said that "he would not take the job unless he was given full control of the State Police in the conduct of the investigation."[2] Whiteman agreed and made sure to inform State Police Lieutenant Colonel George Infante and State Police superintendent William Kirwan that their men would report directly to Fischer.[3]

With so much on the line, however, BCI investigators resisted taking any direction from Fischer or Simonetti and their superiors had little interest in doing so either. Dozens of men had died at Attica and, as Infante and Kirwan knew, many of their own men could face criminal charges if they didn't control this investigation. Within twenty-four hours of arriving at Attica, Tony Simonetti could see that the State Police had closed ranks. As he opined, "independent investigators were required" if he had any hope of examining what troopers might have done wrong.[4] Barring such independent investigators, for which there was no funding allotted, Fischer and Simonetti held a pointed meeting with Lieutenant Colonel Infante, Major John Monahan, Captain Henry Williams, and other State Police personnel to set everyone straight about who was in charge of this investigation.[5] However, this had little effect on the men on the ground.

Fischer and Simonetti, and later Lefkowitz and Simonetti when Fischer left for the bench, never would be able to control the BCI investigators, let alone get them to follow proper procedures. Captain Williams went to great lengths to thwart every state effort to ask thorny questions about the actions of his men.[6] And he went even further than that. In the immediate aftermath of the retaking, Williams took it upon himself to make sure as much evidence as possible was collected that might indicate that a prisoner committed a crime (for example, collecting every baseball bat in D Yard since these could have been used by prisoners as weapons) while also making sure that nothing related to the shooting—shell casings, the weapons themselves—was collected. Even though this was a crime scene, no BCI man made chalk outlines to indicate where bodies had fallen, or made any calculations regarding bullet trajectories vis-à-vis those bodies. Instead, Captain Williams ordered a crew of his men to start a "clean-up operation" of Attica's yards, its storage rooms, and its tunnels as well as other buildings.[7] By 5:00 p.m. on the day of the retaking, Williams's troopers had "completed their assignment."[8]

Troopers collecting evidence as the state's investigation begins *(Courtesy of the* Democrat and Chronicle*)*

Since there was little interest in the governor's camp in seeing state troopers indicted, no one considered removing the BCI, or even just Williams, from the state investigation. Others remarked upon their continued presence at Attica, however. Members of the Goldman Panel wrote directly to Robert Fischer on October 1, 1971, to express their strong feelings that the State Police could not "conduct an objective and impartial investigation of the allegations against state police and correction officers, of post-riot brutality and physical mistreatment of inmates."[9] Clarence Jones and Austin MacCormick of the Goldman Panel went further regarding Captain Williams's involvement. Jones called it "an insult to the public's intelligence; it's ridiculous." MacCormick agreed. "If I were Williams," he said, "I think I'd disqualify myself."[10] The Goldman Panel asked Fischer "to remove him from the assignment as chief of investigators."[11] The president of the state NAACP, Donald Lee, had also called for Williams's removal.[12] Prisoner lawyer Herman Schwartz not only went public with his objections to the Fischer investigation, but he made clear that, legally, the way Williams was running it was "a violation of the inmates' constitutional rights to equal protection under the law."[13]

A few weeks into the start of the investigation, Fischer's own man, Tony Simonetti, also grew increasingly vocal "that it was inappropriate for a State Police official who had been directly involved in the retaking events to play any role whatsoever in their investigation."[14] Williams simply wasn't cooperating with him. When Simonetti asked Williams to turn over all reels of tape that the State Police had recorded, he "made available two reels of eight millimeter film," but refused to turn over the originals. Doing so, Williams said, was unnecessary because they had been "reproduced in their entirety on the two reels furnished."[15] It became clear that none of the materials the BCI needed would be easy to get if it had anything to do with troopers, guns, or shooting. NYSP recalcitrance with Simonetti's office was only a real problem, however, if the state was going to start digging into crimes committed by troopers at Attica. And, at least initially, Fischer and Simonetti had little interest in doing this. When it came time to get the BCI to hand over information it had collected that might be used against prisoners, Simonetti's office had a great deal of cooperation.

Officially, Simonetti's office was tasked with four main areas of investigation: crimes related to the rebellion itself, including the taking of the hostages; deaths that occurred in the prison prior to the retaking; deaths and injuries that resulted from the retaking; and abuses that took place as the prisoners were rehoused. Yet for reasons that many outsiders couldn't quite grasp—since the most death and injury took place during the retaking and after—Fischer asked Simonetti to train his attention first on "the question of conspiracy to cause riot." And then, with equal zeal, his team's resources were to be devoted to investigating all homicides that had occurred prior to the assault—in other words, those that could not have been committed by troopers or COs.[16]

Indeed there were prisoner killings prior to the state's retaking for Simonetti's office to investigate: CO William Quinn had died from the beating he suffered in the initial rioting, and three prisoners were murdered at some point during the uprising.

From the very first day of the uprising, men like Roger Champen had done an extraordinary job of minimizing violence and making D Yard a safe place for all. He and the security team had taken great pains to prevent the sexual coercion, revenge attacks, and drug use that might otherwise have wreaked havoc with almost 1,300 men in a space half the size of a football field. But the longer the rebellion continued, and the more hardened the state's position became, the more suspicion and fear began to take their toll. For prisoners Kenneth Hess and Barry Schwartz, who were accused of treason and taken to a cell in D Block after speaking with reporter Stewart Dan, the rising paranoia had proved deadly.

On Saturday night a prisoner by the name of Sam Liggits, known by his friends as "Bug-Eyed Sam," had been summoned to D Block, along with another prisoner named John Flowers, to tend to some lacerations suffered by detainee Barry Schwartz. When they arrived Schwartz showed them some serious gashes on his arms and feet and told them that his captors had been throwing broken glass on him. While Liggits held a flashlight so that Flowers could see what he was doing, Flowers stitched him up.[17] Sometime later that night, well after Flowers and Liggits had left, a group of elderly and infirm prisoners who had chosen to bunk in D Block since the riot began happened to walk by cell 3 where Bernard Schwartz was being held. These men, shuffling slowly with their arthritis, were literally stopped in their tracks by the gore inside.[18] According to one of them, "I saw a white inmate lying or lied with another inmate on top, half on top of the other man, both covered with blood, the man on the bottom didn't seem to be breathing, the man on the top was breathing like he was gasping for breath. Both men were laying face up, head toward cell doors."[19] Sometime after Liggits and Flowers had left the block Schwartz had again been attacked, and was now dead, and someone had moved him into the same cell with Hess, who had also been stabbed repeatedly.

Although the terrible events unfolding behind the scenes in D Block escaped the notice of everyone outside in D Yard, on Sunday morning one of the state troopers who had been watching D Block noticed that something unusual was happening on one of the tiers. A prisoner was trying to get his attention from an exterior window in D Block. This trooper notified several of his men, including two sergeants, who, in turn, walked closer to the D Block wall. Upon closer inspection he could see that a prisoner had managed to wedge himself into the small opening between the window and the bars that covered it. He was wearing a bloody T-shirt and "what appeared to be a bloody towel or rag around his throat."[20] Although the prisoner was having great difficulty breathing and his voice came out in a rasp, a correction officer also standing there began firing questions at the distressed man. No one there could make out the man's name, something like "Glass," they thought.[21] They could clearly see, though, that he was asking for their help.[22] Unsure what to do, a trooper told the prisoner to lie down, and that they would try to get some assistance. This trooper then dutifully reached a sergeant, who tried to request a vehicle "for the purpose of pulling out the window board," and he was then "told to stand by but nothing ever happened."[23]

The bleeding prisoner was Kenneth Hess. About thirty minutes later, he reappeared at the window and, to the surprise of those troopers still watching, he began climbing up in slow motion, again wedging himself between the window glass and the outside bars but now trying to reach the window on the floor above. According to trooper reports he "appeared to be in extreme difficulty . . . [and] on reaching the second floor, [he] rested on the window and again entered into a conversation [with them]."[24] It began to dawn on the troopers that this man might have been stabbed so they began questioning him about who had attacked him. "He merely shook his head negatively."[25] They watched him leave "the window after a few minutes and [he] was never seen again."[26] Although this incident was quickly reported to state officials, the troopers and COs were, as one put it, "extremely suspicious that he might be walking into a trap and that the man in the window was merely used as bait to get them close to the building."[27] It was not a trap. Three men, Kenneth Hess, his friend Barry Schwartz, and Mickey Privitera—who had been acting crazily in the yard and subsequently were sent to the third tier of D Block for the protection of the men assembled outside—were being held against their will and were in real trouble. By the time the state retook Attica, all three were dead.

It was ironic for the state investigation to focus on these killings with such zeal, when the state had seemed to care little about them as they were happening. Robert Fischer explained that Simonetti's investigation should be oriented first and "primarily toward inmate crimes," because "the initial silence of inmates in this regard has to be broken through early or not at all."[28] As important, he wrote to Attorney General Louis Lefkowitz, the deaths that had happened at the hands of prisoners were "simply more obviously homicides."[29] Because BCI investigators were the ones conducting the legwork of the investigation, there was plenty of "evidence" being found against prisoners.

But just as Simonetti's office knew that the NYSP wasn't being aboveboard turning over evidence it had collected against troopers, it was well aware that the evidence the BCI was collecting on prisoners was highly problematic. For one thing, its interrogations were being conducted without regard to prisoners' legal or civil rights. Even though BCI investigators were repeatedly warned, even by Fischer himself, to make sure prisoners' rights were protected during questioning, they ignored him. The violations of rights were so egregious that as early as September 17, Fischer insisted that Captain Hank Williams order his own investigators to stop all prisoner interviews.[30] He did not. Even Rockefeller later admitted that the BCI had not been "following what appeared to have been a direction by Fischer that Miranda warnings . . . should have been given to inmates before they were interrogated."[31] Rockefeller's lawyer Michael Whiteman also acknowledged that the state police were "proceeding contrary to the directions that had been given . . . that they were conducting interviews with people or doing things they hadn't gotten specific clearance on from Fischer."[32]

Even if Fischer had been able to rein in the BCI investigators, there was still the problem of how Mancusi's COs were treating the prisoners that had been enlisted to help build criminal cases against their fellow prisoners. At least officially, Fischer tried to bring Mancusi in line as well, writing, "As you are aware . . . it is my function to gather evidence in regard to any criminal violations relating to the 'Attica Riots' and assure that these violations are prosecuted according to law. Any attempt by any officer to penalize inmates in any other manner can only interfere with the proper prosecution of those inmates who may have violated the penal code."[33] Mancusi obligingly wrote a memo to his staff that read, in part, "As I have emphasized in the past, despite recent events at this facility, any officer who undertakes any abuse of inmates not only does himself a disservice, but may interfere with proper prosecution of those criminally responsible."[34] As for actually monitoring his own COs' behavior, however, he passed that buck to Deputy Superintendent Leon Vincent. And the violations continued.

Beyond the issuing of internal memos, neither Fischer, Simonetti, nor eventually Lefkowitz, did much to prevent such abuses. The fact was, they relied heavily upon the intelligence that such violations netted them. With few attorneys there to protect the prisoners' right to remain silent, and with even fewer monitors in the prison to make sure that they weren't being threatened, intimidated, and physically hurt, throughout 1971 and into 1972 the Attica investigation proceeded most aggressively.

## 32

# Stick and Carrot

Simonetti paid little attention to the cases of BCI interrogation–related abuse that prisoners repeatedly brought to his attention. The fact was that the endless months of interrogating prisoners were netting his office the very prisoner-witness accounts it would need if it wanted to move to begin indicting prisoners—clearly what the higher-ups wanted. From the earliest days of the investigation, this disinterest in prisoner claims of abuse was mirrored by his boss, Robert Fischer. Back in October of 1971, Fischer had actually asked Governor Rockefeller to contact U.S. Attorney General John Mitchell about the possibility of the Justice Department beginning its own, separate investigation to see if prisoners' claims of abuse and illegal acts of law enforcement had any merit. The Justice Department agreed to take a look.[1] But when the U.S. Justice Department informed Fischer that it had a witness to a terrible assault on an inmate with a Phillips head screwdriver, Fischer "advised that he had no information regarding the incident described by the National Guardsman," and stated firmly that "there has been no medical information brought out which would substantiate any prisoner being wounded in the rear end and by being stabbed with a screwdriver."[2]

Whether they liked to admit it or not, everyone at the Attica investigation was aware that abuse and intimidation were key to persuading Attica prisoners to agree to testify against their own. Consider one witness whom Simonetti's office looked forward to calling in its grand jury case regarding the killing of Barry Schwartz: prisoner Edward Kowalczyk. On the day of the retaking Kowalczyk had been shot seven times, and then was beaten savagely by correction officers—so badly that a National Guardsman intervened on his behalf and got him taken to Meyer Memorial Hospital. But only a day later, while still heavily sedated and clearly in critical condition, he had to deal with BCI investigators. They pointed guns at him, threatened to pull tubes out of him, and said they would poison him. Finally, sick with fear, he agreed to cooperate.[3] He would say that he saw who killed Barry Schwartz.

Simonetti's office also had to know that a combination of abuse and bribery was used to convince Charles "Flip" Crowley to go before the grand jury in another case they hoped to make against one of his fellow prisoners at Attica. On September 17, 1971, Crowley recounted, "I gave an interview under an atmosphere of the most intense terror that I have ever seen. I gave an interview, indeed, to save my life. I felt and knew within myself that had I not spoken to the two officers of the law at the hospital that I would not have been allowed to live."[4]

The two officers who came into Crowley's hospital room told him they knew he'd been having a hard time and were willing to transfer him out of Attica to a "safe location" where he would not be harassed by correction officers or state troopers. In return, though, "they had certain pertinent facts" that they wanted him to confirm for them.[5] When he was unable to do so to their satisfaction, according to Crowley, the officers "proceeded to beat me and they beat me for at least a half an hour. During the course of the beating I was made to crawl around on the floor and shout White Power and kiss their feet . . . this went on for two days."[6] To Crowley's shock, a clergyman had seen the whole thing—but when he begged this man for help, according to Crowley the clergyman just "bowed his head, and walked out and left me there."[7]

Everyone in Simonetti's office presumably would have preferred to get prisoner testimony without such egregious acts of force and intimidation, and indeed, to that end, they had made noises from day one about getting Williams's BCI investigators out of Attica and, instead, hiring their own men to interview prisoners. Ideally, Fischer hoped, Simonetti would have a stable of "NYC detectives who were retired or who could take retirement" to help him conduct the Attica investigation. By November 20, 1971, Fischer had been able to hire nine homicide detectives from the New York City police department.[8] But Simonetti still had to rely heavily on the BCI investigators if he had any hope of getting evidence before a grand jury in a timely manner. As Robert Fischer had bluntly explained, "Herein lies the problem—release of the State Police personnel will slow down the completion of the investigation considerably unless the independent investigative staff can be enlarged somewhat. The net result is that instead of being able to report in the early Fall, the grand jury will not be able to present a complete report until much later."[9]

As a few months turned into almost one and a half years, prisoners continued to endure serious investigative improprieties.

According to one later account of this period in the Attica investigation, the typical prisoner interviews began with investigators trying to get them to identify mug shots of the hundred-plus "pre-selected inmates" against whom the state was seeking evidence.[10] Time and again, the prisoner failed to identify the man whom the investigator had already decided to pursue, and so that investigator would push and push—even telling the witness the name of the man they hoped he'd ID. Given enough pressure, prisoners often would cave, ultimately agreeing that they had, in fact, seen so-and-so committing an illegal act.

Sometimes, though, even leading questions and outright pressuring of prisoners didn't get them to say what the investigators wanted to hear about a given suspect's actions. In these cases a slightly different tactic was employed to get them to cooperate. When one very frightened prisoner was interviewed right after the retaking, he dutifully identified a fellow prisoner whose photo investigators kept trying to get him to name as Roger Champen. Investigators were very interested in gathering evidence against Champ because troopers had marked him on the day of the retaking as a leader of the rebellion. According to this witness, however, Champ was a really good guy—he had actually saved his life in D Yard. His fellow investigators, however, kept pushing this man to say Champ had done something illegal. Ultimately frustrated, one investigator exclaimed in disgust, "I don't want to hear anything about that from them niggers."[11]

When strong-arm tactics still proved ineffective, they switched their approach: should this witness help them, investigators suggested, they would, in turn, help him get paroled.[12] In addition to enticing the witness with the possibility of parole, they also promised to make prison life easier for him in the meantime. As this man later testified, one of Simonetti's own, non-BCI investigators, Ernest Milde, actually put $5 on his commissary account three different times, and he said that this investigator had done the same for at least three other would-be prisoner witnesses.[13]

Prisoners were susceptible to the promise of early release, and in time some were paroled "after cooperating with Fischer's committee."[14] No one from Simonetti's office decried this practice in which "prisoners and ex-prisoners have been subjected to pressure to cajole them into being witnesses for the state."[15] Nor did anyone intervene when the investigators began offering not only parole, but also commuting sentences and granting pardons.[16] State prosecutors merely doubled down on such sweet carrots with some strong sticks. Should a prisoner change his mind later about testifying on behalf of the state, state prosecutors readily reminded him that "the penalty for refusal to testify is 4 years for contempt of court."[17]

Perhaps the greatest incentive for a given prisoner to support prosecutor efforts was neither avoiding a beating nor securing the promise of parole, but was instead the threat of being indicted himself. As stated in a prisoner lawyers' affidavit, many of the Attica investigation's witnesses testified for the state because of, among other things, the "generalized threats of future indictments."[18]

This was exactly why prisoner David Hightower ended up cooperating. Investigators first visited Hightower on September 19, 1971, when he was in bad shape, having been severely beaten during the retaking six days earlier. Genuinely thinking they were there to investigate wrongdoings he might have witnessed, Hightower proceeded to tell them about an incident he claimed to have seen in the hospital in the hours after the retaking—a black prisoner being killed by three correction officers.[19] Not only did the investigators refuse to take this information down, but they also made it clear he was to repeat this story to no one.[20] As Hightower later swore under oath, "The agents from the BCI promised that if I cooperated with them, I would be able to get out of jail quickly; they promised to help me with medical treatment for my eye [but] threatened to indict me for a crime of sodomy that I allegedly committed in the yard if I did not cooperate with them."[21]

Threats, whether overt or subtle, and bribes, whether immediate or promised, worked wonders. Whether or not a prisoner had any knowledge of the event in question or believed that state prosecutors had the wrong man in their sights, they often ended up cooperating. As prisoner rights lawyers pointed out, one such man, Willie Locke, had been interviewed by one of the state's chief investigators, Ernest Milde, "at least five different times during an 18 month period, and . . . he insisted for more than a year that he knew nothing about the death of the two inmates found dead, Hess and Schwartz."[22] However, after being subjected to "unrelenting long drawn out pressure, with a judicious use of both stick and carrot," Locke eventually agreed "to become a half-hearted prosecution witness."[23]

Rather than worry about exactly how Simonetti was building his cases against Attica's prisoners, as 1971 wore on Robert Fischer focused on the fact that, in his view, Rockefeller's office was not giving his investigative effort sufficient funding. It particularly irked him that state funds had also gone to the McKay Commission, and he felt that his investigators' job was much tougher than theirs. Rockefeller's attorney Michael Whiteman agreed that Fischer's request for funding should be "reviewed by Budget and Counsel's Office," and, on July 5, 1972, Fischer finally heard via Robert Douglass that Rockefeller had approved his request for more funding, although it would be limited to the next three months.[24] Eventually, by December of that year, after many back-and-forth battles over his budget, Fischer was able to net the Attica investigation a permanent investigative staff of between ten and twenty men. Meanwhile, the prisoners were trying to cope with the investigation in any way they could.

# 33

# Seeking Help

Fifty-year-old George Jones was so depressed by how he was treated at Attica following the rebellion that at 4:45 a.m. on November 19, 1971, he asked a CO to put him on the sick call list for the next day. Shortly before 6:00 a.m., he "was found hanged in his cell" by his bedsheet.[1]

Most of the men at Attica tried instead to protest all that they were enduring through subtle and small acts of rebellion. They refused to eat or shower, take their medications or get haircuts. One man refused his meals as well as his medications on both October 13 and 14, just as he had done on September 18. On October 16 he again refused his meals. Then, on October 17 yet another prisoner "refused noon meal [and] said he would not eat for 30 days" while scores of others refused showers. By the 20th of that month even more prisoners were declining to eat their evening meal or to take medications and showers. Such quiet and largely individual protests continued well into December.[2]

Other Attica prisoners fought back more publicly by trying to seek help in the legal system. Many individual prisoners tried, for example, to sue the state for damages.[3] By December 14, 1971, 506 Attica prisoners had filed "notices of intent to file claim."[4] Still others exerted pressure on lawyers such as William Hellerstein and Herman Schwartz to keep fighting on their behalf—not to give up after Judge John T. Curtin refused to grant a permanent injunction against prisoners being interrogated without legal counsel and against their physical abuse.

When they had sought this injunction, with *Inmates of Attica v. Rockefeller,* these lawyers were prepared to keep pushing Curtin. For starters, they kept presenting Curtin with additional accounts indicating that prisoners' rights were being violated in the hope that he would again issue at least a temporary injunction. Curtin ultimately did hold hearings on September 30, October 4, and October 5 to consider their new evidence. There he heard testimony from Vincent Mancusi, Clarence Jones in his capacity as a member of the Goldman Panel, Arthur Eve, and six prisoners, including Frank Lott, Roger Champen, and Herbert Blyden. To the prisoners' dismay, though, Curtin still concluded on October 6 he could not issue an injunction, "in view of the steps being taken to protect the inmates' constitutional rights and personal belongings and the absence of evidence of continuation of physical abuse."[5]

And so, prisoners' lawyers filed an appeal with the second circuit. They also tried to take the issue of the men's sixth amendment rights being violated straight to the U.S. Supreme Court. They asked Justice Thurgood Marshall to weigh in, but he wanted the whole court to hear it. The U.S. Supreme Court, however, declined to issue a stay on October 12, 1971.[6]

Attica's men, and their lawyers, didn't give up. Five more prisoners, this time including Jerry "the Jew" Rosenberg, also sought injunctive relief in the court of Judge Curtin, charging that their civil rights were being violated, both because they were still being held in segregation and because they had no legal protections during Fischer's investigation and had been given "no notice of any charges against them."[7] In this instance Judge Curtin issued an order on November 12, 1971, to force Attica's officials to respond to the charges.

And respond they did. Attica's deputy superintendent, Leon Vincent, testified in Curtin's court that "38 convicts at the prison were being held in segregation and denied privileges" because they were a "threat to the institution."[8] But he said that no one's civil rights were being denied because these men "got out in the yard about once a week on the average and had time to walk around it three times before they were led back to their cells."[9] After his testimony Curtin again decided to take some time to make a final decision on these men's fate.[10]

From the perspective of the prisoners and their supporters, Curtin had let them down. In their view this was how things always worked. As they explained it, "this tortuous process of delay, appeals and procedural haggling" was precisely the same type of legal response "that contributed to the atmosphere of total distrust and frustration that led to the uprising of September 1971."[11]

Yet again, these prisoners' pleas to be let out of solitary ultimately went unheeded.

And yet, the prisoners' various legal efforts to get a judge to take their side at Attica had hardly been wasted. On December 1, 1971, the three-judge panel of the Second Circuit Court of Appeals, ruling on Curtin's original denial of injunctive relief—back on September 14—finally issued its decision. Although this higher court "refused to grant a preliminary injunction that would have barred state authorities from questioning all Attica inmates concerning the recent prison uprising until the inmates had consulted lawyers," it did overrule Curtin on the issue of protecting prisoners from physical abuse.[12]

The author of the decision, Judge Walter R. Mansfield, was unequivocal not only that the prisoners had proven they had endured unimaginable abuses, but that such barbarism must stop immediately. Mansfield wrote that the abuse his court had learned of "far exceeded what our society will tolerate on the part of officers of the law in custody of defenseless prisoners," and though these men were incarcerated, they were "still entitled to protection against cruel and unusual punishment by the Eighth Amendment."[13] The appeals court's ruling read as a particular castigation of Curtin's original decision on this issue. Because "prisoners are at the mercy of their keepers," the court opined, "preliminary injunctive relief should have been granted against further physical abuse, tortures, beatings, or similar conduct."[14]

Curtin may well have been relieved that he had been overruled on this issue. Indeed some had speculated at the time that Curtin had written his decision as he had—that there was abuse but then not granting the injunction—so that he would be easily overruled by a higher court. As attorney William Hellerstein saw it, "he gave us a way to appeal it."[15] The truth was that Curtin was between a rock and a hard place when it came to Attica. The very same week he was overruled by the appellate court, Curtin had received a letter from a group calling itself Women in Support of State Correctional Employees, saying that they would hold him "directly responsible for any injuries or deaths to correction employees or inmates at Attica Correctional Facility or any other correctional facility that results from any injunction or decision made by you."[16]

Once he had been overruled by the Second Circuit Court of Appeals, though, he had no choice but to issue an injunction—no matter what COs' wives threatened—and on December 14, 1971, he did. As he stipulated, "defendants, their agents and employees, including State Police and Department of Correctional Services personnel, are immediately prohibited and enjoined from subjecting inmates at the Attica Correctional Facility to physical abuse, torture, beatings or other forms of brutality, from threatening such conduct or from authorizing, sanctioning or permitting such conduct; and it is further ordered that plaintiffs be permitted to maintain as a class action their claim for injunctive relief against brutality."[17]

And yet the abuses continued. A mere two weeks after Curtin's directive to Mancusi, attorneys from the National Lawyers Guild again had to go back to Judge Curtin and ask him to hold Attica's COs in contempt for ignoring his December 14 injunction.[18] They also wanted federal monitors. In hearings held within Attica prison before U.S. Magistrate Edmund Maxwell, much evidence of contempt was heard, including an incident when Richard Clark had tried to read the injunction aloud to fellow prisoners in an elevator ("a guard cursed him with a racial epithet and ordered him to stand with his nose against the rear wall of the elevator . . . [when] Clark refused [he] was then confined to a cell for 24 hours a day").[19] Another incident involved a prisoner being "repeatedly subjected to racial slurs, threats and beatings." Another: Frank "Big Black" Smith had "been cursed, threatened with death, threatened with physical torture and almost constantly harassed by more than one guard."[20] And Maxwell seemed relatively sympathetic to their plight. When prisoners, including Richard Clark, told the judge that four COs had very purposefully "stationed themselves near the thick steel door and barred windows of the room" to intimidate them as they were meeting with him, these COs were "directed to leave by Maxwell."[21]

Although Judge Curtin was more dubious, and deemed these legal claims of contempt "sketchy," he was willing to amend the injunction on December 23 so that it more specifically enjoined prison personnel from "physical abuse, torture, beatings or other forms of brutality, including verbal abuse and racial slurs, from threatening such conduct or from authorizing or permitting such conduct."[22] Regarding the issue of whether the COs were in fact acting in contempt of his order, Curtin stated that he would need more evidence to issue such a directive.[23]

Various jurists' ambivalence toward Attica's prisoners in the fall and winter of 1971 made prisoners vulnerable to the investigation being conducted by the BCI and to the indictments sought by Simonetti's office. Because the courts had failed to put an end to days and months of interrogation techniques that, according to prisoner advocates, "included not only open intimidation, physical torture, threats of indictment and counter-promises of early parole, but also such improper police methods as naming a photo before showing it to a witness for identification," state investigators were, by the close of 1971, well armed with evidence—much of it false, coerced, or corrupt—to take to a grand jury.[24] A mere thirteen months after the start of their investigations, the state was ready to seek criminal indictments against more than sixty prisoners.

# 34

# Indictments All Around

An Attica grand jury had been convened less than three months after the prison's retaking and Simonetti's office was eager to present the evidence it had collected to this body. This grand jury had been seated in the town of Warsaw, which was in the same county as Attica and housed quite a few COs. State officials had defended this choice of site, a mere "10 miles southeast of the Village of Attica," by noting that "there is no provision in the law for a statewide grand jury."[1] Supreme Court Justice Carmen F. Ball of West Seneca was named to preside over this special term of the State Supreme Court in Wyoming.[2]

Within six hours of hearing this news, attorneys for the prisoners from the National Lawyers Guild (NLG) had moved for a change of venue. By late fall of 1971 the NLG had a substantial presence in the area and felt strongly that the men at Attica would not have a fair hearing in Warsaw since the jury would necessarily be all white and its members would undoubtedly be personally acquainted with some of the prison guards. Judge Ball dismissed the request.[3] He also refused to let the NLG lawyers representing prisoners ask vital questions of the prospective jurors about their views on the rebellion or connections to the prison. Thus, when the grand jury first convened on December 8, 1971, not only was it "an all-white jury of 13 men and 10 women," but nine out of the twenty-three "admitted having friends who worked as guards at Attica" and "two of the nine had friends who were held hostage—one of whom was killed."[4] Furthermore, the foreman, Raymond Becker, had been "a close friend of one of the dead hostages" and ran the Attica school bus system, which also employed prison guards.[5]

Of all the crimes that had occurred at Attica, prosecutors were most interested in indicting any prisoner involved with the death of William Quinn, the correction officer who had died from the injuries he had sustained in Times Square on the morning of the rebellion. They were also determined to prosecute the men who had been involved in killing prisoners Barry Schwartz, Kenneth Hess, and Michael Privitera in D Block; and they wanted to charge every prisoner who had been involved in taking a correction officer hostage with the crime of kidnapping. Finally, state officials wanted to levy numerous other charges against prisoners for acts ranging from sexual assault to wielding a makeshift weapon.

To get indictments against these men, Simonetti was depending on the testimony given by prisoners interrogated over the preceding months by BCI and his own investigators. And to help ensure that they cooperated, Simonetti wrote to the chairman of the Wyoming County Board of Supervisors, insisting that "we should make it as simple as possible to get such inmate witnesses into the grand jury to testify and then out of the Court house without chance of exposure to the public or press."[6] The result was that those prisoners who had agreed to testify on the state's behalf were brought to the jury fully hooded so that the public couldn't see who they were and, once they had testified, were immediately transferred to other institutions, as the prisoners put it, "allegedly for their own protection."[7]

Most of the men who had agreed to offer evidence had no intention of backing out—they either were expecting the reward of early release from prison once they had testified, or feared the consequences if they didn't. As one prisoner put it, "I knew that the things I was saying were untrue . . . I knew that I was lying," but once he had agreed to testify, no one bothered him.[8] Another witness said, after the terror he'd experienced at the hands of the troopers in D Yard, by "the time attorney generals, or whoever it was, the BCI came to see me, I would have testified to my mama doing something."[9]

There were a few prisoners who did have second thoughts about lying to the grand jury and tried not to testify after all. When Flip Crowley was about to be called to the witness stand, he became plagued with guilt; as soon as he arrived at the courthouse he asked to see his lawyer, Barbara Handschu, hoping that she could help him get out of testifying. Instead of allowing him to speak to his attorney, however, a state trooper pulled a gun on him, "a very large gun and looked at me, and looked at his partner and said, 'Hey did you see that nigger try to jump out the window? Who did you say you wanted to see?' "[10] Fearing for his life, Crowley cooperated with them. Sure enough, he was later informed that "prior to my coming in, they [members of the parole board] were not disposed to rule favorably . . . in my way, but . . . [after testifying] I come quite highly recommended."[11]

Jiri Newport, another prisoner who later filed an affidavit saying he "had been tricked into testifying for the grand jury," also had second thoughts and tried to contact his lawyer, also Barbara Handschu, to see if she could prevent his being subpoenaed by the grand jury to give testimony that he didn't believe was true.[12] He heard nothing. He complained repeatedly about not having representation. Officials responded that he didn't need a lawyer—nothing he said could hurt him—and that if he "went along with them," in return he would be transferred to Napanoch, a medium security prison, where "it would be much easier" for him to serve his time.[13] Ten days passed, and he still hadn't heard back from Handschu. Newport "became more apprehensive and frightened," then "someone from the Bureau of Criminal Investigation" told him that neither Barbara Handschu nor any other lawyer was going to help him and, because Newport was by now "in a sufficiently scared state of mind to believe the suggestion," he did testify before the grand jury in August 1972.[14] It turned out the letter Newport had asked a CO to mail to his lawyer wasn't sent until the day after he testified.[15]

Even former members of the observers committee were being pulled into the grand jury proceedings. As Arthur Eve wrote to his fellow committee members, "Something of an emergency is developing because some members of the committee have already been called by the Wyoming County grand jury in connection with the Attica indictments."[16] What was most disturbing to him, as well as to prisoner support organizations and lawyers around the state, was that there appeared to be highly "selective presentation of testimony to the grand jury," and that no "witnesses who had given contradictory testimony to the investigators" early on in their probe were being called to testify—so the grand jury didn't even know such contradictions existed.[17]

State prosecutors were particularly careful to not allow any contradictory evidence before the grand jury when trying to make cases against the prisoners accused of murder. With regard to the killing of Barry Schwartz, state investigators spent endless hours grooming four prisoner witnesses, Dallas Simon, Warren Cronan, John Flowers, and Willie Locke, to say that they had seen one of the members of the rebellion's security team, Shango (Bernard Stroble), commit the crime.[18] Given that grudges existed between men in prison, as in any insular community, state investigators didn't always need to use coercion to get one prisoner to turn against another. Johnny Flowers told fellow prisoner Ed Kowalczyk while they both sat in a holding pen waiting to go before the grand jury that he was going to "get" Shango, and was eager to testify against him, simply because "he was pissed at [him] because of an argument" they had had when Schwartz had been removed from D Yard and locked up in the cell.[19]

The jurors never learned that some of the witnesses they heard from had been nowhere near the scenes of the crimes, nor were they told that many of the state's witnesses had told multiple versions of whom they had seen commit these crimes. By December of 1972, little more than a year after it had first been convened, the Attica grand jury was ready to hand down the first of two major sets of indictments.[20] From then on the Attica investigation was awash in funds. While Simonetti may have felt that he'd had to fight tooth and nail to get funding for independent investigators, after the indictments were handed down the amount of money given his inquiry grew exponentially.[21] Records indicate that from April of 1972 to March of 1973 he drew $1,910,000 from state funds; from April of 1973 to March of 1974 his office spent another $2,065,000; and between April of 1974 and March of 1975, it went through another $4,546,000.[22] By 1974 Simonetti would have a full-time and fully funded staff of twenty specially appointed attorneys general, twenty-eight special investigators, and twenty-seven clerks, stenographers, and accountants.[23]

Ultimately, the grand jury sitting in Wyoming County returned forty-two separate felony indictments—the first thirty were filed in December 1972, and twelve more followed—that charged sixty-three prisoners with 1,289 crimes.[24] A journalist for *The Nation* noted, "Despite the fact that ten hostages, as well as twenty-nine prisoners, died from the state's gunfire, the grand jury has not yet found sufficient cause to indict a single trooper or guard."[25]

The state's indictments began with charges for the murders, or attempted murders, of COs (indictment #1 was for the murder of William Quinn; the next indictments were for the attempted murders of hostages Frank Klein and Ron Kozlowski, who were both cut on their necks when the prisoners around them were shot down); and additional murder charges for the killings of prisoners Hess, Schwartz, and Privitera. Then there was a litany of charges: kidnapping, assault, unlawful imprisonment, possession of weapon, sodomy and sexual assault, and more. More than half of these indictments carried a life sentence should the state secure a conviction. And the state, which was very determined indeed to secure those convictions, now began gearing up to prepare for the trials.

Interestingly, other high-level parties also began mobilizing to gather information that might help to make these charges stick. According to a December 20, 1972, memo that the Buffalo office of the FBI received from W. Mark Felt, the acting director of the FBI in D.C. (and later admitted Watergate whistle-blower Deep Throat), had just received a request "for the criminal background of the individuals indicted whose names have been publicly disclosed." No one was to know that the FBI was involved in any way in these cases; Felt stressed discretion, and "cautioned" the Buffalo office "that this matter must be obtained in a most circumspect manner."[26] Pressed to reveal who had made this request, Felt disclosed that it was the vice president, Spiro Agnew, who was "interested in what type of individuals, as to criminal history, were involved."[27]

Between December 1972 and February 1973, any Attica prisoners who were named in the state's blizzard of indictments but had already been released—either via parole or because his sentence had been served—were rounded up, mainly during the Christmas holiday, and were placed in prisons throughout the state to await their arraignment.[28]

To be sure, Simonetti's office had worked around the clock to indict an extraordinary number of prisoners, and by doing so had clearly suggested to the American public that all that had gone wrong at Attica was down to them. But state officials had underestimated how determined those same prisoners were to defend themselves and to make sure that this same public heard their side. In fact, from the moment that the Attica grand jury had been convened back in November of 1971, a massive prisoner defense effort had gotten under way too. It was nowhere near as well funded as the state's Attica investigation, but it was as determined.

PART VII

# Justice on Trial

# ERNEST GOODMAN

*Detroit attorney Ernie Goodman knew of the Attica prisoner uprising of 1971, but he was too busy arguing his civil rights and civil liberties cases to imagine lending his services to any of the sixty-two prisoners indicted in upstate New York.*

*For many years Goodman had been spearheading the legal efforts to ensure that protesters from Mississippi to Milwaukee got a fair trial. Goodman, however, was not what the media would characterize as a "hippie" lawyer. He was older than many of the people now flocking to the legal profession to effect social justice. He was born in 1906 in the tiny town of Hemlock, Michigan, and moved to the big city at the age of five. Life for this Jewish kid was hard. Confined to what was effectively the Motor City's Jewish ghetto, he grew up in a clapboard structure where they often had bedbugs and insufficient heat. Still, the Goodmans held their heads high, kept a kosher house, attended synagogue regularly, and hoped for a better future for their kids. In 1928 Ernie Goodman made his parents proud by getting a law degree from Wayne State College. From that year forward his mission was to fight for social justice through the legal system.*

*In 1937 Goodman was instrumental in forming the National Lawyers Guild (NLG), which was the nation's first racially integrated bar association. Over the decades he would be involved in some of the nation's most important civil rights cases. In the 1930s he worked on the Scottsboro Boys defense. In the 1940s he supported NLG efforts to prosecute Nazis at Nuremberg. In the 1950s he helped represent the Hollywood Ten, the Rosenbergs, and blacklisted artists such as Paul Robeson. In 1951 Goodman joined African American lawyer George Crockett Jr. to form the nation's first integrated law firm. By the 1960s he was immersed in school integration cases as well as in the NLG's efforts to set up offices in the South in order to provide legal support for civil rights activists there.*

*By 1974 Ernie Goodman was trying to slow down a bit, hoping that his lawyer sons would continue the fight. Yet, when he was asked to come defend an Attica prisoner, he just couldn't say no. In Goodman's view Attica was, like Scottsboro, an egregious example of the state's attempt to frame African American citizens.*

## 35

# Mobilizing and Maneuvering

No sooner had the Attica prisoner indictments been announced in December 1972 than it became clear that Special Attica Prosecutor Anthony Simonetti was eager to get these to trial quickly. Knowing this, prisoner supporters stepped up existing efforts to provide a strong defense. Back in the spring of 1972, as prosecutors were presenting evidence before the grand jury, former Attica observer Arthur Eve noted worriedly to the remaining members of the observers committee that two of their biggest priorities would be preparing for the trials and drumming up funds for the defendants' bail and legal defense. With virtually no such monies yet raised to provide help to sixty-two men now facing 1,289 criminal charges—the Attica Brothers, as they were collectively known—this task was daunting.

Back in September of 1971, a number of lawyers had come to Attica from organizations such as the American Civil Liberties Union, the Legal Aid Society, and the National Lawyers Guild and had created an Attica Defense Committee (ADC). The good news was that by December of 1972 there was still a dedicated core of young men and women from the ADC in the area determined to make sure that Attica's indictees had representation.

As dedicated as this group was, though, by 1972 it was comprised of more student volunteers than lawyers who had passed the bar. As significantly, there was no one in charge who could take on the responsibility of coordinating the larger defense effort. The ADC suspected that the state's cases wouldn't be that strong, since so much coercion had gone into securing its indictments. In fact, state prosecutors would eventually drop almost a dozen indictments, even after a trial date had been set, because their evidence was so shaky. Nevertheless, a tightly coordinated defense effort needed to be marshalled, and quickly.

The first major step in doing this was to bring as many lawyers as possible back to upstate New York. The National Lawyers Guild's annual convention in 1973 would be the ideal place to put out a call.[1] The NLG had always been centrally involved in the nation's major civil rights campaigns, including doing important work in the summer of 1964 when it sent sixty-seven attorneys and countless law students to the South to provide legal support for the Freedom Riders and other civil rights initiatives. The NLG had two significant causes to address at the 1973 convention: Wounded Knee and Attica. Assigning lawyers was simple: a line was drawn down the middle of a huge map of the United States, and it was encouraged that "everyone on this side of the line goes to Attica, everyone on this side goes to Wounded Knee."[2] By making sure that every Attica and Wounded Knee indictee had a lawyer, the NLG believed, the state wouldn't be able to turn the defendants against one another to help the state win convictions. In the summer of 1973, the NLG began another so-called summer project and scores of lawyers and law students moved into communal houses in upstate New York—one of the most crowded being located in Victory, near Auburn prison, where the majority of the indictees were being held—and began working together on the broader defense effort. By the fall of 1973, attorneys were arriving from cities around the country, including Chicago, Detroit, San Francisco, Boston, and New York. This network of lawyers and law students would soon be filing myriad pretrial motions as well as beginning the arduous task of investigating the state's claims against the Attica Brothers.

Before any of these efforts could be coordinated, the Attica Defense Committee would need an official director. Dan Pochoda, a lawyer already on the scene in early 1973, contacted his friend Don Jelinek out in California to see if he'd be interested in the job.

Don Jelinek lived in the Bay Area; agreeing to be the legal coordinator of the ADC would mean moving across the country for the indefinite future. But the Attica Brothers were a group of men in dire need of strong legal representation. And so Jelinek arrived at the communal house, in fact a large converted barn, in Victory on March 7, 1973. He quickly realized the challenge he was in for: managing twenty to thirty people, living and working together, all with very different views about how the defense should proceed.

Everyone did agree on one matter: the Attica legal defense effort needed a more formal, more effective, organizational structure. To this end, on September 21, 1973, the Attica Brothers Legal Defense (ABLD) was born. Recognizing the myriad strategic sensibilities and political viewpoints in play, the ABLD was clear in its commitment to doing both the "legal and political work" that needed to be done to help the indicted men and, as important, that "defense funds would be shared" so that all lawyers could work under this one umbrella organization.[3]

The future success of the ABLD hinged on including not just prisoner lawyers, but also local community organizations from the area such as FIGHT and BUILD out of Rochester. The leadership of FIGHT was irked that although they had bailed out many of the Attica prisoners, some of these same men had then been heard criticizing the group for not being radical enough.[4] FIGHT's and BUILD's leaders, including former Attica observer Reverend Scott, needed to be treated with a bit more respect to feel comfortable lending a hand, according to Don Jelinek.[5] By setting up both a "political office" and a "legal office" in New York City, as well as opening official ABLD locations in Berkeley, Rochester, Detroit, Chicago, and Syracuse, the ABLD was able to win the support of these more mainstream organizations, as well as satisfy the radicals.

What the ABLD really needed if it were ever going to take on the state of New York in court was cold hard cash. Four major bar associations offered funds to help the Attica defense: the Association of the Bar of the City of New York, the New York County Lawyers Association, the New York State Trial Lawyers Association, and the New York State Bar Association.[6] But this funding never approached that of the state. ABLD lawyers couldn't even access monies that were legally allotted for public defenders because the judge presiding over the calendar for all of the Attica cases, Carmen Ball, had decided not to release legal fees to any in-state attorneys until their trial had finished and refused to pay any fees to out-of-state attorneys.[7] In Ball's opinion, those lawyers "were contributing their efforts voluntarily with no expectation of reimbursement from the state."[8] And so, although the state had allocated $750,000 for the defense effort (compared with $4,500,000 for the prosecution), by May of 1974, a year into the organized defense efforts, it had yet to release any of these dollars.[9] Given that the ABLD was trying to pay for the legal assistance of eighteen defense attorneys and fund at least twenty-eight investigators, all working around the clock, this was a harsh blow.[10]

Without money for payroll, and with the state routinely refusing to hand over materials expeditiously—even when required by law to do so—the ABLD relied heavily on volunteer labor to track down everything it needed. The prosecutor's office dragged its feet giving the ABLD the names of the many Attica prisoners whom it was relying on as witnesses; so ABLD volunteers spent "some 800-odd hours of office work simply on the identification, classification, and organization of those photographs of Attica inmates."[11]

Fundraising quickly became another full-time job of the ABLD.[12] A key source of funding would come from those Attica Brothers who, having managed bail thanks to community groups such as FIGHT, could travel to campuses and community centers to speak about their defense efforts. Some of the men who had been less visible during the rebellion itself now took an active role in fundraising. One such was Attica Brother Akil Al-Jundi, who was the featured guest at an event at which movement celebrities Amiri Baraka and Afeni Shakur also spoke.[13] Similarly, Frank "Big Black" Smith drew a huge crowd on the campus of Eastern Michigan University on September 12, 1972.[14] Big Black had been paroled in August 1972, was then indicted and released on bail, and, after going back to Brooklyn and getting married, he came to Buffalo determined to work hard on the Attica defense. His talks around the country generated a great deal of support for the Attica Brothers.[15] Even if one of the indicted prisoners couldn't himself show up at a given event, organizations from coast to coast found ways to hold fundraising benefits or vigils on their behalf.[16]

Attica Brothers such as Akil Al-Jundi also approached various groups to suggest how they might help raise money for the defense through their own activities such as "leaflettings, pamphleteering, buying pamphlets, buttons, the holding of bake and cake sales" and "drawing up petitions to be sent to the courts, the Governor of New York State, the President of the United States, State senators, United States senators, Congressmen/women, and the United Nations to help us win."[17]

Even the prisoners who were still locked up, but not facing indictment, tried to assist the Attica Brothers' defense effort. One prisoner wrote to the organization RESIST expressing his concern for the many men now "facing serious charges," and he requested that its newsletter print the ABLD fundraising address "in every issue till the trials are over" as well as give a "grant of $1,000 to the Attica Brothers' Defense Fund."[18] Thanks to suggestions of this nature, a variety of publications ended up helping ABLD fundraising efforts. The Syracuse Attica Coalition, for instance, published a lengthy piece called "Attica Is All of Us," which was chock-full of information on the Brothers, and also promised that "all profits from the sale of this brochure go to the Attica Brothers Defense Fund."[19]

As an organization, the ABLD made regular pitches to anyone it could think of who might give money to help the Attica Brothers. Don Jelinek, legal coordinator of the ABLD, wrote in one November 1973 letter that "help is desperately needed. To mount the kind of defense that is required will take hundreds of thousands of dollars. Please write the largest check that you can. Your contribution is important. ATTICA needs your support."[20] In another instance the ABLD asked very specifically for "$4,575 seed money to begin preparing the defense of those charged with the Attica rebellion of September 1971."[21]

A number of community and religious organizations also made pitches on the ABLD's behalf. The Task Force for Humanity in Criminal Justice implored countless legislators to appropriate more funds to the Attica defense. A few offered support, but others forcefully indicated that they wouldn't consider spending "one dime to help defend these Attica criminals."[22] When New York elected a new governor, Malcolm Wilson, in January 1974, the American Baptist Churches of Monroe Association boldly asked him as well to "use the good services of this office to insure adequate funding for the use of the Attica indictees," but his office was loath to get involved in something so politically charged.[23]

Media celebrities and other wealthy people were more willing than elected officials to make the Attica Brothers a favorite cause. At one fundraising party held in an apartment at 610 West End Avenue, attendees were promised that famed Black Panther Angela Davis would be in attendance.[24] Other Attica bashes were held in swanky New York apartments and in posh houses in Amagansett, Long Island. One, at writer and media personality George Plimpton's house on August 20, 1972, boasted seventy-five guests and had been organized by the wife of Victor Rabinowitz, a lawyer known to take on dissident causes.[25]

By mid-1973, with publicity on the rise and monies finally trickling in from various sources around the country, the ABLD was able to begin its herculean defense effort in earnest. There were by then about fifty-six people on staff who, when possible, were making about $50 a week for their round-the-clock work.[26] In addition to living in the house in Victory, Attica lawyers and volunteer workers also occupied at least five other communal houses in Buffalo. One of these, set up by Chicago-based ABLD lawyers, was referred to as the "Linwood house." It had six huge bedrooms plus a large space on the third floor that everyone called the dormitory because it could sleep nine to ten. At least two dogs roamed freely around the house while Attica defense work went on day and night. Another house on the same street, also filled with ABLD volunteers, was known affectionately as "Little Linwood." On Auburn Street yet another house was filled with Attica lawyers and volunteers, this group primarily devoting its energy to the issue of securing fair juries for the trials. At the house on Mariner Street, Big Black Smith lived with various defense volunteers, and at the communal house on Ashland Street, still other legal volunteers lived and worked around the clock.

There were many tasks that these defense workers had to accomplish quickly, since any of the sixty-two Attica Brothers' trial dates could be set at any time. The ABLD first needed to find and interview witnesses—either to crimes that the Brothers were accused of committing or to crimes committed by law enforcement, since, it was hoped, jurors' attention could be focused on those too. The ABLD also needed to file as many motions as possible, in as short a period of time as possible, both to force the prosecution to turn over critical discovery materials, and also to bury that same prosecution in paperwork. They wanted the state of New York to be forced to defend everything, from the coercive tactics it used with witnesses in building its cases, to the specific charges it had leveled against a given Attica Brother, to the jury pool it was counting on to convict those same men. By the summer of 1974, after nearly a year of working feverishly to file countless discovery motions, motions for dismissal, motions to change venue, and motions to get the Attica Brothers still imprisoned in HBZ released into the general prison population, the ABLD succeeded in its goal of burying the prosecution in paperwork. The stack of papers was so large that Simonetti's office needed a dolly to wheel the papers before the court.[27]

The ABLD was particularly eager to learn the fate of two motions it had filed—one to change the venue of the Attica trials, and the other to force the state to turn over any evidence it planned to use. The ruling on the change of venue turned out to be a partial success. Whereas the judge refused to consider moving the trials to New York City, as some in the ABLD had hoped, he would move them further from the prison to Buffalo in Erie County. Buffalo, at least, was a big city and it had far more racial diversity, as well as a major university. The result of the ABLD's motion for discovery was an even clearer triumph for the defense. This motion, argued for more than five hours before the court on July 10, 1973, was critically important because, as Don Jelinek explained, if "granted by the court," prosecutors would be required "to turn over massive information, facts, documents, and tangible evidence in preparation for the trial."[28]

Whereas the venue motion was argued before Judge Harry Goldman of the now disbanded Goldman Panel, this discovery motion came before Judge James O. Moore—a man completely unknown to the ABLD. To its relief, though, while the Attica defense didn't win access to all of the evidence that the prosecution had, it nevertheless won a remarkable amount. Even better, Judge Moore ordered that the prosecution must copy all of this material, with separate batches for individual lawyers, at its expense. Since the state had levied nearly 1,300 crimes charged in forty-two indictments of sixty-two prisoners, who, in turn, now had at least seventy lawyers working for them, state prosecutors were dismayed by the "many hundreds of copies of everything" they would now have to produce for the defense.[29]

Although it had enjoyed some success with certain key motions, the ABLD also experienced some serious setbacks. For example, its motions to disband the Attica grand jury so that no additional Attica prisoners could be indicted failed.[30] As important, none of its motions to dismiss cases were initially successful either. In one such motion to dismiss more than a dozen indictments, defense lawyers had argued that their clients' "right to a speedy trial [was] denied" and, more serious, that the "Grand Jury [had] used illegally coerced testimony" to indict their clients and, thus, that "the evidence before the Grand Jury was not sufficient to establish offenses charged."[31] None of these arguments swayed the judge.

Attica Brothers such as Big Black took the failure of the ABLD's various motions to dismiss as simple confirmation that the judges were working hand in hand with Special Prosecutor Simonetti "and his political masters, chiefly the former governor of New York, Nelson Rockefeller."[32] Many other Attica Brothers shared this suspicion—particularly those who had been locked up in Auburn's segregation wing since their indictment. Although several of these men had managed to get out of segregation by being paroled or making bail, including Big Black and Champ, most remained. By 1974 over eighty of Attica's men in the HBZ at Auburn had been there for at least nine months, and none of their motions asking to be released to the general population—those who had been indicted or not—were successful. Auburn's superintendent had merely to let the judge know that at least twenty-two former Attica COs (three of whom had been hostages in D Yard), were now working at Auburn and also that forty-two of Auburn's own COs "had been assigned from Auburn to assist in the restoration of order at Attica," to persuade him that it simply wasn't safe for his staff to let the former Attica rebels out of segregation.[33]

The good news was that every person who had come to upstate New York to help in the ABLD defense effort was determined to keep fighting to get all of Attica's men out of segregation and to get all of them who'd been indicted acquitted. There remained, however, significant differences of opinion regarding exactly how this latter fight should be waged.

# 36

# A House Divided

At the very first meeting of lawyers committed to defending the Attica prisoners, in Buffalo on September 13, 1971, it was clear that there were serious tensions—generational, political, cultural, and strategic. Liberal lawyers like Herman Schwartz and William Hellerstein had fought bitterly that evening with younger, more radical law students and lawyers over how best to help the prisoners. As Hellerstein remembered it, he was simply "trying to figure out what we could do legally" to help the men inside, but there was much conflict in the group because others felt that, in addition to legal work, people needed to be organized politically around what was happening to the men in Attica.[1] As Schwartz explained his position, "We were not as interested in the politics as we were in the issue of civil rights and civil liberties unto themselves."[2]

But over the next few years, both legal and political work around Attica did manage to happen in concert, and all lawyers involved with Attica worked hard to do whatever was needed to represent the men behind the walls of Attica and Auburn. Minimizing factionalism was a key motivator when activist and more mainstream lawyers alike came together in 1973 under the auspices of the Attica Brothers Legal Defense. Agreeing to hire one person to coordinate that defense reflected their optimism. Nevertheless, tensions between more mainstream lawyers such as Don Jelinek and the more radical lawyers and young law student activists repeatedly threatened to undermine ABLD cohesion.

By and large, it had been the younger, more radical elements—the forces that had resisted men like Hellerstein and Schwartz in 1971—that had stayed on in Buffalo, both collecting evidence to help the Attica Brothers and also keeping media attention trained on their fate. These men and women had always been suspicious of more "establishment" lawyers, fearing that they would forgo the politically powerful lessons that could be taught and learned from Attica.

This was exactly what lawyers such as former Attica observer William Kunstler thought when he agreed to act as a defense lawyer for the ABLD, as did another self-identified radical attorney, Dennis Cunningham of the People's Law Office in Chicago. As then law student Elizabeth Fink remembered it, defending the Brothers was not just about trying to prove that they hadn't committed a crime, it was also about going on the offensive and investigating the state and its wrongdoings, because "politics belonged in the courtroom."[3] As for the upcoming trials of the Attica Brothers, the key would be to make as much noise as possible about how these men were being railroaded by the state by making sure, for example, that "hundreds of people demonstrated in Buffalo where the trials were to be held."[4]

Because not everyone who had come to Attica to assist the indictees agreed with this view, two defense camps existed at all times. One insisted that the attorneys should mount effective and straightforward legal arguments of the Brothers' innocence only, and one argued that attention should also be trained on the reprehensible actions of the state both in and outside of the courtroom, and where even the illegal acts of prisoners might be defended as justifiable given the broader repression of that same state.[5]

Without question Don Jelinek included himself in the former group. The focus on the politics of Attica, in his view, was mostly just grandstanding and a distraction from the grunt work of filing motions and doing the legal research that would lead to sound arguments in court. Even worse, he feared, such tactics might end up alienating the very jurors the Brothers would be relying on for acquittals. NLG lawyer Ernest Goodman tended to agree with this view and worried as well about the "considerable differences of opinion" among those working on the Attica defense. He, however, felt it important not to draw a line in the sand and, instead, to really think through how cases ought to be handled, the role of the lawyer, the relationship between attorneys, the Brothers and the legal workers, and the correct approach to a 'political' case."[6]

Even the sixty-two Attica Brothers themselves were at times deeply divided over questions of strategy. By 1973 when most of the pretrial work was taking place in the ABLD, clear camps were developing in the prisoner ranks as well.

For example, Big Black was close with some of the more radical attorneys, like Dennis Cunningham, and he argued strongly for making the trials as political as possible. He felt that Attica's main defense struggles should not "be waged in the courtroom" but instead belonged "in the communities and in the street," because the law did not serve "everyone's needs on the same level" and, thus, there was no guarantee of fairness let alone victory in the courtroom.[7] The system needed outside pressure to respond to injustice meaningfully.[8] Big Black was so disillusioned with the more legalistic strategy of men like Jelinek that he came to create his own defense group, the Attica Now Collective (ANC). This group did not break formally from the ABLD but focused its attention on political work. Eventually this group would include Dennis Cunningham as well as another People's Law Office lawyer, Michael Deutsch, and newly minted J.D.s Elizabeth Fink and Joe Heath. The ANC published a newsletter called *Attica News* out of a storefront in the heart of the black area of Buffalo; one of the key missions of this broadsheet was to get word out nationally about the Attica Brothers' cases.[9]

However, Attica Brother Shango Bahati Kakawana, known by the state as Bernard Stroble, did not see things as his fellow indictee Big Black did. Shango had been indicted for the murders of Barry Schwartz and Kenneth Hess. At first he too was deeply suspicious of the state and of his chances within any New York courtroom. Yet as his trial date came closer, he found himself gravitating toward a more traditional defense strategy and would come to rely on Detroit's Ernie Goodman to save him from a devastating sentence. The way Shango saw it, it was impossible to make an effective political point without first winning a legal victory. Further, in his view fighting for one's innocence in the courtroom—through legal channels—*was* political because it was a concrete way for him and the rest of the Attica Brothers to challenge their oppression. "I'll accept A[ttica] N[ow]'s position," he explained in a public exchange with Big Black, "<u>ONLY</u> if they are prepared to give me other means towards securing liberation."[10] All struggles were legitimate, he maintained, and they needed to take place "<u>in the courtroom or wherever oppression exists.</u>"[11]

The Attica Brothers also differed mightily in their opinions of the role that they themselves should play in their own defense efforts. Some, such as Willie Smith, Vernon LaFranque, John Hill, and Charles Pernasalice, were content to have outside lawyers do all of the defense work on their behalf, deferring totally to their judgment. But others felt strongly that they must play an active role in their defense and, although they agreed to have lawyers represent them, they insisted on making any strategic decisions in equal partnership with those attorneys. This was exactly how Big Black, Shango, and Jomo Joka Omowale felt, and they joined with lawyers in their own defense. Legally they had every right to represent themselves, and while more traditional NLG lawyers such as Goodman believed that working alongside pro se–designated clients made court appearances awkward, lengthy, and at times confusing, the more radical lawyers such as Michael Deutsch held that it was crucial to let the Brothers speak for themselves. This way, he said, "we weren't coaching brothers with rhetoric—they came to it on their own."[12]

Whatever their legal standing in their own defense, many of the Attica Brothers came to develop close relationships with their attorneys—including some romantic ones, which generated wholly new tensions between the Brothers awaiting trial. By 1974 there were significant romantic relationships between lawyer Elizabeth (Liz) Gaynes and Jomo, between legal investigator Linda Borus and Shango, and between attorney Barbara Handschu and Mariano "Dalou" Gonzalez. All of these men were still locked up and awaiting trial.

The relationship between Barbara Handschu and Dalou was the first to generate suspicions and tensions among the Brothers. On one occasion a conflict arose when two defendants were overheard besmirching Dalou, suggesting that he was using Handschu to save his own skin and cared nothing for the rest of them. In response, one of Dalou's defenders wrote to some of the other men awaiting trial, "I for one feel that there is nothing Bro. Dalou would do on a personal level that would subordinate the interest of the Brothers/people to his personal interest," but others in the group felt that his relationship with his lawyer suggested otherwise.[13] Attica Brother Richard Clark, for example, was openly hostile to Handschu and, as she reported to Dalou, he "unjustifiably attacked" with some critical words about her promoting women's rights when she should be worrying about the "the real struggle at Attica."[14] Whatever jealousies or suspicions her relationship with Dalou generated, Handschu's myriad motions filed and hours logged on behalf of the other Brothers indicated that she was committed to getting all of them acquitted.

By 1974 virtually all of the Attica lawyers had come to care deeply for the Brothers on a personal level. What the Brothers thought about the lawyers, though, was more varied and fraught. Big Black would go on to have a lifelong friendship with his legal advocates, particularly Elizabeth Fink, and Jomo eventually would marry Liz Gaynes, but Dalou seemed to be much more ambivalent about his relationship with Barbara Handschu. Although Barbara repeatedly expressed to Dalou how passionately she felt about him, writing, "I miss you, perhaps more than you know. Te quiero, b," his replies were more political and practical.[15] As one of his letters to her began, "Power b: With the dialectical understanding evolving in the universe, I greet you with a clenched fist of love, power and solidarity! Palente!" In another, he mostly focused on making sure that she had done something for him (get a letter he wrote on Puerto Rican prisoners to *The New York Times*) and on ensuring that she did not let on to anyone that they were in any kind of romance. To his fellow Attica Brothers, Dalou maintained that Handschu was merely "a comrade at arms," who also facilitated "Y.L.P. [Young Lords Party] communications with me and NYC" and who sent him books that were "meant for the collective," and he signed his letters to her "In struggle: Bro. Dalou."[16]

Another source of tension and suspicion among the Brothers was the fact that some of the Brothers had managed to make bail, and were free to speak around the country and work on their own defenses, while others remained locked first at Auburn in segregation and then in the Erie County courthouse jail, where they were all moved in 1974. Shango, for example, did not make bail and as he languished month after month in a tiny cell awaiting his trial, it infuriated him that other indictees such as Richard Clark and Roger Champen were becoming minor celebrities and seemingly living the good life. Worse, he felt that these bailed Brothers were exploiting the trauma they had all suffered in order to become famous. As he saw it, "the death of the brothers was being opportunized by everyone" and certain men on the outside had begun "backstabbing, lying, exaggerating, distorting the facts, projecting false personality's/politics, etc., etc." merely so they could "win the attention and favor" of outsiders.[17]

This sense of betrayal only became more acute when, just as trials were about to begin in 1974, it was discovered that some of the bailed Brothers, namely Herb Blyden and Roger Champen, had stolen ABLD defense funds to feed drug addictions.[18] Shango blamed them for causing Big Black to break off into his Attica Now group, since Black now worried that the ABLD couldn't be trusted to protect the defense funds he and others would need. In Shango's view, Attica Now had arisen "from the ashes of the burning bank accounts ignited by the greed and lust of so-called Attica brothers Richard Clark, Roger Champen, Herbert Blyden, et. al: media projected 'leaders' of the Attica rebellion." In 1974 Attica Brother Jomo also formed his own defense camp, an organization called Attica Bond to Free Jomo.[19]

By the time the trials got under way, there were four major camps operating within the ABLD—Big Black's Attica Now, Jomo's Attica Bond to Free Jomo, the Friends of Attica Brother Shango group, and those not affiliated with one of these groups who were represented by myriad other attorneys who volunteered their services to the defense.[20] Despite these divisions, the ABLD remained a remarkably effective organization.

In January 1974, a highly respected black lawyer named W. Haywood Burns replaced Don Jelinek—who seemed particularly to raise the hackles of the Attica Now–affiliated lawyers and volunteers—as the ABLD's new legal coordinator.

Burns's background was no more revolutionary than Jelinek's. He had graduated from Harvard, received his law degree from Yale, and then served as federal judge Constance Baker Motley's first clerk as well as general counsel to Martin Luther King's Poor People's Campaign. In addition Burns was one of the founders of the National Conference of Black Lawyers. However, Burns was much more comfortable than Jelinek had been with allowing the Brothers to help shape their own defense strategy; thus, the radical lawyers liked him much better. As a sign of this new cooperative spirit, when Burns took the helm of the ABLD, Big Black became the organization's executive director. Thanks to this new leadership structure, as well as Don Jelinek's hard work throughout 1973 making sure that crucial pretrial work had gotten done (particularly overseeing the filing of an avalanche of motions that would make later defense work both easier and much more effective), the different defense teams were now able to proceed with the trials as they wished and yet remain under the auspices of the ABLD. Every Attica Brother could count on a remarkable and vast network of people in the ABLD who would work both together and separately to make sure every one of them was ready to face state prosecutors when the time came.

# 37

# Laying the Groundwork

Before trials were to begin in the fall of 1974, the Attica Brothers Legal Defense team still had three major tasks to accomplish. First, it needed to ascertain whether there would, in fact, be a trial for every indictee. The prosecution was making noises that it might consider some deals; given that there were nearly 1,300 indictments and eighty-five different groups of charges, and that this was well on "track to be . . . the largest criminal defense effort in American history," any overtures to dismiss indictments would be welcome.[1] Second, if there were going to be trials, the ABLD needed to have completed whatever groundwork could be done ahead of time to make sure that the jury pool would be as representative and reflective of the Brothers as possible. Given the high concentration of prison employees in Erie County, this was a daunting task. Finally, the ABLD needed to make sure that all of its lawyers took advantage of every opportunity that could potentially net the Attica Brothers exculpatory evidence. Under New York State's so-called Rosario rule, they could request state-held evidence; they could also request that their clients have something called Wade hearings prior to the actual trials. The Attica Brothers particularly wanted these latter pretrial hearings because in them the state would have to disclose how it had identified the defendants—whether their procedures had been aboveboard.[2]

Whether all the Attica Brothers would in fact go to trial had been a topic of serious discussion between Attica Special Prosecutor Anthony Simonetti and Don Jelinek in early 1974. Even though Jelinek was no longer serving as ABLD coordinator, he was determined to stay involved. Jelinek and the Attica special prosecutor discussed the possibility of plea deals or even the dismissal of indictments. Jelinek had hoped that his talks with Simonetti would lead to what he later referred to as "the mother of all plea bargains."[3] To Jelinek's frustration, however, Simonetti kept giving him mixed messages about what would be possible for the Brothers.[4]

These discussions first began in February 1974 and involved Victor Rabinowitz, former Attica observer Tom Wicker, and Haywood Burns, as well as Jelinek and Simonetti. Initially, Simonetti intimated that a deal might be struck in which no one indicted for their actions at Attica would serve time (including the troopers, if any, who might be indicted in the future).[5] By March 4, 1974, however, Simonetti was backtracking on the issue of jail time for the prisoner defendants; he suggested instead that individual prisoners be offered deals determined by a judge. Jelinek rejected this outright, playing hardball: "You *know* that dismissals are your only route to avoid indicting *your* people"—meaning that Simonetti would never have to indict state troopers.[6] Simonetti weighed his options, ultimately declaring that any prisoner who was interested in a plea deal would have to make it known by April 29, 1974. Jelinek decided to take the decision to the Brothers themselves by secret ballot.[7] He was leery of recommending a deal since it wasn't clear what the terms would be, and he wasn't persuaded that Simonetti really had the power to make the deals he was hinting at, but he felt the defendants should make their own decision.[8] However, Jelinek had not previously sought advice from any of the Attica Brothers regarding the negotiations that had led to this current deal; this made them suspicious. Big Black announced that if someone wanted to take a plea deal they could, but there would be no secret ballot. And that was the end of that. Trial dates were now a certainty.

And so, beginning in May of 1974, ABLD teams were hard at work to make sure that the Brothers would have the least biased juries possible hearing their cases. The primary leader of this effort was a twenty-four-year-old member of the National Lawyers Guild, Beth Bonora.[9] Bonora had been inspired by a comprehensive 1966 study of juries that suggested a scientific methodology could be used to make sure jury panels were less prejudiced than they otherwise would be when relying on the usual process of selecting eligible voters. She was interested in seeing if this was something the ABLD could use to help the Attica Brothers.

It was well known that even with a careful voir dire during jury selection (the process in which potential jurors were questioned as to their views and potential prejudices), jurors regularly lied "to make themselves acceptable or unacceptable to one side or the other."[10] Jurors' prejudices could matter a great deal to a trial's outcome. Bonora wasn't alone in thinking that it was possible to do research that would, in turn, impact a jury's composition. In 1971 a Columbia sociologist named Jay Schulman had published an article that suggested concrete ways a more open-minded jury could be attained. In one particular 1971 Pennsylvania trial (in which the Harrisburg 8—nuns and priests and a Pakistani journalist, all antiwar activists—were tried for "conspiring to kidnap National Security Advisor Henry Kissinger and blowing up steam tunnels under government buildings in Washington, D.C."), defense lawyers had used so-called scientific jury selection to great effect.[11] That defense team had worked closely with social scientists to analyze the community from which jurors would come as well as "to develop juror profiles for use in jury selection."[12] When these efforts led to a jury that favored dismissal of all charges against the eight defendants, progressive lawyers around the country took notice—particularly Beth Bonora. With the Attica trials looming, her "job was to work with social scientists, attorneys, the many volunteers, and community members to put the jury system under the microscope."[13]

Thanks to the investigative efforts of Bonora and her team, the ABLD managed almost immediately to get a court order to inspect the jury commissioner's records that indicated ways in which the jury selection process was clearly discriminatory. For example, "the qualification process used in the office included handwritten notations about the race of black citizens."[14] After a flurry of filing motions, the newly formed "Fair Jury Project" of the ABLD (usually just called the Jury Project) was able to reconstitute the entire Erie County jury pool: "some 115,000 prospective jurors [were] dumped and a new system instituted."[15]

Needless to say, this was a major victory. However, few in the ABLD were naive enough to think that the next pool would be much better. It was still comprised of Erie County residents—many of whom didn't trust African Americans or prisoners. And so Bonora and her team then began the arduous process, recommended by Schulman's research, of compiling data from surveys of potential jurors that could be used "to select as favorable a jury as possible."[16] Such careful and intensive research into what demographic characteristics generally indicated about a potential juror's viewpoints yielded the ABLD some predictable, and alarming, information, but also some surprises. On the one hand, in any sample of the potential jury pool, "approximately 23% of the people surveyed felt that they could not accept the court's instructions concerning the presumption of innocence," "almost 42% of those surveyed volunteered some form of demeaning racial stereotype in response to a question concerning black people," and "31% of Erie County voters believe that 'radicals' and 'black militants' should be imprisoned solely because of their beliefs, whether or not a violation of law had occurred."[17] Unexpectedly, they also discovered that "*New York Times* readers in Buffalo were not necessarily good choices for the defense."[18]

These kinds of tools for scientific jury selection were already in regular use by prosecutors. As Schulman's guide to successful jury selection explained, similar research was already "regularly conducted by federal and state prosecutors and various commercial investigating services."[19] Such work was much harder for the Attica defense effort, since they had far fewer resources than either group.

It took an enormous amount of both time and money to create a large enough community network to know how a potential juror might view prisoner defendants. If a potential Attica juror was a member of the League of Women Voters, for example, the ABLD Jury Project needed to already have a network in place in that community, which they would canvass to see if anyone knew the juror or shared a mutual acquaintance. Contacts would then be interviewed to determine whether the potential juror had any black friends, had ever used racial slurs, and so forth.[20] Undaunted by what it would take to build these networks and score the demographic characteristics of potential Erie County jurors, the ABLD's legal volunteers got to work. They talked to as many people in the county as they could—meeting them "outside churches, shopping centers, and sports arenas," and surveying them about their affiliations, religion, heritage, habits, and views.[21] In time the ABLD Jury Project managed to sample seven hundred voters from the Buffalo metro area, which had 1,400,000 residents, while keeping the costs down to about "$400.00 in basic research expenses."[22]

The Jury Project's systematic research complemented the ABLD's other massive investigative efforts. Many in the ABLD believed that in order to defend the Attica Brothers successfully, they needed to know as much as possible about what troopers had done at the prison on the day of the retaking and over the subsequent days and weeks, and also who had ordered and overseen their actions throughout that time. They hoped, in effect, to "put the state on trial" in the Brothers' criminal trials, and also, one day, to use this evidence in a civil case against the state. Such evidence of trooper violence could also mobilize people outside the courtroom to support the Brothers.[23] So, while the Jury Project surveyed Buffalo residents to facilitate jury selection, phalanxes of other young ABLD workers began a sustained effort to interview anyone who had been in D Yard on the day of the retaking and the days after.

The most comprehensive interviewing effort involved National Guardsmen, who had not participated in the retaking but who had gone in shortly thereafter to deal with its carnage. The ABLD managed to obtain a list of about five hundred guardsmen who had been called to Attica that day and decided they would send two people "to a Guardsman's house, unannounced, and ask to talk to them . . . [hoping to] document the crimes of the state which we knew existed and were not being investigated by anyone else."[24] In addition to locating the rank-and-file guardsmen who had been in D Yard, these ABLD investigators also wanted to speak with the National Guard physicians who might be able to provide first-hand accounts of the medical impact of the retaking.[25]

The ABLD learned much from the interviews they conducted, including blow-by-blow descriptions of how brutally the State Police had treated the prisoners. However, to their frustration, it was difficult for these witnesses to identify the men who had perpetrated this trauma. The guardsmen usually did not know these troopers' names. Given that three years had passed and that the troopers had deliberately removed their badges on the day of the assault, it was hard for the guardsmen to remember specific faces from the "hundreds of people running around in uniforms—C.O.s, S.T.s [state troopers], Sheriffs, etc." on the day of the retaking.[26] Nevertheless, the project was considered a great success. ABLD workers compiled the interviews, numbered them, and created an index of the forty or so salient points that had been revealed.[27] The ABLD managed to gather crucial information on what briefing and instructions the National Guardsmen had received, their command responsibilities, the way in which medical treatment had been doled out, the gauntlets and beatings they had seen, and how state officials had ordered them not to discuss any of it.[28] By the time they were ready to begin pretrial hearings, the Wade hearings that were allowed them by law, the ABLD attorneys were well armed. They had requested an enormous amount of material from the state via countless discovery motions and had set up a complex system for organizing and analyzing those materials.[29]

Although the ABLD lawyers had little idea which cases the state would decide to try and when, they were already spending a great deal of time in Judge Carmen Ball's courtroom. Virtually every administrative proceeding—particularly the arraignments of the Attica Brothers—packed the courtrooms with ABLD supporters who were often boisterous and were constantly watched by a heavy presence of law enforcement both within the courthouse and on its grounds, which led to a great deal of tension. At Big Black's arraignment, for example, he became so frustrated with the judge's seeming disinterest in what he had to say that he had summarily "ripped up his indictment" and accused Ball of being "a 'full-fledged member of the KKK.' "[30] The courtroom became so charged in proceedings like this that one young woman in attendance noted in a journal she was keeping: "They've changed the water glasses from glass (breakable—a possible weapon) to plastic (almost red in color). Must be at least 50 cops upstairs today. Metal detectors and search downstairs. Each cop has his Billy club. Milling around. Fat bellies. Joking, tense, defensive."[31]

During the various pretrial conferences that followed the contentious arraignments and calendar calls, the atmosphere grew steadily more strained. The Brothers had already waited a long time for the state to decide whether they would even go to trial. Now in these various meetings it became clear that they would not get all the resources they needed to prepare a solid defense—especially if they were representing themselves pro se. At one particularly prickly pretrial conference before Judge Ball, Big Black tried to persuade the judge that he needed money to hire an investigator, reminding him that he had nowhere near the resources to prepare for his own defense as the state had to try to convict him. As he put it, "the only people that had did any work or was authorized to get any money to do any work, had been the state. How can I prepare, really?"[32] "Well, Frank," Ball replied coldly, "these are all problems that you can put on the record in such form as you see fit and they will be reviewed at a proper time."[33] To the judge's surprise, Big Black persisted. "This ain't no joke, Judge. How are you going to tell me that I'm supposed to be ready in 60 days, and the state done took three years Judge; I mean is that a constitutional right, a violation? What do you call this?"[34] This got Big Black nowhere.

The Attica Brothers did have one additional way to strengthen each of their cases before their trials actually began, thanks to two landmark cases, *People of the State of New York v. Rosario* (1961) and *Brady v. Maryland* (1963), decided by the Supreme Court of the United States. These decisions meant that Attica defendants were allowed to challenge prosecutors' prior determination that certain materials were not exculpatory in case they in fact were.[35] The Rosario material they were entitled to included any statements of state witnesses who would testify at the trial, law enforcement forms that might summarize a witness statement, any signed statements by a witness, and the paperwork prepared by a testifying police officer. In addition, the prosecution was obligated to hand over all of that material before a defendant's trial began. Additionally, under the *Brady* decision, "in recognition of the prosecutor's special access to police and other information," the Attica Brothers would be entitled to "any exculpatory evidence" the prosecution might hold.[36] They were also entitled to any evidence that police officer informants had knowingly lied or that its civilian witnesses might have given false statements or been remunerated for acting as a state informant.[37]

However, although "all of these rights are legally absolute," ABLD lawyers couldn't count on getting any of these materials. Simonetti didn't even give them a list of possible witnesses his men might call until "finally threatened with contempt proceedings," and, according to the ABLD, it still took state officials another full year "to comply with repeated court orders by delivering the names of the probable witnesses, as well as other documents to which the defense was obviously entitled."[38] Even when materials were turned over, the ABLD accused the prosecution of supplying "intentionally inaccurate" inmate identification numbers to thwart defense "attempts to locate witnesses."[39] The state dragged its feet so badly on turning over records that Dennis Cunningham wrote directly to Anthony Simonetti on March 8, 1974, to "remind [him] that, among the many aspects of Judge Moore's Discovery Order with which your office has not yet complied is the direction Paragraph 10 regarding disclosure of informers in the defense camp."[40]

The most important legal tool the Attica defendants had when it came to crafting a strong defense turned out to be the Wade hearings. In these pretrial hearings, the state was required to show that the procedures it had used to identify the defendants (e.g., lineups, witness interviews) had been proper and legal.[41] If the investigators' procedures were found to have been "unconstitutionally suggestive," that evidence could be thrown out.[42] The defense could benefit twice over: in order to show that its work was aboveboard, the state had to give up the names of those witnesses who had identified the defendants—giving the ABLD lawyers the access they so desperately wanted to these formerly anonymous witnesses.

## 38

# Testing the Waters

Despite the extraordinary care the ABLD took to prepare for the trials of the Attica indictees, it was allowed to play only a very small role in the first case that made real news, that of Richard Bilello in December 1973. This first case didn't even go to trial because Bilello took a very public plea to charges of kidnapping, coercion, and unlawful imprisonment. Nevertheless, it was a court proceeding that seemed to say to the nation that Simonetti's team was making its cases of prisoner guilt with remarkable ease.

Bilello wanted nothing to do with the ABLD defense effort. A white Attica prisoner with Mafia connections who was already serving a forty-years-to-life sentence for a barroom killing, he saw them as "political lawyers" who "really have no interest in anyone." As he explained at his arraignment, he just wanted his own "good criminal lawyer."[1] It seemed to the ABLD that Bilello refused to put his lot in with the other Attica Brothers because he feared retaliation from his fellow Italian mafiosi for doing so. Yet Bilello also worried about antagonizing the Attica Brothers if he didn't stand with them.[2] So concerned was Bilello about making the wrong choice regarding his own defense strategy—and which prisoners he was, in effect, siding with—that at his arraignment on December 29, 1973, he begged Judge Carmen Ball "for a court order for protection."[3]

Ultimately Bilello decided to take his chances at going it alone before Judge Ball. Although he constituted quite a pathetic figure as he stood before the court, it was clear that Richie Bilello was not at all shy about speaking on his own behalf. When he finally came before Ball, after spending hours in a holding cell with other Attica defendants waiting to be arraigned, he was obviously seething. "This morning I am shabby in appearance, in shackles," he said to the judge. "We have been in shackles since seven-fifteen this morning. It is now one twenty-five your Honor." When the shackles weren't removed Bilello continued more forcefully, "We must be sitting in a room, worse than any animal, the wildest animal in the zoo has no chains on it. . . . We are held worse than convicted people. . . . [Has the state] put us in a place where [we] lose the presumption of innocence before trial?"[4] In addition to pointing out the ugly treatment of the Attica defendants, Bilello also tried to impress upon the judge how few resources any of them had to prepare even a modicum of an effective defense. He was "entitled to one phone call a month," but in order to track down witnesses and try to prepare his case, he would need access to "a phone sometimes three, four times a day."[5]

Ultimately, Bilello's defense was that he couldn't have committed the crimes of which he was accused because he had been in keeplock the entire time of the rebellion. As he put it, "I shouldn't even be in this courtroom" because "I was in a keeplock cell that I had no key to. Twenty-eight cells away from the front door where they were rounding up hostages, or whatever they were doing. And I am in the courtroom indicted for getting hostages. This isn't even logical."[6] He had naively written to state prosecutor Maxwell Spoont, begging him to find the corroborating paperwork: "What I am asking for is your personal investigation as to the effect that I speak of. . . . I shall [then] be able to prove I was in keeplock and I shall be able to prove my innocence."[7] But it soon became clear that no one was ever going to get Bilello his "proof"—certainly not the same prosecutor who was trying to convict him—and, without that, he decided to plead guilty just to get the whole ordeal over with.[8]

Simonetti's office was delighted. If things kept going this way, the future looked bright. The state might not get outright convictions every time, but it could clearly get prisoners to admit criminal wrongdoing at Attica—certainly what Rockefeller had wanted to happen when he launched the Attica investigation.

The future was not so bright for Richie Bilello. On his way to a counseling session at the Clinton Correctional Facility on September 29, 1974, forty-four-year-old Bilello was stabbed repeatedly in the chest and back by another prisoner, mobster Donald Frankos.[9] Although even the FBI knew that this had been a mob hit, state officials still tried to imply that his death might have been on the hands of an Attica rebel, stating suggestively: "there was no way to ascertain whether the stabbing was related to the three-year old Attica Rebellion."[10]

Emboldened by Bilello's guilty plea, Simonetti's office proceeded right away to take an Attica case to trial—one that given its salacious nature might be won easily and also serve to undermine any public sympathy that clearly existed for the prisoner defendants. As ABLD lawyer Michael Deutsch saw it, by choosing to try this case before any of the others, the state was "really, really trying to prejudice the media."[11] African American prisoner William Smith had been charged with first-degree sodomy and the sexual assault of a young white prisoner. He faced a possible thirty-two-year sentence for subjecting "James Schleich to sexual contact by forcible compulsion" and for having "deviant sexual intercourse with James Schleich by forcible compulsion," and the case was to be tried by seasoned prosecutor Brian Malone.[12] Twenty-seven-year-old Willie Smith's defense lawyer hailed from Rochester and was known to specialize in rape and sodomy cases. He was, however, not particularly close to the ABLD and had not partaken of any of their pretrial work—for example, he didn't utilize any of their Jury Project research. Worse, many of the ABLD members did not think much of his attorney; in their view, Smith's attorney was totally incompetent (for example, not making obvious objections when he clearly should have). Still, the state's evidence against Willie Smith was so thin, they remained hopeful.

Jury selection had begun on September 26 for Smith's trial and, without use of the Jury Project, there ultimately would only be one black juror. Still, things didn't go at all well for the prosecution. During the first full week of the trial, for example, investigators from the Bureau of Criminal Investigation were called to the stand and, when asked for the notes they had taken while conducting their interviews of the state's witnesses in this case, they claimed not to be able to do so because "paper shredders had been installed in the prison for use immediately after each prisoner interview."[13] Then, another BCI investigator testified that, for the first time in his seventeen years on the job, "he had been ordered <u>not</u> to take notes during prisoner interviews" because, he admitted, the NYSP wanted to "evade the legal requirement that all such notes be turned over to the defense before a trial as Rosario material."[14] The judge was not at all pleased to hear such testimony and the jurors were bothered by it as well.

Whereas the ABLD felt that this information alone should have led to Smith's case being dismissed—since the evidence the state was relying on was gathered in violation of clear-cut rules and laws—ultimately it was a technical error on the part of the prosecution that undid the state's case against Willie Smith. In short, as ABLD lawyer Elizabeth Fink recalled later, "Brian Malone made a crucial stupid mistake. In sexual cases back then you needed corroboration. There was a statement that Schleich [the victim] had made that they admitted under evidence. But they hadn't read rules on evidence which said that they couldn't use this statement as corroboration."[15] Ultimately Justice Frank R. Bayger felt "the evidence was too flimsy to warrant a jury's consideration" and told the jury pointedly that "the state had failed to provide the necessary corroboration for the testimony of the alleged victim," and on October 9, 1974, he officially dismissed the charge of sodomy and charge of sexual assault against Smith, thus freeing him.[16] When the news broke, throngs of young people gathered outside the courtroom and enthusiastically chanted, "Free the Attica Brothers."[17]

Although the ABLD had every reason to celebrate the outcome of this first official round with the state, the behind-the-scenes story of how victim James Schleich had been used by the state's investigators was heartbreaking. There was little doubt that James Schleich along with his twin brother, John Schleich, had been raped during the first hours of complete chaos in the Attica rebellion. That very day, they had gone straight to the men in charge in D Yard, begging them to find the perpetrators, which they duly set out to do. Even six weeks later, when doctors examined the brothers on October 27, 1971, they still were clearly traumatized from being "forced into anal sodomy the first day of the Attica Riot."[18] What was equally clear, however, was that the victims of this crime had no idea who the men who had hurt them were and, despite knowing this, the state had proceeded with its case—dragging them, and eventually Willie Smith, into a years-long legal ordeal.

In extensive and wrenching testimony, James's brother, John, had told the grand jury the story of what had happened to him and his brother on the morning of September 9, 1971.[19] He had seen his brother dragged away to a bathroom by a group of men and then he too was captured at knifepoint and taken to that same remote location where the two of them were raped by "a group of five or six individuals" for "about 30 to 40 minutes."[20] As much as John Schleich wanted the grand jury to know that he and his brother had endured a terrible assault during the Attica rebellion, however, he had been clear with the BCI well before coming to that grand jury that they couldn't identify their assailants then or later. When they were shown photographs of Willie Smith, neither he nor his brother had ever indicated that Smith was one of their rapists.

John Schleich had nevertheless agreed to testify before the grand jury because he actually hoped it would address the brutality that state troopers had meted out during the retaking. He told these jurors of his dismay and fear when a trooper had grabbed him and aggressively ripped off his St. Christopher medal, and then snatched his "watch and hit that as a baseball bat—or like it was a baseball."[21] John also wanted grand jurors to know just how terrible it was that the state had placed him and his brother somewhere like Attica in the first place. As he told the jury, he had been placed in this maximum security facility at the age of nineteen for a mere parole violation—for the "unauthorized use of a motor vehicle"; his brother had missed his curfew while on parole for the crime of cutting a hole in a convertible top. John had desperately addressed the grand jury: "I want to know if anything ever going to be done about this stuff going on in these prisons? . . . There's a whole lot more kids it happened to. . . . Now, you're the people, you should be able to do something about this. . . . Is that any place for a kid to be, nineteen years old?"[22] Instead of trying to respond to John Schleich's questions, the jurors had instead chosen to indict Willie Smith.

Needless to say, losing this case was a real blow to Simonetti's office.

Still, Assistant Attorney General Simonetti felt hopeful. His team was reasonably confident that it could convince jurors in the next trial up that Vernon LaFranque had used a gas gun to subdue the hostages. Not coincidentally, LaFranque was yet another Attica prisoner who had not worked particularly closely with the ABLD to mount his defense. At his arraignment on December 18, 1972, LaFranque had entered a plea of not guilty. By June 16, 1973, he had retained Don Jelinek so that he might file some motions, but by the time his trial began LaFranque had gone through two more attorneys.[23] Fearing that LaFranque's defense wasn't in very good shape, and knowing that the state's prosecutors were extremely eager to recover from their loss in the Willie Smith case, the ABLD tried its best to stay involved.[24]

On December 19, 1974, the state prosecutors were thwarted yet again. A jury comprised of nine women and three men issued its unanimous not guilty verdict after only half an hour of deliberations. In short, they had been not at all persuaded by the state's witnesses. As an ABLD newsletter explained, "all three witnesses for the state changed their stories several times, and their earlier written statements turned out to be 'lost.' In addition, a former prisoner testified that he saw the state's star witness pull Vernon out of a line of prisoners after the assault and beat him to the ground."[25] Several jurors later told the press "they believed the state's testimony against Vernon had been fabricated."[26]

Two major trial victories were just what the ABLD lawyers needed to marshal the energy to face the series of far more challenging cases just on the horizon. Such victories were a boon to fundraising, and helped attract several prominent people to put their names on fundraising pleas, including political luminaries Bella Abzug, Julian Bond, Noam Chomsky, Daniel Ellsberg, Jessica Mitford, and Charles Rangel.[27]

The next case up would be the most challenging and significant to date for the ABLD—and the state's most important case to win. In January of 1975, the state would try the alleged killers of Attica CO William Quinn.

## 39

# Going for Broke

By 1974 Anthony Simonetti had good reason to feel that his prosecutors could persuade a jury to convict John Hill and Charles Pernasalice—the two young prisoners whom his office had indicted for the murder and second-degree assault of correction officer William Quinn. The case against these two Attica Brothers, the state hoped, would be its most powerful opportunity to justify why it had, to date, focused its energy exclusively on the riot-related actions of prisoners. They had brutally killed a young man for no reason, and his family, prosecutors would show, remained unimaginably traumatized by this horrific act.

Time had moved on for the Quinn family—the baby that Nancy Quinn had been carrying back in September 1971 was now a toddler named Amy, and her eldest daughter, Deanne, was now eight years old. But time had not healed this family. Not having a husband was not easy in the small town of Attica. Nancy was suddenly without an income and had to ask others for help. She felt deep shame every time she had to go to the local bank and ask if she might have some money from the meager Attica Widows fund that well-wishers had set up, or had to ask someone else's family to assist her and her girls in some way. What's more, life as an Attica widow had made her a national curiosity. She was always having to take the phone off the hook to stop the incessant calls from reporters and, as the trial for her husband's killing loomed, reporters began showing up at the house unannounced. Her own feelings about the trial were mixed. On the one hand, a trial meant that she would have to relive the nightmare of her husband's death all over again. Yet if the state indeed knew who had killed her husband, and if it could put those men away, then at least she might be able to feel some closure and begin her life anew.

The two individuals who sat in the courtroom waiting for their trial to begin, however, barely looked like men at all. John Hill, who went by the name Dacajewiah, had been only nineteen years old when the Attica rebellion began. At twenty-two, he still looked like a scrawny kid—although he didn't much resemble the young men his age in the village of Attica familiar to either the Quinn family or to potential jurors. Hill was part Mohawk Indian, he had long hair, and looked very much like what the media had dubbed a "hippie."

That John Hill was now sitting as a defendant in this trial was itself ironic. Hill had been at Attica for less than two months when the rebellion began. The way he saw it, he was hardly a seasoned criminal. As a kid he had robbed a sub shop and had been sent to the juvenile reformatory at Elmira. The only reason that he ended up at that maximum security facility was because, when he turned nineteen, he still had a few months of penance to do. He believed he would be granted parole in October of 1971.[1]

When Hill landed at Attica in August 1971 he had been housed in A Block but he immediately began trying to get moved to the metal shop, hoping to learn a real trade before his release. He wasn't particularly politically active, although he did notice that there were lots of very political people in Attica—"lots of activists coming in from [the] street. Black Panthers. Black Liberation Movement."[2] In the short time that Hill had been at Attica he found himself thinking more about things like discrimination. He couldn't get over the fact that so many of the white COs there were very hostile to the nonwhite prisoners. As he saw it, their racism wasn't at all subtle, but instead very "brutal, right in your face."[3] He had been shocked one day when he watched "as two guys were beaten just for talking in line."[4] When the prison had exploded on the morning of September 9, he was not at all surprised. The place was "thick with rage at the guards there—so many beatings, so many lockdowns, so much solitary."[5] On that morning Hill had been in A Block tunnel—at the epicenter of the riot—and he admitted to being part of the huge group of prisoners that surged through Times Square when William Quinn was so viciously beaten. However, from the day he was indicted, he maintained that he had not stopped to beat any guard, let alone beat him so badly that he would die from his injuries.[6]

John Hill's codefendant had been equally young when he came to

Attica. Charles Joe Pernasalice was part Catawba Indian. Like Hill, he was a slight 125-pound twenty-two-year-old with longish hair, who had landed in Attica after committing a juvenile offense and, in his case, then violating parole. When the Attica rebellion started, nineteen-year-old Pernasalice had been at Attica for merely two weeks.[7] Charley Joe, as he was called, had begun his life behind bars when he was sixteen years old when he tried to run away from his home in Syracuse and stole a bike from a neighbor's garage. For that offense Charley Joe received a two-year sentence at Elmira. When he was almost nineteen, he was finally released on parole and decided to head to California to live with a group of young people in the desert and start a new life for himself.[8] However, he had failed to tell his parole officer that he was leaving the state so when he was later "picked up by the California police for hitchhiking," he was returned to custody in New York and placed in Attica while waiting to hear his fate from the parole board.[9]

No matter how young they were, though, Hill and Pernasalice needed strong representation to face the charges against them. Over the previous years, various ABLD attorneys had made sure that they were properly arraigned and filed motions on their behalf, but for quite some time it remained unclear who would represent them at trial. Ultimately John Hill would be defended by none other than William Kunstler and Margie Ratner, Kunstler's wife. Hill was "amazed and grateful" by his fortune at securing this help.[10] Charley Joe was as thankful when he learned that he would be defended by Ramsey Clark, the former U.S. attorney general, as well as by onetime Attica observer Herman Schwartz and Joe Heath, the ABLD's newly minted lawyer who had been an activist in Vietnam Veterans Against the War.

News of the defense's power team of lawyers sent Simonetti's office into a panic—particularly Louis Aidala, who was scheduled to argue the state's case. They would without a doubt need to bring their A game. Kunstler had already gained a national reputation from his defense of the Chicago 7, and his work in other high-profile cases had shown him to be loud and uncompromising on behalf of his clients. Ramsey Clark was equally famous, but he cut a very different figure in the courtroom. His style was more refined, perhaps even aloof. He was also quiet. Whenever he questioned witnesses, pacing and gesticulating all the while, Clark would stand very close to the stand and, according to one reporter, could "scarcely be heard across the room."[11]

These defense attorneys were set to face a prosecutor who was also

State prosecutor Louis Aidala, left, and prisoners' defense attorney William Kunstler *(Courtesy of the* Democrat and Chronicle*)*

known as "a bit of a showman."[12] Aidala sported "an old fashioned mustache that is curled at each end," and also argued every point loudly with much gesturing and bravado.[13] Aidala had been known to ask witnesses he was questioning to step out of the box so that they might bring the case to life by acting "out the movements of the defendants they have described in their testimony."[14]

Before any of these lawyers could speak to the jury, however, the ABLD insisted on holding a thorough Wade hearing. It was crucially important in this case to make the state explain how it had come to identify Hill and Pernasalice as the men who killed William Quinn, and their lawyers also very much needed the myriad state documents that would be given to them in the process of conducting such a hearing. The Wade hearing for Hill and Pernasalice was presided over by Justice Gilbert King and the courtroom was always full. As one reporter described it, "in the spectator's section sit the relatives of the two defendants . . . others are members of the Attica Brothers Legal Defense organization . . . and one is an Indian spiritual leader named Mad Bear, who wears a feather headdress in court."[15]

The Wade hearing took months to conclude, but from the defense's perspective, the time was well spent. They had learned a great deal to indicate that the state's case against Hill and Pernasalice was shaky at best. It became clear, for instance, that a key state witness had only agreed to testify after being harassed and coached. As important, one prisoner had never been asked to testify before the grand jury even though he indicated that he had crucial testimony that was in fact favorable to the defendants.[16] It also came out that another witness had been interviewed by Attica investigators on February 12, 1973, and made it clear that he didn't want to be there because he had no information to help them. That mattered not. According to this prisoner, investigators told him "to sit down you bastard you will stay until I decide to let you go" and kept on peppering him with leading questions.[17] This same witness said that he then asked for counsel but was informed that he had "no rights."[18]

Another witness stated in affidavits filed in both July and October of 1973 that since his first meetings with the BCI investigators he had "been deeply troubled" by the interrogation methods they had employed—particularly as he had "mounting fear," was under "heavy medications" because he had been shot seven times, and, thus, was in a serious "state of confusion."[19] He had been hounded and threatened by BCI investigators to say that he had seen things that he didn't think he had seen, but he was scared to death that if he did not cooperate, the police would kill him.[20]

Learning that the state's identification of the defendants had often taken place when its so-called eyewitnesses were under serious duress, and that even the statements from some of the state's CO witnesses were contradictory at best, suggested to the defense lawyers that they had a shot at getting this case dismissed. Furthermore, the grand jury had not been able to hear potentially exculpatory material before it indicted Hill and Pernasalice. But Judge King, while not at all pleased with what he had heard over the course of the Wade hearing, maintained that there were insufficient grounds to dismiss the cases outright. Jury selection thus began on January 5, 1975.

By January of 1975 the city of Buffalo was teeming with crowds of young Attica Brothers supporters from all over the country. In explaining the outpouring of support, the National Alliance Against Racism and Political Repression compared Attica to "certain other villages and hamlets" that had "come to represent for peoples of conscience the world over a name imbedded in history for its savagery and intolerable shame. Ludlow and Dearborn and Gastonia, Wounded Knee and Sand Creek, My Lai in South Vietnam and Simchon in North Korea and now Attica—unnoticeable points of geography, not to be found in an Atlas, but never to be forgotten."[21] And though supporters did indeed see Attica in this broader context, they called for immediate and practical redress for those now standing trial. They circulated petitions that demanded "all further criminal proceedings involving the Attica rebellion be immediately ceased," and they held marches throughout Buffalo and the nation on a regular basis.[22] One "March on Buffalo" originated in a "chartered bus leaving Pittsburgh," which cost travelers $10 round-trip and culminated in speeches by "Big Black, Haywood Burns, Angela Davis, [and] William Kunstler."[23] These marches, like an earlier one in Buffalo's Niagara Square, were lively with street theater and huge signs that read "Drop the Charges NOW!," "Stop the railroad," and "Free the Attica Brothers."[24] In all the demonstrations there was a sense among participants that Hill and Pernasalice were facing political trials akin to those "of the Panther 21 in New York, the Chicago 7, the Vietnam Veterans Against the War in Gainesville, Fla., Daniel Ellsberg in Los Angeles, Angela Davis in San Jose, California, [and] Bobby Seale in New Haven, Connecticut."[25] By bringing people out into the streets day after day, the people would make clear that they refused to accept these "governmental attempts to continue this openly political use of courts and prisons" just as they "refused to accept the government's fabrications."[26]

This sort of street activism clearly unnerved Judge Gilbert King. Judge King, described by reporters as "a round-faced man with pink cheeks and

Supporters of the Attica Brothers march *(Courtesy of David Fenton/Getty Images)*

a pink-skinned bald dome," had no doubt that his courtroom's forty-two spectator and press seats would be filled each day and, having the trial covered by *The New York Times,* the *New York Post,* a wire service, and one of Buffalo's two papers, *The Evening News,* might well lead to political theater.[27] The judge in charge of the Attica cases writ large, Carmen Ball, had already taken key steps to make sure this wouldn't happen, ordering tight security in the Erie County courthouse and even authorizing the "hiring of additional security personnel."[28] Anyone who caused a disruption during an Attica proceeding in front of Ball, including a young man who refused to lower his clenched fist in solidarity with the defendants, had been summarily "removed from the courtroom."[29] Rumor had it that seats in the spectator section of the courtroom had been removed so that fewer supporters of the Attica Brothers could attend and, according to one such supporter who waited in line most of the morning and had finally gotten in when others left, "ample distances between the rows of seats supported this theory."[30]

The security measures at the Erie County courthouse were equally unnerving to the many men and women who were summoned to Room 301 as potential jurors. This level of security implied, not all that subtly, that the Attica defendants and their supporters were highly dangerous—not at all helpful for the defense team. Still, William Kunstler had always had remarkable success in front of juries and he was confident that he could, with hard work, secure John Hill's acquittal in front of this one. Also, in part because Ramsey Clark felt it was a good idea, Kunstler was willing to work with the Jury Project in this case.

Unpredictably, however, their willingness to use scientific jury selection techniques backfired. Although investigating potential jurors was not only legal—assuming they weren't harassed, intimidated, or threatened and weren't approached personally—and even though prosecutors also did this regularly, a potential juror told the judge that someone had called him to ask him questions about his views that might shape his objectivity in this case. This accusation halted the jury selection process and the Jury Project members were flabbergasted by this claim, vigorously denied it, and believed that someone from the other side had impersonated them to derail their ability to shape the jury in Hill's and Pernasalice's favor. When the trial resumed Kunstler decided to scrap use of the Jury Project when picking the remaining jurors.[31] In recognition of how biased the Erie County pool was likely to be, Judge King allowed the defense ten more peremptory challenges than the prosecution. The prosecution appealed this decision, however, and these extra challenges disappeared.[32] On February 21, 1975, the jury was sworn in with only two African American members.

The trial began in earnest on February 24. Both men would stand trial together, but the lawyers for each defendant would handle things in their own way. Kunstler was guided by one major premise throughout the trial of his client, whom he called "Dac" in honor of his chosen Indian name, Dacajewiah: the jury must hear as much evidence as possible about the state's ugly actions at Attica rather than focusing exclusively on the he said/he said of the chaotic events leading to William Quinn's death. This was little surprise to anyone who knew William Kunstler since every one of the cases he had taken on in recent years had been very much a political case, and each time he mounted his defense accordingly. However, Kunstler's plan to politicize this case did not sit well with some on Pernasalice's defense team—namely Herman Schwartz, who had been battling fellow Attica lawyers for years now on this very issue of whether politics had any place in the courtroom. Schwartz believed Kunstler was about to make "a dreadful mistake," because they already had a "hostile judge" and this would further prejudice the judge and the "upstate jury" against both defendants. Whatever the jury thought of Hill and his attorney, he worried, they would also think of Charley Joe. Ramsey Clark also "agreed that it shouldn't be a political case," but he felt it was Kunstler's call as to how to handle his own client's defense. Upset, Schwartz tried to have himself dismissed from the case, but the judge wouldn't allow it.[33]

Noting Schwartz's objections, Kunstler proceeded with his plan to bring before the jury examples of trooper brutality, investigator incompetence, and outrageous actions on the part of high-ranking state officials. Kunstler tried to subpoena Nelson Rockefeller himself so that he could tell the jury the Attica story from the top down rather than from the bottom up. Ramsey Clark agreed that having the jury hear directly from Rockefeller might be helpful to both of their cases—particularly since the governor had repeatedly claimed that Quinn had died from being thrown from a second-story window. This would at the very least make it clear that even state officials couldn't get their stories straight regarding what had led to Quinn's death.

Judge King refused to grant this subpoena, going on record that he simply would not allow any evidence having to do with the state's actions at Attica to be introduced into the trial proceedings. The state was not on trial, King admonished the defense. And yet, from Kunstler's point of view, it was—not just rhetorically or polemically, but literally. One key argument that he had hoped to make before the jury was that William Quinn's death, though clearly due to the head trauma he had suffered on the first day of the Attica uprising, would have been entirely preventable had the state not been so negligent in giving him care. It had taken an inordinate amount of time for state officials to move him from the prison to the hospital, even with prisoners begging them to come get him off the mattress and to medical care. And once hospitalized, he had received slipshod care—he had never been moved to intensive care.[34]

Early in the trial it was clear that King wouldn't budge on this matter, or allow any other tack that Kunstler tried. No sooner had King decided against the Rockefeller subpoena than Kunstler asked him to address a more immediate issue: Kunstler felt that the defendants and the prisoners who had agreed to testify on behalf of the defense were being threatened and intimidated by the many law enforcement personnel the judge had positioned around his courtroom, making the defense's job hard to do effectively. These tactics were of "an immoral and illegal nature," Kunstler asserted, and their effect on defense preparation had been "disastrous."[35] Kunstler argued that King needed to arrange for all of the defense witnesses to receive protection as they were ferried to and from the courtroom each day. King denied this motion, too.

As young ABLD attorney Elizabeth Fink saw it, this was actually a very significant loss in the courtroom. She was helping the defense behind the scenes and when she had recently visited Charley Joe Pernasalice in the Erie County jail, it was obvious to her that he had been badly beaten up. He confirmed that he had been hit in the jaw and then choked to unconsciousness by a jailer. Pernasalice's condition was so bad that Fink had immediately demanded an examination by an outside doctor, who confirmed that he had been seriously assaulted. The doctor for the jail, however, took exception to this physician's characterization of Pernasalice's injuries. Judge King remained unmoved when this matter was brought before him. In fact he chastised Charley Joe for the assault he suffered, saying "you precipitated this incident in the jail by your refusal to follow the normal and accepted procedures that are in force . . . the ultimate problem lies with you."[36]

The defense couldn't have been too surprised by King's lack of sympathy for them. Following a possible security breach a year earlier, the ABLD had enlisted technicians from the Spy Shop, "an organization experienced in the means of electronic surveillance," to see if they should be concerned.[37]

These technicians agreed to sign affidavits on behalf of the ABLD indicating that it did appear that their members had been under surveillance by an outside party. Eventually, on February 7, 1975, State Supreme Court Justice James Moore agreed to order an investigation into this possible wiretapping of the ABLD phones. He wrote, "Any intrusion by the government upon the confidential relationship between the defendants in these indictments and their counsel would certainly taint the further proceedings to be had herein."[38] Meanwhile Simonetti's office filed its own affidavit categorically denying any involvement with the FBI in such illegal acts, saying that "the People have no knowledge or information concerning any such hypothetical electronic surveillance; in particular the People have no knowledge or information concerning any electronic surveillance regarding any telephone instrument of the Attica Legal Defense Group."[39] Then, essentially, nothing happened. The attorney general's office didn't even "investigate whether or not any eavesdropping warrants were issued by any court."[40] Kunstler filed a motion before Judge King hoping that he would hold his own evidentiary hearing on this matter, but that motion was also denied.[41]

Recognizing that none of this boded well for his and Clark's chances in defending John Hill and Charley Joe Pernasalice, Kunstler had also appealed to the judge for more time to prepare their defenses. "We have one typewriter, Judge, and we have essentially one legal worker who does typing, who has a part time job in the city, can only come in at certain times. That's the extent of our modest resources."[42] Again, Judge King stated flatly that this was not going to happen.[43] Time and again Kunstler had tried to get a favorable ruling from this judge and had failed, which, over time, led to some serious sparring between them. As one young man in the courtroom observing the trial put it, "The trial often seemed to consist primarily of a conflict between Kunstler and Judge Gilbert H. King . . . [particularly over] the range of permissible evidence . . . [and Kunstler] repeatedly question[ed] the integrity of the judge and the fairness of the trial."[44]

Meanwhile, and with tensions clearly running high between Judge Gilbert King and William Kunstler, the state had begun arguing its case on February 24, 1975. In short, Simonetti's office "hoped to prove that Mr. Hill had struck officer Quinn twice with a wooden object, once while the officer was still standing and once as he lay on the floor," and intended "to prove that Mr. Pernasalice had also hit the officer as he lay on the floor."[45] To that end, Louis Aidala had lined up a total of eighteen witnesses, although he planned to rely on the testimony of five or fewer prisoners and one correction officer.[46] The others, including two more correction officers, might be needed, but since none of them said they had actually seen "either of the defendants hit Quinn," their usefulness was questionable.[47]

The witnesses Louis Aidala had hoped would make his case most strongly had all said, at some point in the last four years, that they could place Hill and Pernasalice near Quinn. First the jury heard from prisoner witness William Rivers that he saw "Hill striking Quinn in the head" two or three times.[48] A week later, Robert Kopec came before the jury, which eagerly listened as he repeated what he had told state investigators in February 1972: that John Hill had actually said to him that he thought he killed a correction officer that morning in Times Square, "because as he was hitting him with a club, he just lost his mind and kept hitting him and hitting him until blood came out of his eyes, ears, and mouth."[49] Aidala felt that the state's best witness was Edward Zimmer. He knew from Zimmer's original testimony before the grand jury that he said he had seen Hill hit William Quinn, and also he claimed to have seen him holding a weapon that was consistent with the injuries Quinn's autopsy indicated had been fatal. As he had testified then, he had seen "John [Hill] with a two by four strike Mr. Quinn in the upper part of his body. Not in the face. Just below his face, sort of across his chest. . . . Then I saw John strike Mr. Quinn again, only this time it was in the face, I can't remember which side."[50] As important, Zimmer had also said then that he had seen Pernasalice—whom he referred to as "Chuck"—at the scene of the assault. As he stated, "John, Chuck, Mario, and the black inmates that I know, and the other ones that I don't know were all kicking and beating the officers after they were already down on the floor."[51] More specifically, he went on, "I seen Chuck with a night stick hit Mr. Quinn, it looked like on the back of the shoulder or across his head. And he didn't move after that."[52]

Aidala hoped that if this jury could just hear testimony from witnesses like Zimmer, his case would be won—particularly since he knew that the testimony he was going to get from the COs who had been in Times Square during Quinn's assault was problematic. They all were willing to say that Hill and Pernasalice had been Quinn's key assailants—eventually—but they hadn't always said this, and Aidala couldn't be sure that the defense wouldn't bring this fact to the jury's attention.

However, Aidala wasn't about to let his whole case hinge on the jury's believing the stories any of his witnesses told. He needed to appeal to the jurors' emotions, needed to make clear to them just how brutal the assault on Quinn had been. After bringing all of his people's testimony before the jury, he called Monroe County pathologist Dr. John Edland as his very last witness.[53] There was a certain irony in the fact that Louis Aidala now hoped to benefit from the testimony of a man whom his higher-ups in the Rockefeller administration had worked so hard to discredit. But calling Dr. Edland made sense given that Aidala wanted graphic testimony. Dutifully the ME took the stand and, accompanied by horrifying images that the state had entered as exhibits, reported how William Quinn had suffered from "massive" bleeding in his stomach, as well as fluid in his lungs. His eyes had also hemorrhaged. Ultimately, he died from fractures to his skull caused by "one or two blows to the forehead."[54] Aidala could see that he had indeed impressed upon the jury how terrible this attack on Quinn had been. To a one they looked sickened and appalled.

Once the defense began its cross-examination of witnesses, however, the prosecution began to run into some trouble. Kunstler and Clark discredited almost every witness that Aidala had called to the stand. Their questioning of prisoner witness William Rivers revealed that he thought he might be transferred, paroled, or even released if he cooperated.[55] More devastatingly, cross-examination of the prosecution's star prisoner witness, Edward Zimmer, revealed that he actually had stated initially to investigators, before they brought him to testify to the grand jury, that he had seen a black man hurting Quinn—a black man who had been kicking him in the face. Later, however, when they asked more about that black man, Zimmer couldn't remember any clear details about what he saw because, he explained to them, "it happened three years ago, I can't remember everything that happened."[56] Kunstler noted wryly to the jurors that it was remarkable how so very recently Zimmer couldn't remember a single useful detail about who did what on the day of Quinn's beating, and now, suddenly in this trial, he could "remember that well."[57] He continued, pulling no punches: Zimmer probably did originally see someone kick Quinn in the face, perhaps even a black man, but this wasn't what the prosecution wanted him to have seen. A kick could not have caused "the injuries the prosecution claimed caused his death," and neither of the men the state had indicted were black. And so, Kunstler went on, not only did the assailant suddenly change, but so did the place where Zimmer had seen that assailant's blow land.[58] What is more, he pointed out to the jury, "the prosecution's Bobbsey Twins" Zimmer and Rivers were so helpful in no small part because these guys had been locked in adjoining cells after the rebellion where they could converse after being interviewed by state investigators, and then were bunked together in the Erie County jail as well as kept at the same motel while prepped for trial. According to Kunstler, "they were a package deal" because the state needed both men to support each other's flawed testimony.[59]

And, as Aidala had feared, Kunstler also made sure to zero in on the limitations of the state's correction officer witnesses. CO Royal Morgan fingered Hill when he took the stand in this trial and yet, on the day after the rebellion started, mere hours after the assault on Quinn actually had taken place, this then twenty-four-year-old CO had made clear to the state's investigators that he had been hit badly, things were very fuzzy, and he didn't know who had hurt his friend. Indeed, when he came upon Quinn, not only was he disoriented and bleeding, but Quinn was already badly injured. At that point Morgan had tried, with the help of Mariano "Dalou" Gonzalez and another prisoner, to get Quinn onto a mattress and to safety.[60] Not only had Morgan made no mention of who had hit Quinn in his original statement to state investigators, but when investigators expressly asked him "at any time during this incident, the entire incident, did you overhear any inmate or any person state who had assaulted officer Quinn?" he had answered with a categorical "No, I didn't. All I heard is that there was an officer that was real bad off and for me to help him and this was when I noticed Quinn on the floor."[61] Yet when this same CO was interviewed again by Simonetti's office later in preparation for the trial, this time he "picked Hill's picture from a series of three identification books."[62]

Kunstler also directed the jury's attention to the testimony of Gordon Kelsey, a correction officer who had been in Times Square with William Quinn when the rebellion began. He too had not identified Quinn's assailants when asked by an investigator right after the retaking. He had answered the question "Did you observe anyone assaulting Mr. Quinn?" with a reply that he did see him go down, "but as to who it was, I couldn't tell you. Like I said, it was, there was many of them."[63] He had elaborated, "They all had their hands in on everything and a lot of hollering and yelling, but as far as who it was, I couldn't say."[64] Then, months later, however, Kelsey changed his tune—telling investigators that he thought it was a white guy who hit Quinn with a two-by-four. Still later, he agreed with prosecutors that the assailant was John Hill, a young man with a noticeably light brown complexion, that had struck Quinn. And that wasn't the end of the waffling. Indeed, according to the state's own records, Kelsey later "retracted the identification" of John Hill, "because Inmate Hill did not have a brush cut" and "he felt the inmate striking Quinn had a brush cut."[65] By trial, though, Kelsey was once again willing to say he had seen Hill deal Quinn a fatal blow. As Kunstler said to the jury, "Of course he is sure, because that's the state's story."[66]

To further cast doubt on the credibility of the prosecution's case against Hill and Pernasalice, the defense called its own CO witness to the stand—a man named Alton Tolbert. Tolbert's testimony was important because although he had claimed to have seen Quinn's killing back in 1971 when interviewed by the BCI, when pushed by the defense, he now admitted that "he had lied to state troopers in 1971 when he volunteered his account" because he wanted to be transferred to a closer prison.[67] He confessed "he had made up the story . . . to ingratiate himself with his superiors and possibly obtain a transfer from Attica."[68] Two months after the Attica uprising Mr. Tolbert had indeed been transferred to Elmira, his hometown.[69] According to reporters covering the trial, when coming clean on the stand, Alton Tolbert "appeared embarrassed and meek" particularly when he admitted that, in fact, he had not seen Mr. Quinn at all on the morning of September 9, 1971."[70] Even though he had claimed to have seen Quinn being hit "with a shovel," this "was a complete fabrication."[71]

The defense's own prisoner witnesses dealt even more blows to the state's case. One prisoner by the name of Everett Burkett (whom Kunstler pointed out had come "forward to tell his story without inducement or promises") was positioned as quite "a heroic figure" because this short, stocky twenty-seven-year-old with a "Van Dyke beard" might well experience some form of retaliation from the state for cooperating with the defense (perhaps having his parole revoked) and yet still agreed to testify for one reason and one reason only: he knew that John Hill could not possibly have killed William Quinn because Hill had been with Burkett the entire morning that first day of the rebellion. Burkett stated firmly, "In that time he had never seen the defendant hit anyone."[72]

Not only did the defense argue, via Burkett, that Hill couldn't have killed William Quinn, it also wanted to show the jury that there were in fact legitimate witnesses to Quinn's beating and none of them had identified either Hill or Pernasalice as the perpetrators. Defense witness Charles Raymond Cratsley testified that he had been right there when Quinn was hit and he "described in graphic detail" how one man had "landed a blow on the forehead." Even though he wasn't sure who that man had been, he said without equivocation that it was neither one of the defendants in this case. This man, a white witness the press noted, struck most observers as a more believable figure than the state's various witnesses had been. As one reporter put it, this witness "contrasted sharply with the prosecution's former inmate witnesses."[73] Unlike them, this man had received no deals to come and testify even though he now had a very menial job working as a dishwasher in a restaurant in Rochester.[74] Kunstler made sure the jury knew that Cratsley had been given nothing but a hotel room and $40 to get himself to the court to testify. As important, he was risking humiliation on the stand because of his low IQ and because he had been originally imprisoned on a rape charge and yet "he still came."[75]

In addition to Cratsley, the defense called two other witnesses who had also identified completely different men, neither Hill nor Pernasalice, as the ones who had fatally beaten Quinn. Kunstler pointed out to jurors that Simonetti's office had been well aware that these men existed, and that they would have told the grand jury this very different version of events had they been called. That they were not called, Kunstler suggested, was deeply unethical. The eyewitness testimony of prisoner Melvin Marshall would have been a problem for the state's case, so the prosecution did not allow him to testify. "He saw Mr. Quinn. He saw him hit on the head by what he thought was a two-by-four or a baseball bat," but "the person he saw was a black person."[76] How certain was Marshall about whom he saw? Well, Kunstler pointed out, he was close enough to see Quinn suffer tremendous bleeding after that hit, but also close enough to yell at the assailant, " 'For Christ's sake, don't kill him,' " which did in fact make him stop.[77] The second witness, Joseph Nance, was even more specific that it couldn't have been Hill or Pernasalice who killed Quinn. This prisoner not only insisted that he saw who beat Quinn, but he had been denied early parole despite his stellar record because he hadn't been willing to say it was Hill. As Kunstler noted, "He saw the wrong people, he didn't see the people they wanted to be seen, so Mr. Nance . . . never got any of these nice benefits." Pushing the point harder, Kunstler went on, "Why would he lie? He doesn't know John Hill . . . what is the motivation for this man?"[78]

Both Kunstler and Clark felt that they had put forward a strong defense of their clients. Clark had, like Kunstler, systematically questioned witnesses in such a way that the light shining through the holes in their testimony was bright indeed. It was challenging to defend two different people in the same trial but it had been surprisingly easy to show just how weak the state's witnesses were. Both attorneys were so confident that the prosecution had been unethical in its efforts to build a case against their clients that they were eager to file motions to dismiss the case before it was time for closing arguments. Arguing his motion with great passion, at times almost yelling, Kunstler said that what "has taken place in this court since the case began on a regular daily basis" has been nothing short of "rank perjury."[79] Not just correction officers had perjured themselves, he suggested, but shaking his head he said bluntly, "I think your honor, what you have in this case throughout, is the fine details planted in witnesses by the state, in what I consider . . . a totally fraudulent prosecution in order to have somebody answer for Mr. Quinn's death."[80]

Clark's motion to dismiss charges—delivered less dramatically—also argued that the state had no credible evidence and that this lack of evidence suggested Charley Joe Pernasalice should go free immediately.[81] Clark declared in wonder, "I have to say that I have never in . . . twenty-four years now at the bar, seen any office of prosecution submit on a charge of murder such inconsequential, insubstantial and insupportable evidence, and I implore you to end this anxiety now and dismiss charges as to Mr. Pernasalice."[82] Clark reminded the jury that only one man claimed to have witnessed Pernasalice commit a violent act against William Quinn and only one other claimed to have even seen him in the area, but neither of these witnesses were at all credible. Two witnesses contradicted each other: Edward Zimmer's testimony that he had seen Pernasalice strike Quinn over the shoulders with a stick didn't fit with Dr. John Edland's statements that Quinn had had no injuries to his shoulders and, even if he had taken such a blow, it would have had nothing to do with Quinn's death.[83] Clark called Zimmer's "by far the vaguest, most contradictory and the most inherently impossible or incredible" testimony in the entire trial. Tom Collins, another prisoner witness who placed Pernasalice on the scene, not only then admitted that he hadn't met Pernasalice until the 10th or 11th of September, but also acknowledged that he hadn't even been in Times Square when the fatal beating took place.[84] Summing up, Clark concluded his argument: "There is no believable evidence to find Charley Joe Pernasalice guilty of any offense other than being an inmate of Attica on September 9, 1971."[85] What is more, he went on to say to the judge, "I am personally so distressed that this young man would be kept living in this staggering anxiety for three years, by the state of New York, on evidence so clearly inadequate."[86]

Judge Gilbert King declined to grant either of the defense's motions.[87] King did not explain his ruling, but did chastise Kunstler for using this trial to try to focus attention on the wrongdoings of the state. "As I have repeatedly held," he said, "we are not here to try prison life in Attica."[88]

When dismissing Clark's motion he was a bit less caustic. While he would not dismiss the charges against Pernasalice, he conceded that he would reserve the right to revisit this motion, and perhaps consider a lesser charge in the future.[89] And indeed, right before the jury left to deliberate, Judge King did dismiss the murder charge against Pernasalice and asked the jury instead to rule on whether he was guilty of second-degree assault and attempted murder. This didn't appease Clark, however. In his view the lesser charge totally missed the point that there was no evidence that Pernasalice had caused Quinn any injury whatsoever.[90]

Clark would try to make this same point again in his closing remarks. He used his last opportunity to speak to the jury to highlight the same weaknesses in the state's case that he had laid out in his motion to dismiss.[91] On March 31, 1975, Ramsey Clark walked the jury through the little testimony that the state had presented against his client and then systematically noted the specific flaws in that testimony: only two witnesses placed his client at the scene and only one of these claimed to have seen him commit an act of violence. Neither witness could possibly have seen what he said he did.[92] The jury must now, Clark implored, set his client free.

In contrast to Ramsey Clark's subdued and relatively short summation, William Kunstler's dramatic closing remarks lasted seven hours and unfolded over the course of two days.[93] Deeply frustrated, Kunstler felt that he had tried time and again in this trial to bring in testimony that would have directly helped his client that the judge simply refused to allow. He believed to his core that the state's actions at Attica, and the testimony of the governor himself, were not only relevant in this trial, but would have persuaded the jury that there was more than a reasonable doubt that John Hill caused William Quinn to die. Trying to contain that frustration, he, like Clark, painstakingly walked the jury through the testimony that it had heard, pointing out the myriad places when the witnesses' stories did not add up and the various reasons why jurors should consider a given witness's testimony to be unreliable because they had been incentivized to give the specific details. He noted with some bitterness that every witness the prosecution brought forward had shown a better memory now at this trial than they had three and a half months earlier at the Wade hearing.[94] Kunstler conceded that one of the correction officer witnesses had himself been traumatized by all that he experienced during the Attica uprising and he confided, "I thought he was troubled."[95] But that alone should have been reason to doubt his testimony.

Kunstler also reiterated his argument that the entire court proceeding had been set up to suggest to jurors that his client was a scary person who needed convicting. As he pointed out, "The jury was escorted by armed guards" and, worse, the judge had made what Kunstler regarded as "openly prejudicial remarks to that jury, that . . . if they were threatened or in any way impeded, they were to report it to the judge . . . to give the jury the idea that they might be imperiled or jeopardized or intimidated by these people."[96] This was absurd, Kunstler insisted; John Hill and Charley Joe Pernasalice had been "among the 'weakest and most vulnerable' possible suspects" and that, he suggested, was why the prosecution settled on them as the perpetrators.[97] "You are sitting in a moment of history," he impressed upon the jurors, imploring them to do the right thing by acquitting his client.[98]

In the state of New York, the prosecution gets the last word in a criminal case. So Louis Aidala, his voice "frequently rising to a shout," had the chance to speak to the jury after both Clark and Kunstler.[99] It was incredible, he insisted, that the defense was trying to discredit witnesses who had, under oath, clearly identified both John Hill and Charles Pernasalice as the killers of Billy Quinn. Regarding the fact that one of his witnesses gave vague testimony regarding the physical characteristics of Quinn's assailant—the best-described feature was that he had "slanty eyes" (a point Kunstler had made much of, Aidala scoffed)—the prosecutor asked jurors to consider whether this description was in fact vague at all.[100] "Ask yourself," he went on, "how many of those [prisoners] may have had slanty eyes?" That will tell you just "how many inmates could have committed this crime."[101] He stressed also that he had brought five men to court who claimed they had seen Quinn hit by the defendants. Despite evidence that at least four of them had been offered a sweeter deal if they gave the specific evidence that they did, Aidala continued to maintain that "there were no promises made to the witnesses."[102]

Regardless of the controversy surrounding the testimony of those witnesses, Aidala ultimately chose to spend little time defending their credibility in his closing remarks. Instead, he sought to win the case emotionally—focusing the jury's attention primarily, and often graphically, on all William Quinn had endured on the morning of September 9, 1971. As the media noted, "often in the course of his remarks, Mr. Aidala showed the jury photographs of Mr. Quinn taken after his death, and of Mr. Quinn's brain," to remind everyone why they were there in court and of the magnitude of the crime for which he now sought justice.[103] At one point in his summation Aidala's finger shot out, pointing at John Hill while the prosecutor shouted that this prisoner had "literally tore away his human brain."[104] Looking over at the defense table with disgust he said, "I wonder if Mr. Kunstler ever once shed a tear for the wife of Mr. Quinn."[105]

Once the arguments for Hill's and Pernasalice's innocence and guilt concluded, the jury shuffled out of the courtroom for lengthy deliberations—twenty-five hours in total. As they left, the defendants and defense attorneys felt optimistic, especially when the four alternate jurors "exchanged 'power handshakes' with the defendants before leaving the courtroom" and one of them, a twenty-five-year-old postal worker, was actually heard saying, "I would acquit both."[106] As the hours dragged on, the defense felt even more heartened; usually lengthy deliberations were "an indication of a close vote favoring acquittal."[107] Surely, the jury would see this whole sordid picture and do the right thing. As John Hill remembered it years later, "I really thought that there was a good chance of acquittal. . . . They had no evidence. Even *Newsweek* said that."[108]

The crowds outside the prison still rallying and protesting on behalf of the defendants weren't quite so confident of the trial's outcome but, for that matter, neither were the scores of police also flanking the courthouse. The result was much tension in the air. Earlier that morning the police had ordered one rally outside the courthouse to disperse, which had resulted in a confrontation and some arrests.[109] During the closing arguments about four hundred more people came to demonstrate outside the courtroom and five were arrested. John Hill, who remained free on bond during the trial, had grabbed a bullhorn during a recess and "implored the demonstrators to heed the directions of the police."[110] Feeling that his chances for acquittal were looking pretty good, it made him nervous to think that clashes between his supporters and the police might now turn jurors against him.

On April 6, 1975, the jury finally reached its verdict.[111] To a one the spectators had grown deathly quiet. The jury forewoman, "one of two blacks on the panel," announced solemnly that John Hill had been found guilty of murder and Charles Joe Pernasalice had been found guilty of second-degree attempted assault.[112] As the defendants stared numbly at the jury, John Hill's pregnant wife sobbed and "the crowded courtroom briefly erupted into pandemonium."[113] When Justice King then "ordered Sheriffs deputies to handcuff the defendants . . . and jail them," the crowd exploded.[114] As utter chaos enveloped the courtroom William Kunstler jumped to his feet demanding to know why they were being remanded

Charles Pernasalice (with hand at mouth, left) and John Hill (right foreground with feathers in hair) and supporters on April 5, 1975, the day before the verdicts were delivered in their trial for the death of guard William Quinn *(Courtesy of the Associated Press)*

before sentencing when real criminals like Watergate's John Mitchell hadn't been, and the crowd roared its agreement. Meanwhile Judge King was shouting for order in his court. It took several hours to clear the courtroom, and long after that ABLD supporters still filled the lawn outside, some in tears, all with a deep sense of foreboding about the many cases still left to go to trial.

This verdict had "stunned" and it seemed a very bad omen for the scores of men who still awaited trial.[115] If the state's case had been this weak against John Hill—so full of contradictions, bribes, and lack of concrete evidence—and yet prosecutors could still manage to send this man to prison, possibly for life, then how little evidence would they need to make the rest of the Attica defendants languish in prison for the rest of their lives as well?

This jury had, in fact, been divided as to whether John Hill and Charley Joe Pernasalice had caused the death of William Quinn. As the first juror who spoke to a reporter explained it, "In the first poll the eight men and four women divided 'roughly in half' on the question of whether the defendants . . . had struck William E. Quinn."[116] This particular juror was himself conflicted. "I felt sorry for the family of Mr. Hill," he explained, "but I also felt sorry for the family of Mr. Quinn. . . . It's not something I'll forget for a long time."[117]

Undoubtedly it had mattered to this jury that its members had never felt any real connection to the defendants. The media also had not taken particularly well to them, although they liked Pernasalice far more than Hill. One paper published typical descriptions: Charles Pernasalice was someone who "smiles a lot and wears a bell on his belt that tinkles when he gets up, as he frequently does, to whisper a suggestion to a defense lawyer," while John Hill was characterized as a man who "seldom moves from his seat facing the jury, and often slumps forward on his elbows over the defense table in a posture of boredom. His face is almost invariably set in an expression of discontent."[118] It wasn't that the media or jury particularly liked Charley Joe either, though. Indeed Pernasalice often tried the patience of the court, coming into court late.[119] When he was late for yet another appearance one morning, Judge King angrily threatened to revoke his bail. Former ABLD coordinator Don Jelinek also felt that these defendants were not respectful enough in the court and, in his view, did not pay "proper homage to the victim."[120] Jelinek feared their "hippie-like" style alone may have turned off working-class jurors from small towns across Erie County.[121]

Others speculated that some of the jurors were put off by Kunstler's litigation style. Of course Aidala was a yeller too, and whenever there was a conflict he and Kunstler would both be "shouting at each other simultaneously."[122] But somehow Kunstler didn't get the same pass for his bombastic style that Aidala did—undoubtedly because he, unlike Aidala, was known as a "Marxist lawyer" and because Kunstler wasn't at all shy about challenging Judge King if he felt that Hill wasn't getting a fair shake. At one point in the trial when Kunstler was trying to make a case that his client had been selectively prosecuted, for example, this discussion got derailed into a debate between him and Judge King over whether the United States was a great country or totalitarian in nature.[123] As one reporter put it, "Showman Kunstler could not resist the temptation to flay witnesses and have a go at State Supreme Court Justice Gilbert H. King." King was clearly hostile to Kunstler as well every time he tried to present a motion or mount a defense of his client that the judge disapproved of. Ultimately, however, it can be argued that the jury had not voted to convict on the evidence before them and thus, probably no lawyer, even one meeker and less of a radical than Kunstler, could have won acquittals. Someone needed to pay for William Quinn's death.

The defense team hoped that they still had a chance to do right by their clients at sentencing. First they tried to vacate the jury verdicts altogether by arguing that there had been selective prosecution of their clients and, as important, because the defense had just learned that "a sheriff's deputy, on duty in the courtroom, had told a radio news reporter early in the trial that 'four or five jurors' had indicated to him that they were ready to convict even before they were empaneled."[124] Although this motion was not successful, it did delay sentencing and it gave time for the defendants to prepare arguments so that King might show some mercy in this phase of their case. John Hill spoke before the judge on May 8, 1975, but when he began his speech the frustration and anger that he felt for having been reimprisoned overwhelmed him. First he accused the jury of racism and of never thinking about the scores of people "murdered by the state" or the "fourteen million Indian peoples who have been killed in the 19th century."[125] The "real" criminals, Hill continued, were in Vietnam and they killed students at Kent State. Then he read a prayer for the Lakota Sioux.[126] Before finishing his speech Hill said passionately, "I just want to tell my people that we will win, we will overcome everything," and then he embraced Kunstler.[127]

Judge King was clearly displeased with John Hill and sentenced him to twenty years to life. As King levied Hill's sentence he looked at him coldly and said that William Quinn had "had a right to continue his life to whatever end it came to. He had a right to continue his life as a husband and a father," and, the judge continued, Hill had taken it upon himself "to make certain he would live no more."[128] Thereafter Hill was removed from the courtroom and taken directly to prison to begin his time. Since he would now be forever branded as Quinn's killer Judge King decided that he shouldn't go back to Attica and sent him instead to Green Haven.[129]

The afternoon's sentencing hearing for Charley Joe Pernasalice went much better than Hill's but not as well as Clark had hoped. For some time Clark argued hard before King that his client should be given probation since there was no evidence whatsoever that he had assaulted Quinn.[130] As important, he argued, this was a young man with a future if the judge could just see his way to being lenient. As he put it to King, "I love this young man, I believe in him. I believe he has enormous worth and potential and I see in him a world of chance, necessity, and free will being cruel to him."[131] Further, he went on, "I believe he can attend Syracuse University in the fall."[132] While the judge was not willing to forgo sentencing Pernasalice entirely, he did give him a relatively light indeterminate sentence not to exceed two years.[133] He then realized that, because of the wording of the penal code, an indeterminate sentence had to be for three years.[134]

After the sentencing, the full weight of this trial loss hit the ABLD. Even though Herman Schwartz was often at odds with the ABLD and its lawyers, he recalled that "the night the verdict came in was one of the bleakest nights I can remember. It was snowing and we went to have supper. The only time I ever saw Ramsey snap at me. We were very tense. We came back to the dimly lit courtroom. It was awful. Guilty of murder. Wails of grief at the courtroom." Michael Deutsch also remembers that moment as a "terrible blow" to the Attica Brothers and the seeming good fortune they had had thus far defending themselves from state prosecutors.[135]

Simonetti's office was as elated as the ABLD was distressed. It had, until now, had a rough go of it in the courtroom with two major losses and then, recently behind the scenes, having had to drop charges against another thirteen prisoners "for insufficient evidence."[136] As one reporter noted, with this victory, "Aidala and other prosecutors made no attempt to hide their satisfaction."[137] Now that they had succeeded in sending John Hill and Charley Joe Pernasalice away for the murder of William Quinn, they were ready to turn their attention to the case of Attica Brother Bernard Stroble, aka Shango. They were prepared to argue that he had brutally murdered fellow prisoner Barry Schwartz in cold blood and, as with Hill and Pernasalice, their goal was to make him pay.

## 40

# Evening the Score

Simonetti's office was delighted to learn that Shango's trial for the murder of fellow prisoner Barry Schwartz would be right after the Hill and Pernasalice win. They had been preparing for this case for several years now, relying heavily on the witness accounts netted by BCI investigators in the immediate aftermath of the Attica rebellion. They were now ready to get to it.

It had been state troopers who had come across the bodies of Barry Schwartz, Kenneth Hess, and Michael Privitera up on a deserted tier of D Block back in 1971. At the time, they were disgusted but they were also deeply relieved that these three ugly killings could not be tied to any State Police or correction officers. Therefore, they worked hard to assist Simonetti's office in figuring out who had committed these heinous acts. These were by no means easy murders to solve, however. The problem the Attica investigators faced in these cases was, in key respects, the opposite of the one they had faced investigating Quinn's death. Quinn had been attacked in the midst of complete chaos, with hundreds of men on the scene and fists flying. However, on the day or days that Schwartz, Hess, and Privitera had been fatally attacked, it was unclear who had been there. As was also true in the Quinn case, however, prosecutors nevertheless forged ahead. By December of 1972 they had decided that several specific men had committed these murders and they were particularly interested in going after one of them: Bernard Stroble, aka Shango Bahati Kakawana.

As one of the heads of rebellion security, along with Big Black, Shango was especially hated by the state troopers who had watched D Yard for days. What is more, Shango was not likely to garner much juror sympathy.

Unlike Hill or Pernasalice, Shango was neither really young, nor had he landed in prison on some juvenile charge or mere parole violation. This was a man who had been arrested in both 1957 and 1958 on felonious assault charges and then, years later, been accused of shooting two police officers in Detroit.[1] The officers had stopped Shango for a traffic violation that he had already paid, and he readily admitted that he had an altercation with them. According to Shango, though, the officers had overreacted when he went into his pocket to get his license and registration and they drew their guns. Acting in self-defense, he said, Shango in turn took out his own gun and began shooting them.[2]

Shango wasn't apprehended at that time because he fled to Chicago in a cab and, from there, went on to New York. No sooner did he get to New York, though, than he got into another altercation with yet another man with a gun—"shooting him in the head during a quarrel in a Bronx pool hall."[3] After this shooting Shango was finally arrested, but not before setting fire to his own apartment to distract the police in the hope that he would get away once more. Eventually Shango was sentenced to twenty to thirty years in prison for manslaughter in New York after first being sent back to Detroit to stand trial there. The deal was that he would serve his New York time at Attica, and then do his time in Michigan.[4]

Shango had lived life as a tough guy—by his own admission, he hadn't always been a good man—but by the time he stood trial for Schwartz's murder, he was both demoralized and chastened. The sheer brutality he had seen in D Yard had affected him profoundly, making him both more cynical and in some ways more humble than he had been before.

He had been singled out for particularly brutal treatment during the retaking. As he remembered, he had unsuccessfully tried to dodge a "fuselage [*sic*] of bullets pouring down from every direction," and was struck three times.[5] The first bullet entered his buttocks and traveled twelve inches up his back to within a hairbreadth of his spine. Two more bullets ripped open his hands. With blood pouring from his wounds he lay still, while all around him he "heard screams . . . infinite screams."[6]

He could barely fathom "the pain, so unreasonably excruciating."[7] Through the raindrops falling into his eyes he "could see the countless number of blood-drenched bodies being carried away."[8] Suddenly a trooper screamed at Shango, "Get up nigger!" but he could only move his arms and the upper part of his body. The trooper demanded that he "move towards the block—crawl!" Shango couldn't do that either; he tried to drag his own body toward A Block, getting hundreds of tiny cuts as he inched along "through blood, glass, dirt and spit until they told me to stop."[9]

In time Shango was thrown into a cell, the floor already slick with blood from the men who had been "beaten and forced into cells before" him.[10] Then began the torture. "One of them set a small piece of paper on fire and threw it at me. I brushed it off," to which another trooper responded, "Don't burn the nigger. Here, let me put out the fire" and thereupon "threw a cup of liquid mixed with filth on me. It smelt like piss and spit."[11] Later another officer flipped a cigarette butt at him saying, "Wake up nigger, we've come to kill you—you ready to die black cocksucker?" and then lifted his gun, cocked the trigger, and aimed it at Shango.[12] "With sadistic enjoyment he said, after clicking the gun once, "I got one bullet in here nigger, now beg. Beg like a nigger. Beg."[13]

Eventually Shango began to heal, although he was kept in segregation in HBZ along with every other man the state had singled out as leaders of the rebellion. Ultimately, the grand jury named him in five separate indictments. By 1975, Shango was facing a life sentence plus fifty-nine years for first degree kidnapping (thirty-four counts, one for each of the hostages), first degree coercion (for Hess and Schwartz), unlawful imprisonment (for Hess and Schwartz), felony murder for Hess, felony murder for Schwartz, and first degree murder for Schwartz. Because of the way that the state had grouped together the kidnapping indictments, Shango's first trial would focus solely on the kidnapping of Barry Schwartz and charge him as well with felony murder and outright murder for his death in D Block. In 1973, when he was indicted, Shango was transported to Buffalo to stand trial.[14]

Shango couldn't believe he was being charged with this murder. He had indeed been patrolling D Block when the brutal killings of Barry Schwartz, Kenneth Hess, and Michael Privitera had taken place. He also thought he knew who had killed them—who had snapped and taken his frustration and paranoia out on helpless fellow prisoners whose worst offense had been talking to a reporter (Hess and Schwartz) and on the unstable Privitera.[15] But he, Shango vehemently maintained, hadn't killed anyone during the rebellion. He had little faith, however, that any jury would believe him.

Although Shango originally had decided to represent himself, as the months wore on he began to grow nervous and decided to contact the ABLD.[16] Attorney Barbara Handschu was assigned to handle his case. Meanwhile, then ABLD director Don Jelinek took a trip to Detroit, Shango's hometown, that would secure him better counsel than he ever could have dreamed of.[17]

Jelinek had taken this 1973 trip eager to persuade lawyers from the Motor City to come to upstate New York to help the ABLD. He particularly hoped to convince Bill Goodman, the son of the famous civil rights lawyer Ernie Goodman, to lend a hand.[18] Jelinek initially had another client in mind for Bill Goodman, but when that man's case was dismissed, he asked him to represent Shango instead.[19] Both Goodman and Jelinek recognized that, given the brutality of the crime he was accused of, Shango would need excellent representation; accordingly, Bill Goodman decided to ask his father to be lead counsel on the case.[20]

Ernie Goodman felt some trepidation. As an out-of-state lawyer, he was unlikely to receive any state funding for his investigation or litigation. Additionally, Goodman was unwilling to stay in a communal home with the decades-younger ABLD workers; therefore he also would have the expense of a hotel room in Buffalo as well as that of the commute back to Detroit on weekends.[21] But after some deliberation, Ernie Goodman agreed to take the case. His firm, Goodman, Eden, Millender, Goodman & Bedrosian, decided to subsidize his efforts. Even better, Haywood Burns, the new director of the ABLD, agreed to help him as co-counsel. As important, when he finally met Shango, he was really taken with him.

As Goodman described him, Shango was "a tall, well built, handsome man, who at the time wore a beard and a mustache which gave him an additional dignified appearance" and he had a certain "dignity" of both "his personality and his posture."[22] Shango was also a forceful presence. On the first day they met, Shango informed Goodman that his name was no longer Bernard Stroble and insisted that all pleadings be changed accordingly. Shango also made clear to Goodman that he would play a central role in his own defense—he too would decide strategy. As Goodman later remarked, with Shango he had "one of the most unusual relationships I've ever had with any client I have ever represented."[23] Ernie Goodman didn't know when he took the case that Shango had grown up in his hometown, but this fact would eventually prove helpful as they "developed considerable community support in Detroit for his defense."[24]

As a defense attorney Goodman made it a practice never to ask a client whether they committed the crime for which they stood trial. This rule held true with Shango.[25] This was strategic: the less he knew, Goodman reasoned, the easier it would be "to develop the defense more from outside sources, from objective evidence, from physical evidence."[26] However,

Bernard "Shango" Stroble (second from right) returns to D Yard with attorneys Ernie Goodman, Haywood Burns, and investigator Linda Borus. *(Photograph by Michael Layman. Courtesy of William Goodman.)*

Shango wasn't willing to let the question of his innocence linger between them. It was vitally important to him that Goodman know that he had not killed anyone during the rebellion. He wrote to Goodman vehemently asserting his innocence: "I can only ask that you believe my innocence. Not as a matter of legal presumption, but as a matter of fact—I am in no way guilty of any murder at Attica."[27] In another letter he reiterated, "I am not guilty of any murder—please believe me."[28] In yet another letter he explained why Goodman's faith in him mattered so much. "I am a very good person, Ernie, this I know deep within. . . . I want to prove myself badly, to all of those especially who think I am such a bad person. . . . I have made some bad mistakes in my life, as we all have. But most of my mistakes have been recorded which makes me look like such a terrible person. I want to deal with this image honestly and correctly and prove it to be wrong. . . . I want to prove many things, but most of all I want to prove that I am a decent and good person."[29]

In time it would become important to Shango not only that Ernie Goodman believed in his innocence, but also that they were friends as well as colleagues in this long battle that they faced together. After one of the many tense meetings they had debating trial strategy, Shango felt compelled to apologize to Goodman as well as to express his fondness for him. "I do hope you understand that there was nothing personal or feelings of dissatisfaction with the work you're doing," he wrote. "On the contrary, you have been a source of great inspiration, hope and strength to me—please understand this. Without you, I'm sure this matter would be almost impossible to deal with."[30]

Although there was certainly tension between Goodman and Shango regarding defense strategy—who should testify, which witnesses should be called, how much should be revealed and held in reserve—on the most important matters, they agreed. They had spent some time early on discussing various possibilities for how to defend Shango, but after the terrible loss in the Hill and Pernasalice trial, both men concurred that this defense would center on the legal particulars not on the case's political implication.

Still, Goodman's trial team devoted considerable energy to managing its public relations both inside the courtroom and out. The team wanted to avoid any perception of "defense spectators as loud and disorderly," which the press portrayed as a "lack of concern about the judicial proceedings."[31] So, for Shango's trial, the ABLD made a deliberate effort to work with various established community groups to "bring black middle class spectators into the courtroom."[32] Outside the courthouse, one young woman, Devon Hodges, was specifically tasked with sending out press releases and both monitoring as well as massaging the media. Hodges had been chair of the English Department at George Mason University and so knew about communications.[33] She had expressed concern that she had neither the contacts nor the budget to forge a good relationship with the media, but was determined to make it happen on $12 a week and much mimeographing. She managed to send out a press release to fifty newspapers each week.[34]

Perhaps the team's best public spokeswoman was Shango's own mother—known affectionately by all as "Ma Stroble." She was a Baptist minister in Detroit, where she had developed a community center in the heart of the city that provided many social services, particularly for children. Both in Detroit and around Buffalo, she became a tireless advocate for her son and a regular presence at all court hearings; perhaps "the single person who was respected and trusted by all the different factions."[35] She acknowledged that her son was no angel, as she phrased it, but she believed him when he said that he hadn't killed anyone at Attica, and was determined that he get a fair trial no matter his past.

To that end, Shango's trial team, and specifically five law students from the University of Buffalo, devoted countless hours to researching the ins and outs of every charge he faced and how these charges might most effectively be countered.[36] For this team there were thousands of pages of witness statements and testimony to wade through in the hope that there were obvious contradictions or competing eyewitness accounts. The good news, one of the student researchers explained about these witnesses, was that "we had the person's original criminal record, we had his grand jury testimony, and we had his Wade hearing testimony. We also had, for some of them, their original interviews with the state police."[37]

It was also vital to make sure that the state's witnesses had not been in any way coerced, so the defense relied heavily on a lead investigator named Linda Borus. A member of the New York City branch of the National Lawyers Guild, Borus had come to Attica right after the retaking. She had seen the hate in troopers' eyes firsthand and had suspected that the state was determined to see the prisoners pay even more than they already had for their rebellion.

Borus had been paying attention when Shango had initially contacted the ABLD for help, and she was one of the first to meet with him about the indictments he faced. At their first meeting, Borus was taken aback in equal measure by how handsome he was and how suspicious of everyone he seemed. Over the next several months, Borus eventually earned his trust and they fell in love with each other. When Ernie Goodman took on Shango's case, Borus offered to help in any way she could to prove his innocence.[38]

The more investigative work that Linda did, the more Goodman became convinced of its value. As he saw it, "One had to understand the whole uprising" to put on a good defense.[39] There was no way to do this "on any narrow basis of just ascertaining who had done what" but doing it more fully was clearly netting the defense dividends.[40] For starters, there seemed to be substantial evidence in this case, as there had been in Hill's and Pernasalice's, that the state's witnesses had been terrorized and coerced. As one state witness described his experience, the most persistent investigators had included Milde and Simonetti, and their "initial approach was with how much time I had left to finish up my time . . . that both inmates and officers alike had praised my actions in helping everyone; how I deserved to be rewarded; how they could insure me my upcoming parole, etc. . . . They believed I could help them, it would be beneficial to me, etc."[41] This particular prisoner admitted that he was tempted by this offer—especially after he was locked up in HBZ "because I wasn't helping them."[42] He was even more tempted to tell them what they wanted to hear when he was sent to another facility, Wende Correctional Facility, and when officers there told him that he was already on an "execution list" because prisoners there thought he had already cooperated with investigators. The prosecutors, he was told, could protect him if he helped them. So this man agreed to talk. But when he told them that he knew who had killed Schwartz, but that it wasn't Shango, an investigator told him bluntly that "they were only interested in convicting Stroble, Champion [Champen], Dalou, Jomo, Frank Smith and Blyden"—precisely the men who were indicted for the murders of Schwartz, Hess, and Privitera.[43]

Trying to nail down as much evidence of state bullying as possible, Goodman's team also wanted a Wade hearing, hoping it would clearly show that the witnesses' "unlawful out-of-court identification" of Shango "was so unnecessarily suggestive as to amount to a denial of due process."[44] For twelve weeks, beginning January 6, 1975, and while the trials of Pernasalice and Hill were in progress, Wade hearings commenced for Shango and four other Attica Brothers: Big Black, Herb Blyden, Roger Champen, and Jomo.[45] With so many defendants and so many defense attorneys as well as prosecutors jammed into his courtroom in Erie County, Judge Joseph Mattina had a lot to contend with. By the time the Wade hearing ended, the transcript numbered 8,412 pages.

The hearing itself took place in a nearly one-hundred-year-old courtroom with no air-conditioning. It was unseasonably hot in the room, and hostilities between the court employees and the defendants who arrived each day were palpable. Judge Mattina was bombarded with stories of investigative impropriety.[46] State witness John Flowers told the court how Ernest Milde had questioned him sometimes for eight hours a day, five days a week for months.[47] Each time they met, Flowers said, Milde pushed and pushed at him to name Shango and the other indictees as killers and made abundantly clear to him, as Flowers now testified, that "If I had any information which was helpful to them, it possibly would be helpful to me."[48] Flowers told the court that Milde "tole me that they knew that Stroble and BB [Big Black] and Champ and Brother Herb and Jomo had committed these murders. And that if I could give the information verifying this that it would be helpful when I went to the Parole Board . . . to show I was interested in helping the state."[49] These words were seductive for a man who wasn't due to get out of prison until at least 1988.[50] Nonetheless,

Flowers did not implicate any others, and he was keeplocked indefinitely.[51] Flowers's terror was made worse by being unable to distinguish between State Police investigators and Simonetti's staff investigators. To him they were "all the same," and given all he had endured on the day of Attica's retaking back in 1971, he feared anyone connected to the New York State Police could really hurt him.[52] When he eventually did agree to testify for the state, Flowers was paroled.

Many of the state's witnesses shared Flowers's experience. Time and again prisoners admitted that they had said what the state wanted to hear "out of fear of prison authorities."[53] The defense lawyers were equally alarmed when they learned that the prosecution had also been exceedingly sloppy, if not outright negligent, in the way that it handled its photo identification process and yet it was being allowed. As Ernie Goodman recalled, "a well-drilled witness unhesitatingly identified the photo [that a prosecutor] handed to him as that of the accused [Shango] as he had looked on September 9 with no beard and a shaved head."[54] The problem for the prosecution was that when that lawyer perfunctorily handed that same photo to the defense so that it might be entered in as evidence, Goodman noted immediately that it wasn't Shango at all. The man in the photograph was actually Jomo. To the state, Goodman mused, "all blacks apparently looked alike."[55]

Further evidence presented at the Wade hearing indicated that the state had heard witness testimony that clearly pointed to someone other than whom they wanted to indict, but they never called these witnesses before the grand jury. At least four prisoner witnesses who testified at the Wade hearing indicated their belief that the death in question had not been caused by those who now stood accused of the crime, but rather had been at the hands of another prisoner altogether: Thomas Hicks. Hicks was the prisoner whose deep intellect had so impressed Attica's teachers back in 1971 and he was also the prisoner who Lieutenant Joe Christian claimed had attacked him as he was trying to rescue the hostages—the attack, he insisted, that prompted his fellow troopers to protect him by spraying that area with pellets and bullets.[56]

In fact, one witness who was now willing to testify that Shango had killed Schwartz not only had initially told state investigator Ernest Milde that he had never seen Shango with any blood on him, but he had then testified at the Wade hearing that he had seen Tommy Hicks with a great deal of blood on him.[57] Similarly, another prisoner who was now going to testify against Shango admitted that, originally, he had told state investigators that he had seen "Hicks with a knife in his right hand and two white hands grasping Hicks' hand, coming from the direction of the bed" and then he saw "Hicks come to the doorway of the cell and wipe a knife or sharp instrument on his shirt or his pants."[58] A third prisoner agreed that he had seen Hicks, not Shango, with shears and blood on him, but he too was now going to be a state witness against Shango.[59]

By the close of the Wade hearing the defense attorneys were disgusted by all that they had heard. In their opinion, Francis Cryan, one of the two prosecutors from Simonetti's office in charge of this case, was simply "dirty."[60] Goodman felt sure he had "proved that the prosecution knew that other person or persons were responsible for that particular crime" and "it was obvious Cryan was implicated in this" since he was the main person deciding which witnesses would be brought before the grand jury.[61]

From his point of view it could not have been any clearer that state witnesses had been coached, manipulated, and bribed to finger his client. Even Cryan himself had, in Goodman's view, admitted as much when he testified on December 18, 1974, that he did "write letters about inmates that had testified." When explicitly asked if the purpose of those letters was to make the parole board look favorably on a given prisoner witness, prosecutor Cryan replied, "Well, I think that speaks for itself."[62] Goodman hoped that Judge Mattina had been paying close attention and that he would, in turn, rule at the close of the Wade hearing that the identification of Shango had not been made properly.

However, Judge Mattina seemed not to hear all that had been testified, or, perhaps, did not believe the prisoners who told tales of fear and coercion. He concluded "there was no tainting of the identification made during the investigation of the deaths of inmates Hess and Schwartz . . . the identification procedure used by state officials was proper."[63]

The trial now was unavoidable. Goodman's team would have to put Shango's fate in the hands of a jury and hope that it could see how this case had been rigged from the start. Even though Goodman couldn't put Cryan himself on trial "as a principle [*sic*] villain in the case," he nevertheless hoped that the jury would have a critical view of the prosecutor's reliance upon, and sanctioning of, shoddy tactics simply to win a case.[64] He would repeatedly remind jurors of "the nature of the investigation, the pressure the state exerted upon people over whom it had absolute control."[65]

That argument would only have an effect if the jury was not already prejudiced against prisoners in general, or Shango in particular. Goodman was worried since it seemed that Judge Mattina was growing harder toward the defense after the Wade hearing. Beth Bonora, from the ABLD's Jury Project, recalled that "the change in the judge's behavior caused grave apprehension in the defense team. Only a week earlier we had cheerfully discussed whether waiving a jury and going to trial before Mattina alone might be the best strategy," because at least at first the judge "had shown respect and sympathy for both Ernie and Shango. Now, he was putting on a cold, hard mask and seemed irritated at the smallest request."[66] As Shango's defense team saw it, the judge's demeanor was crucial: "The tone of a trial is determined in many subtle ways by the judge. His treatment of the parties gives the jury clues to his thoughts, which they incorporate into their evaluation of the evidence."[67]

Beth Bonora and her colleague Eric Swanson were determined to get a jury for Shango that would not be prejudiced or easily swayed by an unsympathetic judge. Ernie Goodman was eager to work with the ABLD Jury Project, which, he could see, had undertaken the herculean tasks of data collection and community network building. The week before Shango's jury selection began was particularly hectic. While defense lawyers busily argued their motion to dismiss indictments, the Jury Project was trying to amass enough information to make sure the defense could pick the best jurors. As Bonora remembered it, "We sent letters to members of the community network alerting them to the start of the case. A meeting was held to decide which of the psychologists used on an earlier Attica murder trial [the Hill and Pernasalice trial] were reliable. Then a meeting was scheduled with those we wanted to use. Data on the current composition of the Erie County jury pool was collected."[68] What they found led Bonora to recommend that Ernie Goodman immediately "file a motion to challenge the entire pool as unrepresentative of young people and women."[69]

He did, and to his surprise Judge Mattina granted the motion. But there was still much work to do.[70] Because Ernie Goodman was the most seasoned lawyer on Shango's team, the plan was that he would begin the voir dire, the questioning of potential jurors, then either Haywood Burns or Shango could step in. The key to a successful voir dire was having solid research from the Jury Project; any answers a potential juror gave could be analyzed in light of the Jury Project's data on juror attitudes. Whatever rating a given juror netted from that analysis would help the defense identify whether he or she should be questioned more closely and carefully.[71] The job of collecting information for the Jury Project seemed never ending. In addition, as soon as anyone on the defense team questioned a juror, the Jury Project team immediately contacted its community network to find out any additional information that might be helpful in gauging whether that individual would or would not be a good pick for the defense.

Even with a relatively good jury pool, picking a sympathetic jury would be no easy task. As Goodman recalled, seeing the first fifty-person panel made the defense "terribly pessimistic": they were "middle class, middle age, elderly, white, mainly men, very few young people, and one black person (possibly two)."[72] They also found that a significant number of the prospective jurors had close relationships with law enforcement agencies—one was "a neighbor of an Attica prosecutor and had even asked him for a ride to court."[73]

Some potential jurors didn't even attempt to hide their contempt and racist views of black people and, yet, in Goodman's view, the judge was trying to shut down the defense's ability to probe their racial prejudices in the voir dire questioning. Goodman finally lost his patience and addressed the judge. "This has been a difficult day for all of us," he began. "I have felt almost a sickness come over me as I have listened to this jury. . . . The defense has a right, and an obligation, to find out how the race of this defendant will affect the jurors . . . [but] you have virtually instructed every juror on that panel how to answer our questions, and you have made it impossible for us to get at their true feelings on this volatile matter."[74]

The second jury panel seemed "just as bad" to Goodman's team, but, thankfully, the third panel was better.[75] The people on this panel appeared to be less prejudiced, even though the lawyers hadn't really been allowed to probe jurors based on their racial views. By then the defense team was well versed in how to most effectively use "the voluminous data" given it by the Jury Project and this had helped them pick a better jury despite the limitations placed on the voir dire process.[76]

By taking seriously the information provided by the Jury Project, Shango's team felt fairly good as the jury selection process drew to a close. To Goodman, the Jury Project had been a godsend. He was surprised at how efficiently the ABLD lawyers had been able to utilize its community network to receive feedback—he "knew very quickly whether a juror was one we would obviously want or one we would obviously reject."[77]

Simonetti's office was upset that the ABLD had been "conducting a telephone interview program with all the prospective Attica jurors to attempt to determine their prejudices in this matter"—particularly since they had to concede that such interviews were "essentially legal."[78]

Just before the final jurors were chosen, however, the prosecution and defense alike were hit with a lightning bolt. One of the ABLD's legal volunteers, Mary Jo Cook, revealed that she was, in fact, an informant for the Federal Bureau of Investigation. The twenty-six-year-old white woman had first come clean to a lawyer on Barbara Handschu's staff, who, in turn, persuaded Cook to go to the press. Her admission, they knew, would have major implications for the myriad cases they were trying to defend, including Shango's, as well as the one they had just lost.[79] John Hill's lawyer, William Kunstler, immediately called his own press conference to insist that, in light of this revelation, the verdict in both his client's and Charley Joe Pernasalice's cases should be overturned.[80] This request was denied.

Judge Mattina agreed to halt Shango's trial in the midst of final jury selection to hold a week-long hearing on the matter of the informant.[81] Testimony revealed that Mary Jo Cook had been an employee of the FBI from June of 1973 until November of 1974. Her boyfriend was already informing for the bureau, while also reporting to someone named Jack Steinmetz at the New York State Police. Since Cook very much needed money, she was excited when asked if she too might want to become an informant.[82] The FBI, it turned out, had a very specific group that they wanted her to infiltrate—Vietnam Veterans Against the War/Winter Soldier Organization.[83] She was given the code name "Jo Leroy" and she made between $50 and $80 each month for her reports.[84] According to Cook, she delivered these reports to her control agent, a Mr. Gary Lash, "in a park or a cemetery that was a really peaceful place."[85] Gary Lash, she insisted, was not just any FBI agent. He had already, in the course of the FBI's official investigation called for by the Justice Department back in 1971, "talked to every witness, hundreds of witnesses, state troopers, guards and other people."[86] Although Mary Jo Cook had been asked, officially, to spy on the VVAW, by September of 1973 she had also become a regular around the offices of the ABLD.

Cook remembered her first Attica defense meeting well. At a storefront on Connecticut Street, they showed a recent documentary by Cinda Firestone about the Attica Brothers, and Big Black as well as John Hill and Charley Joe Pernasalice had all been there.[87] From that moment forward she began volunteering for the Jury Project. She gave Lash everything she could, she testified, "even down to telephone numbers, any little piece of information. . . . I supplied him with details about people that I considered important, whether or not I understood what their importance was."[88] Wondering where that information went, Cook actually asked Lash. "Most of it stayed in Buffalo," he told her, but a summary of it also "went to Washington," which she already knew because, as she testified, "I got a specific telephone call from Washington twice as to the information that I know."[89]

According to Cook, she had, in fact, learned a great deal that the FBI wanted badly to know. For example, during one of the first Attica trials—the one in which Willie Smith was charged with raping John Schleich—she had heard from fellow volunteers "that he had a problem with his lawyer . . . that his lawyer was not working well with the ABLD," among other matters.[90] Additionally, Mary Jo said, she had "received information about Mr. Stroble's defense last summer," whereupon she was called into Judge Mattina's chambers to describe in more detail what she had learned.[91] Perhaps her arrangement with the FBI would have continued indefinitely, but the longer Cook worked for the ABLD, the more sympathetic to the defendants she became and her conscience began to plague her.

What really bothered her, Cook said, were the tactics used by state investigators to build their cases against the Attica defendants. For example, she said, the only reason that they had started their cases against Willie Smith was that they wanted the public to be swayed against all future Attica defendants—get it thinking of them all as deviants.[92] The fact that the Brothers had suffered so much physical abuse also really got to Cook. In fact, she soon became so obsessed with the question of whether there had been atrocities during and after the retaking at Attica that she went to her FBI handlers to ask them what really had happened. On the stand she recalled one meeting with Lash and another agent, "an old Irish Catholic" named Ed, who kept trying to reassure her that there had been no atrocities. "I kept telling them that I knew there had been atrocities at Attica. Their response was a categorical denial."[93]

No denials, though, were able to combat what she had learned from the Attica defendants themselves and, in time, their accounts of torture kept her up at night. By the time Cook was helping the Jury Project, she was already torn. Although she had not admitted it to her FBI handlers, she had actually volunteered there because deep down she actually thought what it was doing "was a good thing."[94]And then her guilt pushed her to admit that she was an informant.[95] According to Cook, she was by no means the only FBI informant in the ABLD, and indeed asserted that there was one still there named Kevin Ryan, so she wanted to do the right thing and tell the ABLD what had been going on.[96]

Even though it was clear from the hearing that Mary Jo Cook had been privy to the defense strategy, and she insisted that she had shared what she knew, she had a hard time proving this and proof is what Judge Mattina wanted. Cook insisted that she "did in fact pass on" the information that she had "obtained from the defense people"—including vital information regarding "the jury project, legal defense strategy, courtroom strategy, communications between lawyers and clients, specific information on defendants' positions and personal problems and the internal structure of the ABLD as a defense effort and how it was coordinated."[97] Mattina, however, wanted corroboration. Although she came to his courtroom with "a large leather briefcase" filled with various reports, that wasn't enough.[98] She would have had even more documents, she explained to the judge, but suspicious fires had broken out both at her residence and at ABLD lawyer Barbara Handschu's office and everything not with her now had been destroyed.[99]

Although Cook had, in Mattina's view, insufficient corroboration that she had passed defense secrets to the FBI, notably, no one in the Bureau denied that Cook was an informant. Cook's control agent, Gary Lash, confirmed that he had been specifically assigned to "security matters" in 1971 and to the VVAW, that Cook reported to him, and that he also knew state policeman Jack Steinmetz. But Lash insisted that "he had never requested Miss Cook to spy on the Attica defense camp."[100] Even when another FBI agent admitted that he too had been placed "in charge of monitoring the Attica defense effort," had also received information on the ABLD, and had even been in contact with prosecutors from Simonetti's office, it seemed to satisfy the judge when he then insisted "that he 'did nothing' with the information."[101] Simonetti's prosecutors James Grable and Charles Bradley confirmed that they had talked with the FBI about the ABLD, but both denied that they used information on the ABLD provided to them by the FBI. That too seemed to satisfy Judge Mattina.[102]

To the stunned reaction of the entire ABLD, Judge Mattina's twelve-page decision concluded that "there was no evidence of governmental interference with the Attica legal defense team" and that Miss Cook's "allegations" were not "supported by her testimony, which I must characterize as general and extremely vague."[103] When *New York Times* columnist and former Attica observer Tom Wicker learned that "the FBI had planted a paid informer among the defense workers" to him it had seemed obvious that the trials, such as Hill's and Pernasalice's, that had just taken place were "not fairly conducted."[104] Not to Judge Mattina, however. The trial against Shango would proceed.

And so jury selection resumed. Jury Project captain Beth Bonora now worried that even the research the defense team was relying on might be tainted. "There was the possibility," she noted, that Cook "had messed with the statistical studies and the resulting info they were getting to pick a jury was faulty." They had no choice, however, but to go forward.[105] Jury selection finally ended on May 15. Opening statements commenced five days later.[106]

Prosecutors Frank Cryan and Daniel Moynihan approached the jury with great confidence. Bernard Stroble, they insisted, had caused "the death of Barry Schwartz by stabbing him with a sharp instrument." In addition, he was charged with kidnapping Schwartz, which allowed the perpetration of the murder.[107]

The state's first witness, prisoner George Kirk, was not that convincing. Kirk's story kept changing on the stand, and at one point he simply broke down and said, "I've had my days mixed up for years, praying I'd forget the entire matter."[108] Watching the prosecution struggle to get Kirk to finger Shango filled defense attorney Goodman with relief. In his view, "the jury realized that this witness was a person that they just couldn't believe."[109]

The state, though, regrouped and called prisoner John Flowers to the stand. Although Flowers also had a hard time telling a coherent story of what he had seen and heard, he did tell the jury something crucial to the prosecution's case—he said that Shango had told him Barry Schwartz was going to be executed for treason. Flowers had been the medic called to Schwartz's cell to sew up the wounds he had suffered when glass was thrown at him after he had been moved to D Block. This was, he claimed, when Shango told him that Schwartz was to be executed.

Prisoner witness Jack Florence also helped to implicate Shango in the murder of Schwartz by placing him at the scene and giving him the same motive—he had killed Schwartz for being a traitor. Florence had testified before the grand jury earlier that he had seen both Schwartz and Hess being led, naked, to D Block by Bernard Stroble and others and that they were accusing these men, most specifically, of "treason." The prosecution had him recount this same story for the jury.[110]

Ultimately, prosecutors needed an eyewitness to Schwartz's murder. Before introducing witnesses willing to testify to this, though, the state first decided to set the scene—to make clear to the jury just how brutal this murder had been. To do this they put a prisoner by the name of Willie Locke on the stand. Locke claimed to have seen the aftermath of Schwartz's alleged execution and told the jury in graphic detail how he had seen "two guys laying on the bed with blood all over them."[111] This was but a prelude, though, for calling prisoner Jimmy Holt. Holt was one of only two witnesses who would tell jurors that he had actually seen Shango stab Schwartz, whereupon "he screamed and fell to the floor."[112]

But Holt's testimony wasn't as strong as the state hoped it would be. In fact, even the prosecution had found it hard to buy this man's testimony. According to an internal memo in 1975 that was addressing the myriad interviews state investigators had done over the years with Jimmy Holt, lead prosecutor Cryan admitted that even he doubted Holt's credibility. As he noted to his colleagues: "Holt related an account of a stabbing which allegedly he witnessed in 42 Company on Saturday night. Holt now informs us that his previous statements concerning these events were based upon what he had heard and not from observations he personally made from the slop sink room in 42 company."[113] Even Holt's testimony about the events leading to those murders—about what had happened in the yard on Friday night—was, in Cryan's opinion, sketchy; "his recollection now of the details of some of these events is somewhat different as to some particulars."[114]

Worse, the prosecutors in Shango's case knew that Jimmy Holt was by no means their only flawed witness. They were also aware, for example, that John Flowers had also told them completely different stories at different times. For example, when he was interviewed by an Organized Crime Task Force investigator in early 1972, Flowers claimed that he had seen Stroble with "several knives down his pants."[115] Two months later, however, when interviewed a second time, he made no mention of having seen Shango at all.[116] By the time he testified before the grand jury in June of 1972, he had yet another account to share—in this case stating that Shango had "what looked like an arsenal of what—knives or screwdrivers, you could see handles sticking out of his belt."[117]

But the prosecution's star witness, it turned out, was to be neither Holt nor Flowers. Cryan and Monyihan instead were counting on a prisoner named Jimmy Ross to make their case. Ross testified that he had seen Stroble in a "black raincoat" with a "pirate's sword," along with four or five men, "put his hand on the man's head . . . then he cut his throat."[118] It appeared to jurors that this witness was very credible. He had obviously been traumatized from having seen this horrific murder. At one point the judge "offered Mr. Ross 'a handful of tissues,'" and while he told this story, "the jury of five men and seven women listened to his testimony with looks of intense discomfort on their faces, their eyes fixed on this slight and frequently inaudible witness."[119]

But whatever ground the prosecution thought it had gained with its alleged eyewitnesses to the murder of Barry Schwartz such as Jimmy Ross was lost almost as soon as Ernie Goodman, at times with his son Bill stepping in to help as well as Haywood Burns and Shango himself, began their cross-examinations and eventually called their own witnesses to the stand.

Ernie Goodman's first blow to prosecutors Cryan and Moynihan's case came during the cross-examination of the state's first witness, George Kirk. Not only was it already obvious that his testimony made little sense since it had changed even as he testified, but, as Goodman pointed out, the state knew this was a totally unreliable witness. For starters, prosecutors knew that this man suffered from mental illness and had been so unstable that even the state couldn't rely on him despite granting him parole for agreeing to testify against Shango. No sooner did he get let out than he skipped town and went to California. When he ran out of money, he was so desperate that "he called the state troopers for funds with which to return."[120]

Goodman then took time to dismantle the credibility of the state's second witness, John Flowers. Unbeknownst to anyone in Simonetti's office, before he had taken the stand for the state, Flowers had already given Shango's defense investigator, Linda Borus, a statement that "became extremely important at his trial, one of the highlights."[121] Written in longhand on yellow legal paper by Flowers himself, "his own statement in his own writing, in his own language," made it clear that he had told the state investigators something completely different from what had happened in order to secure his own parole.[122] So, after Flowers had just testified against Shango as Frank Cryan hoped he would, Goodman then presented him with his own handwritten refutation of that same testimony. According to that statement, Shango had not, in fact, told Flowers that Schwartz was there to be executed. What he had actually said was that it was good Flowers was patching Schwartz up and he was trying to keep things calm. "Look," Shango had really said, "we don't want anybody to get at these people, those who want to hurt them and we are trying to safeguard them and we can't let anybody in here who might do something to them. So we don't want anybody coming in without a pass and that's why it is important that everybody coming in do have a pass."[123] The jury just gaped at this completely different portrayal of what had gone down in D Block on the day in question. Even if they weren't sure which of the accounts to believe, one thing was certain: Flowers "had proven to be a liar" and, as Goodman saw it, that in itself "was really a devastating blow" to the prosecution's case.[124]

Things didn't bode well for the rest of the state's witnesses under Goodman's cross-examination either. Willie Locke, for example, had told the gory tale of throat cutting and seeing the bloody victims on their cots and had, very clearly, put jurors in a mood to make sure that, if Shango had done this horrific crime, he should pay for it. Goodman, however, meticulously walked Locke through the other statements he made to investigators and, most importantly, the testimony he himself had given to the grand jury previously on July 19, 1973. He then asked him directly, "Did you ever see Shango with blood on him at any time?" to which Locke, hanging his head, simply said, "No."[125] Goodman then did the same thing with Jimmy Holt.[126] Very quickly he had Holt admitting in front of the jury not only that it "was difficult for him to remember what he saw and what he heard later, he gets mixed up" but that, in fact, he had actually told the state that someone altogether different than Shango had murdered Schwartz. According to Holt, he had explicitly told state investigators that Tommy Hicks had gone "crazy and kept stabbing" Schwartz until he was dead.[127]

Ernie Goodman, however, most needed to discredit Jimmy Ross, since he had such graphic testimony of Shango actually killing Schwartz. Goodman had to think hard about how he would tackle this particular man on the stand because Ross was already such a pathetic figure. Whatever happened he, Goodman, didn't want to appear to be bullying or belittling this "very thin, small, white, gaunt looking, sallow-faced, pock marked man," this "pitiful object."[128] So rather than push Ross around on the stand, Goodman decided instead to make clear to the jury just how easy it had been for the state's investigator, Ernest Milde, to get Ross to say anything he wanted him to. As Goodman pointed out, Ross "had tried to stay away from him, try not to answer his questions, try not to say what he wanted to say [but] Milde had put things in his mouth, had suggested to him certain answers to certain questions . . . [pushing] again and again to get in something more and more and more and at the same time suggesting what that 'more and more' ought to be."[129] Ultimately Goodman's cross was very successful. As the jury could now see, Milde had suggested so much to Ross that, ultimately, he was willing to make the statement the state wanted him to, under oath, about the killing.[130]

For jurors, however, the question remained: If Shango hadn't killed Schwartz, then who had? Goodman felt fairly certain that the jury would want to have some sense of this before it would be willing to render a not guilty verdict for his client. So he went for the state's jugular, calling four witnesses whose other statements and testimony supported the defense's claim "that the attorney general deliberately—and not by mistake or neglect—deliberately withheld from the grand jury testimony that would show that it was not Shango who killed Schwartz."[131] More specifically, Goodman referred back to what the defense had learned during the Wade hearing: these witnesses had named another man, Tommy Hicks, as the killer but—and this point was key—the state didn't want Hicks to be the murderer because he had already been killed in the retaking.[132]

As proof of these assertions, Goodman noted that Frank Cryan had not brought any witness who identified Hicks as the killer before the grand jury or to this jury. Why? Because at least one of them would have, according to Goodman, "directly contradicted Ross's testimony that Stroble was inside of the cell when this murder took place; it completely eliminates him, and on that testimony he [Cryan] actually had three supporting corroborative witnesses, all of which tend to prove that it was Hicks, not Stroble."[133] Goodman noted that another prisoner reported he had "heard Thomas Hicks say, 'I have cut two dudes' throats,'" and seen Hicks "covered with blood, everywhere, hands, clothing, chest, face, and carrying a straight razor, beige colored, burned handle in his right hand."[134] A third witness—who was also known to the state—had not only "looked in the cell and observed Tommy Hicks cutting a white dude's throat," but had also pointed out that the state's main witness against Shango, Jimmy Ross, hadn't even been there when this murder took place—he had already left the gallery.[135]

Even after decimating the state's witnesses, and showing the ways in which they had, in his view, engaged in prosecutorial misconduct, Goodman couldn't be entirely confident of Shango's chances of acquittal. He had seen what had happened in the Hill and Pernasalice trial, where neither defendant had benefited a whit from the jury's knowing of the state's unsavory deeds, pressuring and bribing of witnesses. Goodman hit upon the only way he might eliminate any doubt that remained in the jurors' minds regarding Shango's innocence: compelling the jury to look carefully at exactly when Schwartz had been killed.[136]

Goodman had spent a lot of time poring over the autopsy that John Edland had done on Barry Schwartz. He was no pathologist, but he was struck by the presence of rigor mortis in Schwartz's body on Tuesday at 5:00 a.m., which certainly suggested that he "had been killed probably not more than thirty hours before the autopsy."[137] This was important. "If that were true," that meant that Schwartz had died after Saturday—the day that prosecutors said Shango had killed him.[138] Goodman began to wonder: if medical evidence indicated that Schwartz didn't die until after Saturday, that meant not only that his client was in the clear, but that troopers might have actually killed Schwartz and Hess during the retaking.[139] Not a single state witness placed Shango anywhere near the murder scene after Saturday.

Goodman was worried about getting Shango to agree that Edland should be their parting shot to the jury; neither was he sure that he could persuade Edland to testify. Goodman decided that he, Shango, and Linda Borus all needed to sit down and decide, together, what the final strategy should be. So he went to the jail. "It was a miserable, horrible day," he recalled. "The depressiveness, the heat, just being within the bars on a beautiful day outside, not being able to smell the air except through those bars . . . was enough to destroy the morale of everybody."[140] They persevered, however, arguing, bantering, and reviewing "everything that was available and the witnesses that were possible."[141]

Whatever strategy they decided upon, Shango asked, would it be enough to convince the jury of his innocence?[142] Goodman couldn't promise that. All he could say was that he felt his "approach to the defense was better, more effective, and less fraught with dangers" than, for example, allowing Shango to testify on his own behalf as he still wanted to do.[143] Shango wanted to speak to clear his own name—but he more desperately wanted "an acquittal on all counts. . . . He wanted no compromise verdict. He wanted and believed he was entitled to a complete acquittal."[144] Maybe Dr. Edland could be the surprise witness that would make all the difference.

At first, John Edland had no interest in testifying in Shango's case. He had over the last four years suffered so much abuse—so much hate mail, so much hostile press—that he wasn't eager again to reenter the fray. He wrote to Goodman, "I would prefer to remain intellectually detached from the prosecution or defense of any of the Attica tragedies."[145] Eventually, however, Goodman persuaded him to explain his autopsy to the jury. The morning that he was to testify, Edland and his wife, "a very concerned and interesting person . . . [who] was terribly supportive of what he was doing," met with Goodman over breakfast to go over what would happen.[146]

When Edland walked into the courtroom that day, the state's surprise was palpable. To Goodman's relief, Edland was a great witness. He didn't come off as coldly intellectual and detached, but as "a straightforward kind of guy, talking in a straightforward type of language that jurors could understand rather than testifying like a professional or an expert witness."[147] This was good because Goodman needed him to explain some rather complicated science having to do with the time of Barry Schwartz's death and the way that rigor mortis manifests in the body. Speaking clearly and without hesitation, Dr. Edland stated that, based on rigor mortis at the time that he had autopsied the victim, "Schwartz had died on Sunday."[148]

Frank Cryan went ballistic. He hopped to his feet and began peppering Edland with questions, all of which seemed somehow sarcastic and disrespectful. At one point Cryan approached Edland with a heavy medical book in hand and tried to suggest that there were many medical experts who would totally disagree with his analysis of rigor mortis vis-à-vis time of Schwartz's death. The more Cryan questioned Edland, the more aggressive he became. However, the prosecutor's bombastic style seemed to backfire. After enduring one particularly aggressive question from Cryan, Dr. Edland finally lost his patience, responding in "such a dramatic, powerful, emotional way," Goodman recalled, that it "knocked all of us back on our feet including the members of the jury."[149] It was as if a long-blocked dam in Edland finally burst. He spoke of how he had been "isolated, tortured, [and put] under extreme pressure" even though his findings had been independently verified and he had autopsied over five thousand bodies in his career.[150] And before he stepped down from the witness box, jurors had seen this man's pain. Earnestly, he said, his voice breaking, he had done "the best job he could," and though others were welcome to disagree with his findings, "he was confident of his conclusions."[151]

As Edland left the stand, the courtroom was hushed. Ernie Goodman was struck by "the tone of his voice, his expression . . . the intensity of his voice, the way he looked directly into Cryan's eyes . . . his whole appearance showed the jury the amount of pressure under which this man had been living simply because he had told what he had seen, with no motivation other than to state the truth."[152]

Perhaps Goodman could have rested his case at that point. He would later concede, "It was the highlight and the most dramatic moment in the whole case for me."[153] However, he had two more defense witnesses to follow Edland on the stand: the first a former prisoner named Albert Victory who was to testify to the positive role Shango had played throughout the rebellion—particularly in trying to ease any tensions in the yard that might erupt between white and black inmates. Then former Attica observer James Ingram testified about Shango's reasoned character in the yard as well as to the broader fears that had led prisoners to detain Schwartz in the first place.[154] It was time for the closing arguments.

On June 25, 1975, the defense made its summation. Goodman walked the jury through the myriad inconsistencies in the state's witnesses' testimony as well as reminded the jury of the many witnesses who had seen something utterly different from what the state claimed had happened. Goodman had hoped that this case would have been dismissed long ago; as far back as the Wade hearing, it was obvious to him how much evidence had been suppressed, so much that it should, in his mind, now "force an acquittal."[155] It seemed incredible to him that the state's entire stable of witnesses in the Attica cases had "all paroled after cooperating."[156] Even more unbelievably, he argued, the state's entire case against Shango rested on the testimony of only one man, Jimmy Ross, who the jury could see "had been used by the prosecution because he was a weak, pitiful figure to establish a case they couldn't get through any other witness."[157] As Goodman made his way to sit down after his long review for the jury, it was clear he was satisfied that he had done all he could. Even the judge, in Goodman's view, despite not having dismissed this case, had been pretty fair to Shango. He had, for example, made sure that Cryan couldn't make any reference to Shango's previous record before the jury and, when Shango came into the courtroom each day, the judge had ensured that "he was brought in by the deputy in a way that people wouldn't see the handcuffs and through the judge's own office and into the courtroom without handcuffs."[158] After Goodman walked the jury through his defense against the murder charge that morning, Haywood Burns summed up the defense's arguments against the charges of kidnapping and felony murder that afternoon.

It was then the prosecution's turn. Cryan's summary took over two hours.[159] He seemed undaunted as he got up to make his own closing arguments. He focused the jury's attention on the sheer depravity of the murder of Barry Schwartz and argued not only that Shango had been there when that murder took place, but that several witnesses believed he had done the crime. Jimmy Ross, he stressed, might be troubled, but he knew what he saw.

When Frank Cryan sat down even Goodman had to concede that, overall, the prosecutor had done a good job in his summation. His witnesses had been so weak and yet he tried valiantly to make their testimony make sense for the jurors. As he put it, Cryan had "dealt with many of the questions that had been raised in our arguments and he dealt with them generally in a fair way."[160] The fact remained that Cryan himself wasn't particularly likable.[161] As Goodman put it, what was "lacking about Cryan and it had been lacking throughout the whole trial is that he is not a concerned human being. You never felt humanity coming out of the man . . . and that was evident in his final argument."[162]

The next morning, June 26, 1975, from 10:10 until 11:28 a.m., Judge Mattina gave his detailed charges to the jury, whereupon it left to deliberate. As it turned out they would be voting only on whether Shango had committed first degree murder. At the eleventh hour the judge responded affirmatively to a motion Goodman had filed earlier to get the kidnapping charge against his client removed, so the felony murder charges were also dropped.[163] Since many of the men awaiting trial were charged under the same indictment, this decision would have serious implications for future cases, because if there hadn't been a kidnapping in this case, there couldn't have been kidnappings in the rest of the cases that the state hoped to try. In fact, with this decision, the judge had kicked the legal moorings that underpinned the state's most dramatic cases yet to be tried right out from under them. Still, Shango was hardly off the hook. The state was charging him with the murder of Barry Schwartz, a charge that could net him a life sentence.

The jury, though, was not going to decide anything quickly. Hours after leaving to deliberate they asked for some trial testimony to be read to them and, then, an hour after that, they adjourned for dinner. After their meal the jurors were back at it but still had much they felt needed to be discussed. At 8:15 p.m. someone came out to ask for some clarification on the judge's charges. By 8:30 p.m. they were again deliberating, and at 8:55 p.m. the jury took its vote.[164]

When the jury emerged from the deliberation room on the evening of June 26, it was utterly silent in the large courtroom. So drained were Goodman and the rest of the defense team that all he could manage was to bury his head in his arms as he waited for whatever the jury had to say. The jury foreperson slowly rose and, in a somber, dispassionate tone stated that the jury had found Bernard Stroble not guilty of murder. When the words sank in, suddenly it was pandemonium. On hearing the verdict Ma Stroble fainted in her seat, right behind her son, whereupon Shango jumped up and tried to attend to her.[165] Goodman wept.[166]

When Ernie Goodman, Haywood Burns, and the rest of Shango's defense team walked out of the courtroom into the dark summer night they were met by scores of ABLD supporters who applauded them as they walked down the stairs. Again, Goodman was overcome. "It was a remarkable feeling," he remembered. "It was a defense that had been able to jointly overpower the state, without money and without expertise in many cases," and yet it had been able to "bring some kind of justice to that courtroom."[167] Everyone assembled felt an integral part of that victory. A chant began to grow louder all around the courthouse: "Attica Means, Fight Back!" and then "Attica Means" from in the street and a slightly muffled, but still powerful, "Fight Back" from inside the Erie County jail, where many Attica Brothers still sat, awaiting their trials.[168]

## 41

# A Long Journey Ahead

In the wake of their embarrassing defeat in the trial of Bernard "Shango" Stroble, Attica Special Prosecutor Anthony Simonetti and his stable of prosecutors lost some faith that the state would necessarily win the cases still slated to go to trial. In every case that had already gone to trial—including in the single one that they had managed to secure convictions, that of Hill and Pernasalice—the ABLD had relentlessly done its homework, and had managed to drum up substantial support in the court of public opinion. The ABLD had, for example, blanketed the recent Erie County fair with colorful, friendly leaflets questioning whether this was indeed a fair county and asking residents to be their best selves when sitting on Attica juries. Thanks to the ABLD it was unlikely that a single potential juror in Buffalo had not at least heard of, if not actually seen, one of these flyers.

Nevertheless, Simonetti and the judge overseeing all of the Attica cases, Carmen Ball, were determined that all remaining cases proceed as quickly as possible. Both men were in fact facing some media criticism that, although sixty-two prisoners had been charged with committing crimes at Attica back in December of 1972 (and some of them, like Shango, had been named in numerous indictments at the same time), by 1975 prosecutors had only managed to bring five cases to trial. A key challenge that Simonetti's team of prosecutors had faced from the beginning was the considerable amount of time it had been forced to expend on responding to the ABLD's strategically deployed blizzard of motions. What is more, the ABLD's myriad motions had at times been granted, which also set back prosecutors—particularly when they were required to dismiss charges against a given defendant altogether. As *The New York Times* noted in November of 1975, charges against twenty-seven defendants had eventually been dismissed for lack of evidence or other legal reasons.[1] Six defendants had passed away while waiting for their trials.[2]

The state still had plenty of Attica defendants left to try, however, and Judge Ball was committed to getting these scheduled as soon as possible.[3] One of the cases still to be tried was that charging several Attica Brothers, including Donald Noble, with the attempted murder of Attica correction officer Michael Smith "by cutting [him] with a sharp instrument" up on the catwalk on September 13, 1971.[4] The fact that Michael Smith himself had told prosecutors that Donald Noble had actually tried to save him from being gunned down on the catwalk on that day, or the truth that Smith's most catastrophic injuries had come not from any homemade prisoner weapon but rather from having been shot numerous times on the day of the retaking, had not stood in the way of their desire to pursue this case against these indictees.

The case they were most eager to get to trial, however, was the so-called leadership indictment, indictment no. 5, which had charged sixteen Attica Brothers—the ones who had been in segregation after having had Xs chalked onto their backs on the day of the retaking—with multiple offenses. Among these men were Big Black Smith, Herb Blyden, Roger Champen, and Shango. Once again Frank Cryan and Daniel Moynihan would represent the state. Judge Ball expected this trial of Attica's most high-profile rebels would last "close to a year" and it would be "the political trial" and "it will take the longest time to try and will probably be the most explosive."[5]

As much as prosecutors would have liked to get on with the leadership indictment—since it was the most involved and would take so much of their energies—first up on the docket was to be the trial for Attica prisoner Jomo Joka Omowale (born Cleveland McKinley Davis), who stood accused of murdering fellow prisoner Kenneth Hess.[6]

Jomo was the son of a North Carolina sharecropper whose family moved to Virginia when he was twelve. His father became one of first African Americans to run a service station in Virginia, but Jomo had little interest in that business. After a few years of hanging around his dad's shop, he went looking for work in Virginia Beach, where he and a friend were arrested for unknowingly transporting moonshine. Their boss had paid them to drive a car across state lines to bring a "delivery" to a customer but had failed to tell them they were running liquor across state lines. Whereas Jomo's white friend was allowed to enlist rather than do time, Jomo was sentenced to five years in Virginia's hellhole of a state penitentiary. When he finally got out on parole, he was a different person—jaded, cynical, and deeply disillusioned about life. Sensing this change in her son's outlook, Jomo's mother tried to give him a fresh start by sending him to live with one of his uncles up north in the Bronx.

By then, though, Jomo felt a whole lot more comfortable hanging around with folks who had experienced the same things he had and, in time, he was spending all of his time with those who skirted the law and was himself committing petty crimes just to get by. Hoping to avoid getting locked up again, he changed his name to Eric Thompson. Before long, he was busted for robbing an auto parts store and he found himself locked up again—this time in Sing Sing. At this prison he underwent another transformation: he devoured every book he could get his hands on in the library and met many other intelligent people on the inside. Thanks to this education, he not only began to rethink his personal direction, but he also began to think about the nation itself in more critical ways. A pivotal moment for him was seeing the electric chair that had executed accused spy Ethel Rosenberg—he swore that he could still see where her urine had stained the concrete. The image haunted him as he tried to make sense of a country that prided itself on free speech and acceptance and yet was all right with electrocuting that mother.

Jomo, now living as Eric Thompson, increasingly questioned the world around him, he also found himself gravitating toward the teachings of Islam. He converted, and it was then that he became Jomo Joka Omowale. He liked the name Jomo because it was a powerful moniker that meant burning spear, snake, or dragon. After becoming a Muslim, Jomo also joined the Black Panther Party for Self-Defense because he found its ideology empowering. Every political group had a following at Sing Sing: the Panthers, the Republic of New Africa, the Five Percenters, and others, and their growing appeal greatly alarmed correction officials. Trying to neutralize the perceived threat, Sing Sing administrators decided to round up the apparent militants and send them, as a group, to Auburn prison. As a defense minister in the Panthers, Jomo was one of those transferred to this new facility. Jomo was also one of those transferred to Attica after his activism during the Auburn uprising of 1970.

When Jomo arrived at Attica he couldn't get over how miserable the conditions were there. He couldn't believe that the men there were so desperate for time outside their cells that they would literally stand outside in the sleet and rain just to catch some fresh air. Jomo was also taken aback by how cold the guards were at Attica. Attica's correction officers barely spoke to the prisoners—preferring instead to convey their wishes with the butt of their batons. In his view, Attica's officers treated the men in their charge like animals that needed neither shelter from the elements nor the camaraderie of conversation. He realized, however, that there was an upside to the COs' attitude toward prisoners. Since they didn't see them as feeling and thinking human beings, they paid no attention whatsoever when prisoners like him wanted to hold political meetings in the yard.

When the Attica rebellion of 1971 began, Jomo was working in the barbershop. Although guards knew him as a militant, in the initial chaotic hours of the riot "he protected [a correction officer named] Heller and civilian staff from harm." When the retaking of Attica commenced, however, Jomo was shot multiple times. He was struck on his upper left arm with shotgun pellets, which, he later explained, "ripped open the inside of my left arm." Jomo was shot six more times in his neck and back. Then he was one of the dozens forced to run through a gauntlet of troopers and COs raining blows down on them. Jomo was suffering from gaping wounds and a collapsed lung. That night, he begged prison officials to take him to a real hospital. They refused. There he remained, in four to five inches of standing water, without sufficiently warm clothes, real food, or even a mattress. He had attempted to keep his wounds clean to avoid infection and to rehabilitate his own lungs by doing intensive breathing exercises in his cell. It was so cold in that cell that Jomo shivered and his wounds continued to bleed. After eventually losing so much blood that he looked near death, and with investigators from the Jones and Pepper commissions now poking around, prison officials finally took Jomo to a hospital in Buffalo for a transfusion. The doctors there were shocked by how severely injured he was.

But in the hospital, the ugly threats and serious harassment from law enforcement continued. During the night, Jomo insisted, "a guy came in and he was acting strange. He had trouble putting the blood unit on the pole" and suddenly Jomo felt a cold liquid entering his arm. He started to hyperventilate, having a terrible reaction to whatever the stranger had given him; hospital staff had to give him something else to stabilize him.[7] Jomo and his roommate worried over who it might have been in his room that night. "No one knew who he was. He wasn't an employee," he later explained.[8] On another occasion, Jomo cowered in his bed as a state trooper walked into his room, looked at him coldly, and then said to the nurse, "This bastard ain't dead yet?" On another occasion a different trooper planted himself next to Jomo's bed and passed the time playing Russian roulette. "He would play with me putting bullets in and taking them out and threatening to shoot me," Jomo recalled, shuddering. "He would click it pointed at my head and then it wouldn't go off."[9] Once Jomo finally left the hospital, he was placed in HBZ.

There his harassment continued, albeit in a different vein. As Attica's narrow halls filled with investigators from the Bureau of Criminal Investigation of the New York State Police and Simonetti's office, Jomo understood that he was going to pay still another price for having rebelled—beyond that of having been shot so many times. And, sure enough, when prosecutors presented cases against him before the Attica grand jury, Jomo ended up with more indictments than any other prisoner.

Ultimately, Jomo found himself facing thirty-four counts of kidnapping as well as four counts of coercion and unlawful imprisonment for taking hostages. He also was charged with kidnapping and murdering Kenneth Hess.[10] The latter case was the more sensational one, and it would be tried first. At least Jomo's murder trial came after Shango's, and this turned out to advantage him quite significantly. Because Judge Mattina had decided in Shango's trial that no kidnapping "in the traditional, legal or actual sense of the word" had taken place in D Yard during the uprising, Judge Ball was forced to bar the prosecution from relitigating the same issue in Jomo's case.[11] In fact, not only did prosecutors have to dismiss felony murder charges against Jomo in his upcoming trial—charges that could only be brought had there been a kidnapping—but they were forced to drop them against Herb Blyden, Frank Smith, and Roger Champen in their pending trials as well.[12]

Jomo, however, still stood charged with the first degree murder of Kenneth Hess. Even though his trial was commencing years after the retaking at Attica, Jomo was still struggling physically and mentally from all he had endured on that day and those following and he worried about his ability to marshal an effective defense. In addition to having flashbacks and nightmares, he was also in a great deal of pain. As important, he had grown unusually fearful and suspicious of people—including those who were trying to help him in the ABLD. This deep wariness of others is what had led him to create his own defense committee—the Attica Bond to Free Jomo.

His defense efforts weren't totally isolated from the ABLD. Over the previous years, while awaiting his trials, he had come to trust at least one of the ABLD lawyers, Elizabeth Gaynes, a great deal. Liz had heard of Jomo during the course of her work with other Attica Brothers who were members of the Black Panthers. Whenever she would ask the other Panther prisoners questions, invariably they would tell her that she needed to speak with Jomo first. While it at times annoyed her, Liz was impressed with how tight this group was in the New York prison system, and how much they revered Jomo. When the ABLD asked her to interview him, she was intrigued.

The day that Liz first met Jomo he was on a list of six prisoners that she was supposed to talk to, but when she walked into his room she was transfixed and stayed longer than she should have. From the moment they began talking she was taken by his political knowledge and analytical mind, and he was also, in her view, an incredibly beautiful man. She could see right away that "he was a brilliant strategist" and, indeed, out of the many Brothers she had already spoken with, she didn't know any who had Jomo's level of perspective on the politics not only of the Attica struggle but also of the struggle against racism in America more generally.[13] In fact, so moved was she by this man that walking out of his room she realized that she had just met her "first real love," and later that night she actually called her mother and said "that this was the guy I was going to marry."[14]

Jomo, it turned out, was equally struck by Liz. She was not only smart, opinionated, and passionate, but was also determined to speak her mind, which Jomo found captivating. Over the coming months, they met again and again to discuss his case and their love affair intensified. The closer they grew, though, the more eyebrows were raised in the larger ABLD community. Over time, tensions began to develop between Jomo and Liz on the one hand, and some of the other Attica defendants who felt that the two of them had isolated themselves. Just as the relationship between Dalou and Barbara Handschu had caused rifts between some of the men awaiting trial, so did the relationship between Jomo and Liz. "Anytime you have a couple and a team it is tricky," recalled Liz Gaynes, but in Jomo's opinion what was really at issue was the fact that Liz was white.[15] He felt compelled to pen a defense of his relationship with Liz and the fact that she was white. He wrote, "A white woman don't ever make a black MAN any less black by standing at his side in trying times, it's just that that woman has committed herself to stand and realizes that their struggle in life is one and the same. . . . So don't think I have copped out on my people or rounded on them for a white woman to hide my face from black struggle."[16]

The other source of tension between Jomo and the rest of the Attica Brothers and the ABLD was his belief in a different approach to his defense. Liz Gaynes agreed with his sense that many of the white lawyers in the ABLD "felt that the Brothers were too stupid to weigh in on their own defenses."[17] Neither she nor Jomo felt that these lawyers would take seriously Jomo's desire to make his case political, and to make it part of the larger political struggle of the Panthers. In Jomo's opinion Attica Brothers such as Shango had forgone politics and "let the lawyers do the job—like a mafia model."[18] Big Black had also said he wanted a more political defense, but Jomo didn't particularly like Big Black and thought he actually was not political at all, describing Big Black's Attica Now Collective as having "no platform. They would always back down. I never felt they were strong."[19]

What irritated Jomo most was his sense that the other Brothers, including Black, were trying to aggrandize themselves at the expense of the less public Brothers and those still locked up. In one letter from the Erie County jail, written in July of 1974, he had called out what he referred to as the "Reactionary Niggers of Attica"—chiding them for speaking "beautifully about things" on the outside, while he and the rest of the Brothers had been left behind within "these walls of pure living hell."[20] In his view, those Brothers on the outside were the darlings of the ABLD, which was reason enough for him to want nothing to do with that organization. Ultimately he did accept some legal help, agreeing to let an attorney by the name of Vincent Doyle represent him as long as Liz Gaynes would be there as well, but he remained suspicious of the ABLD and insisted on his right to tell his own lawyers "how to inject politics into my defense."[21]

Although Jomo had formed his own defense group to raise funds and drum up public awareness of his individual case mainly for political reasons, he was nevertheless a pragmatist.[22] He knew that the ABLD had resources and the ear of the press and the public. He didn't want to alienate this group totally and insisted that he, in fact, wanted "a basic working alliance with ABLD, other defense committees, prison groups, political organizations, etc."[23] To other ABLD lawyers such as Big Black's Michael Deutsch, Jomo's position, while perhaps understandable, was ironic. In his view, when it came time to gear up for Jomo's trial, all-out legal wrangling and maneuvering—not political messaging—soon took center stage.

Vinnie Doyle's primary defense strategy would indeed be more legal than political. In his view it was clear that Jomo was being selectively prosecuted by the state. Despite the preponderance of evidence suggesting that the bulk of the crimes at Attica in September of 1971 had been committed by law enforcement officers—responsible for all of the deaths there save the three prisoners in D Block and CO William Quinn—the state of New York had exclusively, and thus selectively, prosecuted only prisoners. It seemed clear to Doyle that Jomo was one of those being selectively prosecuted. Even the press was now writing pieces about the state's seeming single-minded focus on trying prisoners. Before Jomo's case came to trial, Doyle successfully filed what is known as a Clayton motion, a motion to determine whether the state had singled him out. It would be heard before Judge Ann T. Mikoll.[24]

This hearing was a real turning point for Jomo. He was finally able to get the full story of the abuse he had suffered at trooper hands, and his myriad gunshot injuries from those same members of law enforcement, onto the record, and he was able to show the judge the physical scars that he still bore as a result of that trauma. Prosecutor Charles Bradley recalled one shocking moment in the hearing when suddenly Jomo, "handsome" and a "very big and powerfully built guy," began to describe his scars and then asked the judge for permission just to show her.[25] When she agreed, he looked to Liz Gaynes and asked that she help him, whereupon Gaynes came forward and lifted up Jomo's shirt for the court.[26]

As the hearing came to a close it was clear that Judge Mikoll had been moved by Jomo's story, and the prosecution didn't like it. Even Jomo felt that she might be leaning more toward his side than theirs. Sometimes when he was particularly animated, even "swearing and talking like a Panther," as he put it, the DA tried to silence him but the judge essentially declared that Jomo could speak as he wanted. Jomo's attorney, Vincent Doyle, and the ABLD for that matter, read a deeper significance than a particular fondness into the judge's willingness to let Jomo talk. For years, the state had been bullying the Attica defendants and had, perhaps, finally overplayed its hand with this jurist in Buffalo.

At Judge Mikoll's urging, Vinnie Doyle began settlement discussions with Simonetti's office. Over the past three years state prosecutors had tried to get various Attica brothers to plead out, including several of the men indicted under one major indictment, no. 10, who, it would later turn out, would have their cases dismissed completely because the state lacked enough evidence to proceed. Although Doyle was eager for Jomo to consider a settlement, he knew that it would not be easy to persuade his client to take it. Jomo had from the beginning been hostile to any mention of a plea deal. If he hadn't committed the crime, he reasoned, then he should not say he did just to avoid a longer sentence. Also, Jomo had been very hard on every other Brother who had taken deals, and he was no longer speaking to them.[27]

Simonetti's offer was significant: he would drop the murder charges if Jomo would plead merely to coercion. His sentence would, thus, be four years including time served.[28] Even better, he could take something called an Alford plea, which allowed one to plead guilty while still, officially, proclaiming innocence. In short, Jomo could walk away from this legal nightmare and still not have to concede any wrongdoing.[29] Deep down both Jomo and Doyle felt that the state's willingness to offer this plea had less to do with Judge Mikoll's desires than the fact that Jomo insisted he knew exactly who had shot him on September 13, 1971, while he lay on the ground, injured and bleeding. He had made clear to the prosecution that he was both willing and determined to testify to that effect; the fact that, during the hearing for Jomo's Clayton motion, much of the testimony had corroborated his account meant that state prosecutors had great incentive to settle.[30] Even before Judge Mikoll pressed for a deal, and "prior to any ruling by the court," Simonetti's office made an offer "to drop the charges . . . in return for a plea to a minor offense."[31]

After careful consideration, on October 9, 1975, Jomo pled guilty to coercion—a class D felony that could carry a maximum sentence of seven years but for which he would serve no additional time.[32] Importantly, both to Jomo and to the rest of the ABLD defense effort, "he did not allocate to a specific or named event, date, or victim, but rather stated in open court that although innocent, he was taking his plea solely to enable him to end a prosecution that had been initiated three years before."[33] Yet another case against the Attica Brothers had ended with mud in the state's eye. And yet, just as in Shango's case, thwarting the state's efforts to prosecute did not lead to Jomo's immediate freedom. Despite the plea deal in this case, Jomo still had to return to Attica to finish serving his original time. Something profound had shifted in his relationship with the authorities there, however. It seemed to Jomo that they were far less capricious, and less eager to push him around. When his mother died, for example, Jomo asked to be allowed to attend the funeral in North Carolina. To his surprise, they allowed him to go. As he recalled, "They paid for two officers to come with me. . . . So many people were at the funeral home and the guard took my handcuffs off. . . . I could have run and I did not."[34]

Without question the authorities in the Attica Correctional Facility, the New York State Police, and in the state prosecutor's office were in a far different position by the close of 1975 than when they had first announced prisoner indictments in December of 1972: the state's cases were falling apart, and prisoners who had been vilified in the press were now being written about as the victims of state bullying. Most significantly, on April 8, 1975, *The New York Times* broke a story that rocked the entire New York State Attorney General's Office to its core. Someone inside the Attica investigation had become a whistle-blower.

Malcolm Bell, one of the main prosecutors in Simonetti's office, was now claiming that his colleagues and bosses had worked deliberately and systematically to prevent the prosecution of the troopers and correction officers who had committed crimes at Attica. In fact, he alleged, Simonetti, Frank Cryan, and others had actually tried to cover up these crimes entirely.

Bell had originally raised these shocking accusations against his fellow prosecutors in 1974 as Shango's trial was beginning. But neither judges nor state officials were willing to move on his allegations and, thus, the state proceeded with their cases.[35] By the time Jomo presented his evidence of selective prosecution, these revelations that could support his claims had finally gotten some attention. When Jomo entered his Alford plea, everyone in Simonetti's office felt that they would all suddenly be subject to much more scrutiny. They were correct.

PART VIII

# Blowing the Whistle

# MALCOLM BELL

*Malcolm Bell had entered the practice of law with conventional ambitions. When he left Harvard Law in the 1950s he felt fairly agnostic about politics but was optimistic about the way that the nation was progressing. Indeed it tended to annoy him when, in the 1960s, he saw an increasing number of protests critical of the United States erupting on campuses and city streets. Bell had served two years in the Army—first at Fort McClellan in Alabama and then in Wiesbaden, Germany—and he was a patriot. In 1968 Bell cast his vote for Richard Nixon and unapologetically supported an American presence in Vietnam.*

*By 1971, Bell was divorced and living in Darien, Connecticut. He had worked on corporate litigation at one of Wall Street's most prestigious firms, and was currently doing similar work for another firm uptown. He was, however, restless. He liked the law because it had integrity. But corporate work was not always honorable, and, frankly, he found it tedious. Bell was no radical, but one of the reasons he had been attracted to the law in the first place was to do some good. He was coming to believe, however, that the civil cases he was working on made very little difference in the grand scheme of things.*

*In 1973, Bell found himself wondering if he might try his hand at criminal law. At least it would be more exciting. That August, he saw an intriguing ad in a law journal that would change his life. The Attica investigation had placed a rather cryptic call for "prosecutors." He applied and soon found himself sitting across a desk from Anthony Simonetti in the Attica investigation offices in lower Manhattan. To his astonishment he learned that this was an opportunity to work on one of New York State's largest criminal prosecutions ever. He was offered a modest $28,500-a-year job, and he accepted it with enthusiasm. Bell was to be Anthony Simonetti's chief assistant tasked with collecting and pre-*

*senting evidence to Attica's grand jury of any crimes committed by law enforcement during the retaking and rehousing at Attica. A year into his stint at the Attica investigation, however, he had begun to wonder whether his superiors were in fact as interested in pursuing cases against members of law enforcement as they had been against prisoners. By 1975, Bell would find himself reluctantly at the heart of one of New York's most newsworthy whistle-blowing scandals.*

42

# Joining the Team

From Malcolm Bell's first days on the job at the state of New York's Attica investigation it struck him as odd that so much effort was going into prosecuting prisoners from Attica when "the officers had killed ten times as many people as the inmates had."[1] However, the decision to investigate prisoner crimes before police crimes had been made well before Bell was hired.[2] In 1972, Deputy Attorney General Robert Fischer wrote to his boss, Louis Lefkowitz, that the prisoners' killings of CO Quinn, and that of fellow prisoners Schwartz and Hess, were "more obviously homicides" than the killings of correction officers John Monteleone or John D'Arcangelo.[3] And, as he put it to an attorney from the Justice Department in these early years, any crimes members of law enforcement may have committed against the prisoners while rehousing them after the uprising were "of a lower priority."[4]

There had been pushback on this perspective. In October 1971 the Goldman Panel had noted uneasily that the Attica investigation was concerning itself solely with the prisoners and not with members of law enforcement.[5] Even some of the individuals who had witnessed trooper abuse firsthand, such as National Guard surgeon Dr. John Cudmore, began publicly airing the view that the state's disinterest in trooper crimes was outrageous and unacceptable.[6] State investigators had not even asked Cudmore about the horrific acts he had seen troopers commit until a full two and a half years after Attica's retaking and, as Cudmore pointed out to the press in disgust, it would be hard even to identify one's own children if this much time had passed since you had seen them.[7]

As Malcolm Bell saw it, there wasn't anything wrong, per se, with his bosses investigating and indicting prisoners so zealously. If prisoners had committed crimes at Attica, Bell reasoned, then they should be held accountable. He too began to find it troubling, though, when it seemed that his colleagues were pursuing prisoner cases even when the "the scantness of evidence against the defendants" was quite glaring.[8] It specifically bothered him that the witnesses whom the state relied on to make its cases against prisoners, for example, had clearly changed their stories over time. It also seemed to him that these witnesses' memory of past events was vague at best. He had noticed with some serious discomfort that his colleagues were not above leading and coercing these witnesses to make their cases.[9]

Bell's boss, Simonetti, and his fellow prosecutors were also uncomfortable with the ways in which at least the early evidence in their investigation had been collected—that is, by the investigators from the NYSP's own Bureau of Criminal Investigation—but they felt that they had gotten it back on track. They had not, in their view, done anything inappropriate to make their cases.

And, in the early days, Bell was happy to see it this way as well. In fact, it was a good sign, he thought, that Simonetti would also allow him to work on the so-called shooter cases, the incidents during the Attica retaking in which a member of law enforcement had fired his weapon at a prisoner or hostage without legal justification. Simonetti might have started with the indictment of Attica's prisoners, but he was clearly gearing up to indict troopers and COs too.

Simonetti had, even before Bell's hire, brought a case against a New York State trooper before the Attica Grand Jury in 1972. He had assigned the case to the only African American prosecutor on the team, Ed Hammock—a former New York County assistant district attorney and head of a respected Manhattan narcotics rehab program—but no indictment followed.[10]

Even though Hammock no longer worked in the office and Bell couldn't ask him what had gone wrong with his cases, Bell could see why he might have failed.[11] For starters, precious little groundwork had been done on any case involving a trooper or a CO—even by the time Bell had joined the team. No one had pieced together the evidence secured against members of law enforcement in such a way that an airtight case might be made. Bell had little more than "inconclusive memos about the fatal shooting of two hostages on the catwalks" and "fragmentary memos about the deaths in the Hostage Circle, but there was no coherent story" waiting for him when he was assigned to the shooter cases.[12]

This, however, had advantages. Bell could approach the shooter cases with his mind as open as possible, vowing to work "as hard to find evidence of officers' innocence as of their guilt."[13] And yet, the closer Bell looked at this evidence, and the more he compared the statements that troopers and COs had given to explain their actions with other evidence such as photographs from D Yard, the more apparent it was to Bell that the statements didn't add up. For instance, the troopers who had fired from A and C Blocks insisted that they had aimed only at prisoners who were trying to attack hostages, yet even a novice investigator could see from the photographs that "there were no hostages or anyone else in the direction to which the inmates were running."[14] Countless prisoner witnesses had also made clear that if they had been able to move at all, they had actively fled away from the troopers' fire, certainly not run toward it.

And it wasn't just the evidence that didn't support the troopers' statements, neither "did common sense."[15] One NYSP sergeant who officially admitted to firing at prisoners offered three completely different versions of why he did so. At one point he said the prisoner was about to throw an object at him, but didn't state what it was. In another statement he said that he had been unable to make out exactly what that prisoner had in his hands because there was so much gas in the air and he had been wearing a gas mask. Yet this officer had also claimed on yet another occasion he knew for certain that the inmate had been wielding a Molotov cocktail.[16]

Statements intending to explain how a trooper got shot in the leg in D Yard during the retaking—the only trooper hit by a bullet—also troubled Bell. According to this trooper, State Police Lieutenant Joseph Christian, he had been shot when trying to get to the circle of hostages in D Yard to rescue them.

Armed with two pistols and a shotgun, Christian stated that he had been running toward the hostage circle when a prisoner ran at him with some sort of club and proceeded to hit his helmeted head with that object. Then, in order to save Christian's life, troopers on B Catwalk claimed to have fired their shotguns at this prisoner—in the process not only wounding Christian himself in the leg, but also killing several of the state's own men: the hostages in the circle. According to this scenario, the hostages' deaths, while tragic and terrible, were wholly accidental and unavoidable—and legally justifiable.

Given that so many hostages in that circle had been hit by trooper fire, it was vitally important to Bell that the troopers' accounts be truthful. Yet he was troubled. Joe Christian's own statement, which was supported by a photo taken during the assault, made clear that he was right in front of the hostages when he got shot—and not well off to the side as the troopers had maintained. This could mean that the troopers had been reckless to have fired at that time, and with that much power.[17] As troublingly, at least three of the eight hostages had not been killed by shotgun pellets from B Catwalk; they had been hit by rifle fire—and yet not a single rifle shooter admitted shooting at that area of the yard.

In virtually all of the shooter cases, Bell was not investigating whether the shootings had resulted in death per se; he was trying to determine whether the shots themselves had been justified. Take, for example, the shooting of Sam Melville, the white prisoner who, having been incarcerated for bombing various buildings to protest the Vietnam War, had written the exposé of Attica's profits from its laundry facilities, and had been a leader at the negotiating table. Members of law enforcement were openly thrilled that Melville had perished in D Yard during the retaking, and Bell found the details of this shooting disconcerting. Firstly, according to several witness accounts, Melville had been shot to death while trying to surrender. And then, the trooper who took credit for shooting Melville was a BCI investigator and claimed that he had shot only in self-defense: Melville, he said, had been trying to throw a Molotov cocktail at him. Yet Bell could see from the evidence that no such weapon was located anywhere near Melville.

Time and again, Bell found that trooper claims of having shot prisoners in self-defense had been completely fabricated. This was particularly evident when he closely examined the killing of a prisoner named James Robinson. Robinson had initially been shot by a .270 bullet, which did not kill him outright. Another trooper came upon Robinson lying on the ground, bleeding profusely, and proceeded to riddle the wounded man with shotgun pellets. Because this trooper was shooting at such close range, those pellets went into one side of Robinson's neck and out the other in a spray. To justify this shooting, this trooper took great pains to claim that Robinson had come at him wielding a knife. A gory photograph of the dead man showed a curved sword beside him as proof. Yet Bell quickly recognized two damning facts: first, photos taken seconds before and seconds after Robinson was shot showed him lying in exactly the same position on the pavement and there was simply no way he could

The body of inmate James Robinson lies where he was killed. In the second shot, a weapon has been placed under his hand. *(From the Elizabeth Fink Papers)*

have sprung to his feet after being wounded from the .270 shot, lunged at the trooper, and then lain down in the exact same position between the time the two photos were taken.[18] As troublingly, in the first photo taken of Robinson by troopers there was no sword anywhere near him, but in the second photo—again an image indicating that this man had not moved—there was.[19] Someone else had clearly placed it next to him for that second photograph.

Bell was particularly haunted by two prisoners' deaths: Kenny Malloy and Raymond "Ramon" Rivera. Malloy had been shot twelve times in the head and body, at close range. Rivera, who had been cowering in a hole prisoners had dug under the sidewalk, was similarly pulverized with ten pellets.[20] Piecing together various accounts, Bell learned that at the first sounds of helicopters and gunfire, Rivera had squeezed himself down into this hole to shield himself from the gunfire. Rivera had no firearm, nor any other weapon that could have been construed as a threat to law enforcement. Nevertheless, a state trooper lowered his shotgun into the edge of that hole and fired off a round of buckshot into Rivera's leg whereupon he quickly bled to death.[21] Trying to justify the shooting, this trooper had also claimed that he was acting in self-defense. His own embellishments in his statement, however, soon undid the veracity of this claim. He said that he hadn't used his own weapon, it was a shotgun that he had, fortuitously, taken from a prisoner. He was in fact, he wanted to show, a hero for preventing that prisoner from killing a hostage with the same gun. But it was common knowledge in Simonetti's office that the prisoners in D Yard had had no firearms.

More than the discrepancies and outright lies in the troopers' accounts of their own actions, Bell was alarmed to find as he went deeper into the investigation that higher-ups in the New York State Police seemed to be deliberately hindering his investigation by either not cooperating or, quite literally, concealing evidence. Simonetti had actually warned Bell that "the state police had refused to cooperate . . . withheld evidence . . . and generally obstructed our efforts to learn and prove what had happened," and now he was seeing this firsthand.[22] Back in October of 1971, when the U.S. Department of Justice had opened its own brief inquiry into possible civil rights violations at Attica during the course of the retaking and rehousing—one that ultimately went nowhere—its investigators had also been frustrated by the lack of candor from the State Police and their unwillingness even to provide the statements that troopers had given right after the retaking.[23] For example, when FBI officials asked Henry Williams—the NYSP captain who had helped Major John Monahan orchestrate the assault and the head of Troop A's BCI team who had headed up the initial evidence gathering there—to turn over the trooper statements he had taken, Williams stalled. Their request, he said, "would necessitate some checking on his part," and he never did turn them all over to the Department of Justice.[24]

The truth was, since BCI investigators had tainted the collection of evidence after the retaking, neither Simonetti's office nor the FBI could be certain what evidence even existed. These State Police investigators hadn't, for example, even asked any of the surviving prisoners "what they witnessed . . . while all around them the police were shooting people" and their processing of the crime scenes in D Yard and the catwalks seemed shoddy at best.[25] Captain Hank Williams had requested that the Niagara County sheriff send men in right away to "remove dead and wounded inmates and hostages," and as early as 10:30 a.m. on the 13th, he had those men start a "clean-up operation" that removed "potentially vital evidence from the yards, from storage rooms, from the tunnels and from other unoccupied buildings."[26] This cleanup detail had completed its assignment long before any independent investigator arrived on the scene. [27]

Yet Bell and his fellow attorneys at the Attica investigation suspected that there might be a great deal of evidence that the State Police had collected and simply refused to turn over. Unfortunately, every piece of evidence they managed to force the NYSP to give them seemed compromised in some way. For instance, one batch of statements that BCI investigators had taken from the NYSP troopers who had participated in the retaking read not like objective shooter reports, but more justifications for killing, complete with tales of prisoners rushing at them and trying to kill them.

Bell soon realized that these might not even have been the first statements taken on September 13. There were rumors of "a first generation of handwritten statements" that had been "written on yellow paper"; perhaps the NYSP had instead turned over a second set of "comparatively empty and innocuous" statements that they took on September 15.[28] In Bell's mind this could mean only one thing: someone had decided that those troopers had needed to revise the statements with clearer justification of why they had fired so many rounds and wounded or killed so many people. No one had ever accounted for the actions of NYSP troopers on September 14, which caused Bell to wonder if higher-ups in the State Police had spent that day debriefing their troopers and getting them to write new statements.

This didn't mean that the more fantastical statements were useless to Bell, however. The one thing that they did provide, in a few instances, was evidence of which specific prisoners were shot by which specific troopers and, as important, evidence of which troopers had fired their weapons without justification and thus, in all likelihood, criminally. This would be a valuable start. If Bell could comb through these statements carefully enough, he might find some real leads to follow. If a trooper admitted to shooting a prisoner, for example, and Bell could show that his justification was bogus, then he might have some solid cases to bring to the grand jury.

Other important paperwork was still lacking, however. Each troop that had sent men to Attica had made "blotter entries of personnel and equipment dispatched to Attica," but had made absolutely no record "as to serial numbers of weapons and to whom they were issued."[29] Then, between October and December of 1971 as the BCI had interviewed over a hundred State Police shooters from all over the state, fifteen National Guardsmen, and a group of Wyoming County deputy sheriffs, there was zero effort to link individual weapons to individual shooters in the statements they gave.[30] Worse, one BCI investigator stated that he was told specifically not to conduct "a weapons accountability investigation of those shooters he interviewed."[31] Another stated that "he was assigned by Captain Williams" only "to conduct general interviews of State Police shooters. . . . He was not instructed by Captain Williams or anybody else to conduct a weapons accountability investigation during the interrogation. He was not instructed to obtain serial numbers or otherwise identify the weapon discharged by those shooters he interrogated."[32] Still another trooper had actually started a list of which weapons he was passing out to which troopers on the night of September 9, but then destroyed that list after he found out the next morning that some of the weapons he had listed had then been given to other troopers altogether.[33]

Furthermore, none of the troopers who had fired weapons during the retaking had been asked to fill out a "discharge of firearms" form, which heretofore had been standard procedure, nor had they done any ammunitions accountability paperwork.[34] Bell well knew that weapons and ammunitions accountability were "basic to police procedure," as were things like picking up expended shells and marking their location, and leaving bodies where they had fallen so that key measurements could be taken.[35] None of this had been done.

Adding to Bell's investigative headache was the fact he needed to rely heavily on the NYSP's own photographic and film records of the retaking—but that evidence had been tampered with too.[36] A camera had been filming throughout the rebellion and all through the day of the 13th, recording "the sounds of hundreds of shots," but there was absolutely no footage of anyone actually shooting. Even more damningly, Bell could see "that the state police shortened the tape from approximately six minutes of assault to approximately four minutes of assault before turning it over to the Investigation"[37] One of the men who'd been filming for the State Police blamed the problems with the visual evidence on technical difficulties: "During the first few seconds of the assault, I had the Norelco machine recording but because of the noise and activity, I turned it off."[38] Then, as soon as the rehousing began, and during the exact time the prisoners reported so much torture and abuse taking place, the tape allegedly ran out.[39] Either any visual evidence that might have incriminated a trooper had been excised, or it was never recorded in the first place.[40]

Bell found similar problems with the NYSP's collection of still photographs. He discovered "an amazing series of claimed malfunctions by State Police personnel assigned to photograph the assault in operating their cameras or in having the photographs properly developed."[41] One NYSP photographer on the roof of C Block had taken an entire series of 35mm slides, which were turned over to Bell. However, when Bell's investigator Lenny Brown reviewed them carefully, he could see clearly that "the film as numbered by Kodak show[ed] two gaps in the sequence of photographs taken." Significantly, the first gap was about the time when a trooper would have been "firing his shotgun through the neck of James Robinson in the vicinity of Times Square," and the next was when troopers would have emptied their pistols into prisoner Kenny Malloy.[42] The convoluted explanation offered for the missing photographs was that "all the film packs were first sent from Attica to the New York State Police Photo lab at Troop A headquarters. . . . The color film packs were thereafter . . . sent to the Color Processing Laboratory of the New York State Police at Troop E headquarters," and "Troop E did not . . . number their photographs in the same manner as did Batavia."[43]

The more Bell probed, though, the more apparent it was that a simple difference in numbering or errors on the part of the photo lab techs could not explain what he had before him. Key photos had to have been removed before the State Police turned them over to the Attica investigation. For example, Attica observer and highly respected state senator John Dunne had told prison officials that he had seen prisoner Frank "Big Black" Smith suffering trooper and CO reprisals while laid out naked on a table in A Yard, yet no such pictures were among those the NYSP had given his office. When Bell's investigator, Lenny Brown, finally obtained a photo of this moment not from the State Police but from the individual Monroe County Sheriff's Office employee who had taken the photo, every detail of the story was clearly captured on film: Big Black lay on a table "on his back in A yard balancing a football on his chest," while troopers in the frame hovered over him.[44]

As upsetting as the missing photographs were on their own, the fact that troopers had actively tampered with the photographic evidence seemed worse to Bell. Had he not seen the photo of slain prisoner James Robinson without a sword in his hand, he would never have known that a weapon had been planted in the later photo that the NYSP gave him.[45]

Infuriated but undaunted, Bell pushed on with his investigation. His first order of business was to ask Anthony Simonetti how he might get the State Police to turn over more evidence, and how prosecutors might address the tampering of the evidence they had discovered thus far. Bell recalled that Simonetti had asked him early on, in the fall of 1973, to explore whether they might go after police officials for conspiring to impede their investigation; it seemed like this might now be prudent.[46]

As he considered his options, Bell devised another plan for holding troopers accountable for their shooting spree. The only way a trooper could be legally justified in firing his weapon was if it were demonstrably necessary to save himself or someone else from grievous bodily harm. If a trooper stated that he had fired in the direction of another person when there was no imminent danger, and if Bell could show that "the justifying act had not happened," then he could perhaps indict that trooper on a charge of reckless endangerment in the first degree—a class D felony.[47] To determine whether threats to troopers or hostages had really existed Bell could examine photographs, video, and numerous verbal accounts from nonshooter troopers. Although not officially witnesses to the shooting in the assault, other very credible and totally disinterested people such as Dr. Warren Hanson, who had been brought into D Yard during the rebellion to tend to the sick, shared the view that troopers had exaggerated any threat to their lives or even the lives of the hostages on the morning of September 13, 1971. In Hanson's view, one based both on having come to understand the dynamic between the prisoners and hostages in the yard and then seeing footage of the assault, "for most of the hostages no attempt was made to kill them and . . . when the shooting started, the executioners just dropped down to protect themselves."[48]

While Bell remained committed to going after those who had killed prisoners and hostages, he was equally eager to pursue lesser indictments. As he put it, even if "the highest crime for which most of the admitted shooters could be prosecuted was reckless endangerment," at least that was something.[49]

Even going after reckless endangerment indictments, Bell suspected, was going to be difficult given the grand jury currently sitting in Wyoming County. After all, Hammock had tried to secure trooper indictments and from what he knew of at least one of those cases, the jury's decision to let them slide was ludicrous.[50] Bell marveled: How "could the jury consider the evidence and not indict this trooper?"[51] All he could figure was that this particular grand jury had just been too close to law enforcement to consider indicting any officers.

For this reason Bell was delighted in early 1974 to learn that Simonetti was going to ask Judge Ball to empanel a second grand jury.[52] There was still no guarantee of trooper indictments, but at least they'd get to select new jurors in this Supplemental Grand Jury, and this just might make the difference.[53]

The news that the state of New York was going to convene a second grand jury to assess crimes committed at Attica terrified the Attica defendants, who saw this as yet another attempt to frame them. The ABLD was filled with serious concern as well. The indictments rendered by the original grand jury had taken so much work, and so many resources, and the idea that there would now be a second one to contend with was alarming.

The only group more unnerved by this news was the New York State Police. They knew well that this meant they were soon to be in the Attica investigation's sights and they felt blindsided and not a bit betrayed. From the moment the gas cleared from the air in D Yard, the highest-ranking officials in the state of New York had praised the troopers for their actions at Attica. Governor Rockefeller himself lauded their professionalism and hard work, as had Commissioner Russell Oswald, who had been subjected to much criticism from those same troopers. In an open letter Oswald had written for the January 1972 issue of *Trooper*, the magazine of the New York State Police, he appealed to them: "I am sure that you are as painfully aware of the criticism of both our agencies resulting from the events at Attica as I am. However, I am convinced that when all of the facts are known, both of us can be even prouder of the work of our respective staffs."[54]

And even when Oswald had left the position of commissioner of correctional services in April of 1973, the NYSP still had supporters in high places. Senator Ronald B. Stafford from the 43rd Senatorial District of New York, where Clinton prison was located, responded with "shock and outrage" to the news of a second grand jury convened, possibly, to indict "law enforcement officers."[55] He was disgusted that after "years of intense pressure from radical groups and individuals, a decision was made to capitulate and use our law enforcement personnel as scapegoats for this tragedy."[56] The Police Benevolent Association of the New York State Police also came out swinging and demanded that the state provide troopers a legal fund to defend against possible indictments, claiming that it had already "spent $200,000 of union funds to provide legal assistance" to its members.[57] It also hinted that more monies might be due to address "the mental anguish endured by the troopers and their families," which was "considerable," the PBA president, Patrick J. Carroll, said.[58]

Undaunted by this backlash, Malcolm Bell began building his cases for reckless endangerment and even for murder. Throughout February and March of 1974 he had met with Simonetti and others for shooter conferences, in which the main task was to sort out how many of the 128 shooting deaths and woundings at Attica had not been justified. Bell estimated that there were a minimum of fifty-five shots fired which "could be considered criminal."[59] Simonetti agreed that there was enough evidence to bring at least thirty-two cases against troopers and COs to the grand jury for a range of crimes including "a few attempted murders, a few perjuries, and mostly reckless endangerments."[60] By April of 1974, Bell had managed to identify about seventy State Police and correction officers whom the grand jury might well indict, and, in his view, there were still more cases that could be pursued.[61]

Malcolm Bell began presenting before the new Attica grand jury on May 8, 1974, along with fellow prosecutor Charlie Bradley.[62] Although Bell felt that he had a chance at indicting law enforcement with this grand jury, this new jury had some very close connections to that group. Two of the chosen jurors were aunts of one of the former hostages, Don Almeter. (Another former hostage, Pappy Wald, had actually been considered as a possible juror, although he was dismissed.) In addition, the main State Police lawyer, Bernard "Bud" Malone, had decided that any trooper witness called by the state would help "the prosecution as little as they civilly could," and, accordingly, they were, at times, outright obstructionists on the stand. Still, the jurors seemed interested in hearing why Bell thought that troopers and COs had committed many provable crimes at Attica. Not a few of them eventually wore looks of dismay as they heard about all that the prisoners had suffered on the day of the retaking.[63] Jurors seemed particularly to pale when they heard that one trooper had shot four pellets into a prisoner's thigh and then, as that man writhed on the ground, another trooper became "so irritated by his screaming from the pain of the pellets, [he] fired a shotgun slug through his ankle."[64]

Jurors also seemed taken aback by former Attica hostage Michael Smith's appearance on the stand. Smith exemplified the costs of so much shooting on the day of the retaking. He had been a young CO when he was taken up on the catwalk as the retaking began, and then found himself shot multiple times. For years officials had maintained that Michael's severe wounds—including bullets that had exploded in his abdomen—were accidental; that he had been hit by the fragments of a single bullet intended for one of the prisoners on the catwalk. Prosecutor Bell was able to show the jury that something far more diabolical had taken place: Michael Smith's wound pattern, four bullet holes shot in quick succession and in a straight line, indicated that he had been shot by an automatic weapon and that he may well have been deliberately shot.[65] Only correction officers had wielded weapons that day that could have inflicted this wound pattern—and no correction officer could have mistaken Mike for a prisoner on that catwalk.[66] There was no doubt in Bell's mind that the CO who had shot Michael Smith had committed a crime.

Still, he had to proceed carefully with all of his cases—particularly if the victim had been a prisoner whom jurors had seemed to care little about. He knew there was much inherent sympathy for members of law enforcement on this jury and, if he overplayed his hand, they might balk when it came to voting to indict. A key problem was that the troopers' and COs' accounts of self-defense made for some persuasive testimony. One trooper, for instance, testified on June 13, 1974, that any prisoner who had been struck was absolutely resisting and, indeed, he personally had witnessed prisoners who "refused to cooperate."[67] And so Bell had to show jurors just how unable to resist Attica's prisoners actually were once the shooting began. Most effectively he pressed troopers who claimed to be acting in self-defense to describe the condition of the prisoners they saw all around them that day. Under oath one trooper made clear that there had in fact been "a lot of people screaming" as a result of so much shooting, and that one man, a prisoner who had been shot multiple times in the thigh, was "screaming quite a bit."[68] Bell could see the impact of this testimony on the jury.

After three intense months of Bell presenting evidence to the grand jury, Simonetti called Bell into his office to discuss a three-week recess he had requested from Judge Ball. This was fine with Bell until he realized in the midst of it that this wouldn't be just a short break; Simonetti was suspending only the cases *he* had been presenting and had, in fact, "cancelled the fifteen or so Shooter Case witnesses" that Bell had been planning to call before the jury.[69] Stunned, Bell would plead with his boss to be allowed to continue, to no avail. Although Simonetti had appeared to be fine permitting him to take shooter cases before the grand jury, now Bell's efforts were being halted—in his view, counterproductively delayed—even though there was still much evidence to present.[70]

Bell has a very hard time understanding this. He was well aware that "prosecutors and police were natural allies" and, therefore, it was understandably awkward for them to charge troopers with crimes.[71] But being unsettled by the prospect of indicting troopers was a whole lot different than actively preventing him from doing so—which, Bell realized, was what was happening. Although Simonetti gave no real explanation for this abrupt turn, Bell suspected the chain of command led all the way to former governor Rockefeller.

On August 20, 1974, newly sworn-in president Gerald Ford had nominated Nelson Rockefeller to be the vice president of the United States. Rockefeller had tried to reach the White House many times. He had made a bid for the presidency in 1960, 1964, and 1968, and some thought that he had only resigned as governor of New York to do it again in 1976.[72] Rockefeller would certainly be unhappy if Attica got in the way of his chance to be the vice president, which well could happen if the troopers he had ordered into action were suddenly indicted for murder and other felonies. Confirmation hearings were about to begin, and the Attica investigation, should it be effective, might well make it hard for him to be confirmed.

The subject of Attica would indeed come up many times in these proceedings. Countless witnesses testified about the role the former governor of New York had played at Attica: Representative Bella Abzug, New York assemblyman and observer Arthur O. Eve, Lyndon LaRouche of the U.S. Labor Party, and Curtis Dall of the Liberty Lobby.[73] Even some of the Attica prisoners came to speak.[74]

None of this testimony was kind. Attica Brothers Legal Defense coordinator Haywood Burns and Angela Davis, the former Black Panther leader and now co-chairperson of the National Alliance Against Racist and Political Oppression, both came to the hearings and argued forcefully against confirmation. Among other things, they called attention to the former governor's "moral duplicity" in supporting Nixon's pardon while rejecting all consideration of amnesty for the Attica Brothers. Burns argued, "The case for full and unconditional amnesty for the Attica brothers is as strong in every detail, as the reasons advanced for pardoning Richard Nixon."[75] Rockefeller had indeed recently commended President Ford for forgiving the impeached former president Richard Nixon his sins—even called his pardon "an act of conscience, compassion, and courage."[76] Davis pointed out that somehow, though, he didn't see the lives of more than a thousand people at Attica, "most of whom were black and Puerto Rican, as valuable."[77] She argued that Rockefeller's "support of Richard Nixon's pardon while at the same time being responsible for the Attica massacre" showed "his contempt for equal justice under the law, his callousness and complete willingness to adopt the most lethal and brutal solutions to desperate social crisis born of human misery."[78]

Perhaps Bell's suspicion that his cases were now being sidelined because of Rockefeller's political ambitions was overblown. The former governor in fact had a number of hurdles to overcome in these hearings, including having given major gifts to administration officials such as Henry Kissinger, using his fortune to undermine political opponents, and taking questionable deductions on his federal income taxes. Nonetheless, by waylaying Bell's hearings, there would no indictments of his troopers to cause any media uproar. On December 19, 1974, the former New York governor was confirmed. Bell very much suspected that Rockefeller supporters, including the Republican who succeeded him as governor, Malcolm Wilson, had wanted no chance of Attica making new headlines now—and Bell suspected that someone had made this very clear to his boss.

# 43

# Protecting the Police

Although the state officials would later contest Bell's characterization of the decisions made by the Attica investigative team, something major had changed. In August 1974, when Bell's attempt to seek felony indictments against troopers was suspended, Simonetti explained his decision in a way that gave Bell some hope that his cases were being deferred for an even deeper investigation. According to Simonetti, they would now be trying to make cases against higher-ranking officials in the NYSP for hindering the investigation itself.[1]

The plan had always been to go after the big shooting crimes first, and then to go after those high-ranking members of the NYSP who had made the job of investigating those shooting crimes so difficult by tampering with, or withholding, vital evidence. The fact that key slides had been removed from slide trays, that bullets had gone missing, and that entire swaths of film as well as radio transcriptions no longer existed, suggested that the protection of trooper shooters was being orchestrated from on high. This would also explain why state troopers had descended upon funeral homes after the retaking. A superior would have had to have dispatched these troopers, whom prosecutors had dubbed "night riders," to lean on morticians to contradict Edland's account of how the men had died. At least one undertaker had been pressured to sign a written statement to the effect that there were no bullet holes in John Monteleone even though he had obviously died from a gunshot.[2]

Initially, it appeared to Bell that Simonetti was serious about going after the big fish in the NYSP. Bell estimated that out of the possible thirty or more cases of murder or manslaughter they might have been able to make against law enforcement shooters, only five to seven cases were possible thanks to "the State Police's destruction of evidence (e.g., photos, death scenes) and their failure to collect evidence."[3]

As Bell understood it, Simonetti was planning to present evidence to the grand jury against several ranking officers who had authority over the collection of evidence and who, Simonetti's office felt, had "deliberately hindered the case."[4] Simonetti's main targets in this case included Lieutenant Colonel George Infante, the senior BCI man who had been at Attica right after the retaking as the police were collecting evidence in the yard; Major John Monahan, the Troop A commander who had been in charge of the retaking itself; and Henry Williams, the Troop A BCI captain who had also been instrumental in carrying out the retaking as well as taking trooper statements and collecting evidence when it was over.[5] Their intention was to show that Captain Williams had failed to order the recording of rifle serial numbers or the collection of expended shells, and he had ordered his men to bury evidence behind the prison, and instructed his "BCI interviewers to stop short of asking about assault and brutality that followed" the retaking.[6] Malcolm Bell, for one, believed that Williams should be implicated as well in preventing the Attica investigation from

NYSP Captain Henry Williams outside the prison *(Courtesy of the* Democrat and Chronicle*)*

seeing incriminating photographs or troubling information in the State Police's radio log, in sending the "night riders" to local funeral homes, and in making it so difficult to identify which trooper or troopers had been responsible for the death of prisoner Kenny Malloy.[7]

The state felt it had a lot of damning evidence against Lieutenant Colonel George Infante, as well. If, according to Simonetti's office, Williams was the man who had carried out the cover-up at Attica, then Infante—the highest-ranking BCI officer at Attica on September 13—was its "architect."[8] As they saw it, George Infante had not only been aware of what men like Williams had done to hinder a sound inquiry into trooper actions at Attica, but he also had played his own role in the cover-up. Bell, for example, suspected that Infante, who had supervised "the BCI investigation to determine who fired what weapon," had gone to great lengths to protect at least one of the troopers suspected of killing Kenny Malloy.[9] That trooper claimed that he had acquired the gun used to shoot Malloy from a prisoner in D Yard, but his story later changed. According to Simonetti's office, Infante not only knew this, but he was personally involved in spinning the case.[10] In Bell's view Infante "certainly was aware of all the discrepancies," and as the commanding officer he should have made sure that all deaths were investigated thoroughly.

The Attica investigation felt that it had the evidence to prove that Infante had instead tried to make the problem of this prisoner's death go away. When it was clear that the shooter's initial story wouldn't hold up, that trooper claimed that "a nearby trooper handed him a shotgun." But the gun that he had admittedly used to shoot Malloy and fire several shots into the hole where prisoner Ramon Rivera lay cowering was a pistol.[11] According to an internal report dated September 27, 1971, this trooper gave "six different versions of the incident in Times Square on the 13th" and yet Infante, his main superior, never shared with Simonetti's office any of this evidence that one of his troopers may have committed a crime in D Yard.[12] Later, whenever any prosecutor directly asked Infante about these deaths, all of his "answers seem[ed] evasive, argumentative, and [gave] little if any information."[13]

The deeper Simonetti's team dug, the more Infante's impeding of the investigation looked to them like an outright cover-up of his trooper's crime. First, he had encouraged the trooper, a man he knew to have killed a prisoner, to resign and make himself scarce—which he had difficulty making the trooper do.[14] The man did submit his resignation letter on September 15, 1971, and the head of the NYSP himself, Superintendent William Kirwan, acknowledged this in a September 20, 1971, internal memo. But according to another memo sent on September 28, 1971, the trooper then balked and new pressure had to be exerted on him to go away. What was clear to Simonetti's office was that well before this, and certainly at any time thereafter, Infante, and indeed Kirwan himself, should have turned this trooper's name over to investigators.[15] It was possible that Infante had at least committed perjury and, if so, he should be held accountable.[16]

Simonetti's office managed to get its hands on a number of internal memos that indicated quite a few high-ranking officials had vital information about the killing of Kenny Malloy but had concealed that knowledge. An NYSP inspector named A. L. Bardossi, for example, sent Infante a report regarding the Malloy killing way back on October 6, 1971; two days later, Infante had written another report to Kirwan, the head of the entire state police force, who had been noticeably absent when the Attica retaking went down.[17] Both documents indicated that real work had been done to ensure that the Malloy matter would just disappear.

Even with these memos, as well as other evidence against high-ranking members of the NYSP, it seemed to Bell that Simonetti was now dragging his feet in these "hindering" cases too. Worse, Bell suspected that Simonetti was using the grand jury process to let the people in charge off the hook by granting them immunity.

Under New York law, grand jury witnesses are automatically granted immunity from prosecution for their testimony. Therefore, it had been standard procedure for the Attica prosecutors to ask any member of law enforcement who had shot weapons, or had knowledge of such shooting, to sign a waiver of immunity prior to testifying before an Attica grand jury. Very few troopers willingly signed one for obvious reasons, yet putting someone on the stand without a waiver was always risky for prosecutors. The witness could, of course, reveal nothing of use and still be immunized from prosecution himself. And so prosecutors tried to bargain with such witnesses—if you give us something good, we are willing to put you on the stand without a waiver.[18] Some high-ranking members of the NYSP did willingly sign waivers—including Captain Anthony Malovich, the officer who had led the assault down C Catwalk; Captain John McCarthy, the trooper who led the team into D Yard to rescue the hostages; and Superintendent Kirwan, the head of the NYSP.[19]

Others, such as Major John Monahan from Troop A, who had helped plan and launch the retaking, did not. This could have been a setback to Simonetti's team since what he knew might well be crucial to any case they hoped to build against a member of law enforcement for the actions they engaged in on September 13, 1971. But Malcolm Bell had figured out a way around this. To avoid immunizing Monahan from future prosecution, instead of calling him to the stand Bell would enter as evidence his earlier testimony before the McKay Commission, in which he had said quite a lot that prosecutors felt could now be helpful in making the hindering cases.[20] To Bell's dismay, however, Simonetti did put Monahan on the stand—granting him immunity by default—even though "he had no agreement whatsoever that once he was immunized he would tell anything of value."[21]

John Monahan, the man who, in Bell's estimation, was "at least physically, at the heart of the SP cover-up, was now fully off the hook for anything he may have done to prevent troopers from facing criminal charges."[22] He wrote immediately to Simonetti, reminding him that "evidence exists which tends to establish that it was Monahan's decision not to obtain rifle and shotgun serial numbers from individuals who shot circa 100 people, and that at one point he shared with Lt. Col. Infante the questioning" of one of the troopers who had killed inmate Kenny Malloy. [23] Simonetti was unsympathetic to this argument. And while Bell was still fuming over Simonetti's decision to immunize Monahan, his boss then decided to immunize Captain Hank Williams as well—even though Simonetti had seemed confident earlier that Williams would agree to sign a waiver of immunity.[24] This particularly distressed Bell, since he believed they had already presented ample evidence to the grand jury that directly implicated Williams in the majority of instances where the state's investigation had been actively impeded by the NYSP.[25]

In the course of processing how it was that vital hindering cases had been allowed to implode, Bell eventually came to believe that a serious prosecution of members of law enforcement had in fact been set up to fail from the moment Simonetti had told him to switch his efforts from the shooter cases to cases of hindering the investigation back in August of 1974. Simonetti would have vehemently disagreed with this assessment of his strategic choices, but as Bell carefully deconstructed his work on the hindering cases, he was increasingly persuaded that his boss had sent him before the grand jury with cases that needed much more time and care to develop. In one instance he could remember clearly, he was sent in so unprepared that he "didn't even know how to pronounce the name of the first witness."[26]

Bell also began to feel that Simonetti's demeanor with various politicians whom he had previously held at arm's length was suddenly much more chummy. When asked, Simonetti denied that he was behaving any differently. For instance, although he had been asked to cooperate with the FBI background check on Rockefeller during the confirmation process, Simonetti insisted that this had not made him any less eager to prosecute crimes committed at Attica. Still, Bell thought it significant that he was suddenly no longer invited to meetings, say, with the FBI—surmising that his boss had begun to see him as a fly in the ointment. According to his fellow prosecutor Charles Bradley, it was true that Simonetti no longer trusted Bell. He had even asked Bradley to keep an eye on Bell in court.[27]

Nevertheless, even with his boss now immunizing key officials in the NYSP from prosecution, Bell tried hard to push him to move against others in the NYSP where there remained compelling evidence of wrongdoing. Even before Simonetti put Captain Williams on the stand, Bell had written him a formal letter expressing his concern about the direction in which the investigation seemed now to be going. As Bell put it, "My basic fear, as you know, is that our investigation of a possible cover-up by the State Police may itself become a de facto cover-up."[28] When Simonetti chose not to respond to Bell's letter and continued his plan to immunize Williams with no guarantee of getting anything useful for the prosecution's case in return, Bell's suspicions that the investigation was being sabotaged from within only intensified.[29]

In time it began to worry Bell that Simonetti himself might actually be part of the cover-up. In addition to Simonetti's halting of Bell's shooter presentations to the grand jury, and then his immunizing of Monahan and Williams, Bell suspected that his boss had also protected a trooper who had "watched the whole retaking from the roof of C block and swore he saw none of the scores of shots which were fired where he was looking."[30] Bell had worked hard to prepare a perjury case against this man, spelling out on paper the powerful evidence that he planned to present to the jury—a paper that he then gave to Simonetti to look over. But after he read it, Simonetti did not allow Bell to take it to the jury.[31] Simonetti was, in Bell's view, actively thwarting equal justice under the law.

And yet, Bell still had a hard time wrapping his head around this. He had, after all, managed to bring before the grand jury over nine thousand transcript pages of testimony before things began to deteriorate after August of 1974. And, of course, Simonetti himself had been the one to suggest going after the men with supervisory power in the NYSP. Bell was uncertain what to make of everything that had just happened. But then it soon became clear to him that he was not going to go before the grand jury, which was going to be disbanded. On November 7, 1974, and notably with Rockefeller still not confirmed in Washington, jurors had been told that when they did reconvene, they would have only two weeks of work before them—tops.[32] Bell was thunderstruck. Not only did this grand jury still need to consider indictments in the shooter cases, but it also needed to hear cases relating to law enforcement brutality against prisoners when rehousing them after the retaking. Trying to impress upon Simonetti what a terrible idea it would be for him to disband the grand jury before its work was done, Bell sent his boss another letter—this one ten pages long—on November 13, 1975.[33]

Simonetti had decided to deal with Malcolm Bell by ignoring him. When he failed to respond to Bell's latest letter, Bell finally realized just how isolated he had become and how unlikely it was that members of law enforcement would be prosecuted now—even though many others, not just him, had believed the evidence was there to do so.[34]

# 44

# Smoking Guns

A close look nearly forty-five years later at the Attica investigation's own records—its internal memos, reports, and analyses of everything from ballistics to the locations of where individual prisoners, as well as hostages and troopers, were when the retaking of Attica began—reveals that Simonetti's office did in fact have a remarkable amount of evidence against specific members of law enforcement that did not result in the indictment of those men.

With regard to the possible hindering of prosecution cases, men in Simonetti's office didn't just suspect that the top brass of the NYSP was involved in hiding evidence, they felt they had proof of such acts. The Attica investigation believed, for example, from the interviews it had done, and from the trooper statements that were taken right after the retaking, there was ample evidence that Captain Williams had actively "assisted in setting up the BCI interviews of State Police shooters on 9/13/71," and that, when he did so, the men taking the statements were not "instructed by Captain Williams or anyone else to conduct a weapons accountability investigation during the interrogations [and were] not instructed to obtain the serial number or otherwise identify the weapon discharged by those shooters [they] interrogated."[1] Attica investigators also had evidence from the internal memos and other NYSP documents they had seen that Williams's superior, Lieutenant Colonel Infante, among others supervising the BCI investigation had decided that no one was to "determine who fired what weapon."[2] Further evidence indicated that Major Monahan was also complicit in this: indeed he had expressly said to one of his underlings that discharge of firearms reports wouldn't be necessary.[3] Even NYSP

Chief Inspector John Miller, "the senior [NYSP] officer at Attica [who] was ultimately responsible for this individual accounting," had "decided not to follow that protocol."[4]

Simonetti's office even felt confident it had identified the lower-level troopers who had also covered up evidence at Attica.[5] The BCI investigator from the NYSP who had been "in charge of the Identification Bureau and photographic library," for example, had admitted that "the film had been cut and attempted to be put back together chronologically but not numerically."[6] They also knew exactly who "had deleted State Police slides . . . by removing them from the slide trays before the police turned them over to the Investigation."[7]

As important, Simonetti's prosecutors were also quite certain they knew which troopers had shot their weapons without justification, and thus committed reckless endangerment under the law. Troopers had themselves admitted to the extraordinary amount of times they had shot their weapons and time and again it was obvious that they had no legal justifications for the discharging of even one bullet or pellet. One trooper, J. R. Mittlestaedt, had discharged at least nine shots from his twelve gauge shotgun and admitted to hitting at least three people on B Catwalk.[8] Another trooper, S. D. Sharkey, had hit another three people at least by shooting into D Yard and near Times Square.[9] In fact, Simonetti's team knew that a total of 364 trooper rounds had been fired, and the troopers' justification for these shootings had not been corroborated.

The actions of COs as well were identified as likely or possibly criminal. One CO, Nicholas De Santis, for example, had shot more than twelve rounds from his .45 caliber Thompson. Even if it were true, as he claimed, that all of these shots—six into D Tunnel and six into D Yard—were misses, his firing, in the state's view, might still be deemed reckless.[10] As might the eighteen rounds CO Howard Holt had fired with his .351 rifle, all onto D Catwalk where prisoners stood.[11] On the day of the retaking, correction officers had fired more than seventy rounds into Attica's yards and onto its catwalks, and state prosecutors were able to determine who had fired the vast majority of the shots, even when they seldom knew whom the shots had hit.[12]

Most damningly, Simonetti's office believed it knew exactly which trooper or CO had killed specific prisoners on the day of the retaking. Internal memos suggest that investigators had evidence that trooper James Mittlestaedt shot prisoner James Robinson through the neck "at a range of two to five feet, breaking his neck and killing him instantly."[13] Simonetti's office also indicated that it knew who had killed prisoner Bernard Davis. Davis had died from more than twenty-three gunshot wounds, and one internal memo identified that officer as P. F. Stringham.[14] According to other documents CO Stringham had also likely killed another prisoner—Milton Menyweather.[15] One Attica investigator testified that Paul F. Stringham, armed with his "own personal brownie [*sic*] twelve-gauge shotgun loaded with five deer slugs," had "identified a photo of P-5, Milton Menywether [*sic*] lying on the catwalk to the right of Times Square, as the one he shot."[16]

State investigators in fact had a long list of troopers and COs whom they had evidence had killed or severely wounded prisoners. A trooper named Malcolm Hegeman had himself "identified photo 1C5, of inmate Melvin Ware, as the inmate he shot."[17] They also seemed to know the trooper whose shots had hit prisoner Milton Jones, and that trooper Gregory Wildridge had been reckless with his shooting, as well as hitting several specific prisoners who then perished.[18]

Prosecutors also knew a great deal about the killing of prisoner Tommy Hicks. According to his autopsy and internal investigative memos, Hicks had been "riddled by five bullet wounds from both a .270 rifle and .00 buckshot" and investigators believed they had sufficient evidence to show that the .270 had been "wielded by Trooper Milford Clayson," and that trooper M. [Michael] Grogan was also a likely shooter in this case.[19] Notably, investigators had also linked trooper Clayson to the shooting of prisoners Lorenzo McNeil and William "Taxi Cab" Allen.[20]

New York's Attica prosecutors had far more evidence to work with than the lack of law enforcement indictments implied, even for some of the most high-profile prisoner killings. For instance, although no one was indicted for the killing of L. D. Barkley, the twenty-one-year-old prisoner with the granny glasses whose passionate speech in D Yard had been nationally televised, prosecutor memos suggest that they had some serious leads. For starters there was the testimony and statement of CO Ronald Hollander, who reported that he had fired one solid round "at an inmate in D Yard wearing granny glasses and [a] sweat shirt," and investigators noted his subject "was inmate Elliot Barkley."[21]

Whether it was Hollander's bullet that actually killed Barkley, or that of another CO who had also bragged of his killing and claimed to have kept the glasses on his mantel as a trophy, is not clear in the state's records.[22]

What is clear, however, is that a number of COs knew who had killed this high-profile prisoner and the state also had a number of promising leads to ascertain who that was.

Simonetti's office also failed to take to the grand jury another member of law enforcement, BCI investigator Vincent Tobia, who had actually signed two statements admitting that he had shot a man whom he described as threatening him with a basket of Molotov cocktails. Simonetti's investigators believed that the man who was shot was Sam Melville, Attica's famous white radical prisoner, also known as the "Mad Bomber."[23] The McKay Commission's report from 1972 indicated that the man who shot Melville had indeed admitted to doing so. As that report put it, "He was shot by a law enforcement officer who admitted aiming at him and stated his belief that he was justified in shooting him."[24] The photographic evidence did not support Tobia's claim. Only a jury could actually have determined whether or not this was murder, but lawyers for the prisoners had always felt strongly that Melville had been "murdered in cold blood with his hands in the air in surrender." According to them, in a later civil trial, Tobia "testified proudly that he had indeed killed this famous prisoner."[25]

One of the ugliest prisoner deaths was that of Kenny Malloy, who had been viciously shot at close range. His skull had been riddled with so many bullets that his eye sockets were shredded by the shards of his own bones. Indeed so gruesome was this shooting that one of the two troopers whom investigators knew to be responsible for shooting at this prisoner later spoke of "having nightmares about seeing brains."[26] This trooper, according to an internal investigative report, was a man named Aldo Barbolini. He had shot Malloy with his .357 Magnum Smith & Wesson.[27] The Attica investigation was persuaded that Barbolini also had killed Ramon Rivera, shooting "directly into this tunnel where Rivera fearfully lay."[28]

From the earliest days of the investigation, Simonetti's office had looked closely at Barbolini but all NYSP brass had been making sure that the investigators were told nothing. Significantly, the highest-ranking officials in the NYSP, including Lieutenant Colonel Infante, knew of Barbolini's actions that day and, as Bell saw it, they conspired to cover them up. According to an internal NYSP memo, trooper Barbolini had been asked to resign on September 17, 1971, and, according to a New York state senator who later contacted the Attica investigation about the matter, Barbolini had specifically been told by his superiors "that if he resigned he would not be prosecuted."[29]

Through the rest of 1971, there was much internal discussion of how to deal with Barbolini; the NYSP brass was clearly still worried that his actions might come back to haunt them.[30] In October, Captain Hank Williams had called a fellow NYSP captain to advise him that two members of "Fischer's staff travelled to the residence of former trooper Barbolini to interview him in regard to the investigation."[31] But, because "Barbolini refused to speak to the two investigators," and the brass played dumb regarding what it knew, the Attica investigation limped along with regard to a case against this trooper.[32] Meanwhile, Barbolini, who had only worked as a trooper since May 6, 1968, liked his job and he kept trying to get it back. This clearly wasn't what his bosses had in mind, however, and they shut him down in January 1972.[33] Barbolini wrote again to ask not only to get his job back, but also to have his .357 Magnum Smith & Wesson revolver returned. At that point NYSP chief inspector John Miller personally replied with a curt "no."[34] The gun—which wasn't even legally registered—was potential evidence against the NYSP.[35]

Ironically, had the NYSP brass not expended so much energy on Barbolini in those early days, and had Lieutenant Colonel George Infante not involved himself personally with the internal investigation into this trooper's actions in D Yard, prosecutors might never have known about him. Instead, they wondered what was so interesting about this particular trooper's actions.[36]

Whenever anyone from Simonetti's office asked this question, though, the NYSP responded that this "task of investigating Barbolini" was merely an "administrative issue."[37] No one bought this—particularly since this very trooper, and his actions in D Yard, had been the topic of discussion on September 24, 1971, in the private meeting that was held at Governor Rockefeller's pool house. This was the first of the three meetings in which state officials worked to get the Attica chronology straight.[38]

Another trooper's shots, Simonetti's office suspected, had also contributed to Kenny Malloy's terrible and untimely death. According to an internal memo from state prosecutors, that officer was Gary Van Allen.[39]

Simonetti's office not only believed that it had important evidence regarding who had killed prisoners, it also believed it had evidence relating to whose firing on September 13 had caused hostages to die. Take the case of those COs and civilians who had been shot to death in the hostage circle in D Yard. The story state investigators had been told regarding why troopers had shot so many pellets and bullets into that area was that they had been trying to save fellow trooper Joseph Christian from a prisoner who was attacking him.[40] From the beginning, of his inquiry, Malcolm Bell had seen some real problems in this story, specifically with regard to where exactly Lieutenant Christian was, versus where he claimed to be, when the shooting spree commenced. But even if there were some discrepancies, the real issue was whether the extraordinary number of shots that had been fired into that area were reckless—had this shooting, which had led to hostage deaths and could have killed Christian, been justified.

Simonetti's men painstakingly pieced together exactly where every hostage was in the circle, as well as where gunfire was coming from on the catwalks and in the yard near the circle, and which troopers were specifically assigned to those positions. Christian's rescue detail had included twenty-five regular troopers as well as two correction officers, and investigators discovered to a great degree which of these men were shooting what and where.[41] Lieutenant Kenneth Crounse had shot a round of .00 buckshot while in or near that circle, as had Milford Clayson, Thomas Griffith, and Michael Grogan.[42] So intense was their firepower—at least "14 different shots or 126 pellets [had been] fired in the direction of the hostage circle"—that the investigators marveled that any of the hostages had managed to survive the onslaught.[43]

Quite a few of those shots "were totally unaccounted for in [the] trooper statements," but with the information they had about other shots coming toward the hostage circle from elsewhere in the yard, there were strong indications of who else besides Crounse, Clayson, Griffith, and Grogan might have been responsible for hostage deaths.[44] One trooper, identified in the records as A. Krug, had admitted to firing two rounds of .00 at a prisoner just behind the hostage circle.[45] Another trooper, Jerry O'Hearn, had acknowledged that he too had shot a round of .00 at a prisoner who he alleged was "attempting to stab a hostage."[46] Yet another trooper, William Staples, stated that he had shot a round of .00 "at inmates coming at him with a knife."[47]

Every detail mattered. Prison employees—the state's own—had died in that barrage. Hostages Edward Cunningham, Elmer Hardie, Richard Lewis, and Elon Werner had died on the scene from the .00 pellets that troopers had sprayed into the circle. Hostage Harrison Whalen eventually died at Strong Memorial Hospital. Simonetti's team would have had a difficult time connecting each of these deaths to one specific trooper's shots—especially since unlike bullets, pellets can't be linked back to a specific weapon. Still, they had evidence that jurors might well have deemed the shootings unjustified and, therefore, a felony—reckless endangerment if not manslaughter or murder. There could be no doubt that such shooting had put the hostages in serious jeopardy.[48] As one memo stated clearly, troopers "Crounse, Griffith and Clayson fired a total of fifty-four pellets at their targets in the area of the hostage circle," and, as important, it indicated that the location and direction of fire of the three "are consistent with causing the wounding of the deceased and injured in and immediately near the hostage circle."[49] Trooper Clayson had admitted that he had "fired his shotgun from B catwalk four times at a platoon of armed blacks who were rushing the hostage circle," but not only did Attica's prosecutors conclude that "no such rush occurred," they also determined that "Clayson's four shots (36–48 pellets)" had "likely killed and/or injured a number of hostages and inmates."[50]

Even when investigators were dealing with bullets instead of pellets, it was difficult to tie the deaths of specific men in D Yard to specific troopers. Though investigators knew for certain that hostage Carl Valone had been killed by a .30 caliber slug, and they knew that this came from someone's personal weapon and that these were mostly carried by COs on the day of the retaking, they had no idea whose gun the bullet came from.[51] Several of the hostages had died from troopers shooting rifles—some in the hostage circle, such as civilian Herbert Jones and CO Ronald Werner, and also hostages up on the catwalks, such as John D'Arcangelo.

It was remarkable how much Simonetti's office managed to figure out despite the lack of cooperation and the attempts to block them. With regard to the killing of hostage John D'Arcangelo, for example, they knew the approximate location of the rifle that had killed him and therefore it became a matter of narrowing down who was shooting rifles from that area.[52] In time Attica prosecutors zeroed in on several likely .270 shooters: trooper Frank Panza, trooper Richard Janora, and trooper Steven Sharkey. One internal memo noted that Panza's shots could have hit D'Arcangelo, while another memo speculated that Janora was a more likely candidate.[53] The latter memo noted that Janora had possibly hit two prisoners in addition to D'Arcangelo, and included a statement that "Ballistcs—Consistent with D'Arcangelo."[54] Still another memo suggested that prosecutors also should strongly "consider possibility that SHARKEY's shot . . . may have caused the D'Archangelo [*sic*] fatal injury."[55]

Ironically, it was Sharkey's own convoluted statements that had persuaded prosecutors that his actions may have led to D'Arcangelo's death. In one early interview Sharkey described looking down at the catwalk at the exact spot where D'Arcangelo stood. Then he admitted "firing on the inmates both to the right and to the left of D'Archangelo[*sic*]."[56] Asked whether this hostage was still "on his feet at all after he fired his rounds at these inmates," he answered that he was not.[57] In another statement Sharkey said that he had "looked through the scope and saw the hostage [D'Arcangelo]," and fired his "six rounds in about three minutes."[58] The state even knew which trooper gun fired from C Block had killed D'Arcangelo, but they had no way of proving who had wielded that weapon.[59]

State investigators had quite a bit to go on regarding who had severely wounded hostage Michael Smith. They knew the bullets that had hit Smith had come from a correction officer's gun, and they also knew that, among other officers, COs Ronald Hollander, Howard Holt, and Daniel Clor had been firing from A Block on the morning of the retaking.[60] According to state's records, Hollander and Holt had fired shots from rifles from A Block roof that morning, and Clor had "fired 4 shots, 3 on 'A' catwalk" from that area as well, but it wasn't clear what weapon he had wielded.[61] Whereas Hollander had said he was shooting a .222, and Holt said he had a .351, notably "CO Clor's statement [was] missing" from the pile the NYSP eventually turned over.[62] But Malcolm Bell's main suspect, was not Clor. The man he suspected of shooting Smith had reported that he had a .351 rifle, but, according to Bell, may in fact have been firing "an AR-15 automatic rifle."[63]

Although questions appeared to remain in the minds of Attica's prosecutors about CO Daniel Clor's role in wounding hostage Michael Smith, they had no doubts whatsoever about who had killed hostage John Monteleone.[64] An internal memo explained, "Monteleone had been killed by a .44 Magnum rifle, and this weapon, serial number 10004, was eventually recovered from a correction officer, J. P. Vergamini, who had according to the coroner, gone 'home, got his deer rifle, and came back and shot one of his colleagues' from his position on the third floor of one of the cellblock galleries."[65] Numerous documents from the Attica investigation indicated that everyone knew exactly who had killed John Monteleone—everyone but John Monteleone's family.[66]

Malcolm Bell wasn't sure what he thought about a possible case against Vergamini because he felt that this killing may actually have been accidental. After all, Vergamini himself had never denied that his bullet had hit John Monteleone, but he claimed that he was trying to fire at a prisoner-made barricade. Still, Bell knew that this killing required prosecutorial attention. Even a cursory probe of this shooting had revealed to Bell some troubling details in Vergamini's story. He had insisted that he had been trying to fire at prisoners standing by their handmade barricade but "John Monteleone was seventy feet beyond the barricade" and somehow he was still felled by the bullet he took in the chest.[67] As Bell pointedly put it, seventy feet was not a small margin of error and "the effect was to kill him."[68]

Either way, there was a case here. Even if Simonetti's office didn't want to indict Vergamini for murder, or even manslaughter, there seemed little question that his shooting had been reckless. In order to forestall the possibility of any charge, Vergamini's attorney proposed letting his client "testify to the Supplemental Grand Jury under a waiver of immunity" that there had been much reckless shooting on the day of the retaking so that the state could build other cases with information he would provide.[69] Even this was not to be. As Bell explained, at the "end of the day Tony [Simonetti] did not let me call him to the jury."[70]

By the fall of 1974 it was clear to Malcolm Bell that no matter what evidence his office had against members of law enforcement at Attica, he would not be allowed to present it.

# 45

# Going Public

Malcolm Bell was well aware that his predecessor Ed Hammock had tried and failed to indict troopers before the first grand jury. After he had been there a while, he had watched as fellow prosecutor Frank Cryan also tried unsuccessfully to indict another trooper. As it turns out, however, there were other attempts to indict troopers and COs that Bell did not know about—both before he joined the Attica investigation and after he had been sidelined in it. The Attica investigation had, at some point, tried to indict CO Daniel Clor for murder, manslaughter in the first degree, and manslaughter in the second degree; CO John Vergamini for manslaughter in the second degree and criminally negligent homicide; and trooper Frank Panza for assault in the first degree.[1] They also would try to indict Major John Monahan on the charge of perjury, even though they had immunized him from other possible criminal charges. In each case, however, the first Attica grand juries had voted to No Bill these troopers and COs, which meant that they had declined to indict.

However, even if Bell had known about these attempts to indict members of law enforcement—attempts that Simonetti could certainly point to as proof that he was not ignoring or avoiding cases against law enforcement—his own suspicions of a cover-up at the Attica investigation would likely have persisted.

For some time after he arrived in Simonetti's office, Bell had been told by his boss that the first grand jury was simply too sympathetic to law enforcement to indict—no matter what the evidence. This might well have explained Ed Hammock's earlier disappointment before the grand jury, and this is certainly how Bell understood his colleague Frank Cryan's more recently failed attempt to indict trooper Gary Van Allen for murder, manslaughter in the first degree, and assault in the first degree.[2] Indeed this is a key reason why Simonetti had pushed so hard to get a second Attica grand jury impanelled, and why Bell had been so relieved to learn that he would get to present his cases to a totally new body.[3]

But while Bell certainly had begun to see Simonetti's actions vis-à-vis his cases as his attempt to protect law enforcement, he now began to think that his colleagues who presented before the first Attica grand jury might also have been thwarted from on high. The more he considered his own situation, the more he felt that even before he was told to stop presenting his cases, his boss had made it unnecessarily difficult for him to call the best witnesses, or to utilize the best strategies in front of the jury. Yes, some of his colleagues had been allowed to take law enforcement cases to the grand jury, but Bell wondered if they had really been allowed to make the strongest case they could have. Was it the case that the first grand jury was unwilling to indict troopers and COs because they were biased toward them, or were the cases presented by the prosecution too weak to support? Bell couldn't know for sure, but his suspicions that the prosecutors really didn't want indictments might well have been confirmed by the fact that, according to *Newsday* reporter Edward Hershey, the Attica grand jury had actually voted to indict a trooper whom prosecutors said had killed John D'Arcangelo—but then someone in the Attica prosecution chose not to proceed.[4]

By the close of fall 1974, Bell had begun to worry that he had stumbled upon an outright conspiracy to protect Attica's shooters, one that reached to the highest level of his own Attica investigation as well as to the office of the former governor, Nelson Rockefeller. On December 4, 1974, Bell received a phone call that he believed would allow him to test Anthony Simonetti's commitment to equal justice in the Attica investigation. The caller was a man "with high State Police connections" who was reaching out to Bell because he said he had vital information for the investigation.[5] This evidence, Bell learned, might significantly bolster the hindering cases—those against the highest officers in the NYSP for preventing the Attica investigation from doing its job—as well as the original shooter cases. Two days later Bell met this informant at the Tarrytown Hilton and confirmed the value of his information. This man indicated that key NYSP tapes from the retaking did still exist, though the police had sworn under oath that they did not, because all tapes were routinely recorded over.

Bell typed this good news into a memo for Simonetti. To Bell, however, Simonetti seemed unsettled by this lead, and was not at all eager to use this information. After barely discussing it, Simonetti demanded to know the name of Bell's source. Bell explained that he couldn't reveal that—at least not yet; Simonetti responded that Bell was hereby suspended.[6] To Bell it seemed clear that Simonetti feared such new evidence could make the fire that he had been trying to put out under cases against top NYSP officials suddenly "flame out of control," and he wasn't about to let that happen.[7]

While suspended, Bell contemplated all that had happened in his shop over the previous year, and tried to figure out how to turn things around if that were still at all possible. If he had any hope at all of getting the state of New York to prosecute anyone who wore a badge, Bell finally decided, he would have to go above Simonetti's head—maybe to Attica Judge Carmen Ball, maybe to the attorney general of New York, Louis Lefkowitz, or maybe even to New York's incoming governor, Hugh Carey. And yet, as Bell mulled over this possibility, it dawned on him that it could well put him in harm's way. A great many people had gone to great lengths to make sure that what he knew wouldn't become public. Wouldn't he now be seen as a threat by a whole lot of troopers who had shown themselves to be trigger-happy? Bell decided he would have to both lay low and to resign from the Attica investigation so that he could shine needed light on it.

While at a friend's house Bell penned his resignation letter to Attorney General Lefkowitz. Then he began going through the many Attica investigation documents he had in his possession. In the meantime, just to be safe, Bell also carefully instructed another friend to send all of these many documents to either Tom Wicker at *The New York Times* or to Jack Anderson, a journalist in D.C., should he "end up in, say, a perfectly plausible accident with a truck."[8]

On Tuesday, December 10, Bell sent his letter of resignation to Lefkowitz and laid out precisely what he hoped would happen next: "My objectives have been to see that all the facts which are necessary for the Grand Jury's votes and report are placed before it, and that equal justice applies to inmates and officers. . . . I would like nothing better than to complete the full investigation before the Supplemental Grand Jury, and participate in any trials thereafter. It is clear to me, however that the investigation is being aborted, beyond my power to help."[9] After sending off his letter of resignation to Lefkowitz, Bell also decided to phone Judge Carmen Ball.

It was important to Bell that Ball not disband the grand jury as he knew Simonetti was going to ask him to do.

Judge Ball seemed wholly uninterested in hearing Bell's concerns, and rather than being moved to act, New York's highest-ranking legal official, Lefkowitz, simply accepted Bell's resignation on December 23. Lefkowitz then delivered a copy of Bell's four-page letter to Mr. Justice Carmen Ball and also sent one on to Governor-elect Carey.[10]

Bell's resignation letter set off a firestorm of worry and finger-pointing within the Attica investigation. Prosecutor Charlie Bradley was "surprised that Simonetti did not have a nervous breakdown" in the wake of Bell's "surreal" suggestion that he was overseeing a cover-up.[11] The only saving grace Bradley could see was that "Bell had been an outsider from the very beginning," and therefore maybe no one would pay his allegations much mind.[12] Bell had heard nothing from his former boss so he just assumed that no one had even given one thought to his claim that crimes were being covered up. A full ten days after submitting his letter to Lefkowitz—the same day that the attorney general sent a copy to the governor-elect—Bell finally received a letter from the attorney general which merely accepted his resignation and wished him success in the future.

If Lefkowitz or Simonetti hoped that their highly disgruntled employee would eventually just go away, they were bound for disappointment. As Malcolm Bell waited for some sign that the Attica investigation might reenergize itself, or formally respond to his charges, he thought about ways to take his information to someone who might act. In January of 1975 Bell wrote up a systematic account of what evidence he and his fellow state prosecutors thought they had regarding crimes committed by members of law enforcement at Attica, and exactly what his bosses had done, in his view, to make sure no one was held accountable for those crimes. Underscoring his certainty that troopers and COs were being protected, Bell noted that there were "8,000 pages of testimony in the grand jury proceedings on possible crimes by law officers," pages that the highest-ranking politician in New York should carefully consider.[13] On January 30 he sent his report, eighty-nine typed pages with an additional seventy-one pages of supporting documents, off to now-governor Carey.[14]

Once again, Bell heard nothing. His report had pulled no punches; it was crystal clear that he wanted his charges reviewed right away "in the interest of salvaging the Investigation and completing a proper presentation to the jury, insofar as these objectives are still obtainable."[15] Bell promised the governor that "unless files of the Investigation have [been] destroyed," everything he claimed was fully provable and that the myriad documents that Simonetti and others had in their possession were "evidence of the Investigation's lack of integrity."[16]

And Bell's report had offered Governor Carey specific examples of specific crimes that had been committed by specific troopers. He named names and clearly indicated that his office had plenty of evidence with which to possibly indict many troopers and COs for crimes against prisoners and even their own fellow state employees—the hostages—ranging from reckless endangerment and assault to manslaughter and murder.

Lest the governor feel uncertainty as to why none of the trooper or CO crimes at Attica had been prosecuted, Bell emphasized that higher-ups in the NYSP had actively sabotaged any attempt to do so. He pointed out, for instance, that although reporters from the *Los Angeles Times* and *The New York Times* had managed to listen to the NYSP's radio scanner during and after the assault and had transcribed in rich detail what troopers were saying and doing on the ground during the most crucial hours of the retaking, "there was much not included" in the NYSP's official log of these tapes, which had been "transcribed later back at the Batavia post" by the police themselves.[17] That official log indicated that there were "no messages received between 9:53 and 10:30; it reflects no messages sent between 10:12 and 11:30," and, according to the NYSP officer who had been asked to make that transcript, it was Major Monahan, the man who had led the Attica retaking himself, who "ordered him to compile [that log] sometime after 9/13."[18]

Similarly, deliberate sabotage had taken place with the NYSP photographs. Bell's report explained how Lieutenant Thomas Constantine of the NYSP had admitted that an NYSP sergeant, perhaps on the orders of another lieutenant, had moved certain slides from the slide trays to the academy safe "before the slide trays were turned over to our Investigation."[19] Between this sort of obstruction of justice, and the fact that the State Police had "buried the tents, tables, etc. that had been in D Yard behind the prison before they could be examined for bullet holes," Bell was hopeful that Governor Carey too would see that a cover-up had been attempted and that he would make sure that Attorney General Lefkowitz stepped in so that the Attica investigation could get back on track and operate with integrity. [20] Meanwhile, however, it was clear that Simonetti's office was continuing to handle the NYSP with kid gloves. Even though Lieutenant Constantine had likely seen the murder of prisoner Kenny Malloy, for example, since he "went down C catwalk behind or with Capt.

Malovich's assault force and reached Times Square about the time Malloy was being shot," according to Bell, Simonetti didn't even push him on whether he had.[21]

Bell's document claimed, in no uncertain terms, that there had been a cover-up, straight and simple. So many men had tried to prevent a true accounting of crimes committed at Attica, from the highest offices of the government to the troopers and COs at the local level. Bell pointed out that Rockefeller's office, from the very beginning, had sought to discredit coroner John Edland and his finding that law enforcement bullets had killed hostages.[22] He noted as well that from the earliest days of the investigation until as late as the fall of 1974, Rockefeller attorney Michael Whiteman "was not responding to certain requests for information that A[ttorney] G[eneral] S[imonetti] had made of him" regarding information about the killings in D Yard.[23]

Despite the detailed and dramatic evidence presented in his lengthy report to Governor Carey, again he heard nothing. As one week became two, Bell grew increasingly anxious because he "desperately wanted someone to do something before the second grand jury was discharged."[24] On February 11, 1975, Bell called Carey's office; a secretary confirmed that his report had indeed arrived, but that it "was sitting on the Governor's desk—unread."[25] Bell was disappointed but not surprised and, less than a week later, he "followed the phone call with a letter asking the governor to respond 'with all possible speed.'"[26]

The governor did eventually read Bell's detailed and explosive document, which he immediately shared with both Lefkowitz and Simonetti. The trio needed to figure out if there was any good way to address Bell's charges without opening Pandora's box—without antagonizing NYSP brass as well as many other important political figures in the state. Carey was savvy enough to realize that this document could place his brand-new gubernatorial administration at the epicenter of a public relations nightmare.

Bell, ignorant of Carey's internal deliberations and still hearing no response to his letter, decided that he needed to get a lawyer to figure out his next steps. He secured the services of Robert Patterson, the high-profile attorney who had also been a member of the Goldman Panel—one of the groups that had entered Attica to check on the prisoners after the retaking. Governor Carey's counsel asked Patterson and Bell to sit down with Lefkowitz and Simonetti to see if they might come to some sort of meeting of the minds.[27] That meeting, however, never took place and Bell's conviction grew that his only remaining recourse was to go public regarding this cover-up. When, by March 25—nearly two months after submitting his report—he still had heard nothing from Carey, Bell decided to go to *The New York Times* with his story. He first approached Tom Wicker, who he remembered had been one of the original observers at Attica. Wicker said that he would speak with the metropolitan editor about sending an investigative reporter to talk to him. The next evening reporter Myron Farber showed up at his door to hear Bell's account of what had been happening at the Attica investigation.[28]

Farber knew that he had a powder keg of a story on his hands from the instant Bell revealed it to him. He remained frustrated that Bell was so principled that he would not share any grand jury evidence and wouldn't pubicly name names, but he knew he had enough even without these specifics to make national and even world headlines.[29] At that very moment, Attica was already very much in the news because the jury was deliberating in the John Hill and Charles Pernasalice case.[30]

Myron Farber's story, published in the *Times* on April 8, 1975, pulled no punches, and unsurprisingly created quite a firestorm—especially thanks to the attention that ABLD lawyers brought to it. To them, Bell's allegations were powerful confirmation of what they had always suspected was happening within the Attica investigation.

Ultimately, it fell to Governor Carey, not Attorney General Lefkowitz, to deal with the most immediate fallout from the revelations in the *Times*. Realizing that he had sat on Bell's lengthy and well-documented report that indicated major and outrageous failings on the part of New York State's own, very expensive, Attica investigation, Governor Carey moved into high gear. Behind the scenes, the governor began a feverish attempt to protect his office from a potential public relations disaster. For starters, he requested that Lefkowitz publicly respond to the allegations immediately.[31] As a new governor he simply could not have the citizens of his state, who had been paying the cost of the Attica investigation for almost four years, think that he had ignored evidence that this investigative body was corrupt. Ten days after the story appeared in *The New York Times*, the attorney general appointed former State Supreme Court justice Bernard S. Meyer as a special assistant attorney general "to evaluate the conduct" of New York's official investigation into the retaking of the Attica Correctional Facility and the days and weeks thereafter.[32]

This decision, however, did not exactly keep the press at bay. The media had a field day once it heard who had been appointed to investigate the

Attica investigation. *The Boston Globe* incredulously noted Meyer's lack of "criminal experience."[33] Not only was this man not familiar with criminal law, but, as the *Boston Phoenix* pointed out, the "time limit given Meyer" to complete his investigation was "preposterous."[34]

The time frame that Meyer had been given to complete his investigation was indeed very compressed: he was expected to be done by September 30, 1975, a mere five months later—even though the Attica investigation itself had gone on for nearly four years, presented cases to two grand juries, and indicted sixty-two prisoners whose trials were still in progress. For Malcolm Bell, though, there was once again a modicum of hope. Maybe now all of the state's skeletons would finally be brought out of the closets—and maybe Attica's victims could get some justice. Bell firmly believed that it still wasn't too late.

# 46

# Investigating the Investigation

Democratic governor Carey's selection of Bernard S. Meyer to head up the official inquiry into Bell's charges was highly political. Although Meyer was also a Democrat, notably he was one of the few in New York whom former governor Nelson Rockefeller liked. At the end of Meyer's term as a justice of the New York Supreme Court, then-governor Rockefeller had taken "the 'unusual' step of issuing a statement praising Meyer," publicly recognizing Meyer's "distinguished services to the judicial process," and remarking that it was "most important that the judicial system does not lose . . . a man of outstanding ability, who has rendered great service to the people."[1] Seemingly unconcerned about his connections to Rockefeller, Governor Carey's office assured Meyer that throughout his investigation he would have "the power to examine grand jury minutes, to subpoena witnesses and documents, and to examine under oath any persons with relevant information."[2]

Knowing that he had a tight timeline of only five months, Meyer got right down to business. On the very same day he was appointed to his new post, he received a copy of Bell's so-called "preliminary report" from Carey's office and from Bell's lawyer, Robert Patterson, as well.[3] Within a week, Meyer also received the "first preliminary submissions in response to the Bell report and charges" from Anthony Simonetti, and by June 2 he determined that his investigation would require a budget of at least $330,000.[4] Without this full funding, he insisted, it would be nearly impossible "to hold the September 30th target Date."[5]

From Meyer's point of view, his job was not simply to determine "whether there was a 'cover-up'" but also "whether there was venality."[6]

He also wanted to determine, if he were to discover "deficiencies in the Fischer-Simonetti investigation, why such deficiencies occurred."[7] This was a tall order. It was hard to imagine plowing through the entire paper trail related to the Attica investigation in detail. Although Meyer would later concede that the time allotted had not permitted him to retrace every step the investigation had "during the now four years of its existence," nevertheless, he dutifully tried to do so—not only making sure he had access to all relevant documents, but also asking the public to come forward if they had anything to share that might have important bearing on this case.[8] Meyer and his staff ultimately reviewed "over 33,000 pages of this testimony heard by the two Attica Grand juries" and then "compiled 500 exhibit folders with 1,000 documents with tens of thousands of pages" for further review. Eventually, thirty-seven members of the public (whose identities would be kept confidential in Meyer's report to the governor) offered information that, in turn, generated another ten thousand transcript pages.[9]

Meyer also had numerous meetings with Malcolm Bell. When Bell saw how much pressure this man was under to finish his investigation quickly, he worried that this boded ill for getting at the truth—as did the fact that he had "added eight lawyers to his Commission but only one investigator."[10] As troublingly to Bell, the questions asked of him seemed to suggest they were "questioning Simonetti's mental balance and even asserting negative conclusions about it," rather than looking at the broader systemic problems with the investigation.[11]

In August, six weeks before the deadline, Meyer's commission questioned Vice President Nelson Rockefeller for five hours under oath.[12] And yet, Meyer was at least willing to question Simonetti's boss. The former governor who had ordered the Attica retaking tried his best to offer little useful information. Asked whether he felt, in hindsight, that Robert Fischer should have used the State Police to investigate its own troopers, Rockefeller responded that Fischer was "a man of tremendous integrity and great experience" and "in any case where he felt there could be a conflict of interest . . . he would use somebody else."[13] What is more, the former governor "did not consider the investigation was being conducted by the state police," he said. "I considered the state police simply investigators."[14] Rockefeller was similarly unhelpful on the subject of why the head of the NYSP, William Kirwan, wasn't on the scene during the riot at Attica, nor during the retaking, and why such an important operation had been handed off to the much-lower-ranked Major John Monahan. He couldn't explain why Kirwan wasn't there, and he maintained that this absence hadn't bothered him at all.[15] Still, something important did come out of Rockefeller's deposition: the admission that he had been regularly in touch with the attorney general about the Attica investigation and, what is more, that he "got informal confidential reports from him as to the progress."[16] Rockefeller's testimony, in fact, shattered any illusions that he had not had influence over Lefkowitz, and thus over Fischer, Simonetti, and their men charged with investigating crimes committed by his state troopers and correction officers. He admitted on the record that the attorney general "stayed at the mansion always with me there, and we traveled up and down together, and I saw him down here a great deal. So I was with him a great deal and we would discuss many points."[17] This admission was exactly what Bell had been alleging—that the higher-ups in the Attica investigation were far too close to the very people who had ordered the retaking of Attica to properly investigate it.

Rockefeller's right-hand man at Attica, Robert Douglass, also tried to say little of value, but his deposition was also revealing. Like Rockefeller, Douglass largely avoided the discussion of why Kirwan had not been in charge of the Attica retaking. When pushed to say whether it "seem[ed] strange . . . that the Governor would be represented by four very high officials . . . and yet the assault force would not have in command a Superintendent of State Police," Douglass merely responded that he "didn't form that opinion."[18] However, as in Rockefeller's interview, Douglass admitted that Rockefeller's people had been deeply embedded in the Attica investigation from the very beginning. Although Douglass said he did not recall hearing anything on the day of the retaking about Kenny Malloy's alleged shooter, Aldo Barbolini, who was allowed to resign quietly rather than face potential prosecution, he had "heard much subsequent."[19] Notably, though, no one in the State Police had bothered to tell the investigation prosecutors about this man or what he had done. Douglass was also quite open about the fact that from the earliest days, the top officials in charge of the investigation had "kept the Governor generally informed" regarding the progress of the investigation into the governor's own troopers. Douglass even acknowledged that Robert Fischer had participated in the debriefing at Rockefeller's pool house on September 24, 1971—the same debriefing attended by top men from the NYSP where the Barbolini matter had been discussed.[20] The Meyer Commission lawyer deposing Douglass seemed taken aback by this revelation, asking Douglass "what would have been the point of [Fischer's] sitting in on a conference of the persons responsible for that excessive force if there had been any, if he is supposed to be the independent prosecutor? For example you certainly would not expect him to sit in on a defense counsel conference." Douglass responded that "I didn't ask him to the meeting. I assume the governor did."[21] Either way, he saw no conflict of interest in this situation, nor with the fact that the BCI was investigating its own people.[22]

Bell's allegations of inappropriate relationships among the governor's administration and the investigators were further supported by the testimony of Lieutenant Colonel George Infante. Infante revealed that his own lawyer had "served as an assistant to Governor Rockefeller and the various persons in the Executive Chamber in their dealings with various investigative agencies concerned with Attica."[23] What is more, Infante admitted that this same lawyer had been contacted by Anthony Simonetti when the state prosecutor "was considering giving immunity of some sort to Lt. Colonel Infante."[24] Of course granting immunity to a member of the NYSP whom Simonetti had once dubbed the "architect" of the cover-up at Attica was tantamount to throwing in the towel on any case it might make against law enforcement for its actions there.

More than a month after his deadline, on October 27, 1975, Bernard Meyer finally turned in his final 570-page report to the governor in three volumes.[25] Only the first volume would be released to the public.[26] Governor Carey and Attorney General Lefkowitz made clear that they wished the other volumes to remain undisclosed, citing law "which permits the Governor and the Attorney General to disclose, at their discretion, reports on investigations which they have ordered."[27]

The so-called Meyer Report was detailed and critical, but also a very carefully worded document. Ultimately, Meyer came down quite harshly on the Attica investigation. Not only did the report comment regularly on the Attica investigation's various and often glaring shortcomings, but it specifically called out decisions made by men such as Anthony Simonetti. And yet, to men like Malcolm Bell, as well to Attica's surviving prisoners and hostages, Meyer should have been far harsher on what they saw as the Attica investigation's kid-glove treatment of those who had committed so much harm in D Yard back on September 13, 1971, and for weeks thereafter. Anthony Simonetti's granting immunity to top figures in the potential hindering cases, for example, had been deemed by Meyer merely "a lack of good judgment"; and the NYSP's being placed in charge of investigating its own people from the outset suggested a "possible conflict of interest."[28] The report explained that more police had not been indicted only because of "deficiencies in evidence gathering immediately following the retaking," which then "left so little available to the investigation" to determine whether members of law enforcement were criminally liable or not.[29]

As to Bell's charges of a cover-up at the highest levels of the Attica investigation, Meyer was unequivocal that there had not been any cover-up. The report conceded that there had been some "serious errors of judgment," when it came to how troopers were dealt with by decision makers in the Attica investigation, but there had not, he had decided, been any conspiracy to protect them.[30] The Meyer Report actually went even further than stating that Malcolm Bell's "charge of a cover-up" was "not well founded" (despite Douglass's and Rockefeller's testimony in their depositions for this commission). It also stated that his claims of such a cover-up were "in some parts," based "more on emotion than on fact."[31] Anthony Simonetti might have been a poor prosecutor, or perhaps just in over his head, the report concluded, but he nevertheless had "conducted a detailed and logical investigation of the possibility that his investigation of possible law enforcement crimes may have been deliberately hindered by the State Police."[32] To be sure "many steps should have been taken sooner," but that was the extent of his wrongdoing.[33]

The Meyer Report left Malcolm Bell, and Attica's many victims and survivors, appalled and deeply disheartened.

He compared reading its findings to "being at a holdup and then being told by the investigator, 'the money's gone and the bodies are here, but there wasn't any hold up.' "[34] Bell penned a response in *The New York Times* arguing that Meyer wanted it both ways: although he had to acknowledge that much covering up had happened, he chose to see those acts as unintentional. Therefore, "he did not have to decide who directed it."[35]

Notwithstanding the Meyer Report's unwillingness to support Bell's contention that troopers and COs had been protected, it nevertheless offered some concrete recommendations that set in motion some positive developments for the prisoners who were still awaiting trial. The most important was a call for Governor Carey to appoint "a Special Deputy Attorney General" whose sole purpose would be "to review all convictions, all pending indictments and the evidence relating to possible future indictments with a view to taking, or recommending to the Governor, whatever action he deems appropriate in this wholly unique situation."[36] The report also endorsed trying "to correct the lack of evenhandedness in the State's actions" by continuing to seek indictments against law enforcement personnel "in those cases, if any, involving serious offenses in which there is a reasonable probability of conviction," and possibly giving the NYSP evidence that might allow it to discipline its own employees "whether or not [such was] sufficient for criminal conviction."[37] With regard to justice for Attica's many prisoners who had "sustained serious injuries on September 13, 1971," the commission suggested that they file "a crime victim's compensation claim within, say, one year after passage of the amendment."[38] No mention was made, however, of dismissing the many riot-related criminal charges that Attica's prisoners still faced. In Meyer's view, "amnesty is not the proper solution to Attica-related problems."[39]

Although Bell was disappointed with the report's conclusions, many other New Yorkers who had long thought the Attica investigation a disaster felt it was wonderful news. One of these was Arthur Liman, who had served as the general counsel for the McKay Commission during its extensive investigation into Attica, a longtime critic of the "the grim cycle of accusation and investigation."[40] In his view, "it did not have to happen this way."[41] Liman wrote a personal letter to Hugh Carey after the Meyer Report was released, pointing out that although his commission had warned state officials that "the fair administration of justice required even-handed prosecution," the state's investigation had still proceeded most un-evenhandedly.[42] Liman found it incredible that, despite the findings of the McKay Commission and other Attica investigations, there had indeed been "widespread physical reprisals" against prisoners as well as "inadequate medical care." As revealed in the state's investigation, "not a single indictment had been returned against a state official, a correction officer, or a police officer."[43] In light of the Meyer Report, Liman proposed a brand-new investigation—one that "must clearly focus on identifying those who established and condoned the order of priority that treated offenses by inmates as more serious than the transgressions by the lawmen. Even at this late date, that should not be beyond the faculties or the experiences of lawyers and investigators with a will to do justice."[44]

Other New Yorkers argued against further investigations. The chairman of the McKay Commission, Dean Robert McKay, wrote to the governor that "the time has come to stop the never-ending investigations, closing out this unhappy chapter of our history as quickly and justly as possible."[45] McKay recommended that all further indictments and investigations should be dismissed, "except possibly the one remaining murder indictment," which had charged Mariano "Dalou" Gonzalez with killing fellow prisoner Mickey Privitera in D Block where Hess and Schwartz were also killed.[46]

The public offered still other solutions for proceeding in the wake of the Meyer Report. A group of clergy in Rochester recommended "clemency for all who have been sentenced and dismissal of the remaining indictment."[47] This was exactly what various folks working to defend the Attica Brothers thought as well. As Big Black Smith's Attica Now group stated, "The Brothers' demand for amnesty in 1971 is more compelling for 1976."[48]

Governor Carey committed himself to reviewing all existing cases before deciding how to proceed with the investigation. On the same day that Carey and Lefkowitz released the first volume of the Meyer Report, they announced that Alfred J. Scotti, former chief assistant district attorney of New York County, would be appointed special deputy attorney general as the Meyer Report recommended. Scotti's appointment was big news: not only did it effectively remove Simonetti from any position of influence at the Attica investigation, but it opened up the possibility for a more balanced prosecutorial inquiry in the future.

When Scotti began his probe, the prisoner indictments stood as follows: eight of the sixty-two inmates who had been indicted had pled guilty to get their ordeals over—some had pled right away, others later as their cases wore on. Only two men had been convicted after standing trial, John Hill and Charles Pernasalice, and three others had been acquitted after standing trial: Willie Smith, accused of raping James Schleich; Vernon LaFranque, accused of subduing hostages with a gas gun; and Shango, accused of murdering Barry Schwartz. Meanwhile, charges against thirty-nine prisoner defendants had been dismissed entirely, either because Simonetti's office conceded there was insufficient evidence to go to trial, or because the defendants had not been granted a speedy trial. When Scotti began his investigation cases were still pending against twenty-seven prisoners and one state trooper, Gregory Wildridge, who had been indicted by the second grand jury quite suddenly during the Meyer Commission's investigation.

As far as the New York State Police were concerned, trooper Wildridge's indictment stank of politics. Simonetti's office had clearly scrambled to show that it could indeed indict a trooper once all eyes were upon it. Simonetti asked a prosecutor from his office to persuade the grand jury, just before it was to be dismissed, that Wildridge's actions at Attica "evinced a depraved indifference to human life."[49] Wildridge was charged with reckless endangerment for having fired ten rounds from his shotgun into D Yard, including some into a tent where prisoners were huddled. According to the indictment, Wildridge callously said he had fired so much "to keep up the noise."[50] Wildridge, a thirty-eight-year-old, fourteen-year veteran of the force, was visibly supported by his NYSP fellows. At his arraignment, he was flanked by Captain Hank Williams; and Patrick Carroll of the Police Benevolent Association of the New York State Police told every media outlet he could reach that it was "a travesty of justice to indict a trooper who was risking his life to quell a prison riot."[51] High-powered lawyers from the firm of Hinman, Straub, Pigors & Manning of Albany were ready to defend Wildridge from prosecution. They would argue that Wildridge had been under enormous stress at Attica, "constantly and continuously exposed to tension-filled hours," given "little effective sleep or rest," and subjected to days of "rumors of inmate atrocities"; now the state of New York was "prosecuting him for following orders in the line of duty."[52] Worse, these lawyers argued, their client had been ordered by his superiors to give statements of what he had done during the retaking "without any constitutional warnings," and was "repeatedly forced to give evidence against himself" in the form of his own "coerced written statement."[53]

Simonetti's office must have been pretty shaken up by Bell's letter of resignation and his subsequent detailed and condemning report to the governor because not only was Wildridge indicted in the wake of Bell's departure, but the Attica investigation also chose then to present cases against several other low-level members of law enforcement. According to Scotti's office, Simonetti's office ultimately scurried to present evidence against four troopers and three correction officers before the second grand jury.[54] In that mix was, for example, trooper James Mittlestaedt, whom prosecutors insisted had killed prisoner James Robinson and severely wounded others on the day of the retaking. He faced the possible charges of murder in the second degree, manslaughter in the first degree, attempted murder in the second degree, and attempted manslaughter in the first degree.[55] Similarly, prosecutors had brought evidence to this grand jury against correction officer Nicholas De Santis for reckless endangerment in the first degree. Even though by his own admission he had fired more than twelve rounds from his .45 caliber Thompson into the heavily populated D Tunnel and D Yard on the day of the retaking, he was not indicted.[56] Neither was Mittlestaedt.

When Alfred Scotti stepped into the Attica investigation he could see clearly that getting indictments against troopers and correction officers would be nearly impossible at this late date, in front of a grand jury that was feeling rushed, and with this team of prosecutors. Having looked closely at the evidence, it frustrated him because he could see cases where "the evidence presented to the Grand Jury warranted an indictment," but in one of them, for example, "since that state trooper had already received immunity from the prosecution, prior to my appointment, he cannot now be legally prosecuted."[57] Still, he promised that he would continue to "seek indictments against law enforcement personnel and others in those cases, if any, involving serious offenses, in which there is a reasonable probability of conviction."[58] There were at least two cases against law enforcement that he wanted to pursue, including "one matter [that] involves a possible intentional killing by a state trooper and [another that] involves a possible serious obstruction of the Attica Investigation by a member of the State Police."[59]

However, Scotti did not pursue these cases. Instead, he recommended on February 26, 1976, that the only pending law enforcement indictment, against Gregory Wildridge, be dismissed, and that no reattempts to indict troopers or COs should be undertaken. Although Scotti claimed that "the action we recommend today should not be misconstrued as condoning . . . the brutal acts of some law enforcement," it effectively did just that.[60] The truth was that there was no will to make these cases against law enforcement officers in the wake of the Meyer Report—if ever there had been.[61]

Once it was clear there would be no more trooper or CO indictments, Scotti felt more pressure than ever to take a close look at the remaining cases against prisoners, which everyone now agreed were sloppy at best and, at worst, downright unwinnable. Even when the state had managed to find evidence against the prisoner defendants, its highly questionable provenance made the cases weak if not tainted. In this context, less than three months after having been appointed to assess the existing and potential Attica cases, Scotti recommended dismissing "all pending indictments with the exception of one [Mariano "Dalou" Gonzalez]."[62] Scotti even recommended that the one prisoner defendant who had already pled in a still active indictment be allowed to retract his plea and be cleared.[63] On April 22, 1976, Governor Carey proudly announced, "On Mr. Scotti's recommendation, State Supreme Court Justices Frank R. Bayger (Jan. 26, Feb. 26) and Carmen F. Ball (Feb. 26) dismissed 11 indictments, naming 24 inmates and the only state trooper indicted."[64]

The Attica Brothers and all of their lawyers and supporters were relieved to hear this news, yet it was hard for them not to feel deep bitterness as well. Ernie Goodman wrote a heartfelt letter to his Attica client Shango on February 27, 1976, after having attended one of the hearings in which indictments were vacated.

> I went to Buffalo in the expectation of dismissal. I had anticipated it would be a happy event. I was mistaken. It was bittersweet. Bitter, because Scotti's assumption that belated justice proved the essential fairness of the system, was hypocritical. The reason there was any belated "justice" was only because of the struggle of those who had to fight or die. And the struggle was long and heartbreaking. During its course many wavered, weakened and gave up. Some capitulated. Others, like yourself, stood fast, gained strength and fought back, gaining understanding and support as we revealed the cruel and unconscionable efforts of the State to prove that the leaders of the rebellion were barbarous sadists.[65]

The prisoners and their advocates were angry that they had been put through so much for so long, and sickened that Governor Carey was, in their view, still trying to protect the troopers. Carey insisted that any law enforcement officers the state had been looking to indict would remain unnamed and that their names should only be revealed "if and when disciplinary hearings are undertaken" within their various state agencies. Even Scotti, who originally had recommended the release of all volumes of the Meyer Report, ultimately "endorsed Judge Meyer's suggestion that the second and third volumes should not be made public," undoubtedly because these volumes had grand jury testimony in them that might specifically name troopers and COs who had committed crimes at Attica.[66] Meanwhile, though, the prisoner who the state thought had killed fellow prisoner Mickey Privitera in the midst of the uprising, Dalou Gonzalez, was not going to be afforded any such consideration.[67]

With the dismissal of all but one Attica indictment and with the promise that no indictments would now be sought against troopers, there was no longer any need for the Attica grand juries. And so, Judge Carmen Ball dismissed both panels on March 30, 1976.[68]

## 47

# Closing the Book

Dismissing the remaining indictments as well as the grand juries, however, had not quite ended the Attica headache for Governor Hugh Carey. In fact, in the wake of his April 1976 press conference, which announced that the indictments were being vacated and, thus, the Attica investigation was effectively being dismantled, much of the public, however, thought still more should be done. He received hundreds of letters calling for him to grant executive clemency to all prisoners who had pled or been convicted of an Attica-related offense since they had been so selectively prosecuted and, also, to prevent a later governor from deciding, for whatever reason, to reopen the Attica investigation.[1]

After much deliberation and consultation with Scotti and others, Carey tried once and for all to end any more talk of Attica. On New Year's Eve 1976, Carey called a press conference to make the stunning announcement that he was going to pardon every prisoner who had pled out in an Attica case, grant clemency to every prisoner who had been found guilty in an Attica case, and drop all inquiries into the potentially illegal actions of any state officers and employees at Attica back in September 1971—even disciplinary actions against them would now be off the table. "Attica has been a tragedy of immeasurable proportions," the governor stated, "unalterably affecting countless lives. Too many families have grieved, too many have suffered deprivations, and too many have lived their lives in uncertainty waiting for the long nightmare to end. . . . [The] time has come to firmly and finally close the book on this unhappy chapter in our history as a just and humane state."[2]

Carey explained why he was taking this bold step. In short, all of the inquiries into the recent years of the Attica investigation had persuaded him that "the state, through its highest officials, failed abysmally" by being wholly insensitive to its "constitutional responsibilities" and now, "equal justice by way of further prosecutions is no longer possible."[3] In his view, state officials had bungled the investigation so badly that they had "effectively precluded the possibility" of now bringing anyone to justice for crimes that may have been committed at Attica.[4]

But instead of settling the Attica question for good, the governor's announcement brought it back into the public eye once again. Surprisingly, the most hostile responses came from the people who had dodged the biggest prosecutorial bullet as a result of it: the New York State Police and New York State correction officers. Patrick Carroll of the Police Benevolent Association made major waves in the press, sharing how "appalled" he was to hear that the governor had pardoned Attica's prisoners, and both the PBA and the correction officers union were critical of Carey's statement that he would not pursue disciplinary action against officers who had been on duty at Attica. On behalf of the PBA, Carroll "called the Governor's statement 'a slap in the face' because it suggests that the guards and troopers had in fact committed disciplinary infractions."[5] According to a CO union official, "it leaves a cloud of suspicion over our heads."[6]

The Attica Brothers had a more complicated response. Everyone was relieved that the indictment ordeal was over and that, better still, anyone who had received time as a result of having been indicted would have their records cleared. But there was still much anger over the many years of so many lives that had been spent living in fear of prosecution. They were also angry that even though John "Dacajewiah" Hill was included in the governor's clemency decree—his sentence was commuted—Hill had not immediately been released from prison. Hill wasn't slated to get out until October 23, 1994; the commutation only ensured that he would be eligible for parole in January 1977. Governor Carey would do nothing sooner.[7]

Hill, for one, was relieved that his parole was much nearer. He felt certain that, armed with the Carey decree, he would be released by the parole board within the month. Yet when he appeared before the parole board in January 1977, it did not go as he expected. As the board deliberated, John Hill sat in the prison's visitor's room with his wife, Alicia, and their seventeen-month-old son, John Jr. The board decided that releasing him could possibly lead to "widespread negative community reaction," and they refused to consider his parole again for two more years—the longest interval the board was permitted to wait before having to reconsider his bid for release.[8] When he heard this decision, Hill just shook his head in dismay.[9] In his statement to the press, he was despondent, telling reporters, "If they leave it to the discretion of the parole board, I'll never get out of these penitentiaries. . . . The guards still want revenge for what happened."[10]

The board's reluctance to release Hill only increased the pressure on Carey. To everyone's surprise one of Hill's most vocal supporters became former Attica prosecutor Malcolm Bell. Bell filed a lengthy affidavit supporting Hill, and also made a public statement on his behalf that he was "aware of no circumstances which make the lack of fairness and evenhandedness of the Attica prosecution any less applicable to John Hill than it was to these [other] inmates charged with serious felonies."[11] Multiple grassroots organizations expressed support for Hill with flyers such as "Immediate Amnesty for Dacajewiah," which reminded the public that "Carey may claim he 'closed the book,' but in reality he closed the door on Dacajewiah. . . . We must make the pressure on him to grant amnesty greater than the pressure to continue the cover-up."[12] A faith-based organization, Charter Group for a Pledge of Conscience, urged people to "please write or wire the Governor today demanding that he grant unconditional pardon to John Hill."[13]

In the face of this pressure, Carey's office maintained that it could do nothing.[14] It would be up to Hill's attorneys—now William Kunstler, Margaret Ratner, and Elizabeth Fink—finally to obtain Mr. Hill's freedom via the courts.[15] Notwithstanding the flak Carey received from Hill's supporters and that which he endured from the heads of the organizations representing the State Police and the correction officers, he and the state of New York had done their best to bury the bodies.[16] Bernard Meyer certainly thought he had settled the question of cover-up, Alfred Scotti had ended the Attica investigation, and by offering pardons and clemency, Governor Carey had—at least officially—closed the book on Attica. The state hadn't considered one factor, however: the many hundreds of men who had been wounded and tortured at Attica, and the families of the scores of men who had been murdered, who had not yet had their day in court. They were not going to let the book on Attica be closed until their story was completely and truthfully told. Though it would take almost twenty years from the time that Carey tried to end all matters related to Attica for them to take state defendants to court, take them the prisoners would.

PART IX

# David and Goliath

# ELIZABETH FINK

*When Governor Hugh Carey "closed the book" on Attica, and the criminal trials faded from the headlines, attorney Elizabeth Fink had been living and breathing the fallout from the Attica prison uprising for almost five years. Fink was what activists in America lovingly referred to as a "red diaper baby." She had grown up in the heart of New York City's most intellectual and politically left milieu, and then attended Reed College. An impromptu road trip to Chicago after graduation in the summer of 1968 ignited her own passion for social justice.*

*That August, during the Democratic National Convention, Fink found herself exposed to a most intoxicating experiment in participatory democracy. This moment was transformative for Fink, not only because the demonstrations that rocked that city inspired her deeply and made her feel passionate about the fight against the Vietnam War, but also because she was shaken to her core by the law enforcement violence she saw directed at protesters young and old.*

*When Liz Fink came back to New York she joined the offices of a prominent radical newspaper but soon thereafter her father died and she left to run his business. Feeling some pressure from her mother, who had always wanted her to be an attorney, Fink then enrolled in law school. Armed with a J.D. degree, Fink suspected that she could do some very important political work, fighting the government officials and politicians who were using the courts to squelch dissent.*

*Attica would give her that opportunity.*

*Liz Fink arrived in Buffalo on July 4, 1974, less than two months after she was admitted to the practice of law, and she hit the ground running as a key person in the Attica Brothers Legal Defense (ABLD). On July 5 she first went into Auburn prison to meet with the men there awaiting trials. Soon Fink was one of the main liaisons between the indicted Attica Brothers and the many people working on their behalf. She had become particularly close with fellow Attica lawyers Dennis Cunningham, Michael Deutsch, and Joe Heath. These four worked closely with Big Black Smith and, like him, believed that politics must be central to any defense strategy. Fink was very much aware of the gender politics of the ABLD as well. As much as she liked and admired her male colleagues, she often felt sidelined by them. That is, until the 1980s.*

*In that decade and into the next, Liz Fink would find herself in charge of the highest-profile Attica case to date. Big Black was not about to let the state of New York close the book on Attica and was counting on her to ensure that he and the rest of the prisoners finally had their day in federal court.*

# 48

# It Ain't Over Till It's Over

Although Governor Carey had authority to pardon those who had already been convicted of an Attica crime, he did not in fact have the legal power to pardon anyone in advance of a possible conviction. In other words, while it might have been politically expedient to claim that there now would be no legal actions taken against members of law enforcement for what they had done at Attica, his pronouncement held virtually no weight as "a judicial decision or a legal decision."[1]

Many of Attica's surviving prisoners had actually been trying to make the state of New York accountable for the horror of the retaking via civil actions since 1971. In fact, 508 of them had filed notices of intent to file suit in New York's Court of Claims by December of that year.[2] Undoubtedly there would have been many more, but by law, prisoners who were still incarcerated were not allowed to file these suits—and even those who were released only had a window of three years in which to do so. Then, in 1974, the Court of Claims decided that it would hear no Attica civil case until all of the criminal cases had been dispensed with—which meant that in 1977, in the wake of the Carey pardons, numerous lawsuits related to Attica were finally ready to proceed.[3]

These cases already comprised "one of the largest and most complicated set of claims ever brought against the state," according to one newspaper report.[4] Of course, more suits were now likely to follow, particularly since the Meyer Report had made clear that the state had made many mistakes in its handling of Attica. As the press pointed out, it would now "be very difficult for the state to deny culpability" in the civil arena.[5] Attorney

General Louis Lefkowitz noted tiredly, "With motions and appeals, this could go on for years."[6]

It did go on for years, in part because it was so hard for the prisoners to get their cases heard. The Court of Claims eventually ruled in fourteen prisoner suits that had been filed in the early days after the rebellion, but only nine of these were "resolved in favor of claimant, and 5 were dismissed."[7] As important, even the cases that eventually did win prisoners a damage award took so long to wend their way through the system that some plaintiffs did not live long enough to see the money. This process was in fact so drawn out that one of the Attica plaintiffs wrote to the clerk of the court in March 1983 to remind everyone that his "life has been shortened by the Attica incident," and that if his claim was "not tried soon, neither my witnesses nor myself will be alive for the trial."[8] That plaintiff died the following year, but his estate was finally awarded $164,000 in damages in 1989.[9]

Nineteen eighty-nine would be a good year for a number of Attica prisoners thanks to the decisions of one judge, who was willing to rule that the state was in fact "liable for damages and injuries 'resulting from the intentional use of excessive force.' "[10]And yet, while it was true that nine prisoners, or their estates, eventually were awarded a total of $1.5 million in damages, as one legal scholar noted, for so many others of Attica's surviving prisoners "there was little or no redress."[11]

Still, this wasn't the end of Attica legally. Indeed, as far as New York was concerned, the case most threatening to it had, even at the close of the 1980s, still not been resolved. This case, *Inmates of Attica v. Rockefeller,* had originally been filed in federal district court in Manhattan on September 13, 1974, at the very last minute before the three-year statute of limitations ran out. This class action civil rights suit on behalf of the Attica Brothers—one that had originated in that first injunction against violations of prisoners' rights that lawyers had sought before Judge John T. Curtin back on the night of the Attica retaking—argued that the main officials in charge at Attica, from Governor Rockefeller to John Monahan of the NYSP to various officials at the prison, should be liable for $100 million in damages. They had "violated the rights of prisoners by using excessive force and unrestricted firepower 'calculated to cause unnecessary and inexcusable death, serious injury, terror, and suffering.' "[12]

While the energies of the Attica Brothers and their lawyers were consumed with the defense of the sixty-two men indicted in the criminal courts, this civil case had bounced among various judges in Manhattan.

The first judge recused himself for being too connected with various litigants in the case; the next worked in the same firm that now represented Nelson Rockefeller. Rather than recuse himself and give it to another jurist in New York City, however, the second judge suggested moving the case upstate—bad news for the Attica Brothers.

The deck seemed stacked against the plaintiffs in several ways. First, any legal help they might secure was likely to be in New York City, and they had few resources to manage traveling back and forth to Buffalo. Furthermore, in their desperation to get the case filed by the deadline, the prisoners had originally filed a very general complaint—it listed many "John Does" as defendants because there had not been enough time to figure out who all of the potential defendants might be. Fortunately, an attorney from the National Lawyers Guild in Manhattan decided to take the time to read the McKay Commission's detailed 1972 report and amend the complaint to name specific defendants—shooters, officers, state officials, prison administrators. But then the ball was dropped again.

Back in 1974 when *Inmates of Attica v. Rockefeller* was filed, anyone who was named in a civil case like this one had to be served by a representative from the federal Marshals Service. The key here was that someone from the plaintiff group would have to arrange for a U.S. marshal to serve every potential defendant—not as simple a task as it might seem. In the chaotic years of the criminal defense, this procedure simply did not happen for many of the individuals. By 1979, the only five defendants who had been successfully served and remained in the suit were former governor Nelson Rockefeller, former commissioner of corrections Russell Oswald, NYSP Major John Monahan, former Attica superintendent Vincent Mancusi, and former Attica assistant deputy superintendent Karl Pfeil. Many key figures, from NYSP Lieutenant Colonel George Infante to Attica deputy superintendent Leon Vincent, could breathe a sigh of relief that they had dodged a potentially deadly legal bullet.

When the case was moved to Buffalo, into the court of the Western District of New York, the prisoners' class action suit was assigned to Judge John T. Elfvin. From that day forward, the state's lawyers tried to get Elfvin to dismiss the case but Elfvin denied their motions and made clear that the case would proceed. He insisted on knowing, however, who would be representing the plaintiffs. That was a good question. Officially the Attica Brothers' civil case was being handled by a New York City lawyer named Bob Cantor, but the fact was that it had been hanging around for so long that no one was really in charge anymore. (If someone had been on top of things, Elfvin might not have been able to dismiss the defendants who hadn't been served by a U.S. marshal; an attorney could have argued for more time to serve them.)

Attica Brother Frank "Big Black" Smith was well aware that if there were no lawyers who had the time to commit themselves to this civil case, it would soon be over without any satisfactory results. By this time, Big Black was working in Bob Cantor's office and he could see that this man, alone, would have a hard time taking on a case of this magnitude, especially one that would be argued so far away from Manhattan. Big Black very much hoped that someone else—someone specific—would agree to take on this case: Elizabeth Fink. Fink was a criminal lawyer, not a civil lawyer, but Big Black had seen her in action during the Attica Brothers Legal Defense efforts and had always thought she was just the sort of fighter they all had needed then and still did. Black and his fellow Attica Brother Akil Al-Jundi approached Fink about taking on the Attica civil case. She was flattered, but initially refused; she was recovering from a recent illness, and also working around the clock trying to get another client, Black Panther Dhoruba al-Mujahid bin Wahad (aka Richard Earl Moore), released from prison. The Brothers grew alarmed when Judge Elfvin announced that if the plaintiffs did not commence discovery in this case by February 21, 1981, he would pull the plug.

Fortunately, a pro se clerk in Judge Elfvin's office, Ellen Yacknin, had worried about this possibility for months as she had watched Big Black check in with her again and again to make sure that this case was alive and well. It seemed to her that he needed some help. When Judge Elfvin gave a firm deadline for the plaintiffs to identify their counsel, Yacknin asked the judge if she could try to find some attorneys for the case. Yacknin and Elfvin had a heated debate as he argued for the case to be dismissed and she begged him to give her just a bit more time to find some lawyers. Ultimately, he did allow her to try.[13]

Yacknin's first call was to a local attorney she knew, who declined. She then turned to Prisoner Legal Services, who also said no. Feeling a bit desperate, Yacknin then decided to call every lawyer that she had seen named on the original complaint; each of them also declined to take on the case. Any lawyer worth their salt could see that this was a classic David and Goliath case which would require enormous resources and energy, as well as spending a tremendous amount of time in upstate New York. Every time Ellen Yacknin called another attorney for help she was told the same thing: Call Liz Fink. So she did.

Fink, though, also said no. She explained to Yacknin that she was unusually busy with other cases and, what is more, she was a criminal not a civil litigator. Two days later, however, Yacknin's phone rang. It was Liz Fink, who had talked at length with Big Black Smith; they had decided that they, together, would try this case. Yacknin called it "a very brave thing to do," which was putting it mildly.[14] The state's defendants had hired the best-connected and best-funded lawyers in New York, and the only way that the prisoners might be able to prove their case would be to get the state to turn over evidence in discovery. Given that this case was, at bottom, about murder, torture, and abuse, Fink and Big Black had little doubt that the defense would continue to make every effort to block their access and to continue the now time-honored strategy of insisting that the prisoners, not the state, bore all of the blame for what had happened at Attica.

Nevertheless Fink and Big Black came into Judge Elfvin's court prepared to argue their first discovery motion. As Yacknin recalled, "the other lawyers were blown away."[15] Still, Fink had to fight hard for every single thing the plaintiffs would need to proceed in this case. Not only did defense lawyers persist in trying to have the case dismissed, but they also insisted that the class suing them was invalid. Judge Elfvin seemed to enjoy what he viewed as a game of cat-and-mouse between the defense and the plaintiffs, and he played right along.[16] In an order he issued on Octo-

Frank "Big Black" Smith and Elizabeth Fink, 1981 *(Courtesy of the* Democrat and Chronicle*)*

ber 30, 1979, Elfvin agreed the plaintiffs were, legally, a class—a group who had shared a similar enough experience to stand together as one to seek damages from the state. Then, almost a year later to the day, he changed his mind on this point and revoked the plaintiffs' class certification; it would be another five years before he once again granted the plaintiffs' motion to recertify as a class.[17] To Liz Fink's frustration, this sort of waffling on the judge's part would continue for years, in her view capricious and childish power-tripping.[18]

Fink's biggest fight with Elfvin and the state lawyers alike was trying to get meaningful access to state documents via the discovery process. Unwilling to leave any stone unturned, Fink filed fourteen subpoenas as well as numerous requests for admissions—paperwork that asked specific questions of the defendants that, once answered, could then be accepted as fact as the trial proceeded. For example, she asked: "Do you admit that 39 people were killed on September 13th?" In lieu of a response, the defendants' lawyers from the elite firm of Milbank, Tweed, Hadley & McCloy stalled on her requests and filed their own motions to have her case dismissed. Some of those motions backfired; for instance, the argument that the plaintiffs did not have the resources to litigate the case opened the door for Fink to argue that the entire case was clearly about an imbalance of power and, therefore, that this was all the more reason why it should proceed. She maintained to the judge that she could handle this case even while, behind the scenes, she worried mightily about their limited resources. Fink was almost single-handedly footing the ever-growing cost of the case—dipping into family savings and borrowing money when she could to cover phone bills that averaged $1,500 a month, exorbitant commuting costs, and the staggering amount of money needed to get documents typed, copied, and filed.

No matter how tenacious Fink and Big Black were with their discovery subpoenas, though, the state's lawyers repeatedly denied that they had anything worth seeing. In March 1982, Fink finally got permission to meet with state attorneys at the office of the attorney general in the World Trade Center, where all of the Attica files from the years of criminal litigation were kept. There she and two other lawyers she had known since the ABLD days, Joe Heath, who had worked on the Hill and Pernasalice case, and Michael Deutsch, who also had been central to Big Black's defense team, returned day after day as officials allowed them to see only one box. And so they would argue to see another box. One more container would be brought out the next day, and then the whole tedious process would repeat itself. So the plaintiff lawyers went back to court.

On June 7, 1982, they returned to the World Trade Center armed with a court order and the right to see everything the state had on Attica. Lawyers from Milbank, Tweed joined them to review the documents together. After three days, the defense lawyers, according to Fink, grew bored of the process and left. To their relief, with no defense lawyers on site, and with only one records clerk remaining in that office who was willing to give them fairly free rein, Fink was able to see virtually any document she needed to see despite the state's instructions to allow her access to only selected items.[19] Once she had seen documents that no one outside the Attica investigation had ever seen, including all three volumes of the Meyer Report and countless documents from the state's years-long investigations of prisoners and troopers, Fink felt well prepared to litigate the case.[20]

# 49

# Shining the Light on Evil

Now armed with vital documents to prove their case against prison and police officials as well as against New York's former governor Nelson Rockefeller, Liz Fink and her team were most eager to go to trial. To their dismay, however, Judge Elfvin suddenly allowed the state's lawyers to realize their longtime efforts to remove Rockefeller from the list of named defendants. It was common knowledge that Judge Elfvin was good friends with Rockefeller's attorney in this trial, so close, in fact, that they used to go horseback riding together.[1] Still, the plaintiff lawyers thought that the judge might not protect him this overtly. Fink appealed, but even the appeals court panel slated to consider the motion had to recuse itself since all three judges on it also had close relationships with Rockefeller. Indeed, it took three separate panels of judges to get a ruling on the appeal and, even then, at the end of 1989, the plaintiffs lost their bid to keep Rockefeller in the case.

And so Fink and her team had to move on. They had been requesting trial dates since 1987, but time and again the defendants had found reasons the dates should be moved. In December 1989, Fink again filed papers seeking an immediate trial date; the trial was set to commence on June 5, 1990. But in March of that year the remaining defendants named in the case followed Rockefeller's lead and filed their own motions to be removed from the case, arguing that they too had immunity and thus couldn't be named defendants. Judge Elfvin denied these efforts and confirmed that the plaintiffs' Eighth Amendment claims would be permitted against former commissioner Russell Oswald, "for failure to plan for medical needs in connection with the plan of retaking"; NYSP Major John Monahan, "for his role in supervising the State Police officers who participated in the retaking"; and former Attica officials Superintendent Vincent Mancusi, Assistant Deputy Superintendent Karl Pfeil, and Commissioner Russell Oswald, "all for failure to prevent the acts of retaliation that took place subsequent to the prison retaking."[2]

Word that the civil suit was about to go to trial once again thrust Attica into the national spotlight. It did not escape people's notice that, with this federal trial about to begin in Buffalo, "for the first time the full extent of the killing, brutality and denial of medical care inflicted on the men at Attica [would be] publicly exposed."[3] To make sure this case stayed in the public eye, a newly formed Attica Justice Committee got to work.

The fact that 1991 marked twenty years since the Attica rebellion greatly helped this committee bring attention to the case. Soon, events marking the anniversary and fundraising for the committee sprang up around the country, including "The Attica Prison Rebellion and U.S. Prisons 20 Years Later" in Ann Arbor, Michigan, that showcased speakers Frank "Big Black" Smith and others.[4] Similarly, a "Can't Jail the Spirit" event was held at the Bethlehem Lutheran Church in Oakland, California, on September 13 to commemorate "20 years after the Attica Rebellion, the murder of George Jackson, and the Imprisonment of Geronimo Pratt."[5] An "Attica Rebellion and US Prisons: 20 Years After Attica" event was also held on the campus of Eastern Michigan University; as was an "evening to commemorate the 20th anniversary of the Attica uprising and support the brothers and their families in their federal law suit" at the Canaan Baptist Church in New York City.[6] In addition, lawyers from the New York area sent out their own fundraising letter asking "that each of us contribute $1,000 to this cause either by loaning the money for reimbursement in the event that a favorable verdict or settlement is reached or by contributing the money."[7]

On the eve of the Attica civil trial's opening, the Attica Brothers plaintiffs had an impressive team of lawyers on their side, made up of Liz Fink, Michael Deutsch, and Joe Heath, as well as two other attorneys from the earlier days of the Attica criminal trials, Danny Meyers and Dennis Cunningham. On the defense team were Richard Moot, a third-generation trial lawyer who had been trained at Harvard and now represented Mancusi; Irving C. Maghran represented Pfeil; and John H. Stenger represented Russell Oswald (and, following Oswald's death in March of 1991, his estate).[8] This trio was supported by five more defense attorneys and numerous paralegals.

Though the defense team was far better funded, they were routinely startled by how well the plaintiffs' lawyers argued their case. To the defense's annoyance, it was obvious that attorneys such as Liz Fink were at a great advantage having already spent so many years working on the criminal cases. Her team already knew exactly who had seen abuses taking place at Attica, and thus whom to subpoena. As important, the plaintiff lawyers also had at their disposal the myriad interviews that the ABLD had conducted back in 1971 with the National Guardsmen and doctors who had been at Attica on the day of the retaking. From these older interviews they knew that there were many they could call to testify. Indeed, the attorneys' deep familiarity with Attica meant that they had quite a few disinterested witnesses such as doctors who had tried to assist the wounded in the immediate aftermath of the shooting, National Guardsmen who had witnessed prisoners being tortured following the retaking, and even high-profile former Attica observers. Some of these witnesses, such as observer John Dunne, had reported the horrors he witnessed at the time and yet they had continued—exactly the sort of evidence that could prove the plaintiffs' arguments.[9]

And the plaintiffs also had many former Attica prisoners who themselves could testify as to the trauma they had endured while state officials like Mancusi or Oswald had looked on. Although there were literally hundreds of these men who could have testified, ultimately the plaintiffs' case relied upon just a handful—but their harrowing tales of abuse certainly were sufficient to show just how cruel and callous the state of New York had been at Attica back in September of 1971. The witness list of men from D Yard included Richard Clark, Herbert Blyden, Akil Al-Jundi, Carlos Roche, Jerry Rosenberg, and, of course, Frank "Big Black" Smith.[10]

Unusually, the testimony of these witnesses was recorded in detail because of an earlier indiscretion in Judge Elfvin's personal life. Following an affair between Elfvin and the court reporter, she was no longer allowed to transcribe trials, so they now had to be taped. There was much drama to record throughout this trial—what Elfvin's clerk who had kept this case alive, Ellen Yacknin, called "pure theater in the courtroom."[11] Captured on the tapes were Liz Fink's impassioned statements that, according to Yacknin, "mesmerized the jury," as well as much heated bickering between Judge Elfvin and the various attorneys, which he, at least, seemed to greatly enjoy.[12]

The jury hearing all of this was a virtually all-white, all-working-class group of men and women from upstate New York. This was in no small part because in federal cases the judge questions prospective jurors and

Judge Elfvin, over the strong protests of the plaintiff lawyers, had refused to consider race or a juror's potential racial biases when conducting his voir dire. Nevertheless, the evidence brought to bear in this case left every man and woman in the jury box visibly stunned.

One witness, a medical specialist and a sergeant major in the New York National Guard named David Burke, had been assigned to deal with the many wounded men who covered the yards at Attica. He testified that troopers and COs at Attica had prevented him from loading the ambulances, and that certain Attica staff physicians had treated the prisoners cruelly.[13] One doctor was "speaking to the inmates and saying, you say you're hurt? You're not hurt? We'll see if you're hurt. And he was kicking and hitting them," disregarding their "visible wounds."[14] Sickened at the sight of "more blood, more gunshot wounds, and more injuries that day, than most people see in a typical day of combat. Certainly in Vietnam," Burke as well as his fellow National Guardsman Dr. John Cudmore had tried to stop the abuse—to no avail.[15]

Other disinterested parties corroborated this witness's testimony. Dr. David Breen, who had been a third-year medical resident at the State University of New York at Buffalo in 1971, had headed for Attica in an ambulance "with seven or eight people, including several surgical residents and blood bank technicians" as soon as Mancusi finally called for some doctors.[16] Breen confirmed that Attica's own doctors had been abusive toward the wounded men in the yard. He repeated a story he had originally told years earlier that no one had been interested in hearing at the time: he had seen Dr. Selden Williams near a Spanish-speaking prisoner with a serious gunshot wound to his leg who was hysterical and nearly delirious with pain.[17] While the prisoner kept trying to sit up, the doctor kept trying to force him back down. Finally this wounded prisoner had been "struck on the head with a blunt object by a security guard . . . a very severe blow to the head" while Dr. Williams, according to this witness, just looked on impassively.[18] While on duty in the prison's poorly staffed hospital, Breen had watched as "a number of inmates [were] struck by security personnel, whether they were guards or prison guards or National Guardsmen, I don't know," he said, "but a number of prisoners were struck with clubs and other objects in the process of forcing them to comply with the demands that were being made on them."[19] The witness had been so upset by the trauma that he "made the contact with a newspaperman who put [him] in touch with the federal authorities"—who never did contact him.[20]

When Breen first arrived, he had been stunned to see that absolutely no medical care was being given to the hundreds of wounded prisoners in the yard.[21] Many men needed surgery but the medical facilities at the prison were spartan at best, and disturbingly, there was no "post-operative monitoring or care being provided at all" to those who had to undergo primitive emergency surgery.[22] Without such care, the prisoners had suffered horribly; they faced "respiratory obstruction, urinary tract obstruction, pain, bleeding; [and] a variety of complications [which] may occur following surgery, not the least of which is pain."[23] Yet despite the obvious agony of Attica's many wounded, this then-young medical resident noted, he saw no "meds being administered at all."[24]

A third witness, National Guardsman Dan Callahan, added further detail to the stories of abuse. Callahan testified that he had seen a gravely injured light-skinned black man being seriously hurt by a high-ranking CO: "They forced him to his knees, and at that point, the correction sergeant backed up a short distance and then ran forward and kicked the man in the face. . . . He immediately went limp and his head was hanging down, he was bleeding."[25] That same day, Callahan had also seen "a larger group of inmates who had been undressed. They were lying on their backs with their legs drawn up and shotgun shells had been placed on their knees."[26] Among that group Callahan had been particularly disturbed to see "an inmate who was lying on his back on what looked like a ping pong table, his feet touching the ground. He had been stripped, and a football had been placed either on his chest or on his neck;" and he was crying and begging for mercy.[27]

This man on the table, the jury could clearly see, was none other than Frank "Big Black" Smith, sitting near them in the courtroom flinching as Callahan recounted his nightmare.

Jurors also heard the gruesome account that former Guardsman James O'Day had originally recounted in 1972 to both state officials and federal employees of the Justice Department.[28] O'Day had witnessed a correction officer dump a wounded inmate from his stretcher onto the floor and then demand that the man "move and go down the walkway from Times Square towards C Block."[29] When he was unable to do so, the CO had taken a Phillips head screwdriver and, with "this prisoner . . . lying on his back with his knees up in the air and the guard reached down in the genital area of the rectum and poked this man four or five times and told him to get moving."[30] Even though O'Day's eyewitness account had not, back in 1972, persuaded the U.S. Justice Department that civil rights violations

Prison officials on the catwalk looking down into the yard in the immediate aftermath of the retaking *(From the Elizabeth Fink Papers)*

had taken place on the day of the retaking, Liz Fink very much hoped that O'Day's account would now persuade the jury.

Even if jurors might have doubted O'Day's testimony, the testimony of another state trooper who had participated in the retaking, Gerard Smith, made them suspect that O'Day hadn't seen the worst offenses. Trooper Smith pointed out that the NYSP men had deliberately removed every bit of identifying information—badges, nametags, and so on—so that authorities "couldn't identify what troop or . . . pinpoint the individual in case something happen[ed]."[31] Captain William Dillon of the New York State Police testified that he personally had told troopers to take off their identification and he, of course, was reporting to his superior, defendant John Monahan.[32] Gerard Smith also had terrible stories of prisoner abuse: One prisoner had lain motionless on the pavement, while a trooper "had his gun up to his head and . . . was shooting, the, this gentleman."[33] Some troopers "were going through tent city and different foxholes they [the prisoners] had built and . . . one that I saw explicitly just stuck the rifle into the hole and pulled the trigger and then check[ed] the area out."[34] Smith saw another trooper drop a prisoner "off of C Catwalk into the yard, 15 feet down, and he was already hurt"; meanwhile, other prisoners were "being hit in the head."[35]

As horrible as the stories from these disinterested witnesses were, the testimony from the men who had experienced the abuses firsthand had the greatest impact on the jury. One Attica prisoner had been cowering near the hostage circle, and when he didn't lie down to the liking of a state trooper, he "was shot above the knee."[36] Another prisoner, who had been shot twice, testified to finding himself in the midst of countless bodies on the ground, "like they had those slave ships. . . . There was people packed on top of people. I was pushed, I fell down and I couldn't breathe and somebody was on top of me, I was on top of somebody else, and there was like stacks and stacks of people."[37] He had panicked because he couldn't breathe, but "they was telling us, keep your head down, so I'm trying, I can't breathe, I'm trying to crawl and I'm trying to get the person up off of me."[38]

Later that night, he had found himself in a cell, naked: "There was a lot of hollering and a lot of cells open and they were trying to take people out. . . . I did hear a lot of noise. I heard gunshots. At one point when it was very quiet, then the lights went on, then there was hollering, and then they were shining lights in your face and you know, they shined the light at my face and everybody's face in the cell. They was going from cell to cell doing it."[39] The guards were looking for so-called leaders to bring to HBZ. The prisoner went into shock from his two gunshot wounds, and from the cold air pouring in through the shattered windows.[40]

For the Attica Brothers and their lawyers, it was imperative in this case that the jury should not only be persuaded that reckless torture, abuse, and medical neglect had taken place, but also that the defendants had known about it, had overseen it, and may even have ordered it. Although many of the defendants from the original list had been absolved, either because they hadn't been properly served, or because the judge had allowed them out, Liz Fink believed that key officials could still be linked to the abuse. After all, Commissioner Russell Oswald was in charge of the entire Department of Corrections, Superintendent Vincent Mancusi and his assistant Karl Pfeil had been in charge of the prison from the moment the retaking shooting ceased, and Major John Monahan had been the leader of the NYSP's assault on the prison. The plaintiffs had to show the jury that these individuals had been instrumental in creating the situation that had led to so much suffering and trauma during the retaking, or been liable for not stopping the horrific abuses that continued later.

Numerous witnesses, even when they didn't necessarily intend to help the plaintiffs, provided strong support for the plaintiffs' case. Former Attica observer and New York state senator John Dunne's time on the stand left no doubt that Attica's own prison officials had been all too aware of the abuses taking place on their watch. By 1991 Dunne was serving as the U.S. assistant attorney general for civil rights, appointed by George H. W. Bush, and thus he made a highly credible witness. As Dunne told the jury, on the morning of the retaking he had been touring the facility on a catwalk looking down into the yard, and he had seen "naked men running in a direction toward me through a row of correction officers who were striking them with their batons on buttocks."[41] Dunne and his guide, DOCS deputy commissioner Walter Dunbar, both saw two long lines of correction officers "hitting men."[42] Dunne "was shocked. . . . Horrified. . . . Embarrassed on the part of the establishment," and he told the jury that he had actually told Dunbar "Walter, I am seeing something I shouldn't be seeing and it better stop."[43]

Testimony about the negligence of medical care came from pathologist Michael Baden, who had been tasked with reviewing the findings of John Edland's prisoners' autopsies. Based on those autopsies, Baden was able to assess whether better medical care might have saved lives at Attica.[44] The case of prisoner Sam Melville was indicative: Melville had died of "a shotgun slug that entered the left upper chest and caused his lung to collapse."[45] However, Baden made clear, "if he had been found and identified and diagnosed and treated in a rapid manner, this is the type of wound that could be recovered from."[46]

Equally damning in terms of specific defendants causing, via their orders, specific harm that came to prisoners, the jury heard from troopers whose testimony clearly supported the claim that Monahan was indeed the main man making the retaking decisions on the 13th.[47] Drawing from those accounts Liz Fink argued to the jury that "Monahan had the biggest responsibility," not only because he was the head of Troop A, the main State Police unit from Batavia there to retake the prison from the first day of the uprising, but also because other members of the NYSP had also testified that "he was the operational commander . . . that he was the person in charge."[48] Even though it was a man much higher up the chain of command than Monahan, Lieutenant Colonel George Infante, who had, for example, allowed retaking troopers such as "Mr. Barbolini to resign, rather than to prosecute him with the three counts of first degree, or second degree murder, [that would have] put him in jail for 25 to life," Liz explained to the jury that even he was reporting to Monahan then.[49]

According to Fink, Deutsch, and Heath, however, Monahan was not the only official at fault. Plaintiff attorneys established from witness testimony that some of the most egregious incidents of abuse took place in the yard during the rehousing, and during the night of the assault, when Karl Pfeil was "the highest correctional officer" present.[50] Pfeil admitted that he had seen correction officers in his command "using too much power to put someone down, or that they were cursing or shouting," insisting that he had "told several, be professional, please, keep it down. Do your job more professionally."[51] When pressed, he had to admit that he had left the COs and troopers without supervision, and had not followed up on whether they heeded his warning. Pfeil tried to shift the blame for their actions to his deputy, telling the jury that "I know that Leon Vincent was down there and I assumed he was in charge," but his own testimony that Vincent had been with him in the administration building, not in the yard, undermined that defense.[52] The plaintiffs argued that Pfeil hadn't reined in his own people and, worse, he had "decided to go home in the period immediately following the retaking, when the risk of violence was high."[53] This was a crucial argument: the claim against Pfeil depended not upon his personally and directly participating in any acts of abuse, but on what he did or did not do as the supervisor of the men who did commit these acts.

Throughout the trial, the defense team's strategy had largely focused on trying to discredit witnesses, rather than defending their clients' actions. This strategy tended to backfire, for example when Oswald's attorney, John Stenger, tried to discredit a National Guardsman by drawing attention to his avoiding service in Vietnam. As *The New York Times* reported their exchange:

> Mr. Stenger noted that Mr. Burke had told the jury he had been trained as a combat medic. "But you've never seen any combat, right?" Mr. Stenger asked.
>
> "I beg your pardon?" answered the witness.
>
> "Have you ever seen any combat?" the lawyer persisted.
>
> "I think," Mr. Burke said, "I saw combat that day, sir."[54]

By January 9, 1992, all testimony had been heard, closing remarks from both sides had been delivered, and Judge Elfvin was ready to give the jury its instructions to begin deliberation. The judge's jury instructions, however, were confusing and included inaccurate standards for judging the case. Elfvin told the jury that "the standard was wantonness" but then indicated that context is important. Jurors, he suggested, had to decide if the situation in the yard was riotous, not riotous, or somewhere in between, then apply either a sadistic and malicious standard, a deliberate indifference standard, or some hybrid of the two.[55] The plaintiffs' attorney Michael Deutsch expressed his dissatisfaction to the judge: "We are very troubled by these jury instructions [because] you have created a situation where you juxtapose what you consider normal versus emergency. Now, obviously, it was not normal what was going on here at Attica. . . . But what we are talking about didn't occur where there was still an emergency either—[nothing] that would have justified excessive anything."[56] Deutsch elaborated: "We would ask that it be made specifically clear as to the medical care that it falls within the non-quelling, after the riot was quelled or within a non-emergency situation, and there's [thus] no need to apply any kind of gradated standard on that question" of liability.[57] They had proven under the law, Deutsch insisted, that state officials were negligent in this case and he was not going to sit by while the judge tried to muddy the matter with flawed instructions to the jury.

As Liz Fink saw it, Elfvin's instructions implied to the jury that in order to rule for the plaintiffs "everyone had to be a sadist when that wasn't the standard."[58] She objected as well to the fact that Elfvin characterized Attica to the jury as a facility filled with "dangerous prisoners" when days of testimony had shown clearly that this wasn't "even most of the time the case."[59] Despite the fact that she and her fellow lawyers argued these points through most of the long day, Elfvin was unmoved and Fink had to be content with noting on the record that "we believe you committed a reversible error."[60]

As the jury began its deliberations, a new drama erupted. Judge Elfvin decided to take a vacation to Barbados, explaining that he would read their sealed verdict a month later when he returned.[61] The press was incredulous, and the plaintiff attorneys were furious, that the judge would take a holiday in the midst of a trial as important as this one. Everyone knew that Elfvin usually took this vacation at this time of year but had tried to dissuade him from doing so.

Upon hearing that Elfvin had actually departed for Barbados, Liz Fink and her fellow lawyers tracked him down by phone, pleading once more to get him to come back to Buffalo. All Elfvin said in reply was "They tell me there's a lot of bloviating in the paper this morning. I haven't read it myself, about the fact that the judge is leaving and the jury is continuing deliberations, so I guess you better put it on the record whatever you feel."[62] Michael Deutsch replied, "Judge, I guess what we're concerned about is what happens if you're gone and the jury has a substantive issue that needs to be addressed?"[63] "They cannot be addressed," Elfvin stated bluntly. "Now, if they get stuck in that situation on all four [defendants]," he went on, "the best I can come up with right now is they'd have to wait for me to come back."[64] Joe Heath then erupted. "The fact that substantive issues could not be resolved and the jury deliberations would have to be truncated and they would have to move on, is certainly a problem to us. . . . As you know this is a very serious matter."[65] The judge remained unmoved.

To Elfvin's surprise his own boss, the chief judge of the Western District, Michael Telesca, then got involved.[66] As Telesca recalled, he immediately ordered Elfvin home because over that weekend the jury had a really tough time. The phone system wasn't working so they couldn't contact Elfvin with their questions and, meanwhile, *The New York Times* was asking Telesca for his reaction to Elfvin's having abandoned the case for the beach. So he called Elfvin himself, and they had "a spirited discussion."[67] Elfvin came back to New York the next day.

But Elfvin returned to the courtroom furious and spiteful. He punished the jury for its role in cutting his vacation short by instructing them that they would now "work around the clock to come to a decision."[68] Outraged, the jurors wrote to the judge on January 22, 1992, "We, the Attica jury, feel an urgent need to register a response."[69] These men and women acknowledged the historic significance of the Attica case and the honor they felt to be considering it, but they took their duty as jurors "conscientiously, seriously, diligently, and steadfastly."[70] For many of them, "a good night's sleep had become but a vague and illusive memory of days gone by," and now they suddenly felt "pressured and in a very real sense punished" because they were unwilling to rush their verdict.[71] In closing, they wrote, "Our goal is justice, whether it takes two weeks or two months. . . . The pressure and stress at times seems unbearable, but we continue to persevere."[72]

Judge Elfvin's treatment of the jury, combined with the plaintiffs' evidence against the state officials, did not seem to bode well for the defendants. If one were to lay bets, most would have said that the Attica Brothers would finally be able to hold state officials accountable for all that had been done to them at Attica. And yet the judge's instructions had confused the

Liz Fink and the victorious Attica Brothers outside the courthouse in Buffalo, 1992 *(Courtesy Mike Groll/*The New York Times*)*

jury, and had, additionally, "caused major confusion with the jury sheets [by offering jurors] too many options."[73]

In the end, the jury found that the civil rights of Attica's prisoners had been violated during and after the retaking of the prison but, when it came to deciding which of the four defendants on trial should be held responsible, it was split. Ultimately jurors were only able to agree that one man, Attica's Assistant Deputy Superintendent Karl Pfeil, had been responsible for the acts committed at Attica—they believed he had been "part of the planning and then personally oversaw the brutality."[74] With regard to the responsibility of the other three—Superintendent Mancusi, Commissioner Oswald, who had died in March of 1991, and Major Monahan of the State Police, who had died in 1987—the jury was hung.

Although disappointed that so many defendants had escaped legal censure, Attica's surviving prisoners were still elated that their ordeal had been acknowledged in the verdict against Pfeil and that they would finally be awarded some damages. Importantly, if any defendant was found liable, the state was liable, and this was no small thing. First Assistant Attorney General of New York Richard Rifkin was already telling reporters that he was willing to begin negotiations regarding the "state payment on behalf of Mr. Pfeil."[75] However, when exactly they would receive the money, and how much they would get, was not yet clear. As one newspaper speculated, the issue of damages would be resolved "either through a settlement or a final legal ruling years from now."[76] And yet, so much time had already passed, it was hard to imagine holding on through more delays.

## 50

# Delay Tactics

While the plaintiffs were satisfied, the defendant Karl Pfeil felt the trial had been supremely unfair. In his view, he had been one of the least powerful men in the chain of command at Attica during the rebellion there. Somehow the governor of New York, the commissioner of corrections, his own boss, Vincent Mancusi, and even Major John Monahan, who had actually led the assault on the prison, had not been found liable, but he was. To be sure, both Oswald and Monahan had passed away, but that mattered not. If he was liable, then surely they, or more technically their estates, should have been as well. Though Pfeil couldn't comprehend the reasons for the verdicts, Liz Fink and her team understood just what had led to such a strange outcome in this case and she had every intention of using this knowledge to make sure the other defendants did not, in fact, get off scot-free.

A key reason why so many of the defendants had skated was because of the way the case complaint had been written. In essence, the original complaint had named specific defendants in connection with specific violations—for example, naming Monahan for his role in the assault but not for the reprisals, Mancusi for his role in the reprisals, but not in the neglectful medical care. The jury was asked only to consider if Mancusi was liable for the ugly reprisals; therefore it could not even consider other ways in which each defendant may have been liable for other actions they had or had not taken in 1971.

Determined to leave no stone unturned in this regard, Fink decided to file a key motion "to amend the complaint so as to add causes of action against Defendant Mancusi for failure to provide the plaintiffs with medical care in violation of their constitutional rights and against the estate of Monahan for the reprisals that plaintiffs suffered after the retaking," and filed a similar motion to add in Oswald for the reprisals.[1] In the first motion she argued that "the facts presented during the 1992 liability trial make it clear that there is more than sufficient evidence to support a verdict against Defendant Mancusi for failure to provide medical care and a verdict against the Defendant Estate of Monahan for the reprisals suffered by the plaintiffs."[2] Ultimately Elfvin dodged these motions. Although he eventually ruled that "the verdict against Pfeil should be taken as ascribing responsibility to Pfeil and Oswald and Mancusi for any and all reprisals for which any of them had the requisite . . . involvement" per the Civil Rights Act, it didn't alter the jury's decision and, thus, Pfeil alone remained legally liable.[3]

Pfeil refused to accept the jury's decision in his case.[4] He would try to capitalize on Judge Elfvin's convoluted jury instructions and verdict sheets, arguing in his own appeal that the plaintiffs had failed to show liability because "the special verdict questions were not properly submitted or correctly phrased in accordance with the facts of the case and the applicable law," and, thus, that "jury and counsel misconduct deprived him of a fair trial."[5] What is more, "the passage of over twenty years since the events deprived him of an opportunity to be heard at a meaningful time and in a meaningful manner as is required by due process."[6]

Judge Elfvin was tired of being challenged. He responded firmly: "This court finds that there was sufficient evidence for reasonable jurors to return the verdicts which were rendered against Pfeil. This Court has considered all of Pfeil's other contentions and also finds them to be without merit."[7]

While Judge Elfvin was not willing to let either the plaintiffs or defendant Pfeil revisit the jury's decision, or what had led to it, he also seemed unwilling to move the case forward to determine damages in the wake of that decision. Elfvin's clerk Ellen Yacknin put it bluntly: "Judge Elfvin made decisions to deliberately delay the cases."[8] There were a number of ways to handle the damage awards in the case and Elfvin seemed loath to embark on any of them. There could be negotiations with the state that would result in a settlement of an agreed-upon amount; or there could be a jury trial, or several of them, to determine damages. At one point Judge Elfvin was so frustrated with the plaintiffs' mounting pressure on him to settle the issue of compensation, he threatened to insist upon 1,200 separate damages trials, which would be impossible for their lawyers to handle.[9]

From Liz Fink's point of view, the best thing that could happen for her clients, many of whom by now were very ill or had already died, was to settle this case. Yet even for this to happen, there was much work to be done. She and her team first had to go through "incredible work" to make sure that any potential class member in this class action suit was notified that they had a right to this settlement. As she recalled, "Judge Elfvin made me pay notice to the class in the most expensive way possible. He, for example, ordered that I put a notice in *USA Today*."[10] Then, to facilitate the distribution of monetary awards, the plaintiffs' attorneys had to devise a questionnaire to determine who had suffered exactly which violations of their Eighth Amendment rights—cruel and unusual punishment.[11]

In 1994 a frustrated Liz Fink wrote to Judge Elfvin indicating that they had settled upon six clear categories of damages and that she had all of the information regarding which of the plaintiffs fell into which category:

1. those "who suffered physical reprisals before they were locked in their cells"
2. those "who suffered physical reprisals before they were locked into their cells and who were subjected to mental torture after they were locked in their cells"
3. those "who suffered physical and mental reprisals both before and after they were locked in their cells"
4. those "who were subjected to special and extraordinary physical reprisals before they were locked in and who were subjected to mental torture after they were locked in"
5. those "who were subjected to special and extraordinary physical and mental reprisals both before and after they were locked in"
6. those "who suffered injuries sustained in D Yard who were also subjected to reprisals"[12]

Judge Elfvin's response made it abundantly clear that he still was in no hurry to move forward. In fact, he actively muddied the situation by suggesting, for example, that Pfeil should, now three years after the liability trial, appeal the verdict.[13] Incredulous, Fink penned a scathing letter to the judge reminding him of the extraordinary time and resources her team had put into preparing for the damages trials, which, she noted, had already been scheduled for that November.[14] "Now, suddenly, on the brink of trial," she wrote, "Your Honor unilaterally—and without consent of counsel—has cancelled the scheduled damage trials," and worse, he had invited Pfeil to appeal at this late date.[15] Pulling no punches, Fink declared, "this suggestion is unconscionable and not consistent with fairness and justice."[16]

Despite the fact that there had indeed already been "three years of status conferences concerning the damages issues," and that defendant Pfeil was in the plaintiffs' view now raising a "specious argument that damages upon the reprisals verdict cannot be awarded until after there has been a determination of liability for the assault," the judge still refused to set a date for any damages trials.[17] The years continued to drag on.[18]

Meanwhile, Liz Fink and the rest of her team worked to be sure they would be ready in case they could move Elfvin to begin the damages trials on schedule. They pored over scores of depositions that had been taken which indicated who had been tortured at Attica and in what manner. In one deposition, Akil Al-Jundi (aka Herbie Scott Dean) told how he had been forced to crawl from D Yard to A Yard, and run a brutal gauntlet, and then received an ugly beating from CO Donald Jennings.[19] "Call on your Allah now. See, Allah can't save you," Al-Jundi said Jennings had shouted while landing blow after blow.[20] Al-Jundi endured all of this after suffering a gunshot in the hand during the retaking—from an unjacketed bullet that literally blew out the back of his hand. The wound was so big that one could see daylight through it, and it would eventually require "16 major and 16 minor operations" to heal.[21]

Fink and her team spent untold resources getting many of the Attica Brothers seen by doctors, including psychiatrists, so that there would be a clear and dispassionate assessment of just how much damage had been done to these plaintiffs by officers of the state. Every report that came back made clear that the physical and mental damages these men had suffered were extensive. As one doctor wrote of an Attica prisoner he examined, "He describes being in a cell with four other men without water, food, or clothing for two days or more" and recorded this man's own words: "I know what a person can do to me now, I have become withdrawn and introverted. I want to be left totally alone."[22] Another physician diagnosed a prisoner with suffering severe post-traumatic stress syndrome in addition to physical trauma because this man had been stripped and, as he had described it to the doctor, been "paraded around" naked like a trophy by the State Police who were making all kinds of "obscene statements . . . jokes about penis size, etc."[23]

Liz Fink knew well that it could still be a long time before Elfvin would begin damages trials where she could actually use these depositions or psychiatric reports. She now had years of experience watching Elfvin drag his feet in the original case and thus had no reason to think he would act any differently in the damages phase. Perhaps, she thought, there was a way to settle this directly with the state of New York. After all, when the Pfeil verdict was handed down, First Assistant Attorney General Richard Rifkin had seemed open to discussing this. So in 1992 Fink decided to contact Elfvin's boss, the man who had yanked him back from Barbados, Chief Judge Michael Telesca, to see if he would be willing to help broker a settlement with the state. She assured Telesca, "The defendants have no objection to a settlement process and agree that a judicial intervention might be helpful."[24]

Telesca was well aware that this settlement was going to take political finesse. As he later put it, "I knew that all roads led to Albany. It was going to be a political decision before any money was had."[25] Telesca was not sure that he was the right one to oversee such negotiations so he punted the task to another judge. He explained to the plaintiffs that he would help them manage a settlement if one was brokered, but he felt that Magistrate Judge Edmund Maxwell (a jurist who years earlier had heard testimony from prisoners regarding abuses at Attica) should conduct the actual negotiations and report back to him.[26] Behind the scenes, even though Maxwell was officially in charge, Telesca too "made a number of discreet inquiries and let them know that all I wanted from them was the money. The cases would go away forever. In short, they would be buying a hell of a lot of absolution."[27]

Telesca was having a hard time making any "headway with the state."[28] The biggest barrier to settling with these plaintiffs was "the idea that it would be tantamount to an apology. The state was not about to apologize."[29] He even tried to address this issue head-on, assuring the state, "There will be no apologies (since I knew one wasn't forthcoming)," and yet still he could see they weren't ready to budge.[30] Even the affable Magistrate Maxwell was getting nowhere with the state. So Fink decided that the attorney general's office needed another firm push.

It just so happened that Liz Fink and Michael Deutsch were at this time also working on another case currently being tried in front of Judge Jack Weinstein, "the most impressive judge in the court," as far as Fink was concerned. Weinstein was "one of the top five district judges in the country" and, as important to Fink, "he was Mr. Class Action—he had settled cases related, for example, to Agent Orange."[31] When Fink found herself in front of Judge Weinstein, she broached the subject of the Attica case and asked for his help. Weinstein was reluctant to get involved but she pushed, assuring him that Maxwell would appreciate his help. The next day, Weinstein had to be out of the court so a different magistrate was in charge. Unexpectedly Judge Weinstein arrived with Ken Feinberg, another attorney known for his mediation and settlement skills. Feinberg seemed eager to get involved and offered to take advantage of his regular communication with the attorney general's office to suss out whether the state was really serious about settling. He said, "I will ask Cuomo."[32] This was big news since he was talking about approaching the then governor of New York, Mario Cuomo.

A few days later, according to Liz Fink, Feinberg confirmed that the state had no intention of compromising and also that First Assistant Attorney General Richard Rifkin, whom Fink had been counting on, had no authority to make any deal. When Fink called Rifkin to see if this was true, he was surprised to hear that he had no power to make a deal. He ended the call to look into the situation, and called Fink back almost right away to say, "You're right, I don't."[33]

Demoralized, Fink again turned to Telesca and, with the help of court clerk Ellen Yacknin, managed to get him more overtly and actively involved in trying to seek a settlement. But Telesca also got nowhere with the state and so he decided to lean on Elfvin again, to hold some damages trials. Under pressure from his boss, Judge Elfvin finally scheduled two damages trials: instead of one main trial to decide damages for each Attica prisoner in the class, there would be one trial that would set the highest level of damages a prisoner in the class could get, based on the case of the torture suffered by Frank "Big Black" Smith, and a second trial to set the lowest level of damages a prisoner in the class could receive, based on what an Attica prisoner by the name of David Brosig had suffered on the day of the retaking. Frank Smith's trial was set to begin on May 29, 1997.[34]

## 51

# The Price of Blood

Finally, more than twenty-five years after the smoke had cleared over Attica, a damages trial began on behalf of Attica survivor Frank "Big Black" Smith. But this Attica Brother had not just been waiting for justice to be done. He had worked as Liz Fink's paralegal to bring the original civil rights case to trial in 1991 and had labored since to make sure that all surviving Attica prisoners were told of the class of which they were a part and were informed that damages trials would now begin. He would have to relive everything one more time, in order to make sure the jury knew how barbarically he and his fellow prisoners had been treated in 1971, but this time he would make sure he was really heard.

The damages trials would be quite different from the 1991 trial that determined Karl Pfeil's liability. Entirely new juries had to be constituted, and the issues they would hear were also very different from those in the previous trial. Since liability had already been established, each jury simply had to decide the amount of the monetary award the plaintiff would receive. The idea was that Big Black Smith's trial would set the high end of the damage award—no one in the class would receive more money than he did, and the only men to receive an equal amount would be the Attica Brothers who had already been placed in Category One—those who had suffered the most severe violations of their Eighth Amendment rights.

From the very first day of the trial, it was obvious to the press and jury why Big Black Smith's case had been selected as the benchmark for the high-end damage amount. Liz Fink refused to sugarcoat the brutality at the heart of this case; in her opening statement she also emphasized just how long prisoners like Frank Smith had been fighting to get some justice from the state of New York. That first morning, she told the jurors how Smith had tirelessly "led the fight for justice with the prisoners who are at Attica," even after he was released from prison in August 1973.[1] She reminded the jury that "what this case is about, ladies and gentlemen . . . is torture. . . . This was torture that lasted for hours, that was physical, was race-based, and was psychological. This was torture that was witnessed by others and these witnesses will come in and testify before you about what they saw happen to him and their reactions to what they saw."[2]

Unsurprisingly, the lawyer now representing Karl Pfeil, Mitch Banas, tried to paint a very different picture for the jury. He stated bluntly, "You will hear very little medical proof of what actually happened, injuries actually suffered by Mr. Smith. You won't be hearing about casts or stitches or surgery, what you will hear about are bumps and bruises and bandages."[3] Further, he argued that Smith's injuries "have not prevented him from earning a living, have not diminished his earning capacity, have not significantly impacted the way he lives his day-to-day life, and have not otherwise stopped him from leading a productive life."[4]

But Banas's words seemed absurd from the moment that Big Black took the stand. By now, Big Black was sixty-four years old. He had been fighting to be heard, and for the state of New York to be held accountable for its actions, for much of his adult life; he was going to make sure that the jury understood exactly what had happened to him. Black's testimony transported the jury back to the hazy, gas-choked prison yard where he and hundreds of other men had been forced to strip naked and crawl or stumble across the muddy rutted yard while suffering repeated blows from troopers and COs. He testified quietly,

> I kept hearing my name, I was crawling as everyone was made to do and I kept hearing my name, Where's Big Black, where's Big Black and then eventually someone said, there he is, there's the nigger, we got him now. . . . He came over to me and said, get up nigger, and kicked me and I got up. . . . It was Mr. [Howard] Holt . . . officer I worked for in the laundry. . . . He said, get up nigger and I got up and walked some and he pushed me some and I fell back down and then I got up and I walked across the yard with him pushing me, other officers joined him and they led on the side up to A block tunnel and placed me on the table.[5]

According to Black, the officers kept saying "that I had castrated an officer . . . and they was gonna do it to me." He had pleaded with them,

"I didn't do it, I didn't do anything like that, you all know I didn't do anything like that, why you doing this to me."[6] These men, however, were unmoved. "They say you like to play football, we going to put this football into you, nigger and then we gonna kill you."[7] On the stand, with tears streaming down his face and voice choked up, Black explained to the jurors how these men had shoved a football under his chin and told him that if he let it drop, they would shoot him. His voice choked up as he tried to convey to the jurors what it had felt like to lie on that table for more than five hours being tortured, trying to keep that football from falling, looking beseechingly up to the catwalks where state employees and officials were looking down, and to have known that none of them would intervene to stop his abuse.[8]

As the men on the ground struck him repeatedly in the testicles and shouted threats, the men above "were spitting on me, dropping cigarettes on me and the shell casings from fired weapons was dropped on me and

Frank "Big Black" Smith (on table) and other prisoners were tortured for hours as their fellow prisoners were marched past them. *(From the Elizabeth Fink Papers)*

kicked from the catwalk down onto me. . . . I was scared and they told me not to move, and I would flex my body to make the cigarette fall off me, hopefully, so it wouldn't burn too long."[9] His legs hung over the edge of table for six hours, until they started to go numb. "I kept trying to move them to keep some kind of feeling in them," he explained, but he was terrified of moving too much lest the football fall. Ironically, he recalled, "the football became a part of me. I felt that it was good that the football was there, it gave me something to concentrate on and to deal with how I was feeling. . . . I was afraid that if it wasn't there, if it would fall that they would do something to me."[10]

Looking at the jurors, Big Black wept more as he told them, "I was scared, you know I was afraid, and I kept thinking . . . how could a person say that and do these things to another person, regardless of the fact that I was an inmate."[11] He spoke of the pain he had been in: "My head was hurting and my side was hurting, my back was hurting, my leg was hurting and the most excruciating pain I had was in my testicles. . . . It was a very excruciating pain at that time that I was laying on the table in my genital area."[12]

When he had at last been ordered off of the table, he had been there for over six hours; when he tried to shift his weight, he could hardly move. "I sat up and my legs were dead and, you know, I fell to the ground, to my knees and I tried to get up again, trying to balance myself on the table and I got pushed, I got hit then and I finally got enough strength to get up and to go to the doorway. I was scared, I was beyond scared."[13] Somehow Black managed finally to get himself to the door of A Block, but his heart almost stopped at the sight of "twenty to forty, maybe fifty officers on two sides and in the middle they had glass on the floor and I was told to go through there." Still completely naked, he endured the blows of "ax handles and the baton and pig handles"[14] as he ran this gauntlet. "I was pushed, I was hit, I fell down, I was drugged [dragged]; I went through a lot, lots of licks to my arm, to my leg, to my back, to my head."[15] The pain, Black repeated, had been horrendous. "I mean pain, it's just pain, unbearable pain . . . my testicles . . . my fingers cut and arms and back is sore . . . I'm just, I'm full of pain."[16] There was ugly emotional pain too as he was forced to endure an endless barrage of "vile racial attacks, slurs."[17]

From A Tunnel, Big Black was forced to run through another gauntlet on the way to HBZ where he knew he would be in more danger.[18] When he arrived in Housing Block Z, Black "was knocked to the floor and they was beating me on my arms and on my legs and on my back, they bust my head. . . . I passed out, blacked out, because the next thing I remember, I was in a dark room by myself."[19] By this time he had blood running down his face; yet the ordeal was still far from over.[20] Once he had been placed in a cell, troopers and COs made Black lie on the cold cement floor, still naked, legs spread-eagle. "Open your legs for us nigger, we gonna take it," at least three correction officers were shouting at him as they continued to hit his genitals and began playing Russian roulette at his head.[21]

Finally, someone had put Black on a stretcher, ostensibly to take him out of HBZ to get some medical care for his injuries. "They put me on a stretcher," he recalled for the jury, "and I could remember that first someone came in and put like a little gauze or something on my wound and I was placed on a stretcher and I was taken in the pharmacy's part of the hospital where a bunch of other people was laying all over the floor."[22] Suddenly, though, Big Black was yanked back up to HBZ and, on the way, he was summarily "dumped on the floor [of the elevator] and was made to scoot my buttock up flush against the wall with my feet up on the wall with me laying on my back" while being threatened with more injury.[23] When the elevator doors opened he was told, amid jeers, shouts, and laughter, to run along the hallway to his cell, and was once again beaten along the way.[24] Indeed, Black said, some of the worst pain he had experienced that day was actually in his wrists, which were fractured because he had used them for so many hours to protect himself from the countless vicious blows to his body. His entire body by then was swollen.[25] More than twenty years later, he showed the jury how he still couldn't fully raise his right arm up over his head, his legs still swelled terribly from the damage he had suffered, and he still had burn marks everywhere.[26]

Although he was now once again contained in a cell, Black remained terrified, especially when correction officer Howard Holt came by. As he began praying as hard as he could for some protection, Holt, he told the jury, had pointed a gun at his head to play Russian roulette. While all of this was taking place, Karl Pfeil had passed by and looked into the cell. As Big Black recalled, "Mr. Holt was saying to him this is the person that castrated the officer and Pfeil is looking at me that uh-huh, and we gonna castrate him, oh, he's the one that castrated the officer, yeah, we gonna castrate him too."[27] Seeing that even an Attica supervisor like Pfeil was unmoved to protect him convinced Black that he had no one to help him in this isolated area of the prison and, should he die, no one would know or care. Still, even though Pfeil had merely looked on as Holt played Russian roulette with him, Black remembered, "I'm still praying and hoping that the real truth would come out" because he knew he was innocent.[28] "I didn't do this, and I was hoping someone would understand."[29] As he prayed his urine ran red with blood and both of his fractured wrists dangled limply.[30]

In the courtroom, Black felt good about having finally told his story on the record. But he was also embarrassed by his own tears and his inability to tell it more formally and perhaps clearly. "I think the crying is anger," he tried to explain to the jury.[31] His tears came unbidden, he went on, due to "the fact that I felt violated, helpless. . . . I could be walking the street, I could be driving the car, I cried at night in my bed, it's just something that bothers me."[32]

Multiple physical and psychological evaluations could have corroborated for the jury just how much this ordeal at Attica had scarred Black. He had received thorough evaluations, one well after the first trial had ended, and according to his physician it was obvious that this man still suffered from the horrific torture he had endured in 1971.[33] The doctor's notes read, "He reported that every time he thinks about what actually happened to him at Attica he starts crying; he gets angry; and then he becomes afraid that he will somehow lose control."[34] Notably, to deal with this trauma Big Black had turned first to drugs and then to God, which helped somewhat, but he was by no means healed either psychologically or physically. According to the doctor's report, "His injuries to his urogenital area were such that he urinated blood for about two years" and he still had nightmares, being unable to trust anyone in his life.[35] In the doctor's view it was indisputable that Big Black suffered severe post-traumatic stress disorder and, without question, it was what Black "experienced during the retaking of Attica and more importantly, the psychological and physical torture that he experienced after the prison was retaken that caused him to develop this disorder."[36]

To the plaintiff team's fury, however, Judge Elfvin would not allow Big Black's physician to share his informed conclusions with the jury because if he were "allowed . . . to give his opinion I would have [to have] allowed Mr. Pfeil to bring in his psychiatric expert to the courtroom to give his opinion."[37]

Fortunately, Liz Fink didn't rely solely on medical testimony to persuade the jury that Big Black had been tortured while Karl Pfeil looked on. She also made sure that the jury heard from several of the people who had testified at the liability trial in 1991, including National Guardsman Dan Callahan, who had witnessed some of the torture Black had suffered on the table in A Yard. Other witnesses to the abuses he had suffered included another Guardsman named Ronald Dill, who happened to open the door of the prison hospital and very clearly "saw the brutality committed against him."[38] Black had been on the floor writhing and begging for mercy, saying over and over again, "I didn't do it boss, I didn't do it boss."[39]

By the time the case came to a close on June 4, 1997, this jury was visibly shaken. In her closing remarks, an exhausted Liz Fink tried to stress how important it was for the men and women of the jury to really hear all Black had endured at Attica and every day since. True, she said, "the only thing you can do is give him money. And it doesn't make up for it, but it justifies the fight and it heals and gives you closure. And what money is about, what the monetary award is, is that it compensates Mr. Smith for what was done to him, for the hours he spent being tortured, and it makes an attempt—an attempt, ladies and gentlemen—an attempt to make him whole."[40]

Judge Elfvin once again gave an Attica jury instructions as it headed into deliberations. With every word he uttered, Big Black and his lawyers felt the judge was trying to undermine them. Elfvin opened by telling the jury that this whole trial had been "a very emotional situation for many of the parties involved" and opined that "some of the witnesses were very emotional, wrapped up in this whole matter."[41] He reminded the jurors that the first trial had already established that the prisoners' civil rights had been violated, so now they had to determine whether they were persuaded by the evidence presented to them in *this* trial as to the nature and extent of this violation of rights, and determine how those violations translated into a monetary sum.[42] However, he went on, although jurors accepted that reprisals had taken place at Attica against the prisoners, they still had to "determine whether this plaintiff, Mr. Smith, suffered and/or suffers and/or will suffer the effects of such" and, should they determine that he would get money, "any monetary award of damages must be reasonable."[43]

Big Black and his legal team looked on, stunned. Just as in the first trial, Judge Elfvin was trying to shape the outcome of the jury's deliberations by distorting his instructions by inserting his personal views of the case. They also couldn't believe, given these instructions, that the jury must decide if Black suffered psychological "effects," that Judge Elfvin had prevented the jury from hearing the conclusions drawn by a medical professional about the causes of Black's psychological trauma. As Michael Deutsch noted disgustedly on the record, "Just so the record is clear we do have an exception to the way the Court formulated the instructions as the psychological testimony" because "the defense psychiatrist . . . never came here to testify at all."[44] Elfvin's instructions to the jury that their award must be "reasonable" was equally galling and potentially costly to the plaintiffs. As they pointed out, what is reasonable to one party might well be unreasonable to another.

Notwithstanding Judge Elfvin's attempts to blunt the impact of the evidence and to limit their monetary award, jurors had listened carefully to the testimony and were moved by his ordeal. On June 5, 1997, they awarded Big Black $4 million in damages. It was Elfvin's turn to be stunned. Not only was this amount huge, but it was an amount that, given the structure of damage categories, many other former Attica prisoners would also be entitled to from the state of New York.[45]

On June 23, 1997, soon after this first headline-making award was announced, the second damages trial began for former Attica prisoner David Brosig. Brosig was "selected as an example of a prisoner who suffered the average level of harm common to all of the class members not singled out for special vengeance after the assault."[46] But "the average level of harm" at Attica during the retaking or in subsequent weeks was no easier to hear about than the traumas suffered by Big Black Smith.

Once again Liz Fink opened the trial by highlighting the importance of the jury's job in the case. This time she was flanked not only by Michael Deutsch and Joe Heath, but also by New York City lawyer Danny Meyers, who, like her, had been working on Attica cases for decades now.[47] Here it was, nearly thirty years later, she pointed out, and they still hadn't managed to secure justice for the scores of prisoners who had been so wantonly and horrifically abused. These jurors could help to remedy this, she reminded them, by awarding Attica survivor David Brosig substantial compensation for damages. Fink explained that Brosig was only in Attica in the first place on a minor parole violation. He had gotten into trouble as a kid and then got out, but then failed to report to his parole office.[48] At Attica, she went on, this young man was not only "beaten on several occasions unnecessarily," but was also "subjected to psychological torture, which affected him for the rest of his life."[49] The jurors' task, Fink made clear, was "to determine two things, whether Mr. Brosig suffered reprisals . . . actions which are taken that are sadistic, which are malicious and are for the very purpose of causing harm. And after you determine whether he was subjected to those kind of reprisals, it is your responsibility to set a monetary value, compensatory value on what he should get for those damages."[50]

The jury then heard Brosig's story firsthand. He was a shy man, unused to being in the spotlight, and he spoke quietly. "You couldn't crawl fast enough," he tried to explain to the jurors, shaking his head.[51] "You couldn't crawl too fast with your hands on your head, so the bodies—the people coming through the door started piling up on top of me. . . . I began to feel like I was getting crushed, suffocated. It was like being on the bottom of a giant pile and I know I had to get out of there. It is—I felt that there; that I would suffer—I would get hurt."[52] And so, Brosig went on, his impulse was to try to get up so that he might get some air. As he tried to stand, though, "a state trooper came up and he pointed a shotgun at my head and [said] pretty much the effect of nigger lover, you are going to die . . . and he hit me with the shotgun . . . it was enough to see stars."[53] "We were called nigger lovers," Brosig, who was white, explained. "We were told at times that we deserved to be killed. We were told that we didn't deserve to live, that we were nothing but garbage. Nobody would care." At this point, like Big Black before him, Brosig began to weep. And he too was embarrassed that he was so emotional—the jury heard a muffled "I'm sorry" as he tried to gather himself.[54] Eventually continuing, he told the story of his ordeal after the shooting stopped, being forced to get through the gauntlet of troopers and COs in A Tunnel. "You could hear the sounds of pain of the people being hit and you could hear angry remarks," he said sadly. "Pretty much racial epithets. Nigger, nigger lover . . ."[55]

As in the damages trial for Big Black, Fink made sure that the jurors heard plenty of corroboration of all that David Brosig had experienced from other witnesses. Just as Big Black's jury had, this jury also heard of retaking horrors from men such as observer John Dunne and National Guardsman Daniel Callahan. They also heard medical testimony, and, most movingly, from Brosig's former wife, Gail, about how much this man suffered in the years after the trauma of Attica's retaking.

When Liz Fink made her closing remarks on June 26, she felt that they had done all they could to make it clear in this courtroom that even those who had suffered the least torture at Attica would be permanently scarred. Through her witnesses she had proven that David Brosig had endured a sustained "terror which continued unabated for days and which reappears to this day, twenty-six years later, when he's close to fifty years old."[56] She reminded jurors how Brosig had described "the beatings; the screaming of the inmates, the sounds of sticks on flesh. . . . Here he is, twenty-one years old, naked, vulnerable, terrorized."[57]

Then, after the beatings, there was the period where Brosig had been ordered to stay standing for hours on end and threatened with death if he swayed or fell. "What was the justification for this?" Fink asked the jury, "There wasn't one. . . . They were made to stand because they wanted to terrorize and torture them. They were made to stand there for cruel and unusual punishment; for a malicious reason."[58]

"Imagine the terror," Fink said sadly. "And really, you don't have to stretch your imaginations, because you saw the effects of what happened to him when he testified. You saw him break down."[59] Perhaps worse than anything, "the torture that was inflicted upon Mr. Brosig . . . was not by the actions of law enforcement existing in places where barbarism is the law, but what happened here happened about fifty or so miles away, committed by people who are sworn to uphold the law and the constitution."[60]

In his closing remarks, defense attorney Mitch Banas focused on trying to make the jury question whether any of this horror was really Karl Pfeil's responsibility, even though the original trial had already determined that it was.[61] "Now I'm not here to tell you that nothing happened to Mr. Brosig at Attica on September 13, 1971," he stated in his closing remarks. "Obviously things happened to him. What I am here to do is to try to help you place what he says happened to him in the proper context."[62] That context, Banas suggested, was the utter chaos of a riot and a moment when ordinary people were simply trying to restore some semblance of order. As Banas said in conclusion,

> One of the things that's certainly beyond dispute in this case, is that there were extraordinary conditions prevailing at Attica on September 13th 1971. It was hardly a picnic there. Portions of the prison had been destroyed, Hostages were being held. Violent inmates had weapons that they could use against law enforcement officials . . . yes there was a need to conduct continuous head counts, even if it meant waking inmates up. Obviously, there was a need to strip the inmates and search them for weapons and make them lie down and move on the ground to make room for other inmates in D yard. None of that was retaliatory, and none of it was, in any way, malicious.[63]

"You have to ask yourself," he said in closing to the jury, "what injuries did Mr. Brosig really receive from that? . . . Most of the nightmares Mr.

Brosig testified about were abstract. . . . How often does Mr. Brosig have those nightmares, regardless of what they are about?"[64]

Yet again, though, even with Banas's alternative narrative at their disposal and with equally problematic jury instructions from Judge Elfvin, the jurors hearing this case had been appalled by the treatment that David Brosig had endured as a young man during the retaking of Attica. On July 16, 1997, they awarded him $75,000 in damages.[65]

Now the state was in real trouble. On the high end of the damages scale it was on the hook for $4 million, and on the low end it would have to pay out $75,000 to a class of 1,200 men. The state decided, immediately, to appeal the original liability case because, if that were to be overturned, the damage awards would go away.

As this appeal went forward, Liz Fink and the rest of the plaintiffs' attorneys were worried because they feared that the Second Circuit Court of Appeals would rule in such a way that protected the state from liability for the tens of millions of dollars the two damage verdicts indicated that the prisoners were now owed. They were correct. A three-judge panel of the United States Court of Appeals for the Second Circuit heard this case on July 16, 1998, and decided on August 3, 1999, that "jury verdict in the class liability phase 'failed to establish Pfeil's class-wide liability' " and thus the court "therefore reverse[d] both the liability and damages verdict."[66]

This decision was devastating and deeply ironic. The plaintiffs had argued vehemently that Judge Elfvin was committing "reversible errors" in the way that he had instructed the jury before its deliberation, but in their view these errors only benefited the defense. In this Circuit Court decision, however, the judges saw these same flawed instructions as working unfairly against Pfeil. In fact, Judge Ralph K. Winter wrote, Elfvin's jury instructions had "virtually ensured that the juries in the damages trial would be forced to consider issues of Mr. Pfeil's liability—a violation of the Seventh Amendment's bar on different, successive juries trying the same issue."[67]

In another irony, the court confirmed that Judge Elfvin had also caused serious problems with the jury verdict sheets he had issued. Winter's decision explained that the verdict sheet that the original jury had been given was flawed because the wording "did not require findings sufficient to support class-wide liability or even liability to particular, identifiable plaintiffs."[68] Rather than see this error as, again, benefiting the defense—since, for example, these flawed sheets were, in part, what let many defendants off the hook—in the court's opinion, this error had harmed Pfeil and therefore "the damage awards of Smith and Brosig must be reversed."[69] Pfeil's rights had been additionally violated, the decision went on, because Elfvin had allowed "the damages phase juries to revisit many of the same issues as were considered by the liability jury," and indeed Elfvin was directly chastised in this ruling for causing "confusion" in the damages trials when he "equivocated as to what had actually been established in the liability trial."[70] One of the most alarming aspects of the appeals court's decision, however, was that it "questioned the wisdom of Judge Elfvin in certifying a class action to begin with."[71] If the Attica Brothers were not determined to be a class, then any future attempts to hold anyone liable for their pain would have to be done one by one. Potentially, and unimaginably to lawyers like Liz Fink, justice would have to come via litigating 1,200 separate cases against the state.

Still, the Second Circuit made it clear that those 1,200 men had every right to have their concerns addressed, to come to some sort of resolution with the state of New York, now and not a minute later. Indeed, the decision made clear that "the defendants in this case" had "done all they could—frequently not without the court's acquiescence—to delay resolution" and "that strategy can no longer be tolerated."[72] And, "given the long history of this matter," it concluded, "we direct the district court to give it expedited treatment. We stand ready to exercise our mandamus power [to order a lower court to do this court's bidding] should unreasonable delay occur. We respectfully suggest that the Chief Judge of the district court consider assigning this matter to the judge that is best able to expedite its resolution."[73]

No matter how much it chastised Judge Elfvin, this panel's decision was heartbreaking to every one of the Attica survivors who were still alive as well as to the family members seeking justice for deceased relatives. Liz Fink too was bereft. She had known that Elfvin's jury instructions weakened the plaintiffs' chances of victory, but when the defense had appealed on the grounds that it weakened Pfeil's chances with the jury, she was forced to argue that these problematic instructions had, at worst, been harmless in light of the preponderance of the evidence they had presented of the state's liability. And, according to Ellen Yacknin, Fink was utterly "brilliant in mounting her argument" when she came before the Second Circuit.[74] Still, she was unable to stop that three-judge panel from undoing everything she had fought so hard to win in 1991 and 1997.

Yet giving up was, in Fink's view, not an option—especially considering how much had gone into the trials. At least the Second Circuit had not disputed the facts that the plaintiffs' lawyers had spent years establishing, and it also called for the state to stop dodging its responsibility to resolve this issue with the plaintiffs. It was time, Liz Fink decided, to reapproach Judge Michael Telesca. This time, the state of New York would be brought to the table.

## 52

# Deal with the Devil

By the time the Second Circuit Court upended the Attica civil case victory, it had been nearly three decades since the state had retaken the Attica Correctional Facility with extraordinary force. There was, Liz Fink hoped, still a chance to make the state officials take some responsibility for the trauma caused back in 1971. There was still the possibility that they could force the state to reach a settlement. That would at least be something. And so she called Ellen Yacknin and asked her to ask Judge Michael Telesca of the Western District if he was still willing to try to settle the case. He was. And, as Yacknin reassured the plaintiffs, he was a damned "good settler."[1]

Telesca was a bit incredulous that here he was, this many years later, still trying to get the state of New York to do the right thing. Couldn't the attorney general's office understand what was so obvious to him, which was that these prisoners just weren't going to give up? He knew well that the defendants had spent decades dragging their feet, undoubtedly hoping that because of sheer "lack of momentum it would just go away," but how could they not grasp that this would never happen?[2] The damage awards were, in his view, "so high," and the state could probably have settled for a lot less.[3] Now, this number was out there. Everyone knew what an upstate jury had thought these men's pain and suffering was worth. Now what number would they have to agree to?

Knowing that he had a tough task in front of him, Telesca decided just to start knocking on doors and hope that someone would start talking settlement with him. In his mind, the state might agree to a figure of $15 million. He wasn't quite sure why this number stuck in his head, other than that it was still a lot of money for the state to pay out, but it was a lot less than the two juries had said they should pay. In his view, even $15 million was low when one considered "the horrendous injuries here, horrendous treatment."[4] As he tried to make clear to his counterparts in the governor's office, the Attica case was "the pure definition of what the court had in mind in *Estelle v. Gamble*"—the famous ruling that applied Eighth Amendment protections against cruel and unusual punishment to prisoners.[5]

Deep down Telesca wondered if getting this case back in his hands was exactly what state officials had been hoping for when they appealed the damage awards. "We'll reverse it, make sure Telesca gets it, and he'll wrap this thing up."[6] In short, getting him involved could prove to be "the cheapest way out of it" for the state.[7]

If the Attica plaintiffs were devastated by this decision, Judge Elfvin was made livid by it. "When they ripped the case away from me," the judge recalled, "I angrily took down the photo of Attica I had always had on my wall" and threw it away.[8] True, Elfvin had been the judge on this case since January of 1975 and, for that reason, he had come to feel proprietary about it. He had never liked the idea of settling the case, and had always felt that he should oversee its legal journey. Indeed, he had, in his own words, very much enjoyed the Attica trials and all of the back-and-forths he had engaged in with the plaintiffs' team in particular.[9] Although he thought that Joe Heath "was a jerk" and that "Deutsch was a very heated individual," he had actually liked Liz Fink and got a kick out of what he considered "sparring" with her.[10] That it was just so much sport to him was clear. As Elfvin noted, it disappointed him whenever he would erect some sort of obstacle to trying the case if Fink then didn't push back at him in the way he had hoped "to get things moving."[11]

Although the decision of the Second Circuit made him "very angry" because they had called him out and he thought that their reasoning was "stupid," Elfvin hoped still to be part of the next phase of resolving the case—whatever that should be.[12] At least theoretically the cases could still be retried and he could still oversee them. But that didn't happen. As he recalled, "nobody talked to me . . . I heard nothing, I got angry, and shipped everything off. I was done with it."[13] And, from then on, Attica left "a sour taste" in Elfvin's mouth.[14]

Meanwhile Judge Telesca also felt that he was getting stonewalled—in his case by Governor George Pataki's office. Indeed the first offer he received from the higher-ups was a mere $50,000.[15] But he pushed and pushed. Eventually, to his delight, he managed to get the state to agree to settle with the plaintiffs in the Attica class action suit for $12 million. He was elated. No it wasn't the $15 million he was shooting for. But it was a great deal more than the $50,000 that the state had tried to get away with. He was not, for that reason, at all apologetic when he presented it to Fink and when reporters started calling him following the formal announcement of the settlement on January 4, 2000.

The question now loomed—how would this money be distributed? Telesca also had the power to determine this and, in a most unusual move, he decided that he would invite the many plaintiffs to come into his courtroom and, in their own words, tell him what exactly had happened to them. Not only would he be able to determine the damage awards for each of them, but, as importantly, he would be helping them get all that they had endured on the record.[16] "If the state of the New York wasn't going to offer an apology," he remembered, "I at least wanted them to know what [trauma] they paid their money for."[17] He wouldn't cross-examine these men, or permit others to badger them. He would just let them talk and, ultimately, Telesca recalled, "It was the most fulfilling thing I ever did."[18]

And so, for the next few months in 2000, scores of former Attica prisoners took the stand in Judge Telesca's chambers and, one by one, told the harrowing stories of what they each had experienced in the Attica Correctional Facility in September of 1971 and for nearly thirty years thereafter. Of all the men who spoke before Telesca, Frank "Big Black" Smith struck the judge most profoundly. As he recalled it, "Frank made a very powerful witness when he testified before me. The truth of it all just resonated with him."[19] But the more stories he heard, the more deeply Telesca understood how much all of the men had truly suffered—"They all remembered the same things."[20]

Telesca found himself haunted by the scope of the abuses that took place at Attica and what he heard from one former Attica prisoner in particular. This man had, prior to the retaking, been an exceptionally good basketball player, one good enough that it seemed he had the realistic aspiration of becoming a pro basketball player upon his release. Knowing this, troopers had dragged him from his cell after rehousing him and "with the butts of their guns they crushed the tops of his feet."[21] His mangled feet healed badly, never being properly treated, and now he hobbled like a duck. It sickened Telesca that he "would never be able to give him the money he deserved," but when he tried, apologetically, to explain, this man replied to the judge that it was all right. All he had wanted really to do was to "tell my story . . . I wanted to help my brothers."[22]

Once the stories were recorded, Telesca decided the distribution of funds. He allocated $8 million for the former prisoners and $4 million for the Attica attorneys who had, he acknowledged, funded this case wholly out of their own pockets—particularly out of Liz Fink's pockets—for decades. The specific details of the historic settlement with the state were announced on August 31, 2000. Ultimately Telesca awarded 502 claimants settlement monies, and he divided this group into five clear-cut categories.[23] The first category awarded $6,500 to each of the 260 men who "were beaten, ran the gauntlet, received physical injuries, suffered emotional distress, nightmares, etc., or experienced any combination of these occurrences."[24] The second category included 112 men who would receive $10,000 each for having "received beatings which resulted in broken bones, including broken fingers, broken ribs, loss of teeth, and continue to suffer from emotional distress."[25] Category Three, the ninety-five men who had "received gunshot wounds and/or were singled out for special treatment such as being subjected to more severe, repeated beatings which resulted in a permanent disability and continuing emotional distress," would get $31,000 each. In the fourth category the fifteen men who had "received very severe, multiple beatings, were subjected to acts of torture, or were severely wounded by gunfire, and whose injuries were life-threatening and resulted in serious permanent disability, either physical or emotional," would be given payments of $125,000.[26] And finally, in Category Five were the twenty men named in the class who had died "as a result of gunshot wounds received during the retaking." Each of their heirs would each receive $25,000, except those of one who would get $27,000.[27]

More important than how the state's $12 million would be distributed was Telesca's narrative regarding how this settlement had come to be, and upon what traumas it was based. In the introduction to his lengthy settlement document, Judge Telesca told the story of the Attica rebellion and the long legal battles for justice and accountability that followed the deadly retaking.[28] As important, though, he explained the process by which he had come to know the horrific stories of the retaking. As he noted, "Approximately 200 plaintiffs chose to testify in support of their claims during the period of May through August, 2000. Approximately 160 appeared in person and gave their testimony at the Federal Courthouse in Rochester, New York."[29] These men had come, most at their own expense, from across the country—from New York, and from New Jersey, South Carolina, Ohio, Pennsylvania, Florida, and Minnesota. And Telesca had not only believed what these men told him, but felt that some of the men may actually have "understated the extent of their injuries and how those injuries affected their lives."[30]

Ultimately, the most valuable part of Telesca's order for monetary awards was his "Final Summaries"—the appendix to the order within which he brought to life the horrors that the men at Attica had endured. As *The New York Times* explained it, the two-hundred-page settlement served "as a harrowing encyclopedia" of the traumas suffered during the retaking of the prison—the horrific event just shy of three decades earlier that had left scores dead or wounded, "and countless more psychologically scarred."[31]

Within Category One claims, for example, Telesca not only brought David Brosig's heartbreaking story into the public eye, but he had also done so for scores of other victims. On May 30, 2000, one man explained in excruciating and quiet detail how, on September 13, 1971, he had been "beaten on his head, back, and legs while in D-Yard; was beaten while walking down the A-Yard steps; was beaten for not crawling fast enough while in A-Yard, and was beaten on the head, back, and legs while running the gauntlet. He sustained cuts on his legs from crawling through the glass."[32] Not only had this man not received medical attention, but "he testified that he was afraid to request medical treatment because he saw a prison doctor hitting inmates with a club."[33] And, still in 2000, he suffered terribly "from severe post-traumatic stress disorder, nightmares, flashbacks, and an inability to keep a job."[34]

Telesca not only transcribed the testimony of each man who had come into his courtroom but he made sure it would be readily available to the public. From that day forward, anyone could learn of men such as one who had been "identified as a 'leader' and marked with an 'X' on his back by correction officers."[35] As this man explained what happened then to the judge, "he was forced to strip and was placed against a wall with other 'leaders' and was told, 'Don't worry nigger, it'll be quick and fast,'" whereupon he was beaten so badly that his back was permanently injured.[36] They could also learn about the Attica prisoner who suffered first and second degree chemical burns, as well as lasting emotional trauma from troopers gassing him directly in his face.[37] Another man, one who had only been in Attica one day before the rebellion, was cut by glass, kicked down a flight of stairs, and beaten so badly that "his right shoulder was dislocated and some of the muscles in his right shoulder were torn along with the ligaments in his upper right arm were ripped when he was forcibly lifted by his arms."[38]

The very worst tales told, however, came from the men included in Categories Three to Five. There was the man who had both of his legs riddled with buckshot and then was "beaten on his head, arms, back, and shoulders by correction officers in the A-Gauntlet."[39] Another was still haunted not only from the severe beatings he endured but also from witnessing his best friend being shot and killed. Three decades later, he had told Telesca, "I can still see [his] face every morning. . . . I can't function—I've lost my family—my friends."[40] Still another who was permanently handicapped from the abuse he received had headaches and flashbacks whenever he saw helicopters or policemen. Indeed, virtually every claimant that Judge Telesca heard from "continued to suffer from flashbacks, nightmares, avoidance and severe post-traumatic stress disorder."[41]

And how could it have been otherwise? All of the men had been tortured and the men deemed leaders were not only abused on the way through A Yard but then tortured in the Box. One man being beaten the whole way to HBZ was then "forced to climb a stairway lined with guards holding rifles, plank boards, and night sticks and was struck in the chest, back, legs, arms, feet and head. Once he made it to the top of the stairs, he was kicked so hard in the stomach that he fell down the stairs and was again forced to run the gauntlet up the stairs. He was then placed in a cell (with no mattress or water) and when he attempted to urinate, he discharged pure blood."[42] That particular man, Telesca noted, had suffered permanent damage to his kidneys, was hospitalized for fifty-six days, "and underwent four surgical procedures to correct his bladder function."[43]

The death claims in Category Five were equally poignant, since in these cases it was surviving family members who had come to tell their stories. Josh Melville, the son of the prisoner Samuel Melville, came into Telesca's court on August 7, 2000, to speak "eloquently on behalf of his father."[44] Josh Melville gave Telesca "a series of exhibits consisting of pictures, a forensic ballistic report, and photos of his deceased father in support of his position that his father was intentionally killed by a New York State trooper," and he firmly stated that "his father [had] stood up for injustice, protected the hostages, and was targeted for assassination."[45]

Nearly thirty years after troopers had stormed into Attica with guns blazing, Attica's prisoner victims were able to tell just how brutally and inhumanely they been treated by the state of New York and, as importantly, their stories were believed. They had not only been able to recount the severity and depth of the torture they endured, but they had managed to get some measure of restitution for it. The sums they received were, relative to their injuries and trauma, pitifully low. But the experiences these men shared with Telesca indicated that there was no amount of money that could truly compensate for this level of emotional and physical trauma. As prisoner Howard Partridge mused quietly about his torture at Attica at the hands of a trooper, "I remember those blue eyes. I had never seen so much hatred in anyone's eyes."[46] And, even though they had settled with the state, the state still would not admit to wrongdoing at Attica. And so what the men had gotten wasn't justice. It wasn't even close to justice. But it was the closest thing to justice that these men would ever get.[47]

PART X

# A Final Fight

# DEANNE QUINN MILLER

*By the year 2000 Dee Quinn, the daughter of slain Attica CO William Quinn, had become Dee Quinn Miller, the mother of two young girls and a resident of Batavia, New York. Dee Quinn Miller didn't talk about Attica often, but decades after her father's death, this event still very much shaped who she was. Back in 1971 five-year-old Deanne Quinn had been taught that prison was a place for bad guys. Her dad had become a prison guard at nearby Attica when she was three and a half years old. He had taken this position because it paid better than his job as a social worker. Since she had been told that dangerous men were in Attica, Dee wondered if her father was scared when he went to work. She could see how nervous her mother got anytime the prison's siren blew and how relieved she was when he finally pulled up to the house at the end of his shift.*

*After September 9, 1971, Dee's father never came home again and her life was forever changed. When news broke in January 2000 that Attica's prisoners had just been awarded a multi-million-dollar settlement with the state, Dee Quinn Miller was outraged. She knew that many of those prisoners had been severely beaten during and after the retaking of the prison, but, as so many people she knew saw it, they deserved what they got for having started a riot. They had created the chaos that killed her father. She burned inside wondering why these prisoners were getting restitution for what they had endured at Attica, and yet not one of the former hostages or the families of the slain hostages had received even so much as an apology from the state. Dee Quinn Miller was determined to remedy this.*

# 53

# Family Fury

On January 4, 2000, when Attica's former prisoners finally were awarded some restitution, they were elated. Many others across the country, though, could not fathom what had convinced the state of New York to agree to pay them any money.[1] Perhaps no one was more stunned to hear of this settlement than Attica's former hostages who also had somehow survived the assault on the prison, and the family members of the hostages who had been killed in the retaking. The fact that they still had received nothing from the state—no money, no apology, nothing—and had been largely ignored for the last thirty years was almost too much to take. Although he was thrilled that the prisoners finally had been heard "after 29 years of deceit, cover-up and injustice," former Attica observer and still prominent *New York Times* columnist Tom Wicker summed up the surviving hostage and hostage family's dismay when they heard of the prisoners' settlement. As he put it in a piece he wrote, "But what about the widows and families of the inmates' hostages who were slain that day by indiscriminate state police gunfire? So far, the State of New York has done nothing remotely adequate to compensate these forgotten victims of the bloodiest day in America since the Indian wars."[2]

For decades Attica's surviving guards and widows had all suffered in silence—barely speaking of Attica and hoping that they could get past their ordeals. But the settlement news was like opening a long-festering wound. It was of little surprise that "many correction and State Police officials are upset by the $8 million settlement, saying it is wrong for former prisoners to receive financial benefit because of a riot that they started."[3] But the former hostages also shared this view. Although many of them

Two girls hold a vigil at the memorial to the Attica staff, on the anniversary of the retaking.
*(Collection of the author, undated photo)*

had felt a kinship with the prisoner survivors, at least right after the retaking, that feeling had long since dissipated. "I don't think [they] should get anything," retired correction officer Gary Walker, who was one of the thirty-one hostages, told the *Buffalo News*. "It isn't fair. What happened to them is a lot less than what happened to us. . . . It's a slap in the face to you and to me."[4] Donald Werner, whose brother and uncle were both killed by police gunfire at Attica during the retaking, felt just as Walker did. When he heard of the prisoners' award he was shocked and angrier than he had been for years. "I'm a very, very bitter man," he admitted to reporters.[5] "It will never go away. . . . [I] don't think I've got a good night's sleep since '71."[6]

Many former hostages and surviving family members of hostages first learned of the prisoner settlement on a radio station, WBTA broadcasting out of Batavia, just twelve miles from Attica where so many prison employees now lived. WBTA radio personality John Carberry announced the news as soon as it broke. On that particular Saturday morning's show, he had been planning to spend most of his ninety-minute segment covering Martin Luther King Jr. since the King holiday was around the corner. But no sooner had he read the settlement details than his producer, Deb Horton, got a call from a man she strongly suspected to be an Attica hostage survivor. He was upset. He wanted her to know how badly he and his fellow men "were screwed over by the state of New York."[7]

When the caller hung up, Deb Horton thought about it, and then called him back to ask if he would consider discussing this issue on the air.[8] Then Horton made a decision that would change history. She would dedicate an entire live radio show to news of the prisoner settlement. She would broadcast it from the Signature Café in downtown Attica in the hope that many of the prison employee survivors and their families would attend to share their reactions and tell their stories.[9]

The radio show happened five days after the prisoners' settlement was announced. Deb was nervous about having enough people there to carry the show. To her surprise, however, almost two hundred crowded into the café and "everyone wanted to talk."[10] The one-hour broadcast that she had planned taped for more than two hours.[11] Her husband, local public defender Gary Horton, who had come along that day, was troubled by the stories he heard. Despite what he and the rest of America had assumed, Attica's hostage widows had been left to survive as best they could, alone, and all of them had suffered mightily as a result. Post-traumatic stress clearly plagued many of the hostages who had survived, and their family members had suffered right along with them all of these decades. As remarkable as it might seem, this was the first time any of these people had shared their stories, even with one another.[12] John Carberry was shocked by what was unfolding around him. As he told one fellow writer, "It's one of those rare opportunities as a journalist where you suddenly find something that needs light . . . and it takes off on its own."[13]

That day at the Signature Café was life-altering for many there. When Christine Quinn Schrader, the middle daughter of slain CO William Quinn, had heard that the prisoners had been awarded money, she was "so outraged—outraged and betrayed by our judicial system," that she had decided to come to the café just to vent. Once there, though, Christine was overwhelmed with emotion of a different sort.[14] "For the first time in my life I got to meet some of these other families who had also suffered through this horrific event. It was like a support group, only thirty years too late. As the mayor, hostages, troopers, and family members spoke, I could not help but cry."[15] Christine's mother, Nancy, and her sister Dee Quinn Miller attended too, albeit reluctantly. Miller was also furious that prisoners had gotten money from the state and, frankly, was so mad she wasn't sure she wanted to hear any more about it. Ultimately she decided to go to the café only because, once there, she might learn more. She "wished someone could make them give the money to us since they took our dads' lives."[16]

Dee Miller was surprised by how many people had shown up, and her mother was seeing people that she hadn't laid eyes on in nearly thirty years. It was hard for her even to recognize the survivor families. Nancy Quinn thought she recognized the family of slain CO Edward Cunningham and some of the others, but it was all so overwhelming. For decades now no Attica survivor in her town had discussed anything related to the pain they had endured, and now here they all were in the same room. Suddenly Miller heard people whispering that former Attica hostage Mike Smith, the one who had been shot so badly across the abdomen during the retaking, was also there. She had no idea who Mike Smith was, but some of the others in attendance were clearly apprehensive about him. Miller eventually gleaned that Mike Smith wasn't that popular with the other hostage survivors because they felt that he had been too friendly with the prisoners back when he worked at the prison and, recently, had also made public statements in support of the fact that they had finally gotten restitution from the state. He was also disliked because rumor had it that at some point in the preceding years he too had tried to sue the state for the gunshot wounds he had suffered. Turning against the state, biting the hand that fed so many residents of this area, was considered bad form. As Miller recalled, summing up the ugly gossip about him that filled the air around her that morning, "He wasn't a state boy. They hated him for breaking rank. He was outspoken that the state had shot him. [He was stepping outside the bounds of] the good old boys club that was Attica."[17]

Most of the folks assembled at the Signature Café knew precious little about what had really happened in D Yard after the riot and they had uncritically accepted the state's version of the retaking and rehousing. Dee Miller was one of these. As she later mused, "I knew nothing about Attica."[18] And so, when Mike Smith finally got up to speak—to much eye-rolling and sighing in the group—she found her head spinning. She realized that nothing was as she had thought it to be.[19]

Mike Smith told the group that Attica had needed reforms back in 1971, and that the state had cared so little about the prisoners and about its own employees that it had gone in with guns blazing. The state had known that people would die, Smith said, and it had thereafter abandoned

Hostage survivor Mike Smith
*(Courtesy of the* Democrat and Chronicle*)*

the surviving employees as well as the widows and kids of those who had been killed by State Police gunfire. As Dee Quinn Miller listened to Mike Smith recount his nightmare on the day of the retaking, and of all he had endured since due to his gunshot wounds, tears began rolling down her face. She suddenly saw that the prisoners and COs had both been sacrificed by the state and thus that they weren't each other's enemies.

As Mike Smith spoke about not begrudging the prisoners for standing up to the state and, instead, standing with them so that all could get the restitution that they deserved, Dee Quinn Miller found her preexisting views about the Attica uprising and its aftermath crumbling. She also began to see why Mike "was targeted in the yard."[20] As she put it, "Michael was a real humanitarian and [that is why] he was resented."[21] As the show wrapped up Miller knew she had to meet Mike Smith. She walked over to him, introduced herself, and connected with him right away. As she remembered it, "We hugged each other and we cried."[22]

Dee Quinn Miller drove home after the broadcast overwhelmed by all she had learned. She now better inderstood the prisoners' plight and no longer felt that they should not have received money.[23] But now, her anger burned even hotter than it had before on behalf of the other survivors.

Dee's mother, Nancy, had had to take care of her, her little sister, and the new baby who was born soon after she buried her husband, and the state hadn't compensated her for her trauma. It may have been "just" that the prisoners had been compensated, but to Dee Miller it was *unjust* that her mother still hadn't received even a token payment from the state. As she put it, "I still remain without a father, as do the families of the inmates who were killed."[24]

Although not every hostage or hostage family survivor felt as magnanimously as Dee Quinn Miller and Mike Smith did about the prisoners' right to a settlement, all agreed that the state had treated them abysmally and that it was time for them to come together as a group. A son of slain correction officer Edward Cunningham fumed when he thought about the fact that his mother had been abandoned by state officials despite promises that she would be cared for. "Russell Oswald (then-Commissioner of Correctional Services) came right to our house," the younger Cunningham told a reporter, and "I remember him putting his arm around my mother and saying, 'Helen, we're going to take care of you.' But they never did."[25]

Several months after the show on WBTA, the surviving hostages, widows of hostages, and hostage families decided to come together in an official new organization called the Forgotten Victims of Attica (FVOA)—one that local public defender Gary Horton, radio producer Deb Horton's husband, would provide legal services for pro bono.[26]

The very first meeting, called by former Attica hostage G. B. Smith, took place at the American Legion hall. Notably, Mike Smith wasn't invited.[27] When Gary Horton showed up at this meeting he really wasn't sure about the best way to proceed. Horton had grown up in Batavia and, although his father had been a state trooper, the family had little connection with the regional prison system. Gary Horton had graduated from Hobart College the year that Attica erupted. When he chose a career as a public defender he did learn a little about Attica, but that was only because he was trying to prevent his clients from being sent there.[28] Horton believed to his core that the hostage survivors deserved their day of justice with the state, but it had been hard for him to listen to so much vitriol directed at the prisoners that morning.[29] And yet, Horton was heartened to see that, over time, many of the hostage survivors in Batavia and Attica were beginning to grapple with the hostility they felt toward the prisoners. Some like Don Almeter, G. B. Smith, and Dean Wright would never warm to the idea that the prisoners had received money. As Wright put it to a reporter, "Anyone who was a hostage for one day or one hour deserves at least what Frank Smith [Big

Black] got."[30] Others, however, like Carl Valone's widow, Ann, had worked through their anger. As Ann explained it, "First you get real angry at the inmates. Then you find out they acted more humane than the officials. . . . We've never been able to heal."[31] As the FVOA grew, to between fifty and seventy members, twenty to forty of whom were meeting every Monday night, the group learned to make decisions by consensus. Dee Quinn Miller explained to one reporter: "These are all survivors . . . we each have our own beliefs. [Some] people [said]: 'The [state] troopers were right. They went in. They did their job. They didn't want to kill anybody.' And you have people who say, 'The Troopers sucked. They wanted to kill everybody. They didn't give a rat's ass for anybody's life.' . . . But, you know, we are respectful of everybody's opinion."[32] At the end of the day, Quinn Miller said, what the group wanted most was to be "acknowledged for who we are . . . and for the truth to be told."[33]

The FVOA's most challenging task was figuring out how the employee survivors were going to get their own restitution from the state. Some members clung to the idea that they must first find a way to stop the prisoners from getting their money. The vast majority of members, however, wanted to devote all energies toward getting their own justice.[34] A key step in this direction was to educate the public about what had happened to the hostage survivors after the retaking or, as the daughter of slain hostage Elmer Hardie put it, to let the public "know that everything that should have been done for them wasn't."[35] To that end the FVOA sponsored "a forum on the riot's consequences" at the nearby Genesee Community College on September 26, 2000.

Mounting a successful public relations campaign on their own behalf was the easy part. Figuring out how they could pressure the state to give them damages as well was much more difficult. Debating this question tended to generate serious tensions in the group. The FVOA began discussing this question as Judge Michael Telesca was in his Rochester courtroom hearing prisoners' searing stories of torture in order to decide how he would divvy up their award. Michael Smith as well as the entire family of slain hostage Carl Valone tried to suggest to the broader FVOA group that Telesca's prisoner hearings presented a great opportunity for the organization. The FVOA could take a public stand in support of the prisoners and, in the process, levy enormous PR pressure on the state to offer them a settlement as well. Mike Smith had actually testified on behalf of the prisoners in Telesca's chambers, and Jamie and Mary Ann Valone, the children of Carl Valone, regularly showed up in chambers to show their solidarity with the prisoners. Ellen Yacknin, who had become a senior attorney at the Greater Upstate Law Project in Rochester, was at an event held for the prisoners where she happened to see this trio from the FVOA, and she tried to talk them into joining forces.[36]

Because the FVOA had already decided to make all of its decisions by consensus, however, the organization was clearly not going to work closely with prisoners. Although Mike Smith and the Valones would continue to support Attica's former prisoners, and though Dee Quinn Miller would, in time, come to have a profound relationship with Frank "Big Black" Smith—and even to meet personally with Richard Clark and the other men who had carried her father out of Times Square to safety—the FVOA decided to go it alone. As Gary Horton put it, they decided to "raise money, rent a bus, and walk the halls of Albany to call attention to us. . . . We held small press conferences. We walked office to office."[37] To make the most of its trips to the state capital, Horton asked Jonathan E. Gradess, the head of the New York State Defenders Association, to assist the FVOA. He knew all the players in Albany.[38]

54

# Manipulated and Outmaneuvered

That Attica's surviving hostages and hostage families were left, by 2000, with few options for being heard was itself a product of how badly they had been treated by state officials way back in 1971. Right after the retaking they too had hoped to get justice via the legal system and, like the prisoners, they too had filed many individual claims against the state of New York. State officials, however, worked hard—behind the scenes and via the State Insurance Fund—to make sure that their suits would go nowhere.

As a state employee, any survivor of the Attica retaking, or any widow or dependent of someone killed in the assault, was likely entitled to some sort of state or federal compensation benefit. According to representatives from the state back in 1971, "in the case of an employee who dies in service not as the result of an on-the-job accident, the state provides through the Employees Retirement System a benefit of three times annual salary."[1] There was also the Social Security Death Benefit for the families of the slain hostages as well as various disability benefits, including workman's compensation, for those who managed to survive the assault.[2] Attica's victims were even able to seek benefits such as overtime pay "for all the hours they were in captivity."[3] But while meager Social Security payments did come through for some of them, most had no clear sense of what was happening vis-à-vis the monies they might be owed by their employer, the state of New York.

Right after the retaking, as the dead hostages were being buried and the wounded were healing, all any hostage survivor or family member really knew was that Oswald had promised to take care of them. The commissioner had actually visited some of the wounded COs to assure them that they could take up to six months off and would still get their salary. He said much the same to the CO widows—the state would also make sure they were taken care of.[4] And, sure enough, within a very short period of time state-issued checks began arriving at the houses of the surviving hostages and hostage widows alike.

Eugene Smith was one of the surviving hostages who was thrilled to get his first check of ninety-five dollars since he was still an emotional wreck and was hardly ready to go back into the prison to work.[5] Dee Quinn Miller's mom was equally thankful when she began getting checks for $112 every two weeks.[6] Another Attica widow with a larger family than the Quinns began receiving $230 a month, and she too breathed a sigh of relief.[7] The checks that all of these survivors had been given, ostensibly so that they might buy groceries or pay bills, looked exactly like the checks they had always cashed each month from the prison. However, they were not.[8] Although Oswald had implied that the former hostages were on "a period of authorized leave," and the widows had been told that this money was being given to them simply to ease their burden in a terrible time, all of these survivors were in fact being paid from workman's compensation funds.[9] This would have huge implications for their future.

Receiving payments from the Workers' Compensation Board was not, in itself, odd. When terrible on-the-job events happened, investigators from the bureau were supposed to review the occurrences in question as quickly as possible so that they might "get the facts" necessary to fill out C-62 forms.[10] Then hearings would be held to determine compensation, at which injured workers or widows would be present. But none of the standard procedures were followed with these Attica survivors. After some of the survivors had personal assurances from Oswald that they would be taken care of, "Representatives Robert Knight and Leonard Mann of the State Insurance Fund" tried "to do everything possible to expedite payment" to them.[11] And so, without formally filing for workman's compensation, the checks simply showed up soon after the retaking. Unbeknownst to the recipients, the instant that an Attica survivor or widow signed and cashed one of these checks, under New York state law they had "elected a remedy," which meant that they could no longer sue the state for damages.

This is exactly what Attica's survivors had hoped to do. Although they were grateful for the small checks they had been receiving, hostage survivors and surviving family members were barely making it and thus were also interested in filing damage suits against the state in the Court of Claims. Ultimately there were twenty-eight such individual claims and each sought damages on grounds that the state used excessive force in the retaking, which had led to death and injury, and that the state had failed to protect its own employees on the job.[12] None of these plaintiffs were much aware of what the others were doing. Each was isolated, just trying to get some help for their particular family. Determined to help these individuals, two attorneys out of Buffalo, William Cunningham and Eugene Tenney, began a decade-long process of trying to get these cases to trial. Cunningham's cases, collectively, sought "more than $15 million," and Gene Tenney worked as well to get substantial damages for twenty-two more hostage plaintiffs in his cases.[13]

Clearly, however, state officials had known that they would likely be sued and thus had scrambled to protect themselves by getting checks into the hands of the survivors and widows as soon as possible. State Insurance Fund employee Morris Jacobs went on the record many years later that the state's investigators were well aware that Attica employees could sue and there was speculation about how many would take compensation versus how many would sue.[14] If anyone doubted that the state had tried to stack the odds in its favor, Jacobs noted, one only had to review the procedure that had been followed in all other cases. It seemed that someone must have filled out C-62 forms on behalf of the survivors and widows, and then submitted and approved them before any hearing, which was certainly not the protocol.[15] What is more, whoever filed C-62 forms on behalf of the widows and authorized payments prior to a hearing would have had no official authority to do so.[16]

Even though scores of Attica survivors and widows living in upstate New York had dutifully filed the paperwork necessary to sue the state, it eventually became clear that they were going to have to fight like hell to even have the right to keep their lawsuits alive. The burden fell on their attorneys to show that elective remedy didn't apply.[17] On July 6, 1981, the New York Supreme Court Appellate Division (Third Department) issued a decision that devastated all of the hostage survivors and widows. In the case of *Werner v. State* the court ruled that former hostages or widows who had accepted workman's compensation checks for the period of the uprising and afterward were barred from seeking additional monetary damages from the state.[18] In practical terms this meant that despite thirteen judges having been involved in these hostage cases since 1971, suddenly all of the cases save one were dead in the water.[19]

Back in the awful weeks following the retaking of Attica, Lynda Jones, widow of slain hostage Herbert Jones, just happened to mention to a friend of hers that she had received a check from the state. It also happened that this friend worked for attorney William Cunningham. Since she knew that Lynda Jones had little knowledge of finances let alone dealing with state officials, the friend advised her to stop by Cunningham's office, just to see if there was anything she needed to know about this check before she cashed it.

On October 21, 1971, Jones showed Cunningham the $21 check, which, she explained, officials had told her was for the "four meals the State of New York thought it owed her dead husband for the period during which he had been held hostage by inmates at the Attica prison."[20] Something about this seemed odd to Cunningham. Acting on what he later described as "gut instinct," Cunningham recommended that Lynda not cash the check.[21] What she might do instead, he suggested, was file a lawsuit against the state of New York. If they could show that it "had used excessive force in retaking the prison," she might win a great deal of money.[22] To win, she would have to prove that her husband's death had resulted from "an intentional tort perpetrated by the employer at the employer's discretion."[23]

Although attorney William Cunningham felt that his client was on firm legal ground, Jones's case was dismissed on December 31, 1972—virtually at the same time that the state was handing down its scores of indictments of prisoners.[24] A judge had initially ruled at the state level that she could sue, but the state appealed and that decision was reversed. Since 1971 lawyers for the state, in both the civil and the criminal courts, had been expending a great deal of energy to make sure that neither the prisoner victims nor the hostage victims could be heard. Like the prisoners, however, Lynda Jones was undeterred. Her lawyer appealed the appellate decision and the next December her right to sue was reaffirmed in a highly unusual reversal.[25]

In fact, the Court of Appeals ruling said that "all of the other survivors of the Attica dead, as well as those wounded in the assault, may file suits now," and, what is more, that it expected that "a good number of them will do so, and many may also seek to involve Mr. Rockefeller personally."[26] And so, William Cunningham and Gene Tenney proceeded with all of their hostage survivor and widow cases. Like the prisoners' many civil suits, all of these cases had to be kept on hold until all of the Attica criminal cases were resolved, but Cunningham and Tenney made good use of that time.

For William Cunningham the years between 1973 and 1976 were busy indeed. He was determined to take as many depositions of high-ranking state officials as possible and one of the most important of these, he thought, would be that of Nelson Rockefeller.

To Cunningham's frustration, however, now vice president Nelson Rockefeller was not particularly forthcoming as he sat for his questions on April 22, 1977. Quite predictably he answered the question of whether excessive force had been used with a categorical "absolutely not." And yet, unwittingly, Rockefeller did help Cunningham's case.[27]

Although the former governor laid all responsibility for the retaking at Commissioner Russell Oswald's door, he did acknowledge that he was the one who had insisted on using the State Police for the retaking. On this issue, he said, "I prescribed what should be done to make it possible for him to carry out his order."[28] Significantly, this meant that whatever the State Police proceeded to do at Attica, the governor himself had authorized. What is more, Rockefeller admitted on the record that state officials, including those from his office, the State Police, and the head of the Attica investigation, had in fact met in the wake of Attica to compile a coherent narrative regarding all that had happened at the prison. He also revealed that there was a physical copy of that narrative somewhere. At first when Cunningham asked him about this, Rockefeller stated that he had "made no writings, notes or any memorandum concerning the Attica uprising from September 9 to the 13th and thereafter," and he insisted that the only account ever given to him was verbal.[29] Eventually, though, the former governor admitted that he had "appointed a committee of two to prepare a written report. . . . One was Harry Albright and the other was Eliot."[30] Rockefeller had both seen and reviewed this report.[31]

So, as soon as Governor Hugh Carey ended the Attica investigation and all criminal trials related to the uprising, Cunningham felt pretty good about his chance of getting some restitution for his clients. Lynda Jones's suit came before Judge Robert Quigley of Rochester in October of 1977, and Cunningham was eager to proceed. The trial was recessed almost as soon as it began, however, because lawyers for the New York State Police had decided to fight tooth and nail to prevent Cunningham from using the many trooper statements that had been taken in the immediate aftermath of the retaking. Whereas Cunningham argued forcefully that these statements were essential to his ability to show excessive force, the state brought out the big guns, Attorney General Robert Abrams and Assistant Attorney General John R. Steward, to prevent their use.

There was a great deal at stake here. The only reason Cunningham had gotten his hands on the many hundreds of correction officer and trooper statements in the first place, and knew that they would help his case, was because lawyers for the state had overplayed their hand with the judge in this case.[32] In short, Cunningham had gone to Judge Quigley seeking a *subpoena duces tecum* allowing him to ask the attorney general for any Attica documents that might pertain to his case—much as Liz Fink would do almost a decade later. Predictably the state stalled, and implied that it really had nothing relevant to share. Judge Quigley, however, was getting increasingly frustrated with the defense and, knowing this, Cunningham went to him and told him exactly where these documents were in One World Trade Center. The judge wanted to see for himself what was there before issuing a new order. And so the two of them went to the World Trade Center and spent forty-eight hours combing through file cabinets. They hit pay dirt. After first setting aside the hundreds of parking tickets stuck in those cabinets that state troopers were hoping the attorney general would fix, they located the statements. Once he had these, Cunningham remembered, "I knew I had won."[33]

Armed with these statements Cunningham still had the challenge of figuring out how he "was going to get them into the record."[34] There was really no way to enter them into evidence one at a time, so he made the bold decision to try to enter them all at once. This was a dramatic moment as lawyers for the state immediately jumped up and began their effort to block this move.[35] Cunningham had feared that this would happen and so, the night before, he had asked his secretary to help him get these many statements to a copy shop in Rochester. Once there they asked the shop to close down and he would write them a healthy check as soon as they were done copying the pile. He had already told the judge he would bring the statements back to court, which he then did, but he suspected that this would be the last he saw of them so he made sure he had copies back in his Buffalo office.[36] The state's lawyers managed to halt the trial once again because a higher court now had to rule on the question of whether these statements were admissible. The statements were indeed removed from the plaintiffs, but Cunningham had ample time to study his copies carefully back in his office. This, in turn, gave him a clear trial strategy. "All I had to do was subpoena the troopers who fired," he realized. Even if they had been given immunity in the criminal trials, their immunity did not hold in a civil case.[37]

When the Jones trial finally resumed in November 1978, the state suffered a major blow—Cunningham was going to be able to use "the 'debriefing' statements the guards and troopers made shortly after the riot."[38] But even with statements that placed specific troopers in specific locations engaging in specific acts, these same troopers could still invoke their Fifth Amendment rights—thus not confirming anything that these statements said. As trooper after trooper refused to testify, Cunningham's patience thinned. They wouldn't answer any questions at all, not even basic ones such as whether they had worked at Attica. This was particularly frustrating to Cunningham because he knew from their own statements, just as Malcolm Bell had, exactly who was guilty of excessive use of force. And so he chose his witnesses carefully, including troopers such as Gregory Wildridge and COs like John Vergamini, and high-ranking troopers such as Lieutenant Colonel George Infante. He even tried to bring New York's longtime attorney general Louis Lefkowitz to the stand. Every single one of these men, however, refused to answer his questions.

As infuriated as Cunningham was by this refusal to cooperate, Judge Quigley was even more livid and, to everyone's surprise, the judge slapped these men with contempt of court charges—of the twenty witnesses cited with contempt, eighteen were sentenced to jail.[39] Most of the contempt charges were for refusing to answer questions, but Lefkowitz's charges were for "refusing to produce certain documents and reports."[40] All jail terms ultimately were stayed pending a hearing before another judge, however.[41] Everyone would have to wait to see how the other judge would rule regarding the recalcitrant witnesses' liberal use of the Fifth Amendment.[42]

By November 30, 1978, this question still hadn't been decided, but the standoff between the plaintiff and law enforcement continued.[43] In one remarkable instance, Judge Quigley had ordered a superintendent of the New York State Police to appear in court and state "for the first time the names of 10–12 troopers recommended for disciplinary proceedings."[44] This man was actually supposed to bring into court the letter sent to him by Alfred Scotti, the man Governor Hugh Carey had appointed to resolve the remaining prisoner indictments in the wake of the Bell revelations and the Meyer Report. However, when the NYSP superintendent arrived in court, he did not have the letter and claimed that "he did not understand the instructions."[45] When pushed, he acknowledged that he wanted "to keep those names in confidence."[46] Disgusted with the superintendent, Judge Quigley "leaned back in the cushions of his courtroom chair . . . rolled his eyes, held his temper," and told him icily, "The Court orders you to take yourself to the nearest telephone . . . you are to call your secretary [and] make sure she understands the document you have in mind, and whoever you wish to authorize from your office is to get in a motor vehicle and proceed, within the speed limits, to this court with the document today."[47]

William Cunningham remained tenacious. Rather than relying on trooper admissions, he made sure that some surviving hostages gave their own firsthand accounts of the retaking. This was itself startling testimony for Quigley to hear, and to have on the record, since few in the nation had yet heard what these survivors had in fact endured. And, indeed, it wasn't always easy for Cunningham to get these people to come forward to relive their trauma. Reporters like Tom Goldstein of *The New York Times* found the stories riveting. As he put it, "Some of the surviving hostages have told how they developed nervous conditions, must take medication, often drink heavily and sleep irregularly. The Attica riot brought on 'almost a reverse personality' Richard Fargo, a former guard testified last week. Now, he said, he is 'jumpy, nervous and can't stand to be in crowds.' "[48]

Cunningham's other triumph in this trial was getting Russell Oswald, the former commissioner of corrections, to admit that troopers and COs had indeed used excessive force in the retaking.[49] Oswald began by noting that he couldn't understand why the COs, for example, had "transcended our orders" and shot their weapons during the retaking, but their use of firearms at Attica had, nevertheless, been "reprehensible."[50] When Cunningham pressed, and asked pointedly whether Oswald thought that CO John Vergamini had used excessive force when he shot John Monteleone, Oswald said, "I would say yes."[51] Getting a state official to acknowledge under oath who had shot John Monteleone, a hostage who had later died from that same shot, was huge. For the purposes of this lawsuit it confirmed just how excessive and brutal the shooting during the retaking had been. Of course it also confirmed that state officials were aware who had killed whom at Attica—the very point that Malcolm Bell had been trying to make when he went public back in 1975.[52]

Attorney William Cunningham also made major headway for Attica's hostage victims in general, not just Lynda Jones, when, over the state's objection and after yet another hearing, he was allowed to use grand jury testimony to refresh the recollection of recalcitrant witnesses.[53] This was crucial since it meant that when Cunningham had one trooper from the NYSP on the stand who refused to talk, for example, he was able to put this witness's previous grand jury testimony into the record—evidence that confirmed he had hit four "targets" during the retaking and there was no evidence that any of them had been resisting his authority. Armed with this testimony, Cunningham was able to state for the record, "Well then, we can further presume you killed four people."[54]

Judge Quigley issued his decision in the case of *Jones v. State* on August 31, 1982. It was a scathing denunciation of the way the state of New York, as well as its troopers and COs, had handled the retaking. It had been a long trial—one that had been stalled repeatedly as Cunningham battled the defense for access to the post-retaking statements, volumes 2 and 3 of the Meyer Report, and grand jury minutes. No matter how hard they had tried to conceal evidence, though, lawyers for the state had not managed to prevent Quigley from hearing evidence in his decision. He noted, for example, that "at trial, Major Monahan testified he once had most of the items described in the subpoena, but that he had burned them in the fireplace at his home," an act the judge found appalling.[55] He also made clear that he just didn't believe state witnesses—such as their repeated claim that evidence didn't exist or had been lost. As he put it, "It is incredulous to believe that all copies of the overall plan for the retaking of the Attica Facility are, somehow, 'missing.' "[56] The judge was also infuriated that the highest officials of the NYSP simply would not take responsibility for the retaking—preferring instead to pass the buck regarding who was actually in charge of the retaking. Monahan had admitted to the court that he, "with the assistance of Captain Malovich," had drawn "up a plan for the retaking of the prison," but then he claimed to have "placed Captain Henry Williams in charge of that post and ordered him to stay there" and had "selected Captain McCarthy to be in charge of the rescue crew."[57] Quigley wasn't having it, though. As he wrote in his decision, despite Monahan's attempts to dodge responsibility, "his planning, direction, choice of subordinate leaders and his commands to cease firing were actions that clearly indicate he was functioning in the command position."[58]

Not only did it matter to Quigley that Monahan was responsible for the overly brutal retaking, he found it unconscionable that this man had clearly admitted hearing gunfire after he "gave the cease fire order," and that he knew the "the names of certain troopers who had shot either inmates or hostages," but that he refused to share that information with investigators at the time or the court now.[59] Quigley just couldn't get over how unnecessary the force used during the retaking of Attica had been. He took particular note, for example, of the fact that even General O'Hara of the National Guard had admitted that the gas used in D Yard was so immobilizing, and thus so ineffective for riot control, that he personally had "ordered it out of the inventory of the National Guard," and yet this was exactly what the NYSP had used and then had also used ammunition.[60] Perhaps worse, Quigley noted, O'Hara had testified that "it was the general consensus of opinion by all the officials present that the hostages would be killed one way or another" and indeed that "everybody had that impression."[61]

Quigley was most shocked by the sheer magnitude of firepower that the state had authorized at Attica. The key here, as he saw it, was the nature of the weapons the state had allowed to be used—namely shotguns that dispersed sprays of pellets. Each of these pellets was "approximately the size of a 32-caliber bullet and lethal," wrote Quigley, and the "the total number of pellets fired from shotguns accounted for would be between 2,349 and 3,132 lethal pellets" raining down into D Yard, which, incredibly, was in addition to eight rounds from a .357 caliber, twenty-seven rounds from a .38 caliber, and sixty-eight rounds from a .270 caliber.[62] Of course, he noted, these counts did not even include the bullets showering into this group of inmates and hostages from correction officers and other members of law enforcement not fully accounted for.[63]

"It is the Court's conclusion," Quigley wrote, "that the force used was indeed excessive, and that such conclusion is amply demonstrated in

A sniper on the prison rooftop wears a makeshift gas mask, September 14, 1971. *(Courtesy of the* New York Daily News/*Getty Images)*

the trial record."[64] Excessive firepower was used against people already immobilized by gas, according to high-ranking officials from the National Guard, such as John C. Baker and General Almerin C. O'Hara.[65] Quigley noted, "The evidence [re: excessive force] presented is so overpowering in favor of claimant that the Court does not need to resort to the rule that it may view the evidence in 'the light most favorable to the plaintiff.' . . . Claimant has met her burden of proof and has established a prima facie case."[66] The award? "After a careful review of all the evidence, the Court finds the claimant has been damaged in the sum of $550,000.00 which includes funeral expenses . . . with interest thereon from September 13, 1971 to the date of judgment herein."[67] Lynda Jones would ultimately win $1,063,000 from the state.[68] Unsurprisingly, the state appealed this ruling, but the Appellate Division upheld Judge Quigley on November 4, 1983. The state appealed once again, but in June of 1984 the higher court declined to hear that appeal.[69]

It was perhaps in the context of this huge settlement that Judge John Elfvin was trying to stall the prisoners who were eager to get their civil suit against the state to trial until 1991. It had to have been clear to any jurist following the Jones case that there was abundant evidence that members of law enforcement had used excessive force in D Yard during their assault, and the way the assault force had treated prisoners that day was far worse. Tragically, though, the prisoners themselves knew little of the testimony heard in this case and thus found themselves having to prove many of the same facts all over again in their decades-long court battle. Also unfortunate was the fact that the Jones victory had done nothing to bring justice to the rest of the hostages who continued to suffer their post-Attica trauma individually and alone. That is, until the Forgotten Victims of Attica, in the year 2000, came together to fight as a group to politically shame the state of New York into doing the right thing by all of its victims.

# 55

# Biting the Hand

After the decision came down in *Werner v. State* that the hostage survivors and widows who had "elected a remedy" by cashing their checks from the state couldn't sue, they were left with few options but to pressure politicians in Albany. If they could just get some legislator to hear of the injustice they had suffered, and take up their cause, they might finally get some restitution.

And so, the Forgotten Victims of Attica kept heading to the state capital. Gary Horton explained their goal as forcing a settlement by making it "too uncomfortable politically for them to ignore us."[1] They had some reason to think that the strategy would be successful. Thanks to drumming up support from various state assemblymen, the FVOA received word on June 15, 2000, that the state had given "final legislative approval today to a resolution calling for an annual day of mourning for the 11 prison employees [the hostages slain during the retaking and William Quinn]—but not the 32 inmates [the 29 prisoners killed during the retaking and Hess, Schwartz, and Privitera]—killed" in September 1971.[2] More importantly, several other state legislators had responded to the prisoner settlement (and to the hostage families' dismay at said settlement, expressed in a meeting on April 14, 2000), by proposing some monetary compensation for the widows.

By the close of 2000, state representatives Dan Burling, Charles Nesbitt, and Dale Volker put together legislation that would give each of the eleven widows $50,000—a much lower figure than anyone hoped. Burling originally had proposed $90,000 each, but that figure had been whittled down in budget negotiating sessions. The FVOA rejected the state's first proposed settlement outright. As one newspaper put it, "Those payments have been scoffed at by some survivors as too little too late. Some relatives said they won't cash the checks."[3] Equally significant, the FVOA explained, the widows were by no means the only survivors of Attica. Not only were there others who needed restitution—such as the children of the slain hostages and those hostages who had survived the retaking but had been physically and emotionally damaged by it—but the FVOA had always wanted more than just money: they had rejected the state's offer as much because of "the state's refusal to admit any wrongdoing."[4]

The FVOA worked to build a consensus on a clear list of what it wished the state to do, and crafted a "Five-Point-Plan for Justice."[5] The plan demanded the following:

1. An apology from the New York State government, officially acknowledging culpability for the deaths of hostages, physical injuries to Correction Department employees and emotional trauma suffered by hostages and their families, as well as "the state's duplicity regarding compensation."
2. Opening state records on the riot and its aftermath . . . to provide closure to the families, dispel misinformation given to the public, correct the denial of due process, so the state can learn from its mistakes and to expose the cover-up that the state perpetrated.
3. Counseling for survivors and families.
4. A guarantee that the group can conduct a memorial service outside the prison each Sept. 13.
5. Reparations to group members.[6]

Regarding the last demand, a newspaper noted that "while group spokeswoman Deanne Quinn Miller . . . said no exact figure has been set, some members use the award to Mrs. Jones as a benchmark for widows, with a lesser amount for survivors."[7]

The FVOA took their demands to Albany in the summer of 2000 intending to meet with now governor George Pataki. Instead they were met by the governor's counsel, Jim McGuire; the commissioner of corrections, Glenn Goord; and a team of both senior and junior members of the Governor's Counsel.[8] Undaunted, Dee Quinn Miller, Mike Smith, and Jamie Valone (the son of slain hostage Carl Valone), along with FVOA lawyers Gary Horton and Jonathan Gradess, launched right into their pitch. First, the FVOA hoped that the governor would agree to come to an Attica anniversary event their group was holding the next month at the prison and, second, they hoped that he would consider their list of demands in the meantime. The governor's representatives assured the FVOA members that someone would get back to them within thirty days. Dee Quinn Miller recalled they all left the meeting feeling not only that these people would help them, but that Governor Pataki would actually come to their event.[9]

Yet the thirty-day deadline came and went and the FVOA heard nothing from Pataki's office.[10] And so they began writing follow-up letters—many of them. When they still heard nothing, they decided to switch strategies. After lengthy discussions with attorney Jonathan Gradess, the FOVA decided to draft a document arguing for the need to hold Truth and Reconciliation hearings—similar to what had been held in South Africa in the wake of apartheid—regarding what they had endured at Attica in 1971 and in the decades since.

After submitting their document and again hearing nothing for almost six months, they were surprised to finally get word that the governor would appoint a task force to look into the possibility of holding such hearings. This Attica Task Force, comprised of three members and a chair, was officially constituted on March 13, 2001. According to media sources, "Pataki asked the task force to listen to the group's concerns and make recommendations about resolving those issues."[11] Notably, however, the governor had given the task force "no time table" for doing so.[12]

That this task force was formed at all came as a surprise to FVOA lawyer Gary Horton. When FVOA attorney Gradess first proposed the idea of trying to get a meeting with the Governor's Counsel, and then to go all out for a South Africa–inspired Truth and Reconciliation committee, it had been hard to imagine anyone in Albany actually agreeing to either of those things.[13] However, Gradess had been correct to assume that Governor Pataki had no desire to get in the middle of another Attica-related public relations disaster. Too many governors before him had had to deal with the fallout from Attica and it had never been pretty.

The FVOA had mixed feelings about the Attica Task Force. It was good that the governor's office was doing something to respond. But once the members saw who had been placed on this panel, they weren't at all confident that the state's effort was serious. As Dee Miller put it, "We weren't sure if those on it were there for a stall tactic."[14] How could it bode well if the chair of the task force was none other than Glenn Goord, the current head of the very Department of Correctional Services (DOCS) that had mistreated Attica's survivors and widows back in 1971? Dee Miller personally was incensed that State Senator Dale Volker was also appointed to this task force, since, in her view, he had whined to the media that the Attica widows were ungrateful when they had rejected his proposal to get them each $50,000. Equally worrisome was the fact that Volker, as a Republican politician from Wyoming County, had actually been "present at the Attica disturbance"; it was anyone's guess whose side he was on.[15] The appointment of the second member, former Attica observer Arthur Eve, was not much more reassuring to some FVOA members since he had always been such an outspoken advocate for the Attica prisoners. The final member was cause for some hope: Assemblyman Jeffrion Aubry, a Democrat from Queens, might be more independent as the chairman of the Assembly's Committee on Corrections.[16]

Not only was the Attica Task Force announced to great fanfare, but this body almost immediately met with the FVOA. Dee Quinn Miller, however, felt that this first meeting boded ill for the future of the surviving hostages and the hostage widows. Commissioner Goord seemed openly hostile to them in the meeting, abruptly leaving the room on two or three occasions. In turn, Dee Miller and the other FVOA leaders felt their own hostility grow because they "couldn't agree on anything. [The FVOA] wanted open hearings. The state did not. . . . We were specific and they were vague."[17] Whether the members had been more persuasive than they thought, or the commissioner was under more pressure than they knew, the group unexpectedly received notice just a few weeks later that there would be public hearings on Attica beginning on May 9, 2002, in Rochester and continuing in Albany.

The FVOA had a great deal of work to do before the hearings began. If this was going to be an open hearing at which everyone would be able to get their stories onto the record, it was crucial that people from the group be willing to participate. Dee Quinn Miller and Mike Smith, along with Gary Horton, worked to persuade virtually all of the Attica hostage families that they needed to speak up. This was their long-awaited chance—maybe their only chance—to tell the world what had really happened to the Attica employees during the retaking and after.

The FVOA knew, however, if the state were to settle, they would also need noninterested witnesses who could back up their stories of trauma and neglect, and to corroborate the FVOA's claim that the state had manipulated their members into taking workman's compensation so that they would never be able to sue the state. And for that matter, they would also need people who could really speak to the lengths that state officials had gone to to keep them from getting any restitution for all that they had suffered as a result of the forcible retaking of Attica back in 1971.

For the first point, the attorneys Gene Tenney and William Cunningham could provide ample evidence that excessive force had been used against hostages during the retaking (much of the same evidence that they had presented in Lynda Jones's suit). For the second, Morris Jacobs, the man who had worked for the State Insurance Fund, was willing to testify as to the workman's compensation manipulation. And finally, to the state's undoubted dismay, the FVOA elected to bring whistle-blowing Attica prosecutor Malcolm Bell in to testify to state officials' efforts to cover up their wrongdoing at Attica.

Getting Malcolm Bell involved was no easy decision—particularly for Dee Quinn Miller. She knew that when John Hill, the man convicted of killing her father, had sought to receive clemency from Governor Carey in 1976, Bell had supported his bid. Deep down, Miller wasn't sure what to think about whether Hill really had or hadn't killed her father, but she was nevertheless leery, at least initially, of turning to his lawyer for help. But Mike Smith had, through Frank "Big Black" Smith, made contact with Bell and he persuaded the rest of the group that Bell's testimony would be vital for the FVOA's cause.

Gary Horton, Mike and Sharon Smith, and former hostage John Stockholm and his wife, Mary, all descended upon a quiet and rustic area of Vermont where Bell now lived. He greeted them warmly; he was ready to do anything he could to help the FVOA.[18] Come to Albany, they said. The public hearings would be the FVOA's one shot at making its case that the hostage survivors and widows also deserved restitution from the state of New York.

# 56

# Getting Heard

During the six days of public hearings that the Attica Task Force held between May and August of 2002, eighty-five people came to tell their story. Originally there were only going to be two days of hearings at the Rochester Institute of Technology in May and two days of hearings at the Empire State Plaza in Albany that July, but so many people wanted to be heard that a third set of hearing dates at the Rochester Institute of Technology was added in August as well.

Department of Correctional Services commissioner Glenn Goord opened the first public hearing at RIT's Chester Carlson building on May 9, 2002, by recognizing the "historic public hearings on the plight of correction officers and civilian employees."[1] In these hearings, Goord made clear, the roughly twenty-two people who testified would only be asked for statements, not for evidence. "We will be willing to take each victim and survivor at their word. We will not interrogate the victims or their survivors."[2]

The surviving hostages and family members who testified found their experience emotionally wrenching. They had been talking about Attica in FVOA meetings and had felt support doing so, but to speak formally, with so much at stake, and to the general public, was much harder. John and Mary Stockholm were the first to the microphone. John Stockholm said quietly, "We were repeatedly hurt and disappointed by the poor treatment we received. We were told to take time off after the riot. But no one told us by doing so, we would forfeit our rights to compensation, to sue for remedies. We did not know."[3] His wife, Mary, brought a more personal story to bear. "I did not know how to deal with my husband's mood swings, the night sweats and, worst of all, the silence. At the age of 24, we were expected to get over it, to get on with our lives; which we did, although the events of Attica are just under the surface."[4]

The family members of the late Richard Fargo also made sure that their pain was clearly expressed. Fargo, a hostage, had survived the retaking but had suffered greatly until his death in 1992. His wife, June, spoke of feeling swindled by the state—how they had been called with other hostages to a meeting at a Presbyterian church soon after the prison was retaken, at which Commissioner Russell Oswald had told the surviving hostages to relax, to take time off, and that all would be well. She also noted that they were all "told not to talk about what had happened" to them at Attica.[5] Most importantly, according to June Fargo, taking time off hadn't helped her husband.

> Richard had long-term physical and emotional effects from being held hostage. He took heart and diabetic medicine for 20 years. He had bouts of aggression and anger, and nightmares. He would wake up in the middle of the night with severe chest pains. . . . He tried very hard to put the whole ordeal behind him and he drank too much to do that. Our family lost a happy father and a husband. . . . I never knew what I would find when I got home. I literally shook. . . . Our quality of life was severely impaired . . . we couldn't go into crowds, he was always looking behind him. Panic attacks set in when helicopters flew over our house, which happened frequently. . . . Our life was governed by Richard's moods. . . . He died, still needing counseling, on May 29, 1992. He never got over the fact that his employer could treat him and fellow hostages and widows and survivors so badly.[6]

Testimony from Fargo's daughter Susan echoed her mother's story: "He could become very angry very quickly, or very emotional, crying, choked up, shaking, volatile. I never knew which father I would be coming home to."[7]

Dean Wright, another hostage survivor, also testified that day. He declared that not only had he been lied to by the state officials who said they would take care of the hostages, but he also had been badly used by the state in helping Anthony Simonetti's office make criminal cases against prisoners. He explained how members of the Attica investigation had hounded him to identify prisoners, bombarding him with pictures and peppering him with leading questions. "It got to the point," he said bitterly, "where it didn't make any sense to me . . . they tried to put words in your mouth that he was where he wasn't or was doing something that you didn't see him do."[8]

While the state tried to make Attica all about what the prisoners had done wrong, Wright himself was suffering post-traumatic trauma from his own experiences in D Yard. "Just out of the clear blue sky I'd get the shakes. . . . I still get nervous, I get withdrawn. . . . And it bothers me, because I don't know why I do these things."[9] Despite feeling terrible, Wright had no choice but to go back into the prison to work. When he went back to being a CO, though, "we talked about a lot of things, but the riot was never one of them, and our feelings were never one of them, and our problems were never one of them," and thus his own problems just festered.[10] As the years wore on, Wright felt more and more bitter. He was still furious at the prisoners and he hated the state. "We were wronged by the inmates. They are the ones that caused the riot, we didn't. We were wronged by the state. We were lied to by the state."[11] Wright's son Scott came to the microphone to testify, after seeing his father go through this for years. Scott Wright had one message for the task force: "All of these people should be commended for what they have endured. I feel that the State of New York owes these people an apology."[12]

Before the first day of hearings ended, the task force heard not only from surviving hostages, widows, and children of hostages, but also from the lawyers, William Cunningham and Gene Tenney, who had spent decades trying to seek justice for them in court. Cunningham explained in detail his thirteen-year journey to get some restitution from the state for the widow of Herbert Jones. He made clear how much energy the state had expended on trying to stop this woman from getting any money, going so far as to comb through its many thousands of canceled checks to see if they could prove that Jones had cashed hers. Indeed, Cunningham said disgustedly, "the Attorney General asked for a recess . . . so that the controller could make a further search for the check. They knew Lynda Jones didn't take any funeral expenses. They knew she didn't take a nickel. The judge rightly so, granted a recess. They couldn't find it. To this day, they can't find it. It's because she didn't sign the check."[13] Smiling, he added, "I happen to know where the check is. To this day, I have it."[14]

Even though Jones hadn't taken workman's compensation, as she then testified, five Appellate Division judges had told her that she still couldn't sue. Indeed it wasn't until the Court of Appeals stepped in that she had any chance of being heard in court.[15] And Lynda Jones had been one of the lucky ones, as testimony from attorney Gene Tenney made clear.

As Tenney explained, he had worked on hostage survivor and widow cases for thirty years and he still found it shocking just how manipulative the state had been with his clients for the first twenty of those years. "It was very difficult for me to, as a lawyer, to have judges, esteemed judges who I respected previously, find that these people, these people elected a remedy, as their husbands [lay] in hospitals, as they [lay] in morgues, they [the surviving hostages and widows of the slain hostages] had elected a remedy, an intentional decision to take Workers Compensation."[16] Seeing the look on their faces broke Tenney's heart—particularly since he could still remember so vividly when he first met with them down at Jim Hardie's insurance office in the town of Attica in December of 1971. He had promised them then, "I will do everything in the world I can for you," not knowing how badly the state had already swindled them. Although they hadn't retained Tenney until December 1971, as he noted bitterly, "you can bet your sweet life the State Insurance Fund had all of their lawyers working on this case. And they were working it from the first date. I'm not talking September 13th, I'm talking about September 9th"—something he had found out in a series of hearings in which he later participated.[17] Tenney himself had spent over $100,000 on the survivor and widow cases but, he made clear to the task force, he wasn't requesting compensation for himself. "Whatever you give them is theirs."[18]

Some of the most heart-wrenching testimony came in subsequent days from the widow of John D'Arcangelo and then from hostage Carl Valone's widow and children. D'Arcangelo's widow, Ann Driscoll, recounted that her husband was only twenty-three when he died and their daughter was barely three months old. What is more, her husband had just graduated from college, "majoring in psychology and history. He was my husband, a new father, the bread winner of the family. And most importantly, he was my best friend."[19] And yet, on September 13, 1971, there she was in the basement of some church identifying his bloody body. "My memory of this place," she said quietly, "was that it smelled of blood and dirt."[20]

Ann barely had time to grieve, though, because "a few weeks after the funeral, a group of well-dressed men arrived at my mom's house in Auburn, New York. Commissioner Oswald was one of these men. . . . He handed me John's final pay check and told me that I had to sign these papers that he brought with him. He told me that these were documents that assured us that the State would take care of Julie and me for the rest of our lives. I didn't have a clue that by signing these papers, I would never be able to sue the State. . . . We were 'awarded' $36 a week. And those benefits ended when Julie was 16."[21]

Widow Ann Valone was so angry at Commissioner Goord by the time she was called to the mic that she lashed out at him on the record. Having watched Goord throughout the day it had seemed to her that he looked bored "as people bared their souls."[22] Looking over at him Ann said, "I think [you] people are just listening to us, trying to appease us, show that you are all good guys."[23] With her voice breaking, Ann Valone told how her family "was so traumatized" and that her then ten-year-old son, Carl, her husband's namesake, was particularly scarred by his father's death.[24] "Now if anybody needed counseling in this whole wide world it was my son Carl," she said sadly, but they had no money for such a luxury.[25] Ultimately Carl, her child, had hanged himself.

Carl's sister, Mary Ann Valone, had also been irreparably harmed by the death of her father and, as important, by the state's abandonment of his family. She had been fifteen back in September of 1971. "The kids in my family got so messed up and so bitter and so hostile and so angry, so miserable. And we took it out on my Mom, every single day of the rest of her life. . . . We could not cope with it. We—we could not cope with what happened."[26] After her father's death, Mary Ann was so filled with rage and fear that she could barely function. She found herself hating the state troopers more than anything for wanting "to kill as many black people as they could," but she was also terrified of these troopers so she "ended up leaving New York State as a young girl because I thought the New York State Troopers were going to kill me and throw the gun next to my body."[27]

By the time Mary Ann was an adult she had taken turns hating everyone in her life. "I hated the hostages that lived, I hated the civil rights movement, I hated blacks, I hated God, I hated Correction Officers. I hated my mother, [and] I hated my father because he went to work."[28] Mostly, though, Mary Ann hated herself. "I tried to destroy myself for years because I turned all this anger inside too. I could not figure out who to blame, who is responsible for all this?" She ultimately decided that the prisoners were actually not the ones to blame. As she explained, "I forgave them first. I forgave them a long time ago. They were victims too. . . . After I got a little bit of education, they were the first ones I forgave . . . [but] it took me a long time to forgive God."[29] It was especially hard to forgive God when she learned that her brother, Carl, had killed himself. "My brother was in pain," she said in tears herself. "My brother killed himself, hung himself off the deck of his one hundred twenty five thousand dollar house when he was thirty three years old."[30]

The July and August hearings brought even more trauma to the stand. During the July hearings in Albany, three sons of slain hostage Edward Cunningham testified that their worlds had been turned inside out by his senseless death and the way that state officials handled it. Mark Cunningham spoke of a nagging uncertainty that his dad was even in the grave marked with his name because the state had messed things up so badly that it had to dig up his dad's body to reautopsy it.[31] Mark also tried to express how hard this had been on Edward Cunningham's widow—a mother of many kids who never really recovered. She never stopped calling state officials and trying to be heard, he noted, and because she was never heard, "every day of her life was pretty much anxiety, and depression just filled her life for the whole 28 years before her death."[32]

Mark's brother John, who had only been eight when his father was killed, chose to read a letter written by his mom before her death. "The frustration I and the widows of Attica have felt since the death of our husbands, at Attica, has been extreme. . . . It is difficult to accept the way things were handled, and the outcome for our men and families. . . . The deception and treatment by the state, rumors and misinformation made many years of torture for us. . . . I would like the records to be opened. We should at least be able to know the truth of what happened there at Attica."[33]

Hostage G. B. Smith told the task force in July that he still couldn't believe that the state hadn't even paid them for the entire time they had sat in terror as hostages in D Yard because, other than for eight hours a day, they were, technically, off the clock.[34] And former hostage Gary Walker tried to explain to the task force just how much he and his fellow survivors had suffered. For the "first couple of years," he said, "I broke out in hives constantly because my nerves were shot, I . . . took pills—I did not go back to work for six months because I just could not, and then when I got back I got scared more but I said, well, it is—I got to take care of my family, I got to take care of my kids, I have to have a job."[35]

The cover-up concerning the deaths at Attica had also taken a real toll on many assembled—especially on Don Werner, the brother of slain hostage Ronald Werner. He told the task force about going to the funeral home to see his brother's body. "When we were allowed in the funeral home, I asked Dick Marley, who was a family friend for years," if Ron's throat had been cut. "He looked right at me, says 'Don I am not permitted

A guard in a gas mask speaks to an unidentified hostage lying on a stretcher. *(From the Elizabeth Fink Papers)*

to answer that' . . . this bothered me for a long time. I have never found out really what happened to my brother. . . . I never found out how he was killed."[36] Lest the task force suspect men like Werner of hyperbole, the FVOA made sure that Malcolm Bell also testified, describing in calm and minute detail the state's effort to dodge responsibility for the deaths and injuries at Attica.

Ultimately, the task force was left with no doubt that state officials had swindled the surviving hostages and hostage widows via the workman's compensation system. Morris Jacobs, the former employee of the State Insurance Fund, minced no words when he declared that the state of New York, including "top officials of the State Insurance Fund, as well as the Rockefeller Administration," had "induced the acceptance of Worker's Compensation in order to avoid liability for intentional tort."[37] These officials had "callously manipulated the system" to deny benefits to the widows, had "targeted the Attica widows, by violating an inflexible rule, which is not to approach widows prior to a hearing without the approval of their attorneys," had "intruded on the vulnerable widows within days after the fatalities knowing that the widows were unrepresented by attorneys," and "had been guilty of blatant hypocrisy in initiating and accelerating compensation payments prior to hearing under the bogus pretense that they are befriending and favoring the Attica widows by expediting payments."[38] Ultimately, he insisted, "insensitive bureaucrats" had "maneuvered to victimize the widows a second time by depriving them of seeking alternative, appropriate, legitimate and reasonable redress and indemnification."[39]

By the time the hearings closed in August 2002, there could be no question that the hostage and hostage family survivors of Attica had endured a great deal. Sharon Smith, surviving hostage Mike Smith's wife, gave some of the most jarring testimony. If the state had not sent troopers and correction officers into Attica with guns blazing, Mike would never have received the horrific injuries he had. Worse, this same state then abandoned him in his moment of greatest need.

Sharon explained in graphic detail how "there were four wounds of entry. The bullets . . . seem to have burst into hundreds of small fragments [which] were found all over the peritoneal cavity and quite a few of them were embedded in the pelvis and sacrum. . . . The fragments of the bullets had played havoc in the abdomen. There were about twenty perforations of the ileum which were repaired. At two different places, the ileum was completely torn into small pieces. It was found there were four complete tears in the sigmoid colon. . . . There was a large tear in the dome of the urinary bladder, measuring about five inches. The floor of the pelvis was badly injured. . . . [Some wounds were so big] a fist could be introduced into [them]."[40] Then, as Mike "was still in intensive care fighting for his life," a letter dated September 30, 1971, came to their house indicating that the state hadn't received records that it needed and that if the Smiths didn't file this paperwork immediately, the state would not pay his medical bills. "I was in a panic," Sharon recalled, "[so] I filled out the papers and sent them back without the benefit of legal representation." Little did she know that these documents too related to workman's compensation and thus she was electing a remedy that would prevent her from suing the state later on. Meanwhile, Mike's injuries were so bad that he didn't come home from the hospital for ninety-one days and, even then, "he was transported by ambulance, as he could not walk or sit up. . . . Michael weighed one hundred twenty four pounds."[41] Sharon, who was also taking care of their six-month-old baby, was left in charge of Mike's rehabilitation at home, which was a monumental task. Yet, again, Mike's physical injuries almost paled in comparison to the added injuries he suffered from the state's self-interest and manipulation. As Sharon pointed out, "There was no contact from the state as to his wellbeing until March 13, 1972," and they only called then because a sergeant "wanted him to come by and ID inmates for the criminal prosecution."[42] Later, when Mike wanted to keep the bullets that had been removed from his body, he "had to sign a statement that he would not hold the state [responsible] . . . he would not use the evidence against them. And that was in 1986."[43]

When the hearings ended, everyone who had testified was exhausted and not at all sure what was supposed to happen next. Presumably their stories would move the Attica Task Force to address their list of demands, but as far as anyone could tell, there was no deadline placed upon this body to act. How long would they have to wait to hear from state officials whether their words had in fact mattered? A long time, it would turn out.

# 57

# Waiting Game

In the months following the Attica Task Force hearings the Forgotten Victims of Attica had very little sense of what was supposed to happen next. Dee Quinn Miller reached out to task force member Arthur Eve and, as they became close, learned some disturbing information about the entity that she and other FVOA members were hoping would help them. According to Arthur Eve, the Attica Task Force wasn't particularly cohesive or democratic. In his view, only Dale Volker and Glenn Goord were making the decisions and even the governor seemed out of the loop. Eve shared with Dee Quinn Miller his concern that Commissioner Goord was trying to wrap up this whole inquiry as expeditiously as possible and, since he was maintaining such personal control over the process, it wasn't certain how much justice would be had.

Of course this greatly bothered the FVOA members, especially since they knew that the task force was not facing a deadline and, therefore, no real pressure to make any sort of recommendation to the governor. So Dee Quinn Miller took it upon herself to keep the pressure on by writing regularly to the governor and trying to lean on Goord himself. Every time she spoke with the commissioner, though, she found herself frustrated. In short, she recalled, "they wanted to do it all their way. They were nasty."[1] Growing increasingly concerned that momentum might soon be lost, the FVOA decided on a new tactic: it would try to go public, in hopes that state officials would, in turn, feel embarrassed not to settle with the FVOA.[2]

However, reaching out to the public was expensive and required building powerful networks. Knowing this the FVOA decided to begin with correction officers' unions around the country, asking them to spread word of the fight and, if possible, help the FVOA financially. Within a few months the FVOA had powerful unions such as the New York State Correctional Officers Association & Police Benevolent Association (NYSCOPBA), the California Correctional Peace Officers Association (CCPOA), and other unions from Massachusetts, Pennsylvania, Ohio, and Florida as important allies. From these organizations they received a great deal of publicity as well as monetary support. Bringing in CO unions, particularly NYSCOPBA, had a real cost too. Glenn Goord hated the union and especially disliked its militant president, Rick Harcrow.[3] With the union on the FVOA's side, the organization succeeded in drumming up much public attention and sympathy, but it also served to make negotiations with the task force much more tense.[4]

The FVOA heard nothing from the Attica Task Force for so long that, on February 13, 2003, it decided to issue a report entitled "A Time for Truth," which it hoped would shame Commissioner Goord into offering something. This document began by noting that the task force had not made headway on its study since the hearings had ended six months earlier, and chronicled the sporadic, and dismissive, correspondence that the FVOA had received from state officials.[5] "In a letter of Nov. 18, 2002," the DOCS had assured the FVOA that it planned "to present carefully-considered and well-reasoned recommendations on each of the five points that are as fair as possible to all involved," and yet had also made clear that it wanted no further input from the FVOA.[6] This was unacceptable, the FVOA made clear. Via this report the group was reiterating its "evidence and grievances—in the hope it will be of assistance in finally producing just results."[7] The report provided the public record with a clear "Summary of the Riot Events," as well as a careful exposition of "The Riot's Immediate Aftermath," and made it clear that the FVOA wasn't going to just fade away. "Attica is the ghost that has never stopped haunting its survivors—including both the inmates and the families of the deceased guards and prison personnel," the report noted, and therefore the FVOA was going to insist on some remedy from the state.[8]

To make sure that the task force members would not simply bury this report under a pile of papers, with great fanfare the FVOA also called a press conference. At this event were "representatives of NYSCOPBA (the correction officers union), former correction officials, prison reform advocates, and historians," all loudly stating the importance of the Attica Task Force's doing its job.[9] The FVOA had come to see that bringing the public into its battle with the state was a good strategy. The group even got former New York state senator and Attica observer John Dunne to write an "Open Letter to Families and Friends of the Forgotten Heroes of Attica," which won some attention. As Dunne put it bluntly, "The state, which was instrumental in the violence which resulted in the deaths of dedicated prison guards, has steadfastly denied just compensation to the victims of that violent retaking."[10] And so, "simple justice demands that the state do right by the families and survivors of those loyal and courageous state employees who faithfully held the line and were prepared to make the ultimate sacrifice."[11]

Malcolm Bell had also remained an outspoken supporter of the FVOA in the public sphere. He too wrote an open letter, in this case to Governor Pataki, on July 16, 2003.[12] It was time, he argued, for Pataki to do the right thing. To Bell, "The Forgotten Victims' 'Five Point Plan for Justice'" was "reasonable, responsible, and, under the grim circumstances, modest."[13]

By 2003 the FVOA had amassed many supporters, but one of the most surprising was a group of New York State Police. Since the FVOA had formed in 2000, the Blue Knights, a motorcycle club of New York state troopers, had been holding annual fundraising rides for the group. Heading up this effort was trooper Tony Strollo, whose brother Frank had been a hostage and who himself had participated in the retaking. Strollo was personally conflicted on how that retaking had gone down. In his heart he knew it had been a disaster and that terrible things had happened as a result of it.[14] But he also felt strongly that the state had placed troopers in a terrible situation by sending them into this prison tired, upset, and untrained for what they were expected to do.[15] And so his way of coping was to offer his support to the hostage victims of Attica with this annual ride. In 2003, they stood with NYSCOPBA, the CCPOA, and other unions in support of the FVOA at a rally held in front of the capitol.[16]

DOCS commissioner Glenn Goord noticed that public pressure was mounting and that he would soon have to issue some sort of response to the FVOA's demands. In September of 2003, he sent the group a draft report that outlined what the task force would be recommending to the Pataki administration, including a monetary settlement of $8 million.[17] The $8 million settlement figure was based on what the prisoners had received, with the idea that this amount would be shared by many fewer people in the FVOA, which meant more money for the hostages than what the prisoners had been awarded. Interestingly, the task force explained the difference by reasoning "that most, if not all, of the state workers killed would have remained employed in some capacity. Therefore we believe they are entitled to higher per person awards than inmates received."[18]

As for the other four demands of the FVOA's Five Point Plan, the draft report attempted to dismiss them as unnecessary or problematic. Regarding the release of Attica records, the report explained that "there are no Attica records 'sealed' by order of *any* Governor."[19] Therefore, with the exception of the two volumes of the Meyer Report that a justice of the Wyoming County Supreme Court had confirmed sealed in a decision of May 22, 1979 (like Carmen Ball before him, he had believed the grand jury material they contained to be privileged), there was nothing stopping FVOA members from going to the New York State Archives and looking at any Attica document they liked.[20] The task force did not feel that special provisions for counseling needed to be stipulated, recommending "that FVOA members pay the costs of counseling from any reparations they might receive."[21]

Finally, the task force stated that an apology would not be forthcoming from the state because it was its opinion that "government descends a slippery slope if subsequent administrations believe they have the authority to take their view of today's standards and apply them retroactively to apologize for the decisions of their predecessors whose actions were based upon the prevailing contemporary social standards of an earlier era."[22] By taking the position that state officials in 1971 had "acted in accordance with policies and procedures that were the law and were acceptable at that time," the Attica Task Force was clear that despite what the FVOA had hoped, the state did not see the hearings it had held to be in any way like the Truth and Reconciliation proceedings that had recently taken place in South Africa, where state officials were asked to apologize for actions that may have been legal but were nevertheless immoral.[23]

If Glenn Goord thought that his draft report would be received with relief by the FVOA, he couldn't have been more mistaken. The FVOA "rejected the $8 million payout as an insult," and noted that not a few years earlier the state had mentioned paying widows a total sum of $50 million and the group considered that amount the "starting point in the negotiations."[24] Dee Quinn Miller, Mike Smith, and the rest of the men and women who had been working to keep the FVOA a major priority of the Pataki administration were furious that they had waited for more than a year for a proposal from the state that ignored most of their demands and offered monies that were not at all what the group had in mind. As

Dee Miller recalled, "I wanted 50 million and I wanted the same amount to be given to everyone."[25] Since there ultimately were fifty-two families in the FVOA (totaling 152 claimants), $8 million would be inadequate.[26]

The FVOA responded to the task force's draft report by going public with a detailed forty-page response. Dee and others had heard that the full task force had not been consulted when this draft report was written, which felt even more insulting as a response to their heartfelt and agonizing testimony. Task Force member Arthur Eve apparently knew nothing about the report until the FVOA leaked it to a local newspaper.[27]

The FVOA's response to the task force's draft report was nothing short of scathing. It was published in the form of an open letter to the New York State Legislature on January 13, 2004, and stated clearly that the task force's "Draft Report to the Governor" was offensive to the FVOA.[28] The FVOA responded point by point, beginning with how outrageous it was for the task force to claim an apology was out of order on the grounds that the state had acted within acceptable bounds. "There are not now nor were there in 1971 any prevailing contemporary social standards that would condone the death, injury, pain, anguish and neglect inflicted upon the FVOA by the state of New York."[29] As for the task force's claim that anyone could access state-held records related to the Attica uprising, the FVOA pointed out that not six months earlier "a member of the FVOA, through FOIL (New York state's Freedom of Information Law) application, requested access to specific McKay Commission records held by the State Archives. That request was denied."[30]

The task force's suggestion that they pay for their own counseling was also offensive and out of touch, the FVOA declared, since it "ignores the differing costs of counseling that each member might have based either on the level of treatment needed or on existing insurance benefits . . . [and] further fails to recognize that the children of the hostages—some of whom suffer the most substantial psychological damage traceable to this event—may receive no immediate monetary reparations from the state should their parents still be alive."[31] Not to mention that if counseling monies were going to have to come out of each FVOA member's settlement monies from the state, this was all the more reason to revisit the sum that the state had recommended be awarded to these same members.

Finally, on the issue of state compensation, the FVOA response was equally acidic, accusing the task force of ignoring "the most logical benchmark of fairness, the Jones judgment, and uses instead as a benchmark the settlement [of] inmate litigation against the state."[32] That settlement had come not from a court ruling but rather from prisoners being forced to settle. Arguably, the FVOA noted, their compensation was "insufficient and only a fraction of what might have been awarded had the litigation continued," since, it also pointed out, juries previously had awarded only two of those plaintiffs "over $4 million," and had this been the benchmark, the state's payout would have been "staggering."[33] As important, the FVOA went on, why should the hostages get less than the prisoners had gotten in their settlement just because they weren't asking for attorney fees—since their attorney, Gary Horton, hadn't charged for the work he did for the FVOA? Even though they weren't paying him, the costs of approaching the state for remedy had been high for the FVOA too.[34]

There was one more point about compensation that the FVOA felt crucial. In its draft report the Attica Task Force had recommended taking whatever compensation funds were agreed upon from the budgets of the executive, the Senate, and the Assembly in equal shares. This was a terrible idea, the FVOA maintained: "The FVOA believes that they are owed compensation from the State of New York and that compensation should be funded by the state budget." Otherwise, "this would merely serve to take funding away from various health, education, and social welfare programs currently supported by the legislature. The FVOA does not believe that their suffering should be ameliorated through escalating the suffering of others."[35]

Needless to say, when reporters got wind of the Attica Task Force's draft report, and then heard how hostile the FVOA was to the proposal, they began calling Commissioner Goord and pressured him to explain what the task force might do next to address the FVOA's concerns. To the public he did little more than offer platitudes, repeating his mantra that the state "has a moral obligation" to resolve the Attica dispute.[36] To the FVOA, however, Goord wrote a far more vitriolic reply entitled simply "Commissioners Commentary." It was clear from the opener to the reply that he was angry: "I want to update you on the work of the Attica task force which I chair, now that my discussion draft report on our work has been made public by an anonymous source."[37] He asked members of the FVOA to consider what their answers might be "to several complex questions" that, in his view, had to be resolved before any settlement could be reached between them and the state. If, for example, they now were to receive the same amount of money that Lynda Jones had been awarded, were FVOA members willing as well to pay back the workman's compensation monies they had already received? Or, if they insisted on taking the same sort of settlement as the prisoners had secured, were they prepared to accept that as a final settlement—meaning that the state would not pay their counseling as some separate obligation?[38]

The FVOA refused to get into a back-and-forth argument with Goord. Instead, the group made a fateful decision to go to the powerful California guards' union, the CCPOA, and ask for its help to fund a lobbyist who could provide a direct connection to sympathetic state legislators. The California Correctional Peace Officers Association indeed helped them to secure a lobbyist and, in addition, to fund construction of an FVOA office in Dee Quinn Miller's home so that she could work full-time with Mike Smith and Gary Horton on landing a settlement. With this new financial backing this trio was soon speaking around the country as well as traveling regularly to Albany to meet personally with lawmakers. This travel and PR work was costing the FVOA more money than even the CCPOA was able to offer, so it then turned to other correction officer groups around the country for help. Although NYSCOPBA and the CCPOA had offered the lion's share of the needed funding, many other organizations stepped in to help as well, including the Correctional Peace Officers Foundation (CPOF) and Corrections U.S.A.[39] From selling Attica Anniversary coins to conducting fundraising drives among their own members, these many organizations, along with law enforcement unions in Massachusetts, Pennsylvania, Ohio, and Florida, all worked with the FVOA to pressure Pataki's office into settling.[40]

In the fall of 2004 the FVOA had collected sufficient money to finally pay for a lobbyist. The man they hired, Artie Malkin, normally commanded anywhere from $4,000 to $12,000 a month for his services but agreed to work for much less as long as the FVOA would do much of the scut work—making the calls, writing the press releases, and such—so that all he had to do was glad-hand and negotiate in Albany.[41]

And the FVOA lobbyist was good at doing just that. His credentials were impressive, and he had a client list ranging from the New York State Defenders Association to the Drug Policy Alliance to the American Lung Association, the Police Benevolent Association of the New York State Police, and even Teach for America. This meant that he had major connections in Albany and indeed he had a close relationship with Governor Pataki's counsel, Jerry Connolly, as well as with New York attorney general Eliot Spitzer and even First Assistant Attorney General Richard Rifkin.[42] As Thanksgiving 2004 neared, the FVOA had the sense that something was finally happening in the governor's office. The lobbyist was calling

Dee Miller more frequently to let her know where the governor's office was in terms of a monetary amount for the settlement, and, at these junctures she would run the news by the FVOA members and then, in turn, go back to him with a counterproposal.

Then in December 2004 the FVOA told its lobbyist that a settlement couldn't wait any longer. Frances Whalen, the widow of slain hostage Harrison Whalen, had just died and she was the fourth widow to die since the FVOA had begun its work in Albany. Only seven widows remained who might hope to see restitution from the state and Dee Quinn Miller feared that time was running out.[43] By the end of December 2004 discussions between the FVOA lobbyist and Pataki's counsel were taking place virtually around the clock and, finally, as Dee Quinn Miller put it, they "hammered this out."[44]

On January 14, 2005, the state of New York formally agreed to a $12 million settlement with the hostages who had survived Attica and the family members of the hostages who had not. As a show of good faith, Pataki's office agreed to disperse $2 million to the fifty-two families right away, with the remainder to be worked out at a later date. The FVOA had earned its victory. Or so it seemed.

# 58

# A Hollow Victory

Even though the surviving hostages and hostage widows had finally settled with the state, it was still not clear how the money awarded to them would be distributed. The eventual decision would once again, now thirty-five years later, link their history with that of Attica's surviving prisoners and prisoner widows in powerful and poignant ways.

As a key leader of the Forgotten Victims of Attica, Dee Quinn Miller had learned early on to reach out to anyone who might help her get some sort of justice for families such as hers, and, in turn, she had come to learn much more about what had happened at Attica than she had known before coming to that radio show with such anger in 2000. She had, for example, reached out to Frank "Big Black" Smith and talked for hours on end, so that she might better grasp what had really happened to him. Dee Quinn Miller came to love Big Black and to trust him completely. After talking to him she decided that she should reach out to Judge Michael Telesca to decide how the FVOA settlement should be distributed just as he had done with that of the prisoners.

The more she thought about this, it felt right. After all, Judge Telesca had expressly written in his August 31, 2000, document awarding the prisoner survivors their money that he very much regretted that this settlement still did not help the families of the hostages.[1] And so Dee Miller had actually reached out to Telesca quite early on in the FVOA's battle with the state. Indeed, she had hoped Telesca would help make state officials recognize that the FVOA was serious, and not going to go away, so she had kept in close communication with him throughout 2004 as negotiations intensified. Those negotiations definitely took some heated twists and turns, and Miller came to know, and to trust, Telesca quite well as they had unfolded.

Back on December 18, 2004, for example, the FVOA lobbyist had gotten the state to agree to $10.5 million, but Miller rejected this offer because she had faith that Judge Telesca could lean on First Assistant Attorney General Richard Rifkin on their behalf and get more. As she had waited for a response to the FVOA's rejection of the $10.5 million, however, Dee's faith was tested and indeed the pressures of trying to get a settlement worked out before any more Attica widows died shattered her nerves and landed her in the hospital. From her hospital bed she called the lobbyist, Artie Malkin, in utter anguish. "I just I can't do this anymore!"[2] And in this crucial hour, Dee watched as Telesca worked to help the hostages with as much energy as he had the prisoners. Thanks to the behind-the-scenes pressure levied by Telesca, when the lobbyist went back to the Governor's Counsel and mentioned that Dee was ill, that another widow had just died, and that this had to end now, the state finally agreed to $12 million—the figure that it had also granted the prisoners.[3] At a jubilant Christmas Eve party at a local church, Dee Quinn Miller and Gary Horton gave every-

A guard looks on while one inmate carries another, badly injured, inmate. *(Courtesy of Judge Telesca)*

one the news and the FVOA decided unanimously to accept this offer.[4] As Miller remembered it, "We had the best Christmas we had had in quite a long time."[5]

Although Dee was fairly certain that she wanted Judge Telesca to oversee the way in which the newly awarded $12 million would be dispersed to the FVOA families, she still had some reservations that would have to be addressed. As she explained it, "I had to go see him. . . . Even though Frank Smith thinks he is great I wanted to make sure I thought so too—I wanted to make sure he wasn't biased."[6] When she saw that he had on his desk a heart-wrenching picture of one prisoner helping another, as a trooper looked coldly on, she believed that she had found the right man. As she explained, "His pics in his office spoke volumes. That pic did it for me."[7]

Still, Dee Miller wanted to let the judge know how the FVOA's situation, while similar to that of the prisoners, was not the same. In her view, the dispersal of funds in the hostages' case shouldn't give more to those who had suffered the most physically or even psychologically, as in the prisoner settlement, but in her opinion those families whose men had been killed should receive the highest awards. By 2004 there were so few widows left, she argued, that they should get the most. Needless to say, this was a controversial position to take in the eyes of some of the FVOA members since some, such as Michael Smith, had endured a lifetime of suffering from the wounds received during the retaking. But Dee Quinn Miller was pleased that Judge Telesca at least listened to her point of view and she left her meeting with him feeling that he would be fair and objective.[8]

Miller had to persuade her fellow members of the FVOA that Judge Telesca should be the one to decide who got what in their settlement with the state. The subject of giving Telesca this task had come up on several occasions at various FVOA meetings already and it had been clear that there was some dissent. At one such meeting held five months before the settlement was announced, Gary Horton broached this subject and had gotten a hostile reception.[9] Twenty-nine members had come to this particular meeting and many were uncomfortable when Horton prefaced his remarks that evening by stating that the FVOA members and former Attica prisoner Frank Smith had been on a "common quest for justice."[10] Judge Telesca, who had so clearly helped Frank Smith in his cause, Horton went on, might be a good ally to the FVOA as well. The gathering grew quiet. Some were on board, but others, including former hostages G. B. Smith and Gary Walker, were not. So when this issue was on the table for real in

2005, Miller knew that she had a lot of work to do to build consensus in the group for working with Telesca. Over the next weeks, and over many cups of coffee and lengthy phone calls, she was able to get everyone on board.

When the FVOA announced that it wanted Judge Telesca to apportion their settlement, one of the most conservative members of the Attica Task Force, State Senator Dale Volker, refused to allow him to do so. In Volker's view the FVOA should have no say whatsoever in who would get to apportion the state funds. Undaunted, the FVOA asked its lobbyist, Artie Malkin, to get involved. From him, though, they learned of another roadblock: the governor intended to appoint someone to do this job. Still, though, the FVOA members persisted. For days they met with the governor's lawyer and argued passionately for Telesca to distribute the funds. He was the best choice, they argued, because he had no learning curve. He understood the ins and outs of the Attica retaking and its fallout better than anyone else the governor might appoint. Ultimately, the state agreed to establish the Attica State Employee Victims' Fund, and the governor accepted the FVOA's request to have Telesca handle the settlement. On May 2, 2005, Pataki made that appointment official.

Judge Telesca was grateful to be given this opportunity. In 2003, Big Black had been diagnosed with cancer and had grown increasingly ill, and since then the judge had spent a great deal of time talking with him on the phone. In those conversations Black had expressed his hope that the former hostages and hostage families would also get some justice from the state and he felt that Judge Telesca should be the one to help them get it. He had told the judge, "Take care of the families of Attica prison employees. . . . They are good people, they have had their pain too."[11] And so, if the FVOA was willing to agree to binding arbitration, Telesca decided, then he would do the apportionment.[12]

Notably, there were certain matters over which Telesca had no control that had been decided in the governor's office. To ease the burden on the state budget, the settlement would be paid out over six years. What is more, the deferred payments would not accumulate interest. Also, although it was stipulated that the settlement would be paid out at some point between September and March of each year, no promises of exactly when were made.[13] In a bit of good news, the settlement funds would not be taxed.[14]

Before getting down to business, Judge Telesca first held several meetings with Dee Quinn Miller, Gary Horton, and Mike Smith, as representatives of the FVOA, to make sure he understood what sort of apportionment they had all been imagining. As they spoke he took notes and he couldn't help but notice that there were still some real differences regarding which FOVA members deserved the highest awards. As Dee recalled, "The Judge picked up on it . . . the tensions between me and Mike."[15] Telesca already knew that Dee believed the widows deserved the most money, but Mike Smith argued that they, while profoundly scarred, had not necessarily suffered the most trauma. There was also the thorny question of where the death of William Quinn, Miller's father, fit into all of this. After all, he had not been killed by the state although, in Miller's view, there was no question that, ultimately, he too had died because of state negligence—ironically the same point that attorney William Kunstler had tried to make in front of the jury deciding his client John Hill's fate back in 1975.[16]

To help work through these differences of opinion between FVOA members, Telesca decided to meet with the entire FVOA group on June 13, 2005, in order to get a sense of what everyone else thought should happen. As he had with the former prisoners, he invited them to tell their stories on the record. He made clear that he would also read the Attica Task Force testimony and, if members wanted to, they could tell their stories to him privately and such testimony could be sealed.[17] He instructed every family member to get all of their relevant documentation to him by June 15 so he could begin holding anywhere from four to six days of testimony. His goal was to have the entire matter settled by August 1 to meet the state comptroller's deadline for processing payments. There were now a total of 150 people claiming a piece of this settlement, including, ironically, Lieutenant Joseph Christian, whose rescue mission near the hostage circle on September 13, 1971, had, according to both the McKay Commission report and Malcolm Bell's whistle-blower report, led so tragically to many of the hostages being shot to death by troopers firing from up on the catwalk.[18]

On July 3 Judge Michael Telesca issued his long-awaited order, amended and finalized on July 12, 2005.[19] As this order explained clearly, there were three groups of eligible claimants. There were the families of those correction officers or state civilian employees who died in the course of the Attica retaking—and this was important wording because, by not specifying how they died, it meant that William Quinn could be included in this group.[20] Then there were current or former correction officers or state civilian employees who were "physically attacked, held hostage, or detained by inmates during the riot . . . even if released prior to the retaking of the prison by state forces," or their heirs if they had since died.[21]

Finally, there were current or former correction officers or state civilian employees who had been employed at Attica during the retaking, or any current or former New York State Police employees, who were "shot during the retaking of Attica Correctional Facility by state forces on September 13, 1971," or their heirs if they had since died.[22]

Once Telesca had determined these three groups, he then divided them into six subclasses.[23] There was Category One ($550,000), which included William Quinn and Harrison William Whalen—also described as "those persons who died as a result of injuries inflicted by inmates, [as well as] those persons who were mortally wounded during the retaking on September 13, 1971, and who suffered conscious pain and suffering for a period of 20 or more days."[24] There was Category Two ($500,000), which included hostages Edward Cunningham, John D'Arcangelo, Elmer Hardie, Richard Lewis, John Monteleone, Carl Valone, Elon Werner, and Ronald Werner—also described as "all persons who were either killed instantly during the retaking on September 13, 1971 or died no more than 19 days thereafter from those injuries."[25] Category Three ($380,000) covered former hostages like Michael Smith—"those persons who were severely, but not fatally wounded, as a result of injuries sustained during the retaking on September 13, 1971. For purposes of this subclass, a 'severe' injury is one that required hospitalization for 20 or more consecutive days during the period between September 13 and December 13, 1971, or which resulted in brain damage."[26] Category Four ($225,000) was designated for "those persons who were taken hostage for at least some period during September 9 through September 13, 1971, or persons who participated in the retaking of Attica Prison and who, as a result of beatings received from inmates or injuries sustained from gunfire, received permanent physical injuries that resulted in a complete or partial physical disability." Category Five ($150,000) included "those persons who were taken hostage for at least some period during September 9 through September 13, 1971 and who received significant injuries as a result of gunfire or beatings received from inmates."[27] Finally, Category Six ($100,000) covered "all remaining persons who were held hostage for any period of time during the riot."[28]

In this order, as he had done in the prisoners' order, Telesca also included extensive narrative evidence of the Attica victims as well as that of disinterested parties who could corroborate their testimony—everyone from prisoners to members of law enforcement who had participated in the assault. Telesca had been particularly moved by what he had heard from a former sheriff's deputy from Niagara County who was there on the morning of the retaking. "He was very emotional in describing the shooting that took place and how 'unnecessary it was.' He had trained officers in riot control as a deputy and was a former Marine MP and felt that there was no need to use bullets. Tear gas would have been sufficient to subdue the inmates."[29] Indeed, quite a few men had taken the time to offer corroborating testimony even though they personally "could not share in the settlement fund."[30] And Telesca was glad that so many had, finally, spoken up. As he said in the concluding paragraph of his order, "Hopefully, the survivors and their families of the Attica riots of 1971 will no longer feel 'forgotten' and that those who suffered and continue to suffer will feel some measure of comfort at least from the fact, that the matter is concluded and some measure of justice was served."[31]

Some measure of justice was the best, perhaps, that anyone could have hoped for after almost thirty-five years. As former hostage Ron Kozlowski explained it to reporter Gary Craig, "It doesn't really fulfill what you went through," he said. But, he added, "It's better than nothing."[32] Others, such as FVOA attorney Gary Horton, were also pragmatic about where the FVOA had finally ended up. "I'm not sure what true justice could be in this situation. We're happy we reached this point. Personally, it's further

The inscription on the memorial reads, "In memory of the employees who gave their lives in the riot of September 9–13, 1971," February 2015. *(Courtesy of* The New York Times*)*

than I thought we'd be able to reach."[33] And, as Mike Smith put it, "I don't know if this is justice . . . but this is as close as we're going to get."[34]

To Dee Quinn Miller and to Michael Smith in particular, however, this victory ultimately felt hollow. The fact was that, despite now agreeing to pay out a total of $24 million to the scores of people it had traumatized and to some of the lawyers who had represented them, the state of New York still had not admitted wrongdoing. There was no admission of responsibility, let alone an apology to any prisoner or hostage who had suffered the retaking. The state had managed to keep the survivors of its horrific retaking from knowing the details of that plan and of that day by refusing to bring all of its documents into the public eye as the FVOA had demanded. So many people continued to be protected by keeping these files closed to the public.

As Dee Quinn Miller knew after meeting so many Attica survivors since the FVOA first began its journey, opening the records would not, in itself, bring peace to the victims. Actually, what they learned could well shatter lives in altogether new ways. She wondered if this was particularly true of some of the children of slain hostages she had gotten to know. She worried that some of them might not react at all well, say, to learning who had actually killed their dads.[35] This shouldn't have been the state's call, however. It was wrong that state officials had decided to protect those who had committed crimes at its behest. It was immoral that it was still covering up what actually had happened on its request.

Until the full truth about what had happened at Attica was told, thought Miller, this moment in history would still haunt all of its victims.

EPILOGUE

# Prisons and Power

By 2011, when I found myself staring down at the collected materials that littered the warehouse floor of the New York State Museum, many former Attica prisoners and former Attica hostages, as well as Attica's observers, lawyers, and state officials, had already passed away. Former Attica prisoner Frank "Big Black" Smith lost a grueling battle with cancer in 2004. Former head of the Attica investigation Judge Robert Fischer died in 2005. In 2009, Judge John Elfvin passed away, and by 2012 former Attica observer Tom Wicker, former Attica superintendent Vincent Mancusi, and former Attica hostage Gary Walker had died. In 2016, as this book was going to press, former Attica prisoner Richard X Clark and lawyer Elizabeth Fink passed away.

But even though so many of Attica's participants and witnesses are no longer here, this historic moment has not faded into obscurity. In these pages, their history lives on. They made Attica matter.

However, Attica's legacy—what this moment meant for the history of the United States—remains deeply contested.

Given the brutal way in which the Rockefeller administration ended the Attica rebellion, and in light of the support they received from the president of the United States, readers might be surprised that Attica's immediate impact was to spark some serious reforms of the American criminal justice system. Less than a week after the retaking, the 340 members of New York's Democratic State Committee, including top party politicians such as New York mayor John Lindsay, met on September 19, 1971, at the Hotel Syracuse and called for the immediate implementation of the central demands that had been made during the Attica uprising including greater religious and political freedom, banning censorship of mail and newspapers, and providing more counseling and additional rehabilitation services.[1]

Similar rumblings could be heard in the halls of the New York State Legislature, even before the Jones Committee (the special state panel that had been convened right after Attica to study penal institutions) released its January 1973 report on how to improve prisons.[2] During the 1972 legislative session, the Rockefeller administration, supported by legislators from both parties, was actually proposing various prison reforms, including that prisoners should be allowed to leave prison for a week of educational or vocational training; that they should be permitted temporary leaves from prison for events such as family funerals; and that they be allowed to secure medical care for themselves if the treatment they needed was unavailable at their facility.[3] All also seemed to agree that year that prisoners who had been imprisoned for "comparable crimes" should all be eligible for parole "in roughly the same amount of time."[4]

The upshot of these various proposals and recommendations—which stemmed in no small part from community groups across the state levying enormous pressure on their legislators—was that "over 150 prison reform bills were introduced in the legislature during the 1972 legislative session and eight were passed. The most important of these included the governor's $12 million package of new funds."[5] Not only did prison reform have some real support in the New York State Legislature's 1972 session, but when Governor Rockefeller proposed his budget for 1973, he "exempted the Department of Correctional Services from expenditure restrictions placed on all other state agencies" so that the prison reforms could be funded.

Attica even seemed to positively impact discussions taking place at the federal level. On the floors of Congress, the Pepper Commission, headed by Democrat Claude Pepper, suggested that serious prison reform bills needed to be considered in the wake of what Attica had revealed about the state of America's penal facilities; and Republican senators from New York such as Jacob Javits were also being pressured to bring about real changes in the way that the state's prisons were run. As one constituent wrote to one of Javits's right-hand men, "One Positive Step might be to tie all future LEAA [Law Enforcement Assistance Administration] grants to state and local authorities to an acceptance and implementation by the latter of the reforms contained in the '28 Attica demands.' "[6]

While many scholars and pundits have considered the 1960s the heyday of prisoner rights, and the 1970s the decade of unmitigated backlash, the decade immediately after the Attica rebellion saw vital victories for prisoners across the country in general and at Attica in particular.[7] In the years that followed the uprising, most of the practical proposals the Attica Brothers had fought for were in fact implemented across their state. Right after the rebellion, the Department of Correctional Services requested nearly $2.7 million for the "inauguration of Department-wide inmate food service and clothing programs" that would "permit the Department, for the first time, to provide a nutritious diet to all offenders confined in Correctional Facilities."[8] The department also "asked for nearly $400,000 for the purpose of recruiting and assisting minority group candidates in joining the Department of Correctional Services," and received a grant "to expand day and evening academic/vocational training in selected New York facilities."[9] These requests were important, as was the continuous pressure that the Attica prisoners themselves put on their own administrators to make good on the various promises that had been made. Within a year of the uprising, *The New York Times* reported that reforms had been implemented regarding "clothing, food, visiting privileges, mail censorship, and the number of showers permitted."[10]

In addition to paving the way for the prisoners eventually to "get better food and medical care," the Attica uprising also led to their visiting hours and other privileges being "substantially increased and improved," as well as to their "employment opportunities" being expanded.[11] Following the rebellion Inmate Liaison Committees also were established. These were bodies elected by a vote of the prisoners, intended to help "channel grievances, communications and suggestions from the inmate population to the correctional authorities."[12] The state of New York seemed to take CO training more seriously as well. The Department of Correctional Services, for example, decided to hold a comprehensive "Orientation Training for Correction Officers" at the New York State Police Academy in Albany on December 6–23, 1971, which covered subjects as varied as "Types of Inmates," "Attitudes in Supervision," "Interpersonal Dynamics," "prejudice," and "minority cultures."[13] Thanks to the Attica rebellion, numerous existing grassroots efforts to push for prison reform were newly energized in New York. In November 1971 a large conference was held in Binghamton called "After Attica—What?" and, as important, entirely new prisoner rights organizations were founded, such as Prisoners' Legal Services.[14] Numerous other, older organizations that had long been advocating to humanize New York's prisons, such as the Osborne Association and the

Fortune Society, were also galvanized by Attica. Thanks to their efforts, New York's criminal justice system as a whole became less repressive in the wake of the uprising.

But though Attica reflected the extraordinary power and possibility of prisoner rights activism, at the same time, Janus-like, it also reflected, and helped to fuel, a historically unprecedented backlash against all efforts to humanize prison conditions in America.

One cannot overestimate how much it had mattered—not just to New Yorkers' views of civil and prisoner rights activism, but also to the views of countless other Americans—when state officials stood outside Attica in the immediate aftermath of their assault on the prison and told outrageous tales of prisoner barbarism. The rebellion had been front-page and television news for an entire week and when state officials told the nation that the prisoners—those who had claimed to be clamoring only for better treatment—had slaughtered innocent hostages, many were naturally horrified and disgusted. Activists and protesters, many concluded, had simply gone too far. Indeed, to countless white Americans in particular, Attica suggested that it was now time to rein in "those" black and brown people who had been so vocally challenging authority and pushing the civil rights envelope. It appeared, now, that they weren't legitimate freedom fighters, they were instead just dangerous thugs.[15] As one *Time* magazine reader put it in his October 1971 letter to the editor, "Governor Rockefeller did exactly the right thing. And now let's not have the courts get lenient with these murderous convicts."[16]

Importantly, it wasn't just disenchanted citizens that took this message from the events of 1971. So too did policymakers. The Attica uprising prompted the American Correctional Association (ACA) to conduct a major study of prisons, one that was disseminated widely, which concluded that there was in America by 1971 a "New Type of Prisoner."[17] This new type of prisoner was not only to blame for the ugliness that had happened at Attica, reported the ACA, but he was a regular presence in, and a major threat to, "a majority of prisons and jails in the nation."[18] And, lest there be any doubt about why the nation now faced the threat of this more militant convict, it was because these men had spent the 1960s acquiring "a knowledge—superficially and otherwise—of history, race problems, street fighting and the vocabulary of radicalism" and they now believed they were "a victim of racist society."[19] Most alarming, according to the ACA, this "new breed of politically radical young prisoners" believed that they were "in a 'Holy War' against racist oppressors," which, the organization emphasized, did not bode at all well for the law-abiding citizens of this nation.[20]

This particular understanding of Attica and what it suggested about prisoners would inform how officials across the country dealt with the incarcerated from that year forward. While some enacted reforms in the immediate aftermath of the uprising, other prison wardens and commissioners of correction in California, Connecticut, Vermont, and West Virginia all loudly spoke out against ever again negotiating with prisoners. Force, they insisted, was now a must.[21] In fact, some intimated, simply asserting more authority might be insufficient when it came to dealing with this new breed of militant black prisoner. Perhaps there now needed to be an entirely new sort of penal facility for these men.

No sooner had the smoke cleared over Attica than New York's commissioner of correctional services, Russell Oswald, was pitching exactly this idea to Governor Nelson Rockefeller. According to media reports, Oswald proposed isolating "up to 500 of [the] state's 16,000 inmates to forestall rebellions" in so-called "maxi-maxi" facilities. He argued that there were "certain individuals" who couldn't be allowed to move about in an "open institution."[22] They needed "segregation and intensive help."[23] As Fred Ferretti of *The New York Times* summed it up: "The 'more militant people, the aggressive people' . . . would be concentrated 'so they won't spread their poison' to other inmates."[24] Other departments of correctional services across the country agreed with Oswald's assessment that there was a crisis brewing thanks to black militants in the prisons, and at least one prison administrator was confident that "in the atmosphere that existed in the wake of Attica . . . 'we will be able to do it.' "[25]

That Attica had directly, albeit unwittingly, helped to fuel an anti-civil-rights and anti-rehabilitative ethos in the United States was soon clear to people paying attention to electoral politics across the nation. Any politician who wanted money for his or her district had learned that the way to get it was by expanding the local criminal justice apparatus and by making it far more punitive. The tougher on law and order a district was, the more dollars would come its way.[26] As Republican state senator John Dunne put it bluntly, "As a result of Attica, the public attitude is that we've got to get tougher. That means we've got to put more people in prison. We have not reached the point where as many people as should be in prison, are there."[27]

Dunne had no idea how right he was about the public's expectations.

Notably, for all of the Rockefeller administration's nods to prison reform funding in 1972, the following year Governor Rockefeller added to his reputation of being tough on criminals by passing a set of drug laws that were more draconian than anything that had ever before been on the books.[28] Legislation was enacted that, for example, "created mandatory minimum sentences of 15 years to life for possession of four ounces of narcotics—about the same as a sentence for second-degree murder."[29] These 1973 drug laws were subsequently duplicated across the country, in ever more punitive iterations, over the next two decades. By 1978, for instance, Michigan had passed a so-called "650-Lifer" law that automatically gave life sentences to anyone caught with 650 grams of cocaine. And seemingly overnight, any crime—not just drug crimes—could net someone extraordinary penalties.

Indeed, in the 1980s and the 1990s, politicians passed scores of laws at both the state and federal level that criminalized acts that had previously been legal, as well as passing countless mandatory minimums and so-called truth in sentencing laws that ensured substantially more prison time for any act that was now, or had always been, considered illegal.[30] And by 1990, Republicans were trying to pass a tough-on-crime federal bill that, among other things, would "reduce the number of 'aggravating factors' that are needed for the courts to impose a death penalty."[31] Tellingly, when a less draconian bill was also proposed, the president of the National District Attorneys Association tried to undercut any support for it by saying that the bill looked "like it was drafted by the 'Death Row PAC' at Leavenworth or Attica."[32]

This district attorney need not have worried that anything less harsh would pass. Not only did the Republicans triumph that year but plenty of Democrats also wanted to get even tougher on crime. In 1994 Democrats and Republicans again banded together to pass an even more devastatingly punitive piece of legislation, the Violent Crime Control and Law Enforcement Act. This act was the most comprehensive "tough on crime" bill in American history. Among other things, it earmarked $9.7 billion to fund the building of more prisons. By 1995 the U.S. prison population had topped one million, and was still growing at an unprecedented rate.[33] The fact that so many of these people now in prison had been arrested because they were drug addicts, mentally ill, poor, and racially profiled concerned few if any politicians, whether in a statehouse or in Washington, D.C. Then, to make sure that this now enormous group of the incarcerated did not resist their deteriorating conditions of confinement via the nation's legal system as they had done so effectively both before and after the Attica uprising, in 1996 legislators passed the Prison Litigation Reform Act (PLRA).

The PLRA was a deadly blow to American prisoners. So many prisoner rights victories of the twentieth century had been made possible by the ability of the incarcerated to access federal courts to protect their Eighth Amendment right not to endure cruel and unusual punishment. This new law made it much harder for prisoners to protect themselves legally. For example, it required proof of an actual violation before any decree or injunction could be issued, and it also severely curbed the discretion of the federal courts to render decisions with implications for the system as a whole, and the law actually required them to take the public's safety into consideration when rendering any decision. The act additionally placed a cap on attorney fees and required that a panel of three judges agree before any prisoner could be released from confinement as a result of a lawsuit.[34]

By the time the twenty-first century began, America's War on Crime and War on Drugs had criminalized the nation's poorest neighborhoods—its already most marginalized black and brown communities—to such a degree that the nation descended into an internationally unparalleled crisis known as mass incarceration. While the lies told at Attica—how it had been spun—did not, in some linear way, cause mass incarceration, they had certainly fueled it.[35] Importantly, although the War on Crime had begun six years before Attica, America's dramatic spike in incarceration rates began directly after that rebellion had been quashed.

And, notably, in the age of mass incarceration, the word "Attica" no longer connoted struggle and resistance in the popular imagination—as it had years earlier in the lyrics of John Lennon's "Attica State" or in Sidney Lumet's blockbuster film *Dog Day Afternoon*. Rather, by the 1990s, "Attica"—when it showed up in the lyrics of rappers like KRS-One and Zack De La Rocha, or in an episode of *The Sopranos*, or even in the kids' cartoon *SpongeBob*—had come to mean the worst-of-the-worst criminal.[36]

America by the early twenty-first century had, in disturbing ways, come to resemble America in the late nineteenth century. In 1800 the three-fifths clause gave white voters political power from a black population that was itself barred from voting, and after 2000 prison gerrymandering was doing exactly the same thing in numerous states across the country.[37] After 1865, African American desires for equality and civil rights in the South following the American Civil War led whites to criminalize African American communities in new ways and then sent record numbers of blacks to prison in that region.[38] Similarly, a dramatic spike in black incarceration followed the civil rights movement—a movement that epitomized Attica. From 1965 onward, black communities were increasingly criminalized, and by 2005, African Americans constituted 40 percent of the U.S. prison population while remaining less than 13 percent of its overall population.[39] And just as businesses had profited from the increased number of Americans in penal facilities after 1870, so did they seek the labor of a growing captive prison population after 1970. In both centuries, white Americans had responded to black claims for freedom by beefing up, and making more punitive, the nation's criminal justice system. In both centuries, in turn, the American criminal justice system disproportionately criminalized, policed, and forced the labor of incarcerated, disenfranchised African Americans in ways that wrought incalculable damage both in and outside of America's penal institutions.[40]

Attica's prisoners knew this long history well. This was their history. And this is why they refused to give up until they had effected truly meaningful prison reform. These prisoners felt, just as the state did, that a great deal was at stake in 1971 when they took over the Attica Correctional Facility. If they didn't speak out and demand to be treated like human beings, and if the power of the state to determine the workings of this nation's criminal justice system was allowed to be absolute, the American penal system would eventually be too punitive and inhumane to bear.[41]

And they were correct. A close look at the state of New York in the three decades after Attica's prisoners were silenced clearly shows just how much worse things eventually became. Whereas there were 12,500 prisoners locked in the state's penal facilities in 1971, already so many that facilities like Attica were severely overcrowded, thanks to "changes in sentencing polices and parole release rates," that number more than doubled by 1982.[42] By the close of the 1990s, 72,638 prisoners were locked up in New York prisons, doing enough work for the state prison industries, Corcraft, to generate $70 million of revenue between 1998 and 1999 alone.[43] As the twenty-first century dawned, there were nearly 74,000 men and women, overwhelmingly black and brown citizens of that state, locked in New York penal institutions—all of whom could still be forced to work and none of whom could vote to change the system.[44]

It was clear by the close of the twentieth century that many of the post-rebellion calls for change to New York's prison system had been rolled back the instant that prisoner activism—and thus pressure on the system—was quelled.

Little more than a decade after the Attica uprising, the prison was again in the grips of a serious crisis.[45] By 1982, Attica was so overcrowded that any prisoner programming that still existed fell far short of the number of people who wanted to access it. Once again, there were too many prisoners for the medical care that was available in the facility and that care was, once again, of "poor quality."[46] In fact, there were again so many serious problems at Attica in areas such as "medical care, food service, recreation, visiting, and access to court and legal materials" that many there worried that there might be another explosion.[47] Although there was an Inmate Liaison Committee that could voice concerns to the administration, by the 1980s, prisoners knew that this group had no real power and so they refused to pretend that it did. The superintendent reported that year "that so few prisoners were even interested in running for an ILC position that he cancelled the last election and selected anyone who nominated himself to serve."[48]

At Attica in the 1980s, as before, prisoners who could not be heard eventually lashed out. This time, though, the response was to place them in segregation, and to make that placement far more punitive than it had ever been before. By 1982 "the physical size of this area had more than doubled during the past year and now holds some eighty prisoners," according to the Correctional Association of New York. Worse, prison officials had constructed twenty brand-new segregation cells that were "completely encased by Plexiglas" and that had only small holes for ventilation, which left those imprisoned in them gasping for air and sweltering in the hot summer months.[49] Furthermore, prison officials as well as members of the new correction officers union, NYSCOPBA, had begun clamoring again for the "establishment of a so-called maxi-maxi unit at Attica or a separate maxi-maxi facility."[50] Their model, Great Meadow Correctional Facility, already had one of these, a so-called Involuntary Protection Unit (IPU) for "troublesome" prisoners.[51]

Life was so difficult for Attica's prisoners who landed in its Special Housing Unit (formerly known as HBZ, now called SHU) that one of the mentally ill men incarcerated there killed himself on June 3, 1985. A lawsuit was filed on behalf of the men in that unit against the correction officers, who, the suit insisted, had hounded and taunted this man until he was driven to suicide. In this complaint, which landed on the docket of Judge Michael Telesca, prisoners said that there had been numerous "instances of physical force inflicted by SHU correction officers, the utilization of strip cells [cells in which the prisoner is allowed no clothes or bedding] for punishment purposes, the denial of adequate medical care and adequate physical exercise facilities, unsanitary living conditions, inadequate portions and unsanitary preparation of food, the improper use of Plexiglas shields on the fronts of many SHU cells, inadequate access to the law library and legal research materials, and denial of the right to free exercise of religion."[52]

Forty years after the uprising of 1971, conditions at Attica were worse than they had ever been. According to the Correctional Association of New York, by 2001 "the Department of Correctional Services had cut over 1200 programs providing services to inmates that were there in 1991."[53] By April 12, 2011, there were 2,152 men crammed into this facility, the vast majority of whom were African American and Hispanic, and an overwhelming 21 percent of Attica's prison population that year had been "diagnosed with some level of mental illness."[54] According to the Correctional Association of New York, which surveyed Attica's prisoners, there was still "a noticeably high level of intimidation and fear throughout the facility . . . [and] we received numerous letters describing threats and retaliation for participating in the CA survey."[55] Furthermore, the association noted, "Attica inmates had the highest ratings of all CA-visited prisons for frequency of physical assaults, verbal harassment, threats and intimidation, abusive pat frisks, turning off lights and water, and retaliation complaints—inmates also complained that retaliation materialized in the form of some officers not letting inmates leave their cells for meals."[56]

It is both tragic and deeply ironic that new levels of brutality against America's prisoners have been, at least so far, the most obvious and lasting legacy of the 1971 Attica uprising. Even though the extraordinary violence that took place in 1971 was overwhelmingly perpetrated by members of law enforcement, not the prisoners, American voters ultimately did not respond to this prison uprising by demanding that states rein in police power. Instead they demanded that police be given even more support and even more punitive laws to enforce.

Indeed, the 1960s and 1970s were all about the politics of the ironic. At the Democratic National Convention protests of 1968, Kent State in 1970, and Wounded Knee in 1973, unfettered police power each time turned protests violent, and yet, after each of these events, the nation was sent the message that the people, not the police, were dangerous. Somehow, voters came to believe that democracy was worth curtailing and civil rights and liberties were worth suspending for the sake of "order" and of maintaining the status quo.[57]

But, while it was ironic how voters chose to respond to the violence of the 1960s and 1970s, their response was by no means inevitable. The meaning of the rebellions of that period, and what had actually taken place in them, was actively distorted by the very politicians and state officials whom these protests had targeted. Just as Kent, Ohio, mayor LeRoy Satrom had distorted what had happened at Kent State University, leading to the bloodshed there in 1970, and just as South Dakota governor Richard Kneip had distorted the events that touched off the violence at Wounded Knee in 1973, many state officials and politicians had also actively distorted what had happened at Attica in its immediate aftermath and then tried, thereafter, to cover up subsequent attempts to tell the truth.[58]

And, yet, that truth could not be covered up and contained indefinitely. Not only had the prisoners and hostages who had survived the retaking of Attica never given up their fight to hold the state of New York accountable for the abuses and atrocities committed in September 1971, but they also never stopped insisting that the full story be told and they struggled to make sure that Attica had not been in vain. No matter how repressive the nation became in the wake of the 1971 prison uprising, the men confined in Attica, and in other facilities like it across the country, never stopped fighting for their rights, for their dignity.

Attica's prisoners rose up again a decade later for the same reason as in 1971. On July 21, 1984, almost two hundred men smashed windows and screamed their outrage when a fellow prisoner was shot to death by a tower guard.[59]

Much more recently, they have come together in another dramatic fight to be treated like human beings. On August 9, 2011, twenty-nine-year-old prisoner George Williams was attacked by an Attica sergeant and three correction officers in C Block. Williams was severely wounded, left with "a broken collarbone, two broken legs and other injuries," which required his transport to the Wyoming County Community Hospital in Warsaw.[60] In this case, though, Attica's men didn't riot or rebel within the prison, instead they went public and insisted that the Wyoming County district attorney investigate their claims. Undoubtedly, history told this DA that Attica's men weren't going to let this new case of abuse be ignored. He not only looked into what had happened to Williams, but also then indicted the four correction officers, ultimately charging them with "first-degree gang assault, fourth-degree conspiracy, tampering with physical evidence and official misconduct."[61] The DA said these men had "conspired to assault an inmate in Cell Block C and that following the violent attack, the four prison employees prepared false physical evidence."[62]

The DA's first attempt to indict these men was dismissed on the grounds that the "prosecution had introduced improper evidence in front of the grand jury that heard the case."[63] The DA filed new indictments against three correction officers: Matthew Rademacher, Keith Swack, and Sean Warner; a fourth CO was at the time granted immunity because he had been subpoenaed to testify in front of the grand jury. The three remaining COs faced charges of "first-degree gang assault, a Class B violent felony; tampering with physical evidence, a Class E felony; and official misconduct, a Class A misdemeanor."[64] The outcome of the case against officers Rademacher, Swack, and Warner would not be determined until March of 2015. Its ultimate disposition says a great deal about Attica's complicated legacy.

When the three correction officers from Attica finally went to trial in 2015 they were not lacking for support. Guard unions from around the country had mobilized on their behalf, from virtually the moment they were suspended, and monies poured in to help them defend themselves in court. As NYSCOBPA explained it, COs from Attica and other prisons had created a "new Legal Defense Fund" whose purpose it was "to fight these charges now and in the future."[65] It would, "through the can drives, t-shirts, wristbands, benefits and donations," give the indicted officers the money they needed to hire top counsel and to get the public on their side.[66] Notably, the Forgotten Victims of Attica also sent support their way. A letter from indicted CO Sean Warner to the FVOA noted how "the Forgotten Victims of Attica have been there from the beginning with donations, a kind word, a phone call, and countless letters and support. These men and women have been through so much the past 40 years and are still there at the sides of the current Prison Staff no matter what the circumstances. It is an honor to have these men and women at our sides."[67]

The fact that these men had so much public support of course mattered a great deal to how they would fare in New York's legal system. Their trial began on March 2, 2015, and it ended abruptly in a light plea deal.[68]

The judge had allowed each correction officer to plead guilty to a single charge of misdemeanor misconduct and none of them would have to serve any time in prison.[69] George Williams wept. No matter how hard he had fought to get justice, it still took his breath away that those who had beat him so mercilessly received little more than a reprimand.[70]

Yet the fact that these men had ended up in court charged with a crime at all was important. It was "the first time in the history of New York State that any guard has been prosecuted for brutality against someone in prison," as the Correctional Association of New York correctly noted right after the plea deal.[71] Indeed, that these men had been indicted also reflected perhaps Attica's most powerful legacy—prisoners' determined resistance of repression.

The Attica uprising of 1971 happened because ordinary men, poor men, disfranchised men, and men of color had simply had enough of being treated as less than human. That desire, and their fight, is by far Attica's most important legacy. This is the legacy that led George Williams to refuse to be silent, even though speaking up must have been terrifying given the retaliation he knew he could suffer. This is why he refused to give up even when a local judge tried to dismiss the criminal case against his attackers. This is why he was determined to seek justice in federal court when his attackers received only a reprimand in state court.[72] This is why the Justice Department, in March 2015, began an official investigation into brutality against prisoners at Attica Correctional Facility.[73] Attica's prisoners had refused to stay silent.

That those who have endured Attica have always insisted on speaking out is something that matters. As this book goes to press vital Attica materials at the New York State Archives remain closed to the public. State officials are still denying Freedom of Information Act requests, though there is no legal rationale to do so. Even the Attica documents that filled shelves in the Erie County courthouse in 2006 have since disappeared. But despite state officials' continued efforts to put every roadblock imaginable in the way of journalists, historians, and filmmakers, they have not stopped Attica's history from being written, nor Attica's survivors from telling their story.

From New York in 1971, when nearly 1,300 prisoners stood up against overcrowding and the myriad other injustices that had become policy, to California in 2013, when 30,000 prisoners launched a hunger strike against the repressive conditions in the correction system, to Texas in 2015, when prisoners shut down a major penal facility because of serious abuses,

America's incarcerated people have never stopped struggling against this country's worst and most punitive practices.[74] The Attica prison uprising of 1971 shows the nation that even the most marginalized citizens will never stop fighting to be treated as human beings. It testifies to this irrepressible demand for justice. This is Attica's legacy.

# *Acknowledgments*

Spending almost a decade writing one book means being indebted to so many people that there simply aren't enough pages here to convey my gratitude adequately. I will, however, do my best.

The very first person I must thank is my agent, Geri Thoma, who believed in this book before anyone. Geri, you are not only an incredible literary agent, but you are also my friend. You always cheered me when things looked grim, and you have also celebrated every wonderful research find, every writing breakthrough, and every bit of good news, with such a genuine joy. This has meant everything to me.

I must also thank my editor at Pantheon Books, Edward Kastenmeier—as well as the superstar editors who work with him, Emily Giglierano and Stella Tan. I owe the three of you everything.

I also owe so much to the many people around the country who provided me invaluable Attica-related materials when the State of New York would not.

Without the generosity of Attica lawyer-extraordinaire Elizabeth Fink, this book simply could not have been written. Thankfully for the historical record, and for the sake of Attica's many victims, Liz saved and graciously let me see countless memos, depositions, transcripts, state documents, photographs, videos, and more—a literal treasure trove of Attica's history from 1971 to 2000. My deepest regret today is that Liz passed away before I could hand her a copy of this book. Liz, I hope I got it right . . . I hope I did good.

Attica lawyer William Cunningham shared vital documents from the Lynda Jones civil suit against the state. Dee Quinn Miller shared invaluable resources on the hostages' and hostage families' fight to be heard. Ann Valone, Flo Hoder, and Richard Meisler also shared personal items that helped me to understand

Attica. And then there are those who prefer not to be named—people who were willing to share crucially important materials such as the Attica autopsy reports, personal letters, and more—you know who you are, and thank you for trusting me with those.

I am deeply grateful as well to the following researchers, journalists, and historians: Documentary filmmaker and research dynamo Christine Christopher sent me vital materials and included me in her own research journey as she and David Marshall made their powerful film on the Attica uprising, *Criminal Injustice: Death and Politics at Attica.* Gary Craig of the Rochester *Democrat and Chronicle* very generously offered his time and materials to me; not only is Gary's coverage of the Attica rebellion and its aftermath remarkable, but I am forever indebted to him for working so hard to get his paper's priceless Attica photos included in this book. Peter Wagner of the criminal justice reform organization the Prison Policy Initiative has offered invaluable research assistance over the years. Craig Williams of the New York State Museum let me see and touch those remarkable Attica artifacts that had been hidden from view for so many decades. And finally, my historian friends have shared amazing Attica finds—especially Simon Balto, Daniel Chard, David Goldberg, Trevor Griffey, Caleb Smith, and John David Smith.

Many students have also been incredibly generous with their prison-related sources and their support over the years. Several students have written theses on Attica, and one wrote a paper on the NYC jail riots, all of which taught me so much. Thank you, Jeremy Levenson, Touissant L'Ouverture, Ethan Sachs, and Morgan Shahan. Over the years I relied heavily on the research help given me as well by Katie Mannon, Sarah Miller, and, most recently, Mary Bridget Lee, who, in short, saved my life. Without Mary Bridget helping me to find photos and format the endnotes, this book might well still be a raggedy draft on my Mac. Thank you so much.

Special thanks goes out to the wonderful archivists at the following libraries and research centers for patiently photocopying, microfilming, and otherwise allowing me time to view Attica-related material that proved essential: the Labadie Collection at the University of Michigan, the American Radicalism Collection at Michigan State University, the Walter Reuther Library of Labor and Urban Affairs, Special Collections at Stony Brook, the Rockefeller Archive Center, the New York State Archives, Special Collections at the Bancroft Library at Berkeley, Special Collections at Stanford University, the New York City Archives, Special Collections at Yale University, the Miller Center at the University of Virginia, Pacifica Radio Archives, the Vanderbilt Television Archives, the Gerald Ford Library, the Charles Blockson Collection at Temple

University Library, the Schomburg Center for Research in Black Culture, Special Collections at the University of Rochester, and Special Collections at the University of Buffalo.

I also want to give special thanks to David Swarts, then county clerk at the Erie County courthouse in Buffalo, New York, and to James Conway, then superintendent at the Attica Correctional Facility, for allowing me to view vital uprising-related documents back in 2006.

No matter how many documents and artifacts I finally got to see, I only really understood Attica after listening to the people who had experienced the uprising and its aftermath firsthand. I thank them for so willingly sharing their stories and memories with me—often at great emotional cost to themselves. Thank you so very, very much to: Don Almeter, Herman Badillo, Traycee Barkley, Linda Borus, Charles Bradley, Dan Callahan, Keith Clark, Kevin Clark, James Conway, Mark Cunningham, Jomo Davis, Michael Deutsch, John Dunne, John Elfvin, Arthur Eve, Elizabeth Fink, Elizabeth Gaynes, Bill Goodman, Frank Hall, Rick Harcrow, Jazz Hayden, William Hellerstein, Edward Hershey, Susannah Heschel, John "Dacajewiah" Hill, Flo Hoder, Gary Horton, Clarence Jones, Sarah Kunstler, Larry Lyons, Sue Lyons, Richard Meisler, Josh Melville, Danny Meyer, Deanne Quinn Miller, George Nievez, Margaret Patterson, Carlos Roche, Herman Schwartz, Michael Smith, Sharon Smith, Lewis Steel, John Stockholm, Mary Stockholm, Tony Strollo, Michael Telesca, Ann Valone, Jamie Valone, Mary Ann Valone, Tom Wicker, and Ellen Yacknin.

Malcolm Bell and Joe Heath deserve special thanks. Although Malcolm made clear to me that he could not let me see his original whistleblowing documents, he nevertheless supported me when I stumbled upon them on my own and felt obligated to reveal their explosive contents. Joe offered me tremendous support as well as a keen fact-checking eye. Together these two gave me the strength to make this book brave.

In order to write about Attica I also needed to learn a great deal about American prisons, and about the history of American criminal justice politics and policing, and, to that end, I owe a great many scholars a particular debt. I am grateful for the wisdom of Amanda Alexander, Michelle Alexander, Dan Berger, Doug Blackmon, Ethan Blue Daniel Chard, Robert Chase, Miroslava Chavez Garcia, Dennis Childs, Ta-Nehisi Coates, Mary Ellen Curtin, Khalilah Brown Dean, Alex Elkins, Max Felker-Kantor, Benjamin Fleury-Steiner, Ruth Wilson Gilmore, Marie Gottschalk, Kali Gross, Sarah Haley, Cheryl Hicks, Marc Lamont Hill, Pippa Holloway, Amanda Hughett, James Kilgore, Nora Krinitsky, Regina Kunzel, Talitha Laflouria, Matthew Lassiter, Alex Lichtenstein, Toussaint Losier, Glenn Loury, Ashley Lucas, Lisa Miller, Reuben

Miller, Alan Mills, Nancy Mullane, Dwayne Nash, Jessica Neptune, Michael Lee Owens, Josh Page, Devah Pager, Anne Parsons, Robert Perkinson, Imani Perry, Sherie Randolph, Natalie Ring, Margo Schlanger, Carla Shedd, Jonathan Simon, Jason Stanley, David Stein, Rubia Tapia, Jeremy Travis, Nicole Gonzalez Van Cleve, Vesla Weaver, Bruce Western, Yohuru Williams, Timothy Stewart Winter, and Keeanga Yamatta-Taylor.

To my friends working on other vital periods and topics who have shouted out my work and have given me so much wonderful support throughout this book writing process, thank you: Evan Bennett, Martha Biondi, Charlie Bright, Niambi Carter, Catherine Clinton, Stephanie Cole, Catherine Conner, Nathan Connolly, Jane Dailey, Marcus Daniel, Angela Dillard, Donna Gabaccia, Sarah Gardner, Gary Gerstle, Tiffany Gill, James Green, Julie Green, Cindy Hahamovitch, Grace Hale, Jacqueline Dowd Hall, LaShawn Harris, Lindsay Helfman, Darlene Clark Hine, Patrick Jones, Steve Katrowitz, Robin D. G. Kelley, Robert Korstad, Max Krochmal, Kevin Kruse, Michael Landis, Steven Lawson, Nelson Lichtenstein, Sherrie Linkon, Lisa Lindsay, Nancy Maclean, Austin McCoy, Roberta Meek, Kevin Mumford, Alondra Nelson, Scott Nelson, Liesl Orenic, Chad Pearson, Wendell Pritchett, Barbara Ransby, Jacob Remes, Leah Wright Rigueur, Stacey Robertson, Dan Royles, John Russo, Robert Self, Robert Smith, Tom Sugrue, Peter Thompson, Tim Tyson, Dara Walker, Stephen Ward, Deborah Gray White, and Rakefet Zalashik. Thank you also to Dan Katz and Patricia Jerido for offering me such a warm and welcoming place to stay during those many research trips to New York.

To some scholar-friends I want to say a special thanks.

To my dearest sister-friends Karen Cox, Shannon Frystak, Alecia Long, and Danielle McGuire, thank you for the love, support, and always-needed girls' weekends. To Lisa Levenstein, thank you for being my fiercest ally and steady confidante over this long haul. And to my friend and coeditor Rhonda Y. Williams, as well as to our amazing UNC editor Brandon Proia, thanks for keeping the Justice, Power, and Politics series alive and thriving while I was in the last throes of getting this book to press.

To Khalil Gibran Muhammad: I am not sure that I have spent more time on the circuit talking prisons and policy with anyone than with you and for that I am grateful. You continue to inspire me and I am so very thankful we are friends. And to Kelly Lytle Hernandez: you in particular have pushed me to think about this nation's carceral past in new ways and for that, and our friendship, I am deeply grateful.

To Donna Murch: you are my sister-scholar and co-editor and I thank you for your incredible support—for being a true ally—these last years. And thanks to you and Walter Murch, being in NYC has felt like being home.

To Elizabeth Hinton, Julilly Kohler-Hausmann, and Melanie Newport: you three are not only my heart, but you're also the future of carceral state history. Thank you for pushing the boundaries.

And special thanks to Bryant Simon, whose get-togethers in West Philly kept me sane and motivated, and who connected our families in ways so wonderful. And to Jim Downs, who has always made me feel like a rock star, even when I felt like an exhausted bag of rocks. Peter Logan, thank you for creating the most intellectually engaged and supportive environments any historian could ask for up in the Center for the Humanities at Temple University, and for giving me refuge on the tenth floor.

Beyond the scholars, friends, advocates, and allies who helped me to write this history of Attica, I am also deeply indebted to a number of institutions and organizations: the American Historical Association; the National Endowment for the Humanities; the University of North Carolina at Charlotte; the Rockefeller Archive Center; the New York State Archives; and last but hardly least, the Open Society's Soros Justice Fellowship, which was life-changing. Not only did it allow me a year of leave to conduct book research, but it also introduced me to countless advocates, activists, and fellow scholars working on criminal justice reform. These relationships changed me profoundly and bettered my book immeasurably. Thank you, Adam Cuthbert and Christina Voight, for running such an important program and for bringing us together year after year. Among my fellow Soros recipients whom I haven't already named above, I want to specially acknowledge Neelum Arya, Sujatha Baliga, Michelle Deitch, Shaena Fazel, Mary Heinen, Pippa Holloway, Eric Lotke, Nancy Mullane, and Dee Ann Newell. Each of you is an inspiration.

When it comes to getting this book written, and more specifically written well, let me also thank the godsends who have read drafts of this book and who have helped me, page by page, word by word, to get at the heart of what makes Attica so important. Thank you Terry Bisson, Megan Ritchie Jooste, and particularly Beth Rashbaum for your tremendous patience and hard work with the drafts you waded through. And thank you to the 2014 committee of the J. Anthony Lukas Work-in-Progress Award for naming this manuscript as the finalist for this prestigious prize in 2015. I hope this is the book you all imagined it would be.

Thank you to E.M.W. Beste. Your voice brought this book to life.

In closing, I must somehow find the words to adequately convey to my family just how much it has meant to me that they have given me the time, the space, the love, the encouragement, and the faith that I needed to complete this tome.

To Tamara Smith, you have been there since the earliest days, and you gave so much of your time to help us settle back in Michigan. Love and thanks.

To my Kansas, Colorado, Chicago, California, and Zurich family members—from those who have followed my book-writing saga on Facebook and offered me so much support, to those who have distracted me over wonderful visits these last years, thank you all so much.

To Agnes Spitzer, you know how much I have bent your ear about this book and how much your counsel and presence in my life means to me. You are, and will always be, my soul sister.

To Dan and Betsey Wells, as well as Caroline Wells, Phil Hervey, and Brynne Hervey: You have offered me more love and support than any daughter-in-law/sister-in-law/auntie has a right to ask for. I love you all and thank you.

To my sister, Saskia Thompson, and my niece Isabel LaBarrie Thompson, you have both made these recent years of my life in Philadelphia some of my happiest. I miss living near you both terribly.

To Ann Curry Thompson and Frank Thompson . . . well, you know. You are why I see the world as I do. You are why I hope to help make it a better place. Full stop. I am so grateful that you are my parents.

To Dillon Thompson Erb, Wilder Thompson Erb, Ava Thompson Wells, Kimberly Brink, and Rahshawn (Shawn) Johnson: No mother could ask for more in life than to have it filled with you five incredible human beings. Dillon and Wilder, I am so deeply proud of you both—in fact I am awed by all that you have each accomplished in life. I love you both more than I will ever be able to convey. Ava, I still remember the day I heard I was having a daughter and I have been grateful for each day since. You are brilliant and I am in awe of the kind, generous, and courageous young woman you have become. Kim, you are one of the most extraordinary women I know. Your gentle spirit, fierce smarts, generosity, and ambition all humble me and make me so incredibly glad that you are a part of our family. And Shawn, you have moved mountains. You are one of the sweetest souls I have ever known and you have made our family, and me, complete.

And the last, most profound, thank-you is to Jonathan Daniel Wells. Jon, the support you have offered me to do this book—from the time you have made available to me by taking too much on yourself, to the unconditional love you have given me each and every second of every day, to the faith you had in me that I could actually pull this off—takes my breath away. You are my best friend and partner for life. And now that this book is finally done, I can't wait to begin living that life again with you. I love you.

# Notes

## Abbreviations Used in the Notes

***Attica Task Force Hearing*** Public Hearings Conducted by Governor George E. Pataki's Attica Task Force, Rochester, New York, and Albany, New York, May to August 2002.

***Erie County courthouse*** Document located in Office of the Clerk, Erie County courthouse, Buffalo, New York, visited by author October 2006.

***McKay Report*** New York State Special Commission on Attica, *Attica: The Official Report of the New York State Special Commission on Attica* (New York: Bantam, 1972).

***McKay Transcript*** *New York State Special Commission on Attica Public Hearings Transcript,* Rochester, New York, and New York, New York, April 1972.

***Meyer Commission*** "Special Inquiry into the Attica Investigation, 1975"

***Nixon Tapes*** Richard Nixon White House Recordings, Presidential Recordings Program, Miller Center for Public Affairs, University of Virginia, Charlottesville, Virginia.

***Quigley Order*** Judge Robert M. Quigley, Final Order, *Lynda Jones, Individually and as Administratrix of the Estate of Herbert W. Jones, Jr., Deceased v. State of New York,* State of New York Supreme Court, Appellate Division, Fourth Department, 96 A.D.2d 105 (N.Y. App. Div. 1983), Rochester, New York, August 31, 1982, Archives of William Cunningham.

***Tom Wicker Papers*** Southern Historical Collection, Manuscripts Department, Wilson Library, University of North Carolina, Chapel Hill.

***Walter Reuther Library*** Walter Reuther Library of Labor and Urban Affairs, Wayne State University, Detroit, Michigan.

## A Note About Attica Litigation

There were myriad iterations of the Attica civil case filed on behalf of prisoners, depending on the various named defendants and plaintiffs as well as on when the case was filed over the course of nearly thirty years. The first citation for the case, filed shortly after the rebellion, is *Inmates of Attica et al. v. Rockefeller et al.* By the time the case was finally settled, it was titled *Akil Al-Jundi et al. v. Vincent Mancusi et al.*

## INTRODUCTION · STATE SECRETS

1. Heather Ann Thompson, "How Attica's Ugly Past Is Still Protected," *Time*, May 26, 2015, http://time.com/3896825/attica-1971-meyer-report-release/.

2. Letter. Deputy Attorney General Richard Rifkin to Dr. Heather Thompson. November 12, 2003. Letter in author's possession.

3. Heather Ann Thompson, "The Lingering Injustice of Attica," *New York Times*, September 8, 2011, http://www.nytimes.com/2011/09/09/opinion/the-lingering-injustice-of-attica.html?_r=0.

4. In 2015, when a reporter tried to locate the myriad Attica documents that I had found at the Erie County courthouse, clerks told him that they had no Attica records and never did. Shortly thereafter they called him back and said that they were mistaken—they did in fact have some documents related to Attica that he could see. When this reporter went to view them, though, he was handed one box filled only with prisoner indictments. I was stunned to learn this. All that I saw back in 2006 has apparently been removed. No one seems to know where an entire wall of Attica documents were taken and, in fact, claim no knowledge of their existence. With regard to the artifacts at the New York State Museum, perhaps realizing the controversial nature of the donation they had just received, officials there decided it best no longer to bring scholars such as myself to its warehouse to see them, or to exhibit them to the public in some fashion. Under pressure the museum did return some of these items to the surviving hostages, but the current whereabouts of the majority of its Attica artifacts is unclear. I can only hope that these vital materials that were in Buffalo and in Albany have not been destroyed, and I am deeply grateful that I made copies of some of the items that were most important to the writing of this book.

## PART I · THE TINDERBOX

### 1. NOT SO GREENER PASTURES

1. Forty percent were under thirty, 77 percent came from cities, 80 percent had not graduated from high school, and 63 percent were African American or Puerto Rican.

2. John Thomas Schleich, Testimony, *In the Matter of the Additional, Special and Trial Term of the Supreme Court of the State of New York, Designated Pursuant to the Order of the Appellate Division, Fourth Department.* County of Wyoming, March 21, 1972, Office of the Clerk, document located in Erie County courthouse, Buffalo, New York, visited by author October 2006, 24. Hereafter referred to as Erie County courthouse.

3. Angel Martinez, Testimony, *New York State Special Commission on Attica Public Hearings Transcript*, Rochester, New York, April 13, 1972, 45. Hereafter referred to as *McKay Transcript.*

4. Ibid., 93.

5. Ralph Bottone, Testimony, *McKay Transcript*, April 14, 1972, 691.

6. The New York State Special Commission on Attica, *Attica: The Official Report of the New York State Special Commission on Attica* (New York: Bantam, 1972), 47. Hereafter referred to as *McKay Report.*

7. Martinez, Testimony, *McKay Transcript*, April 13, 1972, 476.

8. William Jackson, Testimony, *McKay Transcript*, April 12, 1972, 82.

9. *McKay Report*, 43–46.

10. David Addison, Testimony, *McKay Transcript*, April 17, 1972, 81.

11. Ibid., 72.

12. Ibid., 75.

13. Cornell Capa, Testimony, *McKay Transcript*, April 17, 1972, 134.

14. Addison, Testimony, *McKay Transcript*, April 17, 1972, 53.

15. Martinez, Testimony, *McKay Transcript,* April 13, 1972, 57. For more on Martinez, see: Jeremy Levenson, "Shreds of Humanity: The Attica Prison Uprising, the State of New York and 'Politically Unaware' Medicine," Unpublished Undergraduate Honors Thesis, Department of Urban Studies, University of Pennsylvania, December 21, 2011, in author's possession, 38.

16. Frank Smith, interview, "Attica Prison Riot," *American Experience: The Rockefellers,* Public Broadcasting Service, 2007.

17. Martinez, Testimony, *McKay Transcript,* April 13, 1972, 66.

18. Jerry Rosenberg, interview, *Voices from Inside: Seven Interviews with Attica Prisoners* (New York: Attica Defense Committee, 1972), American Radicalism Collection, Michigan State University Library.

19. Handwritten note from correction officer B. J. Conway, June 20, 1969, and typed note from correction officer Charles Cunningham regarding staff meeting, June 16, 1969, Attica uprising–related documents kept at the Attica Correctional Facility, Attica, New York.

20. Letter. Rev. Johnnie Monroe to Mr. John R. Cain, Deputy Commissioner, Department of Corrections, March 31, 1969. Box 7b, Folder 29, Franklin Florence Papers, Manuscript and Special Collections, Rush Rhees Library, University of Rochester, Rochester, NY.

21. Letter. John R. Cain to Rev. Johnnie Monroe, FIGHT. April 7, 1969. Box 7b, Folder 29, Franklin Florence Papers, Manuscript and Special Collections, Rush Rhees Library, University of Rochester, Rochester, NY.

22. Dr. Michael Brandriss, Interview Transcript, August 18, 2012, *Criminal Injustice: Death and Politics at Attica,* Blue Sky Project (2012), transcribed by Diane Witzel, original in possession of Christine Christopher.

23. Ibid.

24. Ibid.

25. Ibid.

26. Jackson, Testimony, *McKay Transcript,* April 12, 1972, 110.

27. Ibid., 108.

28. Harold Goeway, Testimony, *McKay Transcript,* April 13, 1972, 383.

29. Ibid., 385.

30. Ralph Bottone, Testimony, *McKay Transcript,* April 14, 1972, 685.

31. The State of New York Special Commission on Attica, "Appendix A: Attica Expenditures Fiscal Year 1971–1972," *McKay Report,* 488.

32. *McKay Report,* 39.

33. Addison, Testimony, *McKay Transcript,* April 17, 1972, 57.

34. Ibid., 86; Manuel T. Murcia, Counsel, Memorandum to "all institutions," Subject: "Religious Correspondence," September 1, 1966, Attica uprising–related documents kept at the Attica Correctional Facility, Attica, New York.

35. Murcia to "all institutions," September 1, 1966.

36. Addison, Testimony, *McKay Transcript,* April 17, 1972, 80.

37. Ibid., 85.

38. Ibid.

39. Jackson, Testimony, *McKay Transcript,* April 12, 1972, 40.

40. Goeway, Testimony, *McKay Transcript,* April 13, 1972, 399.

41. John Stockholm, Testimony, *Public Hearing Conducted by Governor George E. Pataki's Attica Task Force,* Rochester, New York, May 9–10, 2002, 6. Hereafter referred to as *Attica Task Force Hearing.*

42. James E. Cochrane, Testimony, *McKay Transcript,* April 13, 1972, 236.

43. Henry Rossbacher, Supervisor, Testimony, *McKay Transcript,* April 17, 1972, 31.

44. Ibid.

45. Cochrane, Testimony, *McKay Transcript,* April 13, 1972, 293.

46. Ibid., 244.

47. *McKay Report,* 26.

48. Rossbacher, Testimony, *McKay Transcript,* April 17, 1972, 9.

49. Russell G. Oswald, Commissioner, Department of Correctional Services, Memorandum to Nelson A. Rockefeller, Governor, Subject: "Activities Report—February 8, 1973–March 7, 1973," March 7, 1973, Nelson A. Rockefeller gubernatorial records, Departmental Reports, Series 28, New York (State), Governor (1959–1973: Rockefeller), Record Group 15, Box 2, Folder 32, Rockefeller Archive Center, Sleepy Hollow, New York.

50. Addison, Testimony, *McKay Transcript,* April 17, 1972, 62.

51. Samuel Melville, "Anatomy of the Laundry," Attica uprising–related documents kept at the Attica Correctional Facility, Attica, New York. Also see: Samuel Melville, *Letters from Attica* (New York: William Morrow, 1972), 151–52; and Larry Boone, Testimony, *McKay Transcript,* April 17, 1972, 147.

52. Addison, Testimony, *McKay Transcript,* April 17, 1972, 93.

53. Ibid., 94. McGinnis would eventually go even further than this. By 1971 the Department of Corrections had implemented a uniform pay schedule in all correctional facilities and a 5 percent cap on commissary profits.

54. *Stephen Merkle et al. v. Vincent R. Mancusi, Superintendent of Attica Correctional Facility,* Federal Court, Western District of New York, C1970-490, Attica uprising–related documents kept at the Attica Correctional Facility, Attica, New York.

55. *McKay Report,* 129.

## 2. RESPONDING TO RESISTANCE

1. Michael Flamm, *In the Heat of the Summer: From the Harlem Riot of 1964 to the War on Crime and America's Prison Crisis* (Philadelphia: University of Pennsylvania Press, forthcoming); Matthew Countryman, *Up South: Civil Rights and Black Power in Philadelphia* (Philadelphia: University of Pennsylvania Press, 2007).

2. For more on the liberal origins of the war on crime, see: Elizabeth Kai Hinton, *From the War on Poverty to the War on Crime: The Making of Mass Incarceration in America* (Cambridge: Harvard University Press, 2016); Naomi Murakawa, *The First Civil Right: How Liberals Built Prison America* (New York: Oxford University Press, 2014).

3. "Homicide Rate Trends, 1900–1926," Bureau of Justice Statistics, http//bjs.ojp.usdoj.gov/content/glance/tables/hmrttab.cfm.

4. Russell Oswald, *Attica—My Story* (New York: Doubleday, 1972), 194.

5. Ibid., 194.

6. Notably the incarcerated and formerly incarcerated today very much dislike the word "inmate" and prefer to be referred to as "men," "women," or "people," and, if their status as being imprisoned must be specified, most prefer "incarcerated people" or "prisoners." As "incarcerated people" is too wordy, this book refers to Attica's imprisoned as "men," "people" and "prisoners." For more on language, see: Eddie Ellis, "Words Matter: Another Look at the Question of Language," Center for NuLeadership on Urban Solutions, January 2013.

7. Oswald, *Attica—My Story,* 196–97.

8. Ibid., 197.

9. Russell G. Oswald, Commissioner, Department of Correctional Services, Memorandum to Nelson A. Rockefeller, Governor, Subject: "Activity Report—April 8, 1971–May 5, 1971," May 10, 1971, Nelson A. Rockefeller gubernatorial records, Departmental Reports, Series 28, New York (State), Governor (1959–1973: Rockefeller), Record Group 15, Box 2, Folder 32, Rockefeller Archive Center, Sleepy Hollow, New York.

10. Ibid.

11. Ibid.

12. "No. 2 State Aide: Walter Dunbar," *New York Times,* September 16, 1971, 48.

13. Draft of speech to be given at the New York State Bar Center dedication, Albany,

New York, September 24, 1971, Nelson A. Rockefeller gubernatorial records, Speeches, Series 33, New York (State), Governor (1959–1973: Rockefeller), Rockefeller, Nelson A. (Nelson Aldrich), Record Group 15, Box 85, Folder 3471, Rockefeller Archive Center, Sleepy Hollow, New York.

14. Paul D. McGinnis, Commissioner of Correction, "Agency Appraisal Report, 1970," July 15, 1970, Nelson A. Rockefeller gubernatorial records, Departmental Reports, Series 28, New York (State), Governor (1959–1973: Rockefeller), Record Group 15, Rockefeller Archive Center, Sleepy Hollow, New York.

15. Department of Correction Program Meeting Report, September 22, 1960, Present: Paul McGinnis, William Leonard, John Cain, William J. Ronan, Charles Palmer, John Terry, Edith Baikie, Richard Wiebe, William Rand, Nelson A. Rockefeller gubernatorial records, Departmental Reports, Series 28, New York (State), Governor (1959–1973: Rockefeller), Record Group 15, Rockefeller Archive Center, Sleepy Hollow, New York.

## 3. VOICES FROM AUBURN

1. Jomo Davis, conversation with author, Deerfield Correctional Facility, Capron, Virginia, February 16, 2006. At various points in this book this man is referred to by different names. This is the name he goes by now.

2. New York State Senate Committee on Crime and Correction, *The Hidden Society: Annual Report,* 1970, 12.

3. For an eyewitness account of a participant in this Auburn riot, see: Mariano "Dalou" Gonzalez, Interview by Michael D. Ryan, Transcript, W. E. B. Du Bois Library, Special Collections, University of Massachusetts, Amherst, 7–8.

4. James F. Campbell, *Hostage: Terror and Triumph* (Connecticut: Greenwood, 1992), 49–57.

5. New York State Senate Committee on Crime and Correction, *The Hidden Society,* 14.

6. Russell G. Oswald, Commissioner, Department of Correctional Services, Memorandum to Nelson A. Rockefeller, Governor, Subject: "Activities Report—February 25, 1971–March 22, 1971," Nelson A. Rockefeller gubernatorial records, Departmental Reports, Series 28, New York (State), Governor (1959–1973: Rockefeller), Record Group 15, Box 2, Folder 31, Rockefeller Archive Center, Sleepy Hollow, New York.

7. Ibid.

8. Herman Schwartz, telephone conversation with author, July 28, 2004.

9. Frank Lynns, "State Prison Chief Writes to Rebellious Inmates," *New York Times,* February 11, 1971, 36.

10. Oswald Memorandum to Rockefeller, Subject: "Activities Report—February 25, 1971–March 22, 1971," Rockefeller Archive Center.

11. Lynns, "State Prison Chief Writes to Rebellious Inmates," 36.

12. Russell G. Oswald, Commissioner, Department of Correctional Services, Memorandum to Nelson A. Rockefeller, Governor, Subject: "Activity Report—March 23, 1971–April 7, 1971," April 6, 1971, Nelson A. Rockefeller gubernatorial records, Departmental Reports, Series 28, New York (State), Governor (1959–1973: Rockefeller), Record Group 15, Box 2, Folder 31, Rockefeller Archive Center, Sleepy Hollow, New York.

13. Ibid.

14. Oswald, *Attica—My Story,* 37.

15. Russell Oswald, Letter to Frank Walkley, May 11, 1971, obtained through FOIL request #110818 of the New York State Attorney General's Office, 000912.

16. Douglas Robinson, "Abuses Charged in Auburn Prison: Relatives of Prisoners Tell of Beatings and Gassing," *New York Times,* April 23, 1971.

17. Russell G. Oswald, Commissioner, Department of Correctional Services, Memorandum to Nelson A. Rockefeller, Governor, Subject: "Activity Report—March 23, 1971–April 7, 1971," April 6, 1971.

18. Ibid.

19. Russell G. Oswald, Commissioner, Department of Correctional Services, Memorandum to Nelson A. Rockefeller, Governor, Subject: "Activities Report—May 6, 1971–June 2, 1971," June 9, 1971, Nelson A. Rockefeller gubernatorial records, Departmental Reports, Series 28, New York (State), Governor (1959–1973: Rockefeller), Record Group 15, Box 2, Folder 31, Rockefeller Archive Center, Sleepy Hollow, New York.

20. Ibid.

21. Ibid.

22. Ibid.

23. On the transfer of Auburn prisoners to segregation at Attica, see: Oswald Letter to Walkley, May 11, 1971.

## 4. KNOWLEDGE IS POWER

1. Alton Germain, Testimony, *McKay Transcript*, April 14, 1972, 737.

2. Lucien Lombardo, "Attica Remembered: A Personal Essay," *Paideusis: Journal for Interdisciplinary and Cross-Cultural Studies* 2 (1999): 7–14.

3. Ibid.

4. Bernard "Shango" Stroble, Chapter, "Anatomy of a Defense," unpublished book, ed. Ernest Goodman et al., Preliminary Inventory of the National Lawyers Guild Records, 1936–1999, Ernest Goodman Files, Box 67, Series 10, Bancroft Library, University of California, Berkeley.

5. Larry Boone, Testimony, *McKay Transcript,* April 17, 1972, 20.

6. For more on the ways in which Attica's men understood the broader imperative of keeping state power in check within the criminal justice system, see: Heather Ann Thompson, "Lessons from Attica: From Prisoner Rebellion to Mass Incarceration and Back," *Socialism and Democracy* 28, no. 3 (September 2014): 153–71.

7. David Addison, Testimony, *McKay Transcript,* April 17, 1972, 38. Also see: Lawrence Killbrew, Auburn transferee at Attica until January 3, 1972, Testimony, *State of New York Select Committee on Correctional Institutions and Programs,* New York City, February 11, 1972.

8. Jomo Cleveland Davis, conversation with author, February 16, 2006.

9. Elizabeth Gaynes, conversation with author, Long Island, New York, April 8, 2006.

10. *McKay Report,* 130.

11. Russell Oswald, *Attica—My Story* (New York: Doubleday, 1972), 39.

## 5. PLAYING BY THE RULES

1. Larry Boone, Testimony, *McKay Transcript,* April 17, 1972, 27, 150.

2. Attica Liberation Faction, Letter to Russell Oswald, as quoted in: David Addison, Testimony, *McKay Transcript,* April 17, 1972, 95.

3. As quoted in Jeremy Levenson, "Shreds of Humanity: The Attica Prison Uprising, the State of New York and 'Politically Unaware' Medicine," Unpublished Undergraduate Honors Thesis, Department of Urban Studies, University of Pennsylvania, December 21, 2011, in author's possession, 39–40.

4. Attica Liberation Faction to Oswald, *McKay Transcript,* 97.

5. Russell G. Oswald, Commissioner, Department of Corrections, Memorandum to Nelson A. Rockefeller, Governor, as quoted in: David Addison, Testimony, *McKay Transcript,* April 17, 1972, 97. Copy also held at the Walter Reuther Library of Labor and Urban Affairs, DRUM Collection, Subseries 2C National Lawyers Guild: 1963–74, Box 7, Folder 11, Wayne State University, Detroit, Michigan.

Russell G. Oswald, Commissioner, Department of Correctional Services, Memorandum to Nelson A. Rockefeller, Governor, Subject: "Activities Report—June 2, 1971–

July 2, 1971," July 6, 1971, Nelson A. Rockefeller gubernatorial records, Departmental Reports, Series 28, New York (State), Governor (1959–1973: Rockefeller), Record Group 15, Box 2, Folder 31, Rockefeller Archive Center, Sleepy Hollow, New York.

6. Russell G. Oswald, Commissioner, Department of Correctional Services, Memorandum to Nelson A. Rockefeller, Governor, Subject: "Activities Report—June 30, 1971–July 29, 1971," July 30, 1971, Nelson A. Rockefeller gubernatorial records, Departmental Reports, Series 28, New York (State), Governor (1959–1973: Rockefeller), Record Group 15, Box 2, Folder 31, Rockefeller Archive Center, Sleepy Hollow, New York. Also see: Russell G. Oswald, Interview by CBS News correspondent Walter Cronkite, September 21, 1971, Transcript, Dorothy Schiff Papers, Box 4, New York Public Library.

7. Russell Oswald, *Attica—My Story* (New York: Doubleday, 1972), 40.

8. Herbert X Blyden and Akil Al-Jundi, Testimony, Deferred Joint Appendix, *Herbert Blyden et al. v. Vincent Mancus, et al.*, United States Court of Appeals, Second Circuit, 186 F. 3d 252, Docket No. 97-2912, Vol. I, November 11, 1991, in the papers of Elizabeth M. Fink, Brooklyn, New York, A-1-687. Also see: "Folsom Manifesto," in Frank Browning, *Prison Life: A Study of the Exploitative Conditions in America's Prisons* (New York: Harper & Row, 1972).

9. Robert E. Tomasson, "Melville, Attica Radical Dead: Recently Wrote of Jail Terror," *New York Times*, September 15, 1971.

10. Oswald Memorandum to Rockefeller, July 30, 1971.

11. Russell Oswald, Letter to Attica Inmates, July 7, 1971, as quoted in: David Addison, *McKay Transcript*, 106.

12. Ibid.

13. Ibid.

14. Frank Lott, Letter to Russell Oswald, July 19, 1971, as quoted in Addison, *McKay Transcript*, 107.

15. Ibid., 108.

16. Ibid., 110.

17. Ibid., 111.

18. Russell Oswald, Letter to Attica Inmates, undated, as quoted in: Addison, *McKay Transcript*, 111.

19. Second Oswald Letter to Attica Inmates quoted in Addison, *McKay Transcript*, 111.

20. *McKay Report*, 138.

## 6. BACK AND FORTH

1. "August–September, 1971," Agricultural Business Weather Bureau, Historical Databases.

2. James E. Cochrane, Testimony, *McKay Transcript*, April 13, 1972, 290.

3. David Addison, Testimony, *McKay Transcript*, April 17, 1972.

4. For an important recent discussion of George Jackson and the broader California prisoner rights movement, see: Dan Berger, *Captive Nation: Black Prison Organizing in the Civil Rights Era* (Chapel Hill: University of North Carolina Press, 2014).

5. Wallace Turner, "Bingham Charged in Prison Deaths," *New York Times*, September 1, 1971; "Officials Report Racial Angle in San Quentin Break," *New York Times*, August 25, 1971. Also see: Pacifica Radio Reports PM 054 and PM 122 on the killing of George Jackson, in: The Freedom Archives, San Francisco, California, as well as: Television News Archive, Vanderbilt University, Nashville, Tennessee.

6. Conversation #571-10 (rmn_e571b), September 13, 1971, 4:36 p.m.–6:40 p.m., Oval Office; and Conversation #74-2, September 14, 1971, Richard Nixon White House Recordings, Presidential Recordings Program, Miller Center for Public Affairs, University of Virginia, Charlottesville, Virginia. Hereafter referred to as Nixon Tapes.

7. Larry Boone, Testimony, *McKay Transcript*, April 17, 1972, 155.

8. Davis, conversation with author, February 16, 2006.

9. Boone, Testimony, *McKay Transcript,* April 17, 1972, 154.

10. From an August report written by Russell Oswald for Governor Nelson Rockefeller. Copy of report removed from Rockefeller Archives, New York State Archives, by the state of New York, but this quote was reprinted in Oswald's own autobiography. See: Russell Oswald, *Attica—My Story* (New York: Doubleday, 1972), 42.

11. Deanne Quinn Miller, conversation with author, Batavia, New York, August 11, 2004.

12. Henry Rossbacher, Testimony, *McKay Transcript,* April 17, 1972, 14; Addison, Testimony, *McKay Transcript,* April 17, 1972, 38. Also see: *McKay Report,* p. 130.

13. Boone, Testimony, *McKay Transcript,* April 17, 1972, 157.

## 7. END OF THE LINE

1. As quoted in: Russell Oswald, *Attica—My Story* (New York: Doubleday, 1972), 117.

2. As quoted in: ibid., 118.

3. As quoted in: ibid., 119.

4. As quoted in: ibid., 122.

5. Raymond Jordan, Jr., Letter to Russell Oswald, September 8, 1971, FOIA request #110818 of the New York State Attorney General's Office, FOIA p. 000848.

6. Ibid.

7. As quoted in *McKay Report,* 141.

8. Ibid.

9. As reproduced in: Samuel Melville, *Letters from Attica* (New York: William Morrow, 1972), 173–74.

10. Herbert X Blyden, Letter to John R. Dunne, September 8, 1971, FOIA request #110818 of the New York State Attorney General's Office, FOIA p. 001676.

11. Ibid.

12. As reproduced in: Melville, *Letters from Attica,* 173–74.

## PART II · POWER AND POLITICS UNLEASHED

1. Michael Smith, conversation with author, Batavia, New York, August 10, 2004.

2. Ibid.

3. Ibid.

4. Michael Smith, Testimony, *Attica Task Force Hearing,* July 30, 2002, Albany, New York, 197.

## 8. TALKING BACK

1. For more information on the Weather Underground and the Young Lords Party see: Dan Berger, *Outlaws of America: The Weather Underground and the Politics of Solidarity* (Chico, California: AK Press, 2005) and Johanna Fernandez, *When the World Was Their Stage: A History of the Young Lords Party, 1968–1974* (Princeton: Princeton University Press, forthcoming).

2. Chris Mayers, Testimony, *McKay Transcript,* April 14, 1972, 173.

3. Rockefeller Administration, Confidential Memo, "Events at Attica: September 8–13, 1971," 1. This nearly seventy-page so-called Albright-Vestner Report was compiled by Rockefeller's closest aides so that the governor could be briefed on every detail about the upheaval at Attica during the rebellion. The existence of this report was denied for years but in the 1980s it was finally produced under subpoena. This copy was found in the Office of the Clerk, located in Erie County courthouse, Buffalo, New York, when the author visited in October 2006.

4. Investigators James Stephen and F. A. Keenan, State of New York Organized

Crime Task Force Memorandum to R. E. Fischer, Subject: "Interview of Lt. Robert Curtiss," December 9, 1971, Erie County courthouse.

5. Karl Pfeil, Testimony, *In the Matter of the Additional, Special and Trial Term of the Supreme Court of the State of New York, Designated Pursuant to the Order of the Appellate Division, Fourth Department.* County of Wyoming, January 20, 1972, Erie County courthouse.

6. Richard X Clark, *The Brothers of Attica* (New York: Links Books, 1973), 8–9.

7. Chris Mayers, Testimony, *McKay Transcript,* April 14, 1972, 189.

8. Ibid., 191.

9. Rockefeller Administration, Confidential Memo, "Events at Attica: September 8–13, 1971," 2.

10. Investigators Stephen and Keenan Memorandum to Fischer, December 9, 1971.

11. Rockefeller Administration, Confidential Memo, "Events at Attica: September 8–13, 1971," 2.

12. Richard Maroney, Testimony, *McKay Transcript,* April 18, 1972, 397–98.

13. Investigators Stephen and Keenan Memorandum to Fischer, December 9, 1971.

14. *McKay Report,* 152.

15. Rockefeller Administration, Confidential Memo, "Events at Attica: September 8–13, 1971," 2.

16. Maroney, Testimony, *McKay Transcript,* April 18, 1972, 409.

17. Jack Florence, Testimony, *In the Matter of the Additional, Special and Trial Term of the Supreme Court of the State of New York, Designated Pursuant to the Order of the Appellate Division, Fourth Department.* County of Wyoming, January 20, 1972, Erie County courthouse, 17.

18. Ibid., 17–18.

## 9. BURNING DOWN THE HOUSE

1. Chris Mayers, Testimony, *McKay Transcript,* April 14, 1972, 194.

2. Ibid., 195.

3. Ibid.

4. Rockefeller Administration, Confidential Memo, "Events at Attica: September 8–13, 1971," 2.

5. Steven Rosenfeld, Testimony, *McKay Transcript,* April 14, 1972, 219.

6. There is conflicting testimony about who decided the prisoners should be refused rec time and taken back to their cells (see *McKay Transcript* testimonies), and even the governor's office was given a wholly different account of who was where and who said what that morning (see: Rockefeller Administration, Confidential Memo, "Events at Attica: September 8–13, 1971," 3). Taking the testimony of all of the prisoners and correction officers together, however, Curtiss's version seems the more likely. Pfeil testified before a grand jury that he "either gave the order or re-affirmed the order of Mr. Mancusi, that this is what he should do, order that A Block door be locked and personally supervised that that company was locked in on their respective galleries." Pfeil, Testimony, *In the Matter of the Additional, Special and Trial Term of the Supreme Court of the State of New York, Designated Pursuant to the Order of the Appellate Division, Fourth Department.* County of Wyoming, January 20, 1972, 12.

7. Rosenfeld, Testimony, *McKay Transcript,* April 14, 1972, 220.

8. Rockefeller Administration, Confidential Memo, "Events at Attica: September 8–13, 1971," 3.

9. In his memoir, former Attica inmate John Hill (also known as Dacajewiah) asserts that he, Sam Melville, and an unnamed African American prisoner were the three who jumped on Curtiss and began hitting him. As he wrote, "The brother said, 'Fuck you honky,' and punched him in the face dropping him instantly. Sam Melville and I followed suit and kicked the crap out of the Captain and his boys. A black,

white, and red man were unified in one instinctive impulse—to defiantly engage the brutal regime." John Boncore Hill and Sandra Bruderer, *The Autobiography of Dacajewiah: Splitting the Sky, from Attica to Gustafsen Lake* (Canada: John Pasquale Boncore, 2001), 18.

10. Lieutenant Robert Curtiss, Hostage, Statement taken by M. D. Gavin and E. Palascak, September 28, 1971, 4:15 p.m., Erie County courthouse.

11. Richard X Clark, *The Brothers of Attica* (New York: Links Books, 1973), 22.

12. Edward Douglas Zimmer, Testimony, *In the Matter of the Additional, Special and Trial Term of the Supreme Court of the State of New York, Designated Pursuant to the Order of the Appellate Division, Fourth Department.* County of Wyoming, January 20, 1972, Erie County courthouse, 3–4.

13. Investigators James Lo Curto and F. E. Demlar, Memorandum to A. G. Simonetti, Subject: "Quinn Homicide Investigation," October 20, 1971, State of New York Organized Crime Task Force, Erie County courthouse. Also see: Zimmer, Testimony, *In the Matter of the Additional, Special and Trial Term of the Supreme Court of the State of New York, Designated Pursuant to the Order of the Appellate Division, Fourth Department*, 3–4.

14. Harold Goewey, Testimony, *McKay Transcript*, April 13, 1972, 397.

15. Investigators James LeCurto and F. E. Demlar, Memorandum to A. G. Simonetti, Subject: "Quinn Homicide Investigation," October 20, 1971. Also see: Rockefeller Administration, Confidential Memo, "Events at Attica: September 8–13, 1971," 5.

16. Investigators James LeCurto and F. E. Demlar, Memorandum to A. G. Simonetti, Subject: "Quinn Homicide Investigation," October 20, 1971.

17. "The weld itself was defective. The two ends had been butt-welded, so that no more than 1/16" of metal held the two ends of the rod together around its circumference." After this rod had been improperly reconnected, the joint was then "ground smooth, further weakening it." *McKay Report*, 161.

18. Investigators James LeCurto and F. E. Demlar, Memorandum to A. G. Simonetti, Subject: "Quinn Homicide Investigation," October 20, 1971. Also see: Rockefeller Administration, Confidential Memo, "Events at Attica: September 8–13, 1971," 5.

19. Rockefeller Administration, Confidential Memo, "Events at Attica: September 8–13, 1971," 6.

20. Donald Almeter, conversation with author, New Port Richey, Florida, July 3, 2005. Also see: Carol Demare and Sarah Metzgar, "The Attica Uprising 25 Years Ago," *Times Union* (Albany, New York), September 8, 1996.

21. Eugene Smith, Testimony, *Attica Task Force Hearing*, July 31, 2002, Albany, New York, 33.

22. Ibid. 35.

23. Ibid., 36.

24. Ibid., 36.

25. Dean Wright, Testimony, *Attica Task Force Hearing*, May 9–10, 2002, Rochester, New York, 59–63.

26. Nicholas Gage, "Richard Clark," *New York Times*, September 15, 1971.

27. Clark, *The Brothers of Attica*, 23.

28. Royal Morgan, Testimony, *Attica Task Force Hearing*, August 13, 2002, Rochester, New York, 74.

29. Clark, *The Brothers of Attica*, 24.

30. Ibid.

31. Ibid.

32. There are conflicting reports on whether the top official also at that gate was Mancusi or Vincent. The McKay Commission wrote that it was Vincent, and Clark later told Quinn's daughter that it was Mancusi. See: *McKay Report*, 161. Also see: Deanne Quinn Miller, Testimony, *Attica Task Force Hearing*, July 30, 2002, Albany, New York, 184.

33. Investigators James LeCurto and F. E. Demlar, Memorandum to A. G. Simonetti, Subject: "Quinn Homicide Investigation," October 20, 1971.

34. Clark, *The Brothers of Attica*, 25.

35. Gordon Kelsey, Testimony, *In the Matter of the Additional, Special and Trial Term of the Supreme Court of the State of New York, Designated Pursuant to the Order of the Appellate Division, Fourth Department.* County of Wyoming, January 26, 1972, Erie County courthouse.

36. Kelsey, Testimony, *In the Matter of the Additional, Special and Trial Term of the Supreme Court of the State of New York, Designated Pursuant to the Order of the Appellate Division, Fourth Department.* County of Wyoming, January 26, 1972.

37. Richard O. Merle, Testimony, *The State of New York v. John Hill et al.*, Vol. 10, New York State Court of Appeals, Albany, New York, March 7, 1975, 2021–23.

38. Nancy Quinn Newton, Testimony, *Attica Task Force Hearing,* July 30, 2002, Albany, New York, 149.

39. Ibid., 149–50.

## 10. REELING AND REACTING

1. Richard Maroney, Testimony, *McKay Transcript,* April 18, 1972, 400.

2. As described in a publication authored by James A. Hudson, *Slaughter at Attica: The Complete Inside Story* (New York: Lopez Publication, 1971), 34. Copy in the personal archives of Jamie Valone.

3. Rockefeller Administration, Confidential Memo, "Events at Attica: September 8–13, 1971," 11.

4. Ibid., 11; Robert Douglass, Deposition, "Special Inquiry into the Attica Investigation" (hereafter referred to as the Meyer Commission), June 20, 1975, Mineola, New York, 2907, FOIA request #110818 of the New York State Attorney General's Office, FOIA pp. 000253–000254.

5. *McKay Report,* p.188.

6. Major J. W. Monahan, Troop Commander, Memorandum to Superintendent W. E. Kirwin, Subject: "Attica Correctional Facility," September 19, 1971, Investigation and interview files, 1971–1972, New York (State), Special Commission on Attica, 15855-90, Box 86, New York State Archives, Albany, New York, 1.

7. Ibid.

8. Judge Robert M. Quigley, Final Order, *Lynda Jones, Individually and as Administratrix of the Estate of Herbert W. Jones, Jr., Deceased v. State of New York,* State of New York Supreme Court, Appellate Division, Fourth Department, 96 A.D.2d 105 (N.Y. App. Div. 1983), Rochester, New York, August 31, 1982, Archives of William Cunningham, 26, 30. Hereafter referred to as Quigley Order.

9. "State Police/Attica Riot Chronology," New York State Police Headquarters, Albany, New York, in the papers of Elizabeth M. Fink, Brooklyn, New York, 1.

## 11. ORDER OUT OF CHAOS

1. Carlos Roche, Testimony, *Akil Al-Jundi et al. v. The Estate of Nelson A. Rockefeller, Russell Oswald, John Monahan, Vincent Mancusi and Karl Pfeil,* United States District Court, Western District of New York, Buffalo, New York, No. CIV-75-132, October 31, 1991, 1911. Hereafter *Akil Al-Jundi et al. v. The Estate of Nelson A. Rockefeller et al.*

2. John Stockholm, conversation with author, Lehigh Acres, Florida, July 1, 2005.

3. Carlos Roche, Testimony, ibid., 1914.

4. John Schleich, Testimony, *In the Matter of the Additional, Special and Trial Term of the Supreme Court of the State of New York, Designated Pursuant to the Order of the Appellate Division, Fourth Department.* County of Wyoming, March 21, 1972, 11.

5. Ibid., 13.

6. Ibid., 14. Also see: M. Eugene Pittman, M.D. Clinical Physician, Memorandum to John B. Wilmont, Acting Superintendent, Elmira Correctional Facility, November 8, 1971, New York State Archives Investigation and interview files, 1971–1972, New York (State), Special Commission on Attica, 15855-90, Box 84, New York State Archives, Albany, New York.

7. Jack Florence, Testimony, *In the Matter of the Additional, Special and Trial Term of the Supreme Court of the State of New York, Designated Pursuant to the Order of the Appellate Division, Fourth Department.* County of Wyoming, February 2, 1972, 39.

8. Tom Wicker, notes from interview with Roger Champen, undated, Tom Wicker Papers, 5012, Series 1.1, Box 2, Southern Historical Collection, Manuscripts Department, Wilson Library, University of North Carolina, Chapel Hill, 19. Hereafter referred to as Tom Wicker Papers.

9. Ibid.

10. "Inmates in D Yard Survey Statistics," Investigation and interview files, 1971–1972, New York (State), Special Commission on Attica, 15855-90, Box 88, New York State Archives, Albany, New York.

11. Wicker, notes from interview with Roger Champen, undated.

12. "Inmates in D Yard Survey Statistics," New York State Archives.

13. According to Richard X Clark there were about thirty to forty Black Muslims at Attica. See: Richard X Clark, Testimony, *Akil Al-Jundi et al. v. The Estate of Nelson A. Rockefeller et al.*, United States District Court, Western District of New York, Buffalo, New York, No. CIV-75-132, October 25, 1991, 112.

14. As quoted in: "Five Deadly Days," reprinted from the *Democrat and Chronicle* (Rochester, New York), Tom Wicker Papers.

15. Eugene Smith, Testimony, *Attica Task Force Hearing*, July 31, 2002, 39–40.

16. Gary Walker, Testimony, *Attica Task Force Hearing*, July 31, 2002, Albany, New York, 63.

17. Eugene Smith, Testimony, *Attica Task Force Hearing*, July 31, 2002, 37.

18. Walker, Testimony, *Attica Task Force Hearing*, July 31, 2002, 63.

19. Wicker, notes from interview with Roger Champen, undated, 20.

20. Ibid.

21. Ibid.

22. Charles Horatio Crowley, Testimony, *In the Matter of the Additional, Special and Trial Term of the Supreme Court of the State of New York, Designated Pursuant to the Order of the Appellate Division, Fourth Department.* County of Wyoming, May 24, 1972, Erie County courthouse, 45.

23. Mariano "Dalou" Gonzalez, Interview by Michael D. Ryan, 7.

24. Florence, Testimony, *In the Matter of the Additional, Special and Trial Term of the Supreme Court of the State of New York, Designated Pursuant to the Order of the Appellate Division, Fourth Department.* County of Wyoming, February 2, 1972, 47.

25. Frank "Big Black" Smith, Interview by Jennifer Gonnerman, "Remembering Attica," *Village Voice*, September 5–11, 2001.

26. Charles "Flip" Crowley, *In the Matter of the Additional, Special and Trial Term of the Supreme Court of the State of New York, Designated Pursuant to the Order of the Appellate Division, Fourth Department.* County of Wyoming, May 24, 1972, 70.

27. John Schleich, Testimony, *In the Matter of the Additional, Special and Trial Term of the Supreme Court of the State of New York, Designated Pursuant to the Order of the Appellate Division, Fourth Department.* County of Wyoming, March 21, 1972, 19–20.

28. Crowley, *In the Matter of the Additional, Special and Trial Term of the Supreme Court of the State of New York, Designated Pursuant to the Order of the Appellate Division, Fourth Department.* County of Wyoming, May 24, 1972, 64.

29. Carl Rinney, Testimony, *In the Matter of the Additional, Special and Trial Term of the Supreme Court of the State of New York, Designated Pursuant to the Order of the*

*Appellate Division, Fourth Department.* County of Wyoming, March 28, 1972, Erie County courthouse, 33–34.

30. Ibid.

31. Richard X Clark, Testimony, *Akil Al-Jundi et al. v. The Estate of Nelson A. Rockefeller et al.*, October 25, 1991, 131.

32. Ibid., 132.

33. Ibid., 133.

34. George Nieves, Testimony, *Akil Al-Jundi et al. v. The Estate of Nelson A. Rockefeller et al,* United States District Court, Western District of New York, Buffalo, New York, No. CIV-75-132, November 19, 1991, 4652. For a complete list of the fifteen "practical proposals" that the men in D Yard wrote up on September 9, as well as their determination whether each individual demand was "a short range goal" or "something that had to be dealt with later," see Appendix A. Also see: Clark, Testimony, *Akil Al-Jundi et al. v. The Estate of Nelson A. Rockefeller et al.*, October 25, 1991, 137–45.

35. Ibid., 135.

## 12. WHAT'S GOING ON

1. Vincent Mancusi, Testimony, *Akil Al-Jundi et al. v. The Estate of Nelson A. Rockefeller et al.*, United States District Court, Western District of New York, Buffalo, New York, No. CIV-75-132, December 17, 1991, E-9223.

2. Ibid., E-9242–E-9243.

3. Ibid., E-9243.

4. Ibid., E-9244.

5. Russell Oswald, Testimony, in loc. cit., read posthumously into the record on January 2, 1992, 10805.

6. Ibid.

7. Rockefeller Administration, Confidential Memo, "Events at Attica: September 8–13, 1971," 13.

8. Herman Schwartz, Testimony, *McKay Transcript,* April 19, 1972, 498.

9. Russell Oswald, *Attica—My Story* (New York: Doubleday, 1972), 84.

10. Ibid.

11. Herman Schwartz, Personal Diary recorded so that he would remember all that he witnessed and experienced during the Attica uprising, transcript, taped originally on September 12, 19, and 24, 1971. In author's possession.

12. Schwartz, Testimony, *McKay Transcript,* April 19, 1972, 520.

13. Arthur O. Eve, Testimony, *Akil Al-Jundi et al. v. The Estate of Nelson A. Rockefeller et al.*, United States District Court, Western District of New York, Buffalo, New York, No. CIV-75-132, November 6, 1991, 2709.

14. Ibid.

15. Schwartz, Personal Diary, September 12, 19, 24, 1971, 3.

16. All Inmates of Attica Correctional Facility to Richard N. [*sic*] Nixon and Nelson Rockerfeller [*sic*], "Immediate Demands," September 9, 1971, Investigation and interview files, 1971–1972, New York (State), Special Commission on Attica, 15855-90, Box 84, New York State Archives, Albany, New York. Copy of original typed in D Yard complete with handwritten additions by Arthur O. Eve.

17. Richard X Clark, *The Brothers of Attica* (New York: Links Books, 1973), 67.

18. Tom Wicker, Notes from interview with Roger Champen, undated, Tom Wicker Papers.

19. Rockefeller Administration, Confidential Memo, "Events at Attica: September 8–13, 1971," 14.

20. Schwartz, Personal Diary, September 12, 19, 24, 1971, 4.

21. Rockefeller Administration, Confidential Memo, "Events at Attica: September 8–13, 1971," 14.

22. Oswald, *Attica—My Story,* 86.

23. Schwartz, Personal Diary, September 12, 19, 24, 1971, 5.

24. Oswald, *Attica—My Story,* 88.

25. Monahan Memorandum to Kirwan, September 19, 1971.

26. Official Call Log (also known as "the Van Eekeren Tapes"), Headquarters, New York State Police, Albany, in the papers of Elizabeth M. Fink, Brooklyn, New York.

27. Oswald, Testimony, *Akil Al-Jundi et al. v. The Estate of Nelson A. Rockefeller et al.,* read posthumously into the record on January 2, 1992, 10816–17.

28. For a complete list of everyone who came into Attica (time in, time out, and dates), see: "Visitor's Log," Attica uprising–related documents kept at the Attica Correctional Facility, Attica, New York.

29. Technical Sergeant F. D. Smith, New York State Police Memorandum to Major Sergeant Chieco, Subject: "Special Assignment—Attica Correctional Institute," September 9–14, 1971, in the papers of Elizabeth M. Fink, Brooklyn, New York.

30. "WBAI Transcript of Speeches Made in D Yard," March 6, 1972, Investigation and interview files, 1971–1972, New York (State), Special Commission on Attica, 15855-90, Box 84, New York State Archives, Albany, New York. Also see: copy of original typed version of at least portions of Barkley's speech complete with some notations and modifications in the area addressing which observers the inmates wanted called to the prison. Penciled in was the addition of Pablo "Yoruba" Guzman of the Young Lords Party and Huey Newton of the Black Panther Party for Self Defense, L. D. Barkley, "We are Men," speech, investigation and interview files, 1971–1972, New York (State), Special Commission on Attica, 15855-90, Box 84, New York State Archives, Albany, New York.

31. Rockefeller Administration, Confidential Memo, "Events at Attica: September 8–13, 1971," 16.

32. Ibid.

33. "Practical Proposals," copy of original typed list, Investigation and interview files, 1971–1972, New York (State), Special Commission on Attica, 15855-90, Box 84, New York State Archives, Albany, New York.

34. Rockefeller Administration, Confidential Memo, "Events at Attica: September 8–13, 1971," 17; Oswald, *Attica—My Story,* 93.

35. Rockefeller Administration, Confidential Memo, "Events at Attica: September 8–13, 1971," 17.

36. Ibid., 16.

37. Ibid.

38. Ibid.

39. Ibid.

40. There are numerous FBI memos addressed to, or forwarded to, these government officials. See, for example: Federal Bureau of Investigation, Communications Section, Buffalo, Teletype to Director, Domestic Intelligence Section, Stamped: "Included in summary to White House and Attorney General," September 9, 1971. Also see: Domestic Intelligence Division, "Informative Note," September 10, 1971. This summarizes current riot details and then reads: "Information being included in the summary to the White House, the Attorney General, Secret Service and military agencies. Copy being sent to Inter-Division Intelligence Unit, Internal Security and Civil Rights Division of Department." All documents obtained through FOIA request #1014547-000 of the Federal Bureau of Investigation.

41. Albany, Federal Bureau of Investigation, Communications Section Teletype to Director, Buffalo, September 16, 1971, FOIA request #1014547-000 of the FBI.

42. Buffalo Office, Federal Bureau of Investigation, Communications Section Teletype to Director, Domestic Intelligence Division, CC: White House and Attorney General, CC: Mr. Sullivan for the Director, 11:58 p.m., September 9, 1971, FOIA request #1014547-000 of the FBI.

43. Ibid.

44. For one of the most recent histories of the FBI's deliberate destabilization of radical organizations see: Seth Rosenfeld, *Subversives: The FBI's War on Student Radicals, and Reagan's Rise to Power* (New York: Picador, 2013).

45. Domestic Intelligence Division, "Informative Note," September 10, 1971, FOIA request # 1014547-000 of the FBI.

46. Ibid.

## 13. INTO THE NIGHT

1. Malcolm McLaughlin, "Storefront Revolutionary: Martin Sostre's Afro-Asian Bookshop, Black Liberation Culture, and the New Left, 1964–75." *The Sixties: A Journal of History, Politics and Culture* 7, no. 1 (2014).

2. Herman Schwartz, Personal Diary, September 12, 19, and 24, 1971. In author's possession, 7.

3. Richard X Clark, *The Brothers of Attica* (New York: Links Books, 1973), 68.

4. Ibid., 72.

5. Schwartz, Personal Diary, September 12, 19, 24, 1971. 8.

6. Dr. Warren Hanson, interviewed by Joe Heath and John Straithorp, Interview Report Sheet, December 3, 1974, Ernest Goodman Papers, Box 7, Walter Reuther Library of Labor and Urban Affairs, Wayne State University, Detroit, Michigan. Hereafter Walter Reuther Library. Also see: Warren Hanson, Testimony, *McKay Transcript*, April 18, 1972, 289.

7. Dr. Warren Hanson, interviewed by Joe Heath and John Straithorp, Interview Report Sheet, December 3, 1974. Also see: Hanson, Testimony, *McKay Transcript*, April 18, 1972, 289.

8. Hanson, Testimony, *McKay Transcript*, April 18, 1972, 295.

9. Ibid.

10. On the exact location of each hostage in the hostage circle, see: Investigator Joe Mercurio, State of New York Attica Investigation Memorandum to Anthony G. Simonetti, Subject: "Circle Case," July 26, 1974, in the papers of Elizabeth M. Fink, Brooklyn, New York.

11. Hanson, Testimony, *McKay Transcript*, April 18, 1972, 292.

12. Ibid., 295.

13. Clark, *The Brothers of Attica*, 71.

14. Dr. Warren Hanson, interviewed by Joe Heath and John Straithorp, Interview Report Sheet, December 3, 1974.

15. Hanson, Testimony, *McKay Transcript*, April 18, 1972, 297.

16. Ibid., 303.

17. Warren H. Hanson, "Attica: the Hostages' Story," *New York Times*, October 31, 1971.

18. Rockefeller Administration, Confidential Memo, "Events at Attica: September 8–13, 1971," 17.

19. Ibid., 18.

20. Ibid., 19.

21. Larry Lyons, conversation with author, Lehigh Acres, Florida, July 1, 2005.

22. Donald Almeter, conversation with author, July 3, 2005.

23. John Stockholm, conversation with author, July 1, 2005.

24. Clark, *The Brothers of Attica*, 73.

25. Ibid.

26. Ibid., 76.

27. Ibid., 75.

28. Carlos Roche, Testimony, *Akil Al-Jundi et al. v. The Estate of Nelson A. Rockefeller et al.*, October 31, 1991, 1919.

29. Clark, *The Brothers of Attica*, 76.

## 14. A NEW DAY DAWNS

1. Injunction, *Inmates of Attica Correctional Facility v. Nelson Rockefeller, Governor; Commissioner of Correction, Oswald; Vincent Mancusi, Warden,* United States District Court, Western District, New York, September 10, 1971, in the papers of Elizabeth M. Fink, Brooklyn, New York.

2. Ibid.

3. Herman Schwartz, Personal Diary, September 12, 19, and 24, 1971. In author's possession.

4. Ibid.

5. Ibid.

6. Official Call Log, Headquarters, New York State Police, Albany. Date: September 10, 1971. Time: 10:30 a.m.

7. Transmitter Log, September 9–13, New York State Police, Investigation and interview files, 1971–1972, New York (State), Special Commission on Attica, 15855-90, Box 9, New York State Archives, Albany, New York.

8. Russell Oswald, *Attica—My Story* (New York: Doubleday, 1972), 102.

9. Reverend Marvin Chandler, Interview by Laura Hill, May 13, 2009, Rochester Black Freedom Struggle: Online Project, Rare Books and Special Collections, University of Rochester, New York.

10. Xerox of the handwritten note in: Oswald, *Attica—My Story,* 104.

11. *McKay Report,* 267.

12. Schwartz, Personal Diary, September 12, 19, 24, 1971.

13. Ibid.

14. Russell Oswald, Testimony, *Akil Al-Jundi et al. v. The Estate of Nelson A. Rockefeller et al.,* read posthumously into the record on January 2, 1992, 10818.

15. Charles "Flip" Crowley, *In the Matter of the Additional, Special and Trial Term of the Supreme Court of the State of New York, Designated Pursuant to the Order of the Appellate Division, Fourth Department.* County of Wyoming, May 24, 1972, 8–9.

16. *McKay Report,* 269.

17. Schwartz, Personal Diary, September 12, 19, 24, 1971.

18. According to a later investigation there were originally a total of fifty hostages and eleven were released in the initial hours of the rebellion. *McKay Report,* 184.

19. It is unclear who said this. There are conflicting reports. Arthur Eve maintained that Mariano "Dalou" Gonzalez was that person. See: Arthur Eve, Testimony, *Akil Al-Jundi et al. v. The Estate of Nelson A. Rockefeller et al.,* November 6, 1991, 2738. For other descriptions of the event, see: Oswald, Testimony, *Akil Al-Jundi et al. v. The Estate of Nelson A. Rockefeller et al.* Also see: Schwartz, Personal Diary, September 12, 19, 24, 1971.

20. Schwartz, Personal Diary, September 12, 19, 24, 1971.

21. Crowley, *In the Matter of the Additional, Special and Trial Term of the Supreme Court of the State of New York, Designated Pursuant to the Order of the Appellate Division, Fourth Department,* 14.

22. Bernard George Kirk, Testimony, *In the Matter of the Additional, Special and Trial Term of the Supreme Court of the State of New York, Designated Pursuant to the Order of the Appellate Division, Fourth Department.* County of Wyoming, February 17, 1972, Erie County courthouse, 61.

23. Chandler, Interview by Hill, May 13, 2009.

24. Ibid.

25. Ibid.

26. Oswald, Testimony, *Akil Al-Jundi et al. v. The Estate of Nelson A. Rockefeller et al.*

27. As quoted in "Five Deadly Days," reprinted from the *Democrat and Chronicle* (Rochester, New York), Tom Wicker Papers.

28. Dr. Warren Hanson, interviewed by Joe Heath and John Straithorp, Interview Report Sheet, December 3, 1974.

29. Hanson, Testimony, *McKay Transcript,* April 18, 1972, 308.

30. Dr. Warren Hanson, interviewed by Joe Heath and John Straithorp, Interview Report Sheet, December 3, 1974.

31. Wicker, Notes from interview with Roger Champen, undated, Tom Wicker Papers

32. Twenty-six-year-old Barry Schwartz had originally been sentenced to serve time in prison on November 11, 1968. He had been charged with manslaughter in the first degree after a jury determined that he had killed a man and wounded a woman in March of 1967 when he broke into their apartment in Queens, New York. His father, Lester, and mother, Ruth, were divorced and he had a half sister. Since he had been in Attica he had made a number of friends, including D Yard leader Flip Crowley because the two of them "went to counseling sessions together." Kenny Hess had only been in prison since May and would be eligible for parole in six months. This twenty-two-year-old who stood five-eleven and had brown hair and hazel eyes had gone to jail on a charge of grand larceny after getting an honorable discharge from the military and working for a family business, Ed Hess and Sons, in Maine, New York. Hess's greatest weakness was alcohol and speed and this had gotten him into trouble, greatly saddening his two brothers, one sister, and his parents, Edgar and Mary Jane. In Attica Hess made friends with Schwartz. Together they set up a bookie operation in which they sold "pool tickets" to other prisoners. See: Barry Jay Schwartz, Inmate Record Card, October 14, 1994, Ernest Goodman Papers, Accession number 1152, Box 7, Walter Reuther Library; Barry Jay Schwartz, DOB: 4-14-45, Death Certificate, October 14, 1994, Ernest Goodman Papers, Accession number 1152, Box 7, Walter Reuther Library; Kenneth Edgar Hess, Inmate Record Card, October 14, 1994, Ernest Goodman Papers, Accession number 1152, Box 7, Walter Reuther Library; Kenneth Edgar Hess, Death Certificate, October 14, 1994, Ernest Goodman Papers, Accession number 1152, Box 7, Walter Reuther Library.

33. New York State Police Memorandum, Subject: "Stewart Dan, Interview by Sid Hayman, Tony Simonetti, Ed Stillwell, and H. F. Williams, WGR-TV," September 22, 1971, Erie County courthouse.

34. Ibid.

35. Bernard Gaddy, Testimony, *In the Matter of the Additional, Special and Trial Term of the Supreme Court of the State of New York, Designated Pursuant to the Order of the Appellate Division, Fourth Department.* County of Wyoming, May 4, 1972, Erie County courthouse, 42–46.

36. New York State Police Memorandum, Subject: "Stewart Dan, Interview by Sid Hayman et al., WGR-TV," September 22, 1971.

37. Crowley, Testimony, *In the Matter of the Additional, Special and Trial Term of the Supreme Court of the State of New York, Designated Pursuant to the Order of the Appellate Division, Fourth Department,* 39.

38. New York State Police Memorandum, Subject: "Stewart Dan, Interview by Sid Hayman et al., WGR-TV," September 22, 1971.

39. Ibid.

40. Ibid.

41. Gaddy, Testimony, *In the Matter of the Additional, Special and Trial Term of the Supreme Court of the State of New York, Designated Pursuant to the Order of the Appellate Division, Fourth Department,* 49.

## PART III · THE SOUND BEFORE THE FURY

1. Tom Wicker, "Transcribed Personal Notes of Events at Attica Prison and Among the Committee of Observers, September 10–13, '71," Tom Wicker Papers, 5012, Series 1.1,

Box 2, Folder 15. Also see: Tom Wicker, *A Time to Die: The Attica Prison Revolt* (New York: Quadrangle/New York Times Books, 1975), 2–4.

2. Attica Reporter's Notebook (4x8), Tom Wicker Papers, 5012, Series 1.1, Box 2, Folder 14.

3. As described in a publication authored by James A. Hudson, *Slaughter at Attica: The Complete Inside Story.* Also quoted in "Five Deadly Days," reprinted from the *Democrat and Chronicle* (Rochester, New York), Tom Wicker Papers.

4. Wicker, "Transcribed Personal Notes of Events at Attica Prison and Among the Committee of Observers, September 10–13, '71," Tom Wicker Papers. Also see: Wicker, *A Time to Die,* 35.

5. Wicker, "Transcribed Personal Notes of Events at Attica Prison and Among the Committee of Observers, September 10–13, '71," Tom Wicker Papers. Also see: Wicker, *A Time to Die,* 35.

## 15. GETTING DOWN TO BUSINESS

1. According to Minister Farrakhan, he again asked Elijah Muhammad if he could go when it became clear that the situation was deteriorating. Muhammad granted permission, Farrakhan said, and then, when Nelson Rockefeller sent a plane to fetch him and Farrakhan was about to board, Muhammad called and told him not to go so he did not. See: Minister Louis Farrakhan, "Death Stands at the Door," speech, Chicago, Illinois, July 27, 2003, as reproduced in *The Final Call,* May 10, 2010.

2. Johanna Fernandez, *When the World Was Their Stage: A History of the Young Lords Party, 1968–1974* (tentative title) (Princeton: Princeton University Press, forthcoming).

3. According to an FBI memo, a "reliable source advised that BPP Minister of Self Defense Huey P. Newton, contact the secretary of New York State Assemblyman Arthur Eve informing her that he contemplated traveling to Buffalo as requested"; however "no flight arrangements have as yet been made by Newton." See: San Francisco, FBI Memorandum of Communication to Directors Albany, Buffalo, New York City, 5:34 p.m., September 10, 1971. An FBI memo earlier that day assured the Buffalo office that "SF [San Francisco office] will continue to follow this matter with BPP sources and will advise of any definite travel plans obtained." See: San Francisco, FBI Memorandum of Communication to Directors Albany, Buffalo, New York City, 12:02 p.m., September 10, 1971. All documents obtained through FOIA request #1014547-000 of the FBI.

4. Rockefeller Administration, Confidential Memo, "Events at Attica: September 8–13, 1971," 20.

5. Russell Oswald, *Attica—My Story* (New York: Doubleday, 1972), 112.

6. Thomas Wicker, Testimony, *McKay Transcript,* April 18, 1972, 421–22.

7. Ibid., 420.

8. Ibid.

9. Herman Badillo and Milton Haynes, *A Bill of No Rights: Attica and the America Prison System* (New York: Outerbridge & Lazard, 1972), 57.

10. Clarence Jones, conversation with author, New York City, New York, April 21, 2005.

11. Tom Wicker, *A Time to Die: The Attica Prison Revolt* (New York: Quadrangle/New York Times Books, 1975), 43.

12. Ibid.

13. Ibid., 44.

14. Ibid.

15. Clarence Jones, Testimony, *McKay Transcript,* April 19, 1972, 758–59.

16. Ibid., 752.

17. Richard X Clark, Testimony, *Akil Al-Jundi et al. v. The Estate of Nelson A. Rockefeller et al.,* October 25, 1991, 200.

18. Rockefeller Administration, Confidential Memo, "Events at Attica: September 8–13, 1971," 23.

19. John Dunne, conversation with author, Albany, New York, April 3, 2007.

20. Wicker, *A Time to Die,* 47.

21. Wicker, Testimony, *McKay Transcript,* April 18, 1972, 426.

22. Wicker, *A Time to Die,* 50.

23. Ibid., 52.

24. Kirk, Testimony, *In the Matter of the Additional, Special and Trial Term of the Supreme Court of the State of New York, Designated Pursuant to the Order of the Appellate Division, Fourth Department.* County of Wyoming, February 17, 1972, 46.

25. Wicker, "Transcribed Personal Notes of Events at Attica Prison and Among the Committee of Observers, September 10–13, '71," Tom Wicker Papers.

26. Wicker, *A Time to Die,* 63.

27. Ibid.

28. Original note, Tom Wicker Papers, 5012, Series 1.1, Box 2, Folder 15.

29. Copy of paper, Senator Jacob A. Javits Collection, Special Collections and University Archives, Frank Melville Jr. Memorial Library, Stony Brook University, Stony Brook, New York.

30. Wicker, Testimony, *McKay Transcript,* April 18, 1972, 436.

31. Schwartz, Personal Diary, September 12, 19, 24, 1971.

32. Wicker, "Transcribed Personal Notes of Events at Attica Prison and Among the Committee of Observers, September 10–13, '71," Tom Wicker Papers.

33. Ibid.

34. Ibid.

35. Ibid.

36. Ibid.

37. Oswald, *Attica—My Story,* 112.

38. Wicker, "Transcribed Personal Notes of Events at Attica Prison and Among the Committee of Observers, September 10–13, '71," Tom Wicker Papers.

39. Wicker, *A Time to Die,* 99.

40. Ibid., 106.

41. As quoted in: *McKay Report,* 286.

42. Arthur Eve, Testimony, *Akil Al-Jundi et al. v. The Estate of Nelson A. Rockefeller et al.,* November 6, 1991, 2734

43. Mariano "Dalou" Gonzalez, Interview by Michael D. Ryan, 30.

44. Badillo and Haynes, *A Bill of No Rights,* 59.

45. Ibid.

46. John Dunne, handwritten notes of what prisoners wanted, taken down in D Yard during meeting on the night of Friday, September 10, into morning of Saturday, September 11, 1971, Investigation and interview files, 1971–1972, New York (State), Special Commission on Attica, 15855-90, Box 85, New York State Archives, Albany, New York.

47. Albert S. Kurek, "The Troopers Are Coming II: New York State Troopers, 1943–1985," Dee Quinn Miller Personal Papers, 166.

48. Ibid.

49. Official Call Log, Headquarters, New York State Police, Albany, 13.

50. Rockefeller Administration, Confidential Memo, "Events at Attica: September 8–13, 1971," 25.

## 16. DREAMS AND NIGHTMARES

1. George Kirk, Testimony, *In the Matter of the Additional, Special and Trial Term of the Supreme Court of the State of New York, Designated Pursuant to the Order of the Appellate Division, Fourth Department.* County of Wyoming, February 17, 1972, 48.

2. Ibid., 49.

3. Ron Kozlowski, Testimony, *Attica Task Force Hearing,* May 9–10, 2002, Rochester, New York, 171.

4. As quoted in: "Five Deadly Days," reprinted from the *Democrat and Chronicle* (Rochester, New York), Tom Wicker Papers.

5. Wicker, "Transcribed Personal Notes of Events at Attica Prison and Among the Committee of Observers, September 10–13, '71," Tom Wicker Papers. Also see: Wicker, *A Time to Die: The Attica Prison Revolt* (New York: Quadrangle/New York Times Books, 1975), 7.

6. Wicker, Testimony, *McKay Transcript,* April 18, 1972, 450.

7. Ibid., 451.

8. Wicker, "Transcribed Personal Notes of Events at Attica Prison and Among the Committee of Observers, September 10–13, '71," Wicker Papers. Also see: Wicker, *A Time to Die,* 7.

9. Herman Schwartz, Personal Diary, September 12, 19, 24, 1971. In author's possession.

10. Louis James, Original statement (on official letterhead and complete with edits), Tom Wicker Papers, 5012, Series 1.1, Box 2, Folder 15.

11. Wicker, "Transcribed Personal Notes of Events at Attica Prison and Among the Committee of Observers, September 10–13, '71," Tom Wicker Papers. Also see: Wicker, *A Time to Die,* 8.

12. Wicker, Testimony, *McKay Transcript,* April 18, 1972, 454.

13. Schwartz, Personal Diary, September 12, 19, 24, 1971.

14. Clarence Jones, Testimony, *McKay Transcript,* April 19, 1972, 703.

15. Russell Oswald, Testimony, *Akil Al-Jundi et al. v. The Estate of Nelson A. Rockefeller et al.,* read posthumously into the record on January 2, 1992, 10824.

16. Ibid., 10826.

17. Lewis Steel, conversation with author, New York City, April 20, 2004.

18. Clarence Jones, Testimony, *McKay Transcript,* April 19, 1972, 705.

19. "Proposals acceptable to Oswald at this time," original typed copy, Investigation and interview files, 1971–1972, New York (State), Special Commission on Attica, 15855-90, Box 84, New York State Archives, Albany, New York.

20. These would allow for prisoners to have legal counsel during parole hearings. See: *Menechino v. Oswald,* 430 F.2d 403 (2nd Cir. 1970).

21. Robert Douglass, interview, "Attica Prison Riot," *American Experience: The Rockefellers,* Public Broadcasting Service, 2007.

22. San Francisco, Federal Bureau of Investigation Communications Section Memorandum to Directors, Albany, Buffalo, Chicago, New York Subject: "Extremist Matters," 11:15 a.m., September 11, 1971, FOIA request #1014547-000 of the FBI.

23. New York, Federal Bureau of Investigation Communications Section Memo to Directors, Albany, Buffalo, San Francisco, 5:06 p.m., September 11, 1971, FOIA request #1014547-000 of the FBI.

24. Rockefeller Administration, Confidential Memo, "Events at Attica: September 8–13, 1971," 31.

25. Dr. Warren Hanson, Testimony, *McKay Transcript,* April 18, 1972, 334.

26. Ibid., 321–22.

27. Ibid., 322.

28. Ibid.

29. Official Call Log, Headquarters, New York State Police, Albany, 13. Also see: "WBAI Transcript of Speeches Made in D Yard," March 6, 1972, 17.

30. Warren H. Hanson, "Attica: The Hostages' Story," *New York Times,* October 31, 1971.

31. Hanson, Testimony, *McKay Transcript,* April 18, 1972, 316.

32. Rockefeller Administration, Confidential Memo, "Events at Attica: September 8–13, 1971," 31.

33. Wicker, *A Time to Die,* 155.

34. William E. Quinn, September 11, 1971, Certificate of Death, Department of Health, New York State, filed September 21, 1971, Erie County courthouse. Also see: John F. Edland, Autopsy of William Quinn, September 12, 1971, Autopsy #A-339-71, in author's possession; Dr. H. J. Pinsky, Quinn Autopsy X-Ray Findings, Erie County courthouse; Elmer Gordon, William Quinn Laboratory Report, Monroe County Department of Health, Office of the Medical Examiner, September 12, 1971, Erie County courthouse.

35. Rockefeller Administration, Confidential Memo, "Events at Attica: September 8–13, 1971," 30.

36. Wicker, *A Time to Die,* 161.

37. "The Attica Revolt from Start to Finish: A Daily Chronology," Special to the *Buffalo Evening News,* September 14, 1971, Senator Jacob A. Javits Collection, Box 50, Special Collections and University Archives, Frank Melville Jr. Memorial Library, Stony Brook University, Stony Brook, New York. Fred Ferretti, "Amnesty Demand Is Called Snag in Attica Prison Talks," *New York Times,* September 12, 1971.

38. "Summary of Chronology," Investigation and interview files, 1971–1972, New York (State), Special Commission on Attica, 15855-90, Box 88, New York State Archives, Albany, New York.

39. Herman Badillo and Milton Haynes, *A Bill of No Rights: Attica and the America Prison System* (New York: Outerbridge & Lazard, 1972), 59.

40. Wicker, "Transcribed Personal Notes of Events at Attica Prison and Among the Committee of Observers, September 10–13, '71," Tom Wicker Papers.

41. Tiny handwritten note, Tom Wicker Papers, 5012, Series 1.1, Box 2, Folder 15.

42. Wicker, *A Time to Die,* 162.

43. Richard X Clark, *The Brothers of Attica* (New York: Links Books, 1973), 109.

44. Wicker, Notes from interview with Roger Champen, undated, Tom Wicker Papers.

45. Wicker, Testimony, *McKay Transcript,* April 18, 1972, 470.

46. Ibid., 469–70.

47. Wicker, "Transcribed Personal Notes of Events at Attica Prison and Among the Committee of Observers, September 10–13, '71," Tom Wicker Papers.

48. Schwartz, Personal Diary, September 12, 19, 24, 1971.

49. Wicker, Notes from interview with Roger Champen, undated, Tom Wicker Papers.

50. Wicker, "Transcribed Personal Notes of Events at Attica Prison and Among the Committee of Observers, September 10–13, '71," Tom Wicker Papers.

51. Ibid.

52. John Stockholm, conversation with author, July 1, 2005.

53. Wicker, "Transcribed Personal Notes of Events at Attica Prison and Among the Committee of Observers, September 10–13, '71," Tom Wicker Papers.

54. John Dunne, conversation with author, April 3, 2007.

55. Wicker, Testimony, *McKay Transcript,* April 18, 1972, 472.

56. Ibid.

57. Wicker, Notes from interview with Roger Champen, undated, Tom Wicker Papers.

58. As quoted in: Wicker, *A Time to Die,* 172–73, and as recollected by witnesses testifying before the McKay Commission. See *McKay Transcript.*

59. Lewis Steel, conversation with author, April 20, 2004.

60. Rockefeller Administration, Confidential Memo, "Events at Attica: September 8–13, 1971," 32.

61. That Kunstler endorsed the twenty-eight points as the best the prisoners could get is corroborated by a number of sources, including: Arthur Eve, Testimony, *Attica Task Force Hearing,* July 30, 2002, Albany, New York, 81; Wicker, Testimony, *McKay Transcript,* April 18, 1972, 473.

62. Referenced in several different sources. See: Eve, Testimony, *Akil Al-Jundi et al. v. The Estate of Nelson A. Rockefeller et al.*, November 6, 1991; Lewis Steel, conversation with author, April 20, 2004; Wicker, *A Time to Die*.

63. As quoted in Wicker, *A Time to Die*, 174. There is some discrepancy whether it was Eve or Kunstler that announced Quinn's death. Although Eve claims that it was his job to tell the inmates this news and that he was the one who in fact told them, all other witnesses say that it was Kunstler. See: Eve, Testimony, *Akil Al-Jundi et al. v. The Estate of Nelson A. Rockefeller et al.*, November 6, 1991, 2763–64.

64. Charles Ray Carpenter, Testimony, *McKay Transcript*, April 19, 1972, 663.

65. Eugene Smith, Testimony, *Attica Task Force Hearing*, July 31, 2002, 40.

66. Wicker, *A Time to Die*.

67. Oswald, Testimony, *Akil Al-Jundi et al. v. The Estate of Nelson A. Rockefeller et al.*, read posthumously into the record on January 2, 1992, 10828.

68. Ibid.

69. Official Call Log, Headquarters, New York State Police, Albany, 13.

70. Clark, *The Brothers of Attica*, 114.

71. June Fargo, Testimony, *Attica Task Force Hearing*, May 9–10, 2002, Rochester, New York, 118.

72. As quoted in: "Five Deadly Days," reprinted from the *Democrat and Chronicle* (Rochester, New York), Tom Wicker Papers.

73. As quoted in: Paul Jayes, "Kunstler's Arrival Welcome Break in Dull 'Siege of Attica,'" Senator Jacob A. Javits Collection, Special Collections and University Archives, Frank Melville Jr. Memorial Library, Stony Brook University, Stony Brook, New York.

74. Official Call Log, Headquarters, New York State Police, Albany, 13.

75. John and Mary Stockholm, conversation with author, Lehigh Acres, Florida, July 1, 2005.

76. Ibid.

77. Ibid.

78. Ibid.

79. As quoted in: "Five Deadly Days," reprinted from the *Democrat and Chronicle* (Rochester, New York), Tom Wicker Papers.

80. Jack Slater, "Three Profiles in Courage: Mothers Overcome Grief at Deaths of Their Children," *Ebony*, March 1973.

81. Attica Brothers Legal Defense, "Fighting Back! Attica Memorial Book, 1974" (Buffalo, New York), 90.

## 17. ON THE PRECIPICE

1. Copy of statement in: McKay Commission Papers, 15855–90, Box 84, New York State Archives, Albany, New York. Also as quoted in Tom Wicker, *A Time to Die: The Attica Prison Revolt* (New York: Quadrangle/New York Times Books, 1975), 192.

2. Tom Wicker Papers, 5012, Series 1.1, Box 2, Folder 15.

3. Ibid.

4. Attica Reporter's Notebook (4x8), Tom Wicker Papers.

5. Ibid.

6. Rockefeller Administration, Confidential Memo, "Events at Attica: September 8–13, 1971," 34.

7. Attica Reporter's Notebook (4x8), Tom Wicker Papers.

8. Ibid.

9. John Dunne, Transcription of notes taken in observers meetings, FOIA request #110818 of the New York State Attorney General's Office, FOIA p. 001646.

10. Attica Reporter's Notebook (4x8), Tom Wicker Papers.

11. Ibid.

12. Ibid.
13. Ibid.
14. Ibid.
15. Ibid.
16. Ibid.
17. Ibid.
18. Ibid.
19. Ibid.
20. Ibid.
21. Ibid.
22. Ibid.
23. Ibid.
24. Ibid.
25. Ibid.
26. Ibid.
27. As quoted in: Wicker, *A Time to Die,* 208.
28. As quoted in: ibid., 209.
29. As quoted in: ibid., 212.
30. Rockefeller Administration, Confidential Memo, "Events at Attica: September 8–13, 1971," 35.
31. Richard X Clark, *The Brothers of Attica* (New York: Links Books, 1973), 116–17.
32. Arthur Eve, Testimony, *Attica Task Force Hearing,* July 30, 2002, 82.
33. Tom Wicker, Testimony, *McKay Transcript,* April 18, 1972, 485.
34. As quoted in: Wicker, *A Time to Die,* 217.
35. As quoted in: *The Nation,* January 24, 1972.
36. As quoted in: Wicker, *A Time to Die,* 217.
37. Transmission over police radio, 9:40 p.m., September 10, 1971, New York State Police Radio Log, Albany, New York, in the papers of Elizabeth M. Fink, Brooklyn, New York.
38. Rockefeller Administration, Confidential Memo, "Events at Attica: September 8–13, 1971," 34.
39. Russell Oswald, *Attica—My Story* (New York: Doubleday, 1972), 239.
40. Eve, Testimony, *Attica Task Force Hearing,* July 30, 2002, 83.
41. As quoted in: Wicker, *A Time to Die,* 228.
42. As quoted in: ibid., 231.
43. For a full transcript of the hostage interviews, see: "Attica Tape (found at conference table)," transcript, investigation and interview files, 1971–1972, New York (State), Special Commission on Attica, 15855-90, Box 84, New York State Archives, Albany, New York.
44. Ibid.
45. "Speeches Made in D Yard. Sunday, September 12, 1971," March 3, 1972, investigation and interview files, 1971–1972, New York (State), Special Commission on Attica, 15855-90, Box 84, New York State Archives, Albany, New York, 3. Also as quoted in: Wicker, *A Time to Die,* 235.
46. "Attica Tape (found at conference table)," transcript, New York State Archives.
47. The quoted toll at My Lai is not accurate but his point was about the possibility of a massacre at Attica. "Speeches Made in D Yard, Sunday, September 12, 1971," New York State Special Commission on Attica, March 3, 1972, 4–5. Also as quoted in: Wicker, *A Time to Die,* 236–37; "Attica Tape (found at conference table)," transcript, New York State Archives.
48. "Speeches Made in D Yard, Sunday, September 12, 1971," March 3, 1972, New York State Archives, 4–5. Also as quoted in: Wicker, *A Time to Die,* 236–37; "Attica Tape (found at conference table)," transcript, New York State Archives.
49. As quoted in: Wicker, *A Time to Die,* 237.

50. As quoted in: ibid.
51. As quoted in: ibid., 246.
52. "WBAI Transcript of Speeches Made in D Yard," March 6, 1972, 43.
53. For the identity of this man, see: "Speeches Made in D Yard, Sunday, September 12, 1971," New York State Special Commission on Attica, March 3, 1972, 33. Also as quoted in: Wicker, *A Time to Die*, 247.
54. As quoted in: Wicker, *A Time to Die*, 241.
55. "Speeches Made in D Yard, Sunday, September 12, 1971," New York State Special Commission on Attica, March 3, 1972, 28; "WBAI Transcript of Speeches Made in D Yard," March 6, 1972, 41.
56. Wicker, Testimony, *McKay Transcript*, April 18, 1972, 491.
57. As quoted in: Wicker, *A Time to Die*, 250.
58. "WBAI Transcript of Speeches Made in D Yard," March 6, 1972, 28.
59. Ibid.
60. As quoted in: "Five Deadly Days," reprinted from the *Democrat and Chronicle* (Rochester, New York), Tom Wicker Papers.
61. As quoted in: ibid.
62. As quoted in: ibid.
63. As quoted in: ibid.
64. Mary Stockholm, Testimony, *Attica Task Force Hearing*, May 9–10, 2002, Rochester, New York, 18.
65. As quoted in: "Five Deadly Days," reprinted from the *Democrat and Chronicle* (Rochester, New York), Tom Wicker Papers. Also see: John Stockholm, Testimony, *Attica Task Force Hearing*, May 9–10, 2002, Rochester, New York, 11.
66. Tom Wicker, "4 Days of Attica Talks End in Failure," *New York Times*, September 14, 1971.
67. Oswald, *Attica—My Story*, 246.
68. Ibid.

## 18. DECIDING DISASTER

1. Robert D. Quick, Testimony, *Akil Al-Jundi et al. v. The Estate of Nelson A. Rockefeller et al.*, United States District Court, Western District of New York, Buffalo, New York, No. CIV-75-132, December 13, 1991, E-8702.
2. Albert S. Kurek, "The Troopers Are Coming II: New York State Troopers, 1943–1985," Dee Quinn Miller Personal Papers, 166, 167.
3. Technical Sergeant F. D. Smith, New York State Police Memorandum to Major Sergeant Chieco, Subject: "Special Assignment—Attica Correctional Institute," September 9–14, 1971, in the papers of Elizabeth M. Fink, Brooklyn, New York.
4. Governor Nelson Rockefeller, Statement for Immediate Release, September 12, 1971, Nelson A. Rockefeller gubernatorial records, Press Office, Series 25, New York (State), Governor (1959–1973: Rockefeller), Record Group 15, Box 49, Folder 1065, Rockefeller Archive Center, Sleepy Hollow, New York.
5. Charles "Flip" Crowley, Testimony, *In the Matter of the Additional, Special and Trial Term of the Supreme Court of the State of New York, Designated Pursuant to the Order of the Appellate Division, Fourth Department.* County of Wyoming, May 24, 1972, 17.
6. Charles Ray Carpenter, Testimony, *McKay Transcript*, April 19, 1972, 639.
7. Clarence Jones, conversation with author, April 21, 2005. Also see coverage of John Dunne's views. Dunne reportedly "said he believed the final decision was not dictated by the governor but, rather, it was arrived at by his chief aide and counsel, Robert R. Douglass and Commissioner Oswald." Ralph Blumenthal, "Dunne Supports Attack on Attica: But Senator Says That Governor Should Have Gone There," *New York Times*, September 30, 1971.

8. Rockefeller Administration, Confidential Memo, "Events at Attica: September 8–13, 1971," 37.

9. Ibid., 38.

10. Ibid., 39.

11. *McKay Report*, 342.

12. In a 1991 article, reporter John O'Brien wrote that "in retaking Attica, state police disregarded a preset plan for regaining control of a prison rebellion. The plan, Operation Plan Skyhawk, called for the National Guard to retake the prison with minimal violence, and prohibited the type of weaponry used at Attica." See: John O'Brien, "The Scars of Attica," *The Post-Standard* (Syracuse, New York), September 3, 1991.

13. Vincent Mancusi, Testimony, *McKay Transcript*, New York City, April 28, 1972, reproduced in: 90-2287, 2289, 2291, Plaintiff-Appellees' Appendix, 2408, in the papers of Elizabeth M. Fink, Brooklyn, New York.

14. Francis X. Clines, Joseph Lelyveld, Michael Kaufman, and James Marham, "The Attica Revolt: Hour-by-Hour Account Traces Its Start to Misunderstanding," *New York Times*, October 4, 1971, Julius Epstein Collection, Box 16, "Attica" folder, Hoover Institution Archives, Stanford, California.

15. As quoted in: *McKay Report*, 329.

16. Clines et al., "The Attica Revolt: Hour-by-Hour Account Traces Its Start to Misunderstanding."

17. Quigley Order, *Lynda Jones v. State of New York*, 96 A.D.2d 105 (N.Y. App. Div. 1983), August 31, 1982, 49–50.

18. Robert Quick, questioned by attorney Elizabeth Fink, *Akil Al-Jundi et al. v. The Estate of Nelson A. Rockefeller et al.*, United States District Court, Western District of New York, Buffalo, New York, No. CIV-75-132, December 13, 1991, E-8758.

19. O'Brien, "The Scars of Attica."

20. Nelson A. Rockefeller, Deposition, *Lynda Jones, Individually and as administratrix of the estate of Herbert W. Jones, Jr. v. State of New York et al.* (Claim No. 54555); and *Elizabeth M. Hardie, Individually and as administratrix of the estate of Elmer S. Hardie v. State of New York et al.* (Claim No. 54684), State of New York Court of Claims, April 22, 1977, 47.

21. Herbert Blyden, Speech, Transcript, September 12, 1971, investigation and interview files, 1971–1972, New York (State), Special Commission on Attica, 15855-90, Box 84, New York State Archives, Albany, New York.

22. Ibid.

23. Michael Smith, conversation with author, August 10, 2004.

24. Tom Wicker, Notes from interview with Roger Champen, undated, Tom Wicker Papers.

25. Arthur Eve, Account of the Attica rebellion, Tom Wicker Papers, 5012, Series 2.2, Box 15, Folder 146.

## PART IV · RETRIBUTION AND REPRISALS UNIMAGINED

1. Tony Strollo, conversation with author, Albany, New York, July 12, 2004.

2. Ed Hale, "Ex-Trooper, Gun Expert Recalls Horror of Attica," *Times Adirondack*, October 30, 1988.

3. Tony Strollo, conversation with author, Albany, New York, July 12, 2004.

## 19. CHOMPING AT THE BIT

1. "Five Deadly Days," reprinted from the *Democrat and Chronicle* (Rochester, New York), Tom Wicker Papers, 23.

2. Russell Oswald, Interview by Walter Cronkite, transcript, "Oswald and Attica,"

*New York Post,* September 25, 1971, Dorothy Schiff Papers, Box 4, New York Public Library.

3. Ibid.

4. Ibid.

5. Tom Wicker, "Nominee Was Burnished by Attica's Fire," *San Jose Mercury News,* January 30, 1990.

6. Rockefeller Administration, Confidential Memo, "Events at Attica: September 8–13, 1971," 39.

7. Rockefeller Administration, Confidential Memo, "Events at Attica: September 8–13, 1971," 39.

8. Captain A. T. Malovitch, Memorandum to Major John Monahan, Subject: "Attica Prison Disorder," September 21, 1971, in the papers of Elizabeth M. Fink, Brooklyn, New York.

9. Live Broadcast Script, WROC-TV, September 13, 1971. WROC-TV was the flagship station in Rochester in 1971.

10. Monahan Memorandum to Kirwan, September 19, 1971; Rockefeller Administration, Confidential Memo, "Events at Attica: September 8–13, 1971," 42.

11. Daniel Callaghan, conversation with author, New Port Richey, Florida, July 5, 2005. For more on Operation Plan Skyhawk, also see: *McKay Report,* 364.

12. Gerard Smith, Testimony, *Akil Al-Jundi et al. v. The Estate of Nelson A. Rockefeller et al.,* United States District Court, Western District of New York, Buffalo, New York, No. CIV-75-132, November 19, 1991, 4023.

13. John Kifner, "Four Kent State Students Killed by Troops," *New York Times,* May 4, 1970.

14. Arthur Eve, Interview by Christine Christopher, November 12, 2011, *Criminal Injustice: Death and Politics at Attica,* Blue Sky Project (2012), transcribed by Diane Witzel.

15. Callaghan, conversation with author, July 5, 2005.

16. Ibid.

17. Ibid.

18. Vincent Mancusi, Testimony, *The Additional Special and Trial Term of the Supreme Court of the State of New York designated pursuant to the Order of the Appellate Division Fourth Department,* dated November 1, 1971, Proceedings Before the Grand Jury, State of New York Supreme Court: County of Wyoming, August 15, 1972, 77–78, included in: *Akil Al-Jundi et al. v. The Estate of Nelson A. Rockefeller et al.,* Plaintiff's-Appellant Brief Index, 90-2287, 2289, 2291, United States Court of Appeals for the Second Circuit.

19. Ibid.

20. Robert Quick, Testimony, *Akil Al-Jundi et al. v. The Estate of Nelson A. Rockefeller et al.,* December 13, 1991, E-8729.

21. There is some discrepancy regarding the exact number of troopers to be used in the assault between the notes compiled for the governor's office and memos later circulated by the New York State Police. See: Captain A. T. Malovich, Memorandum to Troop Commander, Troop A, Subject: "Attica Detail—September 13, 1971," September 17, 1971, in the papers of Elizabeth M. Fink, Brooklyn, New York.

22. *McKay Report,* 351.

23. Gerard Smith, Testimony, *Akil Al-Jundi et al. v. The Estate of Nelson A. Rockefeller et al.,* November 19, 1991, 3943, 4028.

24. There was so much finger-pointing after the retaking of Attica regarding why highly emotional correction officers had participated in the retaking that it is hard to sort out exactly what directive had been given them by Vincent. After the retaking, the governor's office claimed that it had been crystal clear with Vincent that his men were not to participate, and in turn Vincent insisted that he instructed his men of this fact, but there is no corroborating evidence that he in fact did spell this out for them.

25. Vincent Mancusi, Testimony, *Akil Al-Jundi et al. v. The Estate of Nelson A. Rockefeller et al.*, December 17, 1991, 9537.

26. Sue Lyons, conversation with author, Lehigh Acres, Florida, July 1, 2005. In 1971 she was married to another correction officer named Roger.

27. "Five Deadly Days," reprinted from the *Democrat and Chronicle* (Rochester, New York), Tom Wicker Papers, 23.

28. Ibid.

29. AAG James Grable, State of New York Organized Task Force Memorandum to AAG Anthony Simonetti, Subject: "Report on Weapons Accountability Investigation—State Police .270 Rifles at Attica. Buffalo Office," April 8, 1974, in the papers of Elizabeth M. Fink, 5.

## 20. STANDING FIRM

1. "Five Deadly Days," reprinted from the *Democrat and Chronicle* (Rochester, New York), Tom Wicker Papers, 24.

2. Perry Ford, Testimony, *McKay Transcript*, April 24, 1972, 1456–57.

3. Rockefeller Administration, Confidential Memo, "Events at Attica: September 8–13, 1971," 43. Italics are author's.

4. This word is underlined in the reproduction of this message to the inmates made by the governor's office. Rockefeller Administration, Confidential Memo, "Events at Attica: September 8–13, 1971," 43.

5. Ibid.

6. As quoted in: Charles Ray Carpenter, Testimony, *McKay Transcript*, April 19, 1972, 668.

7. As quoted in: ibid.

8. As quoted in: ibid., 669.

9. Frank Wald, *McKay Transcript*, April 24, 1972, 1390.

10. Mariano "Dalou" Gonzalez, Interview by Michael D. Ryan, 31.

11. Ibid.

12. When Senator Dunne had learned the night before that the assault on D Yard was to take place the very next morning, "he argued for and obtained a pledge that at 7 a.m., before the resort to violence . . . one last appeal would be made to the inmates for a settlement." Tom Wicker, "Nominee Was Burnished by Attica's Fire," *San Jose Mercury News*, January 30, 1990.

13. Attica Reporter's Notebook (4x8), Tom Wicker Papers.

14. Ibid.

15. Arthur Eve, Notes on the day-by-day events of the riot, Tom Wicker Papers, 5012, Series 1.1, Box 2, 4.

16. As quoted in: Blumenthal, "Dunne Supports Attack on Attica," *New York Times*, September 30, 1971.

17. Tom Wicker, "Transcribed Personal Notes of Events at Attica Prison and Among the Committee of Observers, September 10–13, '71," Tom Wicker Papers, 18.

18. Tom Wicker, Handwritten notes about Monday morning, Tom Wicker Papers, 5012, Series 1.1, Box 2, Folders 12–23.

19. Ibid.

20. Rockefeller Administration, Confidential Memo, "Events at Attica: September 8–13, 1971," 44.

21. Ibid.

22. Ibid.

23. Ibid.

24. Frank "Big Black" Smith, Testimony, *Akil Al-Jundi et al. v. Estate of Nelson A. Rockefeller et al.*, United States District Court, Western District of New York, Buffalo, New York, No. CIV-75-132, October 22, 1991, 23, in: Deferred Joint Appendix Volume I

of VI (Pages A-1–A-687), *Herbert X. Blyden, Big Black, Also Known As Frank Smith et al., v. John S. Keller et al.,* United States District Court for the Western District of New York, August 3, 1999.

25. Wicker, Notes from interview with Roger Champen, undated, Tom Wicker Papers.

26. Ibid.

27. Jameel Abdul Raheem, Testimony, *Akil Al-Jundi et al. v. Estate of Nelson A. Rockefeller et al.,* United States District Court, Western District of New York, Buffalo, New York, No. CIV-75-132, November 1, 1991, 2121; James Diggs, Testimony, *Akil Al-Jundi et al. v. The Estate of Nelson A. Rockefeller et al.,* United States District Court, Western District of New York, Buffalo, New York, No. CIV-75-132, November 19, 1991, 4782.

28. Frank Wald, *McKay Transcript,* April 24, 1972, 1390.

29. Ibid., 1355.

30. Michael Smith, conversation with author, August 10, 2004.

31. Ron Kozlowski, Testimony, *Attica Task Force Hearing,* May 9–10, 2002, 173.

32. Rockefeller Administration, Confidential Memo, "Events at Attica: September 8–13, 1971," 47.

33. "War at Attica: Was There No Other Way?," *Time,* September 27, 1971, 24.

34. Rockefeller Administration, Confidential Memo, "Events at Attica: September 8–13, 1971," 45.

35. Ibid.

36. Michael Smith, Testimony, *Attica Task Force Hearing,* July 30, 2002, 199.

37. For material on the Conservation Corps helicopter surveying the scene, see: "A Nation of Law? (1968–1971)," transcript, *Eyes on the Prize: America's Civil Rights Movement, 1954–1985,* Public Broadcasting Service, 1987.

38. Transmitter Log, September 9–13, New York State Police, investigation and interview files, 1971–1972, New York (State), Special Commission on Attica, 15855-90, New York State Archives, Albany, New York.

39. "Five Deadly Days," reprinted from the *Democrat and Chronicle* (Rochester, New York), Tom Wicker Papers, 25.

40. Eugene Smith, Testimony, *Attica Task Force Hearing,* July 31, 2002, Albany, New York, 42.

## 21. NO MERCY

1. "Five Deadly Days," reprinted from the *Democrat and Chronicle* (Rochester, New York), Tom Wicker Papers, 25.

2. Ibid.

3. Roche, Testimony, *Akil Al-Jundi et al. v. The Estate of Nelson A. Rockefeller et al.,* October 31, 1991, 1932. Hostage Michael Smith corroborates that this is indeed what some of the inmates thought. "I recall inmate speculation that it may be an official helicopter making reference to Rockefeller coming to Attica." See: Michael Smith, Testimony, *Attica Task Force Hearing,* July 30, 2002, Albany, New York, 200–201.

4. Roche, Testimony, *Akil Al-Jundi et al. v. The Estate of Nelson A. Rockefeller et al.,* October 31, 1991, 1933.

5. Ibid.

6. Decision and Order, Appendix 1, Category One Claimants, *Akil Al-Jundi et al. v. Vincent Mancusi et al.,* United States District Court, Western District of New York, Buffalo, New York, No. CIV-75-132, August 28, 2000, 168.

7. Raymond Scott, Interview by Laura Hill, Transcript, July 11, 2008, Rochester Race Riots Interviews, Rare Books and Special Collections, University of Rochester, New York, 33.

8. Quigley Order, *Lynda Jones v. State of New York,* 96 A.D. 2d 105 (N.Y. App. Div. 1983), August 31, 1982, 46–47.

9. Governor Nelson Rockefeller and Michael Whiteman, Counsel to the Governor, Proclamation for Immediate Release, September 13, 1971, Nelson A. Rockefeller gubernatorial records, Press Office, Series 25, New York (State), Governor (1959–1973: Rockefeller), Record Group 15, Box 49, Folder 1066, Rockefeller Archive Center, Sleepy Hollow, New York; Governor Nelson Rockefeller and Michael Whiteman, Counsel to the Governor, Executive Order No. 51 for Immediate Release, September 13, 1971, Nelson A. Rockefeller gubernatorial records, Press Office, Series 25, New York (State), Governor (1959–1973: Rockefeller), Record Group 15, Box 49, Folder 1066, Rockefeller Archive Center, Sleepy Hollow, New York; Transmitter Log, September 9–13, New York State Archives.

10. About half of the troopers sent in to retake Attica did not fire their weapons, which means that the extraordinary barrage of bullets expended that day were fired by a very specific group of men.

11. Quick, Testimony, *Akil Al-Jundi et al. v. The Estate of Nelson A. Rockefeller et al.*, December 13, 1991, E-8787-E-8788. Also see: Gerard Smith, Testimony, *Akil Al-Jundi, et al. v. The Estate of Nelson A. Rockefeller et al.*, November 19, 1991, 3917.

12. William K. Dillon, Statement taken by Malcolm Bell, Organized Task Force Offices, Buffalo, New York, April 26, 1974, Erie County courthouse, 77.

13. Gerard Smith, Testimony recounting testimony given previously on April 2, 1974, *Akil Al-Jundi et al. v. The Estate of Nelson A. Rockefeller et al.*, November 19, 1991, 3920.

14. Tony Strollo, conversation with author, July 12, 2004.

15. Captain G. J. Dana, Memorandum to Detail Commander, Subject: "Rifle and Shotgun Accountability—Attica Prison Detail," New York State Police, Troop A Station Headquarters, September 19, 1971, in the papers of Elizabeth M. Fink, Brooklyn, New York.

16. Monahan Memorandum to Kirwan, September 19, 1971.

17. Quigley Order, *Lynda Jones v. State of New York*, 96 A.D.2d 105 (N.Y. App. Div. 1983), August 31, 1982, 68–69.

18. Ibid.

19. Ibid., 56; *Elizabeth M. Hardie, Individually and as administratrix of the estate of Elmer S. Hardie, v. State of New York et al.* (Claim No. 54684), State of New York Court of Claims. Also: Russell Oswald, Testimony, *Lynda Jones, v. State of New York et al.* (Claim No. 54555), State of New York Court of Claims, June 5, 1979, 96.

20. Tony Strollo, conversation with author, July 12, 2004.

21. Albert S. Kurek, "The Troopers Are Coming II: New York State Troopers, 1943–1985," Dee Quinn Miller Personal Papers, 168.

22. "Five Deadly Days," reprinted from the *Democrat and Chronicle* (Rochester, New York), Tom Wicker Papers, 26.

23. Kozlowski, Testimony, *Attica Task Force Hearing*, May 9–10, 2002, 175–76.

24. Ibid., 175–77.

25. Ibid., 175–76.

26. It was very clearly a fellow correction officer who had shot Mike Smith, not a state trooper, because "the police did not have machine guns." See: Malcolm Bell, Testimony, *Attica Task Force Hearing*, July 30, 2002, Albany, New York, 18.

27. Michael Smith, Testimony, *Attica Task Force Hearing*, July 30, 2002, 202.

28. Michael Smith, Corroborating Testimony, p. 3. Decision and Order, Appendix 4, *Akil Al-Jundi et al. v. Vincent Mancusi et al.*, United States District Court, Western District of New York, Buffalo, New York, No. CIV-75-132, August 28, 2000. Final Summaries.

29. Michael Smith, Corroborating Testimony, 3. Decision and Order, Appendix 4, *Akil Al-Jundi et al. v. Vincent Mancusi et al.*, August 28, 2000. Final Summaries.

30. "Five Deadly Days," reprinted from the *Democrat and Chronicle* (Rochester, New York), Tom Wicker Papers, 25.

31. "War at Attica: Was There No Other Way?," *Time,* September 27, 1971, 24. Watkins's story of being saved by the inmate is also in "Convict Saved His Life," *New York Post,* September 14, 1971, Dorothy Schiff Papers, Box 4, New York Public Library.

32. John Hill, Telephone conversation with author, May 31, 2005.

33. Ibid.

34. Edward Kowalczyk, also known as Angelo Martin, Affidavit, *People of the State of New York v. Shango Bahati Kakawana (Indicted as Bernard Stroble),* 407 F.Supp. 411 (1976), October 12, 1974, Ernest Goodman Papers, Accession number 1152, Box 6, Walter Reuther Library.

35. Decision and Order, Appendix 1, Category One Claimants, *Akil Al-Jundi et al. v. Vincent Mancusi et al.,* August 28, 2000, 184.

36. Kowalczyk, also known as Angelo Martin, Affidavit, *People of the State of New York v. Shango Bahati Kakawana (Indicted as Bernard Stroble),* 407 F.Supp. 411 (1976), October 12, 1974, Ernest Goodman Papers.

37. See videotaped account of assault: "September 9–13, 1971: New York State Troopers Kill 39 Men in Raid to End Attica Prison Uprising," *Democracy Now,* September 11, 2003, www.democracynow.org.

38. Decision and Order, Appendix 1, Category One Claimants, *Akil Al-Jundi et al. v. Vincent Mancusi et al.,* August 28, 2000, 88.

39. Tony Strollo, conversation with author, July 12, 2004.

40. Gerard Smith, Testimony, *Akil Al-Jundi et al. v. The Estate of Nelson A. Rockefeller et al.,* November 19, 1991, 3912.

41. Ibid., 3817.

42. Gene Anthony Hitchens, Corroborating Testimony, 7. Decision and Order, *Akil Al-Jundi et al. v. Vincent Mancusi et al.,* United States District Court, Western District of New York, Buffalo, New York, No. CIV-75-132, August 28, 2000. Appendix 4.

43. Ibid.

44. "A Nation of Law? (1968–1971)," transcript, *Eyes on the Prize,* 1987.

45. Jomo Davis, conversation with author, Deerfield Correctional Facility, Capron, Virginia, February 17, 2006.

46. Carlos Roche, Testimony, *Akil Al-Jundi et al. v. The Estate of Nelson A. Rockefeller et al.,* October 31, 1991, 1937, 1958.

47. Jameel Abdul Raheem, Testimony, *Akil Al-Jundi et al. v. The Estate of Nelson A. Rockefeller et al.,* November 1, 1991, 2103.

48. Decision and Order, Appendix 1, Category One Claimants, *Akil Al-Jundi et al. v. Vincent Mancusi et al.,* August 28, 2000, 18.

49. Ibid., 38.

50. Ibid.

51. Ibid., 48.

52. Ibid., 183.

53. Ibid., 103.

54. Ibid., 185.

55. Gerard Smith, Testimony referencing statement Smith gave in 1974, *Akil Al-Jundi et al., v. The Estate of Nelson A. Rockefeller et al.,* November 19, 1991, 3909.

56. Decision and Order, Appendix 1, Category One Claimants, *Akil Al-Jundi et al. v. Vincent Mancusi et al.,* August 28, 2000, 186.

57. Ibid., 19.

58. Ibid., 32.

59. As quoted in Francis X. Clines, Joseph Lelyveld, Michael Kaufman, and James Marham, "The Attica Revolt: Hour-by-Hour Account Traces Its Start to Misunderstanding," *New York Times,* October 4, 1971, Julius Epstein Collection, Box 16, "Attica" folder, Hoover Institution Archives, Stanford, California.

60. As quoted in: ibid.

61. "The Battle of Attica: Death's Timetable," *New York Post,* September 14, 1971, Dorothy Schiff Papers, Box 4, New York Public Library.

62. William Maynard, Testimony, *Akil Al-Jundi et al. v. The Estate of Nelson A. Rockefeller et al.,* United States District Court, Western District of New York, Buffalo, New York, No. CIV-75-132, November 19, 1991. Jomo Joka Omowale reports that it was a CO shooting them in this last incident, Maynard says it was a trooper.

63. Decision and Order, Appendix 1, Category One Claimants, *Akil Al-Jundi et al. v. Vincent Mancusi et al.,* August 28, 2000, 52.

64. Ibid., 181.

65. Dean Wright, Testimony, *Attica Task Force Hearing,* May 9–10, 2002, 65.

66. Robert Curtiss, Testimony, *McKay Transcript,* April 24, 1972, 1327–28.

67. Larry Lyons and John Stockholm, conversation with author, Lehigh Acres, Florida, July 1, 2005.

68. Mercurio, Attica Investigation Memorandum to Simonetti, Subject: "Circle Case," July 26, 1974.

69. Regarding which troopers shot at prisoners near the hostage circle to protect Christian, see: Attica Investigator Leonard Brown, Testimony, regarding testimony of Arthur Kruk, *The Additional Special and Trial Term of the Supreme Court of the State of New York designated pursuant to the Order of the Appellate Division Fourth Department,* dated November 1, 1971, Proceedings Before the Grand Jury, State of New York Supreme Court: County of Wyoming, August 10, 1972, Wyoming County Courthouse, Warsaw, New York, 2–7. Notably, later investigative interviews with two troopers revealed that they had immediately managed to subdue the prisoner who had attempted to strike Lieutenant Christian, allegedly Tommy Hicks, by knocking him down with the butt of a gun. If that was the case, then the barrage of bullets shot into the hostage circle that killed so many hostages had been completely unnecessary. See: Bell, Testimony, *Attica Task Force Hearing,* July 30, 2002, 27–28.

70. Decision and Order, Appendix 1, Category One Claimants, *Akil Al-Jundi et al. v. Vincent Mancusi et al.,* August 28, 2000, 12.

71. His original words, testifying on behalf of his damages claim on July 5, 2000, were: "I could see all this blood just running out of the mud and water. That's all I could see." Judge Michael Telesca referred to this testimony in his summation by saying: "Everywhere he looked he saw only blood and water." Decision and Order, Appendix 1, Category One Claimants, *Akil Al-Jundi et al. v. Vincent Mancusi et al.,* August 28, 2000, 48.

72. *Attica,* film written and directed by Cinda Firestone, April 1974.

73. Ibid.

74. Transmitter Log, September 9–13, New York State Police, New York State Archives; Captain A. T. Malovich, Memorandum to Troop Commander, Troop A, Subject: "Attica Detail—September 13, 1971," September 17, 1971, in the papers of Elizabeth M. Fink. Regarding which troopers were shooting into A Yard, see: Dillon, Statement taken by Malcolm Bell, Organized Task Force Offices, Buffalo, New York, April 26, 1974, 54–55.

75. Dennis Cunningham, Michael Deutsch, and Elizabeth Fink, "Remembering Attica Forty Years Later," *Prison Legal News* 22, no. 9 (September 2011).

76. Twenty-six died right away and three others clung to life for a few more days before perishing. Rockefeller Administration, Confidential Memo, "Events at Attica: September 8–13, 1971," 50.

77. *Attica,* Firestone, 1974.

78. As quoted in: *McKay Report,* 501.

79. "Names and Badge Numbers of Officers in Hostage," document, Attica uprising–related documents kept at the Attica Correctional Facility, Attica, New York. Also see: H. Shapiro and M. B. Spoont, Confidential Memo, Attica Investigation, November 1, 1971, in the papers of Elizabeth M. Fink, Brooklyn, New York.

80. As quoted in: *McKay Report,* 501.

81. "Names and Badge Numbers of Officers in Hostage," document, Attica uprising–related documents kept at the Attica Correctional Facility, Attica, New York.

82. Dr. Gene Richard Abbott, Testimony, *Attica Task Force Hearings,* May 9–10, 2002, Rochester, New York, 189–90.

83. As quoted in: New York State Special Commission on Attica, *McKay Report,* 501.

84. "Names and Badge Numbers of Officers in Hostage," document, Attica uprising related documents kept at the Attica Correctional Facility, Attica, New York.

85. Rockefeller Administration, Confidential Memo, "Events at Attica: September 8–13, 1971," 50.

86. As quoted in New York State Special Commission on Attica, *McKay Report,* 502–3.

87. For ballistics concerning Melvin Ware, see: Decision and Order, Appendix 2, Category V Death Claims, *Akil Al-Jundi et al. v. Vincent Mancusi et al.,* United States District Court, Western District of New York, Buffalo, New York, No. CIV-75-132, 113 F.Supp.2d 441 (2000), August 28, 2000, 3. Regarding testimony of Malcolm Hegeman, see: Attica Investigator James Stephen, Testimony, *The Additional, Special and Trial Term of the Supreme Court of the State of New York,* State of New York Supreme Court: County of Wyoming, Wyoming County Courthouse, Warsaw, New York, October 25, 1972, 7.

88. Decision and Order, Appendix 2, Category V Death Claims, *Akil Al-Jundi et al. v. Vincent Mancusi et al.,* No. CIV-75-132, 113 F.Supp.2d 441 (2000), August 28, 2000, 5. According to state investigator Malcolm Bell, Donald Girvin admitted shooting this inmate. Bell, *Preliminary Report on the Attica Investigation,* 19.

89. Ibid., 7.

90. As quoted in: *McKay Report,* 498–99.

91. Details of the shot that killed Sam Melville come from Malcolm Bell's discussion with Dr. George Abbott regarding the original autopsy Abbott conducted on Melville. Autopsy also in author's possession. See: FBI, Memorandum regarding interview with Donald Goff of the Correctional Association, October 21, 1971, FOIA request #110818 of the New York State Attorney General's Office; Decision and Order, Appendix 2, Category V Death Claims, *Akil Al-Jundi et al. v. Vincent Mancusi et al.,* No. CIV-75-132, 113 F.Supp.2d 441 (2000), August 28, 2000.

92. Decision and Order, Appendix 2, Category V Death Claims, *Akil Al-Jundi et al. v. Vincent Mancusi et al.,* No. CIV-75-132, 113 F.Supp.2d 441 (2000), August 28, 2000, 3. Michael Baden, Autopsy of Thomas Hicks, September 16, 1971, Ernest Goodman Papers, Accession number 1152, Box 6, Walter Reuther Library of Labor and Urban Affairs. For information about who shot Hicks, see: Memorandum regarding Trooper Milford J. Clayson, FOIA request #110818 of the New York State Attorney General's Office, FOIA p. 001547. Remarks: "Possible hit P#12, (Lorenzo McNeil), P#26 (Thomas Hicks)."

93. John F. Edland, Autopsy of Thomas Hicks, September 14, 1971, in author's possession.

94. The National Guardsman was Franklin Davenport. A report later released by the McKay Commission said that Hicks was dead during the retaking. See: *McKay Report,* 396–97.

95. John O'Brien, "The Scars of Attica," *The Post-Standard* (Syracuse, New York), September 3, 1991.

96. Investigator Michael McCarron, State of New York Attica Investigation Memorandum to Anthony Simonetti, Subject: "Interview of Larry Barnes, ACF #26589," January 30, 1975, FOIA request #110818 of New York State Attorney General's Office.

97. Melvin Marshall, Interview by Christine Christopher, transcript, September 10, 2011, *Criminal Injustice: Death and Politics at Attica,* Blue Sky Project (2012), 34.

98. James J. Peppard Jr., "Attica Inmate Alleged to Have Met Death After Peace," *Daily Messenger,* October 1, 1971. Also see reports on this in: "Attica Leaders Killed After Assault," *Georgia Straight* 5, no. 21 (December 16, 1971); "Attica Leaders Assassinated,"

*Fifth Estate* 6, no. 15 (October 14, 1971). Eve was intensely relieved when he saw that one of the most outspoken of the prisoner leaders from his own district, L. D. Barkley, was still alive. He said to Robert Garcia, who was standing closest to him, "that's L.D . . . at least he's alive." Frank Lott also saw him. "L.D. was alive. . . . He was right off the A Block area with his nose down in the grass." See: Eve, Notes on the day-by-day events of the riot, Tom Wicker Papers, 5; "Five Deadly Days," reprinted from the *Democrat and Chronicle* (Rochester, New York), Tom Wicker Papers, 25.

99. Decision and Order, Appendix 2, Category V Death Claims, *Akil Al-Jundi et al. v. Vincent Mancusi et al.*, No. CIV-75-132, 113 F.Supp.2d 441 (2000), August 28, 2000, 2.

100. Marshall, Interview by Christopher, transcript, September 10, 2011, *Criminal Injustice*, 36.

101. Rockefeller Administration, Confidential Memo, "Events at Attica: September 8–13, 1971," 53.

102. John Dunne, Testimony, *Herbert X. Blyden et al. v. Vincent Mancusi et al.*, United States Court of Appeals, Second Circuit, 186 F. 3d 252, Docket No. 97-2912, Vol. II, December 3, 1991, A-886.

103. State of New York notes on John Dunne, FOIA request #110818 of the New York State Attorney General's Office, FOIA pp. 0011631 and 212076; Tom Wicker, "Nominee Was Burnished by Attica's Fire," *San Jose Mercury News*, January 30, 1990.

104. Tom Wicker, "In the Nation: A Man of Character," *New York Times*, January 29, 1990.

105. Handwritten notes about Monday morning, Tom Wicker Papers.

106. Ibid.

107. Ibid.

108. "A Nation of Law? (1968–1971)," transcript, *Eyes on the Prize*, 1987.

109. Rev. Marvin Chandler, Interview by Hill, May 13, 2009.

110. Tom Fitzpatrick, "Bill Kunstler's Worst Day—Hearing the Guns of Attica," *Chicago Sun-Times*, October 6, 1971, as reprinted in *Penal Digest International* 1, no. 5 (October 1971).

111. Ibid.

112. Wicker, Notes from interview with Roger Champen, undated. Tom Wicker Papers.

## 22. SPINNING DISASTER

1. John Dunne, Transcription of notes taken in observers meetings, FOIA request #110818, FOIA p. 001669.

2. "Five Deadly Days," reprinted from the *Democrat and Chronicle* (Rochester, New York), Tom Wicker Papers, 25.

3. Appendix 6: "Supplemental Materials on Nelson Rockefeller by Attica Brothers Legal Defense," as contained in: Attica Brothers Legal Defense, Statement, Nelson A. Rockefeller Vice Presidential Confirmation Hearings, House of Representatives, 93rd Cong., 2nd sess., *Congressional Record* 120 (November 26, 1974), Ron Nessen Papers, Box 25, Folder "Rockefeller, Nelson—Confirmation Hearings," Gerald R. Ford Presidential Library, Ann Arbor, Michigan, 1177.

4. "War at Attica: Was There No Other Way?," *Time*, September 27, 1971, 24.

5. Michael Whiteman, Testimony, Meyer Commission, June 12, 1975, 1817, FOIA request #110818 of the New York State Attorney General's Office, FOIA p. 000801.

6. Russell Oswald, Statement, September 13, 1971, Nelson A. Rockefeller gubernatorial records, Press Office, Series 25, New York (State), Governor (1959–1973: Rockefeller), Record Group 15, Box 49, Folder 1066, Rockefeller Archive Center, Sleepy Hollow, New York.

7. Ibid.

8. Harry W. Albright Jr. and Eliot N. Vestner Jr., Memorandum to the Governor,

Subject: "The Throat Slitting Story and Atrocity Stories," Appendix 2 in Rockefeller Administration, Confidential Memo, "Events at Attica: September 8–13, 1971."

9. Ibid.

10. Ibid.

11. Ibid.

12. Arthur Eve, Notes on the day-by-day events of the riot, Tom Wicker Papers, 5.

13. Ibid. Not only did Dunbar report that the man on the table was responsible for the castration to these elected officials, but he also later testified to this before the Pepper Commission. See: *Elizabeth M. Hardie, Individually and as administratrix of the estate of Elmer S. Hardie v. State of New York et al.* (Claim No. 54684), State of New York Court of Claims. Also: Russell Oswald, Testimony, *Lynda Jones v. State of New York et al.* (Claim No. 54555), State of New York Court of Claims, June 5, 1979, 122. All documents in possession of author.

14. Eve, Notes on the day-by-day events of the riot, Tom Wicker Papers, 5. See also: *Elizabeth M. Hardie, Individually and as administratrix of the estate of Elmer S. Hardie v. State of New York et al.* (Claim No. 54684), State of New York Court of Claims. Also: Russell Oswald, Testimony, *Lynda Jones v. State of New York et al.* (Claim No. 54555), State of New York Court of Claims, June 5, 1979, 122.

15. Albright and Vestner, Memorandum to the Governor, Subject: "The Throat Slitting Story and Atrocity Stories."

16. Edmond Pinto, "The Attica Report: An AP News Special," Dorothy Schiff Papers, Box 4, New York Public Library.

17. Albright and Vestner, Memorandum to the Governor, Subject: "The Throat Slitting Story and Atrocity Stories."

18. Associated Press wire bulletin, Senator Jacob A. Javits Collection, Special Collections and University Archives, Frank Melville Jr. Memorial Library, Stony Brook University, Stony Brook, New York.

19. As quoted in: *McKay Report*, 457.

20. "Death Penalty Possible in Slaying of Hostages," *New York Times*, September 14, 1971, Dorothy Schiff Papers, Box 4, New York Public Library.

21. As referenced in: *McKay Report*, 456.

22. "37 Die as Police Guards Storm Attica Prison," Fort Scott, Kansas, *News and Courier*, September 14, 1971.

23. Stephen Isaacs, "Attica Prison Retaken, 37 Slain," *Washington Post*, September 14, 1971.

24. In Morgantown, West Virginia, readers of *The Dominion News* were informed that "nine hostages were killed by inmates" at Attica the day before. Likewise, residents of Harlingen, Texas, who read the *Valley Morning Star* learned that "nine hostages were found dead—slain by inmates," and Michiganders who lived in the small town of Holland also read that "rebel convicts killed nine civilian employees at the Attica State Prison" in their paper, *The Holland Evening Sentinel*. From Augusta, Maine, to rural Pennsylvania, Americans were told in no uncertain terms by their trusted media sources that "rebellious convicts" had "murdered" nine guard hostages in cold blood. See: "Hostages Are Murdered," *Kennebec Journal*, September 14, 1971; "Nine Prison Hostages Found Dead," *Bucks County Courier Times*, September 13, 1971. More locally, in Buffalo the *Buffalo Evening News* opined that it was fortunate that although "New York State has virtually abandoned the death penalty, persons convicted of killing Attica hostages could be sentenced to the electric chair" because, in the wake of the Auburn rebellion, the state legislature had amended the law eliminating capital punishment to make an exception for "the slaying of a civilian employee of a prison." In: "The Attica Revolt from Start to Finish: A Daily Chronology," Special to the *Buffalo Evening News*, September 14, 1971.

25. H. Vozka, Nashville, Tennessee, Telegram, September 15, 1971, and W. T. Combs, Fresno, California, Telegram, September 14, 1971, both in Attica uprising–related documents kept at the Attica Correctional Facility, Attica, New York.

26. Dr. and Mrs. Derkasch, Valley Stream, New York, Telegram, September 13, 1971, and Mr. and Mrs. Marshall, Louisville, Kentucky, Telegram, September 14, 1971. Both in Attica uprising–related documents kept at the Attica Correctional Facility, Attica, New York.

27. E. C. Johnson, Chicago, Letter to the Editor, *Time*, Monday, October 4, 1971; Elizabeth M. Keating, Jacksonville, Letter to the Editor, *Time*, Monday, October 4, 1971; Jim Griffith, Cincinnati, Letter to the Editor, *Time*, Monday, October 18, 1971.

28. Clarence Jones, conversation with author, April 21, 2005. Also see: John Dunne, Leo Seferetti, and Clarence Jones, Episode 4.6, *The David Frost Show*, September 27, 1971.

29. John J. O'Conner, "Attica in the News," *New York Times*, September 15, 1971. Also see: Lewis Steel, conversation with author, April 20, 2004.

30. C. J. Callahan. Rochester, New York, Letter to the Editor, *Time*, Monday, October 18, 1971.

31. Tom Murton, "The Atrocity at Attica," *Penal Digest* 1, no. 4 (September 1971); N. Mastrian, "Reply to Rhetoric of Right," *Penal Digest* 1, no. 5 (October 1971).

32. "The Awesome Attica Tragedy," *Crisis*, November 1971, 299–30; Winston E. Moore, "My Cure for Prison Riots," *Ebony*, December 1971, both in the Schomburg Center for Research in Black Culture, New York Public Library.

33. Henry Bellmon, Statement, Senate, 92nd Cong., 1st sess., *Congressional Record* 117s (September 14, 1971), Ron Nessen Papers, Box 25, Folder "Rockefeller, Nelson—Confirmation Hearings," Gerald R. Ford Presidential Library, Ann Arbor, Michigan, 31719–20.

34. Ibid.

35. Herman Badillo, Statement, House of Representatives, 92nd Cong., 1st sess., *Congressional Record* 117s (September 15, 1971), 31990.

36. "War at Attica: Was There No Other Way?," *The Nation*, September 27, 1971.

37. Draft of speech to be given at the New York State Bar Center dedication, Albany, New York, September 24, 1971. Nelson A. Rockefeller. Record Group 15, Series 33: Speeches. Box 85, Folder 3471, Rockefeller Archive Center, Sleepy Hollow, New York.

38. Nelson A. Rockefeller, Press Release, September 13, 1971, Nelson A. Rockefeller gubernatorial records, Press Office, Series 25, Record Group 15, Box 49, Folder 1066, Rockefeller Archive Center, Sleepy Hollow, New York.

39. Appendix 6: "Supplemental Materials on Nelson Rockefeller by Attica Brothers Legal Defense," as contained in Attica Brothers Legal Defense, Statement, Nelson A. Rockefeller Vice Presidential Confirmation Hearings, House of Representatives, 93rd Cong., 2nd sess., *Congressional Record* 120 (November 26, 1974), 1177.

40. Richard Nixon, Daily Diary, September 13, 1971, The White House, Washington, D.C. Information courtesy of Peter Balonen-Rosen.

41. Ibid.

42. Conversation #571-6 (rmn_e571b), September 13, 1971, 3:47 p.m.–4:16 p.m., Oval Office, Present: Richard Nixon and Clifford Hardin, Nixon Tapes, 10:27–10:35. Also: Conversation #571-1C (rmn_e571a), September 13, 1971, Oval Office, Nixon Tapes, 1:01:37; Conversation 571-10 (rmn_e571b), September 13, 1971, Oval Office, Nixon Tapes, 1:09:50.

43. Conversation #571-6 (rmn_571b), September 13, 1971, 4:36 p.m.–4:16 p.m., Oval Office, Present: Richard Nixon and Clifford Hardin, Nixon Tapes, 10:38–4:16.

44. Conversation #571-10 (rmn_e571b), September 13, 1971, 4:36 p.m.–6:00 p.m., Oval Office, Present: Richard Nixon, H. R. Haldeman, and Charles Colson, Nixon Tapes, 1:10:07–1:10:16.

45. Ibid., 1:10:40–1:10:54.

46. Nixon, Daily Diary, September 13, 1971. Information courtesy of Peter Balonen-Rosen.

47. Conversation #008-113 (rmn_e008c), September 13, 1971, 1:31 p.m.–1:38 p.m.,

Oval Office Telephone, Present: Richard Nixon, Nelson Rockefeller, Nixon Tapes, 1:17:46–1:18:24.

48. Ibid., 1:19:25–1:19:28 and 1:22:01–1:22:03. For another contemporaneous story regarding hostages killed before the retaking, see the following headline: Leonard Katz, "Attica: Two Hostages Slain Before Showdown," *New York Post*, September 14, 1971, Dorothy Schiff Papers, Box 4, New York Public Library.

49. Conversation #008-113 (rmn_e008c), September 13, 1971, 1:31 p.m.–1:38 p.m., Oval Office Telephone, Present: Richard Nixon, Nelson Rockefeller, Nixon Tapes, 1:19:31–1:19:33.

50. Ibid., 1:19:40–1:19:44.

51. Ibid., 1:20:08–1:20:27.

52. Ibid., 1:23:35–1:23:50.

53. Ibid., 1:23:50–1:23:53.

54. Ibid., 1:24:09–1:24:11.

55. June Fargo, Testimony, *Attica Task Force Hearing*, May 9–10, 2002, Rochester, New York, 22.

56. Parole Officer Lumen V. Brown, Memorandum to Commissioner Dunbar, Commissioner James Morrow, Superintendent Vincent Mancusi, Deputy Superintendent Leon Vincent, and Deputy Superintendent Wilson Walters, Subject: "Monitoring Attica Correctional Facility," November 5, 1971, Attica uprising–related documents kept at the Attica Correctional Facility, Attica, New York.

57. Paula Krotz, Testimony, *Attica Task Force Hearing*, May 9–10, 2002, Rochester, New York, 120.

58. Ibid., 120.

59. Krotz, *Attica Task Force Hearing*, May 9–10, 2002, 121.

60. Sharon Smith, Testimony, *Attica Task Force Hearing*, July 30, 2002, Albany, New York, 212–13.

61. Ibid.

62. Jennifer Gonnerman, "Remembering Attica," *Village Voice*, September 5–11, 2001.

63. Ibid.

64. Ibid.

65. Ann Driscoll, Testimony, *Attica Task Force Hearing*, May 9–10, 2002, Rochester, New York.

66. Ann Valone, conversation with author, Batavia, New York, October 17, 2004.

67. Mary Ann Valone, Testimony, *Attica Task Force Hearing*, July 31, 2002, Albany, New York, 131.

68. Ann Valone, conversation with author, October 17, 2004.

69. Ibid.

70. Ibid.

71. Mary Ann Valone, Testimony, *Attica Task Force Hearing*, July 31, 2002, 131.

72. David Shipler, "Lack of Data on Inmates' Fates Scored by Prisoners' Families," *New York Times*, September 15, 1971.

73. Frances X. Clines, "Attica Residents Inclined to Doubt Autopsy Findings," *New York Times*, September 17, 1971.

74. "List of Prisoner Dead," *New York Times*, September 16, 1971.

75. Ibid.

76. Ibid.

## 23. AND THE BEAT GOES ON

1. "Five Deadly Days," reprinted from the *Democrat and Chronicle* (Rochester, New York), Tom Wicker Papers, 26.

2. Ibid.

3. Major Frank Hall, Interview by Christine Christopher, transcript, September 17, 2011, *Criminal Injustice: Death and Politics at Attica,* Blue Sky Project, 2012.

4. John O'Brien, "After 20 Years, Attica's Scars Run Deep," *Seattle Times,* September 8, 1991.

5. "Five Deadly Days," reprinted from the *Democrat and Chronicle* (Rochester, New York), Tom Wicker Papers, 26.

6. Ibid.

7. Dr. Michael Brandriss, Interview Transcript, August 18, 2012.

8. Ibid.

9. "Injuries State Police Personnel," Teletype, Investigation and interview files, 1971–1972, New York (State), Special Commission on Attica, 15855-90, Box 84, New York State Archives, Albany, New York.

10. Jeremy Levenson, "Shreds of Humanity: The Attica Prison Uprising, the State of New York and 'Politically Unaware' Medicine," Unpublished Undergraduate Honors Thesis, Department of Urban Studies, University of Pennsylvania, December 21, 2011, in author's possession, 44.

11. John Stainthorp, Attica Brothers Legal Defense, "National Guard and Medical Workers: Report on Interviews," January 8, 1975, in the papers of Elizabeth M. Fink, 5–6.

12. John Dunne, Transcription of notes taken in observers meetings, FOIA request #110818, FOIA p. 001671.

13. "Injuries State Police Personnel," Teletype, Investigation and interview files, 1971–1972, New York (State), Special Commission on Attica, 15855-90, Box 84, New York State Archives, Albany, New York.

14. David Breen, Testimony, *Akil Al-Jundi, et al. v. The Estate of Nelson A. Rockefeller, Russell Oswald, John Monahan, Vincent Mancusi and Karl Pfeil,* United States District Court Western District of New York, Buffalo, New York, No. CIV-75-132, November 14, 1991, 4033–36.

15. Stainthorp, Attica Brothers Legal Defense, "National Guard and Medical Workers," January 8, 1975, 8.

16. Ibid.

17. U.S. Department of Justice, Federal Bureau of Investigation Memorandum, March 24, 1972, Buffalo, New York, FOIA request #1014547 of the FBI.

18. Stainthorp, Attica Brothers Legal Defense, "National Guard and Medical Workers," January 8, 1975, 4.

19. Ibid., 3.

20. Ibid.

21. Ibid.

22. Ibid.

23. Ibid., 8.

24. Breen, Testimony, *Akil Al-Jundi, et al., v. The Estate of Nelson A. Rockefeller et al.,* November 14, 1991, 4033–36.

25. "Assembly Resolution to Impeach Governor Nelson A. Rockefeller for His Wrongful and Unlawful Conduct in Connection with the Handling of the Attica Correctional Facility Inmate Rebellion," January 25, 1972, as contained in: Arthur Eve, Statement, Nelson A. Rockefeller Vice Presidential Confirmation Hearings, House of Representatives, 93rd Cong., 2nd sess., *Congressional Record* 120 (November 26, 1974), 307.

26. Levenson, "Shreds of Humanity," 46.

27. Edward Kowalczyk, also known as Angelo Martin, Affidavit, *People of the State of New York v. Shango Bahati Kakawana (Indicted as Bernard Stroble),* 407 F.Supp. 411 (1976), October 12, 1974, Ernest Goodman Papers.

28. Ibid.

29. Goldman Panel to Protect Prisoners' Constitutional Rights, Report, Investigation and interview files, 1971–1972, New York (State), Special Commission on Attica, 15855-90, Box 9, New York State Archives, Albany, New York, 12.

30. Ibid.

31. John W. Cudmore, Testimony, *Akil Al-Jundi, et al. v. The Estate of Nelson A. Rockefeller, Russell Oswald, John Monahan, Vincent Mancusi and Karl Pfeil,* United States District Court Western District of New York, Buffalo, New York, No. CIV-75-132, December 4, 1991, 6736.

32. Ibid., 6727.

33. Stainthorp, Attica Brothers Legal Defense, "National Guard and Medical Workers," January 8, 1975, 6.

34. Ibid.

35. Cudmore, Testimony, *Akil Al-Jundi et al., v. The Estate of Nelson A. Rockefeller et al.,* December 4, 1991, 6736.

36. Breen, Testimony, *Akil Al-Jundi et al., v. The Estate of Nelson A. Rockefeller et al.,* November 14, 1991, 4055.

37. Perry Ford, Testimony, *McKay Transcript,* April 24, 1972, 1474.

38. Stainthorp, Attica Brothers Legal Defense, "National Guard and Medical Workers," January 8, 1975, 13.

39. Ibid., 12. Also see: U.S. Department of Justice, Federal Bureau of Investigation Memorandum, March 24, 1972, Buffalo, New York.

40. U.S. Department of Justice, Federal Bureau of Investigation Memorandum, March 24, 1972, Buffalo, New York. In this FBI memo the name of the Guardsman is redacted but other documents identify him as James O'Day. In 1991, when he was then a high school biology teacher in North Tonawanda near Buffalo, O'Day came forward with his story in a local paper. See: John O'Brien, "The Scars of Attica," *The Post-Standard* (Syracuse, New York), September 3, 1991.

41. Stainthorp, Attica Brothers Legal Defense, "National Guard and Medical Workers," January 8, 1975, 16.

42. Ibid.

43. Ibid.

44. Ibid.

45. Ibid.

46. Ford, Testimony, *McKay Transcript,* April 24, 1972, 1495–96.

47. Dan Callahan, conversation with author, New Port Richey, Florida, July 5, 2005.

48. Ibid.

49. Gerard Smith, Testimony, *Akil Al-Jundi et al. v. The Estate of Nelson A. Rockefeller et al.,* November 19, 1991, 3925, 3936.

50. Arthur Eve, Notes on the day-by-day events of the riot, Tom Wicker Papers, 5.

51. Ibid.

52. Elizabeth Fink, conversation with author, Brooklyn, New York, June 26, 2007.

53. Callahan, conversation with author, July 5, 2005.

54. Ibid.

55. Ibid.

56. Stainthorp, Attica Brothers Legal Defense, "National Guard and Medical Workers," January 8, 1975, 12.

57. Callahan, conversation with author, July 5, 2005.

58. Ford, Testimony, *McKay Transcript,* April 24, 1972, 1505; Stainthorp, Attica Brothers Legal Defense, "National Guard and Medical Workers," January 8, 1975, 9.

59. Jack Florence, Testimony, *In the Matter of the Additional, Special and Trial Term of the Supreme Court of the State of New York, Designated Pursuant to the Order of the Appellate Division, Fourth Department.* County of Wyoming, February 2, 1972, 108.

60. Callahan, conversation with author, July 5, 2005.

61. Ibid.

62. Jameel Abdul Raheem, Testimony, *Akil Al-Jundi et al. v. The Estate of Nelson A. Rockefeller et al.,* November 1, 1991, 2102.

63. "A Nation of Law? (1968–1971)," transcript, *Eyes on the Prize,* 1987.

64. Dennis Cunningham, Michael Deutsch, and Elizabeth Fink, "Remembering Attica Forty Years Later," *Prison Legal News* (September 2011).

65. Ibid.

66. Ford, Testimony, *McKay Transcript,* April 24, 1972, 1473.

67. Cudmore, Testimony, *Akil Al-Jundi et al. v. The Estate of Nelson A. Rockefeller et al.*, December 4, 1991, 6699.

68. Stainthorp, Attica Brothers Legal Defense, "National Guard and Medical Workers," January 8, 1975, 9.

69. Ibid.

70. Jennifer Gonnerman, "Remembering Attica," *Village Voice,* September 5–11, 2001.

71. Monahan Memorandum to Kirwan, September 19, 1971.

72. Callahan, conversation with author, July 5, 2005.

73. Goldman Panel to Protect Prisoners' Constitutional Rights, Report, New York State Archives, 14.

74. Ford, Testimony, *McKay Transcript,* April 24, 1972, 1476. On this issue of how long troopers and correction officers continued shooting after the retaking was over, prisoner testimony, from numerous sources, is unequivocal that guns were being discharged well into the night of the 13th. One man reported that prisoners locked in cells were shot by officers and that he very clearly "heard gunshots." See: Jameel Abdul Raheem, Testimony, *Akil Al-Jundi et al. v. The Estate of Nelson A. Rockefeller et al.*, November 1, 1991, 2109.

75. Ibid., 1482–83.

76. Ibid., 1483–84.

77. Ibid., 1489–90.

78. Carlos Roche, Testimony, *Akil Al-Jundi et al. v. The Estate of Nelson A. Rockefeller et al.*, November 1, 1991, 2077.

79. "Assembly Resolution to Impeach Governor Nelson A. Rockefeller for His Wrongful and Unlawful Conduct in Connection with the Handling of the Attica Correctional Facility Inmate Rebellion," January 25, 1972, as contained in: Arthur Eve, Statement, Nelson A. Rockefeller Vice Presidential Confirmation Hearings, House of Representatives, 93rd Cong., 2nd sess., *Congressional Record* 120 (November 26, 1974), 307. Also see: *Inmates of Attica Correctional Facility v. Nelson Rockefeller et al.*, September 10, 1971, 748–49.

80. Donald Almeter, conversation with author, July 3, 2005.

81. Ford, Testimony, *McKay Transcript,* April 24, 1972, 1491.

82. Jack Florence, Testimony, *In the Matter of the Additional, Special and Trial Term of the Supreme Court of the State of New York, Designated Pursuant to the Order of the Appellate Division, Fourth Department.* County of Wyoming, February 2, 1972, 113.

83. "Assembly Resolution to Impeach Governor Nelson A. Rockefeller for His Wrongful and Unlawful Conduct in Connection with the Handling of the Attica Correctional Facility Inmate Rebellion," 313.

84. Alton Slagle, "Medic: Guns Killed Hostages," New York *Daily News,* September 15, 1971.

85. Dr. Michael Brandriss, Interview Transcript, August 18, 2012.

86. Ibid.

87. Ibid.

88. Ibid.

89. "Assembly Resolution to Impeach Governor Nelson A. Rockefeller for His Wrongful and Unlawful Conduct in Connection with the Handling of the Attica Correctional Facility Inmate Rebellion," 313.

90. Ibid.

91. For the various dates and times during which officials were at Attica in the immediate aftermath of the retaking, see Official Call Log, Headquarters, New York State Police, Albany.

92. "Attica Aftermath: Problems and Progress," *New-Gate News,* Department of Correctional Services, Central subject and correspondence files, 1959–1973, New York (State), Governor (1959-1973: Rockefeller), Record Group 15, Box 2, Folder 31, Rockefeller Archives, New York State Archives, Albany, New York.

93. Cunningham, Deutsch, and Fink, "Remembering Attica Forty Years Later."

94. Herman Schwartz, Personal Diary, September 12, 19, 24, 1971. In author's possession.

95. William Hellerstein, telephone conversation with author, November 8, 2011. Schwartz, Personal Diary, September 12, 19, and 24, 1971.

96. Hellerstein, telephone conversation with author, November 8, 2011.

97. Ibid.

98. Schwartz, Personal Diary, September 12, 19, 24, 1971.

99. Hellerstein, telephone conversation with author, November 8, 2011.

100. Ibid.

101. Karl Pfeil, Testimony, *Akil Al-Jundi et al. v. The Estate of Nelson A. Rockefeller et al.,* 9768.

102. Schwartz, Personal Diary, September 12, 19, 24, 1971.

103. Ibid.

104. Ibid.

## PART V · RECKONINGS AND REACTIONS

1. This and all subsequent quotations in this section are from: Robert Douglass, Interview, "Attica Prison Riot," *American Experience,* 2007.

## 24. SPEAKING UP

1. Rockefeller Administration, Confidential Memo, "Events at Attica: September 8–13, 1971," 53.

2. As quoted in: Bernard S. Meyer, Special Deputy Attorney General, *Final Report of the Special Attica Investigation,* October 27, 1975, Printed reports and studies, 1955–1958, 1975–1982, New York (State), Governor, B0294-82, Container 1, New York State Archives, Albany, New York, 57.

3. As quoted in: ibid.

4. Meyer, *Final Report of the Special Attica Investigation,* October 27, 1975, New York State Archives, 46. Indeed Simonetti was almost immediately a central presence at Attica, which would prove important as the later state investigation of what had happened at Attica got under way. State Police, for example, noted his comings and goings as in this entry from the police radio log: "September 14th: 12:06 Car 1035: DA Simonetti." From "State Police Radio Log of Troop A Headquarters," Investigation and interview files, 1971–1972, New York (State), Special Commission on Attica, 15855-90, Box 9, New York State Archives, Albany, New York. Also see: Whiteman, Testimony, Meyer Commission, June 12, 1975, 1629, FOIA request #110818, FOIA p. 000652.

5. State of New York, Executive Chamber, Press Release, September 15, 1971, Nelson A. Rockefeller gubernatorial records, Press Office, Series 25, New York (State), Governor (1959–1973: Rockefeller), Record Group 15, Box 49, Folder 1066, Rockefeller Archive Center, Sleepy Hollow, New York.

6. "Five Deadly Days," reprinted from the *Democrat and Chronicle* (Rochester, New York), Tom Wicker Papers, 25; Michael A. Baden and Judith Adler Hennessee, *Unnatural Death: Confessions of a Medical Examiner* (New York: Random House, 1989), 210.

7. John F. Edland, Monroe County Medical Examiner, Memorandum to Mr. Gor-

don Howe, Monroe County Manager, Subject: "Deaths from Attica Emergency," September 22, 1971. Document in author's possession.

8. "Five Deadly Days," reprinted from the *Democrat and Chronicle* (Rochester, New York), Tom Wicker Papers, 25.

9. John T. Edland, Autopsy of William Quinn, September 12, 1971, Autopsy #A-339-71.

10. Lawrence Van Gelder, "Worst Day of My Life," *New York Times,* September 15, 1971.

11. Gene Richard Abbott, Testimony, *Attica Task Force Hearing,* May 9–10, 2002, Rochester, New York, 194–95.

12. "Five Deadly Days," reprinted from the *Democrat and Chronicle* (Rochester, New York), Tom Wicker Papers, 25.

13. Abbott, Testimony, *Attica Task Force Hearing,* May 9–10, 2002, 194–95.

14. Abbott, Testimony, *Attica Task Force Hearing,* May 9–10, 2002, 194–95.

15. Autopsy of John Monteleone (identified as #8), September 14, 1971, Autopsy #A-343-71. Other autopsies such as that of hostage John D'Arcangelo can also be found in the Ernest Goodman Collection. See: Dr. Abbott, Autopsy of John D'Arcangelo, Autopsy #A-347-71; and John D'Arcangelo, Death Certificate. All above from the Ernest Goodman Collection, Accession number 1152, Box 7, Walter Reuther Library.

16. Autopsy of John Monteleone (identified as #8), September 14, 1971, Autopsy #A-343-71; Dr. Abbott, Autopsy of John D'Arcangelo, Autopsy #A-347-71; John D'Arcangelo, Death Certificate.

17. Autopsy of Elliott J. Barkley (identified as Prisoner #17), September 14, 1971, Autopsy #A-355-71, in author's possession.

18. Autopsy of Samuel Melville (identified as Prisoner #13), September 14, 1971, Autopsy #A-366-71, in author's possession.

19. Ibid.

20. Edland Memorandum to Howe, September 22, 1971.

21. "Examiner Surprised by Attica," *Democrat and Chronicle* (Rochester, New York), December 10, 1971.

22. Autopsy of Barry J. Schwartz (identified as Prisoner #22), September 14, 1971, Autopsy #A-351-71, in author's possession.

23. Autopsy of Michael Privitera (identified as Prisoner #23), September 14, 1971, Autopsy #A-352-71, in author's possession.

24. Abbott, Testimony, *Attica Task Force Hearing,* May 9–10, 2002, 194–95.

25. Edland Memorandum to Howe, September 22, 1971.

26. "Conflicting Reports from Inside," *Medical World News,* 3, as quoted in: Jeremy Levenson, "Shreds of Humanity: The Attica Prison Uprising, the State of New York and 'Politically Unaware' Medicine," Unpublished Undergraduate Honors Thesis, Department of Urban Studies, University of Pennsylvania, December 21, 2011, in author's possession.

27. V. R. Mancusi, Superintendent, Western Union Telegram to Medical Examiners, John Edland, September 14, 1971.

28. News clipping, *Rochester Times-Union,* undated, in author's possession.

29. Ibid.

30. "Conflicting Reports from Inside," *Medical World News,* 3, as quoted in: Levenson, "Shreds of Humanity."

31. Edland Memorandum to Howe, September 22, 1971.

32. Arthur Eve, Statement, Nelson A. Rockefeller Vice Presidential Confirmation Hearings, House of Representatives, 93rd Cong., 2nd sess., *Congressional Record* 120 (November 26, 1974), 300.

33. Whiteman, Testimony, Meyer Commission, June 12, 1975, 1610, FOIA request #110818, FOIA p. 000633.

34. "A Nation of Law? (1968–1971)," transcript, *Eyes on the Prize,* 1987.

35. "Amnesty: Governor Contradicted," *New York Post,* September 15, 1971, Dorothy Schiff Papers, Box 4, New York Public Library.

36. Nelson Rockefeller, Deposition, Meyer Commission, August 8, 1975, Mineola, New York, 8681, FOIA request #110818 of the New York State Attorney General's Office, FOIA p. 000428.

37. Gene Spagnoli, "Autopsies Leave Governor Silent," New York *Daily News,* September 15, 1971, Dorothy Schiff Papers, Box 4, New York Public Library.

## 25. STEPPING BACK

1. Robert Douglass, Deposition, Meyer Commission, September 4, 1974, 17, FOIA request #110818, FOIA p. 000182.

2. John F. Edland, Monroe County Medical Examiner, Memorandum to Mr. Gordon Howe, Monroe County Manager, Subject: "Deaths from Attica Emergency," September 22, 1971. Document in author's possession.

3. Ibid.

4. Douglass, Deposition, Meyer Commission, September 4, 1974, 20, FOIA request #110818, FOIA p. 000185.

5. Ibid., FOIA p. 000675.

6. Ann Valone, conversation with author, October 17, 2004.

7. McCandlish Philips, "Semblance of Outward Normality Returns to Attica as Some Policemen Depart," *New York Times,* September 16, 1971.

8. Michael Whiteman, Testimony, Meyer Commission, June 12, 1975, 1701, FOIA request #110818, FOIA p. 000685.

9. *McKay Report,* 459.

10. As partially quoted in Alton Slagle, "Medic: Guns Killed Hostages," *Daily News,* September 15, 1971, and fully quoted in: Annette T. Rubenstein, "Attica, 1971–1975," Pamphlet, Charter Group for a Pledge of Conscience, New York City, December 1975, 17. This fifty-eight-page detailed overview of the Attica rebellion and its implications was drafted by supporters and attorneys for the Attica prisoners indicted for their role in the Attica rebellion. The writing of this account seems to have been prompted by the possibility that there might be renewed attention to the role that the New York State Police played in the retaking of Attica after revelations by Malcolm Bell (see part 8). In the New York State Coalition for Criminal Justice Records, 1971–1986, Series 9: Issues File, Box 1: Attica Aftermath, 1971–1974, Folder 1, M. E. Grenander Department of Special Collections and Archives, State University of New York, Albany, New York.

11. *McKay Report,* 459, 461.

12. Ibid.

13. Gene Spagnoli, "Autopsies Leave Governor Silent," New York *Daily News,* September 15, 1971.

14. Conversation #571-1A (rmn_e571a), September 13, 1971, 12:37 p.m.–2:58 p.m., Oval Office, Present: Richard Nixon, Bob Dole, Alexander Haig, H. R. Haldeman, Nixon Tapes, 4:18.

15. Conversation #571-6 (rmn_e571b), September 13, 1971, 3:47 p.m.–4:16 p.m., Oval Office, Present: Richard Nixon, Clifford Hardin, Nixon Tapes, 10:38–10:54.

16. Conversation #571-1A (rmn_e571a), September 13, 1971, 12:37 p. m.–2:58 p.m., Oval Office, Present: Richard Nixon, Bob Dole, Alexander Haig, H. R. Haldeman, Nixon Tapes, 4:55–5:28.

17. Ibid., 5:29–5:34.

18. Conversation #277 (rmn_e277a), September 15, 1971, 1:05 p.m.–2:10 p.m. Executive Office Building, Present: Richard Nixon, H. R. Haldeman, Nixon Tapes, 58:00–59:00.

19. Ibid., 57:35–57:38.

20. Ibid., 58:13–58:29.

21. Ibid., 58:34–58:39.

22. "Amnesty: Governor Contradicted," *New York Post*, September 15, 1971, Dorothy Schiff Papers, Box 4, New York Public Library.

23. Fred Ferretti, "Autopsies Show Shots Killed 9 Attica Hostages, Not Knives; State Official Admits Mistake," *New York Times*, September 15, 1971; Stephen D. Isaacs, "NY Prison Head Says Gunshots Killed Hostages," *Washington Post*, September 15, 1971.

24. Ferretti, "Autopsies Show Shots Killed 9 Attica Hostages, Not Knives"; Isaacs, "NY Prison Head Says Gunshots Killed Hostages."

25. Rockefeller Administration, Confidential Memo, "Events at Attica: September 8–13, 1971," 56.

26. Ibid.

27. Stephen D. Isaacs, "Attica Report: Whose Credibility Is in Question?," *Washington Post*, September 13, 1971.

28. S. Thran, "Attica Coverage Sloppy, Incomplete," *St. Louis Journalism Review* 2, no. 7 (December 1971), 5.

29. Edmond Pinto, "The Attica Report: An AP News Special," Dorothy Schiff Papers, Box 4, New York Public Library.

30. Ibid.

31. Ibid.

32. Ibid.

33. J. Linstead, "Attica/Where Media Went Wrong," *Chicago Journalism Review* 4, no. 11 (November 1971), 9.

34. Levin and Garrett, "Attica Chronology," Draft, *New York Post*, Dorothy Schiff Papers, Box 4, New York Public Library.

35. Dorothy Schiff, Internal Memorandum to Paul Sann, Subject: "Our 45-page Attica 'Chronology,'" Dorothy Schiff Papers, Box 4, New York Public Library.

36. Ibid.

37. Dorothy Schiff, Note to Paul Sann, Subject: "Attica Prisoners," November 26, 1971, Dorothy Schiff Papers, Box 4, New York Public Library.

38. Isaacs, "Attica Report: Whose Credibility Is in question?," as reproduced and referred to during hearings: House of Representatives, 92nd Cong., 2nd sess., *Congressional Record* 118 (September 13, 1972), 30549.

39. Michael A. Baden and Judith Adler Hennessee, *Unnatural Death: Confessions of a Medical Examiner* (New York: Random House, 1989), 211.

40. *McKay Report*, 461.

41. Baden and Hennessee, *Unnatural Death*, 211.

42. Ibid.

43. Ibid.

44. Ibid.

45. Edland Memorandum to Howe, September 22, 1971.

46. Ibid.

47. Ibid.

48. Baden and Hennessee, *Unnatural Death*, 212.

49. A Dr. Muhtseen Veznedaroglu also conducted one of the autopsies, that of a hostage, but it is unclear whether he too was at this meeting. See: *McKay Report*, 458. Regarding the meeting, see: Edland Memorandum to Howe, September 22, 1971.

50. Edland Memorandum to Howe, September 22, 1971.

51. Baden and Hennessee, *Unnatural Death*, 212.

52. Ibid.

53. Ibid., 213.

54. In 2012 when this author and filmmaker Christine Christopher began reexamining the death of L. D. Barkley they asked Dr. Gene Richard Abbott, the pathologist who originally autopsied Barkley, to review the records again in light of Baden's claim. Unequivocally Abbott said that there is no way, based on the evidence in this

autopsy and his original study of that body, that this was a "tumbling" or accidental shot.

55. McCandlish Phillips, "Prison Chaplain at Guards Funeral, Asks Separate Facility for Revolutionaries," *New York Times,* September 17, 1971.

56. Letter to Dr. Edland, undated and unsigned, John Edland Personal Files, in author's possession.

57. Lawrence Van Gelder, "Worst Day of My Life," *New York Times,* September 15, 1971.

58. As quoted in: Rubenstein, "Attica, 1971–1975," 18.

59. See examples of how this story was also picked up around the country: *Holland Evening Sentinel* (Holland, Michigan), September 17, 1971, and *Coshocton Tribune* (Coshocton, Ohio), September 17, 1971.

60. William Farrell, "Rockefeller Lays Hostages' Deaths to Troopers Fire," *New York Times,* September 17, 1971.

61. "Amnesty: Governor Contradicted," *New York Post,* September 15, 1971. Also see: Nelson Rockefeller, Press Conference Transcript, September 15, 1971. Printed reports and studies, 1955–1958, 1975–1982, New York (State), Governor, B0294-82, Container 1, New York State Archives, Albany, New York, 68–71.

62. Nelson Rockefeller, draft of speech for New York State County Officers' Assoc. Annual Banquet, Monticello, New York, September 16, 1971, Canceled. Also see: Persico, Memorandum to the Governor, Subject: "County Officers Speech, September 16, 1971," September 15, 1971. Both in: Nelson A. Rockefeller gubernatorial records, Speeches, Series 33, New York (State), Governor (1959–1973: Rockefeller), Rockefeller, Nelson A. (Nelson Aldrich), Record Group 15, Box 85, Folder 3465, Rockefeller Archive Center, Sleepy Hollow, New York.

63. Len Katz, New York *Daily News* Internal Memo, Dorothy Schiff Papers, Box 4, New York Public Library.

64. Nelson Rockefeller, Statement to Press following Edland revelations, Transcript, in: Bernard S. Meyer, *Final Report of the Special Attica Investigation,* October 27, 1975, New York State Archives.

65. James A. Wechsler, "A Superb Job?," *New York Post,* September 17, 1971, Willoughby Abner Collection, Box 16, Folders 16–27, Walter Reuther Library.

66. Ibid.

67. Frank Lynn, "Lindsay Criticizes Governor on Attica," *New York Times,* September 18, 1971, Dorothy Schiff Papers, Box 4, New York Public Library.

68. Ibid.

69. Philip D. Carter, "High Officials Absent as Attica Buries Hostages," *Washington Post,* September 16, 1971.

70. Ann Driscoll, Testimony, *Attica Task Force Hearing,* May 9–10, 2002, 146.

71. Carter, "High Officials Absent as Attica Buries Hostages."

72. Ibid.

73. Joseph Lelyveld, "Findings Shock Families of Hostages," *New York Times,* September 15, 1971.

74. Francis X. Clines, "Attica Residents Inclined to Doubt Autopsy Findings," *New York Times,* September 17, 1971.

## 26. FUNERALS AND FALLOUT

1. Francis X. Clines, "Attica Residents Inclined to Doubt Autopsy Findings," *New York Times,* September 17, 1971.

2. David Shipler, "Lack of Data on Inmates' Fates Scored by Prisoners' Families," *New York Times,* September 15, 1971.

3. "Racial Strife Is Hinted in Attica Prison Violence," Hayward, California, *The Daily Review,* September 14, 1971.

4. Howard Coles, WSAY Radio Program, CD #23, Howard Coles Collection, Rochester Museum and Science Center, Rochester, New York.

5. Jack Slater, "Three Profiles in Courage," *Ebony,* March 1973.

6. Traycee Barkley, sister of slain Attica inmate L. D. Barkley, conversation with author, Rochester, New York, July 14, 2011.

7. Slater, "Three Profiles in Courage."

8. Barbara Campbell, Inmates' Kin Critical: For Families of Inmates, Word Is Late," *New York Times,* September 18, 1971.

9. Ibid.

10. Ibid.

11. As quoted in a publication authored by James A. Hudson, *Slaughter at Attica: The Complete Inside Story* (New York: Lopez Publication, 1971). Copy in the personal archives of Jamie Valone.

12. Campbell, "Inmates Kin Critical."

13. Vincent Mancusi, Western Union Telegram, to John Edland September 17, 1971, John Edland Personal Files, in author's possession.

14. Listing of where bodies were to go: John Edland Personal Files, in author's possession.

15. Illegible, possibly "Hawk," Memo to Mancusi, Investigation and interview files, 1971–1972, New York (State), Special Commission on Attica, 15855-90, Box 84, New York State Archives, Albany, New York.

16. "The Attica Prisoners' Statement," *Georgia Straight* 5, Perkins Bostock Library, Duke University, Durham, North Carolina, p. 17.

17. Murray Schumach, "Slain Attica Leader Is Eulogized," *New York Times,* September 20, 1971.

18. Ibid.

19. "Remember Attica, Remember Attica, Remember Attica," Memorial Service of Slain Attica Inmates, Franklin Florence Papers, Box 7b, Rare Books, Special Collections, and Preservation, University of Rochester Library, Rochester, New York; Schumach, "Slain Attica Leader Is Eulogized."

20. Eric Pace, "Another Attica Prisoner Dies, Bringing Toll to 42," *New York Times,* September 26, 1971.

21. Ibid.

22. Ibid.

23. Ibid.

24. "Blacks Here Have Plans to Bury Any Bodies Unclaimed at Attica," *New York Times,* September 19, 1971.

25. "Attica Dead Honored, Families Aided at Apollo Benefit Headlined by Aretha Franklin and Sponsored by Urban League," *New York Amsterdam News,* December 25, 1971, B8.

26. "Cornell University Students Collect $700.00," *New York Amsterdam News,* December 25, 1971, B7.

27. "Attica Fund Gives $1,964 to Families," *Democrat and Chronicle* (Rochester, New York), November 7, 1971.

28. "Fact Sheet #2 from Attica," Attica guard newsletter, September 16, 1971, Lieutenant H. Steinbaugh Papers, in author's possession; "Thank You from Families," full-page ad in the *Attica Pennysaver,* September 29, 1971, Lieutenant H. Steinbaugh Papers, in author's possession.

29. "Thank You from Families."

30. Philip D. Carter, "High Officials Absent as Attica Buries Hostages," *Washington Post,* September 16, 1971.

31. McCandlish Phillips, "Prison Chaplain at Guards Funeral, Asks Separate Facility for Revolutionaries," *New York Times,* September 17, 1971.

32. "Guard's Burial Delayed," *New York Times,* September 17, 1971

33. "6 Attica Hostages Buried: Families Are Not Present," *New York Times*, September 19, 1971.

34. David K. Shipler, "Guards Come from Afar," *New York Times*, September 18, 1971.

35. "Fact Sheet #2 from Attica."

36. Shipler, "Guards Come from Afar."

37. Ibid.

38. McCandlish Phillips, "Tragedy Weighs Heavy on Townsmen," *New York Times*, September 15, 1971.

39. Phillips, "Prison Chaplain at Guards Funeral, Asks Separate Facility for Revolutionaries."

40. "A Guard Dies, Raising the Attica Toll to 43," *New York Times*, October 10, 1971.

41. William M. Kunstler, Letter to Mrs. Ann Valone, October 26, 1971, Mrs. Ann Valone Papers.

42. Ibid.

43. Ibid.

44. Ibid.

45. Ibid.

46. Ibid.

47. "Oswald Pays Visit to Attica Widows," *Courier Express* (Buffalo, New York), November 16, 1971, Investigation and interview files, 1971–1972, New York (State), Special Commission on Attica, 15855-90, New York State Archives, Albany, New York.

48. June Fargo, Testimony, *Attica Task Force Hearing*, May 9–10, 2002, Rochester, New York 23–24.

49. Ibid.

## 27. PRODDING AND PROBING

1. Herman Schwartz, Personal Diary, September 12, 19, 24, 1971. In author's possession.

2. Schwartz, Personal Diary, September 12, 19, 24, 1971.

3. "Lawyers to Meet Attica Prisoners," *New York Times*, September 17, 1971.

4. Schwartz, Personal Diary, September 12, 19, 24, 1971.

5. State of New York, Executive Chamber, Press Release, September 14, 1971, Nelson A. Rockefeller gubernatorial records, Press Office, Series 25, New York (State), Governor (1959–1973: Rockefeller), Record Group 15, Box 49, Folder 1066, Rockefeller Archive Center, Sleepy Hollow, New York.

6. Annette T. Rubenstein, "Attica, 1971–1975," Pamphlet, Charter Group for a Pledge of Conscience, New York City, December 1975.

7. Schwartz, Personal Diary, September 12, 19, 24, 1971.

8. Richard A. Fowler, Bureau of Staff Development, "Summary and Evaluation of the Monitoring Operation at Attica State Correctional Facility from 9/14/71 to 11/12/71," Investigation and interview files, 1971–1972, New York (State), Special Commission on Attica, 15855-90, Box 84, New York State Archives, Albany, New York. Also see: "Fact Sheet #2 from Attica," September 16, 1971, Lieutenant H. Steinbaugh Papers.

9. Schwartz, Personal Diary, September 12, 19, 24, 1971.

10. Goldman Panel to Protect Prisoners' Constitutional Rights, Report, New York State Archives.

11. Ibid.

12. James D. Bradley, MD, Letter to Russell Oswald, November 17, 1971, Investigation and interview files, 1971–1972, New York (State), Special Commission on Attica, 15855-90, Box 84, New York State Archives, Albany, New York.

13. Dr. Lionel Sifontes, Interview by FBI agents Vincent Plumpton Jr. and Sylves-

ter B. Smith, October 20, 1971, FOIA request #110797 of the New York State Attorney General's Office, FOIA p. 000053.

14. Ibid., FOIA p. 000054.

15. Ibid.

16. Ibid., FOIA p. 000056.

17. As quoted in Jeremy Levenson, "Shreds of Humanity." Also see: original data in: Goldman Panel to Protect Prisoners' Constitutional Rights, Report, New York State Archives.

18. *McKay Report*, 464.

19. Richard A. Fowler, Bureau of Staff Development, "Summary and Evaluation of the Monitoring Operation at Attica State Correctional Facility from 9/14/71 to 11/12/71," New York State Archives, 7.

20. "Two Groups Term State Attica Panels 'Whitewash' Units," *New York Times*, October 4, 1971, Dorothy Schiff Papers, Box 4, New York Public Library.

21. Austin MacCormick, Letter to Nelson Rockefeller, December 2, 1971, Nelson A. Rockefeller gubernatorial records, Ann C. Whitman, Gubernatorial, Series 35, Whitman, Ann, New York (State), Governor (1959–1973: Rockefeller), Record Group 4, Box 13, Folder 283, Rockefeller Archive Center, Sleepy Hollow, New York.

22. Ibid.

23. Goldman Panel to Protect Prisoners' Constitutional Rights, Report, New York State Archives, 4–5, 10–11, 12.

24. Rubenstein, "Attica, 1971–1975."

25. Goldman Panel to Protect Prisoners' Constitutional Rights, Report, New York State Archives, 18.

## 28. WHICH SIDE ARE YOU ON?

1. James Foreman, Postscript, *The Making of Black Revolutionaries: A Personal Account* (Washington, D.C.: Open Hand Publishing, 1985).

2. Angela Y. Davis, "Lessons: From Attica to Soledad," *New York Times*, October 8, 1971.

3. John Darnton, "Nixon Repeats Support for Governor's Action," *New York Times*, September 17, 1971; Barry Straus, "March Commemorates Prisoners; Mayor Refuses Permit for Paraders," *Cornell Daily Sun* 87, no. 12 (September 17, 1971); Daniel Margulis, "Cornell Students Demonstrate," *Cornell Daily Sun* 87, no. 10 (September 15, 1971).

4. Richard Phalon, "800 in Albany Protest the Attica Assault," *New York Times*, September 24, 1971.

5. Ibid.

6. "Demonstrators in Albany Oppose Attica 'Massacre,'" *The Cornell Daily Sun* 87, no. 17 (September 24, 1971); Phalon, "800 in Albany Protest the Attica Assault."

7. Rockefeller, Deposition, Meyer Commission, August 8, 1975, 8746, FOIA request #110818, FOIA p. 000550.

8. Russell G. Oswald, Commissioner, Department of Correctional Services, Memorandum to Nelson A. Rockefeller, Governor, Subject: "Activities Report—December 16, 1971–January 14, 1972," January 19, 1972, Nelson A. Rockefeller gubernatorial records, Departmental Reports, Series 28, New York (State), Governor (1959–1973: Rockefeller), Record Group 15, Box 2, Folder 32, Rockefeller Archive Center, Sleepy Hollow, New York.

9. Rockefeller, Deposition, Meyer Commission, August 8, 1975, 8746, FOIA request #110818, FOIA p. 000550.

10. Russell G. Oswald, Commissioner, Department of Correctional Services, Memorandum to Nelson A. Rockefeller, Governor, Subject: "Activities Report, February 10, 1972 through March 10, 1972," Nelson A. Rockefeller gubernatorial records, Depart-

mental Reports, Series 28, New York (State), Governor (1959–1973: Rockefeller), Record Group 15, Box 2, Folder 32, Rockefeller Archive Center, Sleepy Hollow, New York.

11. "3 Held in Protest Against Governor," *New York Times,* December 15, 1971.

12. Phalon, "800 in Albany Protest the Attica Assault."

13. John Darton, "Protesters Staging Rallies as Prison Dispute Widens," *New York Times,* September 16, 1971.

14. Ibid.

15. "Teach-Ins on Prison Set for 28 College Campuses," *New York Times,* October 5, 1971.

16. John Darnton, "Protests Mount, Prayers Offered," *New York Times,* September 18, 1971.

17. Eric Pace, "'Sick' Crank Calls Harass Widows of Attica Guards," *New York Times,* September 29, 1971.

18. Official Call Log, Headquarters, New York State Police, Albany, September 9, 1971, 6:30 p.m.

19. Ibid., September 10, 1971, 10:43 p.m.

20. Murray Schumach, "Unfounded Rumors Still Cause Fear and Uncertainty at Attica," *New York Times,* September 18, 1971.

21. Murray Schumach, "Memories of Riot Are Evident as Attica Village Board Meets," *New York Times,* September 25, 1971.

22. Official Call Log, Headquarters, New York State Police, Albany, September 9, 1971, 2:45 p.m.

23. Oswald, Memorandum to Rockefeller, Subject: "Activities Report—November 1, 1971–December 15, 1971," Nelson A. Rockefeller, Gubernatorial. Series 28. Departmental Reports. Department of Correction, 1960, 1963–1964, 1970–1971. Record Group 15, Series 28. Box 2. Folder 31. Rockefeller Archive Center. Sleepy Hollow, New York.

24. Herman Schwartz, Personal Diary, September 12, 19, 24, 1971.

25. Oswald, Memorandum to Rockefeller, Subject: "Activities Report—October 1, 1971–October 31, 1971," Rockefeller Archive Center.

26. Peg Savage Gray, "1971 Prison Disturbances," April 20, 1972, Report compiled for the Select Committee on Crime, House of Representatives, Congress of the United States, Investigation and interview files, 1971–1972, New York (State), Special Commission on Attica, 159855-90, Box 90, New York State Archives, Albany, New York.

27. Ibid.; Alton Slagle, "Medic: Guns Killed Hostages," New York *Daily News,* September 15, 1971.

28. Gray, "1971 Prison Disturbances."

29. Ibid.

30. "N.Y. Guards Threaten to Lock Cells," *Washington Post,* September 23, 1971.

31. Gray, "1971 Prison Disturbances."

32. Ibid.

33. Howard K. Smith, "Riot Occurred Earlier This Week," CBS Evening News, September 24, 1971.

34. Jerry Wurf, AFSCME President, "Attica," *The Public Employee,* October 1971, Willoughby Abner Collection, Box 16, Folder 16-27, Walter Reuther Library, 2.

35. Ibid.

36. "AFSCME Demands Reforms in N.Y. Prisons—NOW!!," *The Public Employee,* October 1971, Willoughby Abner Collection, Box 16, Folders 16–27, Walter Reuther Library, 8; Wurf, "Attica," 2.

37. Bill Hamilton, AFSCME Public Affairs Director, "We Tried to Tell Them but Got No Response," *The Public Employee,* October 1971, Willoughby Abner Collection, Box 16, Folder 16-27, Walter Reuther Library, 8.

38. Russell G. Oswald, Commissioner, Department of Correctional Services, Memorandum to Nelson A. Rockefeller, Governor, Subject: "Activities Report, February 10, 1972, through March 10, 1972," Rockefeller Archive Center.

39. "N.Y. Guards Threaten to Lock Cells." *Washington Post,* September 23, 1971.

40. Russell G. Oswald, Commissioner, Department of Correctional Services, Memorandum to Nelson A. Rockefeller, Governor, Subject: "Activities Report—December 16, 1971–January 14, 1972," Rockefeller Archive Center.

41. Russell G. Oswald to Nelson A. Rockefeller, January 19, 1972.

42. Joseph Lelyveld, "Black Prison Guards Deplore Racial Imbalance in Penal Chain of Command," *New York Times,* October 24, 1971.

43. Ibid.

44. Ibid.

45. "Fact Sheet #2 from Attica," September 16, 1971, Lieutenant H. Steinbaugh Papers.

46. Ragged spiral bound notebook with handwritten notes and addresses where to send word. Found in a cell that was dismantled by guards and subsequently taken as evidence by New York State Police. Part of collection of materials handed over to New York State Museum in 2011. Author viewed these artifacts in warehouse of New York State Museum, October 2011.

47. Ibid.

48. Goldman Panel to Protect Prisoners' Constitutional Rights, Report, New York State Archives.

49. John Stainthorp, Attica Brothers Legal Defense, "National Guard and Medical Workers," January 8, 1975, 12.

50. Goldman Panel to Protect Prisoners' Constitutional Rights, Report, New York State Archives.

51. Vincent R. Mancusi, Letter to James D. Bradley, M.D., November 10, 1971, Investigation and interview files, 1971–1972, New York (State), Special Commission on Attica, 15855-90, Box 84, New York State Archives, Albany, New York.

52. James D. Bradley, M.D., Correction Medical Director, Memorandum to Walter Dunbar, Executive Deputy Commissioner, Subject: "Inspection at Attica Facility," November 23, 1971, Investigation and interview files, 1971–1972, New York (State), Special Commission on Attica, 15855-90, Box 84, New York State Archives, Albany, New York.

53. Ibid.

54. Eric Pace, "Visiting Day at Attica Stirs New Charges of Brutality," *New York Times,* September 30, 1971.

55. "Fact Sheet #2 from Attica."

56. Ibid.

57. Transferee Lists, undated, Investigation and interview files, 1971–1972, New York (State), Special Commission on Attica, 15855-90, Box 9, New York State Archives, Albany, New York.

58. Memorandum, Subject: "Status of Attica Riot Transfers," September 23, 1971, Investigation and interview files, 1971–1972, New York (State), Special Commission on Attica, 15855-90, Box 9, New York State Archives, Albany, New York.

59. "Institution Status Report—Attica Inmates 9/30/71," Investigation and interview files, 1971–1972, New York (State), Special Commission on Attica, 15855-90, Box 9, New York State Archives, Albany, New York.

60. Fred Ferretti, "Legal Aid Files Suit on Behalf of Clinton Inmates," *New York Times,* October 30, 1971.

61. Ibid.

## 29. DUCKS IN A ROW

1. Joseph Persico, Speech, Draft, September 22, 1971, Nelson A. Rockefeller gubernatorial records, Speeches, Series 33, New York (State), Governor (1959–1973: Rockefeller), Rockefeller, Nelson A. (Nelson Aldrich), Record Group 15, Box 85, Rockefeller Archive Center, Sleepy Hollow, New York.

2. Hugh Morrow, Statement for Nelson Rockefeller, Draft, September 17, 1971, Nelson A. Rockefeller gubernatorial records, Speeches, Series 33, New York (State), Governor (1959–1973: Rockefeller), Rockefeller, Nelson A. (Nelson Aldrich), Record Group 15, Box 85, Sleepy Hollow, New York.

3. Conversation #571-1, September 13, 1971, 12:37 p.m.–2:58 p.m., Oval Office, Present: Richard Nixon, Robert Dole, Alexander Haig Jr., H. R. Haldeman, Nixon Tapes.

4. Spiro T. Agnew, "The 'Root Causes' of Attica," *New York Times,* September 17, 1971.

5. John N. Mitchell, Attorney General, Statement Concerning Campus Disorders, Special Subcommittee on Education, Committee on Education and Labor, House of Representatives, May 20, 1969.

6. Morrow, Statement for Nelson Rockefeller, Draft, September 17, 1971.

7. Rockefeller, Deposition, *Lynda Jones v. State of New York et al.* (Claim No. 54555) and *Elizabeth M. Hardie v. State of New York et al.* (Claim No. 54684), State of New York Court of Claims, April 22, 1977, 47. Also see: Robert Douglass, Testimony, Meyer Commission, June 20, 1975, FOIA request #110818 of the New York State Attorney General's Office, FOIA p. 000295.

8. Whiteman, Testimony, Meyer Commission, June 12, 1975, 1726, FOIA request #110818, FOIA p. 000710.

9. Ibid., FOIA p. 000691.

10. Rockefeller, Deposition, *Lynda Jones v. State of New York et al.* (Claim No. 54555) and *Elizabeth M. Hardie v. State of New York et al.* (Claim No. 54684), State of New York Court of Claims, April 22, 1977, 47.

11. Rockefeller, Deposition, Meyer Commission, August 8, 1975, 8746, FOIA request #110818, FOIA p. 000468.

12. Douglass, Testimony, Meyer Commission, June 20, 1975, FOIA request #110818, FOIA p. 000349.

13. Harry Albright Jr. and Eliot Vestner Jr., Memorandum to the Governor, Subject: "Sources of Attica Chronology," in: Rockefeller Administration, Appendix 3, Confidential Memo, "Events at Attica: September 8–13, 1971."

14. Ibid.

15. Whiteman, Testimony, Meyer Commission, June 12, 1975, 1619, FOIA request #110818, FOIA p. 000642.

## PART VI · INQUIRIES AND DIVERSIONS

### 30. DIGGING MORE DEEPLY

1. John Darnton, "Nixon Repeats Support for Governor's Action," *New York Times,* September 17, 1971.

2. John Darnton, "Protests Mount, Prayers Offered," *New York Times,* September 18, 1971.

3. Marilynn Bailey, "Statewide Coalition Urged to Support Prison Reform," *Democrat and Chronicle* (Rochester, New York), November 12, 1971.

4. Fred Ferretti, "Congressional Committee Also Plans Investigation," *New York Times,* September 16, 1971, Senator Jacob A. Javits Collection, Box 50, Special Collections and University Archives, Frank Melville Jr. Memorial Library, Stony Brook University, Stony Brook, New York.

5. Arthur Eve, Memorandum to Members of the Attica Observers Committee, Subject: "Next Meeting," October 12, 1971, Franklin Florence Papers, Rare Books, Special Collections, and Preservation, University of Rochester Library, Rochester, New York.

6. Ibid.

7. These included: Arthur Eve, Herman Badillo, Robert Garcia, and some other prison reformers who decided to join this group such as David Rothenberg. Naomi Burns, Letter to Members of the Observers Committee, May 11, 1972, Franklin Florence Papers, Rare Books, Special Collections, and Preservation, University of Rochester Library, Rochester, New York.

8. John Dunne, Testimony, U.S. House Select Committee on Crime, September 27, 1971, 33522.

9. State of New York Select Committee on Correctional Institutions and Programs, New York City, February 11, 1972.

10. Russell G. Oswald, Memorandum to Superintendents of Correctional Facilities and State Institutions and Directors of State Hospitals, Subject: "List of Committees," October 28, 1971, Attica uprising–related documents kept at the Attica Correctional Facility, Attica, New York.

11. Hugh R. Jones, Report Number One, investigation and interview files, 1971–1972, New York (State), Special Commission on Attica, 15855-90, Box 90, New York State Archives, Albany, New York.

12. Eric Pace, "Attica Inmates Tell of Running a 'Gauntlet,'" *New York Times,* September 19, 1971.

13. Hugh R. Jones, Report Number One.

14. Ibid.

15. Ibid.

16. Russell G. Oswald, Commissioner, Department of Correctional Services, Memorandum to Nelson A. Rockefeller, Governor, Subject: "Activities Report, August 23, 1972–September 20, 1972," Central subject and correspondence files, 1959–1973, New York (State), Governor (1959–1973: Rockefeller), Record Group 15, Box 2, Folder 32, Rockefeller Archives, New York State Archives, Sleepy Hollow, New York.

17. Ibid.

18. William Ferrell, "House Committee Confers with Rockefeller on Attica," *New York Times,* September 18, 1971.

19. Ibid.

20. Congressmen Claude Pepper and Frank Brasco, Interview, *Attica Aftermath,* NBC News, Attica, New York, September 18, 1971, NBCUniversal Archives, Clip #5112474568_s05, Roll 3.

21. Ibid.

22. Ferretti, "Congressional Committee Also Plans Investigation."

23. Pace, "Attica Inmates Tell of Running a 'Gauntlet.'"

24. Select Committee on Crime, Hearings, House of Representatives, 92nd Cong., 1st sess. (Washington, D.C.: U.S. Government Printing Office, 1972), November 20, 30, December 1, 2, and 3, 1971.

25. Ibid.

26. "2 Inmates to Testify in Attica Court Room," *Courier Express* (Buffalo, New York), December 9, 1971; Investigation and interview files, 1971–1972, New York (State), Special Commission on Attica, 15855-90, New York State Archives, Albany, New York.

27. William Ringle, "House Crime Unit to Visit Attica to Quiz Prisoners," *Democrat and Chronicle* (Rochester, New York), December 3, 1971.

28. Select Committee on Crime, Hearings, House of Representatives, 92nd Cong., 1st sess. (Washington, D.C.: U.S. Government Printing Office, 1972), November 20, 30, December 1,2, and 3, 1971.

29. Morton Minz, "NY Prisons Official Finds No Red Conspiracy at Attica," *Washington Post,* undated, Senator Jacob A. Javits Collection, Box 50, Special Collections and University Archives, Frank Melville Jr. Memorial Library, Stony Brook University, Stony Brook, New York.

30. Michael Whiteman, Testimony, Meyer Commission, June 12, 1975, 1809, FOIA request #110818, FOIA p. 000793.

31. Commissioner Oswald, Address to the Select Committee on Crime, House of Representatives, Congress of the United States, November 30, 1971, Washington, D.C., Attica Correctional Facility Archive.

32. Fred Ferretti, "Badillo Decries Attica 'Inaction': Tells House Panel Promises Have Not Been Honored," *New York Times,* December 2, 1971, 61.

33. Paul L. Montgomery, "2 Attica Inmates Tell U.S. Panel Brutality and Harassing Persist," *New York Times,* February 26, 1972, 59.

34. Ibid.

35. Appendix C: "Continuing Questions About Nelson Rockefeller," as contained in: Nelson A. Rockefeller Vice Presidential Confirmation Hearings, House of Representatives, 93rd Cong., 2nd sess., *Congressional Record* 120 (November 26, 1974), 1090; "Two Groups Term the State's Attica Panels 'Whitewash' Units," *New York Times,* October 4, 1971.

36. Nelson A. Rockefeller, Governor, and Ronald Maiorana, Press Secretary, Press Release, September 16, 1971, State of New York, Executive Chamber, Senator Jacob A. Javits Collection, Box 6, Attica Prison Riot, 1971–1972, Special Collections and University Archives, Frank Melville Jr. Memorial Library, Stony Brook University, Stony Brook, New York.

37. Nelson Rockefeller, Speech, International Downtown Executives Association, Hilton Hotel, New York City, New York, September 21, 1971, Nelson A. Rockefeller gubernatorial records, Speeches, Series 33, New York (State), Governor (1959–1973: Rockefeller), Rockefeller, Nelson A. (Nelson Aldrich), Record Group 15, Box 85, Folder 3466, Rockefeller Archive Center, Sleepy Hollow, New York.

38. Ibid.

39. Arthur Liman, Attica Diary, Draft, January 13, 1972, Arthur L. Liman Papers (MS 1762), Group 1762, Series 1, Box 1, Folder 5, Manuscripts and Archives, Yale University Library, New Haven, Connecticut, 1–2.

40. New York State Special Commission on Attica, Press Release: "Attica Commission Completes Investigation: To Release Report to Public September 13th," Investigation and interview files, 1971–1972, New York (State), Special Commission on Attica, 15855-90, Box 88, New York State Archives, Albany, New York.

41. *Ludington Daily News* (Ludington, Michigan), October 21, 1971.

42. *McKay Report,* xvi.

43. Whiteman, Testimony, Meyer Commission, June 12, 1975, 1822, FOIA request #110818, FOIA p. 000806.

44. New York State Special Commission on Attica, Meeting Minutes, Present: McKay, Marshall, Carter, Rothschild, Broderick, Wadsworth, Wilbanks, Henix, and Rossbacher, November 1971, Investigation and interview files, 1971–1972, New York (State), Special Commission on Attica, 15855-90, Box 88, New York State Archives, Albany, New York.

45. Ibid.

46. Ibid.

47. Commissioner Oswald, Letter to Mancusi, January 7, 1972, Attica Correctional Facility Archive.

48. Liman, Attica Diary, January 13, 1972, 13.

49. Prisoner-written document found in Lieutenant H. Steinbaugh Papers, in author's possession.

50. Ibid.

51. Ibid.

52. Tom Wicker, Notes from interview with Roger Champen, undated, 24, Tom Wicker Papers.

53. Ibid.

54. Michael T. Kaufman, "Leader in Attica Revolt Calls Inquiry 'Whitewash,'" *New York Times,* April 20, 1972.

55. Ibid.

56. Jim McAvey, "Effort Made to Prevent Probe by Special Panel," *Courier Express* (Buffalo, New York), December 23, 1971, Investigation and interview files, 1971–1972, New York (State), Special Commission on Attica, 15855-90, New York State Archives, Albany, New York; "Suit Seeks Halt to Attica Probe," *Democrat and Chronicle* (Rochester, New York), December 23, 1971.

57. Liman, Attica Diary, January 13, 1972, 16.

58. Ibid.

59. New York State Coalition for Criminal Justice Records, 1971–1986, Series 9: Issues File, Box 1: Attica Aftermath, 1971–1974, Folder 1, M. E. Grenander Department of Special Collections and Archives, State University of New York, Albany, New York; New York State Special Commission on Attica, Press Release, "Attica Commission Completes Investigation: To Release Report to Public September 13th," New York State Archives.

60. New York State Coalition for Criminal Justice Records, 1971–1986, Series 9: Issues File, Box 1: Attica Aftermath, 1971–1974, Folder 1, M. E. Grenander Department of Special Collections and Archives, State University of New York, Albany, New York; New York State Special Commission on Attica, Press Release: "Attica Commission Completes Investigation: To Release Report to Public September 13th," New York State Archives.

61. New York State Special Commission on Attica, Press Release: "Attica Commission Completes Investigation: To Release Report to Public September 13th," New York State Archives.

62. Robert McKay, Letter to Nelson Rockefeller, April 1, 1972, Nelson A. Rockefeller gubernatorial records, Ann C. Whitman, Gubernatorial, Series 35, Whitman, Ann, New York (State), Governor (1959–1973: Rockefeller), Record Group 4, Box 13, Folder 305, Rockefeller Archive Center, Sleepy Hollow, New York.

63. Ibid.

64. New York State Special Commission on Attica, Press Release: "Attica Commission Completes Investigation: to Release Report to Public September 13th," New York State Archives.

65. Whiteman, Testimony, Meyer Commission, June 12, 1975, 1783, FOIA request #110818, FOIA p. 000767.

66. Michael T. Kaufman, "Doctor Testifies on Attica Abuses," *New York Times*, April 28, 1971. Also see: Dr. John W. Cudmore, Testimony, *McKay Transcript*, April 27, 1972, 2181–2250; John Cudmore, Louis Futterman, Ronal Dill, and James O'Day, *McKay Transcript*, April 27, 1972, 2250–2349.

67. Cudmore, Testimony, *McKay Transcript*, April 27, 1972, 2313–14.

68. New York State Special Commission on Attica, Press Release: "Attica Commission Completes Investigation: To Release Report to Public September 13th," New York State Archives.

69. Ibid.

70. McKay Commission, Press Conference Statement, September 13, 1972, New York University School of Law, Investigation and interview files, 1971–1972, New York (State), Special Commission on Attica, 15855-90, Box 88, New York State Archives, Albany, New York.

71. *McKay Report*, 329.

72. Senator Javits, Statement on McKay Commission Report on Attica, undated, Senator Jacob A. Javits Collection, Box 6, Special Collections and University Archives, Frank Melville Jr. Memorial Library, Stony Brook University, Stony Brook, New York.

73. Brian Conboy, Memorandum to Senator Jacob Javits, Subject: "McKay Report re Attica," September 13, 1973, Senator Jacob A. Javits Collection, Box 50, Special Collections and University Archives, Frank Melville Jr. Memorial Library, Stony Brook University, Stony Brook, New York.

74. Michael McCarron, State of Attica Investigation Memorandum to Anthony Simonetti, New York City Office, May 10, 1974, in the papers of Elizabeth M. Fink, Brooklyn, New York.

75. Conboy, Memorandum to Javits, Subject: "McKay Report re Attica," September 13, 1973.

76. Ibid.

77. Ibid.

78. Louis Lefkowitz, Robert Fischer, and Gerald Ryan, Subpoena (Duces Tecum) to Citizens Committee, Robert McKay, Chairman, Arthur Liman, counsel, Ordered to appear September 14, 1972 at 10:00 a.m., Signed September 1, 1972, Investigation and interview files, 1971–1972, New York (State), Special Commission on Attica, 15855-90, Box 88, New York State Archives, Albany, New York.

79. "Attica Study Commission Vows Grand Jury Won't Get Its Files," *Washington Post,* September 14, 1972.

80. "Battle Continues on Attica Records," *New York Times,* October 18, 1972. There would be long-term ramifications of this decision—namely that many decades later even the Attica survivors would be prevented from seeing these files because they had been ordered protected in this hearing.

81. Whiteman, Testimony, Meyer Commission, June 12, 1975, 1843, FOIA request #110818, FOIA p. 000807.

## 31. FOXES IN THE HEN HOUSE

1. New York State Coalition for Criminal Justice Records, 1971–1986, Series 9: Issues File, Box 1: Attica Aftermath, 1971–1974, Folder 1, M. E. Grenander Department of Special Collections and Archives, State University of New York, Albany, New York.

2. As quoted in Bernard S. Meyer, *Final Report of the Special Attica Investigation,* October 27, 1975, New York State Archives, 63.

3. As quoted in: ibid., 63, 97.

4. As quoted in: ibid., 65.

5. As quoted in: ibid., 64.

6. Ibid., 66.

7. "Attica Assignment Mutual Aid Request form," Summary of total assignments of Niagara County Sheriff's Office September 9–13, 1971, September 14, 1971, FOIA request #110818 of the New York State Attorney General's Office, FOIA p. 000152.

8. Ibid.

9. As quoted in: Rockefeller, Deposition, Meyer Commission, August 8, 1975, 8841, FOIA request #110818, FOIA p. 000563.

10. Eric Pace, "Officer in Inquiry at Attica Scored," *New York Times,* October 2, 1971.

11. Goldman Panel to Protect Prisoners' Constitutional Rights, Report, New York State Archives.

12. WCBS News, Copy Transcript, Sunday October 3, 1971, 11:15 p.m., Dorothy Schiff Papers, Box 4, New York Public Library.

13. James Clarity, "Attica Prisoners Opposing a Double Role in the Inquiry," *New York Times,* October 6, 1971.

14. As quoted in: Meyer, *Final Report of the Special Attica Investigation,* October 27, 1975, New York State Archives, 66.

15. Special Agents, Lee Mason and Carl Underhill, FBI Memorandum, October 21, 1971, Attica, New York, Buffalo File 44-592, FOIA request #110818 of the New York State Attorney General's Office, FOIA p. 000157.

16. Meyer, *Final Report of the Special Attica Investigation,* October 27, 1975, New York State Archives, 124. There were in fact two investigators assigned to the retaking

from the outset including Michael McCarron, but they were given virtually no support and pressure was coming their way to get the job done.

17. Investigator T. J. Sullivan, Organized Crime Task Force Memo to Robert Fischer, Subject: "Interview with John Flowers: 2/18/72," February 22, 1972. Also see: John Flowers, Testimony, *In the Matter of the Additional, Special and Trial Term of the Supreme Court of the State of New York, Designated Pursuant to the Order of the Appellate Division, Fourth Department.* County of Wyoming, June 11, 1972, Erie County courthouse, 8–9.

18. Frederick Berry, Interview, Attica Investigation, State of New York Organized Crime Task Force, September 22, 1971, 1:45 p.m., Erie County courthouse.

19. Warren Cronan, Interview, Attica Investigation, State of New York Organized Crime Task Force, February 22, 1971, Erie County courthouse. Handwritten Statement from Cronan attached.

20. Sergeants Fay Scott and Edward Qualey, Interview, Attica Investigation, State of New York Organized Crime Task Force, Buffalo Office, October 29, 1974, Erie County courthouse.

21. Ibid.

22. Ibid.

23. Ibid.

24. Ibid.

25. Ibid.

26. Ibid.

27. Rockefeller Administration, Confidential Memo, "Events at Attica: September 8–13, 1971," 38. Also see: Correction Office Don Jennings, Interview, Attica Investigation, State of New York Organized Crime Task Force, November 14, 1974, Erie County courthouse.

28. Robert Fischer, Letter to Louis Lefkowitz, June 14, 1972, as quoted in: Meyer, *Final Report of the Special Attica Investigation,* October 27, 1975, New York State Archives, 124–25.

29. Ibid.

30. Handwritten notes, FOIA request #110818 of the New York State Attorney General's Office, FOIA p. 001217.

31. Rockefeller, Deposition, Meyer Commission, August 8, 1975, 8704, FOIA request #110818, FOIA pp. 000346–000451.

32. Whiteman, Testimony, Meyer Commission, June 12, 1975, 1634-1635, FOIA request #110818, FOIA pp. 000657–000658.

33. Robert E. Fischer, Deputy Attorney General, Memorandum to Superintendent Mancusi, October 1, 1971, State of New York Organized Task Force, Attica uprising–related documents kept at the Attica Correctional Facility, Attica, New York.

34. Leon J. Vincent, Deputy Superintendent Attica Prison, Memorandum to All Employees, October 1, 1971, Attica uprising–related documents kept at the Attica Correctional Facility, Attica, New York.

## 32. STICK AND CARROT

1. This investigation uncovered much evidence of prisoner abuse but ultimately did not pursue any civil rights cases on behalf of the prisoners.

2. FBI notes in the matter of allegation of National Guardsman and inmate abuse with screwdriver, April 10, 1972, File: Buffalo 44-592, FOIA request #1014547-001 of the FBI, September 28, 2009.

3. Edward Kowalczyk, also known as Angelo Martin, Affidavit, *People of the State of New York v. Shango Bahati Kakawana (Indicted as Bernard Stroble),* 407 F.Supp. 411 (1976), October 12, 1974, Ernest Goodman Papers, Walter Reuther Library.

4. Charles "Flip" Crowley, Testimony, Wade Hearing, *People of the State of New*

*York v. Shango Bahati Kakawana (Indicted as Bernard Stroble),* 407 F.Supp. 411 (1976), January 22, 1975, 586–87, 595–98, 628–31, as quoted in: Annette T. Rubenstein, "Attica, 1971–1975," Pamphlet, Charter Group for a Pledge of Conscience, New York City, New York, December 1975. Transcripts for Attica Wade Hearings can also be found in the Ernest Goodman Papers, Series IV, Subseries A: Trial Records, Boxes 24–32, Walter Reuther Library.

5. Ibid.

6. Ibid.

7. Ibid.

8. Robert E. Fischer, Memorandum to Dunham, June 5, 1972, as reported in: Meyer, *Final Report of the Special Attica Investigation,* October 27, 1975, New York State Archives, 79.

9. Fischer, Memorandum to Attorney General Lefkowitz, June 14, 1972, as quoted in: Meyer, *Final Report of the Special Attica Investigation,* October 27, 1975, New York State Archives, 102.

10. Rubenstein, "Attica, 1971–1975."

11. From Wade Hearing, *People of the State of New York v. Shango Bahati Kakawana (Indicted as Bernard Stroble),* 407 F.Supp. 411 (1976), 407 F.Supp. 411 (1976), February 20, 1975, 3152–54. As quoted in: Rubenstein, "Attica, 1971–1975."

12. From Wade Hearing, *People of the State of New York v. Shango Bahati Kakawana (Indicted as Bernard Stroble),* 407 F.Supp. 411 (1976), February 20, 1975, 3229–31; 3225–26, as quoted in: Rubenstein, "Attica, 1971–1975."

13. Ibid., 3229–31.

14. Rubenstein, "Attica, 1971–1975,", 31.

15. William M. Kunstler, Ted L. Wilson, Edward Kowalczyk, and Barbara Handschu, Annexed Affirmations (affidavits), September 5, 1973, in: *People of the State of New York v. Dacajewiah, Indicted as John Hill,* Transcript, 49 A.D.2d 1036 (1975), and *People of the State of New York v. Mariano Gonzalez,* 43 A.D. 2D 793 (N.Y. App. Div. 1973), Erie County courthouse.

16. *Attica News,* Attica Now Collective, April 1972, Lieutenant H. Steinbaugh Papers, in author's possession.

17. Ibid.

18. Kunstler, Wilson, Kowalczyk, and Handschu, Annexed Affirmations (affidavits), *People of the State of New York v. Dacajewiah, Indicted as John Hill,* Transcript, 49 A.D.2d 1036 (1975), and *People of the State of New York v. Mariano Gonzalez,* 43 A.D. 2D 793 (N.Y. App. Div. 1973), September 5, 1973.

19. David Hightower, Affidavit, Attica Investigation, State of New York Organized Crime Task Force, November 29, 1974. Ernest Goodman Papers, Accession number 1152, 10/14/94. Box 7, Walter Reuther Library.

20. Ibid.

21. Ibid.

22. Wade Hearing Vol. XXIII, *People of the State of New York v. Shango Bahati Kakawana (Indicted as Bernard Stroble),* 407 F.Supp. 411 (1976), 5424–29, 5434–50 quoted in: Rubenstein, "Attica, 1971–1975."

23. Ibid.

24. Palmer, Memorandum to Dunham and Whiteman, June 22, 1972, as quoted in: Meyer, *Final Report of the Special Attica Investigation,* October 27, 1975, New York State Archives, 98.

## 33. SEEKING HELP

1. "Attica Con Hangs Self in Cell," *Courier Express* (Buffalo, New York), November 20, 1971, Investigation and interview files, 1971–1972, New York (State), Special Commission on Attica, 15855-90, New York State Archives, Albany, New York.

2. Information from the record book kept by Lieutenant Steinbaugh, correction officer at Attica Correctional Facility. Book was personal accounting of inmate haircuts, pants, shaves, soap, shirts, showers, recreation, meals, and who refused to participate in any of these. Lieutenant H. Steinbaugh Papers, in author's possession.

3. "Inmates to Seek Injury, Property Redress," *Courier Express* (Buffalo, New York), December 9, 1971.

4. "506 Convicts Sue the State," *Courier Express* (Buffalo, New York), December 15, 1971.

5. *Inmates of the Attica Correctional Facility et al. v. Nelson Rockefeller, Governor, State of New York, et al.*, United States Court of Appeals, Second Circuit, 453 F.2d 12, Argued November 5, 1971, decided December 1, 1971.

6. 92.S.Ct.35 Supreme Court of the United States. *7 Males of Attica Correctional Facility v. Governor Nelson Rockefeller, et al.* Application No. A-385. October 12, 1971.

7. "Attica Ruling Is Reversed," *Courier Express* (Buffalo, New York), November 13, 1971, Investigation and interview files, 1971–1972, New York (State), Special Commission on Attica, 15855-90, New York State Archives, Albany, New York.

8. "Attica Aide Explains Why 38 Inmates Are in Isolation," *Courier Express* (Buffalo, New York), December 2, 1971, Investigation and interview files, 1971–1972, New York (State), Special Commission on Attica, 15855-90, New York State Archives, Albany, New York.

9. Ibid.

10. Ibid.

11. *Attica News*, Attica Now Collective, April 1972, Lieutenant H. Steinbaugh Papers, in author's possession.

12. *Inmates of the Attica Correctional Facility et al. v. Nelson Rockefeller, Governor, State of New York, et al.*, United States Court of Appeals, Second Circuit, 453 F.2d 12, argued November 5, 1971, decided December 1, 1971.

13. Ibid.

14. Ibid.

15. William Hellerstein, telephone conversation with author, November 8, 2011.

16. "Attica Women Tell Judge Isolation Must Continue," *Courier Express* (Buffalo, New York), December 6, 1971, Investigation and interview files, 1971–1972, New York (State), Special Commission on Attica, 15855-90, New York State Archives, Albany, New York.

17. *Inmates of the Attica Correctional Facility, Mariano Gonzales, et al. v. Nelson Rockefeller, Governor, State of New York, et al.*, Western District Court, Buffalo, New York, December 14, 1971.

18. Jim McAvey, "Federal Monitors for Attica Asked," *Courier Express* (Buffalo, New York), December 31, 1971, Investigation and interview files, 1971–1972, New York (State), Special Commission on Attica, 15855-90, New York State Archives, Albany, New York.

19. McAvey, "Federal Monitors for Attica Asked."

20. Ibid.

21. Jim McAvey, "Guards' Treatment Rough, 2 Attica Convicts Tell Court," *Courier Express* (Buffalo, New York), December 14, 1971.

22. David L. Norman, Assistant Attorney General, Civil Rights Division, United States Department of Justice Memorandum to Acting Director, Federal Bureau of Investigation, October 31, 1972. Attached is Curtin Order received by U.S. Attorney's office. John T. Curtin, Order, *Inmates of the Attica Correctional Facility, Mariano Gonzalez, et al. v. Nelson Rockefeller, et al.*, CIV 1971-410, August 1, 1972, Western District Court, Buffalo, New York.

23. McAvey, "Federal Monitors for Attica Asked."

24. As quoted in: Annette T. Rubenstein, "Attica, 1971–1975," Pamphlet, Charter Group for a Pledge of Conscience, New York City, New York, December 1975.

## 34. INDICTMENTS ALL AROUND

1. David Prizinsky, "Justice Ball to Preside at Enquiry of Attica Riot," *Courier Express* (Buffalo, New York), November 4, 1971, Investigation and interview files, 1971–1972, New York (State), Special Commission on Attica, 15855-90, Box 85, New York State Archives, Albany, New York.

2. In the state of New York, the "Supreme Court" is merely a general jurisdiction court where trials take place—both civil and criminal.

3. Richard J. Roth, "Scope of Grand jury Probe Hinted During Impaneling," *Courier Express* (Buffalo, New York), November 30, 1971, investigation and interview files, 1971–1972, New York (State), Special Commission on Attica, 15855-90, Box 85, New York State Archives, Albany, New York.

4. Ibid.

5. Carolyn Micklem, "Updates on Attica Defense," undated, New York State Coalition for Criminal Justice Records, 1971–1986, Series 9: Issues File, Box 1: Attica Aftermath, 1971–1974, Folder 1, M. E. Grenander Department of Special Collections and Archives, State University of New York, Albany, New York; Annette T. Rubenstein, "Attica, 1971–1975," Pamphlet, Charter Group for a Pledge of Conscience, New York City, December 1975. Also see this point made in: Malcolm Bell, *The Turkey Shoot*, 106.

6. Attorney General Simonetti, Letter to Mr. Elwood Kelly, Chairman, Wyoming County Board of Supervisors, December 16, 1971, Erie County courthouse.

7. Ibid.; *Attica News*, Attica Now Collective, April 1972, Lieutenant H. Steinbaugh Papers, in author's possession.

8. As quoted in: Rubenstein, "Attica, 1971–1975."

9. Wade Hearing, *People of the State of New York v. Shango Bahati Kakawana (Indicted as Bernard Stroble)*, 407 F.Supp. 411 (1976), 596, as quoted in: Rubenstein, "Attica, 1971–1975."

10. Charles "Flip" Crowley, Testimony, Wade Hearing, *People of the State of New York v. Shango Bahati Kakawana (Indicted as Bernard Stroble)*, 407 F.Supp. 411 (1976), January 22, 1975, 628–31, in: Rubenstein, "Attica, 1971–1975."

11. As quoted in: Crowley, Testimony, Wade Hearing, *People of the State of New York v. Shango Bahati Kakawana (Indicted as Bernard Stroble)*, 407 F.Supp. 411 (1976), January 22, 1975, 628–31, in: Rubenstein, "Attica, 1971–1975,"

12. Jiri Newport, Affidavit, *People of the State of New York v. Mariano Gonzalez*, Supreme Court of New York, Appellate Division, Fourth Department, 43 A.D. 2D 793 (N.Y. App. Div. 1973), January 24, 1973, Erie County courthouse.

13. Ibid.

14. Ibid.

15. Ibid.

16. Arthur O. Eve, President, and David Rothenberg, Secretary, Memorandum to Attica Observer Committee Members, April 11, 1972, Franklin Florence Papers, Rare Books, Special Collections, and Preservation, University of Rochester Library, Rochester, New York.

17. As quoted in: Rubenstein, "Attica, 1971–1975."

18. Dallas Simon, Statement, Interview by Investigator Ernest Milde, Attica Investigative Office, Buffalo, New York, February 19, 1975, Erie County courthouse; Warren Cronan, Interview, Attica Investigation, February 22, 1971. Handwritten Statement from Cronan attached.

19. Joe Heath, Letter to Bernard "Shango" Stroble, November 24, 1973, Ernest Goodman Papers, Accession number 1152, Box 7, Walter Reuther Library.

20. William M. Kunstler, Annexed Affidavit, June 14, 1974, and Patrick Baker, Annexed Affirmation (affidavit), June 7, 1974, *People of the State of New York v. Dacajewiah, Indicted as John Hill*, Erie County courthouse.

21. As quoted in: Bernard S. Meyer, *Final Report of the Special Attica Investigation,* October 27, 1975, New York State Archives, 79.

22. Background Paper for Statement Calling for Dropping of Indictments, New York State Coalition for Criminal Justice Records, 1971–1986, Series 9: Issues File, Box 1: Attica Aftermath, 1971–1974, Folder 1, M. E. Grenander Department of Special Collections and Archives, State University of New York, Albany, New York.

23. Ibid.

24. Document in: New York State Coalition for Criminal Justice Records, 1971–1986, Series 9: Issues File, Box 1: Attica Aftermath, 1971–1974, Folder 1, M. E. Grenander Department of Special Collections and Archives, State University of New York, Albany, New York; Rubenstein, "Attica, 1971–1975."

25. David J. Rothman, "You Can't Reform the Bastille," *The Nation,* March 19, 1973.

26. W. Mark Felt, Acting Director, FBI, Memorandum to SAC, Buffalo, Subject: "Indictments," December 20, 1972, FOIA request #1014547-001 of the FBI, September 28, 2009.

27. Ibid.

28. *Attica: Chronology of Events, 1971–1974,* Attica Brothers Legal Defense, Buffalo, New York, Joseph A. Labadie Collection, Special Collections Library, University of Michigan, Ann Arbor, Michigan.

## PART VII · JUSTICE ON TRIAL

### 35. MOBILIZING AND MANEUVERING

1. Bill Goodman, Interview, *Speaking Freely: Bill Goodman,* National Lawyers Guild, June 3, 2013.

2. On February 27, 1973, two hundred Oglala Lakota (Sioux) activists and members of the American Indian Movement (AIM) began a protest in Wounded Knee, South Dakota, demanding that the U.S. government make good on treaties from the nineteenth and early twentieth centuries. They remained for seventy-one days in a standoff with law enforcement. Ultimately the protest ended after much gunfire, some deaths, and many of the protesters arrested. On the NLG Attica strategy, see: Goodman, Interview, *Speaking Freely: Bill Goodman,* National Lawyers Guild, June 3, 2013.

3. Donald Jelinek, *Attica Justice: The Cruel 30-Year Legacy of the Nation's Bloodiest Prison Rebellion, Which Transformed the American Prison System* (Jelinek Publishers, 2011), 240.

4. Ibid., 237.

5. Ibid., 235.

6. Fred Ferretti, "4 Bar Groups Give Legal Aid to Inmates at Attica," *New York Times,* October 26, 1971.

7. Annette T. Rubenstein, "Attica, 1971–1975," Pamphlet, Charter Group for a Pledge of Conscience, New York City, December 1975, 36.

8. Leonard J. Klaif and Dennis Cunningham, Petition to Judge Carmen F. Ball, Subject: "In the Matter of the Application for payment of legal fees and expenses incurred on behalf of the Attica brothers Legal Defense between December 1972 and July 1974," *Additional Special and Trial Term of the Supreme Court, State of New York, County of Erie,* Filed October 24, 1974, request denied October 24, 1974, New York State Coalition for Criminal Justice Records, 1971–1986, Series 9: Issues File, Box 1: Attica Aftermath, 1971–1975, M. E. Grenander Department of Special Collections and Archives, State University of New York, Albany, New York.

9. Background Paper for Statement Calling for Dropping of Indictments, New York State Coalition for Criminal Justice Records, 1971–1986, State University of New York, Albany, New York.

10. In: New York State Coalition for Criminal Justice Records, 1971–1986, Series 9: Issues File, Box 1: Attica Aftermath, 1971–1974, M. E. Grenander Department of Special Collections an Archives, State University of New York, Albany, New York.

11. Rubenstein, "Attica, 1971–1975," 39.

12. "Proposed Budget—1974. Attica Brothers Legal Defense," in the papers of Elizabeth M. Fink, Brooklyn, New York.

13. "Testimonial to a Revolutionary Activist," Flyer, Committee to Support Attica Brother Akil Al-Jundi, in the papers of Elizabeth M. Fink, Brooklyn, New York.

14. Flyer, American Radicalism Collection, Special Collections, Michigan State University, East Lansing, Michigan.

15. Flyer, Joseph A. Labadie Collection, Special Collections Library, University of Michigan, Ann Arbor, Michigan.

16. Flyer, American Radicalism Collection, Special Collections, Michigan State University, East Lansing, Michigan.

17. Herbie Scott Dean aka Akil Al-Jundi, "An Autobiographical Synopsis," September 11, 1973, in the papers of Elizabeth M. Fink, Brooklyn, New York.

18. Salvador Agron, Attica Correctional Facility, Letter to Andrew Himes, April 24, 1973, Resist Collection, Watkinson Library, Trinity College, Hartford, Connecticut.

19. Syracuse Attica Coalition, "Attica Is All of Us," Syracuse, New York, 1973, Rare Books Collection, Department of Special Collections, Stanford University, Stanford, California.

20. Donald Jelinek, Attica Legal Defense and Legal Coordinator, Fundraising Letter, November 22, 1973, American Radicalism Collection, Special Collections, Michigan State University, East Lansing, Michigan.

21. Louis M. Rabinowitz, Foundation, Fundraising Letter, March 27, 1973, in the papers of Elizabeth M. Fink, Brooklyn, New York.

22. Carol Bellamy, representing the 23rd District, wrote to Irene Jackson: "I assure you that I agree with the sentiments in your letter and I do support the proposed supplemental budget items." Carol Bellamy Letter to Irene Jackson, May 13, 1974, New York State Coalition for Criminal Justice Records, 1971–1986, Series 9: Issues File, Box 1: Attica Aftermath, 1971–1974, Folder 1, M. E. Grenander Department of Special Collections and Archives, State University of New York, Albany, New York; Edwyn E. Mason, 48th District representative, Letter to Irene Jackson, May 8, 1974, New York State Coalition for Criminal Justice Records, 1971–1986, Series 9: Issues File, Box 1: Attica Aftermath, 1971–1974, Folder 1, M. E. Grenander Department of Special Collections and Archives, State University of New York, Albany, New York.

23. In: New York State Coalition for Criminal Justice Records, 1971–1986, Series 9: Issues File, Box 1: Attica Aftermath, 1971–1974, Folder 1, M. E. Grenander Department of Special Collections and Archives, State University of New York, Albany, New York.

24. "Ex-Attica Inmate Indicted in Slaying of Guard in Riot," *New York Times*, December 17, 1972.

25. Enid Nemy, "Party on LI Assists Attica Defense," *New York Times*, August 21, 1972.

26. Michael Deutsch, conversation with author, Chicago, Illinois, June 27, 2005.

27. Jelinek, *Attica Justice*, 211.

28. Ibid., 223.

29. Ibid., 255.

30. Notice of Petition, *Attica Brothers v. Additional Special November 1971 Grand Jury*, 45 A.D.2d 13 (N.Y. App. Div. 1974), seeking "judgment quashing the Grand Jury Panel under CPLR Article 78," Erie County courthouse.

31. "Memorandum of Law in support of Attica Brothers notice of motion to dismiss the indictments," *People of the State of New York v. Armstrong et al.*, New York Supreme Court, Special and Trial Term, Erie County, 76 Misc.2d 582 (N.Y. Misc. 1973), November 16, 1973.

32. Writ of Prohibition, *Big Black, also known as Frank Smith v. Carmen F. Ball*, Supreme Court of State of New York, Appellate Division, Fourth Department, 51 A.D.2d 684 (1976), October 14, 1975.

33. Walter Dunbar and Robert Henderson, Deposition, January 21, 1974, Erie County Courthouse, Erie County, Buffalo, New York, 100–101.

## 36. A HOUSE DIVIDED

1. William Hellerstein, telephone conversation with author, November 8, 2011.

2. Herman Schwartz, conversation with author, July 28, 2004.

3. Dennis Cunningham, Michael Deutsch, and Elizabeth Fink, "Remembering Attica Forty Years Later," *Prison Legal News* (September 2011).

4. Ibid.

5. Donald Jelinek, *Attica Justice: The Cruel 30-Year Legacy of the Nation's Bloodiest Prison Rebellion, Which Transformed the American Prison System* (Jelinek Publishers, 2011), 171. For more on the strong merits of defending the cases of this period in history, particularly cases in which black radicals were on trial, see: Sherie M. Randolph, *Florynce "Flo" Kennedy: The Life of a Black Feminist Radical* (Chapel Hill: UNC Press, 2015).

6. Ernie Goodman et al., "Anatomy of a Defense," unpublished book, Preliminary Inventory of the National Lawyers Guild Records, 1936–1999, Ernest Goodman Files, Box 67, Series 10, Bancroft Library, University of California, Berkeley.

7. Frank "Big Black" Smith and Bernard "Shango" Stroble, "Different views on Defense," two letters written to the NLG to explain divergent views, February 24, 1975, Sidney Rosen Papers, 1921–1980, Box 1, Folder 8, Walter Reuther Library.

8. Ibid.

9. Ibid. One issue of *Attica News* was published seven months after the retaking and it updated the public on legal actions, medical conditions of prisoners still inside, and so forth. *Attica News*, Attica Now Collective, April 1972, Lieutenant H. Steinbaugh Papers, in author's possession.

10. Frank "Big Black" Smith and Bernard "Shango" Stroble, "Different views on Defense," February 24, 1975.

11. Ibid.

12. Michael Deutsch, conversation with author, June 27, 2005.

13. See letters from Baba to Bro. Williams and from Bro. Baba to Bro. Jomo. Letters intercepted by second officer Scott Pedalty in HBZ, who called CO E. Schmidt and turned them over on May 19, 1972. The letters were in an envelope concealed in a newspaper and had "evidently been brought into the institution by other than prescribed channels." CO Scott Pedalty, Memorandum to CO E. Schmidt and Sgt. Conners, Memorandum to E. Montanye, superintendent, both in the papers of Elizabeth M. Fink, Brooklyn, New York.

14. Barbara Handschu, Letter to Mariano "Dalou" Gonzalez, undated, in the papers of Elizabeth M. Fink, Brooklyn, New York.

15. Ibid.

16. Mariano "Dalou" Gonzalez, Letter to Barbara Handschu, May 8, 1972, in the papers of Elizabeth M. Fink, Brooklyn, New York.

17. Bernard "Shango" Stroble, Letter to Ernie Goodman, undated, Ernest Goodman Papers, Accession number 1152, Box 6, Walter Reuther Library.

18. Frank "Big Black" Smith and Bernard "Shango" Stroble, "Different views on Defense," February 24, 1975.

19. Ibid.

20. Jelinek, *Attica Justice*, 304.

## 37. LAYING THE GROUNDWORK

1. Donald Jelinek, *Attica Justice: The Cruel 30-Year Legacy of the Nation's Bloodiest Prison Rebellion, Which Transformed the American Prison System* (Jelinek Publishers, 2011), 206.
2. Ibid., 254.
3. Ibid., 271.
4. Ibid.
5. Ibid., 275.
6. Ibid., 286.
7. Ibid., 288.
8. Ibid., 289.
9. Ibid., 218.
10. National Jury Project, *The Jury System: New Methods for Reducing Prejudice. A Manual for Lawyers, Legal Workers, and Social Scientists* (Cambridge, Mass.: The Project, 1975), 32.
11. Beth Bonora, "We'd Only Just Begun: The Origins of Trial Consulting," Newsletter (San Francisco: Bonora Roundtree, 2012).
12. Ibid.
13. Ibid.
14. Ibid.
15. Ibid.
16. National Jury Project, *The Jury System*, 31.
17. Memorandum, "Why the Community is Involved in the Attica Jury selection," Ernest Goodman Papers, Accession number 1152, Box 7, Walter Reuther Library.
18. Jelinek, *Attica Justice*, 307.
19. National Jury Project, *The Jury System*, 36.
20. Ibid., 37.
21. Ibid., 47.
22. Ibid., 48.
23. John Stainthorp, Attica Brothers Legal Defense, "National Guard and Medical Workers," January 8, 1975, 1.
24. Ibid.
25. "National Guard and Medical Workers: Report on Interviews," typed draft, undated, in the papers of Elizabeth M. Fink, Brooklyn, New York.
26. Stainthorp, Attica Brothers Legal Defense, "National Guard and Medical Workers," January 8, 1975, 16.
27. "National Guard and Medical Workers: Report on Interviews," typed draft, undated.
28. Ibid.
29. Jelinek, *Attica Justice*, 241.
30. Flo Hoder, Personal Trial Notes, Oakland, California, sent to author by Ms. Hoder.
31. Ibid.
32. Pretrial conference before Carmen Ball on indictments 5 and 15, June 19, 1974, in: *The People of the State of New York v. Frank Smith, aka "Big Black."*
33. Ibid.
34. Ibid.
35. *The People of the State of New York v. Luis Manuel Rosario*, Court of Appeals of the State of New York, 9 N.Y.2d 286 (1961), argued January 19, 1961, decided March 23, 1961; *Brady v. Maryland*, United States Supreme Court, 373 U.S. 83 (1963), argued March 18–19, 1963, decided May 13, 1963.
36. Annette T. Rubenstein, "Attica, 1971–1975," Pamphlet, Charter Group for a Pledge of Conscience, New York City, December 1975, 37.

37. Ibid.
38. Ibid.
39. Ibid., 38.
40. Dennis Cunningham, ABLD, Letter to Anthony Simonetti, CC: Hon. James O. Moore, March 8, 1974, in the papers of Elizabeth M. Fink, Brooklyn, New York.
41. *United States v. Wade,* United States Supreme Court, 388 U.S. 218 (1967), argued February 16, 1967, decided June 12, 1967.
42. Ibid.

## 38. TESTING THE WATERS

1. See coverage of Bilello in court in *Buffalo Evening News,* June 13, 1973. Letter. Richard Bilello to Frank (Big Black) Smith. Printed in: *Attica News.* September 12, 1974. Vol. 2. No. 10.
2. Ibid.
3. Flo Hoder, Personal Trial Notes, sent to author by Ms. Hoder.
4. Indictment #5, Bilello Arraignment, *People of the State of New York v. Richard Bilello,* Court of Appeals of the State of New York, 31 N.Y.2d 922 (1972), December 29, 1972.
5. Ibid.
6. *People of the State of New York v. Richard Bilello,* Transcript, January 30, 1973, 25.
7. Richard Bilello, Letter to Maxwell Spoont, Special Attorney General, January 8, 1974, FOIA request #110818 of the New York State Attorney General's Office, FOIA p. 001040.
8. *People of the State of New York v. Richard Bilello,* Transcript, January 30, 1973, 7.
9. "Inmate from Attica Slain at Dannemora," *New York Times,* October 30, 1974, 21.
10. Ibid.
11. Michael Deutsch, conversation with author, June 27, 2005.
12. Documents in: Erie County courthouse.
13. Annette T. Rubenstein, "Attica, 1971–1975," Pamphlet, Charter Group for a Pledge of Conscience, New York City, December 1975, 39.
14. Ibid.
15. Elizabeth Fink, conversation with author, June 26, 2007.
16. "Metropolitan Briefs: Attica Defendant Wins Acquittal," *New York Times,* October 10, 1974, 51.
17. Ibid.
18. Memo: Department of Correctional Services, Elmira Correctional Facility. From: John Wilmont, Acting Superintendent to Vincent Mancusi. Re: Statement by Dr. Eugene Pittman, M.D. regarding John Schleich and James Schleich, November 8, 1971, investigation and interview files, 1971–1972, New York (State), Special Commission on Attica, 15855-90, New York State Archives, Albany, New York.
19. John Schleich, Testimony, *In the Matter of the Additional, Special and Trial Term of the Supreme Court of the State of New York, Designated Pursuant to the Order of the Appellate Division, Fourth Department.* County of Wyoming, March 21, 1972, 12.
20. Ibid.
21. Ibid., 22.
22. Ibid., 24.
23. Indictment no. 35, *The People of the State of New York v. Vernon LaFranque,* State of New York Supreme Court: County of Erie, November 14, 1974, Erie County courthouse.
24. Ibid.
25. Newsletter, Joseph A. Labadie Collection, Special Collections Library, University of Michigan, Ann Arbor, Michigan.

26. "Attica Trial Ends in Victory: Brother Acquitted: Jurors Denounce Prosecution, Evidence Called Fabrication," *Workers' Power* 112 (January 16–29), 1975.

27. Newsletter, Joseph A. Labadie Collection, Special Collections Library, University of Michigan, Ann Arbor, Michigan.

## 39. GOING FOR BROKE

1. Donald Jelinek, *Attica Justice: The Cruel 30-Year Legacy of the Nation's Bloodiest Prison Rebellion, Which Transformed the American Prison System* (Jelinek Publishers, 2011), 305; John "Dacajewiah" Hill, telephone conversation with author, May 31, 2005.

2. Hill, conversation with author, May 31, 2005.

3. Ibid.

4. Ibid.

5. Ibid.

6. Ibid.

7. Jelinek, *Attica Justice,* 305.

8. Michael Kaufman, "Reporter's Notebook: Attica Trial Something of an Anti-climax," *New York Times,* March 30, 1975.

9. Ibid.

10. Hill, conversation with author, May 31, 2005.

11. Kaufman, "Reporter's Notebook: Attica Trial Something of an Anti-climax."

12. Ibid.

13. Ibid.

14. Ibid.

15. Mary Breasted, "Attica Hearings Are Under Way," *New York Times,* December 2, 1974.

16. *People of the State of New York v. Dacajewiah, Indicted as John Hill,* Transcript, vol. 10, Supreme Court of the State of New York, Appellate Division, Fourth Department, 49 A.D.2d 1036 (1975), March 7, 1975, 1987–88.

17. Ted L. Wilson, Affirmation (affidavit), "Supplemental Motion for Discovery and for a Protective Order," *People of the State of New York v. Dacajewiah, Indicted as John Hill,* 49 A.D.2d 1036 (1975), and *People of the State of New York v. Mariano Gonzalez,* 43 A.D.2D 793 (N.Y. App. Div. 1973), February 14, 1973, Erie County courthouse.

18. Ibid.

19. Edward Kowalczyk, Affirmation (affidavit), "Supplemental Motion for Discovery and for a Protective Order," *People of the State of New York v. Dacajewiah, Indicted as John Hill,* 49 A.D.2d 1036 (1975); *People of the State of New York v. Mariano Gonzalez,* 43 A.D.2d 793 (N.Y. App. Div. 1973), July 11, 1973, Erie County courthouse.

20. Kowalczyk, also known as Angelo Martin, Affidavit, *People of the State of New York v. Shango Bahati Kakawana (Indicted as Bernard Stroble),* 407 F.Supp. 411 (1976), October 12, 1974, Ernest Goodman Papers.

21. Michael Myerson, "Attica: 2 Years Later in Memoriam and Solidarity," undated draft, National Alliance Against Racism and Political Oppression, Box 39, Folder 17: Attica Draft for Brochure, Schomburg Center for Research in Black Culture, New York Public Library.

22. Ibid.

23. National Alliance Against Racism and Political Oppression, Box 39, Folder 21: Attica Correspondence, Schomburg Center for Research in Black Culture, New York Public Library.

24. Flyer, Joseph A. Labadie Collection, Special Collections Library, University of Michigan, Ann Arbor, Michigan.

25. Annette T. Rubenstein, "Attica, 1971–1975," Pamphlet, Charter Group for a Pledge of Conscience, New York City, December 1975.

26. Ibid.

27. Kaufman, "Reporter's Notebook: Attica Trial Something of an Anti-climax."

28. Frederick M. Marshall, Administrative Judge, 8th Judicial District, Letter to Michael A. Amico, Erie County Sheriff, May 17, 1974, Erie County courthouse.

29. Carmen F. Ball, Affidavit, *People of the State of New York v. Dacajewiah, Indicted as John Hill,* 49 A.D.2d 1036 (1975), October 22, 1974, Erie County courthouse.

30. Richard Meisler, "An Attica Trial," personal typewritten account of the Hill and Pernasalice trial, 1–2, given to the author by Mr. Meisler.

31. Jelinek, *Attica Justice,* 308.

32. "Appeals Court Lets 2 in Attica Trial Get Extra Challenges," *New York Times,* January 19, 1975, 49.

33. Herman Schwartz, conversation with author, July 28, 2004.

34. Michael T. Kaufman, "Prosecutor Rests in the Attica Case: Defense Wants State to Pay Its Witnesses' Expenses—Pathologist Testifies Not on Critical List," *New York Times,* March 18, 1975, 27.

35. William Kunstler, Affirmation (affidavit), "Supplemental Motion for Discovery and for a Protective Order," *People of the State of New York v. Dacajewiah, Indicted as John Hill,* 49 A.D.2d 1036 (1975); *People of the State of New York v. Mariano Gonzalez,* 43 A.D. 2d 793 (N.Y. App. Div. 1973), August 29, 1973, Erie County courthouse.

36. *People of the State of New York v. Dacajewiah, Indicted as John Hill,* Transcript, vol. 16, Supreme Court of the State of New York, Appellate Division, Fourth Department, 49 A.D.2d 1036 (1975), December 10, 1974, 151.

37. Don Jelinek, ABLD, Letter to Judge James O. Moore, affidavit attached, undated, Erie County courthouse.

38. As quoted in: Stuart Cohen, ABLD, Letter to Judge James O. Moore, Subject: "Wiretap order," March 18, 1974, in the papers of Elizabeth M. Fink, Brooklyn, New York.

39. Maxwell B. Spoont, Special Assistant Attorney General of the State of New York, "Affidavit in Opposition to Motion for Discovery Alleged Electronic Surveillance Material," *People of the State of New York v. William Bennett et al.,* Supreme Court, Additional Special and Trial Term, Erie County, 75 Misc.2d 1040 (N.Y. Misc. 1973), November 13, 1973.

40. Cohen Letter to Judge Moore, Subject: "Wiretap order," March 18, 1974, Erie County courthouse.

41. *People of the State of New York v. Dacajewiah, Indicted as John Hill,* Transcript, vol. 17, 49 A.D.2d 1036 (1975), November 18, 1974.

42. Kunstler to judge on issue of resources: *People of the State of New York v. Dacajewiah, Indicted as John Hill,* Transcript, vol. 16, Supreme Court of the State of New York, Appellate Division, Fourth Department, 49 A.D.2d 1036 (1975), March 17, 1975, 3310.

43. Ibid.

44. Meisler, "An Attica Trial," 3.

45. Mary Breasted, "Killing at Attica Laid to 'Others,'" *New York Times,* February 24, 1975.

46. This testimony constituted eighty pages of trial transcript. See: *People of the State of New York v. Dacajewiah, Indicted as John Hill,* Transcript, vol. 33, 49 A.D.2d 1036 (1975), March 31, 1975, 4656.

47. Mary Breasted, "Attica Murder Trial Judge Bars Testimony on Police Prison Attack," *New York Times,* February 26, 1975.

48. William Rivers, Testimony, *People of the State of New York v. Dacajewiah, Indicted as John Hill,* Transcript, vol. 13, 49 A.D.2d 1036 (1975), March 5, 1975, 1515.

49. Robert Kopec, Testimony, Exhibit: Kopec, Interview by Investigator Palascak, February 1, 1972, 2909, *People of the State of New York v. Dacajewiah, Indicted as John Hill,* Transcript, vol. 14, 49 A.D.2d 1036 (1975), March 13, 1975. Kunstler is referring to this testimony.

50. Edward Douglas Zimmer, Testimony, *In the Matter of the Additional, Special and Trial Term of the Supreme Court of the State of New York, Designated Pursuant to the Order of the Appellate Division, Fourth Department.* County of Wyoming, January 5, 1972, Erie County courthouse.

51. Ibid.

52. Ibid.

53. Michael T. Kaufman, "Jury Starts Deliberations in the Case of 2 Accused," *New York Times,* April 4, 1975.

54. Kunstler to judge on issue of resources, *People of the State of New York v. Dacajewiah, Indicted as John Hill,* Transcript, vol. 16, 49 A.D.2d 1036 (1975), March 17, 1975, 3186–87.

55. Michael T. Kaufman, "Former Prisoner at Attica Testifies He Saw Inmate Strike Two Correction Officers with a Club," *New York Times,* March 5, 1975.

56. Kunstler to the Judge, *People of the State of New York v. Dacajewiah, Indicted as John Hill,* Transcript, vol. 17, 49 A.D.2d 1036 (1975), March 17, 1975, 3426.

57. Ibid.

58. Ibid., 3425.

59. Kaufman, "Former Prisoner at Attica Testifies He Saw Inmate Strike Two Correction Officers with a Club.".

60. Royal Morgan, Interview, September 15, 1971, transcribed by Marie T. Kaminski on January 9, 1974, in the papers of Elizabeth M. Fink, Brooklyn, New York.

61. Ibid.

62. Royal Morgan, interviewed by Investigator T. J. Sullivan, February 1, 1972, Erie County courthouse.

63. Gordon Kelsey, interviewed by Investigator N. E. Minklein, September 12, 1971, Attica Investigation Files, Erie County courthouse.

64. Ibid.

65. Investigators James Lo Curto and F. E. Demler, Organized Crime Task Force Memorandum to Attorney General Anthony Simonetti, Subject: "Quinn Homicide Investigation," October 20, 1971, Erie County courthouse.

66. Kunstler to the Judge, *People of the State of New York v. Dacajewiah, Indicted as John Hill,* Transcript, vol. 17, 49 A.D.2d 1036 (1975), March 17, 1975, 3401–3403.

67. Robert Hanley, "Guard Who Lied About Attica May Be Disciplined by the State," *New York Times,* March 21, 1975.

68. Ibid.

69. Ibid.

70. Michael T. Kaufman, "Ex-Guard at Attica Admits He Falsely Blamed Inmate," *New York Times,* March 20, 1975.

71. "State to Dismiss Guard Who Lied," *New York Times,* May 14, 1975.

72. Michael T. Kaufman, "Attica Defense Rests as Inmate Says He Saw Hill Hit No One," *New York Times,* March 26, 1975.

73. Michael T. Kaufman, "Witness Unable to Identify 2 at Attica," *New York Times,* March 21, 1975.

74. Ibid.

75. William Kunstler, Summation, *People of the State of New York v. Dacajewiah, Indicted as John Hill,* Transcript, vol. 25, 49 A.D.2d 1036 (1975), April 2, 1975, 5062.

76. Ibid., 5055.

77. Ibid.

78. Ibid., 5071.

79. Kunstler to the Judge, *People of the State of New York v. Dacajewiah, Indicted as John Hill,* Transcript, vol. 17, 49 A.D.2d 1036 (1975), March 17, 1975, 3401.

80. Ibid., 3393.

81. *People of the State of New York v. Dacajewiah, Indicted as John Hill,* Transcript, vol. 17, 49 A.D.2d 1036 (1975), 3456.

82. Ibid., 3482.
83. Ibid., 3465.
84. Ibid., 3463. Clark also refers to vol. 6, pages 2109 and 2114, of the trial transcript.
85. "Attica Verdict: Guilty," *Time,* April 14, 1975.
86. *People of the State of New York v. Dacajewiah, Indicted as John Hill,* Transcript, vol. 17, 49 A.D.2d 1036 (1975), 3457.
87. Ibid., 3509.
88. Ibid., 3508.
89. Ibid.
90. Ibid., 3481.
91. Eighty transcript pages, *People of the State of New York v. Dacajewiah, Indicted as John Hill,* Transcript, vol. 33, 49 A.D.2d 1036 (1975), March 31, 1975.
92. Ibid.
93. Jelinek, *Attica Justice,* 310.
94. William Kunstler, Summation, *People of the State of New York v. Dacajewiah, Indicted as John Hill,* Transcript, vol. 24, 49 A.D.2d 1036 (1975), April 1, 1975, 4920.
95. Ibid., 4832.
96. Ibid., 4869.
97. Breasted, "Killing at Attica Laid to 'Others.'"
98. Kunstler, Summation, *People of the State of New York v. Dacajewiah, Indicted as John Hill,* Transcript, vol. 24, 49 A.D.2d 1036 (1975), April 1, 1975, 4731.
99. Michael T. Kaufman, "Prosecution in Summation, Calls Killing of Officer in Attica Prison Revolt 'Cowardly,'" *New York Times,* April 3, 1975.
100. "Attica Verdict: Guilty," *Time.*
101. Ibid.
102. Ibid.
103. Kaufman, "Prosecution in Summation, Calls Killing of Officer in Attica Prison Revolt 'Cowardly.'"
104. Ibid.
105. Ibid.
106. Michael T. Kaufman, "Jury Starts Deliberations in the Case of 2 Accused," *New York Times,* April 4, 1975.
107. William Claiborne, "2 Guilty in '71 Attica Death," *Washington Post,* April 6, 1975.
108. Hill, conversation with author, May 31, 2005.
109. Kaufman, "Jury Starts Deliberations in the Case of 2 Accused."
110. William Claiborne, "'Vicious Attack' Cited by Attica Prosecutor," *Washington Post,* April 3, 1975.
111. Michael T. Kaufman, "Attica Jury Convicts One of Murder, 2nd of Assault," *New York Times,* April 6, 1975.
112. "Attica Verdict: Guilty," *Time.*
113. Kaufman, "Attica Jury Convicts One of Murder, 2nd of Assault"; Claiborne, "2 Guilty in '71 Attica Death."
114. Claiborne, "2 Guilty in '71 Attica Death."
115. Ibid.
116. Michael T. Kaufman, "Attica Juror Says Panel Fixed Guilt After 12 Hours of Study," *New York Times,* April 7, 1975.
117. Ibid.
118. Kaufman, "Reporter's Notebook: Attica Trial Something of an Anti-climax."
119. *People of the State of New York v. Dacajewiah, Indicted as John Hill,* Transcript, vol. 7, 49 A.D.2d 1036 (1975), 3795.
120. Jelinek, *Attica Justice,* 308–9.
121. Ibid.
122. Mary Breasted, "Attica Drama Unfolds in Back Rows and Halls as Well as on Stand," *New York Times,* March 4, 1975.

123. *People of the State of New York v. Dacajewiah, Indicted as John Hill,* Transcript, vol. 29, 49 A.D.2d 1036 (1975), December 10, 1974, 5689–91.

124. Michael T. Kaufman, "Motions Delay Attica Killers' Sentencing," *New York Times,* May 8, 1975.

125. John "Dacajewiah" Hill, Statement before sentencing, *People of the State of New York v. Dacajewiah, Indicted as John Hill,* Transcript, vol. 32, 49 A.D.2d 1036 (1975), May 8, 1975, 5979.

126. Ibid., 5983.

127. Ibid., 5988

128. *People of the State of New York v. Dacajewiah, Indicted as John Hill,* Transcript, vol. 32, 49 A.D.2d 1036 (1975), May 8, 1975, 5990.

129. Ibid., 5994.

130. Ibid., 5995.

131. Ibid.

132. Ibid., 6001.

133. Ibid., 6006.

134. Ibid., 6013.

135. Deutsch, conversation with author, June 27, 2005.

136. William Claiborne, "Former Inmate to Go on Trial in New Attica Case," *Washington Post,* April 7, 1975.

137. Ibid.

## 40. EVENING THE SCORE

1. Sandy McClure, "Detroit's 'Meanest Man' Recalled by One of His Victims," *Detroit Free Press,* December 5, 1982.

2. Linda Borus, conversation with author, Detroit, Michigan, June 15, 2005.

3. McClure, "Detroit's 'Meanest Man' Recalled by One of His Victims."

4. Ibid.

5. Shango (Bernard Stroble), draft chapter, "Shango: The Anatomy of a Defense," unpublished book, ed. Ernest Goodman et al., National Lawyers Guild Records, 1936–1999, Ernest Goodman Files, Box 67, Series 10, Bancroft Library, University of California, Berkeley.

6. Ibid.

7. Ibid.

8. Ibid.

9. Ibid.

10. Ibid.

11. lbid.

12. Ibid.

13. Ibid.

14. Charles Bradley, Order, Subject: "Transfer Bernard Stroble, in State Prison in southern Michigan, to Erie County Holding Center at Buffalo for trial," February 5, 1976, Erie County courthouse.

15. The state's indictments suggested that because Hess was still alive on Sunday, after Shango had tried to kill him on Saturday, Jomo Joka Omowale then told Privitera to kill him. Subsequently, they argued, it was Mariano "Dalou" Gonzalez who then fatally stabbed Privitera. Francis X. Clines, "12 Inmates Named in Attica Charges," *New York Times,* December 19, 1972.

16. Attica Defense Committee, Letter to Bernard Stroble, undated, in the papers of Elizabeth M. Fink, Brooklyn, New York.

17. Ernest Goodman, Taped and transcribed account of Shango trial, undated, Ernest Goodman Papers, Accession number 1152, Box 6, Tape 1, Walter Reuther Library, 3. Intention of account was to, eventually, be in a book: "Shango: The Anatomy of a

Defense." This manuscript was represented by Zipporah W. Collins of Berkeley, California. Ultimately, the cost of publishing made Goodman drop the idea. See: Ernest Goodman, Letter to Zipporah Collins, May 7, 1986, Ernest Goodman Papers, Accession number 1152, Walter Reuther Library.

18. Ernest Goodman, Taped and transcribed account of Shango trial, undated, Ernest Goodman Papers, Accession number 1152, Box 6, Tape 1, 4, Walter Reuther Library.

19. Ibid., Tape 1, 5.

20. Ibid., Tape 1, 6.

21. Ibid., Tape 2, 17, and Tape 3, 2.

22. Ibid., Tape 1, 8.

23. Ibid.

24. Ernest Goodman, Chapter, "Shango: The Anatomy of a Defense."

25. Ernest Goodman, Taped and transcribed account of Shango trial, undated, Ernest Goodman Papers, Accession number 1152, Box 6, Tape 5, 2, Walter Reuther Library.

26. Ibid.

27. Bernard "Shango" Stroble, Letter to Ernest Goodman, November 15, 1974, Ernest Goodman Papers, Accession number 1152, Box 6, Walter Reuther Library.

28. Ibid., undated.

29. Ibid.

30. Ibid., November 4, 1974.

31. Devon Hodges, Chapter on Media and Publicity, "Shango: The Anatomy of a Defense."

32. Donald Jelinek, *Attica Justice: The Cruel 30-Year Legacy of the Nation's Bloodiest Prison Rebellion, Which Transformed the American Prison System* (Jelinek Publishers, 2011), 321.

33. Borus, conversation with author, June 15, 2005.

34. Hodges, Chapter on Media and Publicity, "Anatomy of a Defense."

35. Goodman, Chapter, "Anatomy of a Defense."

36. These students were: John Stuart, Hugh Brantley, Glen Davis, Howie Sasson, and Lowell Jacobs. See: Stuart, Chapter, "Shango: The Anatomy of a Defense."

37. Ibid.

38. Borus, conversation with author, June 15, 2005.

39. Ernest Goodman, Taped and transcribed account of Shango trial, undated, Ernest Goodman Papers, Accession number 1152, Box 6, Tape 2, 3, Walter Reuther Library.

40. Ibid.

41. Letter to Bernard "Shango" Stroble, undated, author unknown but clearly an inmate who served in the role as medic in prison during the uprising. Likely John Flowers, Ernest Goodman Papers, Accession number 1152, Box 7, Walter Reuther Library.

42. Ibid.

43. Ibid.

44. Judge Joseph Mattina, Memorandum, Subject: "Indictments for 1. Alleged kidnapping of Hess and Schwartz, 2. Death of Hess, 3. Death of Schwartz," undated, Erie County courthouse.

45. Ernest Goodman, Taped and transcribed account of Shango trial, undated, Ernest Goodman Papers, Accession number 1152, Box 6, Tape 2, 15, Walter Reuther Library.

46. Ibid., Tape 4, 8–9.

47. John Flowers, Testimony, Wade Hearing, *People of the State of New York v. Shango Bahati Kakawana (Indicted as Bernard Stroble)*, 407 F.Supp. 411 (1976), 2957. As referenced in: Hugh Brantley, Memorandum to attorneys and Pro Se defendants in indictments 38–42, 6, and Attica Brothers Trial Office. Subject: "Testimony of John

Flowers and original BCI interview, statements, and Wade Hearing testimony February 19, 1975." Date: April 14, 1975. Document from: Defense prep notes, Haywood Burns Papers, Schomburg Center for Research in Black Culture, New York Public Library. Transcripts for Attica Wade Hearings can also be found in the Ernest Goodman Papers, Series IV, Subseries A: Trial Records, Boxes 24–32, Walter Reuther Library.

48. Ibid., 2971–72.

49. Ibid., 2972.

50. Ibid.

51. Ibid., 2986.

52. Ibid., 2955.

53. Jelinek, *Attica Justice,* 323.

54. Annette T. Rubenstein, "Attica, 1971–1975," Pamphlet, Charter Group for a Pledge of Conscience, New York City, December 1975, 21.

55. Ibid.

56. Ibid., 32.

57. Details of potentially exculpatory testimony in: "Memorandum of law in support of Motion to Dismiss," Statement of Facts, *People of the State of New York v. Shango Bahati Kakawana, Indicted as Bernard Stroble,* State of New York Additional and Special Trial Term, State of New York Supreme Court: County of Erie, March 27, 1975, Ernest Goodman Papers, Accession number 1152, Box 7, Walter Reuther Library. Also see: Leon Holt, Testimony, *In the Matter of the Additional, Special and Trial Term of the Supreme Court of the State of New York, Designated Pursuant to the Order of the Appellate Division, Fourth Department.* County of Wyoming, December 12, 1972; and Jake Milde, Testimony, *In the Matter of the Additional, Special and Trial Term of the Supreme Court of the State of New York, Designated Pursuant to the Order of the Appellate Division, Fourth Department.* County of Wyoming, May 11, 1972. Both documents located in the Erie County courthouse. See Transcripts for Attica Wade Hearings in the Ernest Goodman Papers, Series IV, Subseries A: Trial Records, Boxes 24–32, Walter Reuther Library.

58. Details of potentially exculpatory testimony in: "Memorandum of law in support of Motion to Dismiss," Statement of Facts, *People of the State of New York v. Shango Bahati Kakawana, Indicted as Bernard Stroble,* March 27, 1975. Also see: Holt, Testimony, *In the Matter of the Additional, Special and Trial Term of the Supreme Court of the State of New York, Designated Pursuant to the Order of the Appellate Division, Fourth Department,* December 12, 1972, and Milde, Testimony, *In the Matter of the Additional, Special and Trial Term of the Supreme Court of the State of New York, Designated Pursuant to the Order of the Appellate Division, Fourth Department,* May 11, 1972. See collection of Wade Hearing transcripts where Goodman learned of much inconsistent state witness testimony in the Ernest Goodman Papers, Walter Reuther Library.

59. Ibid.

60. Ernest Goodman, Taped and transcribed account of Shango trial, undated, Ernest Goodman Papers, Accession number 1152, Box 6, Tape 4, 11, Walter Reuther Library.

61. Ibid.

62. Wade Hearing, *People of the State of New York v. Shango Bahati Kakawana (Indicted as Bernard Stroble),* Transcript, 407 F.Supp. 411 (1976), December 18, 1974, Ernest Goodman Papers, Accession number 1152, Box 6, Walter Reuther Library, 2492–93.

63. Judge Mattina, Memorandum, Subject: "Indictments for 1. Alleged kidnapping of Hess and Schwartz, 2. Death of Hess, 3. Death of Schwartz," Erie County courthouse.

64. Ernest Goodman, Taped and transcribed account of Shango trial, undated, Ernest Goodman Papers, Accession number 1152, Box 6, Tape 4, 12, Walter Reuther Library.

65. Ibid., Tape 5, 8.

66. Beth Bonora and Eric Swanson, Chapter, "Shango: The Anatomy of a Defense."

67. Ibid.

68. Ibid.

69. Ibid.

70. Ibid.

71. Ibid.

72. Ernest Goodman, Taped and transcribed account of Shango trial, undated, Ernest Goodman Papers, Accession number 1152, Box 6, Tape 7, 2, Walter Reuther Library.

73. Bonora and Swanson, Chapter, "Shango: The Anatomy of a Defense."

74. Ibid.

75. Ernest Goodman, Taped and transcribed account of Shango trial, undated, Ernest Goodman Papers, Accession number 1152, Box 6, Tape 7, 4, Walter Reuther Library.

76. Jelinek, *Attica Justice*, 320.

77. Ernest Goodman, Taped and transcribed account of Shango trial, undated, Ernest Goodman Papers, Accession number 1152, Box 6, Tape 7, 6, Walter Reuther Library.

78. Memo admitted into evidence: 4.28.75, in Erie County courthouse.

79. Ernest Goodman, Taped and transcribed account of Shango trial, undated, Ernest Goodman Papers, Accession number 1152, Box 6, Tape 10, 10, Walter Reuther Library.

80. Kunstler and Clark had worried from the moment that a juror had claimed that someone from the Jury Project had contacted him personally—an illegal action—that someone from the defense side had in fact called this man in an attempt to prevent them from using the Jury Project altogether. With the knowledge that Mary Jo Cook had been working for the FBI and the ABLD at this time, there was a serious concern that she had in fact made the call. The implications of this were enormous since the last two jurors chosen for this trial, nos. 11 and 12, led the jury to vote for conviction when many on the panel had serious doubts. Author's telephone conversation with Joe Heath, November 21, 2015. Also see: Bonora and Swanson, Chapter, "Anatomy of a Defense."

81. Ernest Goodman, Taped and transcribed account of Shango trial, undated, Ernest Goodman Papers, Accession number 1152, Box 6, Tape 7, 11, Walter Reuther Library.

82. Mary Jo Cook, Testimony, *People of the State of New York v. Shango Bahati Kakawana (Indicted as Bernard Stroble)*, Transcript, 407 F.Supp. 411 (1976), April 21, 1975, Erie County courthouse; also FOIA request #110818, FOIA pp. 001224–001419.

83. Ibid., 22–23.

84. Ibid., 26.

85. Ibid., 32.

86. Ibid., 39–40.

87. Ibid., 37–38.

88. Ibid., 42, 46.

89. Ibid., 66.

90. Ibid., 101–2.

91. Tom Goldstein, "Court Told of Spying on Attica Defense," *New York Times*, April 22, 1975.

92. Cook, Testimony, *People of the State of New York v. Shango Bahati Kakawana (Indicted as Bernard Stroble)*, Transcript, 407 F.Supp. 411 (1976), April 21, 1975, Erie County courthouse, 159; also FOIA request #110818, FOIA pp. 001224–001419.

93. Ibid., 39.

94. Ibid., 40.

95. Ibid., 159–60.

96. Ibid., 62, 193.

97. Ibid., 100.

98. Goldstein, "Court Told of Spying on Attica Defense."

99. Cook, Testimony, *People of the State of New York v. Shango Bahati Kakawana (Indicted as Bernard Stroble),* Transcript, 407 F.Supp. 411 (1976), April 21, 1975, Erie County courthouse, 177; also FOIA request #110818, FOIA pp. 001224–001419.

100. Ibid., 412; also: Goldstein, "Court Told of Spying on Attica Defense."

101. Tom Goldstein, "Attica Prosecutor's Appearance on FBI Issue Put Off by Court," *New York Times,* April 29, 1975.

102. Cook, Testimony, *People of the State of New York v. Shango Bahati Kakawana (Indicted as Bernard Stroble),* Transcript, 407 F.Supp. 411 (1976), April 21, 1975, Erie County courthouse, 818; also FOIA request #110818, FOIA pp. 001224–001419; also: Goldstein, "Court Told of Spying on Attica Defense."

103. Tom Goldstein, "Judge Rules FBI Did Not Interfere in Attica Defense," *New York Times,* May 7, 1975.

104. Tom Wicker, "A Middle Course," *New York Times,* April 29, 1975.

105. Bonora and Swanson, Chapter, "Shango: The Anatomy of a Defense."

106. Ernest Goodman, Taped and transcribed account of Shango trial, undated, Ernest Goodman Papers, Accession number 1152, Box 6, Tape 8, 12, Walter Reuther Library.

107. Indictment #38: Blyden, Champen, Smith, Thompson, Stroble, *People of the State of New York v. Shango Bahati Kakawana (Indicted as Bernard Stroble),* Transcript, 407 F.Supp. 411 (1976), August 31, 1973.

108. Tom Goldstein, "Wide Impact Seen in Attica Verdict: Some View Acquittal as Sign of Collapse of Prosecution in Four Other Cases," *New York Times,* July 13, 1975, 20.

109. Ernest Goodman, Taped and transcribed account of Shango trial, undated, Ernest Goodman Papers, Accession number 1152, Box 6, Tape 9, 10, Walter Reuther Library.

110. *In the Matter of the Additional, Special and Trial Term of the Supreme Court of the State of New York, Designated Pursuant to the Order of the Appellate Division, Fourth Department.* County of Wyoming, Appellate Division, Fourth Department, February 2, 1972, Haywood Burns Papers, Box 4239, Schomburg Center, New York Public Library, 70.

111. Willie Locke, Testimony, *People of the State of New York v. Shango Bahati Kakawana (Indicted as Bernard Stroble),* Transcript, 407 F.Supp. 411 (1976), June 13, 1975, 2836, 2847.

112. Summary of various statements given by James Holt, Obtained by defense from Rosario and Wade materials, Haywood Burns Papers, Box 4239, Schomburg Center for Research in Black Culture, New York Public Library.

113. Assistant Attorney General Frank Cryan, Department of Law: Attica Investigation Memorandum to Hess and Schwartz File, Subject: "Interview of James Holt," January 9, 1975, Erie County courthouse.

114. Ibid.

115. T. J. Sullivan, Organized Crime Task Force Memorandum to Robert Fischer, Subject: "Interview of John Flowers on February 18, 1972," February 22, 1972, Erie County courthouse.

116. James Stephens and Frank Keenan, Organized Crime Task Force Memorandum to Robert Fischer, Subject: "Interview with John Flowers on November 1, 1971," November 4, 1971. No mention of Stroble then.

117. Flowers, Testimony, *In the Matter of the Additional, Special and Trial Term of the Supreme Court of the State of New York, Designated Pursuant to the Order of the Appellate Division, Fourth Department.* County of Wyoming, June 11, 1972, 12.

118. Jimmy James Ross, Testimony, *People of the State of New York v. Shango Bahati Kakawana (Indicted as Bernard Stroble),* Transcript, 407 F.Supp. 411 (1976), July 26, 1973, 35, 39.

119. Mary Breasted, "Attica Witness Tells of Slaying," *New York Times,* June 10, 1975.

120. Rubenstein, "Attica, 1971–1975," 51, 48.

121. Ernest Goodman, Taped and transcribed account of Shango trial, undated, Ernest Goodman Papers, Accession number 1152, Box 6, Tape 10, 1, Walter Reuther Library.
122. Ibid., Tape 10, 2–3.
123. Ibid., Tape 10, 10.
124. Ibid.
125. Willie Locke, Testimony, *People of the State of New York v. Shango Bahati Kakawana (Indicted as Bernard Stroble)*, Transcript, 407 F.Supp. 411 (1976), 2875.
126. Summary of various statements given by James Holt, Obtained by defense from Rosario and Wade materials, Haywood Burns Papers, Box 4239, Schomburg Center for Research in Black Culture, New York Public Library.
127. Ibid.
128. Ernest Goodman, Taped and transcribed account of Shango trial, undated, Ernest Goodman Papers, Accession number 1152, Box 6, Tape 10, 14, 16, Walter Reuther Library.
129. Ibid., Tape 12, 1.
130. Ibid., Tape 12, 3.
131. Rubenstein, "Attica, 1971–1975," 43.
132. Ibid.
133. Ibid., 44, 47.
134. Ibid., 43.
135. Ibid., 44.
136. Ernest Goodman, Taped and transcribed account of Shango trial, undated, Ernest Goodman Papers, Accession number 1152, Box 6, Tape 12, 17, Walter Reuther Library.
137. Ibid., Tape 5, 3.
138. Ibid.
139. Ibid., Tape 2, 7.
140. Ibid., Tape 13, 4.
141. Ibid., Tape 13, 5.
142. Goodman, Chapter, "Anatomy of a Defense."
143. Ibid.
144. Ibid.
145. John Edland, Letter to Ernest Goodman, August 20, 1974, Ernest Goodman Papers, Accession number 1152, Box 7, Walter Reuther Library.
146. Ernest Goodman, Taped and transcribed account of Shango trial, undated, Ernest Goodman Papers, Accession number 1152, Box 6, Tape 13, 6, Walter Reuther Library.
147. Ibid.
148. Ibid., Tape 13, 7.
149. Ibid., Tape 13, 9.
150. Ibid.
151. Ibid., Tape 13, 8–9.
152. Goodman, Chapter, "Shango: The Anatomy of a Defense."
153. Ernest Goodman, Taped and transcribed account of Shango trial, undated, Ernest Goodman Papers, Accession number 1152, Box 6, Tape 13, 10, Walter Reuther Library.
154. Ibid.
155. Rubenstein, "Attica, 1971–1975," 32.
156. Ibid., 31.
157. Ernest Goodman, Taped and transcribed account of Shango trial, undated, Ernest Goodman Papers, Accession number 1152, Box 6, Tape 12, 5–6, Walter Reuther Library.
158. Ibid., Tape 8, 7.

159. Case Docket, *People of the State of New York v. Bernard "Shango" Stroble,* Erie County courthouse.

160. Ernest Goodman, Taped and transcribed account of Shango trial, undated, Ernest Goodman Papers, Accession number 1152, Box 6, Tape 13, 15, Walter Reuther Library.

161. Ibid.

162. Ibid.

163. Ibid., Tape 12, 6. A charge of felony murder can be applied when someone is committing a felony and, in the process, someone else dies. Their death does not have to be intentional, and can be accidental, but nevertheless the defendant is liable for that death.

164. Case Docket, *People of the State of New York v. Bernard "Shango" Stroble,* Erie County courthouse.

165. Ernest Goodman, Taped and transcribed account of Shango trial, undated, Ernest Goodman Papers, Accession number 1152, Box 6, Tape 13, 18, Walter Reuther Library.

166. Ibid., Tape 13, 19.

167. Ibid., Tape 13, 20.

168. Ibid.

## 41. A LONG JOURNEY AHEAD

1. "Charges Dropped in Attica Deaths," *New York Times,* November 14, 1975.

2. For the state of things according to Judge Ball as of November 8, 1974, see: Carmen F. Ball, Letter to Honorable Richard J. Bartlett, Subject: "Status report of cases involved with Attica uprising," November 8, 1974, Erie County courthouse.

3. Tom Goldstein, "Felony Charges Are Dismissed Against 13 in Revolt at Attica," *New York Times,* November 28, 1975, 41.

4. Attica Indictment sheet, December 15, 1972, Erie County courthouse.

5. Judge Carmen Ball, "Status of Outstanding Cases," Typed Report, January 10, 1975, Erie County courthouse.

6. Ball Letter to Bartlett, Subject: "Status report of cases involved with Attica uprising," November 8, 1974.

7. Jomo Davis, conversation with author, February 17, 2006.

8. Ibid.

9. Ibid.

10. Indictment no. 5, "Answer in Opposition to defendant's motion for a separate trial," undated, *People of the State of New York v. Eric Jomo Thompson,* Erie County courthouse.

11. Carmen Ball, Memorandum to Blyden, Champen, and Smith, Subject: "Defendants Motion to Dismiss Indictments 38 and 41," November 13, 1975, Erie County courthouse.

12. Ibid.

13. Elizabeth Gaynes, conversation with author, April 8, 2006.

14. Ibid.

15. Ibid.

16. Jomo Davis, Letter to Rafiki, August 6, 1974, Erie County jail, in: "Awakening of a Dragon," a booklet outlining Jomo's political philosophies, publishing some of his letters, and outlining his thoughts on his legal defense, in the papers of Elizabeth M. Fink, Brooklyn, New York.

17. Gaynes, conversation with author, April 8, 2006.

18. Jomo Davis, Letter to the "Reactionary Niggers of Attica," July 1, 1974, Erie County Jail, in: "Awakening of a Dragon."

19. Ibid.

20. Ibid.

21. Ibid.

22. Attica Bond to Free Jomo: For the defense of Attica Brother Jomo Omowale Eric Thompson a/k/a Cleveland Davis, Box 620, Ellicott Station, Buffalo, New York, October 31, 1974, in: "Awakening of a Dragon."

23. Davis, Letter to the "Reactionary Niggers of Attica," Free Jomo Publicity Booklet, July 1, 1974, Erie County jail.

24. "Motion to dismiss indictment Nos. 38-1973, 39-1972, 41-1973 on grounds of selective enforcement," *People of the State of New York v. Eric Thompson (aka Jomo Davis),* New York Supreme Court: Erie County, September 1975.

25. Charles Bradley, conversation with author, Sleepy Hollow, New York, July 15, 2004.

26. Ibid.

27. Jomo Davis, conversation with author, February 17, 2006.

28. Jelinek, *Attica Justice,* 325.

29. Ibid.

30. Edward M. Wayland, Counsel for Cleveland Jomo Davis, Letter to Helen F. Fahey, Chair, Virginia Parole Board, December 29, 2004, Cleveland Jomo Davis Personal Papers.

31. Ibid.

32. Tom Goldstein, "An Attica Inquiry Yields an Indictment," *New York Times,* October 10, 1975.

33. Wayland Letter to Fahey, December 29, 2004, Regarding: "Supplemental Information regarding charges stemming from 1971 Attica uprising."

34. Jomo Davis, conversation with author, February 17, 2006.

35. Ernest Goodman, Taped and transcribed account of Shango trial, undated, Ernest Goodman Papers, Accession number 1152, Box 6, Tape 10, 10, Walter Reuther Library.

## PART VIII · BLOWING THE WHISTLE

### 42. JOINING THE TEAM

1. Malcolm Bell, updated edition (in draft) of *The Turkey Shoot,* Chapter 6, 2. In possession of Malcolm Bell.

2. Emerson Moran, aide to Fischer, Notes, State of New York Department of Law, in: Bernard S. Meyer, *Final Report of the Special Attica Investigation,* October 27, 1975, New York State Archives, 124.

3. Robert Fischer, Letter to Louis Lefkowitz, June 14, 1972, as quoted in: Meyer, *Final Report of the Special Attica Investigation,* October 27, 1975, New York State Archives, 125.

4. Meyer, *Final Report of the Special Attica Investigation,* October 27, 1975, New York State Archives, 128.

5. As quoted in: ibid., 6. Also see: Goldman Panel to Protect Prisoners' Constitutional Rights, Report, New York State Archives.

6. Michael T. Kaufman, "Guard Cites Delay of His Attica Testimony," *New York Times,* April 10, 1975.

7. Ibid.

8. Bell, updated edition of *The Turkey Shoot* (in draft), Chapter 6, 11.

9. Ibid.

10. Ibid., 2.

11. Meyer, *Final Report of the Special Attica Investigation,* October 27, 1975, New York State Archives, 81.

12. Bell, updated edition of *The Turkey Shoot* (in draft), Chapter 6, 2.

13. Ibid., Chapter 1, 5.
14. Bell, *The Turkey Shoot,* 50.
15. Ibid.
16. Investigators M. J. McCarron and J. Stephen, State of New York Organized Crime Task Force Memorandum to Assistant Attorney General Simonetti, Subject: "Sgt. Anthony J. Marchione," February 16, 1974, in the papers of Elizabeth M. Fink, Brooklyn, New York. Also see: statements of Marchione dated September 15, 1971, and interview done with Marchione by Attica investigator James Stephen. James Stephen, Testimony, *Proceedings before the Supplemental Grand Jury of the Additional, Special, and Trial Term, convened pursuant to the order of Governor Nelson A. Rockefeller,* Special and Trial Term of the Supreme Court of the State of New York, Appellate Division, Fourth Department, Wyoming County Courthouse, Warsaw, New York, November 7, 1973.
17. Bell, *The Turkey Shoot,* 143.
18. Correspondence from Malcolm Bell to author, December 5, 2015.
19. Bell, *The Turkey Shoot,* 112.
20. Investigators McCarron, Dolan, and Peo, State of New York Organized Crime Task Force Memorandum to Anthony Simonetti, Subject: "List of Deceased hostages and inmates, indicating location of wounds and caliber of weapon," December 20, 1971, in the papers of Elizabeth M. Fink, Brooklyn, New York.
21. Bell, Testimony, *Attica Task Force Hearing,* July 30, 2002, 44–45.
22. Bell, *The Turkey Shoot,* 61.
23. FBI Memorandum, October 23, 1971, File: Buffalo 44-592, FOIA request #110818 of the New York State Attorney General's Office, FOIA p. 000157.
24. Ibid.
25. Bell, updated edition of *The Turkey Shoot* (in draft), Chapter 6, 5–6.
26. "Attica Assignment Mutual Aid Request form," Summary of total assignments of Niagara County Sheriff's office from September 9–13, 1971, September 14, 1971, FOIA request #110818 of the New York Attorney General's Office, FOIA p. 000152.
27. Ibid.
28. Malcolm Bell, *Preliminary Report on the Attica Investigation,* January 29, 1975, p. 31. This is the whistle-blowing report that Bell penned and gave copies of to his bosses, Judge Ball, and Governor Hugh Carey only. This document has never been seen by the public. Document located in the Erie County courthouse, Office of the Clerk. Copy in author's possession.
29. Nick Savino, State of New York Attica Investigation Memorandum to Anthony Simonetti, Subject: "Weapons Accountability," July 10, 1974, in the papers of Elizabeth M. Fink, Brooklyn, New York.
30. Nevertheless, some links were clear. Investigators, for example, did know which trooper's pistols had shot prisoner Kenny Malloy and whose had put a .38 bullet into prisoner Willie West, and more. Correspondence from Malcolm Bell to author, December 5, 2015.
31. As quoted in: Meyer, *Final Report of the Special Attica Investigation,* October 27, 1975, New York State Archives, 9–10. By Malcolm Bell's count there were 111 shooters, including COs and Park Police.
32. Meyer, *Final Report of the Special Attica Investigation,* October 27, 1975, New York State Archives, 9–10.
33. Information from Trooper Frank Lavier as described in: Savino, State of New York Attica Investigation Memorandum to Simonetti, Subject: "Weapons Accountability," July 10, 1974.
34. Bell, *The Turkey Shoot,* 179.
35. Ibid., 58.
36. Ibid., 59.
37. Malcolm Bell, Affidavit, *People of the State of New York v. John Hill,* Additional

Special and Trial Term of the Supreme Court of the State of New York: County of Erie, Filed June 28, 1978.

38. Sergeant P. S. Chamot, New York State Police Memorandum to Major S. A. Chieco, Director of Training, Subject: "Attica Disturbance—participation in September 9 through 13, 1971," State Police Academy, October 5, 1971, in the papers of Elizabeth M. Fink, Brooklyn, New York.

39. Technical Sgt. F. D. Smith, New York State Police Memorandum to Major S. A. Chieco, Director of Training, Subject: "Special Assignment—Attica Correctional Institute September 9 through 14 1971," State Police Academy, October 6, 1973, in the papers of Elizabeth M. Fink, Brooklyn, New York.

40. Bell, *The Turkey Shoot*, 259.

41. Malcolm Bell, Affidavit, *People of the State of New York v. John Hill*, filed June 28, 1978.

42. Ibid.

43. Special Agents Lee Mason and Carl Underhill, FBI Memorandum, October 27, 1971, Attica, New York, Buffalo File 44-592, FOIA request #110818 of the New York State Attorney General's Office, FOIA p. 000093.

44. Bell, Affidavit, *People of the State of New York v. John Hill*, filed June 28, 1978.

45. Bell, *The Turkey Shoot*, 59.

46. Ibid., 61.

47. Ibid., 72.

48. Dr. Warren Hanson, Interviewee #941, Interview by John Stainthorp and Joe Heath, Investigative Report Sheet, November 3, 1974, Ernest Goodman Papers, Accession number 1152, Box 7, Walter Reuther Library. After the retaking, many used the term "executioner" for those prisoners who surrounded the hostages on the catwalk. During the retaking itself, most prisoners saw this as a role they were playing in order to dissuade the state from sending in troopers to retake the prison with force.

49. Bell, Affidavit, *People of the State of New York v. John Hill*, filed June 28, 1978, 7.

50. When a grand jury votes not to indict someone, they issue a "No Bill."

51. Bell, *The Turkey Shoot*, 64.

52. Ibid., 73.

53. Ibid., 107.

54. As quoted in: "Troopers Praised for Attica Action," *New York Times*, January 7, 1972.

55. Press Release: "Stafford Assails Attica Indictment," FOIA request #110797 of the New York State Attorney General's Office, FOIA p. 000184.

56. Ibid.

57. Francis X. Clines, "Attica Troopers Seek State Aid to Pay for Their Legal Counsel," *New York Times*, April 26, 1975.

58. Ibid.

59. Bell, *The Turkey Shoot*, 92.

60. Ibid.

61. Ibid., 93.

62. Charles Bradley was one of the prosecutors soon thereafter arguing the state's ill-fated case against Shango.

63. Bell, *The Turkey Shoot*, 142.

64. Ibid.

65. Ibid., 119.

66. Ibid.

67. Edward Vincent Qualey, Testimony, *Proceedings before the Supplemental Grand Jury of the Additional, Special, and Trial Term, convened pursuant to the order of Governor Nelson A. Rockefeller*, Special and Trial Term of the Supreme Court of the State of New York, Appellate Division, Fourth Department, Wyoming County Courthouse, Warsaw, New York, June 13, 1974, Erie County courthouse.

68. Ibid.

69. Bell, *The Turkey Shoot,* 152.

70. Ibid., 147.

71. Ibid., 88–89.

72. "A 16-Year Political Career with White House in Mind," *New York Times,* December 20, 1974.

73. Nelson A. Rockefeller Vice Presidential Confirmation Hearings, Senate, 93rd Cong., 2nd sess., *Congressional Record* 120 (September 23–26, 1974), 295–349, 533–45, 631–73.

74. Ibid., 546–84.

75. Haywood Burns, Legal Coordinator, Attica Brothers Legal Defense, Statement, ibid., 424.

76. Angela Davis, Co-Chairperson of the National Alliance Against Racist and Political Oppression, Statement, ibid., 349.

77. Ibid.

78. Ibid.

## 43. PROTECTING THE POLICE

1. Bernard S. Meyer, *Final Report of the Special Attica Investigation,* October 27, 1975, New York State Archives, as quoted in: Malcolm Bell, Affidavit, *In the Matter of the Application of Hugh L. Carey, Governor of the State of New York, for a judicial determination as to the publication of Volumes 2 and 3 of the Final Report of Bernard S. Meyer, Special Deputy Attorney General, evaluating the conduct of the investigation by the Special Prosecutor into the retaking of Attica Correctional Facility on September 13, 1971, and related events subsequent thereto,* State of New York Supreme Court: County of Wyoming, Index No. 15062, filed October 25, 2013, decided April 24, 2014.

2. Malcolm Bell, *The Turkey Shoot,* 185.

3. Malcolm Bell, Affidavit, *In the Matter of the Application of Hugh L. Carey, for a judicial determination as to the publication of Volumes 2 and 3 of the Final Report of Bernard S. Meyer,* Index No. 15062, filed October 25, 2013, decided April 24, 2014.

4. Bell, *The Turkey Shoot,* 175.

5. Malcolm Bell, *Preliminary Report on the Attica Investigation* , 27.

6. Bell, *The Turkey Shoot,* 218.

7. Bell, *Preliminary Report on the Attica Investigation,* 49.

8. Ibid., 41.

9. Assistant Attorney General James Grable, State of New York Organized Crime Task Force Memorandum to Assistant Attorney General Anthony G. Simonetti, Subject: "Report of Weapons Accountability Investigation—State Police .270 rifles at Attica," Buffalo Office, April 8, 1974, in the papers of Elizabeth M. Fink, Brooklyn, New York.

10. Investigator James Lo Curto, State of New York Attica Investigation Memorandum to Anthony G. Simonetti, Subject: "Rivera-Malloy Cover-up," July 10, 1974.

11. Ibid.

12. Ibid.

13. Investigator Nick Savino, State of New York Attica Investigation Memorandum to Anthony Simonetti, Subject: "Weapons Accountability," July 22, 1974, in the papers of Elizabeth M. Fink, Brooklyn, New York.

14. Locurto, State of New York Attica Investigation Memorandum to Simonetti, Subject: "Rivera-Malloy Cover-up," July 10, 1974. Years later, this trooper was still fighting what he believed was an involuntary resignation. Matter of *Barbolini v. Connelie* 68 A.D. 2d 949 (1979).

15. Locurto, State of New York Attica Investigation Memorandum to Simonetti, Subject: "Rivera-Malloy Cover-up," July 10, 1974.

16. Ibid.

17. FBI Memorandum, October 23, 1971, File: Buffalo 44-592, FOIA request #110818, of the New York State Attorney General's Office, FOIA p. 000157.

18. Bell, *The Turkey Shoot,* 205.

19. Ibid.

20. Ibid., 206.

21. Bell, *Preliminary Report on the Attica Investigation,* 140; Bell, *The Turkey Shoot,* 207.

22. Bell, *Preliminary Report on the Attica Investigation,* 40.

23. As quoted in: Malcolm H. Bell, State of New York Memorandum to Attorney General Anthony Simonetti, October 17, 1974, in Bell, *Preliminary Report on the Attica Investigation,* 45.

24. Bell, *The Turkey Shoot,* 217.

25. Bell, *Preliminary Report on the Attica Investigation,* 49.

26. Bell, *The Turkey Shoot,* 158.

27. Ibid., 164; Charles Bradley, conversation with author, July 15, 2004.

28. As quoted in: Bell, State of New York Memorandum to Simonetti, October 17, 1974, in Bell, *Preliminary Report on the Attica Investigation,* 46.

29. As quoted in: ibid., 46.

30. Bell, *Preliminary Report on the Attica Investigation,* 44.

31. Ibid.

32. Bell, *The Turkey Shoot,* 236.

33. Ibid., 237.

34. Bell, *Preliminary Report on the Attica Investigation,* 4, 5.

## 44. SMOKING GUNS

1. All above from: James Grable, State of New York Organized Crime Task Force Memorandum to Simonetti, Subject: "Report of Weapons Accountability Investigation—State Police .270 rifles at Attica," April 8, 1974. For more on Williams's view on accountability and Infante's role vis-à-vis weapons accountability and the BCI investigation, see: Savino, Attica Investigation Memorandum to Simonetti, Subject: "Weapons Accountability," July 22, 1974.

2. Grable, State of New York Organized Crime Task Force Memorandum to Simonetti, Subject: "Report of Weapons Accountability Investigation—State Police .270 rifles at Attica," April 8, 1974.

3. All above from ibid.

4. Grable, State of New York Organized Crime Task Force Memorandum to Simonetti, Subject: "Report of Weapons Accountability Investigation—State Police .270 rifles at Attica," April 8, 1974; also see John C. Miller's testimony before the grand jury on August 10, 1972, in: Savino, State of New York Attica Investigation Memorandum to Simonetti, Subject: "Weapons Accountability," July 12, 1974.

5. Malcolm Bell, *Preliminary Report on the Attica Investigation.*

6. Leonard Polakiewicz, New York State Special Commission on Attica Memorandum to Arthur Liman, Subject: "State Police, Troop E, photographs," March 10, 1971, Investigation and interview files, 1971–1972, New York (State), Special Commission on Attica, 15855-90, Box 92, New York State Archives, Albany, New York.

7. Malcolm Bell, *The Turkey Shoot,* 198.

8. Grid of personnel and shots fired, FOIA request #110818 of the New York State Attorney General's Office, FOIA pp. 000813–000818.

9. Ibid.

10. Ibid.

11. Ibid.

12. Ibid.

13. Bell, *Preliminary Report,* 17.

14. Decision and Order, Appendix 2, Category V Death Claims, *Akil Al-Jundi et al. v. Vincent Mancusi et al.*, No. CIV-75-132, 113 F.Supp.2d 441 (2000), August 28, 2000, 3. Also see: "Analysis of Correction Officers Rounds Extended," October 18, 1971, FOIA request #110818 of the New York State Attorney General's Office. Also see: Grid of personnel and shots fired, FOIA #110818, FOIA pp. 000813–000818.

15. Regarding the testimony of Paul Stringham, see: Attica Investigator James Stephen, Testimony, *In the Matter of the Additional, Special and Trial Term of the Supreme Court of the State of New York, Designated Pursuant to the Order of the Appellate Division, Fourth Department.* County of Wyoming, October 24, 1972, Erie County courthouse, 4–6; On the killings: "Five Deadly Days," reprinted from the *Democrat and Chronicle* (Rochester, New York), Tom Wicker Papers; Decision and Order, Appendix 2, Category V Death Claims, *Akil Al-Jundi et al. v. Vincent Mancusi et al.*, No. CIV-75-132, 113 F.Supp.2d 441 (2000), August 28, 2000, 6.

16. Ibid.

17. For ballistics concerning Melvin Ware, see: Decision and Order, Appendix 2, Category V Death Claims, *Akil Al-Jundi et al. v. Vincent Mancusi et al.*, No. CIV-75-132, 113 F.Supp.2d 441 (2000), August 28, 2000, 3. Regarding the testimony of Malcolm Hegeman, see: Stephen, Testimony, *In the Matter of the Additional, Special and Trial Term of the Supreme Court of the State of New York, Designated Pursuant to the Order of the Appellate Division, Fourth Department.* County of Wyoming, October 25, 1972, 7.

18. Wildridge was in fact indicted, but charges were dropped upon the dissolution of the grand jury. "Possible Hostile Inmate Threats" memorandum, FOIA request #110818 of the New York State Attorney General's Office, FOIA pp. 000813–000818. Also see: Investigator Michael McCarron, State of New York Attica Investigation Memorandum to Anthony G. Simonetti, May 10, 1974, in the papers of Elizabeth M. Fink, Brooklyn, New York.

19. All above from: McCarron, State of New York Attica Investigation Memorandum to Simonetti, May 10, 1974.

20. Shooter File #4058, FOIA request #110818 of the New York State Attorney General's Office, FOIA p. 001547.

21. "Circle Case." Notes of August 9, 1974. Papers of Elizabeth M. Fink, Brooklyn, New York. Also see: "Possible Hostile Inmate Threats" memorandum, FOIA request #110818, FOIA pp. 00813–00821.

22. My conversations with several former COs and persons connected to them indicated that they knew who was responsible for L.D.'s death and it was a CO, but not Hollander. Although they said his name, and though all agreed that this was the man who had killed Barkley, in no small part because he had been proud of it and had kept his glasses as a souvenir, I have nothing but their hearsay statements that this was indeed the killer.

23. Vincent Tobia, Statements, from author conversation and follow-up email with Joshua Melville, March 2015.

24. *McKay Report*, 398.

25. Dennis Cunningham, Michael Deutsch, and Elizabeth Fink, "Remembering Attica Forty Years Later," *Prison Legal News* (September 2011).

26. Bell, *Preliminary Report on the Attica Investigation*, 33.

27. According to ballistics this was serial number K 890342.

28. For information on ballistics and Barbolini's weapon, see: "Evidence Receipt—Scientific Laboratory. New York State Police. Re A. R. Barbolini. Shield # 2781," FOIA request #110818 of the New York State Attorney General's Office, FOIA p. 000993. For who shot Rivera, see: Bell, *Preliminary Report on the Attica Investigation*, 17.

29. Bell, *Preliminary Report on the Attica Investigation*, 123.

30. Captain A. P. O'Neill, Memorandum to Director of Personnel, Division Headquarters, Subject: "Barbolini, Aldo R. Cease Active Duty," September 17, 1971, Filed, September 22, 1971; "Resignation requested or accepted," FOIA request #110818 of the

New York State Attorney General's Office, FOIA p. 001420; Headquarters, SP, Memorandum to Major R. M. Kisor, Troop commander, Troop F, Subject: "Effective 10:30 a.m., September 17, 1971, this member respectfully submits his resignation from the Division of State Police," September 17, 1971, FOIA request #110818 of the New York State Attorney General's Office, FOIA p. 000958.

31. Captain A. T. Malovitch, New York State Police Memorandum to J. W. Monahan, Subject: "Information Regarding Interview of Former Trooper A. R. Barbolini," October 26, 1971, FOIA request #110818 of the New York State Attorney General's Office, FOIA p. 000966.

32. Ibid.

33. Chronology of Barbolini correspondence and actions vis-à-vis the New York State Police, Untitled memo, undated, FOIA request #110818 of the New York State Attorney General's Office, FOIA p. 000965. Also see: John C. Miller, Deputy Superintendent, Letter to Aldo Barbolini, January 17, 1972, FOIA request #110818, FOIA p. 000990.

34. From FOIA request #110818 of the New York State Attorney General's Office, FOIA p. 000979.

35. Investigator R. W. Horn, Forensics Section, New York State Police Memorandum to First Deputy Superintendent W. C. Miller, Subject: "Correspondence Aldo R. Barbolini," July 7, 1972, FOIA request #110818 of the New York State Attorney General's Office, FOIA p. 000981

36. James Locurto, State of New York Attica Investigation Memorandum to Anthony Simonetti, Subject: "Rivera-Malloy Cover-up," July 30, 1974, in the papers of Elizabeth M. Fink, Brooklyn, New York.

37. Ibid.

38. Nelson Rockefeller, Deposition, Meyer Commission, August 8, 1975, 8704, FOIA request #110818, FOIA p. 000445.

39. Bell, *Preliminary Report on the Attica Investigation*, 17.

40. Regarding which troopers shot at prisoners near the hostage circle to protect Christian, see: Attica Investigator Leonard Brown, Testimony regarding testimony of Arthur Kruk, *In the Matter of the Additional, Special and Trial Term of the Supreme Court of the State of New York, Designated Pursuant to the Order of the Appellate Division, Fourth Department.* County of Wyoming, August 10, 1972, Erie County courthouse, 2–7. Notably, later investigative interviews with two troopers revealed that they had immediately managed to subdue the prisoner who had attempted to strike Lieutenant Christian, allegedly Tommy Hicks, by knocking him down with the butt of a gun. If that was the case, then the barrage of bullets shot into the hostage circle that killed so many hostages had been completely unnecessary. See: Bell, Testimony, *Attica Task Force Hearing*, July 30, 2002, 27–28.

41. Mercurio, Memorandum to Simonetti, Subject: "Position of Hostages in Circle Prior to Shooting (in the papers of Elizabeth Fink)," July 30, 1974.

42. Ibid.

43. Ibid.

44. Ibid.

45. Ibid.

46. Ibid.

47. Ibid.

48. Investigators suspected that because of the poor weapons accountability of the NYSP, there were a number of possibilities as to which trooper's buckshot or bullet killed hostages on September 13, 1971. One report stated that "troopers likely responsible for killings in hostage circle" included "Lt. Kenneth Crounse, Inv. V. Tobia, Sgt. R. Stout, Sgt. P. Zelinski, Troopers: G. Wildridge, D. Girvin, T. Griffith, R. Miller, M. Clayson, L. Lang, Captain W. Dillon, Troopers R. Pacek, P. Lawatsch." State of New York Attica Investigation. Memorandum. To: Anthony G. Simonetti From: Inv.

Michael McCarron. May 10, 1974, in the papers of Elizabeth M. Fink, Brooklyn, New York.

49. Information on various shooters in area of hostage circle in: Internal Attica Investigation Memo, "Hostage Circle—Conclusions," 4. Also see: Mercurio, Memorandum to Simonetti, Subject: "Position of Hostages in Circle Prior to Shooting," July 30, 1974. Both in the papers of Elizabeth Fink.

50. Accounting of shooters and rounds, Internal memo, FOIA request #110818 of the New York State Attorney General's Office, FOIA p. 000821; Quote regarding Clayson from: Bell, *Preliminary Report,* 22.

51. Spoont, Confidential Memo to Shapiro Subject: "Attica Investigation," Albany, New York, November 1, 1971.

525. Rockefeller Administration, Confidential Memo, "Events at Attica: September 8–13, 1971."

53. All above from: McCarron, State of New York Attica Investigation Memorandum to Simonetti, May 10, 1974.

54. State of New York Organized Crime Task Force Memo, Subject: Richard Janora. February 6, 1974, in the papers of Elizabeth M. Fink, Brooklyn, New York.

55. Organized Crime Task Force Internal Memorandum, Distributed to Simonetti, Flierl, Bell, Fitzgerald, Grable, Perry, Schechter, Nitteraurer, Dr. Baden, A. Hoppe, Subject: "S. D. Sharkey," February 6, 1974, in the papers of Elizabeth M. Fink, Brooklyn, New York.

56. James Stephen, Testimony, *In the Matter of the Additional, Special and Trial Term of the Supreme Court of the State of New York, Designated Pursuant to the Order of the Appellate Division, Fourth Department.* County of Wyoming, October 31, 1972, 17–18.

57. Ibid.

58. Regarding interview with trooper Steven Sharkey, see: ibid., 7, 16.

59. Grable, State of New York Organized Crime Task Force Memorandum to Simonetti, Subject: "Report of Weapons Accountability Investigation—State Police .270 rifles at Attica," April 8, 1974.

60. All above from: McCarron, State of New York Attica Investigation Memorandum to Simonetti, May 10, 1974.

61. Information on troopers, correction officers, their weapons, and their locations, obtained through FOIA request #110818 of the New York State Attorney General's Office, FOIA pp. 00081–000821; State of New York Attica Investigation. Memorandum. To: Anthony G. Simonetti From: Inv. Michael McCarron. May 10, 1974, in the papers of Elizabeth Fink.

62. Mercurio, Memorandum to Simonetti, Subject: "Position of Hostages in Circle Prior to Shooting (in the papers of Elizabeth Fink)," July 30, 1974.

63. Bell, *The Turkey Shoot,* 119; Grid of personnel and shots fired, FOIA #110818, FOIA pp. 000813–000818.

64. Investigators McCarron, Dolan, and Peo, Organized Crime Task Force Memorandum to Anthony Simonetti, December 20, 1971, in the papers of Elizabeth M. Fink, Brooklyn, New York.

65. See: Dr. G. Richard Abbott, Testimony, *Attica Task Force Hearing,* May 9–10, 2002, 189–90. The correction officer who shot Monteleone gave a statement to state officials regarding the shooting on September 18, 1971, and it was taken into evidence and used as an exhibit 3-644 in later litigation on behalf of guard families. See: Quigley Order, *Lynda Jones v. State of New York,* 96 A.D.2d 105 (N.Y. App. Div. 1983), August 31, 1982.

66. Regarding documents indicating that the .44 Magnum was Vergamini's, see: Bell, *Preliminary Report on the Attica Investigation,* January 29, 1975, 18. Also see: "Analysis of Correction Officers Rounds Extended," October 18, 1971, FOIA request #110818 of the New York State Attorney General's Office. About the death of Monteleone, see: Rockefeller Administration, Confidential Memo, "Events at Attica: September 8–13, 1971," 49. This office gave a statement regarding the shooting of this weapon on Sep-

tember 18, 1971, and it was taken into evidence by state investigators and was used as an exhibit (3-644) in later litigation on behalf of guard families. See: Quigley Order, *Lynda Jones v. State of New York,* 96 A.D.2d 105 (N.Y. App. Div. 1983), August 31, 1982, 54.

67. Bell, Testimony, *Attica Task Force Hearing,* July 30, 2002, 15.

68. Ibid.

69. Bell, *Preliminary Report on the Attica Investigation,* 18.

70. Ibid.; and Bell, *The Turkey Shoot,* 116, 355.

## 45. GOING PUBLIC

1. Notice of No Bill, Exhibit C, *People of the State of New York v. Gregory Wildridge,* State of New York Supreme Court: County of Wyoming, December 19, 1975, Erie County courthouse.

2. Ibid.

3. His optimism might well have been justified. When Simonetti had told him to stand down on his cases, for example, Bell later learned from five jurors that they would have indicted if they been "given a proper chance." See: Malcolm Bell, Affidavit, *In the Matter of the Application of Hugh L. Carey, for a judicial determination as to the publication of Volumes 2 and 3 of the Final Report of Bernard S. Meyer,* Index No. 15062, Filed October 25, 2013, decided April 24, 2014.

4. Edward Hershey, "Attica Trooper Indictment: Papers Never Filed," *Times Union* (Albany, New York), April 23, 1974; "Did Attica Indict a Trooper?," *Democrat and Chronicle* (Rochester, New York), April 24, 1974; FOIA request #110797 of the New York State Attorney General's Office, FOIA pp. 000487–000490.

5. Malcolm Bell, *The Turkey Shoot,* 275.

6. Ibid., 277.

7. Ibid., 276.

8. Ibid., 281.

9. Ibid., 286

10. Bernard S. Meyer, *Final Report of the Special Attica Investigation,* October 27, 1975, New York State Archives, 26.

11. Charles Bradley, conversation with author, July 15, 2004.

12. Ibid.

13. Bell, *The Turkey Shoot,* 294

14. Robert Lenzner, "Probe of Attica Riot Takes New Turn," *Boston Globe,* April 20, 1975.

15. Malcolm Bell, *Preliminary Report on the Attica Investigation,* 4

16. Ibid., 5.

17. Ibid., 35.

18. Malcolm Bell, Memorandum to Anthony Simonetti, Subject: "Moran 'L.A. Times' Radio Log dated 5/8/72," November 15, 1974, in Bell, *Preliminary Report on the Attica Investigation,* 132–33.

19. Bell, *Preliminary Report on the Attica Investigation,* 29, 107–8.

20. Ibid., 114.

21. Ibid., 125, 12.

22. Ibid., 34.

23. Ibid.

24. Diane Dumanoski, "Attica: Covering Up for the Cops," *Boston Phoenix,* May 13, 1975.

25. Ibid.

26. Ibid.

27. Bell, *The Turkey Shoot,* 303.

28. Ibid., 308.

29. Ibid., 313.

30. Ibid., 314.

31. Myron Farber, "Chief Prosecutor on Attica Accused of Jury Cover-Up," *New York Times*. April 8, 1975, Morris Gleicher Papers, Accession number UP001536, Box 7, Folder 20, Walter Reuther Library.

32. Hugh L. Carey, Governor, Press Release, State of New York, Executive Chamber, December 31, 1976, Press Releases, 1921–1948, 1954–1958, 1976–2006, New York (State), Governor, 13688-82, Box 2, Folder 394, New York State Archives, Albany, New York.

33. Lenzner, "Probe of Attica Riot Takes New Turn."

34. Dumanoski, "Attica: Covering Up for the Cops."

## 46. INVESTIGATING THE INVESTIGATION

1. As quoted in: Vincent R. Johnson, "Judge Bernard S. Meyer: first merit appointee to the New York Court of Appeals," *Albany Law Review* 75, no. 2 (December 2011).

2. "N.Y. to Re-examine Attica Investigation," *Boston Globe*, April 14, 1975.

3. Bernard S. Meyer, *Final Report of the Special Attica Investigation*, October 27, 1975, New York State Archives, 33.

4. Ibid., 29.

5. Ibid.

6. Ibid., 27–28.

7. Ibid.

8. Ibid.

9. The public, to this day, still cannot access all of these materials collected by Meyer. See: Heather Ann Thompson, "How Attica's Ugly Past Is Still Protected," *Time*, May 26, 2015.

10. Malcolm Bell, *The Turkey Shoot*, 331, 333.

11. Ibid., 335.

12. Ibid., 338.

13. Rockefeller, Deposition, Meyer Commission, August 8, 1975, 8660, FOIA request #110818, FOIA p. 000407.

14. Ibid., August 8, 1975, 8671, FOIA request #110818, FOIA p.000418.

15. Ibid., August 8, 1975, 8668, FOIA request #110818, FOIA p. 000415.

16. Ibid., August 8, 1975, 8808, FOIA request #110818, FOIA p. 000530.

17. Ibid., August 8, 1975, 8811-8812, FOIA request #110818, FOIA pp. 000533–000534.

18. Douglass, Deposition, Meyer Commission, September 4, 1974, 2933, FOIA request #110818, FOIA p. 000280.

19. Ibid., FOIA p. 000284.

20. Ibid., FOIA p. 000293.

21. Ibid., FOIA p. 000298.

22. Ibid., FOIA p. 000347.

23. George Infante, Testimony, Meyer Commission, August 25, 1975, Mineola, New York, 10, 751, FOIA request #110818 of the New York State Attorney General's Office, FOIA p. 000369.

24. Infante, Testimony, Meyer Commission, August 25, 1975, 10, 760, FOIA request #110818, FOIA p. 000378.

25. Bell, *The Turkey Shoot*, 339.

26. Until 2015 when highly redacted versions of volumes 2 and 3 were also ordered released. Nick Reisman, "Schneiderman's Office Releases Unsealed Attica Documents," *State of Politics*, May 21, 2015; Hugh L. Carey, Governor, Press Release, State of New York, Executive Chamber, December 22, 1975, New York State Coalition for Criminal Justice Records, 1971–1986, Series 9: Issues File, Box 1: Attica Aftermath, 1971–1974, Folder 12, M. E. Grenander Department of Special Collections and Archives, State University of New York, Albany, New York.

27. Carey, Press Release, State of New York, Executive Chamber, December 22, 1975.

28. Meyer, *Final Report of the Special Attica Investigation,* October 27, 1975, New York State Archives, 1.

29. Ibid.

30. Ibid., 2.

31. Ibid., 5.

32. Ibid., 4.

33. Ibid.

34. Bell, *The Turkey Shoot,* 345.

35. Ibid., 348.

36. Meyer, *Final Report of the Special Attica Investigation,* October 27, 1975, New York State Archives, 6.

37. Ibid., 7.

38. Ibid.

39. Ibid., 11.

40. Arthur Liman, Letter to Governor Hugh Carey, April 15, 1975, New York State Coalition for Criminal Justice Records, 1971–1986, Series 9: Issues File, Box 1: Attica Aftermath, 1971–1974, Folder 1, M. E. Grenander Department of Special Collections and Archives, State University of New York, Albany, New York.

41. Ibid.

42. Ibid.

43. Ibid.

44. Ibid.

45. Robert B. McKay, Press Release, January 14, 1976, New York State Coalition for Criminal Justice Records, 1971–1986, Series 9: Issues File, Box 1: Attica Aftermath, 1971–1974, Folder 12, M. E. Grenander Department of Special Collections and Archives, State University of New York, Albany, New York.

46. Ibid.

47. "Let Clemency End the Attica Tragedy," *Democrat and Chronicle* (Rochester, New York), April 10, 1976, New York State Coalition for Criminal Justice Records, 1971–1986, Series 9: Issues File, Box 1: Attica Aftermath, 1971–1974, Folder 12, M. E. Grenander Department of Special Collections and Archives, State University of New York, Albany, New York.

48. Frank "Big Black" Smith, National Director, *Attica Now,* Fundraising Letter, Attica Brothers Trial Office, Winter 1976, Rosenberg Collection, Box 1, Folder 6, Walter Reuther Library.

49. Gregory Wildridge Indictment, "Reckless Endangerment in the First Degree," *People of the State of New York v. Gregory Wildridge,* October 10, 1975, Erie County courthouse. Class D felony. Max sentence of seven years.

50. Ibid.

51. Tom Goldstein, "Trooper Accused of Reckless Use of Shotgun in Attica Uprising," *New York Times,* October 11, 1975.

52. The above all in aid of: "Motion to dismiss indictment pursuant to Sections 210.20 1 b and 210.30 of Criminal Procedure Law and for Inspection of All Grand Jury Minutes," Omnibus Motion Pursuant to Article 255 of the Criminal Procedure Law, *People of the State of New York v. Gregory Wildridge,* State of New York Supreme Court: County of Wyoming, December 19, 1975, Erie County courthouse, 4–5.

53. Ibid., 6.

54. "Attica Grand Juries Vote 'No Bill' on 7," *New York Times,* December 20, 1975, 30.

55. Notice of No Bills, Exhibit C, *People of the State of New York v. Gregory Wildridge,* State of New York Supreme Court: County of Wyoming, December 19, 1975, Erie County courthouse.

56. Ibid.

57. Alfred Scotti, Special Attorney General, Statement Made in Court before the Honorable Judge Frank Bayger, February 26, 1976, as quoted in: Bell, *The Turkey Shoot,* 365.

58. Ibid.

59. Ibid.

60. Ibid.

61. Hugh Carey, Governor, Press Release, State of New York Executive Chamber, April 22, 1976.

62. Martin J. Mack, Affirmation (affidavit), *In the Matter of the Application of Hugh L. Carey, for a judicial determination as to the publication of Volumes 2 and 3 of the Final Report of Bernard S. Meyer,* Index No. 15062, Filed October 25, 2013, decided April 24, 2014.

63. Statement of Alfred Scotti, Special Attorney General, Statement Made in Court before the Honorable Judge Bayger, February 26, 1976, as quoted in: Bell, *The Turkey Shoot,* 365.

64. Carey, Press Release, State of New York Executive Chamber, April 22, 1976.

65. Ernest Goodman, Letter to Bernard "Shango" Stroble, February 27, 1976, Ernest Goodman Papers, Accession number 1152, Box 6, Walter Reuther Library.

66. Carey, Press Release, State of New York Executive Chamber, April 22, 1976.

67. Ibid.

68. "Attica Probe by New York Comes to End," *New York Times,* April 1, 1976.

## 47. CLOSING THE BOOK

1. New York State Coalition for Criminal Justice, Letter to Governor Hugh Carey, December 3, 1975; New York State Coalition for Criminal Justice, Letter to Governor Hugh Carey, February 13, 1976. Both in: New York State Coalition for Criminal Justice Records, 1971–1986, Series 1: Coalition Administration, 1975–1984, Box 1: Attica Clemency Legislation, M. E. Grenander Department of Special Collections and Archives, State University of New York, Albany, New York; Statement in: Joseph A. Labadie Collection, Special Collections Library, University of Michigan, Ann Arbor, Michigan.

2. Governor Hugh Carey, Press Release, State of New York, Executive Chamber, December 21, 1976, New York State Archives.

3. Ibid.

4. Ibid.

5. Tom Goldstein, "Trooper and Guard Assail Carey on Clemency in Attica Revolt," *New York Times,* January 1, 1977.

6. Ibid.

7. Carey, Press Release, State of New York, Executive Chamber, December 21, 1976.

8. Tom Goldstein, "New York State Still Faces Lawsuits Despite Carey's Attica Clemency Stand," *New York Times,* January 24, 1977.

9. Ibid.

10. Ibid.

11. Malcolm Bell, Affidavit, *People of the State of New York v. John Hill,* filed June 28, 1978, 41–42.

12. "Immediate Amnesty for Dacajewiah," Flyer, New York State Coalition for Criminal Justice Records, 1971–1986, Series 1: Coalition Administration, 1975–1984, Box 1: Attica Clemency Legislation, M. E. Grenander Department of Special Collections and Archives, State University of New York, Albany, New York.

13. Charter Group for a Pledge of Conscience, Flyer, New York, New York State Coalition for Criminal Justice Records, 1971–1986, Series 1: Coalition Administration, 1975–1984, Box 1: Attica Clemency Legislation, M. E. Grenander Department of Special Collections and Archives, State University of New York, Albany, New York.

14. "Attica Figure's Bid for Parole Denied Despite Clemency," *New York Times*, January 19, 1977.
15. Ibid.
16. Malcolm Bell, *The Turkey Shoot*, draft, Chapter 1, 3.

## PART IX · DAVID AND GOLIATH

### 48. IT AIN'T OVER TILL IT'S OVER

1. Mark K. Benenson, lawyer of Herman Holt, statement during testimony of Herman Holt, November 3, 1978, *Hardie v. State of New York* and *Jones v. State of New York*, 1495, FOIA request #120209 of the New York State Attorney General's Office, FOIA p.000072.
2. "Claims Against State Mount," *New York Times*, December 15, 1971.
3. Stephen Light, "The Attica Litigation," *Crime, Law, and Social Change* 23, no. 3 (1995): 215–34.
4. Tom Goldstein, "New York Still Faces Lawsuits Despite Carey's Attica Clemency Stand," *New York Times*, January 24, 1977.
5. As quoted in: ibid.
6. As quoted in: ibid.
7. Light, "The Attica Litigation," 215–34.
8. Ibid.
9. Ibid.
10. "Inmates, Relatives, Win in Attica Suit," Associated Press, News Clipping, American Radicalism Collection, Special Collections, Michigan State University, East Lansing, Michigan.
11. Light, "The Attica Litigation," 215–34.
12. Ibid.
13. Ellen Yacknin, conversation with author, Rochester, New York, October 16, 2004.
14. Ibid.
15. Ibid.
16. Judge John T. Elfvin, conversation with author, Buffalo, New York, August 9, 2004.
17. Judge John T. Elfvin, Memorandum and Order, Granting Plaintiffs Motion for Class Certification, October 30, 1979, Vol. I, A-191; Judge John T. Elfvin, Memorandum and Order, Revoking Class Certification, October 27, 1980, Vol. I, A-244; Judge John T. Elfvin, Memorandum and Order, Granting Plaintiff's Motion for Recertification of Class, June 24, 1985, Vol. I, A-257, all in: Deferred Joint Appendix, *Herbert Blyden et al. v. Vincent Mancusi et al.*, 186 F. 3d 252, Docket No. 97-2912.
18. See: John T. Elfvin, Memorandum and Order Denying Defendant Estate of Nelson A. Rockefeller Motion to Decertify the Class, Deferred Joint Appendix, *Herbert Blyden et al. v. Vincent Mancusi et al.*, 186 F. 3d 252, Docket No. 97-2912, Vol. I, April 2, 1987, A-282.
19. Elizabeth Fink, conversation with author, Brooklyn, New York, February 23, 2014.
20. Ibid.

### 49. SHINING THE LIGHT ON EVIL

1. Elizabeth Fink, conversation with author, February 23, 2014.
2. *Akil Al-Jundi et al. v. Vincent Mancusi et al.*, United States Court of Appeals, Second Circuit, 186 F. 3d 252, Docket No. 97-2912, argued July 16, 1998, decided August 3, 1999, 5.

3. Dennis Cunningham, Michael Deutsch, and Elizabeth Fink, "Remembering Attica Forty Years Later," *Prison Legal News* (September 2011).

4. In: American Radicalism Collection, Special Collections, Michigan State University, East Lansing, Michigan.

5. George Jackson was the prisoner-writer who had inspired many in the prisoner rights movement and who was killed by guards at San Quentin in 1971; Geronimo Pratt was a high-ranking member of the Black Panther Party who was wrongfully convicted of a murder in 1972 and whose conviction was vacated in 1997. From American Radicalism Collection, Special Collections, Michigan State University, East Lansing, Michigan.

6. In: American Radicalism Collection, Special Collections, Michigan State University, East Lansing, Michigan.

7. Ibid.

8. When Oswald died in 1991, this attorney represented his estate.

9. Elizabeth M. Fink, Affirmation (affidavit), Regarding Plaintiff's Petition for a Writ of Mandamus, Deferred Joint Appendix, *Akil Al-Jundi et al. v. Vincent Mancusi et al.*, United States Court of Appeals, Second Circuit, 186 F. 3d 252, Docket No. 97-2912, Vol. III, November 8, 1995, in the papers of Elizabeth M. Fink, Brooklyn, New York, A-2090-2109.

10. Ibid.

11. Ellen Yacknin, conversation with author, October 16, 2004.

12. Ibid.

13. David Burke, Testimony, *Akil Al-Jundi et al. v. The Estate of Nelson A. Rockefeller, Russell Oswald, John Monahan, Vincent Mancusi and Karl Pfeil,* United States District Court, Western District of New York, Buffalo, New York, No. CIV-75-132, November 1, 1991, 61.

14. Ibid., 67.

15. Ibid., 70, 79.

16. Dr. David Breen, Testimony, ibid., 4033–34.

17. Ibid., 4053.

18. Ibid., 4053.

19. Ibid., 4053.

20. Ibid., 4079.

21. Ibid., 4033–34.

22. Ibid., 4053.

23. Ibid.

24. Ibid.

25. Daniel Callahan, Testimony, Deferred Joint Appendix, *Akil Al-Jundi et al. v. Vincent Mancusi et al.*, United States Court of Appeals, Second Circuit, 186 F. 3d 252, Docket No. 97-2912, Vol. II, November 27, 1991, in the papers of Elizabeth M. Fink, Brooklyn, New York, A-861.

26. Ibid., A-862.

27. Ibid.

28. United States Department of Justice, FBI Memorandum, Subject: "Unknown victims, Attica, Summary punishment, Civil rights," Buffalo, New York, March 24, 1972, FOIA request #1014547-001 of the FBI, September 28, 2008.

29. Ibid.

30. Ibid.

31. Gerard Smith, Testimony, *Akil Al-Jundi et al. v. The Estate of Nelson A. Rockefeller et al.*, No. CIV-75-132, November 14, 1991, 3920.

32. Captain William Dillon, Testimony, ibid., 6255.

33. Gerard Smith, Testimony, *Akil Al-Jundi et al. v. The Estate of Nelson A. Rockefeller et al.*, No. CIV-75-132, November 14, 1991, 3897.

34. Ibid., 3909.

35. Ibid., 3912.

36. George Colcloughey, Testimony, *Akil Al-Jundi et al. v. The Estate of Nelson A. Rockefeller et al.*, United States District Court, Western District of New York, Buffalo, New York, No. CIV-75-132, November 19, 1991, 4631

37. Jameel Abdul Raheem, Testimony, *Akil Al-Jundi et al. v. The Estate of Nelson A. Rockefeller et al.*, No. CIV-75-132, November 1, 1991, 2102.

38. Ibid., 2103.

39. Ibid., 2109.

40. Ibid.

41. John Dunne, Testimony, Deferred Joint Appendix, *Akil Al-Jundi et al. v. Vincent Mancusi et al.*, 186 F. 3d 252, Docket No. 97-2912, Vol. II, December 3, 1991, A-886.

42. Ibid., A-887.

43. Ibid.

44. Michael Baden, Testimony, Deferred Joint Appendix, *Akil Al-Jundi et al. v. Vincent Mancusi et al.*, United States Court of Appeals, Second Circuit, 186 F. 3d 252, Docket No. 97-2912, Vol. II, December 10, 1991.

45. Ibid., A-968.

46. Ibid., A-969.

47. George Infante, Testimony, *Akil Al-Jundi et al. v. The Estate of Nelson A. Rockefeller et al.*, United States District Court, Western District of New York, Buffalo, New York, No. CIV-75-132, December 16, 1991, E-8968.

48. Ibid., E-8989.

49. Ibid., E-8991.

50. Karl Pfeil, Testimony, Deferred Joint Appendix, *Akil Al-Jundi et al. v. Vincent Mancusi et al.*, United States Court of Appeals, Second Circuit, 186 F. 3d 252, Docket No. 97-2912, Vol. II, December 19, 1991, A-1302.

51. Ibid.

52. Ibid.

53. *Akil Al-Jundi et al. v. Vincent Mancusi et al.*, 186 F. 3d 252, Docket No. 97-2912, Argued July 16, 1998, Decided August 3, 1999, 6.

54. William Glaberson, "Echoes of Violence: Attica's Story Retold in Court," *New York Times*, December 10, 1991.

55. *Akil Al-Jundi et al. v. Vincent Mancusi et al.*, 186 F. 3d 252, Docket No. 97-2912, Argued July 16, 1998, decided August 3, 1999, 7.

56. Deferred Joint Appendix, *Akil Al-Jundi et al. v. Vincent Mancusi et al.*, 186 F. 3d 252, Docket No. 97-2912, Vol. II, January 9, 1992, A-1471.

57. Ibid.

58. Ibid., A-1472.

59. Ibid., A-1474.

60. Ibid., A-1616.

61. Andrew Yarrow, "Attica Jury Still Out, but Judge Plans Holiday," *New York Times*, January 15, 1992.

62. For a transcript of the drama before Elfvin's vacation departure, see: Attorneys' exchanges with Judge Elfvin, Deferred Joint Appendix, *Akil Al-Jundi et al. v. Vincent Mancusi et al.*, 186 F. 3d 252, Docket No. 97-2912, Vol. III, January 14, 1991, A-1627.

63. Ibid., A-1627.

64. Ibid., A-1627.

65. Ibid., A-1632.

66. Judge Michael Telesca, conversation with author, Buffalo, New York, August 13, 2004.

67. Ibid.

68. Ibid.

69. Jury, Outraged letter to Judge John Elfvin, January 22, 1992, in: Deferred Joint Appendix, *Akil Al-Jundi et al. v. Vincent Mancusi et al.*, 186 F. 3d 252, Docket No. 97-2912, Vol. III, January 14, 1991, A-1748–49.

70. Ibid.
71. Ibid.
72. Ibid.
73. *Akil Al-Jundi et al. v. Vincent Mancusi et al.*, 186 F. 3d 252, Docket No. 97-2912, Argued July 16, 1998, Decided August 3, 1999, 15.
74. Cunningham, Deutsch, and Fink, "Remembering Attica Forty Years Later."
75. William Glaberson, "Unanswered in Attica Case: High Level Accountability," *New York Times*, February 6, 1992.
76. Ibid.

## 50. DELAY TACTICS

1. Elizabeth M. Fink, Affirmation (affidavit), Notice of Plaintiff Motion to Amend Complaint, *Akil Al-Jundi et al. v. Vincent Mancusi et al.*, United States Court of Appeals, Second Circuit, 186 F. 3d 252, Docket No. 97-2912, Vol. III, March 1, 1995, in the papers of Elizabeth M. Fink, Brooklyn, New York, A-1931.
2. Ibid., A-1932.
3. Ibid., A-1827.
4. Motion for Judgment as a Matter of Law, Deferred Joint Appendix, *Akil Al-Jundi et al. v. Vincent Mancusi et al.*, United States Court of Appeals, Second Circuit, 186 F. 3d 252, Docket No. 97-2912, Vol. III, January 16, 1992.
5. John T. Elfvin, Order and Memorandum, Deferred Joint Appendix, *Akil Al-Jundi et al. v. Vincent Mancusi et al.*, United States Court of Appeals, Second Circuit, 186 F. 3d 252, Docket No. 97-2912, Vol. III, A-1751.
6. Ibid., A-1760.
7. Ibid.
8. Ellen Yacknin, conversation with author, October 16, 2004.
9. Ibid.
10. Elizabeth Fink, conversation with author, February 23, 2014.
11. See: "Attica Questionnaire," Deferred Joint Appendix, *Akil Al-Jundi et al. v. Vincent Mancusi et al.*, 186 F. 3d 252, Docket No. 97-2912, Vol. III, A-2080–89.
12. Elizabeth Fink, Letter to Judge John T. Elfvin, Subject: "Lists of the appropriate six categories and the living plaintiffs who fall into each list," April 22, 1994, in: Deferred Joint Appendix, *Akil Al-Jundi et al. v. Vincent Mancusi et al.*, 186 F. 3d 252, Docket No. 97-2912, Vol. III, A-2090–2109.
13. John Elfvin, Letter "to all counsel," November 17, 1994, in *Akil Al-Jundi et al. v. Vincent Mancusi et al.*, 186 F. 3d 252, Docket No. 97-2912, argued July 16, 1998, decided August 3, 1999.
14. Elizabeth Fink, Letter to Judge Elfvin, December 2, 1994, in *Akil Al-Jundi et al. v. Vincent Mancusi et al.*, 186 F. 3d 252, Docket No. 97-2912, Vol. III, A-1829.
15. Ibid.
16. Ibid., A-1831.
17. Ibid.
18. During the years between the liability trials and the damages trials countless motions were filed to get this case going. See: Notice of Motion of Plaintiffs Setting Date for Immediate Damages Trials and Excluding Issues of Liability, Deferred Joint Appendix, *Akil Al-Jundi et al. v. Vincent Mancusi et al.*, 186 F. 3d 252, Docket No. 97-2912, Vol. III, January 26, 1995, A-1805; Irving Maghran filed his own opposition to this motion: Deferred Joint Appendix, *Akil Al-Jundi et al. v. Vincent Mancusi et al.*, 186 F. 3d 252, Docket No. 97-2912, Vol. III, February 13, 1995, A-1840; Oral Argument on Plaintiffs Motion Setting Date for Immediate Damages Trials and Excluding Issues of Liability, Deferred Joint Appendix, *Akil Al-Jundi et al. v. Vincent Mancusi et al.*, 186 F. 3d 252, Docket No. 97-2912, Vol. III, February 24, 1995, A-1847; Petition for Writ of Mandamus of Plaintiff, Deferred Joint Appendix, *Akil Al-Jundi et al. v. Vincent Mancusi et al.*, 186

F. 3d 252, Docket No. 97-2912, Vol. III, June 20, 1995, A-1875; Honorable John T. Elfvin, Response to Plaintiff's Petition for a Writ of Mandamus, Deferred Joint Appendix, *Akil Al-Jundi et al. v. Vincent Mancusi et al.*, 186 F. 3d 252, Docket No. 97-2912, Vol. III, October 25, 1995, A-2066; Second Circuit Court Order Denying Plaintiff's Petition for a Writ of Mandamus, Deferred Joint Appendix, *Akil Al-Jundi et al. v. Vincent Mancusi et al.*, 186 F. 3d 252, Docket No. 97-2912, Vol. III, November 16, 1995, A-2113.

19. Herbie Scott Dean, aka Akil Al-Jundi, Deposition, Deferred Joint Appendix, *Akil Al-Jundi et al. v. Vincent Mancusi et al.*, 186 F. 3d 252, Docket No. 97-2912, Vol. III, August 10, 1994, 11.

20. Ibid., 28.

21. Ibid., 45.

22. David J. Barry, MD, Report on patient Ezell Vance, Deferred Joint Appendix, *Akil Al-Jundi et al. v. Vincent Mancusi et al.*, 186 F. 3d 252, Docket No. 97-2912, October 12, 1994, A-2158–60.

23. Also: Stephen S. Teich, MD, Report on Daniel Sheppard, Deferred Joint Appendix, *Akil Al-Jundi et al. v. Vincent Mancusi et al.*, 186 F. 3d 252, Docket No. 97-2912, October 13, 1994, A-2151–56.

24. Elizabeth Fink, Letter to Honorable Michael A. Telesca, Chief Judge, Rochester, New York, Deferred Joint Appendix, *Akil Al-Jundi et al. v. Vincent Mancusi et al.*, 186 F. 3d 252, Docket No. 97-2912, February 25, 1992, A-1823.

25. Michael Telesca, conversation with author, August 13, 2004.

26. Honorable Michael A. Telesca, Letter to Counsel, February 26, 1992, A-2110.

27. Telesca, conversation with author, August 13, 2004.

28. Ibid.

29. Ibid.

30. Ibid.

31. Fink, conversation with author, February 23, 2014.

32. Ibid.

33. Ibid.

34. *Akil Al-Jundi et al. v. Vincent Mancusi et al.*, United States Court of Appeals, Second Circuit, 186 F. 3d 252, Docket No. 97-2912, argued July 16, 1998, decided August 3, 1999, 9.

## 51. THE PRICE OF BLOOD

1. Deferred Joint Appendix, *Akil Al-Jundi et al. v. Vincent Mancusi et al.*, 186 F. 3d 252, Docket No. 97-2912, Vol. V.

2. Plaintiffs Opening Statement, Frank Smith Damages Trial. Deferred Joint Appendix, *Akil Al-Jundi et al. v. Vincent Mancusi et al.*, 186 F. 3d 252, Docket No. 97-2912, Vol. IV, May 29, 1997, A-2323–25.

3. Mitch Banas, Statement, Deferred Joint Appendix, *Akil Al-Jundi et al. v. Vincent Mancusi et al.*, 186 F. 3d 252, Docket No. 97-2912, Vol. IV, May 29, 1997, A-2333.

4. Ibid., A-2912.

5. Frank Smith, Testimony, Deferred Joint Appendix, *Akil Al-Jundi et al. v. Vincent Mancusi et al.*, 186 F. 3d 252, Docket No. 97-2912, Vol. IV, May 29, 1997, A-2353–54.

6. Ibid., A-2355–56.

7. Ibid., A-2356.

8. Ibid., A-2357.

9. Ibid., A-2359.

10. Ibid., A-2366.

11. Ibid., A-2363.

12. Ibid., A-2365.

13. Ibid., A-2371–72.

14. Ibid., A-2373.

15. Ibid., A-2374.

16. Deferred Joint Appendix, *Akil Al-Jundi et al. v. Vincent Mancusi et al.*, 186 F. 3d 252, Docket No. 97-2912, Vol. II, Bl.

17. Frank Smith, Testimony, Deferred Joint Appendix, *Akil Al-Jundi et al. v. Vincent Mancusi et al.*, 186 F. 3d 252, Docket No. 97-2912, Vol. IV, May 29, 1997, A-2376.

18. Ibid., A-2378.

19. Ibid., A-2380.

20. Ibid., A-2381.

21. Ibid., A-2383.

22. Ibid., A-2384.

23. Ibid., A-2386.

24. Ibid., A-2389.

25. Ibid., A-2393.

26. Ibid.

27. Ibid., A-2396.

28. Ibid., A-2399.

29. Ibid.

30. Ibid., A-2137.

31. Ibid., A-2367.

32. Ibid.

33. Richard G. Dudley, Jr., MD, Medical Report: Psychiatric Evaluation of Frank "Big Black" Smith, Deferred Joint Appendix, *Akil Al-Jundi et al. v. Vincent Mancusi et al.*, 186 F. 3d 252, Docket No. 97-2912, November 11, 1994, A-2132.

34. Ibid., A-2134.

35. Ibid., A-2137.

36. Ibid., A-2140.

37. John Elfvin instructions to the Jury, Deferred Joint Appendix, *Akil Al-Jundi et al. v. Vincent Mancusi et al.*, 186 F. 3d 252, Docket No. 97-2912, Vol. V, A-3071.

38. Ronald Dill, Testimony, Deferred Joint Appendix, *Akil Al-Jundi et al. v. Vincent Mancusi et al.*, 186 F. 3d 252, Docket No. 97-2912, Vol. IV, A-2326.

39. Testimony related to Big Black's treatment on the day of the retaking in D Yard, Deferred Joint Appendix, *Akil Al-Jundi et al. v. Vincent Mancusi et al.*, 186 F. 3d 252, Docket No. 97-2912, Vol. V, A-3032.

40. Plaintiffs Closing Statement, Frank Smith Damages Trial. Deferred Joint Appendix, *Akil Al-Jundi et al. v. Vincent Mancusi et al.*, 186 F. 3d 252, Docket No. 97-2912, Vol. V, June 4, 1997, A-3036.

41. John Elfvin instructions to the Jury, Deferred Joint Appendix, *Akil Al-Jundi et al. v. Vincent Mancusi et al.*, 186 F. 3d 252, Docket No. 97-2912, Vol. V, A-3086.

42. Ibid., A-3066.

43. Ibid., A-3067.

44. Ibid., A-3078.

45. Verdict, Deferred Joint Appendix, *Akil Al-Jundi et al. v. Vincent Mancusi et al.*, 186 F. 3d 252, Docket No. 97-2912, Vol. V., June 5, 1997, A-3086.

46. Dennis Cunningham, Michael Deutsch, and Elizabeth Fink, "Remembering Attica Forty Years Later" *Prison Legal News* (September 2011).

47. Plaintiffs Opening Statement, Brosig Damages Trial. Deferred Joint Appendix, *Herbert Blyden et al. v. Vincent Mancusi, et al.*, 186 F. 3d 252, Docket No. 97-2912, Vol. V, June 23, 1997, A-3161.

48. Ibid., A-3163–64.

49. Ibid., A-3164–65.

50. Ibid., A-3166–67.

51. Ibid., A-3180.

52. Ibid.

53. Ibid., A-3181.

54. Ibid., A-3195.
55. Ibid., A-3198–99.
56. Ibid., A-3594.
57. Ibid., A-3596.
58. Ibid., A-3598–99.
59. Ibid., A-3600.
60. Plaintiffs Closing Statement, Brosig Damages Trial. Deferred Joint Appendix, *Akil Al-Jundi et al. v. Vincent Mancusi et al.*, 186 F. 3d 252, Docket No. 97-2912, Vol. V, June 26, 1997, Vol. V, A-3591.
61. Defense, Closing Statement, Deferred Joint Appendix, *Akil Al-Jundi et al. v. Vincent Mancusi et al.*, 186 F. 3d 252, Docket No. 97-2912, Vol. V, A-3614.
62. Ibid., A-3615.
63. Ibid., A-3617–22.
64. Ibid.
65. Case Verdict, Deferred Joint Appendix, *Akil Al-Jundi et al. v. Vincent Mancusi et al.*, 186 F. 3d 252, Docket No. 97-2912, Vol. V, A-3663.
66. Mark Hamblett, "Attica Civil Rights Verdict Overturned," *New York Law Journal* August 4, 1999.
67. Ibid.
68. *Akil Al-Jundi et al. v. Vincent Mancusi et al.*, United States Court of Appeals, Second Circuit, 186 F. 3d 252, Docket No. 97-2912, argued July 16, 1998, decided August 3, 1999, 14.
69. Ibid.
70. Ibid.
71. Hamblett, "Attica Civil Rights Verdict Overturned."
72. *Akil Al-Jundi et al. v. Vincent Mancusi et al.*, United States Court of Appeals, Second Circuit, 186 F. 3d 252, Docket No. 97-2912, argued July 16, 1998, decided August 3, 1999, 14.
73. Ibid.
74. Ellen Yacknin, conversation with author, October 16, 2004.

## 52. DEAL WITH THE DEVIL

1. Ellen Yacknin, conversation with author, October 16, 2004.
2. Michael Telesca, conversation with author, August 13, 2004.
3. Ibid.
4. Ibid.
5. Ibid.
6. Ibid.
7. Ibid.
8. John Elfvin, conversation with author, August 9, 2004.
9. Ibid.
10. Ibid.
11. Ibid.
12. Ibid.
13. Ibid.
14. Ibid.
15. Yacknin, conversation with author, October 16, 2004.
16. Telesca, conversation with author, August 13, 2004.
17. Ibid.
18. Ibid.
19. Ibid.
20. Ibid.
21. Ibid.

22. Ibid.

23. Michael A. Telesca, Decision and Order, Final Approval of Settlement and Distribution of Settlement, *Akil Al-Jundi et al. v. Vincent Mancusi et al.*, United States District Court, Western District of New York, Buffalo, New York, 113 F.Supp.2d 441 (2000), No. CIV-75-132, August 28, 2000, 7.

24. Ibid.

25. Ibid.

26. Ibid.

27. Ibid.

28. Ibid.

29. Ibid., 8.

30. Ibid., 8.

31. David Chen, "Compensation Set on Attica Uprising," *New York Times*, August 29, 2000.

32. Telesca, Decision and Order, Final Approval of Settlement and Distribution of Settlement, Final Summaries. *Akil Al-Jundi et al. v. Vincent Mancusi et al.*, 113 F.Supp.2d 441 (2000), No. CIV-75-132, August 28, 2000.

33. Ibid.

34. Ibid.

35. Ibid.

36. Ibid.

37. Ibid.

38. Ibid.

39. Ibid.

40. Ibid.

41. Ibid.

42. Ibid.

43. Ibid.

44. Ibid.

45. Ibid.

46. Ibid.

47. Yacknin, conversation with author, October 16, 2004.

## PART X · A FINAL FIGHT

### 53. FAMILY FURY

1. David W. Chen, "NY Agrees to Settle Lawsuit over Attica Prison Riot in '71—$8 Million Awarded to 1,281 Inmates, Who Must Approve Deal," *Dallas Morning News*, January 5, 2000; "Attica Inmates Receive Money from Settlement," *San Diego Union-Tribune*, December 3, 2000; "Attica Riot Settlement on Way to Inmates," *St. Petersburg Times*, December 3, 2000.

2. Tom Wicker, "Public Needs to Know How State Has Treated Widows, Survivors of 1971 Attica Riot," *The Daily News* (Batavia, New York), August 29, 2000.

3. Dan Herbeck and Michael Beebe, "An American Tragedy Defying Closure—A Judge's Allocation of $8 Million Among 502 Former Inmates Abused—After the 1971 Attica Prison Riot Underscored the Difficulty of Putting 'A Dollar Value on Human Suffering,'" *Buffalo News*, August 29, 2000.

4. Herbeck and Beebe, "An American Tragedy Defying Closure."

5. Jim Memmott, "Attica's Pain Still Lingers for Many," *Democrat and Chronicle* (Rochester, New York), January 9, 2000.

6. Ibid.

7. Gary Craig, "Lawyer Fought Long, Hard for Attica Hostages, Kin," *Democrat and Chronicle* (Rochester, New York), September 13, 2005.

8. Ibid.
9. Ibid.
10. Ibid.
11. Ibid.
12. Ibid.
13. Ibid.
14. Christine Schrader Quinn, Testimony, *Attica Task Force Hearing,* July 30, 2002, 172.
15. Ibid.
16. Dee Quinn Miller, conversation with author, August 11, 2004.
17. Ibid.
18. Ibid.
19. Ibid.
20. Ibid.
21. Ibid.
22. Ibid.
23. Herbeck and Beebe, "An American Tragedy Defying Closure."
24. Ibid.
25. Jim Memmott, "The Attica Aftermath," *Democrat and Chronicle,* September 26, 2000.
26. Wicker, "Public Needs to Know How State Has Treated Widows, Survivors of 1971 Attica Riot."
27. Dee Quinn Miller, conversation with author, August 11, 2004.
28. Gary Horton, conversation with author, Batavia, New York, August 12, 2004.
29. Ibid.
30. Jennifer Gonnerman, "Remembering Attica," *Village Voice,* September 5–11, 2001.
31. Clyde Haberman, "No Solace for Widow of Attica," *New York Times,* February 22, 2000.
32. Gonnerman, "Remembering Attica."
33. Ibid.
34. Horton, conversation with author, August 12, 2004.
35. Memmott, "The Attica Aftermath."
36. Ellen Yacknin, conversation with author, October 16, 2004.
37. Horton, conversation with author, August 12, 2004.
38. Ibid.

## 54. MANIPULATED AND OUTMANEUVERED

1. "Statement of Abe Levine: Director of the State Office of Employee Relations," Press Release, State of New York Executive Chamber, September 24, 1971, Investigation and interview files, 1971–1972, New York (State), Special Commission on Attica, 15855-90, Box 93, New York State Archives, Albany, New York.
2. Ibid.
3. "39 Ex-Attica Hostages Seeking Special Benefits," *New York Times,* October 31, 1971.
4. David Staba, "Survivors, Families Cope with Attica Riot After Three Decades," *Niagara Falls Reporter,* May 14, 2002.
5. Richard Fabian, Testimony, *Ardith Monteleone v. New York State Attica Correctional Facility,* Supreme Court of New York, Appellate Division, Third Department, 141 A.D.2d 938 (N.Y. App. Div. 1988), January 22, 1986, 3023.
6. Jennifer Gonnerman, "Remembering Attica," *Village Voice,* September 5–11, 2001.
7. Staba, "Survivors, Families Cope with Attica Riot After Three Decades."

8. Ibid.
9. Ibid.
10. Richard Fabian, Testimony, *Ardith Monteleone v. New York State Attica Correctional Facility,* 141 A.D.2d 938 (N.Y. App. Div. 1988), January 22, 1986, 3066.
11. "Fact Sheet #2 from Attica," September 16, 1971, Lieutenant H. Steinbaugh Papers.
12. Dennis Cunningham, Michael Deutsch, and Elizabeth Fink, "Remembering Attica Forty Years Later," *Prison Legal News* (September 2011).
13. "Attica Hostages Pressing Law Suits," *New York Times,* January 20, 1976.
14. Morris Jacobs, Deposition, January 26, 2001, 26, taken by Gary Horton for FVOA, in author's possession.
15. Ibid., 35.
16. Ibid.
17. William Cunningham, telephone conversation with author, October 18, 2004.
18. *Werner v. State of New York,* Court of Appeals of the State of New York, 53 N.Y.2d 346 (1981), argued June 1, 1981, decided July 6, 1981.
19. Cunningham, Deutsch, and Fink, "Remembering Attica Forty Years Later."
20. Tom Wicker, "Justice for One: A Widow's Attica Lawsuit," *New York Times,* March 22, 1985.
21. Ibid.
22. Ibid.
23. Cunningham, Deutsch, and Fink, "Remembering Attica Forty Years Later."
24. "Court Bars Claim for Attica Victim," *New York Times,* December 31, 1972.
25. Cunningham, Deutsch, and Fink, "Remembering Attica Forty Years Later."
26. Tom Wicker, "Attica Reopened," *New York Times,* January 4, 1974.
27. Nelson Rockefeller, Deposition, *Lynda Jones v. State of New York et al.* (Claim No. 54555) and *Elizabeth M. Hardie v. State of New York et al.* (Claim No. 54684), State of New York Court of Claims, April 22, 1977, 40.
28. Ibid.
29. Ibid., 46.
30. Ibid., 48.
31. Ibid., 49.
32. William Cunningham, telephone conversation with author, October 18, 2004.
33. Ibid.
34. Ibid.
35. Ibid.
36. Ibid.
37. Ibid.
38. Tom Goldstein, "Echoes of the 1971 Attica Uprising Haunt Courtroom in Damages Suit," *New York Times,* November 24, 1978.
39. *Lynda Jones v. State of New York et al.* (Claim No. 54555) and *Elizabeth M. Hardie v. State of New York et al.* (Claim No. 54684), Hearing transcript, Vol. XIV, State of New York Court of Claims, October 20, 1978, William Cunningham Papers; John Pauley, "Troopers in Attica Retaking to Be Named Today," *Buffalo Courier-Express,* November 2, 1978.
40. Cunningham, Deutsch, and Fink, "Remembering Attica Forty Years Later."
41. Bob Buyer, "'Truth' Asked as Hearing on Attica Closes," *Buffalo Evening News,* November 30, 1978.
42. Goldstein, "Echoes of the 1971 Attica Uprising Haunt Courtroom in Damages Suit."
43. Nancy Monaghan, "Contempt Ruling Delayed in Attica Suit," *Democrat and Chronicle* (Rochester, New York), November 30, 1978.
44. John Pauley, "Troopers in Attica Retaking to Be Named Today."

45. Janis Marston, "Leader of State Police Fails to Produce Letter," *Times Union* (Albany, New York), November 2, 1978.

46. Ibid.

47. Nancy Monaghan, "Names of Troopers Remain a Secret," *Democrat and Chronicle* (Rochester, New York), November 3, 1978.

48. Goldstein, "Echoes of the 1971 Attica Uprising Haunt Courtroom in Damages Suit."

49. William Cunningham, telephone conversation with author, October 18, 2004.

50. Russell Oswald, Testimony, *Lynda Jones v. State of New York et al.* (Claim No. 54555) and *Elizabeth M. Hardie v. State of New York et al.* (Claim No. 54684), Hearing transcript, William Cunningham Papers, 144–45.

51. Nancy Monaghan, "Oswald: 'To Say I Am to Blame Is an Outrage,'" *Democrat and Chronicle* (Rochester, New York), undated, William Cunningham Papers.

52. Remarkably, no one in the news media and no one in the Monteleone family ever heard this testimony though.

53. Major Blake Muthig, Testimony, *Lynda Jones v. State of New York et al.* (Claim No. 54555) and *Elizabeth M. Hardie v. State of New York et al.* (Claim No. 54684), Hearing transcript, William Cunningham Papers, 22.

54. Lew Plumley, Testimony, *Lynda Jones v. State of New York et al.* (Claim No. 54555) and *Elizabeth M. Hardie v. State of New York et al.* (Claim No. 54684), Hearing transcript, William Cunningham Papers, 142, 87–101.

55. Quigley Order, *Lynda Jones v. State of New York,* 96 A.D.2d 105 (N.Y. App. Div. 1983), August 31, 1982, 26.

56. Ibid., 75.

57. Ibid., 29.

58. Ibid.

59. Ibid., 34.

60. Ibid., 47.

61. Ibid., 49.

62. Ibid., 52.

63. Ibid., 56.

64. Ibid., 76.

65. Ibid.

66. Ibid., 79.

67. Ibid., 83.

68. William Cunningham, telephone conversation with author, October 18, 2004.

69. Wicker, "Justice for One: A Widow's Attica Lawsuit."

## 55. BITING THE HAND

1. Gary Horton, conversation with author, August 12, 2004.

2. "Assembly Approves Day of Mourning for Attica Guards," *New York Times,* June 15, 2000.

3. Ibid.

4. David Staba, "Survivors, Families Cope with Attica Riot After Three Decades," *Niagara Falls Reporter,* May 14, 2002.

5. Ibid.

6. Ibid.

7. Ibid.

8. Dee Quinn Miller, telephone conversation with author, May 7, 2006.

9. Ibid.

10. Ibid.

11. "Assembly Approves Day of Mourning for Attica Guards."

12. Ibid.
13. Horton, conversation with author, August 12, 2004.
14. Dee Quinn Miller, telephone conversation with author, May 7, 2006.
15. Andrew Tilghman, "Attica Victims Seek Justice, Relief," *Times Union* (Albany, New York), July 28, 2002.
16. Staba, "Survivors, Families Cope with Attica Riot After Three Decades."
17. Horton, conversation with author, August 12, 2004.
18. Ibid.

## 56. GETTING HEARD

1. Gene Warner, "Echoes of Attica," *Buffalo News,* May 9, 2002.
2. *Attica Task Force Hearing,* May 9–10, 2002, Rochester, New York, 4.
3. John Stockholm, Testimony, ibid., 12.
4. Mary Stockholm, Testimony, ibid., 20.
5. June Fargo, Testimony, ibid., 23–24.
6. Ibid., 24–25.
7. Susan Fargo, Testimony, ibid., 28.
8. Dean Wright, ibid., 67–68.
9. Ibid., 68.
10. Ibid., 69.
11. Ibid., 72.
12. Scott Wright, Testimony, ibid., 76.
13. William Cunningham, Testimony, ibid., 80.
14. Ibid.
15. Ibid., 83.
16. Gene Tenney, Testimony, Attica Task Force Hearings, May 9–10, 2002, Rochester, New York, 93.
17. Ibid., 96.
18. Ibid., 97–98.
19. Ann Driscoll, Testimony, ibid., 144.
20. Ibid., 146.
21. Ibid., 147.
22. Ann Valone, Testimony, ibid., 153.
23. Ibid., 155.
24. Ibid., 158.
25. Ibid., 160.
26. Mary Ann Valone, Testimony, *Attica Task Force Hearing,* July 31, 2002, Albany, New York, 106–7.
27. Ibid., 111.
28. Ibid., 112.
29. Ibid., 117–18.
30. Ibid., 126.
31. Mark, John, and James Cunningham, Testimony, ibid., 5.
32. Ibid., 6.
33. Ibid., 12–13.
34. Eugene "G. B." Smith, Testimony, ibid., 52.
35. Gary Walker, Testimony, ibid., 71.
36. Don Werber, Testimony, ibid., 77–78.
37. Morris Jacobs, Testimony, *Attica Task Force Hearing,* July 30, 2002, Albany, New York, 98.
38. Ibid., 99.
39. Ibid., 100.

40. Sharon Smith, Testimony, ibid., 215–16.
41. Ibid.
42. Ibid., 218–19.
43. Ibid., 215–16.

## 57. WAITING GAME

1. Dee Quinn Miller, telephone conversation with author, May 7, 2006.
2. Ibid.
3. Rick Harcrow, conversation with author, Batavia, New York, August 12, 2004.
4. Dee Quinn Miller, telephone conversation with author, May 7, 2006.
5. Forgotten Victims of Attica, "A Time for Truth," report, February 13, 2003, in author's possession.
6. Ibid.
7. Ibid.
8. Ibid.
9. Scott Christianson, "Attica Hostages and Kin Demand Reparations and Apology," *Independent Media Center,* February 21, 2003.
10. John R. Dunne, Statement, "Open Letter to Families and Friends of the Forgotten Heroes of Attica," September 11, 2002, in author's possession.
11. Ibid.
12. Letter, Malcolm Bell to Honorable George A. Pataki, July 16, 2003.
13. Ibid.
14. Tony Strollo, conversation with author, Albany, New York, February 16, 2004.
15. Ibid.
16. "NYSCOPBA Shows their support for the Forgotten Victims of Attica," about rally at the capitol, New York State Correctional Officers & Police Benevolent Association, 2003, www.nyscopba.org website, accessed February 24, 2004, copy in author's possession.
17. This money would go to the hostage survivors and widows and also to Joe Christian, who had been wounded during the retaking, shot by one of his own men. Even though there had been much controversy surrounding Christian's story of why shots had been fired near him during the retaking, the task force had determined that "his injury was indistinguishable from those of the other victims." See: Attica Task Force, Report to the Governor, Draft Report, September 2003, 11.
18. Ibid., 12.
19. Ibid., 16.
20. *Hugh L. Carey v. State of New York,* New York Supreme Court: County of Wyoming, 92 Misc. 316 (1977), decided November 29, 1977, as referenced in: Attica Task Force, Report to the Governor, Draft Report, September 2003, 18.
21. Attica Task Force, Report to the Governor, Draft Report, September 2003, 22; Forgotten Victims of Attica, Letter to New York State Legislature, Subject: "Draft report circulated by Glenn Goord to members of Task Force," January 13, 2004.
22. Attica Task Force, Report to the Governor, Draft Report, September 2003, 22; Forgotten Victims of Attica, Letter to New York State Legislature, Subject: "Draft report circulated by Glenn Goord to members of Task Force," January 13, 2004.
23. Attica Task Force, Report to the Governor, Draft Report, September 2003, 22; Forgotten Victims of Attica, Letter to New York State Legislature, Subject: "Draft report circulated by Glenn Goord to members of Task Force," January 13, 2004.
24. Tom Precious, "Pataki to Ask Aid for Staff in Attica Riot—$12 Million Would Go to About 50 Families," *Buffalo News,* January 14, 2005.
25. Dee Quinn Miller, telephone conversation with author, May 7, 2006.
26. Ibid.

27. Ibid.
28. The Forgotten Victims of Attica, Letter to New York State Legislature, Subject: "Draft report circulated by Glenn Goord to members of Task Force," January 13, 2004.
29. Ibid.
30. The issue of accessing state files regarding the Attica uprising was a more complicated matter than either the task force or the FVOA fully understood. Not only were volumes 2 and 3 of the Meyer Report—and presumably all materials that were used to create them—sealed by not one but two judges, but all records related to the extensive investigation into Attica that the McKay Commission had conducted were also sealed—in this case because Arthur Liman had fought hard, and successfully, to keep these records out of the hands of those trying to prosecute prisoners back in 1972. So the only records that were theoretically available to the FVOA were those held in the attorney general's office at the World Trade Center and in off-site storage but it was unclear which of these documents would in fact be disclosed.
31. Attica Task Force, Report to the Governor, Draft Report, September 2003, 22; Forgotten Victims of Attica, Letter to New York State Legislature, Subject: "Draft report circulated by Glenn Goord to members of Task Force," January 13, 2004.
32. Attica Task Force, Report to the Governor, Draft Report, September 2003, 7; Forgotten Victims of Attica, Letter to New York State Legislature, Subject: "Draft report circulated by Glenn Goord to members of Task Force," January 13, 2004.
33. Attica Task Force, Report to the Governor, Draft Report, September 2003, 7; Forgotten Victims of Attica, Letter to New York State Legislature, Subject: "Draft report circulated by Glenn Goord to members of Task Force," January 13, 2004.
34. Forgotten Victims of Attica, Letter to New York State Legislature, Subject: "Draft report circulated by Glenn Goord to members of Task Force," January 13, 2004.
35. Ibid.
36. Precious, "Pataki to Ask Aid for Staff in Attica Riot."
37. Goord, "Commissioner's Commentary."
38. Ibid.
39. For more information on these organizations, see their websites: http://cpof.org/ and http://www.cusa.org/.
40. Dee Quinn Miller, email to author, February 17, 2014.
41. Dee Quinn Miller, telephone conversation with author, May 7, 2006.
42. Dee Quinn Miller, email to author, February 17, 2014.
43. See: Ethan Sachs, "A State and Its Prison: The Attica Riot of 1971 and Untold Stories Since," University of Michigan, Senior Honors Thesis, April 2, 2012.
44. Dee Quinn Miller, telephone conversation with author, May 7, 2006.

## 58. A HOLLOW VICTORY

1. Forgotten Victims of Attica, "A Time for Truth," Report, February 13, 2003.
2. Dee Quinn Miller, telephone conversation with author, May 7, 2006.
3. Ibid.
4. Ibid.
5. Ibid.
6. Ibid.
7. Ibid.
8. Ibid., June 21, 2005.
9. Author's notes, Forgotten Victims of Attica, meeting, August 9, 2004.
10. Ibid.
11. Ibid.
12. Michael Telesca, conversation with author, August 13, 2004.
13. Dee Quinn Miller, telephone conversation with author, June 21, 2005.

14. Melissa Long, "Settlement for Forgotten Victims of Attica," WROC-TV, May 13, 2005.

15. Dee Quinn Miller, telephone conversation with author, June 21, 2005.

16. Ibid.

17. Ibid.

18. See: New York State Special Commission on Attica, *McKay Report,* 391–93, and Bell, *Preliminary Report on the Attica Investigation.*

19. "Attica State Employees Victims' Compensation Fund Amended Order. This Order, and Schedule A attached hereto, are amended for the sole purpose of correcting the spelling of some of the claimants' names and, in all other respects, the Order and Certification issued by this Court on July 12, 2005 remain unchanged," United States District Court, Western District of New York.

20. Ibid.

21. Ibid.

22. Ibid.

23. Ibid.

24. Ibid.

25. Ibid.

26. Ibid.

27. Ibid.

28. Ibid.

29. Decision and Order, *Akil Al-Jundi et al. v. Vincent Mancusi et al.,* 113 F.Supp.2d 441 (2000), No. CIV-75-132, August 28, 2000. Final Summaries.

30. Ibid.

31. Ibid.

32. Gary Craig, "Attica Victims Split $12M," *Democrat and Chronicle* (Rochester, New York), July 18, 2005.

33. Ibid.

34. Long, "Settlement for Forgotten Victims of Attica."

35. Gary Horton, conversation with author, August 12, 2004. Also see prologue of this book regarding why this author chose to reveal all information that was available to her.

## EPILOGUE · PRISONS AND POWER

1. "Democrats Back Demands," *New York Times,* September 19, 1971.

2. "Rockefeller Offers Package for Prison Reform," *New York Times,* April 2, 1972.

3. Ibid.

4. Ibid.

5. Gerald Benjamin and Stephen Rappaport, "Attica and Prison Reform," *Proceedings of the Academy of Political Science* 31, no. 3, 200–13, 1974.

6. Gary Gold, Letter to Brian Conboy, Subject: "Federal legislation to implement the 28 Attica Demands,'" September 15, 1971, Senator Jacob A. Javits Collection, Box 6, Special Collections and University Archives, Frank Melville Jr. Memorial Library, Stony Brook University, Stony Brook, New York.

7. It was in 1972 that prisoners' right to the "reasonable opportunity to pursue their faith" was confirmed by the U.S. Supreme Court in *Cruz v. Beto.* In 1976 the court similarly supported prisoners' right to medical care in *Estelle v. Gamble.* Perhaps most significantly, thanks to the many successful legal actions taken by prisoners around the country in the wake of Attica, by 1983 "eight states had their prison systems declared unconstitutional and 22 other states had facilities operation under either a court order or consent decrees." What is more, Attica sparked a tremendous amount of civil rights activism in the nation's court system even after the 1970s. Whereas prisoners had filed

only 218 civil rights suits in 1966; in 1980, even as civil rights activism in the streets seemed to have disappeared, prisoners filed a record 12,718 civil rights actions in courts across America. In 1985 they filed 18,863 suits, and by 1995 they filed a record 41,679 civil cases in state and federal courts. That mattered on the ground. It meant that by 1985 a full "forty-two states had their correctional systems or facilities encumbered by the courts in some way," which, in effect, meant that someone was watching how prisoners were being treated in those jurisdictions. See: *Cruz v. Beto* 405 U.S. 319 (1972); *Estelle v Gamble* 429 U.S. 97 (1976). For one of the most remarkable cases of this in Texas, see: Robert Chase, *Civil Rights on the Cell Block: Prisoners' Rights Movements and the Construction of Carceral States, 1945–1995*, manuscript in preparation for the University of North Carolina's "Justice, Power, and Politics" series. For another detailed history of prisoner rights activism, see: Dan Berger, *Captive Nation: Black Prison Organizing in the Civil Rights Era* (Chapel Hill: University of North Carolina Press, 2014); Table 1. Prisoner petitions filed in U.S. district court by federal and state inmates, 1980–2000. Data source: Administrative Office of the U.S. Courts, Report of the Proceedings of the Judicial Conference of the United States, in John Scalia, BJS Statistician, "Prisoner Petitions Filed in U.S. District Courts, 2000, with Trends 1980–2000," January 2002, NCJ 189430. It is also interesting to note that in 1983, 9,938 general civil rights actions were filed, whereas 18,477 prisoner civil rights actions were filed.

8. Russell Oswald, Memorandum to Rockefeller, Subject: "Activities Report—October 1, 1971–October 31, 1971," Rockefeller Archive Center.

9. Ibid.

10. Paul Montgomery, "Attica Prisoners Have Gained Most Points Made in Rebellion," *New York Times*, September 12, 1972.

11. "Since Attica: The Past Year of Penal Reform," Government Document, April 19, 1973, New York Public Library.

12. Ibid.

13. On training COs better: New York State Department of Correctional Services, Program: "Orientation Training for Correction Officers," New York State Police Academy, Albany, New York, December 6–23, 1971, Investigation and interview files, 1971–1972, New York (State), Special Commission on Attica, 15855-90, Box 93, New York State Archives, Albany, New York.

14. For information on this large conference for prison reform, see: "After Attica—What?," Program, New York State Conference on Prison Reform, Binghamton, New York, November 5–6, 1971, Senator Jacob A. Javits Collection, Box 6, Special Collections and University Archives, Frank Melville Jr. Memorial Library, Stony Brook University, Stony Brook, New York. Information in this collection also on a "National Conference on Prisoner Rights" in Chicago post-Attica. For other post-Attica events, actions, and organizations, see: Michele Hays, "The New York Prison System—A Generation After Attica," *Verdict: National Coalition of Concerned Legal Professionals* 7, no. 3 (July 2001).

15. Hazel Erskine, "The Polls: Politics and Law and Order," *Public Opinion Quarterly* 38, no. 4 (Winter 1974–1975).

16. Letters, *Time*, October 4, 1971.

17. For information on the American Correctional Association study and report, "New Type of Prisoner," see: Robert Gruenberg, draft news story, *Chicago Daily News*, 1971, Dorothy Schiff Papers, Box 4, New York Public Library.

18. Ibid.

19. Ibid.

20. Ibid.

21. Peter Kihss, "Prison Leaders in 8 States Support Assault at Attica," *New York Times*, September 16, 1971.

22. Michael T. Kaufman, "Oswald Seeking Facility to House Hostile Convicts," *New York Times*, September 29, 1971.

23. Ibid.

24. Fred Ferretti, "Facility for Militants Urged," *New York Times,* September 23, 1971.

25. Ibid.

26. Monies had already been flowing to American cities for more punitive policing and to expand prisons thanks to the Law Enforcement Assistance Act of 1965 and the Safe Streets Act of 1968, but the bulk of funding for what became the largest criminal justice system in American history also postdates this rebellion.

27. Richard L. Madden, "US Will Study Charges of Mistreatment at Attica," *New York Times,* October 21, 1971.

28. For more on the origins of the Rockefeller drug laws, see: Julilly Kohler Hausmann, "The Attila the Hun Law: New York's Rockefeller Drug Laws and the Making of a Punitive State." *Journal of Social History* 44, no. 1 (2010): 71–95. Also her forthcoming book with Princeton University Press on this same subject. For more on the drug wars of other decades, see: Matthew Lassiter, "Impossible Criminals: The Suburban Imperatives of America's War on Drugs," *Journal of American History* 102, 110, 1 (2015), 126–140; Donna Murch, "Crack in Los Angeles: Crisis, Militarization, and Black Response to the Late Twentieth-Century War on Drugs," *Journal of American History* 102, no. 1 (2015): 162–73.

29. Madison Gray, "A Brief History of the Rockefeller Drug Laws," *Time,* April 2, 2009.

30. Being homeless, for example, had not, until this punitive turn, been regarded by law enforcement as inherently leading to criminal acts. Increasingly over the last four decades, laws have been passed that have made it a crime for homeless people to sleep in public spaces or to panhandle. Other acts once considered merely antisocial, such as spitting or urinating in public, also began to lead to arrest. For more on this new level of criminalization, see: "Criminalizing Crisis: The Criminalization of Homelessness in U.S. Cities," a report by the National Law Center on Homelessness & Poverty, November 2011. Also see: Charles G. Koch and Mark V. Holden, "The Overcriminalization of America," Politico.com, January 7, 2015.

31. Michael Isikoff, "Bush Promises Veto of Crime Bill," *Washington Post,* September 13, 1990.

32. Ibid.

33. Christopher J. Mumola and Allen J. Beck, "Prisoners in 1996," Bureau of Justice Statistics Bulletin, June 1997, NCJ 164619.

34. Prisoner Rights Primer: Syllabus, Justice 294, Dr. Tom O'Connor, North Carolina Wesleyan College.

35. The history of America's punitive turn in the latter third of the twentieth century is much larger than Attica—although the Attica rebellion, and as important the state's response to it, very much fueled and solidified that turn. As I have argued previously, the War on Crime, which would, in turn, lead to the War on Drugs and to the United States incarcerating more of its population than any other country, began in 1965 when President Lyndon Johnson created the Office of Law Enforcement Administration and passed the Law Enforcement Administration Act. Historians have begun to flesh out the contours of the carceral state and we continue to learn more about why this nation embraced such harsh penal policies after 1965, why it became the world's largest jailer, and what this punitive turn meant for our communities, our economy, and our very democracy. See: Heather Ann Thompson, "Why Mass Incarceration Matters: Rethinking Urban Crisis, Labor Decline, and Political Transformation in Postwar America," *The Journal of American History* (December 2010). Also see the powerful essays on the history of the carceral state in special issues of the *Journal of American History* edited by Heather Ann Thompson, Khalil Gibran Mohammad, and Kelly Lytle Hernández (June 2015) and the *Journal of Urban History* edited by Heather Ann Thompson and Donna Murch (Fall 2015). Also see recent new comprehensive histories of the origins of the carceral state such as Elizabeth Kai Hinton, *From the War on Poverty to the War on Crime:*

*The Making of Mass Incarceration in America* (Cambridge: Harvard University Press, 2016); Naomi Murakawa, *The First Civil Right: How Liberals Built Prison America* (New York: Oxford University Press, 2014); Marie Gottschaulk, *Caught: The Prison State and the Lockdown of American Politics* (Princeton: Princeton University Press, 2014); Dennis Childs, *Slaves of the State: Black Incarceration from the Chain Gang to the Penitentiary* (Minneapolis: University of Minnesota Press, 2015); and Kelly Lytle Hernández, *City of Inmates: Conquest and the Rise of Human Caging in Los Angeles* (Chapel Hill: UNC Press, forthcoming).

36. John Lennon wrote "Attica State" in 1971 and released it on his *Some Time in New York City* album that same year. Sidney Lumet's *Dog Day Afternoon* came out in 1975. Decades later see: "C.I.A. (Criminals in Action)" by KRS-One, Zack De La Rocha, and the Last Emperor; see the thirteenth episode of season one of *The Sopranos,* "I Dream of Jeannie Cusamano"; and see the episode of *SpongeBob* called "Missing Identity."

37. For more on the ways in which prison gerrymandering in the age of incarceration has distorted America's democracy by counting the bodies of black prisoners who can't vote as census population, which, in turn, increases the voting power of whites, see: Heather Ann Thompson, "How Prisons Change the Balance of Power in America," *The Atlantic,* October 7, 2003, http://www.theatlantic.com/national/archive/2013/10/how-prisons-change-the-balance-of-power-in-america/280341/. Also see the myriad reports on this phenomenon done by the Prison Policy Initiative, http://www.prisonersofthecensus.org/.

38. For more on this history of criminalization of black spaces in the South after the Civil War as well as disfranchisement and convict leasing, see: Edward L. Ayers, *Vengeance and Justice: Crime and Punishment in the 19th-Century American South* (New York: Oxford University Press, 1984); Mary Ellen Curtin, *Black Prisoners and Their World, Alabama, 1865–1900* (Charlottesville: University of Virginia Press, 2000); Alex Lichtenstein, *Twice the Work of Free Labor: The Political Economy of Convict Labor in the New South* (New York: Verso, 1996); David M. Oshinsky, *"Worse Than Slavery": Parchman Farm and the Ordeal of Jim Crow Justice* (New York: Free Press, 1997); Karin Shapiro, *A New South Rebellion: The Battle Against Convict Labor in the Tennessee Coalfields, 1871–1896* (Chapel Hill: University of North Carolina Press, 1998); Talitha L. LeFlouria, *Chained in Silence: Black Women and Convict Labor in the New South* (Chapel Hill: University of North Carolina Press, 2015); Robert Perkinson, *Texas Tough: The Rise of America's Prison Empire* (New York: Picador, 2010); Sarah Haley, *No Mercy Here: Gender, Punishment, and the Making of Jim Crow Modernity* (Chapel Hill: UNC Press, 2016). On the criminalization of black spaces in the North and West, see: Kali Nicole Gross, *Colored Amazons: Crime, Violence, and Black Women in the City of Brotherly Love,* 1880–1910 (Durham: Duke University Press, 2006); Khalil Gibran Muhammad, *The Condemnation of Blackness: Race, Crime, and the Making of Modern Urban America* (Cambridge: Harvard University Press, 2011); Cheryl Hicks, *Talk with You Like a Woman: African-American Women, Justice, and Reform in New York, 1890–1935* (Chapel Hill: UNC Press, 2010); Donna Jean Murch, *Living for the City: Migration, Education, and the Rise of the Black Panther Party in Oakland, California* (Chapel Hill: UNC Press, 2010); Kelly Lytle Hernández, *Migra!: A History of the U.S. Border Patrol* (Oakland: University of California Press, 2010); Miroslava Chávez-García, *States of Delinquency: Race and Science in the Making of California's Juvenile Justice System* (Oakland: University of California Press, 2012).

39. Paige M. Harrison and Allen J. Beck, "Prisoners in 2005," Bureau of Justice Statistics Bulletin, US Department of Justice, November 2006, NCJ 215092; "Race and Hispanic Origin in 2005," Population Profile of the United States, US Census Bureau.

40. For two of the most important books on felon disfranchisement in the nineteenth and twentieth centuries, see: Pippa Holloway, *Living in Infamy: Felon Disfranchisement and the History of American Citizenship* (New York: Oxford University Press,

2013); and Jeffery Manza and Chris Uggens, *Locked Out: Felon Disenfranchisement and American Democracy* (New York: Oxford University Press, 2008).

41. For more on the ways in which Attica's prisoners understood the consequences of not fighting for better rights, see: "Lessons from Attica: From Prisoner Rebellion to Mass Incarceration and Back," in special issue: "Mass Incarceration and Political Repression," coedited by Mumia Abu-Jamal and Johanna Fernández, *Socialism and Democracy,* #66, vol. 28, no. 3 (December 2014).

42. The Correctional Association of New York, verdict, "Attica, 1982: An Analysis of Current Conditions in New York State Prisons" (New York, September 1982).

43. Ibid.

44. Ibid.; *Verdict: National Coalition of Concerned Legal Professionals* 7, no. 3 (July 2001).

45. The Correctional Association of New York, Verdict, "Attica, 1982: An Analysis of Current Conditions in New York State Prisons," 5.

46. Ibid., 9, 11.

47. Ibid.

48. Ibid., 15.

49. Ibid., 20, 21.

50. Whereas Attica's COs had belonged to AFSCME Council 82, in 1998 they broke away and became part of the much more conservative New York State Correctional Officers & Police Benevolent Association, NYSCOPBA. The Correctional Association of New York, Verdict, "Attica, 1982: An Analysis of Current Conditions in New York State Prisons," 23.

51. Ibid.

52. Decision and Order, *George Eng et al. v. Harold Smith et al.,* United States District Court, Western District of New York, No. CIV-80-385, January 29, 1988.

53. Roger Wilkins, "Since Attica, the Significant Changes Have Been Rhetorical," *New York Times,* April 20, 1975; Michele Hays, "The New York Prison System—A Generation After Attica," *Verdict: National Coalition of Concerned Legal Professionals* 7, no. 3 (July 2001).

54. The Correctional Association of New York, "Attica Correctional Facility: 2011," Prison Visiting Project Report, April 2011.

55. Ibid.

56. Ibid.

57. The reality was that protesters weren't the ones who physically attacked sixty-three reporters during the Democratic National Convention in 1968, nor was it students who shot, killed, and maimed so many at Kent State in 1970. Likewise it wasn't the Native American protesters who surrounded FBI agents and began firing M-16 automatic weapons and throwing M-79 gas grenades into the town of Wounded Knee. And as indicated earlier, ordinary state violence defined Attica. But the spin that both liberal and conservative politicians put on such protests suggested otherwise. Americans had listened closely when the Democratic governor of South Dakota, Richard Kneip, had called members of the American Indian Movement "'terrorists' and 'hoodlums' and accused them of 'creating a climate of fear, hatred, and reprisals.'" And Americans had listened equally intently to Mayor LeRoy Satrom, a longtime Democrat, when he offered his personal analysis of the blood that was shed in his city of Kent. Not only had this state official attributed the clash of May 4, 1970, to a "subversive element" among the students, but he assured the public that, should there be any more unrest, he would again send in the National Guard and he "would not send them out without loaded weapons." See: John William Sayer, *Ghost Dancing the Law: The Wounded Knee Trials* (Cambridge: Harvard University Press, 2000); 127; *Dennis Banks et al. v. Richard Kneip, Governor of South Dakota et al.*: Class Action for Deprivation of Constitutional Rights Under Color of Law, Feb. 1973. 2 folders, Box 11, Wounded Knee Legal Defense/Offense

Committee Collection, Minnesota Historical Collection; Satrom quoted in: *New York Times,* June 13, 1970, 23.

58. See: James Munves, *The Kent State Coverup* (Bloomington: iUniverse, 2001); Laurel Krause and Mickey Huff, "Uncovering the Kent State Cover-Up," *Counterpunch,* September 27, 2012; Stew Magnusen, *Wounded Knee 1973: Still Bleeding: The American Indian Movement, the FBI, and Their Fight to Bury the Sins of the Past* (Sioux Falls, SD: Courtbridge Publishing, 2013).

59. Joseph Berger, "Attica Inmates End Night Long Protest of Shooting," *New York Times,* July 22, 1984.

60. Paul Mrozek, "Four Prison Guards Charged in Attack on Attica Inmate," New York *Daily News,* December 14, 2011.

61. Ibid.

62. Ibid.

63. Paul Mrozek, "Three Attica Guards Re-Indicted on Gang Assault Charges," New York *Daily News,* January 24, 2013.

64. Ibid.

65. Jason Ziolkowski, Attica CCS, Letter to "friends," New York State Correctional Officers & Police Benevolent Association, undated.

66. Ibid.

67. Sergeant Sean Warner, Letter to "my NYSCOPBA Brothers and Sisters," New York State Correctional Officers & Police Benevolent Association, undated.

68. Tom Robbins, "A Brutal Beating Wakes Attica's Ghosts," *New York Times,* February 28, 2015.

69. Tom Robbins and Lauren D'Avoliomarch, "3 Attica Guards Resign in Deal to Avoid Jail," *New York Times,* March 2, 2015.

70. Ibid.

71. "CA Says Attica Guards' Plea Deal in 2011 Gang Assault Is Historic, Not Justice," March 3, 2015, Correctional Association of New York, http://www.correctionalassociation.org/news/ca-responds-to-attica-guards-plea-deal-in-2011-gang-assault.

72. Dan Herbeck, "Former Attica Prisoner's Attorney Pledges to Push Forward with Federal Lawsuit," *Buffalo News,* March 7, 2015.

73. Tom Robbins, "Feds Open Attica Investigation," *The Marshall Project,* May 17, 2015.

74. Sarah Childress, "After Riot, Feds End Contract for Private Texas Prison," *Frontline,* Public Broadcasting Service, March 17, 2015.

# *Index*

Page numbers in *italics* refer to illustrations.

## ABOUT THE AUTHOR

HEATHER ANN THOMPSON is a historian at the University of Michigan. She has written on the history of mass incarceration, as well as its current impact, for *The New York Times*, *The Atlantic*, *Time*, *Salon*, *Dissent*, *New Labor Forum*, and *The Huffington Post*, as well as numerous scholarly publications. She served on a National Academy of Sciences blue-ribbon panel that studied the causes and consequences of mass incarceration in the United States and has given congressional staff briefings on this subject. Thompson is also the author of *Whose Detroit?: Politics, Labor and Race in a Modern American City* and editor of *Speaking Out: Protest and Activism in the 1960s and 1970s.*

## A NOTE ON THE TYPE

This book was set in Minion, a typeface produced by the Adobe Corporation specifically for the Macintosh personal computer and released in 1990. Designed by Robert Slimbach, Minion combines the classic characteristics of old-style faces with the full complement of weights required for modern typesetting.

*Composed by North Market Street Graphics,*
*Lancaster, Pennsylvania*

*Printed and bound by Berryville Graphics,*
*Berryville, Virginia*

*Designed by Cassandra J. Pappas*

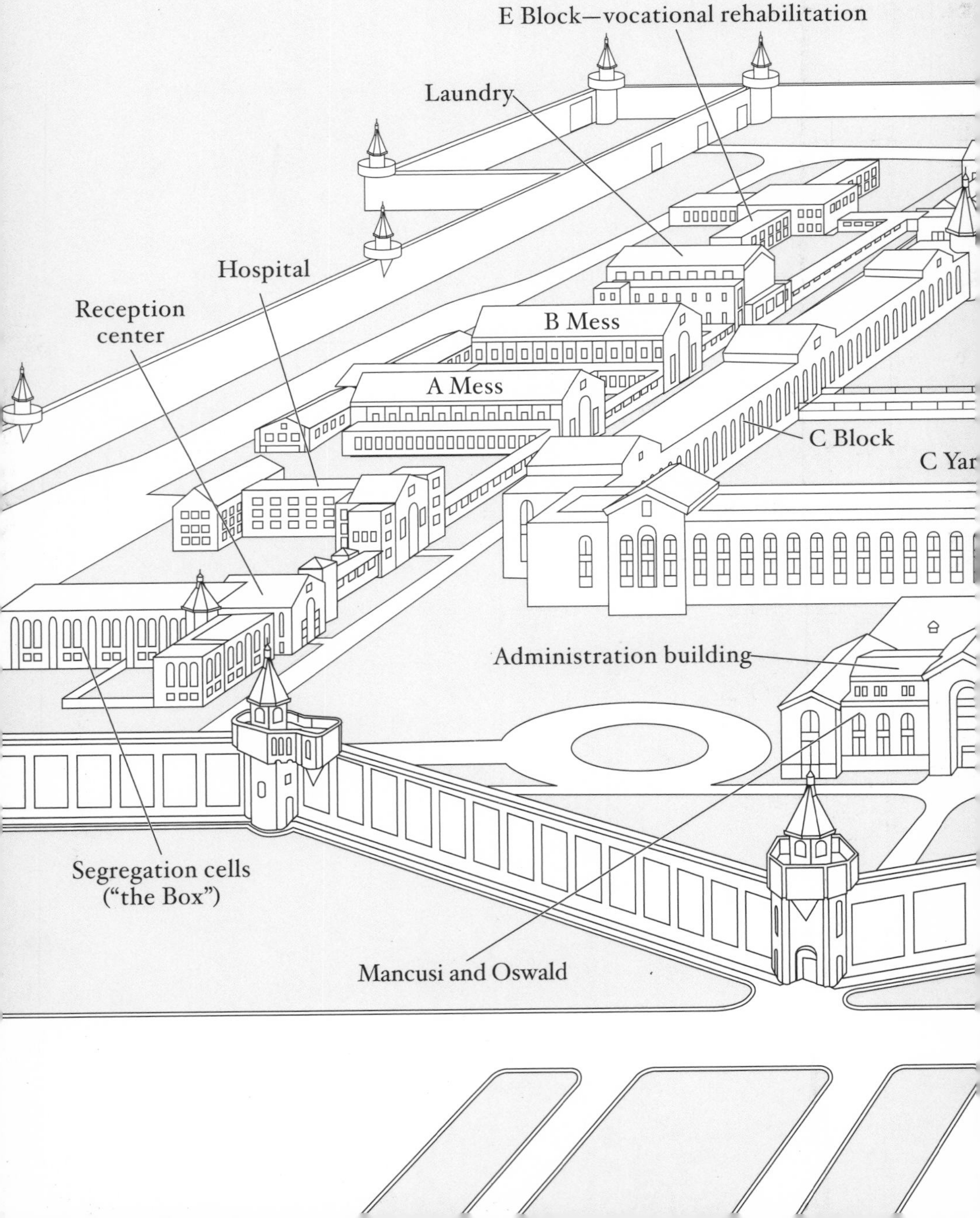

E Block—vocational rehabilitation

Laundry

Hospital

Reception center

B Mess

A Mess

C Block

C Yar

Administration building

Segregation cells ("the Box")

Mancusi and Oswald